The Matt Busby C

MANCHESTER UNIT

MATCH BY MATCH

DESERT ISLAND FOOTBALL HISTORIES

CLUB HISTORIES:

Title	ISBN
ABERDEEN: A CENTENARY HISTORY 1903-2003	1-874287-49-X
ABERDEEN: CHAMPIONS OF SCOTLAND 1954-55	1-874287-65-1
ABERDEEN: THE EUROPEAN ERA – A COMPLETE RECORD	1-874287-11-2
BRISTOL CITY: THE MODERN ERA – A COMPLETE RECORD	1-874287-28-7
BRISTOL CITY: THE EARLY YEARS 1894-1915	1-874287-74-0
CAMBRIDGE UNITED: THE LEAGUE ERA – A COMPLETE RECORD	1-874287-32-5
CAMBRIDGE UNITED: 101 GOLDEN GREATS	1-874287-58-9
THE STORY OF THE CELTIC 1888-1938	1-874287-15-5
CHELSEA: CHAMPIONS OF ENGLAND 1954-55	1-874287-94-5
COLCHESTER UNITED: GRAHAM TO WHITTON – A COMPLETE RECORD	1-874287-27-9
COVENTRY CITY: THE ELITE ERA – A COMPLETE RECORD	1-874287-51-1
COVENTRY CITY: AN ILLUSTRATED HISTORY	1-874287-59-7
DUNDEE: CHAMPIONS OF SCOTLAND 1961-62	1-874287-86-4
DUNDEE UNITED: CHAMPIONS OF SCOTLAND 1982-83	1-874287-71-6
HISTORY OF THE EVERTON FOOTBALL CLUB 1878-1928	1-874287-14-7
HALIFAX TOWN: FROM BALL TO LILLIS – A COMPLETE RECORD	1-874287-26-0
HEREFORD UNITED: THE LEAGUE ERA – A COMPLETE RECORD	1-874287-91-0
HUDDERSFIELD TOWN: CHAMPIONS OF ENGLAND 1923-1926	1-874287-88-0
IPSWICH TOWN: THE MODERN ERA – A COMPLETE RECORD	1-874287-43-0
IPSWICH TOWN: CHAMPIONS OF ENGLAND 1961-62	1-874287-63-5
KILMARNOCK: CHAMPIONS OF SCOTLAND 1964-65	1-874287-87-2
LUTON TOWN: THE MODERN ERA – A COMPLETE RECORD	1-874287-05-8
LUTON TOWN: AN ILLUSTRATED HISTORY	1-874287-37-6
MANCHESTER UNITED'S GOLDEN AGE 1903-1914: DICK DUCKWORTH	1-874287-96-1
THE MATT BUSBY CHRONICLES: MANCHESTER UNITED 1946-69	1-874287-92-9
MOTHERWELL: CHAMPIONS OF SCOTLAND 1931-32	1-874287-73-2
NORWICH CITY: THE MODERN ERA – A COMPLETE RECORD	1-874287-67-8
PETERBOROUGH UNITED: THE MODERN ERA – A COMPLETE RECORD	1-874287-33-3
PETERBOROUGH UNITED: WHO'S WHO?	1-874287-48-1
PLYMOUTH ARGYLE: THE MODERN ERA – A COMPLETE RECORD	1-874287-54-6
PLYMOUTH ARGYLE: 101 GOLDEN GREATS	1-874287-64-3
PLYMOUTH ARGYLE: SNAKES & LADDERS	1-874287-82-1
PORTSMOUTH: FROM TINDALL TO BALL – A COMPLETE RECORD	1-874287-25-2
PORTSMOUTH: CHAMPIONS OF ENGLAND – 1948-49 & 1949-50	1-874287-38-4
THE STORY OF THE RANGERS 1873-1923	1-874287-95-3
THE ROMANCE OF THE WEDNESDAY 1867-1926	1-874287-17-1
STOKE CITY: THE MODERN ERA – A COMPLETE RECORD	1-874287-76-7
STOKE CITY: 101 GOLDEN GREATS	1-874287-55-4
POTTERS AT WAR: STOKE CITY 1939-47	1-874287-78-3
TOTTENHAM HOTSPUR: CHAMPIONS OF ENGLAND 1950-51, 1960-61	1-874287-93-7
WEST HAM: FROM GREENWOOD TO REDKNAPP	1-874287-19-8
WEST HAM: THE ELITE ERA – A COMPLETE RECORD	1-874287-31-7
WIMBLEDON: FROM SOUTHERN LEAGUE TO PREMIERSHIP	1-874287-09-0
WIMBLEDON: FROM WEMBLEY TO SELHURST	1-874287-20-1
WIMBLEDON: THE PREMIERSHIP YEARS	1-874287-40-6
WREXHAM: THE EUROPEAN ERA – A COMPLETE RECORD	1-874287-52-X

WORLD CUP HISTORIES:

Title	ISBN
ENGLAND'S QUEST FOR THE WORLD CUP – A COMPLETE RECORD	1-874287-61-9
SCOTLAND: THE QUEST FOR THE WORLD CUP – A COMPLETE RECORD	1-897850-50-6
IRELAND: THE QUEST FOR THE WORLD CUP – A COMPLETE RECORD	1-897850-80-8

MISCELLANEOUS:

Title	ISBN
RED DRAGONS IN EUROPE – A COMPLETE RECORD	1-874287-01-5
THE BOOK OF FOOTBALL: A HISTORY TO 1905-06	1-874287-13-9
FOOTBALL'S WAR & PEACE: THE TUMULTUOUS SEASON OF 1946-47	1-874287-70-8

The Matt Busby Chronicles

MANCHESTER UNITED 1946-69
MATCH BY MATCH

Series Editor: Clive Leatherdale

Jim Brown

DESERT ISLAND BOOKS

First Published in 2004

DESERT ISLAND BOOKS LIMITED
7 Clarence Road, Southend on Sea, Essex SS1 1AN
United Kingdom
www.desertislandbooks.com

British Library Cataloguing-in-Publication Data
A catalogue record for this book is available from the British Library

ISBN 1-874287-53-8 (Cased)
ISBN 1-874287-96-1 (Paper)

Printed in Great Britain
by 4Edge Ltd

~ Contents ~

~ *Acknowledgements* ~

I wish to thank everyone who has helped me with this book. I am especially grateful to Brian Tabner, Brian Hodges, Richard Whitehead, Richard Owen, Barry Hugman, Alan Shury, Barry Dunne, Donal Cullen, Iain McCartney, Colin Farmery, and Roger Wash.

The advent of the Premiership has generated unprecedented media interest in football, and the depth and quality of football match reports has been commendable. It was not always the case. Fifty years ago it was sometimes hard to find a match report of a Manchester United game, other than in the Manchester newspapers or the North-West editions of the nationals. Many hours have been spent at the British Newspaper Library at Colindale trying to track down goal-scorers, line-ups, and facts about games in the 1940s and 1950s.

Thankfully, the Library has a remarkable collection of provincial newspapers, not to mention the now fast-dying Saturday evening sports editions (Pinks or Greens). The staff at Colindale are thanked for their invaluable help and assistance.

Mark Wylie, the curator at Old Trafford, kindly gave me access to the club's records and scrapbooks, and I would like to thank him and Nicola Struthers for their help and assistance.

There have been hundreds of books written about Manchester United over the years. In researching and writing these chronicles I have used a number of them, including *Winners and Champions* by Alec Shorrocks, *The Tommy Taylor Story* by Brian Hughes, *Matt, United and Me* by Jimmy Murphy, *Viollet* by Roy Cavanagh and Brian Hughes, *Roger Byrne* by Iain McCartney, *Father of Football* by David Miller, *The Lawman* by Bernard Bale, *Sir Matt Busby* by Rick Glanville, *Soccer At The Top* by Matt Busby, *The United Alphabet* by Gart Dykes, *Manchester United in Europe* by David Meek and Tom Tyrell, *Blessed* by George Best, *Back Page United* by Stephen F Kelly, *A Strange Kind of Glory* by Eamonn Dunphy, and most importantly *Manchester United: A Complete Record* by Ian Morrison and Alan Shury.

My publisher and editor, Clive Leatherdale, gives me wonderful support and encouragement and the confidence to approach football book projects without fear.

Finally thanks to my wife Doreen for her support and encouragement in what has been a long but satisfying project.

~ *Prelude* ~

At the outbreak of the Second World War in 1939, Manchester United were not considered to be one of England's top football clubs. Since the club's arrival in the League as Newton Heath in 1892, they had divided their time equally between the First and Second Divisions. In fact, since relegation in 1931 United had only spent two seasons in the top flight.

Their golden period had been in the years immediately prior to the Great War. Under the shrewd management of Ernest Mangnall, and inspired by the greatest player of the era, Billy Meredith, United had won the League twice, in 1908 and 1911, and the FA Cup in 1909.

The inter-war years had been depressing, notwithstanding the benefits of a move in 1910 to a large, new stadium at Old Trafford. The club suffered continual financial crises and were perennially yo-yoing between the top two divisions. They suffered relegation in 1922, 1931, and 1937, and were hidden deep in the shadows of Manchester's premier club, City, who reached (but lost) the FA Cup final in 1926 and 1933, but defeated Portsmouth 2-1 in the 1934 final.

Coincidentally, City's right half that day was a 24-year-old Scotsman called Matt Busby. City went on to win the First Division title in 1937 before themselves suffering the ignominy of relegation twelve months later – the first and (to date) only club to be demoted the season after being champions.

In 1938, United secretary Walter Crickmer came up with what was a novel idea of the time for developing young footballers. Along with United's chief scout, Louis Rocca, he helped form the Manchester United Junior Athletic Club (MUJAC). The MUJACs, as they became known, were run by a committee that included schoolteachers and instructors able to spot talented young footballers amongst their pupils. Chairman James Gibson said the aim was 'a United team composed of Manchester players'. In 1939 the MUJACs won the Chorlton League and began to produce players for the club's senior sides. The scheme would be the forerunner of the club's highly effective youth programme that would, after the War, make United the biggest club in England.

In March 1941 a German Luftwaffe air raid on the Salford Docks and Old Trafford industrial area left the Old Trafford stadium in flames. When the smoke finally cleared, United's home was left a smouldering ruin. The main stand was virtually burnt down with the dressing rooms destroyed. As the ground was totally unusable, neighbours City came to the rescue, allowing United to play their home games at Maine Road (each club played their respective home matches on alternate Saturdays).

As the War neared its conclusion, the Manchester United board decided to seek a manager – hoping to progress from the situation whereby the team was picked by a desk-bound secretary and which trained only haphazardly.

Matt Busby's considerable talent as a player was well-known in Manchester. He had played for City between 1928 and 1936 as a stylish wing-half. He won a Cup winners' medal with them in 1934, and a Scottish cap in 1933, before joining Liverpool in 1936 for a fee of £8,000.

Busby had spent the War as a physical training instructor, where he refined his ability to organise and direct training methods. Like many footballers in the armed services, he had guested for other clubs and made eight wartime appearances for Scotland, several times as captain. With peace on the horizon, Liverpool offered him a five-year contract as player-coach and assistant to George Kay, who was manager at the time. After being interviewed by James Gibson, Busby opted to accept the United job instead, feeling that it offered greater potential. Anfield felt betrayed by his decision.

On 19 February 1945, Company Sergeant-Major Instructor Matt Busby was publicly confirmed as Manchester United's new manager. The appointment, for five years, would date from one month after his demobilisation. His salary would be £750 per annum and he would be manager in more than name only.

Soon after the German surrender in May 1945, Busby was asked to take a star-studded British Army side to Italy, Greece and Egypt, for the purpose of entertaining battle-weary troops who had been starved of top-class football for so long.

In the southern Italian town of Bari, Busby met up with Jimmy Murphy, against whom he had played before the War. Busby offered him a job at Old Trafford. It wouldn't be easy, Busby explained. Old Trafford was a bombed wreck of a ground and there was no prospect of playing games there in the foreseeable future. United were also heavily in debt. Money would not be available to buy players. They would have to work with what they found and develop young players themselves. That would be Murphy's task. Impressed by Busby's quiet assurance, he accepted without hesitation. Murphy was 35. He had been a classy player with West Brom, winning 22 Welsh caps. During the summer of 1939 he had been transferred to Swindon Town, for whom as it turned out, he never kicked a ball.

The deal as Busby outlined it was that Murphy would run United's reserve team and coach the youngsters on Tuesday and Thursday nights at the club's training ground, The Cliff, in Lower Broughton. Busby would take care of the first team on Saturdays and both would share the day-to-day training. Busby had no revolutionary ideas about physical conditioning. Keeping fit was a simple business: for the first hour the players would lap the pitch, gradually increasing the pace from a jog to three-quarter speed for a couple of laps, ending with, perhaps, three or four flat out gallops.

Matt Busby had not really fulfilled himself in League football. One FA Cup medal and a solitary peacetime game for Scotland were scant rewards for his talent. His years at Manchester City had been, as often as not, frustrating. Liverpool had provided a relatively obscure stage for a player of his potential.

With Old Trafford a bomb-damaged ruin, Manchester United FC was administered from a small office in James Gibson's Cornbrook Cold Storage depot. Busby shared this office with Walter Crickmer, a young assistant Les Olive, and a typist borrowed from Gibson's business.

When Busby started work, in October 1945, United were in sixteenth position in the Northern League and plenty of players were still in the armed forces. The first side he named, against Bolton Wanderers at Maine Road, was: Crompton, Walton, Roach, Warner, Whalley, Cockburn, Worrall, Carey, Smith, Rowley, Wrigglesworth. United won 2-1 with goals from Johnny Carey and Harry Worrall.

This was a makeshift side, deprived of the services of most of the better players on United's books, who had yet to return from wartime service. Missing from that first Busby team were players who would subsequently distinguish themselves in United's colours, such as Pearson, Mitten, Morris, Chilton, and Aston. One by one they would drift back from the forces, but it would take until the beginning of the following season – when the Football League proper would resume – before Busby could send out the team he wanted. Meanwhile, he assessed his situation and improvised with team selection to such good effect that United finished the 1945-46 season, the last before the league structure recommenced, fourth in the League North table.

Chapter One

The Maine Road Era (1946-49)

LEAGUE DIVISION 1	**1946-47**
Division 1	Runners-Up
FA Cup	Fourth round

Optimism was high on Manchester University's Fallowfield playing fields in July 1946 as United's players assembled for pre-season training. The winning ways during the second half of the 1945-46 season had pleased manager Matt Busby and, with the majority of the players called up during the War now back in the fold, an improvement on the fourteenth place achieved in the last peacetime season in 1938-39 was the least Busby expected.

The players were soon made aware that Old Trafford was a long way from being suitable for First Division football – due to the aerial bombing it sustained in 1941 – and the club would continue to share the Maine Road ground of their arch rivals Manchester City. United would pay City a rent of £3,000 per annum, an arrangement that would continue until 1949, when the Old Trafford stadium would be able to accommodate enough spectators to make it worthwhile to return. In the meantime, both sides' reserve teams would play their games at Old Trafford.

United announced that they were unable to issue season tickets for Maine Road in the coming season, and the 1,000 or so supporters who had bought season tickets seven years previously would have their money refunded. Two weeks into that – the 1939-40 season – football had been suspended for the duration of the conflict. United had promised each season ticket holder free tickets for the 'first season of normal football'. Many supporters, however, now insisted that they did not want their money back and would wait for 'normal' service to be resumed at Old Trafford.

Another pressing issue was the lack of training kit. Matt Busby made appeals in the press and the club programme for fans to donate clothing coupons, and trainer Tom Curry also asked players to hand over their coupons. The club had just enough match-kit to clothe the four teams that they operated, and the appeals enabled the club to acquire the necessary training gear.

DID YOU KNOW?

In 1963 Denis Law scored three goals against Gordon Banks in three games for three separate teams – for United (FA Cup final), for Scotland and for Rest of the World.

Despite these off-field problems, Busby and assistant Jimmy Murphy prepared for the opening game against Grimsby Town on 31 August, the start of a fixture list replicated from that of 1939-40.

The War had in one way or another wreaked havoc with the plans of most football clubs. Established senior players, like Busby and Murphy, were too old to resume their careers. Many promising youngsters never had the opportunity to come through the ranks. This is what encouraged those clubs who could afford to – and some which could not – to buy players. This option did not exist for United. Busby was better off than some, worse off than others.

Busby's squad was an amalgam of various types. There were a group who had played first-team football for United before 1939. These included Jack Rowley (now aged 25), Johnny Carey (27), Stan Pearson (27), Jimmy Hanlon (27), Allenby Chilton (27) and Jack Warner (34). Others like Charlie Mitten (25), John Aston (24), Johnny Morris (22) and Henry Cockburn (22) – who had come through MUJACS – had been blooded when service duties permitted in wartime football. Other than Rowley, who had cost £3,000 as a 17-year-old from Bournemouth in 1937, the only player to have cost a fee was the veteran Scot Jimmy Delaney, whom Busby bought from Celtic for £4,000 in February 1946 to add pace to United's right flank.

The reserve team reflected the ageing playing staff, with the majority of players over 25, among them pre-War veterans such as Bert Whalley (34) and Billy Wrigglesworth (33).

The players were back in full-time training, all except the remarkable Cockburn, who was still working as a textile engineer's fitter, and Joe Walton, a promising young right-back who was a plumber.

United started the season with a bang. After a 2-1 home win over Grimsby at Maine Road, they travelled to London for two games in four days. Both Chelsea and Charlton were put to the sword and the normally hard-nosed London press were unanimous in their praise of the style and quality of the visitors. Henry Cockburn's performances had the newspapers tipping him for England honours, and national team boss Walter Winterbottom, a former United player, could not have failed to be impressed when he watched him at Stamford Bridge. The other star of the London games was goalkeeper Crompton, who saved penalties from England players Tommy Lawton (Chelsea) and Don Welsh (Charlton), but otherwise had little to do.

An unchanged side recorded a 5-0 home win over Liverpool. A more patient 1-0 win against Middlesbrough meant that United boasted a 100 per cent record after five games, their best start since 1908. The fans were impressed and over 65,000 watched the Boro game, an increase of 20,000 on the number who watched the opening game of the season.

The bubble had to burst, however, and after Chelsea had grabbed a point at Maine Road, the run came to an end with a 2-3 defeat at Stoke. This sparked a run of eight games with only one victory, 5-2 over an ageing Arsenal side, for whom 34-year-old Cliff Bastin – a pre-War England international – made his final Gunners appearance. By early November, United lay fifth.

Apart from a shock home defeat by Sunderland – who would be the only side to lower the flag at Maine Road – the overall home form was outstanding, with seventeen wins and 61 goals in 21 matches. October saw the return of Johnny Morris from Army duty in India. A lightly built, curly-haired inside-forward with excellent ball control and a deadly finish, Morris had been on United's books as a junior in 1939. Aged 23, Busby threw him into the first team, the final piece of the dream forward line of Delaney, Morris, Rowley, Pearson and Mitten which was to perform so brilliantly for the club.

Another key player to get his break was John Aston, also on United's books since before the War. Aston, 25, returned from being a Royal Marine Commando in 1946 and played his first game as an inside-forward against Chelsea in September, following some outstanding reserve-team games. He failed to impress and had to wait until Christmas for another opportunity, this time as a full-back. With injury hitting all the club's full-backs, Aston was forced to play there at Grimsby. He would be United's regular left-back for the next seven seasons and win seventeen England caps.

A number of other players got their chance in the winter of 1946-47, including full-back Harry Worrall, who had been at the club since 1937, goalkeeper Cliff Collinson, who made seven appearances deputising for the injured Jack Crompton, and centre-forward Ronnie Burke who, despite scoring nine goals in thirteen games, could only ever get a game if one of the dream forwards was injured.

In September, Henry Cockburn became United's first post-War England international when, after just six peacetime League games, he was chosen to face Northern Ireland in Belfast. In an experienced side including Frank Swift, Tommy Lawton, Raich Carter and Wilf Mannion, Henry Cockburn did well in the 7-2 win and retained his place for subsequent games against Eire and Wales. The latter game was played at Maine Road and although England won 3-0 Cockburn struggled and was subsequently dropped in favour of Blackpool's Harry Johnston. Cockburn had, however, achieved international status while working full-time in an Oldham mill. As the only United player to be selected for England in the first post-War season, he was envied by certain better-known colleagues who failed to win caps during the campaign.

The poor away form puzzled Busby and Murphy, and it would ultimately cost United the League title. Between August and Easter the Reds won only once away from home and failed to beat mediocre teams such as Brentford, Grimsby, Huddersfield and Bolton. Wolves, their closest rivals in the championship race, won ten away games, whilst Liverpool, the champions, won twelve.

United were rarely far off the title pace and achieved some excellent results at home, including comprehensive wins over high-flying Blackpool and Wolves. Over 67,000 turned up for the latter game which, with two Easter victories over Leeds and a win at Portsmouth, put United back into contention, behind title favourites Wolves. A narrow defeat at Anfield however, together with Wolves' inexplicable slip-up, opened the door for Liverpool to seize the championship in a final day shoot-out at Molineux.

United's final game saw Jack Rowley score a hat-trick to take his League tally to 26 goals, overtaking Sandy Turnbull's record of 25, which had stood since 1908.

Although Liverpool won the title, for the first time in 24 years, it was Manchester United's vibrant style of play which captured the public's imagination. In fact, almost two million spectators paid to watch United and City at Maine Road over the course of the season. City, who ended it by winning promotion from the Second Division, attracted their share of Manchester's football-hungry population, but more – well over one million – came to worship Busby's team. The crowds congregated in droves up and down the country to see United wherever they played: home and away they attracted the highest aggregate attendances in the First Division. Maine Road did, however, host United's smallest ever post-War crowd in February 1947, when under 8,500 watched a midweek afternoon game with Stoke that had to be re-arranged because of FA Cup commitments. Work, together with freezing cold weather, kept the crowd down.

One of the worst winters in memory caused hundreds of games to be postponed. With midweek games banned by the authorities in order to safeguard vital industrial production, re-arranged games had to be played on Saturdays. As a result, the season was eventually extended into mid-June to recover the backlog.

United were permitted to pay their players a bonus (quaintly called talent money) for finishing second in the league. League regulations, however, restricted the sum to £220 for the whole team. It is not clear how United distributed the princely total but it is unlikely that any single player received more than £20.

The FA Cup turned out to be a damp squib for United. Following a 3-0 win in the Bradford Park Avenue mud, another Second Division side, Nottingham Forest, caused the shock of the fourth round by winning 2-0 at Maine Road.

In the reserves, United's mixture of old-timers and young bucks, captained by Bert Whalley and coached by Jimmy Murphy, won the Central League championship.

Match of the Season 1946-47

United 3 Wolverhampton 1

Division One, 5 April 1947

Easter Saturday 1947 was a key day in the First Division title race, with the top four teams opposing each other. At Anfield, third-placed Liverpool met second-placed Blackpool. Wolves, the leaders, travelled to Maine Road to face fourth-placed United. Ted Vizard's Wolves had lost only twice in an eighteen-game league run stretching back to November. Their team was settled and included three England international half-backs – Billy Wright, Stan Cullis and Tom Galley – plus several players tipped for international honours in the near future, such as wingers Jimmy Mullen and Johnny Hancocks, and centre-forward Dennis Westcott who, with 29 goals, headed the Division One scoring charts.

Wolves had beaten United 3-2 in a thriller at Molineux earlier in the season, but the return game was hard for the pundits to predict, especially in the light of United's daunting home record, which made visitors fear to tread.

DID YOU KNOW?

Manchester United goalkeeper Dave Gaskell played Rugby Union for Orrell RFC after retiring from soccer.

United, on the other hand, apart from the surprise FA Cup defeat to Forest, had lost only twice in thirteen games since mid-December. On both occasions, at Highbury (2-6) and Derby (3-4), Crompton had been absent through injury and his deputy Bill Fielding, signed from Bolton in January, had not inspired confidence among his defenders. The team was unchanged from the side that had drawn 2-2 at Huddersfield the previous week, with Jimmy Hanlon, a survivor of three years in a German concentration camp, and Ronnie Burke continuing to deputise for the injured Johnny Morris and Charlie Mitten.

The windy weather did not deter the expectant spectators and the Maine Road gates were closed fifteen minutes before the kick-off. Massive queues were locked outside, with the biggest crowd of the season, 67,204, inside.

United started by penning the old gold shirts into their own half. The game was played at a frenetic pace and Wolves' breathless defenders hung on during the first half-hour. Their goalkeeper Bert Williams rushed ten yards out of his goal to head clear from United's buzzing centre-forwards. A goal was almost inevitable and arrived on 24 minutes when Hanlon netted with a twenty-yard shot after Burke's good work.

Eight minutes after half-time the contest sparked into life when the prolific Westcott escaped from Chilton for the only time and equalised with a left-foot shot. Two minutes later United regained the lead when Jack Rowley raced half the length of the field to score a wonder goal. Soon afterwards a Delaney cross deflected off Stan Cullis's head and Jack's precise shot clinched both points (two points for a win operated in the Football League until 1981).

United's heroes were the lanky Chilton – who won most of his aerial duels against Westcott – and Carey, who although unable to match the diminutive Mullen for pace, nevertheless kept him on a tight rein with shrewd positional play and a cool head.

Defeat cost Wolves the leadership, as Blackpool won at Liverpool to leapfrog to the top. United were back in the title hunt, level with Liverpool and, although they were five points behind Blackpool, they – like Wolves and Liverpool – had five games in hand. Wolves, despite their defeat, remained favourites for the title.

LEAGUE DIVISION 1	**1947-48**
Division 1	Runners-Up
FA Cup	Winners

Following the prolonged first post-War campaign, the close season of 1947 was the shortest in memory. United kicked off on 23 August with a 2-2 draw at Middlesbrough, coming from two down thanks to a brace of Jack Rowley headers.

The season started like the previous one, with United looking invincible in their first three games. After a 2-0 win over champions Liverpool in the opening home game, football writer Alf Clarke commented that 'this season, in my opinion, may be an outstanding one'. His words were to prove prophetic.

Three days later FA Cup holders Charlton were thumped 6-2, with Rowley netting four to make it seven goals in three games. In addition, United hit the bar five times and Charlton's goalkeeper Sam Bartram received glowing praise for numerous saves.

But the Reds failed to win any of their next nine games and slumped to eighteenth. Rowley's goals dried up, wingers Mitten and Delaney were both dropped, and the defence went to pieces. Sheffield United and Grimsby – the Mariners heading for relegation – lowered the flag at Maine Road. The previous season's bad habit of losing to poor teams looked to be repeating itself.

Delaney's form was a mystery. At one stage he approached Matt Busby with a view to leaving the club, but Busby persuaded the popular Scot to persevere.

With Manchester City back in the top division, a massive 72,000 crowd watched the first post-War Manchester derby in September. It was a poor game that left Johnny Carey limping on the wing. The injury kept the skipper out for three weeks. Further injuries to Joe Walton and Jimmy Hanlon stretched the squad to the limits. New faces Harry Worrall and Joe Dale – a winger signed in the close season from Witton Albion – got chances but failed to make them tell. Local young goalkeeper Ken Pegg also earned his opportunity when Jack Crompton took a knock in November. But Pegg's two appearances were all that he would make in four years on the club's books.

The turning point came at Wolves on 1 November. The previous week, goals from Rowley and the restored Delaney had given United a 2-0 win over Aston Villa. Wolves, previously unbeaten at home, took the lead but were ripped apart 6-2. Missing the recently retired

Stan Cullis in defence, and entering a period of transition, Wolves slumped to their biggest home defeat for thirteen years.

United's five draws in the next six games, including three at home, impeded the recovery, but anyone who witnessed the 4-0 thrashing of Chelsea at Stamford Bridge must have wondered how United were not in the title chase. A Christmas double over Portsmouth, and a 5-0 thumping of second-placed Burnley on a mud-heap pitch, had many pundits tipping the Reds for a good Cup run.

The third round of the FA Cup handed United a tie at Aston Villa, and 59,000 fans witnessed an epic. United conceded a goal after thirteen seconds but led 5-1 at half-time. Villa roared back and scored three goals, only for Stan Pearson to clinch the tie 6-4 two minutes from time. Spectators and the press were ecstatic. *The Daily Despatch* reporter was unrestrained, describing it as 'Mafeking Night, Armistice Day and VE Day rolled into one'.

The following day's Cup draw put both Manchester clubs at home. City were paired with Chelsea, whilst United would play Liverpool. FA rules did not permit United's game to be played at Maine Road on any other date, so a new venue had to be found. The choice, Goodison Park, appeared to favour opponents Liverpool. But Busby told his players that the big, wide-open pitch would suit United's style of play and that Everton's 'neutral' fans would cheer for United. The bookmakers saw it the same way, installing United as joint favourites to win the trophy.

Beforehand, United entertained Arsenal, the League leaders, in front of an English League record crowd of 83,260. The Gunners stifled the game and, despite United hitting the woodwork three times, a point apiece was the outcome.

At Goodison Park, another massive crowd saw the gates closed half an hour before the kick-off, with almost 75,000 inside and another 10,000 locked out. Liverpool started strongly, Aston cleared off the line, Done missed a good chance, and then the tide turned. Three United goals in seven minutes demoralised Liverpool. Their famous future manager, Bob Paisley who played that day, described United as one of the best post-War teams he had ever seen. The United board also sensed that a special team was in the making, the press reporting that the players received a £4-a-man bonus for the win. That bonus would be increased to £6 for the fifth round. If United were still in the Cup, bonuses would rise round by round, until £20 per man was on the table if they won at Wembley.

DID YOU KNOW?

In August 1963, Harry Gregg saved Ted Phillips' penalty for Ipswich. It was his first miss for three years, and a week later Gregg saved another from the same player.

Another First Division side, holders Charlton, beckoned in round five. With Manchester City drawn at home to Preston, another ground switch was necessary, the choice falling on Huddersfield's Leeds Road. Before the tie, United's sixteen-game unbeaten run ended at Sheffield United, who overcame an injured goalkeeper and an early goal to win 2-1. United's debutant goalkeeper, Berry Brown, on leave from the RAF, could not be faulted and in fact saved a penalty.

Only 33,000 watched the Cup-tie at Leeds Road, put off by heavy overnight rain and the fear by many that they would not gain admission. Charlton requested an early kick-off, in order to catch a return train back to London, and the game started at 1.55pm. United forced seven corners in the first 25 minutes and went ahead through Jack Warner's deflected shot.

Goalkeeper Sam Bartram stood between United and a large victory. Mitten finally beat him again near the end to make it 2-0, but Charlton's fans chaired Bartram off the pitch at the end.

The quarter-final draw paired United at home to Preston, victors over Manchester City. Two weeks before the tie, United and Preston warmed up with a 1-1 draw at Maine Road. A 2-0 win at Stoke helped put Busby's men into an even better frame of mind.

Over 74,000 crammed into Maine Road for the Cup-tie. Preston lined up with debutant goalkeeper Jack Hindle, standing in for the injured Jimmy Gooch. United welcomed 'find of the season' John Anderson back from injury, and a 4-1 win propelled United into a Hillsborough semi-final against Derby. Pearson's hat-trick then clinched United's first ever visit to Wembley, but United were helped by two goalkeeping errors by Jock Wallace. Blackpool's 3-1 win over Tottenham meant it would be an all-Lancashire final for the first time since 1933.

In the six-week gap before the Wembley appointment, United faced a hectic League programme, including five games in 24 days before the final. Arsenal looked uncatchable, but the runners-up position was within United's grasp. In fact, George Allison's Gunners, inspired by the signing of the veteran wing-half Joe Mercer, were so far ahead that they were officially declared champions on 10 April, with four games still left to play.

By this time, United were in second place, having lost only twice in thirteen games since the Bramall Lane defeat. Interest in United reached unprecedented levels during this spell, with over 72,000 packing Maine Road for league games with Bolton and Manchester City. This ensured that United's average attendance exceeded 54,000, a figure the club would not emulate for almost twenty years. Despite the atmosphere, United succumbed 0-2 to struggling Bolton and were held 1-1 by City. Several reserves got run-outs in this period, including blond full-back John Ball, Scottish half-back Tommy Lowrie, and forward and schoolteacher Laurie Cassidy.

Wembley tickets were like gold dust. On the Monday after the semi-final, the club received 30,000 applications for its quota of 12,000 tickets, with fans travelling long distances to push their applications through the club's letter-box. Some even delivered them to the homes of Matt Busby and secretary Walter Crickmer.

A week before Wembley, United dismissed Chelsea 5-0, and defeat the following Saturday was unthinkable. Busby had only one selection problem. Should he pick the experienced Jack Warner, or stick by John Anderson, who had made an impact after coming into the side in December, following the death of his wife two months earlier. Busby, normally a cautious man, gambled by playing the younger Anderson, a gamble, which would pay off (see Match of the Season).

United's superb football had been rewarded by the selection of Pearson and Cockburn for England, and Delaney for Scotland, for the annual battle at Hampden Park two weeks before the final. Pearson's selection was long overdue, whilst Cockburn's return was the result of a run of consistent form. Rowley, Morris and Aston, however, had not done enough to nudge the selectors, although Rowley scored two goals for the Football League (v the League of Ireland) four days later.

Aston would be called up to the squad for a friendly against Italy in Turin, but did not play. Cockburn did, and was part of a 4-0 victory which England stars Billy Wright and Stan Mortensen later declared was the greatest display in which they had ever taken part. The Italians, notionally world champions by dint of having won the last World Cup in 1938, were expected to win in front of a partisan 85,000 crowd. Frank Swift, England's goalkeeper, was one hero, with numerous flying saves. Stan Mortensen was another, scoring a phenomenal goal to silence the vociferous Italian supporters.

Following the Wembley victory, United still had two league games remaining, the first of them at Blackpool four day later. Busby's team lost 0-1, but rounded the season off with a 4-1 home win over relegated Blackburn, clinching second place on goal-average.

Match of the Season 1947-48

United 4 Blackpool 2

FA Cup final, 24 April 1948

This was one of the great Wembley finals. United twice came from behind to ensure Matt Busby's first trophy for United and cement his reputation. But the result could so easily have gone the other way.

With ten minutes left it was anybody's Cup. United had trailed twice, but twice pulled level. Suddenly Blackpool's England centre-forward Stan Mortensen – who had scored in every round – fired at goal from outside the area. Crompton dived to his right, clutched the ball, and threw it to John Anderson. Anderson passed to Pearson, who fired low from 25 yards. The ball flew in off a post – while at the other end Mortensen was still walking out of the penalty area.

Blackpool, in their changed white shirts, having been close to leading for the third time, were now losing for the first time. Within another three minutes Anderson's shot spun off defender Kelly's head and curved into the top of the net. 4-2. No other team had ever twice come from behind to win a Wembley final.

Whilst United's route to Wembley had been tough – with every opponent from the First Division and only one game played in Manchester – Blackpool's progress had been against lower division teams, including Colchester United, a non-league side. For the final, manager Joe Smith had dropped inside-forward Jimmy McIntosh, scorer of five Cup goals, in favour of former Japanese PoW Alex Munro.

One United fan arrived at Euston with six crates of beer on a trolley: 'We will win and there won't be any beer in London tonight, so I've brought my own – just to make sure I get a drink.'

Chilton felled Mortensen for a penalty, despite newsreels showing the trip to be outside the area. Eddie Shimwell converted. United levelled when Robinson and Hayward left Delaney's centre to the other, allowing Rowley an easy goal. Blackpool went ahead again when evergreen Stanley Matthews directed a free-kick to Kelly, whose pass enabled Mortensen to shoot past Crompton.

Blue-shirted United's second equaliser came when Kelly handled, Morris took the free-kick, and Rowley's header beat Robinson.

LEAGUE DIVISION 1	**1948-49**
Division 1	Runners-Up
FA Cup	Semi-finals

Trouble was brewing at Manchester United during the summer of 1948. A small coterie of players had been unhappy that the players only received £20 a head bonus for winning the FA Cup. It was well known that Blackpool had been on £100 a man, and that two years previously Derby's players had all received a gold watch for winning the Cup.

Back in Manchester for pre-season training, that small group grew larger as the more vociferous among them expounded their views. Many of the players were approaching 30 and their careers were winding down. The club's coffers were full with the proceeds of the Cup run, not to mention record League crowds – so why couldn't the players have a bigger share? Busby himself picked up a year's salary, £1,750, as a bonus for the Wembley victory.

A deputation led by Morris, Mitten and Chilton presented their case to Busby. The manager reminded them of the rules regarding bonuses and said his hands were tied. He also pointed out that players enjoyed plenty of perks, including free golf, trips to the boxing at Belle Vue, and outings to Blackpool and Colwyn Bay in the summer. The players, however, wanted cash, and two days before the start of the season threatened to strike if no concessions were made.

The fans, unaware of these arguments, were bemused by United's start to the season, when Derby came to Maine Road and won 2-1. The protracted row about bonuses had drained several players' emotions and left a sour taste in Busby's mouth. His relationship with Morris, the perceived ring-leader, would never recover. On the field, wins at Blackpool and at Highbury promised better things, only for the Seasiders to visit Maine Road for the return and win 4-3.

The consensus was that the side lacked the rhythm of the previous season and lacked the authority of the recent past. The attack spluttered, and the usually prolific Rowley scored only one goal in the first nine games. His brace against Villa sparked a purple patch of nine goals in ten games that earned him his first England cap, but following a hat-trick in a 4-1 win at Middlesbrough, he failed to find the net in the next seven league games.

United's defence generally looked solid. Only Blackpool in that 3-4 home defeat, Wolves, on a slippery surface at Molineux, and Arsenal in the Charity Shield at Highbury, scored more than two against the Reds. John Anderson's form, however, looked shaky, and by November the strong tackling Billy McGlen had made the No 6 shirt his own – Cockburn switching to right-half.

The patchy form persisted into October, with home draws against Charlton and Burnley, and defeats at Stoke and Sunderland, causing United to slip to twelfth. A 6-1 win at struggling Preston, however, sparked an eighteen-match unbeaten league and cup run which put the Reds not only into a strong league position but also into the quarter-finals of the FA Cup.

Their main rivals in the title race were Portsmouth, Derby, and newly promoted Newcastle. All three were faced in successive games in December, and United came out of them with honours. A 1-1 home draw with Newcastle attracted 73,000 to Maine Road, and a week later United became the first team to come away from Fratton Park with a 2-2 draw, thanks to McGlen's late goal. Top-of-the-table Derby, on the Saturday before Christmas, saw their unbeaten record in tatters. The physical Ronnie Burke netted twice in a 3-1 win.

Five clean sheets over Christmas and New Year confirmed that the defence was in good health, and a 6-0 hammering of Third Division Bournemouth saw the FA Cup trail off to a good start. The prize for beating the Cherries was a home draw with Second Division Bradford Park Avenue. A massive crowd of 82,771, a record Cup crowd outside a final, did not faze Bradford who took a first-half lead and bustled the Reds out of their stride. Charlie Mitten levelled to set up extra-time, when Bradford's John Downie might have settled the tie.

The replay was a rough affair played on a foggy, icy pitch. Without the injured Morris and Delaney, United could only force another 1-1 draw. The second replay against Bradford was staged at Maine Road on the Monday afternoon. The official gate was 70,434, but thousands more clambered over the walls or gained illegal entry at the turnstiles. In view of the need for post-War industrial recovery, the Ministry of Labour asked local factories the next day to account for the number of workers who had taken time off.

The kick-off was preceded by a lecture for the players from referee Blythe, and thereafter it was clear that Bradford's luck had run out. United won 5-0 to set up a tie with giant-killers Yeovil Town who, under the tutelage of Alec Stock, had beaten First Division Sunderland. As the Yeovil tie was played on the following Saturday, it meant United contested four Cup-ties in fourteen days. Another mammoth crowd, 81,565, meant that almost 250,000 had watched the three home ties. The men from Somerset were overwhelmed 8-0, with Rowley becoming the first United player ever to score five goals in a game (including a sixteen-minute hat-trick).

Despite losing their unbeaten run at Aston Villa the following Saturday, United progressed to the Cup semi-final by a solitary goal against Hull. Behind the scenes, however, trouble was brewing.

The club announced that Johnny Morris had been transfer-listed at his own request. At the time, little explanation was given. Media coverage was restricted to guessing who might buy him and for how much – maybe a British record. Liverpool were the early favourites but Morris said no, leaving the door open for Derby to break the record and pay £24,000 for the youngest and one of the most skilful players in Busby's team.

Since the pre-season arguments about bonuses, Busby and Morris had endured an uneasy relationship, and training-ground incidents allowed resentment to fester. Morris was injured in December, but when fit again was left out. Matters boiled over after the first Bradford game, when Morris stormed off the training pitch, despite Busby's threats of dire consequences. Within three hours, Busby told the press Morris was available for transfer.

This was the first major crisis of Busby's managerial life and he was determined not to be undermined. Two weeks later – whilst Morris was still a United player – Busby paid Bradford Park Avenue £18,000 for inside-forward Johnny Downie, who had been a thorn in United's side in the marathon Cup-tie.

Downie made an instant impact with goals in his first two games. But as he was Cup-tied, he was ruled out of the Wolves semi-final. United were unlucky to lose the semi (see Match of the Season), but many fans and pundits insisted that, with Morris, United would have prevailed, and in the final beaten Second Division Leicester as comfortably as Wolves eventually did.

After the semi-final defeat, United lay seventh, burdened by a fixture backlog. They faced twelve games in 31 days in which to overhaul leaders Portsmouth, which proved too tall an order. Defeats at Birmingham and Huddersfield left United fighting it out for second place. A win at Newcastle set up a 3-2 last-day victory over champions Portsmouth to clinch second place for the third year running. That game brought the curtain down on the three-year tenancy at Maine Road, where United had so often played memorable football.

DID YOU KNOW?

When United beat Benfica 5-1 in the Stadium of Light in 1966, it constituted Benfica's first home defeat in the European Cup for nine years.

On the international scene, John Aston won six England caps at left-back and Cockburn was recalled for five caps at left-half. Jack Rowley, despite competition from Mortensen, Lawton and Newcastle's Jackie Milburn, won two caps – scoring on his debut, a 6-0 win over Switzerland. Stan Pearson also won two caps, and Morris was selected for two internationals after his move to Derby – he scored three goals and was at the pinnacle of his career.

On Cup final eve, Johnny Carey was presented with the Footballer of the Year trophy, voted by the Football Writers Association. It was only the second year of the award and Carey followed Stanley Matthews – who had won the inaugural vote – by polling nearly 40 per cent of the votes. His award was a popular choice.

Match of the Season 1948-49

Wolverhampton 1 United 0

FA Cup, semi-final replay, 2 April 1949

United returned to Hillsborough, and to the same dressing room, one year after their memorable semi-final victory over Derby. Whilst their recent football was not as flowing as twelve months previously, the fans were confident that United would be too strong for Wolves.

Morris's departure and Downie's ineligibility meant Busby had a crucial decision to make at inside-right. He selected the 1948 Cup final hero John Anderson, who had been out of the side since November. It was another Busby gamble, but Anderson had Cup experience and could score goals.

Stan Cullis was in his first season as manager at Molineux and had made little change to the side he had inherited. Wolves' greatest threats were still posed by the fast but tiny wingers Hancocks and Mullen, and at centre-forward Jesse Pye had more than adequately replaced Dennis Westcott.

Over 62,000 watched the first clash, a physical match with several players crocked. Wolves scored when Chilton's poor back-pass was intercepted by Hancocks, who centred for Sammy Smyth. United equalised in the first half when Mitten lobbed Bert Williams.

DID YOU KNOW?

In 1957-58 United played Shamrock Rovers in the European Cup. Without floodlights, the light was so bad in Dublin that the half-time interval was dispensed with.

Wolves had serious injuries to full-backs Kelly and Pritchard, which left both of them as passengers. United's Cockburn was concussed and Rowley had to play with a bloody head wound. John Anderson looked uncomfortable out of position.

Wolves' hero was goalkeeper Bert Williams. In the last minutes of extra-time 'the Cat' pulled off several fine saves as weary Wolves hung on. Their defence weathered the storm of United's attack, which mustered fourteen corners to Wolves' three.

A week later the teams replayed at Goodison Park. Wolves replaced their injured full-backs, and Busby moved Rowley to inside-right in place of Anderson. Ronnie Burke wore No 9.

A 72,000 crowd saw another fast and exciting game, with United on top in the first half but, once again, repelled by Williams. After half-time, however, the balance of the game tilted Wolves' way. With five minutes left, everyone seemed resigned to yet more extra-time, but it was then that Wolves scored the only goal.

Pye, perhaps offside, collected the ball on the right flank. Aston, Carey and Chilton hesitated but the linesman's flag stayed down. Pye's cross from the by-line was parried upwards by Crompton, and Smyth headed in the loose ball.

United had failed to score for the first time in fourteen Cup-ties, and had missed chances to win this one. Privately the players felt that Morris's absence had made all the difference. Publicly the fans blamed the officials for allowing Wolves an offside goal. Busby refused to blame anyone and in the following week's programme notes was magnanimous. He wrote: 'I do not wish to complain. We are sportsmen – let us remain so.'

In the final, Stan Cullis's team beat Leicester 3-1.

CHAPTER TWO

CHAMPIONS AT LAST (1949-52)

LEAGUE DIVISION 1	**1949-50**
Division 1	Fourth
FA Cup	Quarter-finals

In the summer of 1949 Matt Busby and Jimmy Murphy surveyed their ranks of young players. They concluded that, although the reserves had won the Central League in 1948, there was little in the way of exciting talent pushing through. Murphy went further, insisting that not a single player in the reserves was good enough for the first team. Behind their frustration at the near misses in both League and Cup in 1949, lay worries about the future.

The old scout Louis Rocca, the man responsible for discovering and nurturing many of the 1948 side, was feeling his age, and Busby drafted in Joe Armstrong as chief scout. A tiny man with a thatch of grey hair and a laughter-lined face, Armstrong was a charmer. Over the coming years he would turn his charm on the mothers of many talented schoolboys, convincing them that their sons would benefit from joining United. His appointment was as vital as any that Busby made in his managerial career.

Armstrong's brief was to lure the best young talent in the country to Old Trafford – United's home once again. Once there, Murphy and trainer Bert Whalley would select the pick of the crop. Armstrong's charm, and eye for talent, ensured that over the next two decades United secured more than their fair share of the cream. The first three starlets to arrive in 1949 were schoolboy internationals Dennis Viollet, Jeff Whitefoot (from England), and Jackie Blanchflower (Northern Ireland). Before the season was over, Whitefoot would become United's youngest ever first-team player.

The season opened at Derby, where a Rowley goal gave United the points. The following Wednesday night saw the re-opening of Old Trafford after the three-year exile at Maine Road. The crowd and the team celebrated with a 3-0 house-warming win over Bolton. The main stand was all-seater but remained uncovered, and was flanked by the two corner roofs which had survived the bombs. As building materials gradually became available, further work was carried out and the main stand roof was completed in 1951. Facing the main stand, the United Road terraces were covered, but those behind each goal were not. The capacity, 55,000, was substantially smaller than Maine Road, which meant that gate receipts at big games would suffer. Over 42,000 converged on Old Trafford for the Bolton game and the congestion meant thousands missed the kick-off.

One notable omission was the transfer-listed Allenby Chilton. His wife's health had been causing some concern and a move back to his native north-east looked possible. Another possible motive for his transfer request was the barracking he had received. A section of the United support enjoyed pouring scorn on the ungainly centre-half, forgetting his solid commitment to the cause. His deputy, Sammy Lynn, who had been at the club since 1935, took over the No 5 shirt. A few weeks later, Chilton asked to come off the list and was soon back at the heart of the defence.

United did not lose any of their first eight games, recording their best ever unbeaten start. The run included a 2-1 win over Manchester City, when Henry Cockburn became the first United player to be sent off since the War, following an altercation with City's Billy Linacre. Cockburn, a player with a reputation for sportsmanship, was upset by the decision, which earned a one-game suspension.

The run was terminated by a 0-1 defeat at Burnley. A week later, Sunderland became the first post-War visitors to win at Old Trafford – thanks to the dazzling skills of Len Shackleton and Ivor Broadis – but that only sparked another nine games without defeat. The sequence included a 4-0 win at Aston Villa and a 3-0 victory over unbeaten leaders Wolves, which went some way to avenging the previous season's semi-final defeat.

Busby had experimented at inside-forward, initially with 17-year-old Brian Birch for one game, then Ted Buckle, who played seven games without scoring, before giving Tommy Bogan – a summer signing from Preston – an extended run. None of these adequately replaced Johnny Morris, and by February Johnny Downie had re-claimed his place.

Goalkeepers also caused Busby some sleepless nights. First, Jack Crompton, married on the morning of the home game with Charlton, broke his wrist. Reserve Berry Brown had been sold to Doncaster, which left Irishman Sonny Feehan and Mancunian Joe Lancaster to fight it out during Crompton's absence. Looking ahead, Busby signed 18-year-old Ray Wood from Darlington and gave him a debut against

Newcastle. In all, Crompton missed nineteen games and, although his deputies did not let the side down, none were ready for an extended run in First Division football.

Brown's departure was one of several as the management culled reserve and fringe players to raise funds and make space for other youngsters. At a time when the British record fee was £26,000, Ronnie Burke joined Huddersfield for £16,000, Buckle moved to Everton for £6,000, and John Anderson signed for Nottingham Forest.

The last game of 1949 saw United win at Maine Road to record their first double over City since 1909. United had picked up seven points out of eight over the festive period, which left them trailing leaders Liverpool by two points.

The FA Cup third round awarded Southern League Weymouth a trip to Old Trafford, and although the part-timers held out for half an hour, United ran out 4-0 winners. Three weeks later United faced a sterner test at Watford, where a record crowd of over 32,000 saw United scramble through, thanks to a late Rowley goal.

The fifth-round draw paired United with Division One rivals Portsmouth. Following a 3-3 draw at Old Trafford, United won the replay 3-1 to progress to a quarter-final at Chelsea.

Meantime, in the league United were going from strength to strength and briefly headed the table after a 1-0 home win over Chelsea in mid-January. They suffered defeat at Stoke the following week but two wins and a draw meant they went into the Stamford Bridge tie looking down from on high.

The talk now was of the 'double'. Jack Crompton had returned in goal a week earlier after a three-month absence, and United were at full strength for the quarter-final. Over 70,000 watched United's 'double' hopes shredded. Crompton was at fault for the first goal, when he misjudged a soft shot, and Roy Bentley scored a second ten minutes from time to earn a semi-final tie with Arsenal.

Four days later, Aston Villa paid the price, crushed 7-0 at Old Trafford. Player of the season, and ever-present, Charlie Mitten set a Football League record by scoring three penalties and added another goal for good measure. A 3-2 win at Middlesbrough sent United four points clear of Liverpool with ten games remaining. Was this to be the year that United would seize the elusive championship?

Incredibly, they won only one of their remaining ten games, and that was the final match. In nine games they netted just five goals. United finished fourth, three points behind champions Portsmouth, who won the crucial game at Old Trafford 2-0. United that day were without Aston and Carey – on international duty (league games were not postponed for international call-ups in those days) – and Busby gave debuts to full-back Tom McNulty and Jeff Whitefoot – the youngest ever United League player at sixteen years 105 days.

In their final game, United beat Fulham 3-0, but a combination of foul weather, the FA Cup final being broadcast on the radio, and the anticlimax felt by the fans kept the crowd down to 11,968 – the lowest Saturday home gate since 1935.

The season's end had a silver lining. The club had been invited to tour the USA for six weeks, and on 2 May the United party set off from Southampton aboard the *Queen Mary*. One player was destined not to return.

Match of the Season 1949-50

Portsmouth 1 United 3

FA Cup, 5th round replay, 15 February 1950

Portsmouth, like United, had lost a Cup semi-final twelve months previously, a result that ultimately cost them the League and Cup 'double'. For the current tie, originally at Old Trafford, they were lying fourth, two places below United. Demand for tickets was intense and 40,000 were sold within three hours of going on sale. High winds and pelting rain did not deter over 53,000 fans, including 6,000 from the south coast.

Injury to leading scorer Duggie Read forced Pompey boss Bob Jackson to switch Jack Froggatt from outside-left to centre-forward, with 36-year-old Cliff Parker – a survivor of Pompey's 1939 FA Cup winning team – coming in on the left. United were unchanged from the 3-2 win over Burnley with fourth-choice goalkeeper Joe Lancaster between the sticks.

Len Phillips hit the post for Pompey early on, whereupon United scored twice. First goalie Butler punched a cross to Mitten, then Pearson headed in Mitten's corner. When Pearson took a knock on his ankle and was confined to the wing, Pompey seized the initiative. Ike Clarke poached a goal from close range and Parker headed in Peter Harris's cross to level. Mitten restored United's lead from the spot after Ferrier handled, but another penalty, after Chilton handled, allowed Ferrier to square the tie at 3-3.

DID YOU KNOW?

In February 1953 Jack Crompton was taken ill at Sunderland. Without any reserve goalie, United had to play Johnny Carey in goal for 90 minutes. The game ended 2-2.

After the match, hundreds of Pompey fans surrounded the team bus to congratulate the players before dashing to catch their transport back south.

The replay at Fratton Park on the following Wednesday afternoon was played in a frenzied atmosphere. It seemed the whole of Portsmouth had skipped school or work, citing sick relatives and bouts of smallpox. The gates were locked with almost 50,000 inside, just 300 below the ground record, whilst thousands outside were treated to a match commentary by a local police inspector.

Pompey were unchanged, but Busby decided to replace the inexperienced Lancaster with Sonny Feehan in goal. Johnny Downie also came in for Stan Pearson, who thereby missed his first game through injury since the War. Downie would prove to be the match winner, setting up Mitten's opener before hitting a scorcher from Rowley's knockdown to make it 2-0 midway through the first half. Peter Harris, outstanding on Portsmouth's right wing, pulled a goal back from a tight angle before half-time, but Delaney confirmed what was only Pompey's second home defeat in two years with a fierce shot.

Afterwards the Pompey manager conceded that the better team had won: 'The players are naturally disappointed but never mind, we must have a good crack at the league. We've still got a good chance of winning the championship again.' Prophetic words indeed, as Portsmouth duly reclaimed their league crown.

LEAGUE DIVISION 1	**1950-51**
Division 1	Runners-Up
FA Cup	Quarter-finals

Busby must have regretted taking his team to the USA in the summer. Not only did they look jaded when the new season began, but while the party were in New York at the end of the eleven-match tour, Charlie Mitten signed for Colombian club Sante Fe of Bogota.

Mitten had been contacted by Stoke's England centre-half Neil Franklin, who was about to sign for the same club. He persuaded Mitten to travel to Colombia, where several big clubs had left their national association to form a new league. As such they were outside the jurisdiction of FIFA, and were no longer bound to abide by its rules and regulations, especially regarding transfers.

Mitten was tempted not just by the money (the club was rumoured to be offering a large signing-on fee and £5,000 a year, compared to the £750 paid by United at the time), but also by the passion for soccer in Colombia and the high standard of living available for footballers. Busby was horrified when he heard the stories and tried to persuade Mitten to think again, but Charlie, a keen gambler, saw his opportunity to make a killing.

Mitten signed for Sante Fe, then rejoined the United team in New York to inform the shocked Busby, who reminded him that he was under contract. Mitten, however, insisted that he was a free agent. What Busby had overlooked was that Colombia was outside FIFA. The normal punitive contract laws of football did not apply and there was nothing that Busby could do. He had lost arguably the best uncapped winger in England. Mitten – 61 goals in 161 games – was at the peak of his career, and United would not receive a penny.

To add to Busby's problems, rumours were rife that the Colombians were also wooing John Aston and Henry Cockburn, both with the England World Cup squad in Brazil. Aston expressed his loyalty to the Reds, but Cockburn was only persuaded after Busby imposed his powerful personality on the international.

Billy McGlen claimed Mitten's No 11 shirt at the start of the season but, after press rumours of an interest in Wolves' tiny winger Johnny Hancocks, Busby secured the more modest acquisition of Bolton's Harry McShane. The veteran winger had recently given Johnny Carey a tough game, but his arrival was only a stop-gap measure. Reluctant to over-spend, Busby allowed full-back John Ball, Carey's understudy, to move to Burnden Park. Ball would go on to play 200 games for Bolton in Division One whilst McShane played just 50 games.

There were two other new arrivals that summer. One was USA international captain Eddie McIlvenny, who had emigrated after being freed by Wrexham in 1948. He had starred for his adopted country as they reached the last four in the World Cup, beating England 1-0 on the way. The Scots-born player was at wing-half in United's opening two games, but was never again in the reckoning in three more years at the club.

After the previous season's goalkeeping predicament, Busby paid £11,000 for Queen's Park Rangers' 28-year-old Reg Allen. The former prisoner of war was well-known to Busby from his Army days, and had been on Busby's wanted list for two years. McIlvenny's place went to 21-year-old Don Gibson, who made a strong impression and was a virtual ever-present.

United's early-season form was patchy. Delaney struggled and goals were hard to come by. Behind the scenes, questions were asked about the wisdom of the USA tour. McShane's arrival in September helped to boost a misfiring attack and United crept into the top four before losing 0-3 at leaders Arsenal, a game which convinced Busby that his team needed further surgery.

Within weeks Jimmy Delaney was sold to Aberdeen. At the age of 36 his best days were past him, and other younger players such as Cliff Birkett, Frank Clempson and Brian Birch were knocking on the door. Seventeen-year-old Birkett, a former schoolboy prodigy, debuted in the first home defeat of the season against Newcastle in early December, and a week later scored the winner in a 3-2 victory at Huddersfield. In that game Busby switched John Aston from full-back to centre-forward, not only to replace the flu victim Jack Rowley, but also in an attempt to reinforce United's goal-threat. The move paid off: Aston netted fourteen league goals in 22 games as United surged on an unbeaten run in the second half of the season.

A miserable Christmas saw bogey teams Bolton and Sunderland both win at Old Trafford. That meant three successive home defeats – United's worst run since 1934 – and it dropped them to ninth. For the first time, Busby was under some pressure. There was speculation about him losing his job and he went public to deny the rumours.

A 4-1 FA Cup win over Oldham sparked a run of seven straight wins to silence the critics. Among the victims were leaders Tottenham, second placed Middlesbrough, and FA Cup holders Arsenal in a memorable fifth round FA Cup-tie. In fact, United dropped only four league points between New Year's Day and the end of the season, and lost only once, at Stoke. Despite their surge, United were unable to overhaul Arthur Rowe's Tottenham and finished four points adrift – runners up for the fourth time in five seasons. That wretched Christmas had proved fatal.

United's extraordinary league run makes the FA Cup quarter-final defeat at Birmingham inexplicable. Second Division Birmingham had done their homework and refused to allow United to settle, once they had scored after 21 seconds through Jimmy Higgins. In a hard, physical game, Pearson and Birkett were given a rough time – Birkett was stretchered off ten minutes from time and numerous other United players required medical treatment. Many felt that United's younger players had been unable to find the extra resources to cope with the physical and mental demands of this sort of Cup-tie.

The loss of Mitten and Delaney had been a major blow to Busby. To his credit, he tried to replace them from within the club's ranks before turning to the transfer market. His belief in home-grown talent was as strong as ever and, as the season ended, he and Jimmy Murphy sensed that a golden seam of talent was close to being mined. Jeff Whitefoot and centre-half Mark Jones were teenagers, given a taste of first-team football when international duty or injuries occurred. In the reserves, youngsters such as Roger Byrne, Jackie Blanchflower and Dennis Viollet were flexing their muscles, and would be pushing for a chance in the near future.

Mark Jones, a tall, commanding stopper type of centre-half would have to wait several years before completely ousting Chilton. The veteran centre-half, now 32, was finally rewarded for his consistent domestic displays with an England cap in November, a 4-1 victory over Northern Ireland.

The Mitten saga had dropped from the headlines, but behind the scenes the news filtered back that he was homesick. His wife, Betty, and children returned to Manchester after only six months. Publicly, Mitten put on a brave face, but in December he wrote to local newspaper reporter Alf Clarke, telling him that he would be returning to England when his contract expired in the summer and was hopeful of a warm welcome. Two months later he wrote again, saying that he had rejected an improved offer from Santa Fe for a further year and was returning to England to face the music. The verdict of the Football Association would influence United's stance.

DID YOU KNOW?

In 1961, 17-year-old goalkeeper Ronnie Briggs conceded six goals on his debut at Leicester and seven at Sheffield Wednesday in the FA Cup in his third game.

Match of the Season 1950-51

United 2 Tottenham 1

Division One, 13 January 1951

A miserable Christmas, with defeats to Sunderland (twice) and Bolton, left United down in ninth. Arthur Rowe's newly promoted Spurs' eight straight autumn wins had taken them to the top. The only side to have lowered their colours since September were Huddersfield.

Rowe had coached in Hungary before the War and introduced new tactics into the English game. Dubbed 'push and run', it involved players 'pushing' the ball to a colleague and 'running' into space to take a return. It required more passing and patience than was the traditional English style, but less room for individual flair. In his first season, 1949-50, Rowe took Spurs to the Second Division title. They were now threatening to become the first club to win the two titles in succession since Everton in the early 1930s.

A solid defence was marshalled by England full-back Alf Ramsey and Billy Nicholson. Speedy wingers Les Medley and Sonny Walters scored almost as many goals as did centre-forward Len Duquemin. A Channel Islander, Duquemin was now injured. At White Hart Lane in September, 60,000 saw Walters' first-half goal give Spurs the points. The contrast in styles made for a fascinating and thrilling contest.

Busby continued with John Aston at centre-forward, for the England left-back had responded with six goals in six games.

Spurs scored when United keeper Reg Allen looked unsighted and new England cap, Baily's shot squeezed under his body. Four minutes later Ted Ditchburn seemed to have gathered Carey's long ball, only for Brian Birch to bundle the goalie and the ball over the line.

The winning goal was vintage Rowley. He set off on an electrifying run, leaving Harry Clarke and Ramsey in his wake before hitting the ball past Ditchburn. Ramsey's red face may partially explain his later distaste for wingers.

It was the Reds' first home win in seven, and they lost only one of their subsequent sixteen league games. Tottenham lost only two more games on the way to their first ever League title.

LEAGUE DIVISION 1	**1951-52**
Division 1	Champions
FA Cup	Third round

At the start of the 1951-52 season, Matt Busby had little reason for optimism. In five seasons at the club he had delivered only one trophy (the FA Cup) and the immediate post-War promise had not really been fulfilled. United were still respected, but they were not feared like the 1948 team had been. Busby's best hope was that United would not lose ground. Remarkably, they won the championship for the first time since 1911.

Always loath to use the transfer market, Busby procrastinated over the right-wing position. Jimmy Delaney had not been suitably replaced and Busby finally plumped for Birmingham's Johnny Berry, whom he had admired for two years since scoring a beauty at Old Trafford. For £25,000 United acquired a fast, brave and direct winger who had guts and an eye for goals.

Charlie Mitten returned from Colombia, desperate to re-start his career. First, however, he had to plead his case. He allegedly returned having cleared a profit of £3,500 – more than he could earn in three years in the domestic game. The Football Association came down hard, fining him £250 and suspending him until the end of the year, during which time he could receive no wages. He was forbidden even to train with any club until 1 November. The football establishment wanted to make an example of him and United followed suit by placing him on the transfer list – their prodigal son had to be sacrificed. In early December, Mitten was transferred to First Division Fulham for £20,000 and in January he recommenced his career. United had got a good fee, but had lost a skilful winger who had thrilled the crowds, many of whom were upset at his departure.

Nine games into new season, United, with only one defeat, were top of the table. Jack Rowley, back in his favourite centre-forward position, had already scored fourteen goals, including three hat-tricks, equalling his tally for the whole of the previous campaign. Ernie Bond, a £300 signing from Lancashire non-league side Leyland Motors, was a revelation at outside-left, and for a time solved the left-wing headache. John Aston, who had undergone cartilage surgery in the summer, missed most of the first half of the season but was adequately covered by Billy Redman. The good form earned England caps for Cockburn (his thirteenth) and Chilton (his second) against

France at Highbury. The 2-2 draw was judged a poor team performance and neither player excelled. Both were among six players dropped for the next international, and neither would play for their country again.

A patchy autumn saw Preston and Sunderland (again) win at Old Trafford. November defeats at Chelsea and at home to leaders Portsmouth dumped the Reds down to seventh. A week later, for a trip to Anfield, Busby rang the changes. Reg Allen (an ever present since his arrival) and Don Gibson made way for Jack Crompton and debutant 18-year-old Jackie Blanchflower. Aston was 'rested', having played just twice since his operation, and Rowley was restored at centre-forward. The most significant change was at left-back, where Busby unveiled Roger Byrne. The Gorton youngster had been groomed in the reserves for two years, and his mature display in the 0-0 draw at Liverpool convinced many of his promise.

A week later, in a 3-1 win against Blackpool, the wheels were well and truly back on track. Blanchflower returned to the reserves and Tommy McNulty was promoted to right-back, allowing Carey to move to right-half. The combination gelled and the team started to climb the table, notching up notable wins against Arsenal (3-1 at Highbury) and West Brom (5-1 at home). In the last game of 1951, an Old Trafford full house of 55,000 saw bogey team Bolton beaten 1-0, a result that left United top of the League.

On paper, a home FA Cup third-round tie with Hull City looked a formality. Former England midfield maestro Raich Carter had other ideas, however, and masterminded a shock 2-0 win for the struggling Second Division side. It was the first time United had failed to reach the fourth round since 1939, but it meant an all-out effort on the championship with no distractions.

Solid home form, including a repeat of the previous season's win over challengers Spurs, and successive away wins at Preston, Derby and Sunderland, strengthened United's grip on the leadership. With eight games remaining they had a two-point lead over Arsenal, with Spurs and Pompey a further three points back. Then they stumbled, losing 2-3 at Huddersfield, the bottom club, a late goal curtailing United's run of sixteen unbeaten league games.

A week later, with Stan Pearson and Jack Rowley on international duty at Hampden Park, United slipped again, losing 0-1 at Portsmouth, who became the only side to do the double over the Reds. Ironically, Pearson scored twice as England beat the auld enemy 2-1.

The ship was rocking now, with United's noses in front of Arsenal and Portsmouth only by goal-average. Busby made subtle changes. Reg Allen returned in goal and Aston was switched to left-back, with Roger Byrne given the No 11 shirt, allowing Rowley to again revert to centre-forward.

The changes paid off in a glorious Easter period. A 1-1 draw at Burnley on Good Friday and thumping wins over Liverpool (4-0) and Burnley (6-1) lifted United a point clear of Arsenal and four ahead of Spurs, in what was now – with three games left – a three-horse race. Arsenal pulled level with United following a win over Stoke, as the Reds were held 1-1 at Blackpool, but two days later Arsenal lost at West Brom while United beat Chelsea 3-0 in an emotional night at Old Trafford. United would be champions unless Arsenal could beat them by at least 7-0 the following Saturday.

Arsenal were aware of the magnitude of their task as they arrived at Old Trafford but were determined to make a game of it. They had missed out on a League and Cup double, but faced Newcastle in the Cup final the following Saturday. Their manager, Tom Whittaker, had already sent a congratulatory telegram to Busby, who was taking no chances. He named an unchanged side, with Byrne at No 11 after his six goals in five games since being switched from left-back. Arsenal's slim hopes were dashed in the eighth minute, when Rowley scored, and by half-time Pearson and Byrne had given United an impregnable lead. Rowley added two more to take his season's tally to 30 and end the season as he started it, with a hat-trick. Pearson scored the sixth goal amid noisy celebrations.

After 41 years, and for the third time in their history, United were League champions. Busby had stuck to his principles and been rewarded with his first title.

Match of the Season 1951-52

United 3 Chelsea 0

Division One, 21 April 1952

With two games remaining, United and Arsenal were level on 53 points. On this Monday night, as the Reds faced Chelsea, the Gunners travelled to the Hawthorns to play West Bromwich Albion. Depending on results, everything might hinge on a winner-takes-all showdown for the title between United and Arsenal five days hence.

DID YOU KNOW?

For entertaining football in 1959-60 United were the team to watch. In 21 away games they scored 49 league goals and conceded 50.

Busby named an unchanged side, after the 2-2 draw at Blackpool. Meanwhile, Chelsea manager Billy Birrell and his team were celebrating their First Division safety, following a 4-1 home victory over Burnley. It had been a strange season for the Londoners. They had beaten United at Stamford Bridge in November and reached the FA Cup semi-final before losing in a replay to Arsenal. All too often, they would collapse against average teams; a recent 1-7 thrashing at Villa Park being a good example. In Roy Bentley and 19-year-old Bobby Smith, they boasted one of the best strike-forces in the division, but the defence had too many off-days. United still harboured memories of the Cup defeat in 1950, but on paper had little to fear against a side who had not won at Old Trafford since 1920.

With so much at stake, United started nervously. Even when Stan Pearson netted in the 23rd minute with a 25-yard shot, the side did not look comfortable. Only when the killer second goal arrived just before half-time did the points seem assured. Johnny Carey strode upfield and let fly with his left foot from 30 yards. The ball soared past goalkeeper Robertson and hit the back of the net so hard it bounced out to the penalty spot with Robertson still unmoved. The crowd's ovation lasted several minutes: they recognised the great captain's role on a triumphant night in the club's history. Half-time reports that Arsenal were 0-2 down at the Hawthorns only confirmed to everyone that United were champions.

When Henry Cockburn's shot flew in off McKnight's body for the third goal, little Henry's leap for joy said it all. There could and should have been further goals, so superior were United to their opponents. Attention now focused on the scoreboard, where updates from the Arsenal game were being posted.

Meanwhile, Chelsea goalie Bill Robertson grabbed Byrne's ankles, but Byrne missed the ensuing penalty. At the final whistle, the loudspeaker relayed the news from West Bromwich – Arsenal had lost. The Chelsea players magnanimously congratulated their opponents. The crowd invaded the pitch as the players dashed for the tunnel. Minutes later the champions were quaffing champagne in the communal bath. Before long, congratulatory telegrams were received from Arsenal's manager Tom Whittaker and captain Joe Mercer.

CHAPTER THREE

EMERGENCE OF THE BABES (1952-55)

LEAGUE DIVISION 1	**1952-53**
Division 1	Eighth
FA Cup	Fifth round

It is not unusual for champions to quickly go off the boil. In 1938, for example, Manchester City were relegated twelve months after winning the title. After the euphoria, it is hard to re-motivate, and players suffer the equivalent of a hangover. By mid-October relegation was on the cards, but Busby implemented changes – including the blooding of several 'babes' – that ensured United rallied to finish eighth.

With eleven games played, United had lost six and won two. They were kept off the bottom rung only by neighbours City, who had made an even worse start – irrespective of the fact that they had inflicted their first post-War victory over the Reds.

United's problems were manifold. First, goalkeeper Reg Allen's injuries meant he played only twice, the second time in a 2-6 thumping at Wolves, which many said shattered his confidence so much that he never played for United again. Young Ray Wood did his best, but ultimately Busby plumped for his old faithful, Jack Crompton, whose presence in goal steadied the defence through the autumn. Second, Rowley's goals dried up, and a long absence through injury saw John Aston reinstated at centre-forward with mixed results. Third, and crucially, several of the 'old guard' were on the downhill slope. Carey looked leg-weary, Cockburn could not shake off bronchitis, and his pace suffered. And while Pearson scored sixteen goals, he was not as consistent as he once was.

Confidence improved dramatically, once a 5-0 win at Preston lifted United out of the drop zone, and Busby felt free to experiment. By Christmas he had called upon 24 different players. Reserves Frank Clempson, Don Gibson, Harry McShane and Ernie Bond were given a chance. From the youth set-up, Irish winger Jackie Scott, centre-half Mark Jones, centre-forward Eddie Lewis and wing-half Jeff Whitefoot had varying degrees of success. Seventeen-year-old Lewis enjoyed a dream debut, scoring in a 1-3 defeat at West Brom, and by the end of the season had scored seven goals in ten starts.

DID YOU KNOW?

United goalkeeper Reg Allen spent three years in a Japanese prisoner-of-war camp in World War Two.

Lewis was just one of a unique bunch of youngsters growing up fast at Old Trafford. Whilst the first team struggled, Busby's youth team excited gasps of admiration. No sooner did they start to break into the first team than the press latched onto the nickname 'Busby Babes'. A week after Lewis, Busby unveiled two more 17-year-olds – left-winger David Pegg and inside-forward John Doherty – in a 3-2 home win over Middlesbrough. At Anfield, the 20-year-old (almost a veteran in this nappy-clad team) full-back Bill Foulkes was blooded in direct opposition to the legendary Billy Liddell and accounted himself well. Lewis, Foulkes and Doherty were used sparingly, but Pegg quickly became a fixture on the wing.

The name on everybody's lips, however, was Duncan Edwards. United had signed the Dudley-born youngster in 1952 after his outstanding displays for England schoolboys, when his sheer physical strength had bludgeoned the opposition. When only fifteen he had played in a public trial and all those present predicted a glittering career for the young wing-half. He made his debut, aged sixteen, in a 1-4 home defeat by Cardiff at Easter and did not disgrace himself.

Fourteen games from October to mid-January brought only one defeat. United were up into the top six. The League title was not yet beyond them, and in the Cup Isthmian League Walthamstow Avenue would not impede further progress.

Bolton ended United's eight-game unbeaten run at a gloomy Burnden Park in front of 46,000. FA Cup dreams were extinguished at Second Division Everton, and successive league losses to Wolves (0-3 at home) and at Stoke further dashed championship hopes. Jack Rowley returned from injury in February and celebrated with a brace in a 3-1 home win over Aston Villa, his first home goals of the season. Rowley, too, was no longer as nimble as he once was, and in early March Busby paid £30,000 for Barnsley's No 9, Tommy Taylor. With Rowley moving to inside-right, Taylor debuted by netting twice in a 5-2 demolition of high-flying Preston in front of the biggest crowd of the season – 54,000.

With little at stake, the season fizzled out. That gave Busby the opportunity of blooding Dennis Viollet, a Manchester-born 19-year-old former England schoolboy. Viollet impressed in a 2-1 win at

Newcastle, in which Taylor's two goals brought his tally to seven in eight games, and United fielded their sixth goalkeeper of the season. With all three senior goalies injured, amateur Les Olive – the club's assistant secretary – took over and earned rave reports. Two outfield players also pulled on the green jersey during the season. At home to Bolton, Reg Allen broke a finger and Jack Rowley took over. At Sunderland in February, Jack Crompton went down with flu on the morning of the game. It was too late to despatch a replacement, so Johnny Carey donned the green jersey in a 2-2 draw.

On the final day, United crashed to their worst defeat since the War, 0-5 at Middlesbrough. It was the first time the Teesside club had beaten United in thirteen matches. It was a sad end to Carey's playing career – he shortly became manager at Blackburn.

New signings Tommy Taylor and Johnny Berry had both settled in, and were rewarded with international caps on England's summer tour of South America.

United's eighth place was their lowest post-War finish, but it had been a season of transition. Nine youngsters had been given their debuts as the great side of 1948 began to be dismantled. Duncan Edwards played just one first-team game but helped United win the newly inaugurated FA Youth Cup. Early in the season, after Busby had faced criticism at the club's AGM, he had boasted of £200,000-worth of talent in the reserve and youth teams. He hoped a good run in the new competition would substantiate his claims and he was proved correct.

United reached the two-legged Youth Cup final, where they faced Wolves. Before an enthralled 21,000 Old Trafford crowd, United won the first leg 7-1. They then drew 2-2 at Molineux in the return. Only Pegg, Edwards and Lewis of the victorious side had first-team experience, but others such as Albert Scanlon, Eddie Colman and Liam Whelan, would not be far behind them.

Match of the Season 1952-53

Walthamstow Avenue 2 United 5

FA Cup, 4th round replay, 5 February 1953

A squeaky 1-0 win at Millwall in the third round set up a home tie with crack East London amateurs Walthamstow Avenue, top of the Isthmian League. Nine months earlier a 100,000 Wembley crowd had watched them lift the FA Amateur Cup for the first time. Their team boasted two personalities in England cricketer Trevor Bailey and England amateur's centre-forward Jim Lewis, plus three other amateur internationals in Stratton, Young and Saunders.

At Old Trafford the Isthmian Leaguers put up a brave rearguard action with goalkeeper Gerula the hero, so much so that at the end the 1,000 Avenue fans chaired him off the field. Eddie Lewis had scored his sixth goal in seven United games just before half-time, heading in Rowley's cross. Walthamstow, in their blue and white hooped shirts, had only two shots all game, but in one of them Jim Lewis scored from Harper's free-kick.

The result caught the attention of the national press and the replay was arranged for Highbury on the Thursday afternoon. Many rubbed their hands at the prospect of a major giant-killing.

A 2pm start meant many Londoners quit work at lunchtime to converge on Highbury, which was unprepared for the numbers demanding admission. It was later estimated that 30,000 entered the ground *after* the kick-off, with many missing United's first four goals.

That salvo, inside the first half-hour, brought three goals in a five-minute spell. Rowley crossed from the right for Pearson to nod into the far corner; Eddie Lewis netted with his left foot following Berry's corner; and Carey and Pearson sent Rowley through for the third. When Stratton nudged Pearson in the air, Byrne added a fourth from the spot.

The amateurs refused to fold, and a minute before the interval Jim Lewis was floored by Chilton and scored from the penalty spot.

With half an hour remaining, Walthamstow's Lewis scored again, guiding home Stratton's free-kick, and United were wobbling. Twice the amateurs came close to a third: Lewis fired over from twenty yards and Cockburn blocked Bailey's shot on the line. But the next goal fell to United, Gerula misjudging a swirling cross from Rowley under his crossbar.

LEAGUE DIVISION 1	**1953-54**
Division 1	Fourth
FA Cup	Third round

The summer of 1953 was a memorable one for the whole country. The Queen was crowned in June, on the day it was disclosed that Mount Everest had been climbed by Edmund Hillary and Sherpa Tensing. Legendary jockey Gordon Richards finally won the Derby, and Stan Matthews got his FA Cup winners' medal. England's cricketers regained the Ashes in spectacular fashion at the Oval.

Manchester United made their worst start since 1930 – four draws and four defeats in eight games. Carey had gone, new skipper Stan Pearson was injured on the opening day, and Matt Busby was feeling the heat. Eight goals were shipped in the first three games, whereupon Busby axed Crompton, Gibson and Pegg in favour of Ray Wood, Tom McNulty and Jeff Whitefoot. Bill Foulkes shortly replaced Aston at right-back and even with the return of Pearson results improved only marginally.

With the glut of youthful talent on the books, no close-season signings had been necessary, but Reg Allen and Johnnie Downie left to join Altrincham and Luton respectively.

In late October, United travelled north for a friendly with Kilmarnock. Pearson and Jack Rowley made way for Dennis Viollet and Jackie Blanchflower. United won 3-0 but a broken jaw for Henry Cockburn took the gloss off the result. Three days later, at third-placed Huddersfield, Busby retained Viollet and Blanchflower, and filled Cockburn's place with Duncan Edwards. The 'new look' side contained seven players aged 21 or under, and though the game ended goalless Busby was satisfied by the performances of the young guns in what was later recognised as a pivotal game. The same eleven held Arsenal to a 2-2 draw, demolished Cardiff 6-1 at Ninian Park, and humbled Blackpool 4-1. The 'Busby Babes' had arrived.

Allenby Chilton had assumed the captaincy from Pearson and ushered the young team through the transformational period with inspiration and panache. The other old hand, Jack Rowley – who retained his left-wing place against the challenge of Pegg – provided a wise head among the eager young forwards.

Defeat at Chelsea in December was the first for two months and provided a lesson. The Londoners set out to intimidate the kids and succeeded. Busby's doubts about playing too many youngsters resurfaced, but Jimmy Murphy convinced him to stick to his instincts. The outcome – four wins over Christmas to lift United into the top six.

It was asking much to expect consistency from such a young side, and January saw the team exit the FA Cup after a 3-5 thriller in the Burnley mud. Two weeks later Bolton's wily veterans won 5-1 at Old Trafford, but Busby was by now committed to his course. The message was clear to the United old-timers. In February, Stan Pearson was transferred to Bury. Cockburn, resigned to life in the shadow of Edwards, asked for a move, as did McShane and McNulty. Aston struggled to recover from his shoulder injury, and once fit could not displace Foulkes at right-back. Instead, he took over from the injured Tommy Taylor at No 9 for the final few games. In the summer of 1954 Aston was diagnosed with tuberculosis and spent seventeen months in a sanatorium. Aged 33 his playing career was over and he would later join the coaching staff.

Duncan Edwards, Dennis Viollet and Jackie Blanchflower were revelations. After a dozen first-team games, 17-year-old Edwards was selected for the England Under-23s, along with Ray Wood and Jeff Whitefoot. Before the end of the season he was in the England B team with many commentators suggesting he should be in the full international side. A sub-standard performance in a 1-3 defeat at Arsenal, when the selectors were watching, probably cost him the distinction of being the youngest England international of all time.

The frail-looking Viollet was a gifted inside-forward with electric pace. He scored eleven goals in 29 games after displacing Pearson and always seemed to be in the right place at the right time. He was rewarded with a game for 'Young England' in the annual fixture against 'Old England' on Cup final eve.

Blanchflower, brother of Northern Irish star Danny, lacked pace but was a battler whose shooting left goalkeepers with stinging fingers. He notched thirteen goals and, with Tommy Taylor bagging 22, United were hardly lacking in the goalscoring department.

Roger Byrne, now settled at left-back after his virtuoso performances on the left-wing, won his first England cap in April against Scotland, and kept that position throughout the disappointing World Cup finals in Switzerland. Taylor recovered from his end-of-season injury to win two caps during the World Cup, but was far from fully fit and failed to make an impression. The press made strong cases for the inclusion of Johnny Berry, Ray Wood and Allenby Chilton in the England squad, but all three were to be disappointed.

DID YOU KNOW?

Manchester United's 'Babes' won the FA Youth Cup in each of the first five seasons of the competition.

It had been a tumultuous season for English football. In November the great Hungarians had overwhelmed England 6-3 at Wembley. Seven months later, during the warm up for the World Cup, Hungary won 7-1. No United players took part in either game, but the backlash would benefit their young stars, as the selectors jettisoned the old guard in an effort to catch up with Continental sides who had overtaken England since the War.

The domestic season ended with United fourth, earning 'talent' money, an extra bonus paid to the top four clubs. United finished nine points adrift of the champions, Wolves, but had the satisfaction of beating Stan Cullis's men in a tight game in March.

The youth team retained the FA Youth Cup, with Bobby Charlton, Wilf McGuinness and Shay Brennan joining Edwards, Colman and Pegg. Wolverhapton were again beaten in the final, this time 5-4 on aggregate.

Match of the Season 1953-54

United 4 Blackpool 1

Division One, 21 November 1953

In the autumn of 1953 Blackpool were arguably the strongest side in England. They had won the FA Cup the previous May, with Stan Matthews finally gaining his first winners medal. Their sluggish start to the league campaign had been cured by four successive victories, including a 4-1 thumping of pace-setters West Brom, which had lifted the Seasiders into the top six. Four of Blackpool's finest – Matthews, Stan Mortensen, Ernie Taylor and captain Harry Johnston – would play for England against Hungary four days after visiting Old Trafford, with a fifth, Tommy Garrett, a reserve. In addition, George Farm, Hugh Kelly and Allan Brown were either in or on the verge of the Scotland team.

Matthews was rested for this game but the rest of Blackpool's England contingent endured a taste of what awaited them against the Magyars at Wembley. At a fog-shrouded Old Trafford, Busby's boys ripped them apart.

DID YOU KNOW?

In 1946, United skipper Johnny Carey played against England twice within three days – for Northern Ireland (losing 2-7) and then the Republic of Ireland (0-1).

Busby selected an unchanged side for the fourth game running, following a 6-1 demolition of Cardiff the previous Saturday. Seven of the side were no older than 21. The old hands, Chilton and Rowley, appeared revitalised by the inclusion of the babes and Rowley was happy to switch to the left flank to allow Tommy Taylor to lead the line. This game would give everyone an opportunity to compare Taylor to Stan Mortensen, his main rival for the England No 9 shirt. Taylor had managed just six goals to date, whilst Mortensen headed the division's scoring list with fifteen.

Despite Matthews' absence, over 51,000 – the biggest Old Trafford attendance of the season – saw United pin their opponents in their own half. But it was Blackpool who took the lead when South African left-winger Bill Perry latched onto Garrett's clearance, waltzed around Foulkes, and finished with a shot that seemed to take Wood by surprise. Six minutes later Taylor equalised with a header from Rowley's cross after Berry had beaten six men in a jinking crossfield run.

Two more goals arrived before half-time. While Blackpool defender Fenton was off the field injured, United made their numerical superiority tell. First, Viollet took a pass from Rowley, evaded Johnston's lunge, and slammed the ball home. No sooner had Blackpool kicked off than Taylor finished off another slick move.

Seven minutes into the second half, Taylor completed his first United hat-trick, when Farm could only parry Berry's shot and Taylor won the race for the loose ball.

United's other heroes were the wing-halves, Jeff Whitefoot and Duncan Edwards. Edwards had to mark inside-forward Ernie Taylor, and despite Taylor having the upper hand early on, thereafter the 17-year-old Edwards dominated the tussle.

Blackpool were hampered by Fenton's leg injury, which forced him to limp on the wing for the second half, but this was a day when the young babes of United were unstoppable.

LEAGUE DIVISION 1	**1954-55**
Division 1	Fifth
FA Cup	Fourth round

Matt Busby had been satisfied with his young team's performances in the second half of the previous season, and as the 1954-55 season approached intuitively knew his strongest eleven. Tommy Taylor and Roger Byrne returned from England's World Cup campaign in Switzerland. Byrne had been one of few successes, whereas Taylor's role as a dual centre-forward with Bolton's Nat Lofthouse had not brought out the best in the semi-fit United leader. Injury forced Taylor to miss the start of the campaign and 22-year-old Welshman Colin Webster deputised. Webster, a winger, had made only one previous appearance, but now scored four goals in six games.

The rest of the side picked itself and United dazzled for the first three months. Despite losing at home to Portsmouth on the opening day, five straight victories sent them to the top of the League. The critical London press resorted to superlatives after a 2-0 win at White Hart Lane, with Edwards tipped for a place in the England team.

Defeat in the Manchester derby by a resurgent City, with Don Revie pulling strings as a Hungarian-style deep lying centre-forward, was United's first reverse in nine games, but a week later the wheels came off at Molineux.

The team's winning ways meant more international call-ups. Wood, Foulkes, Byrne (all England) and Blanchflower (Northern Ireland) were missing as Wolves ran riot in the last twenty minutes to win 4-2. Two more youngsters, Ian Greaves and Paddy Kennedy, filled the vacancies at full-back – the latter was never spotted again – and veterans Jack Crompton and Henry Cockburn came in for Wood and Blanchflower. It was to be Cockburn's last first-team game, and the fourth goal was credited to him; two weeks later he was sold to Bury, thus ending a distinguished career at Old Trafford.

Tommy Taylor was soon fit and hitting the headlines with his goalscoring exploits. He scored nine in four games in October, including four in a 5-2 win over Cardiff and two at Chelsea a week later. United's main problem, in a season where there was no outstanding league sides, was consistency. The home form after Christmas was a mystery. Having gone unbeaten since the opening day, the Reds now lost four out of six, among them a 0-5 reverse in the Manchester derby. Many blamed the heavy pitches, but Busby made no excuses.

DID YOU KNOW?

In April 1953, on account of a crippling injury crisis among their goalkeepers, United were forced to play assistant secretary and amateur goalie Les Olive in two matches.

Don Gibson had displaced Whitefoot at right-half in October, but otherwise the team was unchanged. In February another old favourite departed when 34-year-old Jack Rowley joined Third Division Plymouth as player-manager. There was not just one ready-made replacement for Rowley but two. David Pegg and another youth product, Albert Scanlon, fought over the No 11 shirt.

A month after Rowley's departure, Allenby Chilton joined Grimsby on a similar basis. Chilton, 36, had played 175 consecutive games at centre-half, but like Rowley there was a young starlet, Mark Jones, whom Busby could confidently fill his boots. Chilton's role in helping the development of the Babes was acknowledged by Busby.

Three more youngsters were thrown into the first team during the final weeks of the season. With Jackie Blanchflower injured, another Irishman, Liam Whelan, impressed in a 2-0 win at Preston. Salford-born Geoff Bent deputised at left-back when Roger Byrne was injured. Twenty-one-year-old wing-half Freddie Goodwin earned a call-up for five games when Edwards was absent and never appeared on the losing side.

The departure of Chilton, Cockburn and Rowley meant the transformation from the old to the new was complete. Roger Byrne, the new club captain and England's regular left-back, was maturing into a great defender. Whilst not the best of tacklers, he was quick and clever and could rarely be passed. He dispossessed clinically, and going forward he was as dangerous as most wingers.

Like Johnny Carey beforehand, Byrne projected a definable sense of Manchester United. The new mood, however, was different. As embodied by its captain, the team had a swagger and arrogance, displayed in a world that was changing as youth began to assert itself. In Byrne's case this was demonstrated each time he came up against old-style heroes like Tom Finney and Stan Matthews. Byrne developed a habit of stalking them, never intimidated by their reputation and generally prevailing in his personal tussles.

Apart from Byrne, England caps were at this time in short supply at Old Trafford. Wood and Foulkes were quickly jettisoned, and Taylor – despite netting twenty goals in 30 games – could not oust the tried and tested Nat Lofthouse.

Duncan Edwards, though, enjoyed a memorable season. In November he was playing for the England youth team, but by April he had won his first full cap in a 7-2 win over Scotland at Wembley, becoming the youngest England international of the century at eighteen years and 183 days. Assured displays during the close-season overseas tour cemented his place in the England team alongside luminaries such as Billy Wright, Stan Matthews and Don Revie. He was already being hailed as the most outstanding English footballer of his generation.

Another memorable moment for Edwards came in the New Year's Day fixture against Blackpool at Old Trafford when he scored his first senior goal. Don Davies ('an Old International') in *The Guardian* described it thus:

'Darting forward, he put every ounce of his prodigious strength into a mighty, uninhibited swipe. There was a sharp crack of boot on leather – a veritable detonation, this – and a clearing of the atmosphere by a blurred object, which first soared over Farm's upraised arms then dipped suddenly and passed in under the crossbar. A scene of great commotion followed. Spectators hugged each other, then threw their heads back and brayed their approval. Edwards leaped and gambolled like a soul possessed, until his adoring colleagues fell upon him and pinned him down with their embraces.'

By the season's end Edwards had scored five more goals, after Busby tried him at inside-left. He also netted a hat-trick for England Under-23s as an emergency centre-forward against Scotland.

For the third year running, Edwards was part of the unbeatable FA Youth Cup winning team – he was often pulled out of the first team to ensure the juniors progressed. A strong team, including Bobby Charlton, Eddie Colman and Wilf McGuinness, struggled to beat Chelsea in the semi-final but thrashed West Brom 7-1 over two legs in the final. Many criticised Busby for allowing Edwards, a full cap, to play for the youths, but Busby retorted that he was eligible and desperate to play.

Match of the Season 1954-55

Chelsea 5 United 6

Division One, 16 October 1954

By October 1954, Manchester United were the most talked about club in the country. A month earlier they had wowed the London press corps with a 2-0 win at White Hart Lane, in which 17-year-old Duncan Edwards shone like a beacon.

Chelsea were an enigmatic team and the butt of music-hall jokes. They had been members of the First Division since 1930 but until 1954 had only finished in the top half once. Former Arsenal and England centre-forward Ted Drake had become manager in 1952 and after a close shave with relegation in his first season had rebuilt the side around experienced players like Ron Greenwood, Roy Bentley and Ken Armstrong, with promising youngsters such as Peter Sillett, Bobby Smith and Frank Blunstone blossoming in their company.

In 1953-54 the Blues took three points off United, and a fourteen-game unbeaten run earned a final placing of eighth, their best since 1936. Drake's penchant for amateurs led him to sign the stars of Walthamstow Avenue's 1953 Cup run, Jim Lewis and Derek Saunders. Another, Seamus O'Connell of northern amateurs Bishop Auckland, made his debut in this game.

Chelsea had only lost three league games to date, but too many draws left them back in ninth. O'Connell in place of Stubbs at inside-left was the only change from the side that lost 0-1 at Huddersfield. United were at the time a point behind leaders Sunderland, and fielded the same eleven which beat Cardiff a week earlier.

The first fifteen minutes gave no clues as to the outcome, although both defences looked shaky. Viollet then put United ahead, courtesy of a deflection. Chelsea swept in front when elementary errors let in the amateurs O'Connell and Lewis.

Johnny Berry set up goals for Taylor and Viollet before half-time to restore United's advantage. Within eight minutes of the second half, Berry had created two more goals, for Taylor and Viollet, and at 5-2 the contest looked over.

Chelsea's Ken Armstrong headed in Eric Parson's corner, only for Jackie Blanchflower to reply in kind a minute later. Being three goals in arrears seemed to inspire Chelsea. O'Connell tapped in Chelsea's fourth and then completed his hat-trick when Parson's header came off the bar to his feet. There were still fourteen minutes left and some of the crowd had lost count of the score. In the end, Ray Wood's save from Saunders' free-kick clinched the points for United.

Drake's Chelsea were to be virtually unbeatable in the second half of the season and lifted the title for the first time in the club's history. In a non-vintage season, however, their total of 52 points equalled the lowest ever in a 42-match Division One campaign.

CHAPTER FOUR

THE GLORY YEARS – I (1955-58)

LEAGUE DIVISION 1	**1955-56**
Division 1	Champions
FA Cup	Third round

As the 1955-56 season started, few pundits tipped United for the championship. The consensus was 'you win nothing with kids': they would need another year or two to gain the required experience. Those kids might, however, be a good bet for the FA Cup. The experts were to be proved wrong on all counts as the Busby Babes romped home in the League but exited the FA Cup at the first hurdle to a Second Division side.

With so many talented youngsters, Matt Busby deemed it unnecessary to sign anyone in the summer of 1955. The only transfer activity saw the sale of Busby's son-in-law Don Gibson to Sheffield Wednesday for £8,000. Gibson had been a regular the previous season, but Busby had faith in England Under-23 international Jeff Whitefoot and Salford-born right-half Eddie Colman.

Injuries to Taylor, Berry, Viollet and Edwards hampered the early weeks. After eight games United had lost three, were mid-table and seemed to be fulfilling the experts' predictions. Eddie Lewis and Colin Webster were inadequate replacements for the goal-king Taylor, and Freddie Goodwin could hardly replace man-mountain Edwards – hospitalised with influenza.

Taylor's return in mid-September sparked an upsurge. He netted eleven goals in ten games as United went unbeaten for eight and marched to the top of the table in early November. At home, the team notched six straight wins, but on their travels they were more vulnerable. Only two away wins were recorded before Christmas Eve and the fans questioned United's championship credentials after recent defeats at Bolton and Portsmouth – the latter through conceding two goals in the last two minutes.

Busby tinkered with the line-up. Whitefoot had lost form, and after a first and last appearance by 21-year-old Walter Whitehurst, the diminutive Colman claimed the No 4 shirt and kept it for the next two years. Seventeen-year-old Wilf McGuinness, another Manchester lad, was given two games as Edwards' deputy and starred in a 4-3 win over Wolves. At inside-forward, Viollet's injury gave opportunities to Liam Whelan and the injury-ravaged John Doherty, who later filled in when Blanchflower was injured. On the left wing, David Pegg was back in favour and kept out Albert Scanlon.

Blackpool and Sunderland were United's nearest challengers, but once United went top after beating Birmingham 2-1 in mid-December they stayed there, despite blips at Charlton and Preston after Christmas. After nine 'derby' games without a win, the hoodoo was broken at Old Trafford on New Year's Eve. Interest in the game was so enormous that an estimated 15,000 fans were locked out.

A shock 0-4 defeat at Bristol Rovers ended United's involvement in the FA Cup, but at least – in that tired expression – it allowed the team to concentrate on the title race. Seven league wins out of eight put United six points clear by early March. The team seemed to relish the ice and snow that blighted the first two months of 1956, and the nimble-footed youngsters seemed to skate over the treacherous surfaces like ballet dancers. United completed the double over Stan Cullis's Wolves and hammered defending champions Chelsea 4-2 at Stamford Bridge. The wonderful home record meant only three sides would escape with so much as a draw.

United travelled to Newcastle on Easter Monday needing a win for the title, but the Magpies held the Reds 0-0. Five days later United would host second-placed Blackpool, the only side who could overhaul them. Busby missed the game because of his mother-in-law's death in Scotland.

Despite torrential rain, a crowd of 62,522 – Old Trafford's biggest post-War attendance – packed in to witness the championship confrontation. After 90 seconds the United fans were silenced when the evergreen Stan Matthews set up Dave Durie's goal. By half-time the Seasiders still led 1-0. Early in the second period Taylor went off for treatment to a head injury and whilst he was absent United won a penalty, converted by Berry. With ten minutes remaining, the winger created the second goal for Taylor. United were champions and a pitch invasion ensued. A win and a draw from their remaining two games extended United's unbeaten run to fourteen games. This left them eleven points clear of second-placed Blackpool and equalled the record margin of success. The trophy was presented at the final home game, against Portsmouth, and an open-topped bus ride through the crowded streets of Manchester preceded a civic reception.

DID YOU KNOW?

Jimmy Delaney holds the unique record of winning Cup winners' medals in England (with United), Scotland (Celtic) and – aged 40 – in Northern Ireland (Derry City).

United had proved themselves to be one of the strongest teams of the English post-War era, playing with determination and ability which, blended with the brashness of youth, made them irresistible. Busby's philosophy of trying to play football at all times was unchanged from the day he took over the club. Many teams tried to kick United out of their stride, but the players always let their football do the talking.

With Ray Wood in goal, Busby possessed a goalkeeper both agile and reliable. In front of him were two other internationals, Byrne and Foulkes – who in January was replaced by another outstanding newcomer, Ian Greaves. The half-back line of Colman, Jones and Edwards picked itself, once Colman arrived on the scene. Of the five forwards (United at this time played a tradition WM formation), Berry, Taylor, Viollet and Pegg were virtually ever-present, whilst Whelan and Doherty shared the No 8 duties in Blanchflower's absence. Taylor scored 25 goals, leading the line with power and finesse. His partner, Viollet, who scored twenty, was deadly when the openings materialised. The wingers Berry and Pegg were creators of the highest quality. The average age of the team was 22.

Wood, Byrne, Edwards, Taylor and Berry all won full caps for England, whilst Pegg and Viollet earned Under-23 honours. Blanchflower and Whelan also won full caps for their countries in what was an extraordinary season for the Reds. Strangely, no United player appeared in the top seven in the Footballer of the Year poll, which Blackpool's Stan Matthews topped.

Success for United's reserves in the Central League, together with that of the youth team in the FA Youth Cup – for the fourth successive year – reminded rivals how difficult it would be to halt United in the near future. Youngsters like Bobby Charlton, Alex Dawson and Mark Pearson would be knocking on the first-team door, making an already powerful team even stronger.

United's next challenge, however, would be in the European Cup. In the competition's inaugural season, champions Chelsea had been pressurised by the football authorities not to enter. Busby, however, had no intention of taking instructions in this way and began to prepare for European football.

Match of the Season 1955-56

United 4 Wolverhampton 3

Division One, 8 October 1955

Wolverhampton Wanderers were arguably one of the top sides in Europe in the period just before the European Cup was inaugurated in 1956. They had been English champions in 1954 and would have retained their title in 1955 but for a calamitous finish, which saw them squander a five-point lead over Chelsea in the last eleven games.

Manager Stan Cullis had recognised the importance that European football would play, inviting top Continental sides to Molineux for floodlit friendlies. Spartak Moscow and Honved – the Hungarian Army side brimming with internationals who had twice humiliated England in 1953 – were beaten by Wolves in front of capacity crowds and a national TV audience.

Although Cullis's team arrived at Old Trafford in eleventh place, it was a false position. Wolves had played two games fewer and were only two points behind fourth-placed United. Their nine games had seen them score 29 goals, nine of them at Cardiff and seven at home to Manchester City, with ace striker Roy Swinbourne notching fourteen. The Wolves team was virtually unchanged for the last two years, apart from at left-half, where tough tackling Eddie Clamp had taken over from Ron Flowers.

For Busby, Bill Foulkes failed to obtain leave from National Service, Geoff Bent, who had deputised for Byrne – on England duty the previous week – continued, and Byrne played at right-back. Seventeen-year-old Wilf McGuinness was given his debut at left-half and John Doherty stood in for the injured Blanchflower.

Games between these two clubs were generally rip-roaring affairs and this was no exception. Wolves had the upper hand in a pulsating first half played in glorious autumn sunshine and were unlucky to go in at half-time a goal down. Four minutes before the break David Pegg's shot had been deflected past goalkeeper Bert Williams by England captain Billy Wright.

United looked stronger in the early exchanges of the second half but Wolves soaked up the pressure and twice caught United napping. First, Jimmy Mullen's corner was headed in by the amateur Bill Slater – on the day the best player on the park – then, seven minutes later, Swinbourne swept home a clever pass from Peter Broadbent.

DID YOU KNOW?

On 30 November 1957, against Tottenham Hotspur, Matt Busby sent out a United side comprising eleven home-grown players for the first time.

Trailing 1-2, United were up against it, but equalised when Taylor's shot swerved in the air, struck a bemused Williams on the head, and rolled into the net. No wonder the England goalkeeper threw his cap into the net in disgust.

Three minutes later the snarling Wolves went ahead again, as Ray Wood failed to collect a Wilshaw cross and Swinbourne kneed the ball past him. United's unbeaten home record now looked likely to fall, but with six minutes left Byrne swung over a free-kick from the right and Doherty somehow swept the ball home.

Four minutes later United completed their dramatic comeback. Berry's curling corner-kick was headed on by Mark Jones, and put away by Taylor in a goalmouth melee. Many spectators thought Jones had scored but Taylor later claimed the goal, capping a wonderful day for the centre-forward who had given his England captain Wright such a torrid time. Afterwards, the ever-sporting Wright praised United's fitness and stamina – attributes normally associated with Wolves – but now allied to United's skill and speed.

LEAGUE DIVISION 1	**1956-57**
Division 1	Champions
FA Cup	Runners-Up
European Cup	Semi-finals

Season 1956-57 resumed with United, for once, clicking quickly into gear, recording ten victories in an unbeaten first twelve games. The rest of the First Division could only look on in awe as United extended their unbeaten run to 26 games in total, scoring 32 goals of which Viollet netted ten and Whelan nine.

The side was unchanged for nine games until Mark Jones's injury allowed Crewe-born Ronnie Cope a debut in a 2-1 win at Arsenal. A week later, internationals meant Byrne, Edwards and Taylor missed the home game with Charlton. One of the deputies, 18-year-old Bobby Charlton, celebrated his debut with two goals in a 4-2 win.

In the meantime, the first European Cup had commenced, to the annoyance of the Football League. Busby was anxious to ensure that the extra fixtures did not affect United's league form, which would otherwise have provided ammunition to the critics. Following their first trip to the Continent – a 2-0 midweek win in Brussels against Anderlecht – United returned to thrash Sheffield Wednesday 4-1 on the Saturday.

The return with Anderlecht was played under floodlights at Maine Road, as were United's next two European Cup-ties. Old Trafford was committed to installing lights, but they would not be ready for use until later in the season. On a miserably wet night, 43,000 fans roared United to a record 10-0 win over the Belgian champions.

In the second round, United were paired with West Germany's Borussia Dortmund. After a first half which saw United take a 3-0 lead, the Germans kept the tie open with two late goals. Three days later the 26-match unbeaten league run was ended by Everton, 5-2 winners at Old Trafford. The result also wrecked a 32-match unbeaten home run, extending back to March 1955, when ironically Everton had also been the visitors.

United suffered only two more defeats before the end of the year – at Bolton and Birmingham – and progressed to the third round of the European Cup by virtue of a hard-earned 0-0 draw in Dortmund. Domestically, the goals continued to flow and Christmas victories over Cardiff and Portsmouth consolidated United's lead at the top of Division One.

DID YOU KNOW?

Between 1951 and 1955, Allenby Chilton made 175 consecutive League and Cup United appearances. That constituted a club record until beaten by Steve Coppell.

The games came thick and fast in the New Year, but Busby resisted the opportunity to rest players and fielded his strongest eleven at every opportunity. Five league wins out of six saw 25 more goals scored. The only blip was a defeat at Hillsborough, the Reds' first post-War defeat there, coming just three days after the long, tiring but satisfying trip to Bilbao. Manchester City were thumped 4-2 at Maine Road and in-form Arsenal were swatted 6-2.

The FA Cup trail had started at Hartlepool, where a record crowd saw the home team recover from 0-3, only to lose in a seven-goal thriller. Wrexham were beaten 5-0 in Wales, Everton 1-0 at Old Trafford, and Third Division giant-killers Bournemouth 2-1 at Dean Court. The south coast club, managed by Freddie Cox – a noted Cup-hunter in his Arsenal days – had knocked out Wolves and Spurs on the way to the quarter-finals. United looked set to join their list of victims when the Cherries took the lead against ten men, Jones having gone off with a leg injury. However, Duncan Edwards, switching to centre-half, proved almost a team in himself, and two goals by Berry – the second a dubious penalty – put United into the semi-finals.

A week into March and the treble was still on, but suddenly the doubts started creeping in. In the run up to the FA Cup semi-final at Hillsborough, vital points were dropped to Aston Villa and Wolves, but United booked their appointment at Wembley by brushing aside Birmingham. Again Berry found the net, this time against his former club, who had reached the final the previous year. Bobby Charlton, deputising for the injured Viollet, scored the other goal, his tenth in ten games. Jones's injury at Bournemouth was more serious than first thought and Blanchflower grabbed the opportunity and put in some classy performances as a stand-in stopper.

Three days after Hillsborough, United's bogey side, Bolton, officially opened the Old Trafford floodlights but the party went flat with the Trotters going home with both points.

The next hurdle lay in Madrid, where United faced defending champions Real in the first leg of the semi-final in front of a 125,000 crowd. Real won 3-1 but displayed an ugly, cynical aspect at the Bernabeu Stadium. Tommy Taylor was especially singled out for harsh treatment. Argentinian forward Di Stefano scored the second goal, and although Taylor pulled a goal back, a late Mateos effort gave Real a handsome advantage for the second leg.

United flew home to face a fixture pile-up which required four games in the fourteen days. Taylor's return from injury spurred the side to wins at Luton and Burnley, and on Easter Saturday Sunderland were slaughtered 4-0. United were champions.

Busby could therefore rest nine players against Burnley on Easter Monday, but his team still won 2-0, with young Alex Dawson scoring on his debut. United's final points total – 64 – was the highest in the First Division since 1931, when Arsenal accumulated 66.

Real arrived in Manchester for Old Trafford's first ever European Cup-tie and the noise generated by 65,000 United fans was almost as intimidating as twice that number in the Bernabeu. Busby hoped that United could repeat the feat achieved against Bilbao, but Real were in a different class and cruised into a 2-0 lead with goals from French international Raymond Kopa and Di Stefano. This left United 1-5 down and facing a hopeless task. Unfortunately, Real were much too wise for the young Busby Babes. In the second half, however, inspired by Tommy Taylor's swashbuckling performance, United levelled the scores on the night with goals from Taylor and Charlton, but it was all in vain. United's first European expedition was over.

Jones and Viollet were unable to recover from their injuries, so Busby stuck with the same side against Aston Villa at Wembley ten days later. United were clear favourites, having scored 141 goals in all competitions – in the process becoming the first Division One side since Manchester City in 1936-37 to score 100 league goals in a season. As for Villa, they were a mid-table side whose strength was in defence. The pundits said luck would have to intervene for Villa to stop the Reds becoming the first side in the twentieth century to win the double. And luck did intervene.

With six minutes gone, the Wembley injury jinx struck when Ray Wood was charged by Villa's McParland. His cheekbone fractured, the dazed Wood returned later to 'play' on the wing. Blanchflower went in goal but could do nothing about McParland's two second-half goals as Villa made their numerical superiority tell. In a last gamble, Busby sent Wood back into goal and pushed Edwards into attack. Taylor headed in Edwards' corner and the Reds forced five corners but all was in vain. United's 'double dream' lay in ruins.

United's success meant Byrne, Edwards and Taylor were regulars in an England team preparing for the World Cup in Sweden. David

Pegg also won his first cap. Edwards was second in the Footballer of the Year award behind Tom Finney. Byrne was fourth.

Match of the Season 1956-57

United 3 Athletic Bilbao 0

European Cup, quarter-final, 2nd leg, 6 February 1957

Frank Taylor of the *News Chronicle* described this as the greatest night Manchester soccer fans had ever seen. Demand for tickets led Walter Crickmer, United's secretary, to announce that he could have sold between 300,000 and 400,000 tickets for the tie.

The first leg had been played in wintry conditions, with the soggy San Mames pitch described by Roger Byrne as the worst he had ever seen. Athletic Bilbao, who had lost only one home game in three years, had eliminated the Hungarians of Honved in the previous round. They now led 3-0 at half-time, but Taylor and Viollet closed the deficit. Bilbao scored two more goals before Liam Whelan made it 5-3 five minutes from time, finishing off a snaking 40-yard run.

Looking ahead to the second leg at Maine Road, Ferdinand Daucik, the Czech manager of Bilbao, warned that no one ever scored three against his team. His confidence seemed justified in a frustrating first half. The Reds were too eager, missed a couple of early chances, and Bilbao's experienced players slowed the game down.

Three minutes before the interval Edwards' shot rebounded off Garay, the Bilbao defender, for Viollet to net. After 70 minutes Taylor at last found a way past Garay. A swerve to the right made space for a left-foot shot that hit a post. A minute later Taylor did it again. This time the ball went just inside the upright.

A third-match replay in Paris now looked likely, but five minutes from time Taylor squared the ball to Berry, whose right foot did the rest. All United had to do was play out time, but they almost let it slip when a sloppy back-pass from Foulkes was almost missed by Wood. The goalkeeper grabbed the ball just in time.

Daily Express reporter Henry Rose, who would die at Munich, wrote: 'My hands are trembling as I write. My heart still pounds. And a few hours have passed since, with 65,000 other lucky people, I saw the greatest soccer victory in history, ninety minutes of tremendous thrill and excitement that will live for ever in the memory. Salute to the eleven red shirted heroes of Manchester United.'

LEAGUE DIVISION 1	**1957-58**
Division 1	Ninth
FA Cup	Runners-Up
European Cup	Semi-finals

Following United's two successive League championships, the bookmakers were reluctant to take bets on three in a row. Busby had built the best post-War English football team and had yet more young starlets banging on the door. Important though the European Cup would later become, winning three titles in a row – as Herbert Chapman's Huddersfield and Arsenal had done before the War – was Busby's holy grail. His young team were wiser for having chased the 'treble' in 1956-57, and Busby felt with another twelve months experience there was no limit to what they could achieve.

Before the season started, however, the club had to fend off Italian interest in Tommy Taylor and Matt Busby. Impressed by Juventus's swoop for Leeds' John Charles – for a British record fee of £65,000 – Inter Milan made overtures to Taylor. Busby fumed, denying that a similar fee could prise away his centre-forward. Taylor was sent into hiding and Busby announced he was going nowhere. By all accounts Taylor wanted to go, but the club, in those days, had total control of players' contracts.

Within weeks, the speculation switched to Busby and the Italian Federation's desire to appoint him as their national coach. Busby said no, as he had the previous year when Real Madrid tried to lure him with a £100,000 a year salary.

On the pitch, Busby named an unchanged side for the first nine league games and the team went unbeaten for the first six. There were handsome wins at Leicester (3-0) and Blackpool (4-1), and at home to Everton (3-0), Manchester City (4-1) and Leeds (5-0). Then things went wrong. United lost three of their next four games – 0-4 at Bolton, 1-2 at home to Blackpool, and 1-3 at Wolves, although United did have four players out with flu.

For a few weeks the champions lost their focus and Wolves took over at the top. Busby refused to panic during a fraught autumn. The composition of his young side was always changing and he was never afraid of making tough decisions. His ambitions seemed focused on horizons way beyond anyone else's. In October, John Doherty was sold to Leicester and soon afterwards Jeff Whitefoot joined Grimsby. Eddie Colman was rested for three games after being laid low by flu, and responded by demanding a transfer. Once Colman was back in, replacing Freddie Goodwin, it was Goodwin who wanted a move.

Following further home defeats, to Tottenham and Chelsea, Busby acted. For the first time in almost five years he paid for an incoming player. £25,000 – a world record fee for a goalkeeper – secured the signature of Doncaster's Northern Ireland international Harry Gregg. Gregg debuted at home to Leicester, with four players dropped. Gregg replaced Ray Wood, Kenny Morgans – an 18-year-old from the youth team – replaced Johnny Berry, Bobby Charlton came in for Liam Whelan, and Albert Scanlon for David Pegg. Leicester were thumped 4-0, Charlton and Scanlon found the net, and United strung together an unbeaten sequence of seven games to storm back into the title race.

United had progressed in the European Cup, eliminating on aggregate Irish champions Shamrock Rovers 9-2 and Dukla Prague 3-1. In mid-January a 2-1 home win over Red Star set the scene for a tough second leg in Belgrade in early February.

In the FA Cup, Workington led the Reds 1-0 at half-time on an icy Cumberland pitch, but a Viollet hat-trick ensured that United went through. Ipswich were similarly swatted in round four. In the league, Bolton were thrashed 7-2, Charlton netting a hat-trick, and Arsenal were beaten 5-4 at Highbury. Those twelve goals in two games left United third, six points behind leaders Wolves, but Cullis's team were due at Old Trafford three days after the trip to Yugoslavia.

In Belgrade, United looked home and dry at half-time, leading 3-0, and 5-1 overall. Red Star stormed back to level at 3-3 but United held out in a niggly game to progress to the semi-finals for the second successive season.

The BEA Elizabethan aircraft, which carried the United team, officials and journalists, stopped to refuel at snowbound Munich on the way home. On its third attempt to take off, the plane careered off the runway. In one instant, the greatest team in Britain was wiped out. Roger Byrne, Geoff Bent, Eddie Colman, Mark Jones, Duncan Edwards, David Pegg, Liam Whelan and Tommy Taylor lost their lives, as did secretary Walter Crickmer, trainer Tom Curry, and coach Bert Whalley. Duncan Edwards lingered for fourteen days after the crash before succumbing. Matt Busby lived. For a while he was unaware of the fate of his team. To survive his physical injuries was one thing, but to overcome the mental pain, and pledge to rebuild Manchester United, quite another.

DID YOU KNOW?

Between February 1938 and November 1957, United stayed unbeaten in 47 home league games against London opponents.

In Jimmy Murphy, United had the man to hold the bridge while Busby recuperated in a Munich hospital. Murphy knew how Busby operated, he knew his principles and, despite the tragedy, the Manchester United story rolled on. Fate decreed that Murphy missed the Belgrade trip. He was in Cardiff, managing the Welsh team in a World Cup qualifier against Israel.

Although the following Saturday's much-awaited league clash with leaders Wolves was postponed, football had to go on and it did. Harry Gregg and Bill Foulkes, who had dragged the dead and dying from the aircraft, were the only survivors capable of playing immediately. Murphy signed Blackpool's veteran inside-forward Ernie Taylor, who Busby had almost signed pre-Munich, and Aston Villa's Stan Crowther. United were given dispensation from the FA to play both new signings in the FA Cup fifth round tie with Sheffield Wednesday, despite their being Cup-tied.

A crowd of 60,000 crammed into Old Trafford thirteen days after the disaster to see a patched-up United beat Sheffield Wednesday 3-0, thanks to two goals from reserve full-back Shay Brennan and one from Alex Dawson. On a night of high emotion, the roar when the teams emerged was deafening, but the stadium was soon hushed for the minute's silence. United were so unsure of who was going to play that the line-up in the black-edged programme was left blank.

Three days later, 67,000 saw a 1-1 draw with Nottingham Forest. The pick-and-mix team won only one further league game, at Sunderland on Good Friday. Wolves profited from United's tragedy: when they arrived at Old Trafford for the re-arranged game in the last week of the season they were already champions and twenty points ahead of the Reds, who would finish ninth. Wolves won 4-0.

The eleven players who ran out against Sheffield Wednesday were largely those who represented the club through the final weeks and carried the club to Wembley for the second successive season. Crash survivors Bobby Charlton and Kenny Morgans returned to play their part, and at the end of April, Dennis Viollet returned to first-team action. The injuries of two other survivors – Johnny Berry and Jackie Blanchflower – were so serious they would never play again. Ray Wood, his confidence shattered, would play only one further game for

United, although a move to Huddersfield a few months later restored his self-belief.

It is said that a wave of national sympathy bore United to Wembley. Somehow the makeshift team beat West Bromwich Albion after a replay, and overcame Second Division Fulham in the semi-final, also at the second attempt. At Wembley, the whole country it seemed – Bolton apart – was rooting for the Reds, and for the second year running United's goalkeeper was injured in controversial circumstances. After 55 minutes Bolton were leading 1-0 when Gregg caught the ball and was heavily charged by Nat Lofthouse. Ball and man were forced over the goal-line. In those days goalkeepers were afforded little protection and were considered fair game for physical contact of this kind. Nowadays, such 'goals' are outlawed; then, they were usually allowed, as in this case. The goal stood and Bolton won 2-0. In reality United, watched by a pale and frail Busby, were outgunned from start to finish, and Bolton deserved their triumph.

The European Cup semi-final with AC Milan was an anticlimax, although a 2-1 first-leg advantage gave hope that United could reach the final. Minus Bobby Charlton, on England duty, they slumped 0-4 in the San Siro. Milan would lose in turn, to Real Madrid in the final.

Match of the Season 1957-58

Arsenal 4 United 5

Division One, 1 February 1958

Although those present could hardly know it, they were watching the last performance on British soil by the great Busby Babes. Five days later, five of the side that performed with such panache at Highbury lay dead or dying in the ashes of the Munich air disaster.

United were unbeaten in eight League and Cup games, which had seen them creep up to fourth, only six points behind leaders Wolves. Two weeks previously, a 7-2 thrashing of Bolton had taken United's goal tally to 68 and silenced lingering doubts about their ability to challenge for their third successive title. On the flanks, Kenny Morgans and Albert Scanlon continued to keep out the more experienced Berry and Pegg whilst super-kid Bobby Charlton's nine goals in ten games was enough to depose Liam Whelan from the side.

Arsenal, on the other hand, were in a state of turmoil. A shock FA Cup defeat at Third Division Northampton had piled pressure on manager Jack Crayston, and it needed a win at Leicester the previous week – their first away win since October – to ease the strain on the Highbury boss. Crayston had made changes: Jack Fotheringham and Gerry Ward had replaced Bill Dodgin and Cliff Holton.

United wore their all-white change kit and both sides wore black arm-bands as a mark of respect for United director George Whittaker who had died that morning at the club's hotel.

By half-time United led 3-0 and the capacity 64,000 crowd anticipated a heavy defeat. Duncan Edwards had opened the scoring with a fierce low shot. The speedy Scanlon then ran 70 yards and outstripped the Arsenal defence before crossing for Charlton. Two minutes before the interval Tommy Taylor slotted home number three after being set up by Morgans.

The first fifteen minutes of the second half were goalless, but then Arsenal scored three goals in three breathtaking minutes to level the scores. Gregg was powerless to stop a David Herd thunderbolt, then Jimmy Bloomfield scored two in quick succession to leave the Arsenal fans pinching themselves. The first came from Groves' knock-down; the second from Nutt's cross, allowing Bloomfield to dive full-length to head in off the post.

With the momentum of the game dramatically changed, United's babes dug deep. Viollet headed them back in front from Scanlon's cross. Then Taylor netted from a tight angle for his sixteenth goal in 25 games, only for Derek Tapscott to respond for Arsenal. The home side pressed for a fifth goal but United held out.

The Times described events beautifully, 'the thermometer was doing a war-dance. There was no breath left in anyone. The players came off arm in arm. They knew they had finally fashioned something of which to be proud.' Arsenal defender Denis Evans summed up his feelings, 'everyone was cheering. Not because of Arsenal, not because of United. Just cheering because of the game itself. Because it was. No one left until five minutes after the game. They just stood cheering.'

CHAPTER FIVE

THE REBUILDING YEARS (1958-63)

LEAGUE DIVISION 1	**1958-59**
Division 1	Runners-Up
FA Cup	Third round

In the summer of 1958 Matt Busby headed for Switzerland for further recuperation from his injuries – by this time mental as much as physical. He had seriously considered retiring from the game, feeling in some way responsible for the deaths of so many talented young men. He had always gone to great lengths to reassure parents that the club would look after their sons. Now he felt he had somehow let them down, almost abused their trust. Busby's wife, Jean, convinced him that the 'lads' would have wanted him to carry on, rebuild the team, and finish the job.

After his return to England, Busby and his assistant Jimmy Murphy set about the task of massive team-rebuilding, but Busby took one day off to visit Buckingham Palace with his family to receive the CBE for his services to soccer.

United, in an unprecedented gesture, were invited by UEFA to participate as guest entrants to the European Cup. In the first round they were paired with Swiss club Young Boys of Berne. The Football Association granted permission, only for the Football League to intervene and prohibit United from taking part. Despite the wave of sympathy for the club, this did not extend to the Football League chairmen, who vetoed the plan on the grounds that Wolves were the League champions and, according to the rules, Manchester United were ineligible. United had to abide by the decision, but it left a lot of bitterness at Old Trafford.

Inevitably, there was much pre-season transfer speculation, with names like veteran England winger Tom Finney and a prolific young goalscorer by the name of Brian Clough strongly linked to United. Remarkably, Matt Busby had not bought a single player between March 1953 (Tommy Taylor) and November 1957 (Harry Gregg). Busby believed that with his matchless scouting system and thorough indoctrination, he could rear his own players, and his record supported this seemingly idle boast. In fact, Busby was suspicious of players whose characters had been formed at other clubs. His experience in the years following Munich confirmed these views.

When the 1958-59 season kicked-off, no signings had been made. The only changes to the Cup final side were the return of Albert Scanlon on the left wing and the introduction of Wilf McGuinness in place of Stan Crowther. Crowther had allegedly caused 'trouble' in training sessions and Busby wanted him out – he would join Chelsea before Christmas. McGuinness's form was so good he was picked for England after fewer than ten United games and won two caps. Scanlon had recovered from serious head injuries at Munich and would play a major part in the successful rebuilding season.

Former goalkeeper Jack Crompton, who had been 'lent' to the club by Luton after Munich, now signed up as first-team trainer, taking over from the deceased Tom Curry.

In some quarters United were tipped as possibles for relegation, especially in view of the disastrous post-Munich league run. However, the team quickly gelled, with Bobby Charlton netting eight goals in five games, including an opening-day hat-trick in a 5-2 mauling of Chelsea. After ten games United had lost only two and were in the top six. In late-September Busby made his first signing when paying Sheffield Wednesday a British record fee of £45,000 for Albert Quixall. It broke the previous record by £10,000 and was seen by many as a gamble. Quixall, an England international, replaced Ernie Taylor, who had plugged a gap after the crash but who would be on his way to Sunderland by December. Quixall was one of the modern stars: immaculate hair and the shortest of shorts – long before they became fashionable. He had been a teenage prodigy – debuting at seventeen and playing for England at twenty. An excellent passer, full of creativity, he was not however a heavy scorer.

Money was tight. United had been under-insured for those killed and permanently injured at Munich – and some of the Quixall fee had to be recouped. Colin Webster was sold to Swansea for £7,500 in October, despite being a first-team regular. A further £7,000 was raised from Ernie Taylor's sale. Crowther, who had cost £18,000 in February, was sold for £10,000. Goalkeeper Ray Wood, restricted to one game – and that because Gregg was on international duty – turned down moves to Coventry and Southend.

Crash survivors Berry and Blanchflower hoped to start light training, although Blanchflower still limped and suffered with his right arm. Realisation slowly dawned that neither would ever play again.

DID YOU KNOW?

United first appearance on BBC's Match of the Day was in September 1964 – a 1-2 defeat at Fulham's Craven Cottage.

Bobby Charlton was becoming a star. Both he and Gregg were regularly besieged by autograph hunters. Gregg, following his performances for Northern Ireland in the World Cup in Sweden – he was voted the goalkeeper of the tournament – would be United's first choice for some time. Charlton, now an England regular, was the new golden boy of English soccer.

A dramatic slump saw United win only two games in thirteen in the autumn, and with the team down to fourteenth something had to change. Some critics argued for a big-name centre-forward in the Tommy Taylor or Nat Lofthouse mould. Such players, however, were rare and expensive. Busby persisted with the stocky Alex Dawson. He also resigned as Scottish team manager, a ex-officio role he had undertaken for matches against Wales and Ireland that autumn.

A shattering 3-6 defeat at Bolton was brightened by the debut of winger Warren Bradley, who only played because Viollet was injured. Bradley gave England left-back Tommy Banks a roasting and set up all three United goals. The following week, after a relaxing break at Blackpool, Viollet returned at centre-forward in place of Dawson and Joe Carolan replaced Ian Greaves at left-back, and this proved to be the turning point of the season.

The side was virtually unchanged thereafter, and although United lost 0-3 in the FA Cup at Norwich in the third round, the league form was daunting. The team won eight games in a row, and sixteen out of eighteen to push themselves into the title race.

Bradley, an England amateur international, had signed with two other Bishop Auckland players, ostensibly to strengthen the reserves. A schoolteacher by profession, he signed part-time forms in November and made a dramatic impact with his non-stop running and accurate crosses. He also chipped in with twelve goals in 24 games and completed a fantastic rise to stardom by winning three full England caps at the end of the season.

By February, United's transformation was complete when they beat Wolves, the leaders, 2-0 at home to pull level on points. A last-minute goal from Charlton had sealed the win and some parts of the press called for England manager Walter Winterbottom to select the complete United forward line. A week later he was a spectator at

Highbury to see United stumble, losing to third-placed Arsenal. Nevertheless, Scanlon, Charlton and McGuinness were called up for the Under-23s and Viollet for the Football League.

Going into Easter, United – with five straight wins following the Highbury defeat – were one point behind Wolves in a two-horse race. On Good Friday, United leapt to the top by blitzing Portsmouth 6-1, but the following day blew their advantage by losing 2-4 at Burnley. It was a damning setback, for Wolves did not lose another game and romped to the title with a six-point cushion.

Although United lost their final game, at Leicester – only their third league reverse since mid-November – they had taken massive strides since Munich. They were just not good enough to outpace Stan Cullis's no-nonsense side. Wolves probably had a better-balanced team, while United – despite a forward line that netted 103 goals – could be brittle in defence.

With three games remaining, Bobby Charlton needed one goal to equal Jack Rowley's 1952 United record of 30 in a season, but the goal would not come and Rowley's record remained intact. Only Chelsea's Jimmy Greaves and Tottenham's Bobby Smith scored more goals than Charlton, who was by now an England regular.

The season saw the end of United's domination of the FA Youth Cup. Despite beating Wolves in the quarter-final, they lost 1-4 on aggregate to Blackburn in the semis. None of the team had first-team experience, although Nobby Stiles, Johnny Giles, Nicholson, Gaskell and Moir would in time become first-team regulars.

Match of the Season 1958-59

Preston 3 United 4

Division One, 13 December 1958

The late 1950s were Preston's golden years of the twentieth century. From their point of view, it was a shame that those years coincided with Manchester United's and Wolves' best years. Preston finished third behind United in 1956-57 with 56 points, then a year later were second to Wolves with 59 points. Their success, under experienced manager Cliff Britton, was attributed to a solid defence built around unspectacular players like goalkeeper Fred Else, full-backs Willie Cunningham and Joe Walton, and centre-half Joe Dunn. Tommy Docherty was one of the best wing-halves in the League, and up front they had a blistering strike-force. England legend Tom Finney had been transformed into a centre-forward and built a strong partnership with Tommy Thompson. Finney netted 54 goals in two seasons, whilst Thompson's 63 earned an international call-up. At fortress Deepdale, only three games had been lost in two seasons.

Despite the sale of Docherty to Arsenal in the close season, the 1958-59 campaign started well for Preston, with only one defeat in the first nine games. A 2-0 win at Old Trafford in October sent them top. However, when Thompson went off the boil and Finney got injured, Preston's results suffered.

A week before United's visit to Deepdale, a 2-1 win at Tottenham had lifted Preston into fourth place and a rare tussle was anticipated with Manchester's Reds. Finney was injured, Dennis Hatsell deputised, and Thompson returned to the side.

United's three straight wins had lifted them from fifteenth to ninth. They were unchanged for the fourth game in a row, with newcomer Joe Carolan – a product of Dublin's Home Farm club – at left-back, and amateur winger Warren Bradley keeping out Alex Dawson.

Bradley opened the scoring after Albert Quixall had bamboozled the home defence and set up a tap-in. Hatsell was proving to be a handful for Ronnie Cope, and the Preston man's two goals in nine minutes seemed to have turned the game around. The first stemmed from a long ball from Dunn; the second was a lob over the heads of Gregg and Carolan.

United equalised from Bradley's pass early in the second half and it remained 2-2 until the closing minutes. Then, first Scanlon, and a minute later Charlton, scored to put United in control. Else, the hero of the earlier victory at Old Trafford, blocked Scanlon's fierce shot but the ball squirmed over the line. Thompson headed a third for Preston from a free-kick two minutes from time.

The Empire News described this as one of the finest games at Deepdale for many seasons and eulogised about United's inside-forward trio of Quixall, Viollet and Charlton.

The defeat was only Preston's third at home all season, but after Christmas they lost five successive games at Deepdale, and with Finney increasingly absent with injury they slumped to twelfth.

LEAGUE DIVISION 1	**1959-60**
Division 1	Seventh
FA Cup	Fifth round

For the first time in five seasons, by the time 1959-60 entered the home straight Manchester United were not in contention for honours. The FA Cup home defeat to newly promoted Sheffield Wednesday ended United's dreams at a time when they were becalmed in mid-table in the First Division.

For the third season in four, United's attack scored over 100 goals but at the other end their defence conceded 80, the worst by any United team since the dark Division Two days of 1933-34.

Mind you, fans certainly got their money's worth. Over 40,000, on average, viewed United's away games, with the gates locked at many grounds – including 66,000 at Stamford Bridge, 47,000 at Burnley, and 62,000 at White Hart Lane. United scored 49 goals in 21 away games, conceding 50, which meant virtually every game witnessed an avalanche of goals. Thumping wins at Forest (5-1), Chelsea (6-5), Blackpool (6-0) and Fulham (5-0) were countered by numbing defeats at Newcastle (3-7), Arsenal (2-5) and Preston (0-4). United's yo-yo form was best illustrated in the Christmas double-headers against pacesetters Burnley. Well beaten at Old Trafford on Boxing Day, United travelled to Turf Moor and hammered the champions-elect 4-1.

Having been outscored by Bobby Charlton the previous campaign, Dennis Viollet ended with 32 goals in 36 games, breaking Jack Rowley's club record and earning full England recognition. Viollet's strength was his speed, and Charlton paid tribute: 'Everything he does is carried out so swiftly that opponents have no time to recover.'

Charlton had, by his own high standards, a poor season. Dropped by England after a Wembley defeat by Sweden in October, his domestic form suffered and Busby rested him for four games in December. He bounced back after Christmas and in March was switched with some success to outside-left. He earned an England recall and ended the season with eighteen goals.

England, like United, were entering another new era. After 21 years with Wolves, and thirteen seasons in an England shirt, captain Billy Wright had retired from both domestic and international football. The national side's summer tour of South America had been a disaster, with three defeats in four games, and England's international reputation had been severely dented.

DID YOU KNOW?

In 1959, United's Warren Bradley was selected to play for England after only 24 games for United, in the same season he had won an England amateur cap.

Busby saw where the weaknesses in his team were, but kept his views to himself. Most pundits reckoned the team needed strengthening at full-back and centre-half. Ian Greaves, a stalwart after Munich, had struggled: following the opening two games, both lost, he was axed and replaced by Ronnie Cope. A month later, with the defence still leaking goals, and United on the wrong end of a 1-5 home result to Spurs, Busby swapped Cope and centre-half Bill Foulkes.

In September, Busby admitted he had submitted bids for seven players and it was rumoured that among his targets were Blackpool's pair of young defenders Jimmy Armfield and Roy Gratrix, and Leicester's tall England Under-23 international centre-half Tony Knapp. Another to catch his eye was Arsenal's Scottish forward David Herd, whose father Alex had played alongside Busby before the war. Arsenal rejected Busby's advances, but he would come back for Herd later. United announced profits of £26,000 and had over £120,000 in the bank available for the right players.

Busby's main target was Rangers' Scottish international full-back Eric Caldow. Caldow was one of the fastest backs around, and when the clubs agreed a fee of £25,000 the press reported that the transfer was concluded. Caldow, however, dragged his heels and the deal fell through. He would remain at Ibrox for the rest of his career, which was terminated in 1963 when, in the Scotland v England international, he broke a leg in a challenge from Bobby Smith.

Busby, under rare pressure, insisted he was not prepared to buy players who were no better than those already at the club, and that he had another tranche of youngsters close to first-team action. In this category he included a young Irish winger, Johnny Giles – who debuted in the Spurs debacle – youth team wing-halves Jimmy Nicholson and Norbert Stiles, and a dazzling inside-forward called Nobby Lawton. To illustrate the point, United's reserve team were running away with the Central League title, for only the second time since 1947, and were attracting five-figure crowds to Old Trafford. In other words, Busby was asking for patience from his critics.

Defenders Cope, Foulkes and Carolan were virtual ever-presents and the fans got used to a defence prone to capsize, but which was generally camouflaged by a dazzling attack.

Busby, however, was not complacent. After a 1-2 defeat at Everton in early December he read the riot act. Four internationals were axed. Gregg carried the can for sloppy Everton goals, and England men McGuinness, Bradley and Charlton also lost their first-team places. Charlton had looked stale and off-colour, but quickly regained his place and by the end of the season rejuvenated his career by moving to outside-left, a switch which persuaded England boss Walter Winterbottom to select him in the No 11 shirt. By the time of the Scotland v England fixture in April, Italian club AC Milan were pursuing Charlton and had a £70,000 bid rejected by Busby.

McGuinness, however, would not be so lucky. For several weeks he had been playing through pain in his shinbone, even though X-rays had not revealed any problem. He could not train, but continued to play after being on the treatment table all week. As a result, his form suffered. Desperate to regain his place, McGuinness had cortisone injections from the club doctor and played for the reserves at Stoke. Early in the game he broke his leg – he had been suffering from a stress fracture and the break would ultimately end his playing career. Bradley, a professional for just over a year, was never again a first-team regular, but stayed at United until 1962 when he signed for Bury. His star fell almost as fast as it had risen.

In his first full season, Albert Quixall failed to impress everyone. His form had been patchy, goals few, and it was apparent that the big transfer fee weighed heavily on his shoulders. Dennis Viollet, however, supported his teammate: 'If there is a better forager and schemer in England I haven't seen him.'

Dave Gaskell got another run in goal, but after six games was back in the reserves following the drubbing at Newcastle – he did however earn a place in the England Under-23 squad. The Newcastle game was the swansong of another pre-Munich babe, wing-half Freddie Goodwin, who could not emerge from the shadow of Duncan Edwards and was transferred to Leeds. Goodwin's demise was signalled by the arrival of Maurice Setters, a key Busby target. Bandy-legged Setters had impressed many with his gritty performances for West Brom and England Under-23s, and his crew-cut hairstyle gave him the impression of a tough nut, which he was. He was a ball-winner and, with his verbal urgings, an extra captain on the field. At £30,000 he would prove to be an outstanding signing.

Injuries to Viollet and Quixall in the final weeks opened the door for Alex Dawson and Johnny Giles, and both took their opportunity.

Viollet's goalscoring feats were not missed and the robust Dawson scored eleven goals in the last ten games to lift United to a final position of seventh.

Burnley were crowned champions following a ding-dong battle with Wolves, who had some compensation by winning the FA Cup. The highlight of season was, however, Real Madrid's 7-3 victory over Eintracht Frankfurt in the European Cup final at Hampden Park. It was widely acclaimed as the finest football display of all time and left many domestic critics wondering how far English clubs had slipped so far behind the fabulous Madrid side, which had now won the trophy five years in succession. Wolves, England's representatives, were dumped at the quarter-final stage by Barcelona (2-9 on aggregate) and looked well short of challenging the best.

Busby wanted his team to sample crack European opposition and in the autumn organised home and away friendlies with Real Madrid. Over 63,000 watched Puskas, Di Stefano and the rest run riot at Old Trafford, winning 6-1. In the return, United, with a gutsy display, ran Real close before losing 5-6. The sporting Spanish fans cheered United off the pitch at the end. In a speech at a banquet later that night the Real chairman, Santiago Bernabeu, told the assembled audience that, 'Mr Busby is the greatest man I have ever met in football.'

Another outstanding United youth team – which included emerging youngsters such as Nicholson, Stiles, Phil Chisnall, Ian Moir and Irish-born goalkeeper Ronnie Briggs – were beaten by Preston in the semi-final of the FA Youth Cup.

During the season, the Professional Footballers Association (PFA) started making noises about industrial action. They were aggrieved that the players' maximum wage was still only £20 – the clubs had rejected a proposal to increase it to £25 in 1958. It became public knowledge that United were paying all their professional players (whichever tier they played in) the maximum of £20 per week. The first-team bonus was £4, but only £2 for playing for the reserves. At that time, United's Central League team were in such winning form that they frequently picked up £22 a man against the £20 of a losing first-teamer.

The PFA, fronted by their chairman, the Fulham forward Jimmy Hill, threw down the gauntlet, demanding not only the abolition of the maximum wage but also the age-old retain and transfer system, which effectively enslaved the players to their clubs. The whole issue would resurface with dramatic effects the following season.

DID YOU KNOW?

The crowd of 82,771 at the FA Cup fourth round tie with Bradford Park Avenue in 1949 is the second biggest FA Cup crowd outside the final.

Match of the Season 1959-60

Chelsea 3 United 6

Division One, 2 September 1959

Only Wolves and Chelsea came close to emulating United's success with youth players. Chelsea boss Ted Drake only rarely resorted to the transfer market, for instance paying £22,000 for Coventry's England international goalkeeper Reg Matthews in 1956. His youth policy unearthed Jimmy Greaves, Peter Brabrook, Bobby Tambling, Barry Bridges and Ken Shellito. Winning his first cap on the summer tour of 1959, Greaves was already a star. His 54 League goals in his first two seasons spoke for themselves.

Drake's Ducklings, as the press dubbed them, were blighted by a porous defence which kept them in the bottom half in recent seasons. But anyone watching Chelsea would see goals. In 1958-59 they had scored 77 and conceded 98. Chelsea had kicked off 1959-60 with a 4-4 home draw against Preston. Four days later they visited Old Trafford in the first game of a double-header and hung on, protecting an early Greaves goal. After seventeen games without a win at United – stretching back to 1920 – Chelsea had now won twice in three seasons.

Interest in the return at Stamford Bridge was enormous. The gates were closed with over 66,000 inside, the largest since the Pensioners' championship season, and the club later received 1,000 letters from fans complaining that, although they got in, they could not see.

Chelsea drew first blood when Gregg parried Frank Blunstone's shot and Greaves scored. Within nine minutes United were 3-1 ahead, and all three goals stemmed from Matthews failing to deal with crosses from United's wingers, Bradley and Scanlon. Before half-time Peter Sillett's 40-yard free-kick sailed over Gregg's head. After the break, Viollet slid in goal number four, and further goals from Bradley and Viollet emphasised United's domination. A late Peter Sillett penalty was scant consolation for a glum home crowd.

Man of the match Viollet said: 'What a wonderful experience. I rate [it] the finest exhibition of football by a United team in which I have ever played. I felt proud to be captain.'

LEAGUE DIVISION 1	**1960-61**
Division 1	Seventh
FA Cup	Fourth round
League Cup	Second round

In mid-October 1960 things looked bleak for Manchester United. After eleven games the Reds were one place above the drop zone, with 27 goals already conceded. After a 3-5 hammering by champions Burnley, Busby knew that he had to take action. His priority was a defender to plug the gaps. Then, having found him, an unbeaten home run of sixteen league games helped pull United up into a final placing of seventh.

This was a season marred by injuries, a goalkeeping crisis and finally, stability in defence after two years of inconsistency. Three defenders who played in the opening-day defeat by FA Cup finalists Blackburn were quickly dropped. Right-back that day, Ronnie Cope, played a few games in his preferred centre-half position but lost his place when Busby switched Bill Foulkes from full-back to pivot in October. Left-back Carolan was scapegoated for the heavy defeat at Everton and was shown the door to Brighton. Youth-team product Frank Haydock started the season at No 5 but lost his place after a tortuous afternoon against Spurs' international Bobby Smith.

Foulkes' inspired conversion saved United a fortune. Busby had pursued several top centre-halves, including Swansea's Mel Nurse and Dundee United's Ron Yeats. He had offered £35,000 for Nurse but the deal foundered on Swansea's insistence that Alex Dawson switch to Vetch Field. Yeats would later sign for Liverpool and captain them to the League and Cup under Bill Shankly.

Shay Brennan, a post-Munich hero, was another conversion. In his case he switched from a wing-half into a right-back. However, Busby wanted to strengthen the left side. He earmarked Huddersfield's Ray Wilson, a young England left-back playing for Huddersfield in Division Two, but Wilson was injured at an inopportune time. Then Bubsy switched his sights to West Ham's Noel Cantwell. Cantwell reminded many of fellow Irishman Johnny Carey, with his cultured distribution and gentlemanly approach. Like Carey he was captain of Eire. He did not come cheap, however, and cost United £29,500, a British record fee for a full-back. After defeat in Cantwell's debut at promoted Cardiff, the Reds went eight games without defeat. These included a first away win at Blackburn, followed by a second at Chelsea.

DID YOU KNOW?

In October 1954, Chelsea's amateur debutant Seamus O'Connell scored a hat-trick in his side's 5-6 defeat by United.

Before Cantwell's arrival, Busby had experimented with Maurice Setters at right-back, which allowed another home-grown player, 18-year-old Nobby Stiles, to be given a debut at right-half. Stiles' all-action style immediately endeared him and he became a virtual ever-present, switching to inside-forward after Christmas. His fellow wing-half was Jimmy Nicholson, another teenager given his spurs. Nicholson's form was inconsistent but he played over 30 games and won Irish international honours.

Setters regained his right-half place in December and, following Viollet's injury, was appointed captain. Over Christmas, Setters man-marked two of the country's most prolific goalscorers, Chelsea's Jimmy Greaves and Manchester City's Denis Law. Stiles' form over the next few years, however, would eventually see the hard-tackling Devon-man become surplus to requirements.

Rumours abounded that Arsenal's David Herd was on his way to Old Trafford. In October, when the Gunners signed pay-rebel George Eastham from Newcastle, Herd's departure from Highbury looked inevitable, but nothing happened. Further rumours linked United with other big centre-forwards – Derek Kevan of West Brom and Blackburn's Derek Dougan. The juiciest gossip, however, had United linked to an end-of-season move for Welshman John Charles. Charles, who excelled at centre-half or centre-forward, had joined Italian club Juventus from Leeds in 1957.

Injuries hit the club badly, with Mark Pearson out of action until November, and wing-wizard Johnny Giles breaking a leg at Birmingham the same month. Two weeks after Giles' injury it was Viollet's turn. He had not been at this best – his England place had gone to Tottenham's Bobby Smith – but he had still scored ten goals in eighteen games. At Cardiff he collided with goalkeeper Vearncombe and broke his collarbone, which would keep him out for four months.

The most serious injury, however, was sustained by Harry Gregg. His dislocated shoulder against Tottenham in January was more serious that at first appeared. It effectively ended his season, although he did return for two games in March before suffering a relapse. With reserve goalkeeper Dave Gaskell also injured, Busby gave a debut at Leicester to third-choice Ronnie Briggs. The game was a nightmare for the tall Belfast-born 17-year-old, with United whipped by one of the surprise teams of the season. Contemporary match reports apportion little blame to the youngster, but his confidence was undoubtedly shaken. The game also allegedly marked the day that Busby got tough. According to Eamonn Dunphy's book *A Strange Kind of Glory,* Busby boarded the coach after the match to discover the card school playing for high stakes – as much as a week's wages. He let the culprits know exactly what he thought by flinging the cards out of the coach window.

Worse was to come, however. A week later United drew at Sheffield Wednesday in the FA Cup fourth round, but collapsed in the replay. Poor Briggs was at fault for three goals and Busby immediately acquired England amateur goalkeeper Mike Pinner from Queen's Park Rangers on a short-term contract. Pinner's experience steadied the ship until Gaskell was fit enough to resume.

Recent bad defeats forced Busby and Murphy to reassess the players. They concluded that Pearson, Dawson and Nicholson fell short of the club's exacting standards, and that the acclaimed youth policy would take some years before yielding players of pre-Munich calibre. In the short term, if the club hoped to quickly regain its position at the summit of English football, then Busby had to spend and spend big. Cantwell's signing would be the first of many.

Busby himself was hospitalised in February for further surgery on his back, leaving Jimmy Murphy in control of club affairs. Needing to convalesce, Busby was out of action until the summer and inevitable questions were posed whether he would ever return, although at 52 he was not old in managerial terms. One story refuted by United chairman Harold Hardman was that Busby was joining the board and Johnny Carey was returning as manager.

In the last month of the season Giles and Viollet returned from injury and United signed off with a flourish – five wins and two draws in the final seven games. Viollet scored his second hat-trick of the season, against Burnley, and Charlton's club form reflected the enormous impact he was having on an England team enjoying their best period of the post-War era. The national team, which largely picked itself, won six out of six, scoring 32 goals, including a 9-3 win over Scotland at Wembley. Charlton scored seven goals from the left wing for his country and created a host more. England's good form continued on an end-of-season tour, with a draw in Portugal and a 3-2 win in Italy, before the run ended with defeat in Austria.

Off the field, the Professional Footballers Association took their grievances to the brink, and in January 1961 a players' strike looked inevitable. The Football League clubs finally capitulated and the maximum wage was abolished. A new dawn was breaking and First Division Fulham set the hares chasing by offering England captain Johnny Haynes £100 a week, five times the previous maximum wage.

The summer of 1961 saw the arrival at Old Trafford of a promising youngster from Belfast by the name of George Best. Those who saw the scrawny kid on arrival did not give him much chance of survival in the fierce and competitive atmosphere at United.

Match of the Season 1960-61

United 2 Tottenham 0

Division One, 16 January 1961

During the winter of 1960-61, one football team stood head and shoulders above the rest, Tottenham Hotspur. They dominated the domestic scene as no other English team had done in the twentieth century, eclipsing even the feats of Manchester United in 1956-57.

Manager Bill Nicholson had created an awesome team since taking over as manager in 1958. Inheriting players like Danny Blanchflower, Bobby Smith and Cliff Jones, 'Billy Nick' used the transfer market to great effect. In the summer of 1959 he signed Scottish international wing-half Dave Mackay, a bruising but creative wing-half, and a goalkeeper Bill Brown, from Dundee. Soon afterwards, another Scot, inside-forward John White, and Les Allen, a natural goalscorer, were added to the squad. Nicholson rejuvenated the career of winger Terry Dyson and defenders Maurice Norman and Peter Baker, and Spurs nearly won the championship in his first full season. Burnley pipped them by two points.

Spurs started the 1960-61 season by winning their first eleven games and remaining unbeaten until mid-November. When they arrived at Old Trafford they had lost just once, at Sheffield Wednesday, and were ten points clear at the top of the league.

Tottenham reserves Ken Barton and John Smith came in for their only appearances of the season in place of the injured Baker and Jones. United were unchanged for the fifth successive game.

The Monday night fixture, originally scheduled for the Saturday but postponed because of fog, saw United outplay Spurs from start to finish. It seemed the whole of Manchester wanted to see the classy Londoners, who had not lost in six games. Over 65,000 turned up and were treated to a classic.

In an electric atmosphere, Nobby Stiles put United in front, after skilful play from Albert Quixall. Just before half-time, Harry Gregg dislocated his shoulder and had to leave the field for treatment. As substitutes were not allowed, centre-forward Alex Dawson pulled on Gregg's green jersey. Gregg returned to the fray, his arm in a sling, and took Dawson's place at centre-forward. But the Irishman back-heeled a pass to Mark Pearson for United's second goal seventeen minutes from the end.

Tottenham's defeat had no lasting effect on their title aspirations and, although they lost a further five league games, they still won the championship by eight points. By beating Leicester 2-0 at Wembley, Spurs became the first team to win the League and Cup double in the twentieth century.

LEAGUE DIVISION 1	**1961-62**
Division 1	Fifteenth
FA Cup	Semi-finals
League Cup	Did not enter

The early 1960s saw massive change, not only in football but also in the fabric of British society. The baby-boomers were becoming teenagers and for the first time that generation wanted their voice heard. Pop music in the shape of the Beatles and Bob Dylan was radical and in some ways revolutionary. In English football, too, the times they were a'changing.

Tottenham Hotspur had won the 'double' in 1961, playing stylish football, influenced by their captain Danny Blanchflower, one of the game's great thinkers. Before them, Burnley had also won the League playing cultured Continental-style football under Jimmy Adamson, their captain, and Jimmy McIlroy, a graceful schemer. These two sides were expected to be the main contenders for honours in 1961-62. Manchester United were some pundits' choice, on the strength of the fine end-of-season run the previous campaign.

Noel Cantwell had been reared in the West Ham Academy of Football and had strong ideas about the way the game should be played. He was horrified by the training methods and lack of tactical preparation at United when he arrived in 1960. He set out to improve things and in time would get results.

In the summer of 1961 Busby finally signed David Herd from Arsenal for £38,000, a large fee, but seen as a bargain over the next few years. Herd's arrival raised doubts over the futures of former babes Alex Dawson and Pancho Pearson, but the player ultimately to make way was Viollet, a former school pal of Herd.

Viollet's fall from grace was sudden and spectacular and shocked many supporters. In September, despite a patchy start to the domestic season, he was called up to replace England captain Johnny Haynes in England's World Cup qualifier against Luxembourg at Highbury. England won 4-1, but the fans and press crucified the England players' pathetic performance. Viollet, winning his second and what would be his last cap, came in for some vitriolic abuse, despite scoring one of the goals. His club form seemed to be affected and, although at some time or another in a miserable autumn, almost all of his teammates were dropped, when Viollet was 'rested' he disappeared from first-team contention completely.

DID YOU KNOW?

On 1 February, 1958 a crowd of 18,991 watched the reserve game with Wolves at Old Trafford. They had come for vouchers for the Sheffield Wednesday Cup-tie.

According to Eamonn Dunphy in *A Strange Kind Of Glory*, it was no secret around Manchester that Viollet had a penchant for ladies and the nightlife. Dunphy believes Busby tolerated it for a time but then lost patience. When a good offer came in, he decided to release Viollet. In January, after two months in the reserves, with little prospect of a recall, he joined Second Division Stoke, whose manager, Tony Waddington, had recently re-signed Stanley Matthews and was building an experienced side geared for promotion. United banked £22,000 which, added to the £20,000 raised from the surprise sale of Alex Dawson to Preston and the £16,000 proceeds of Cope and Bradley's sale to Luton and Bury respectively, boosted Busby's war chest for the big signing he had in mind.

With the exception of Bobby Charlton, playing superbly at outside-left, a position he allegedly hated, all of the forwards endured periods of poor form in the autumn and found themselves dropped at one time or another.

Herd scored three goals in his first three games, then failed to net until the end of November. The strong start, with only one defeat in the first nine games, and another good home win over Tottenham, masked weaknesses that were exposed in a ten-game run without a win; the worst sequence since the War. Home defeats – after a whole year unbeaten at Old Trafford – to mediocre sides like Wolves, Birmingham and Bolton – were not appreciated by the faithful. Four straight away defeats left United in 21st place by early December. The scores – at Arsenal (1-5), Ipswich (1-4) and Everton (1-4) – were bad enough, but the performances were even worse.

Busby continually shuffled the pack. In November, Quixall and the combative Stiles, earning a hard-man reputation, were the latest to be axed. Jimmy Nicholson returned, Nobby Lawton got an extended run at inside-left, and another youth product, 19-year-old Phil Chisnall, came in at outside-right.

Injuries did not help matters. Gregg hurt his shoulder again and Noel Cantwell picked up a mystery bug. This opened the door for another young Irishman, Tony Dunne. The small, fast full-back would keep Cantwell out of the first team for a year and go on to be a first-team regular for twelve seasons.

The outside-right position was an additional headache for Busby. Albert Quixall's form was patchy, Warren Bradley had lost form and moved on, and although 18-year-old Ian Moir dazzled with his ball skills in four appearances, he was style without substance. Busby admitted that he needed a traditional right-winger. Amongst the names canvassed were Huddersfield's Mike O'Grady, Swindon's rising star Mike Summerbee, and Southampton's hot prospect Terry Paine. In the meantime, Chisnall played nine games without ever convincing that he was the answer.

The shocking home form – United had lost six out of thirteen by January – was forgotten when the FA Cup started. United's Cup run started with a fortuitous home win over Bolton. The fog was so bad that many fans didn't see the late goals that carried United through. The weather also played its part against Arsenal in round four, with United adapting better to the paddy-field conditions.

Over 65,000 squeezed into Old Trafford to see another titanic clash with First Division Sheffield Wednesday in round five. Both sides missed chances to win and, in a defining replay, United soaked up incredible pressure to snatch victory.

In retrospect, the Cup run was a watershed for United. The new team was beginning to take shape but could achieve no consistency in the League. In the one-off atmosphere of Cup-ties, however, they were proving difficult to beat. At Preston in the quarter-finals, United again lived dangerously, with Alex Dawson getting an early opportunity to show Busby he had been wrong to sell him. United survived and sneaked through the replay.

At Hillsborough in the semi-final, United would lose to Tottenham, who were heading for a second successive FA Cup triumph, but were not disgraced by a Spurs team strengthened by the arrival in January of Jimmy Greaves, whose sojourn in Italy with Milan had been short and unsatisfying.

Following the semi-final disappointment, United's season petered out. Inconsistency was confirmed by victories over the top two – Ipswich and Burnley – but failure to win any of their last three home games. They ended up fifteenth.

Upstarts Ipswich won the championship in their first ever season in the top flight, and Spurs – still in most people's eyes the best side in the country – won the FA Cup final 3-1, beating Burnley, who fell between the twin stools of League and Cup. England went off to Chile for the World Cup with only one United player – Bobby Charlton.

This reflected United's waning power as a top English club. Only one other United player, Shay Brennan, made the initial squad of 40 players selected for Chile, from which the final travelling party of 22 was chosen.

Match of the Season 1961-62

United 5 Ipswich 0

Division One, 7 April 1962

With less than a month to go, there was an unlikely name heading the top division. Ipswich, in their very first season in the top flight, were leading the pack into the last lap. Admittedly, they were only a point ahead of second-placed Burnley, who had four games in hand, and few Fleet Street soccer pundits expected the upstarts to lift the title. In sleepy Suffolk, however, the locals were convinced their team was going see off the challenge of the big clubs – Burnley, Tottenham and Everton – who were breathing down their necks. More importantly, their manager, Alf Ramsey, the former Tottenham and England full-back, was certain the title was going to Ipswich.

It seemed extraordinary: after all, a team only voted into the Football League in 1938, and with no big-name players, had upset the big guns from the start of this amazing season. United had already been battered by the East Anglian whirlwind, losing 1-4 at Portman Road in November, and all the so-called top clubs had succumbed to Ramsey's unlikely heroes. Tottenham, holders of the League and Cup 'double', had already lost home and away to their former player's unorthodox team.

Ramsey's secret was shrewd, unorthodox tactics. He employed two wingers, Stephenson and Leadbetter, playing deep and confusing opposing full-backs. The wingers played diagonal balls up to two strikers, Ray Crawford and Ted Phillips, and the deadly duo revelled in the service. Ramsey had also been lucky with injuries, and fielded a virtually unchanged side throughout the season. The team had cost less than £30,000 to assemble, and several players, especially the ancient-looking Leadbetter, were dismissed as too old.

Ipswich arrived at Old Trafford unbeaten since January and raring to claim the 'double' over United, who were still hung over from their FA Cup semi-final defeat by Tottenham a week earlier. Busby's men had not won a league game for six weeks.

DID YOU KNOW?

In April 1965 Noel Cantwell was invited to become Irish Member of Parliament in his hometown constituency in Cork.

Goalkeeper Gaskell and 'find' of the season Nobby Lawton had been injured in the 3-4 midweek defeat at Leicester in midweek, and Ronnie Briggs and Johnny Giles deputised. Earlier in the season Ray Crawford had become Ipswich's first England international, but the 32-goal forward was now injured winning his second cap against Austria in midweek. Dermot Curtis deputised.

Torrential Manchester rain had rendered the Old Trafford pitch a bog, and perhaps caused the attendance to drop to 24,000. Ipswich – hampered by an early muscle injury to Elsworthy – were never in the game. Albert Quixall was in the sort of form which four years previously had made him Britain's costliest player. He scored two early goals – the second a 25-yard effort which Ipswich keeper Roy Bailey barely saw. United flitted across the boggy surface as if on skates, and Charlton – fresh from the England game – was at the heart of much of United's dominant play.

Early in the second half, Quixall completed his hat-trick and United refused to slacken. Bailey made several sharp saves and Charlton and Sammy McMillan hit the woodwork. Then, as the minutes ticked away, first Setters and then Stiles had time to finish with smart shots. The outcome was United's biggest home win since August and Ipswich's biggest defeat of the season.

Ipswich confounded their critics, yet again, and recovered their composure, whilst nearest rivals Burnley lost their nerve. Ramsey's team won the title by three points. Less than twelve months later, he was appointed the full-time manager of the England team and the rest, as they say, is history.

LEAGUE DIVISION 1	**1962-63**
Division 1	Nineteenth
FA Cup	Winners
League Cup	Did not enter

Despite the removal of the maximum wage in 1961, several top British players were still tempted to play in Italy. Among these were England internationals Jimmy Greaves, who would return to Tottenham after a few unhappy months, Gerry Hitchens, a success at Inter Milan, and Joe Baker, who experienced mixed fortunes at Torino. Torino had also signed Scottish international Denis Law from Manchester City.

Law had not enjoyed the 1961-62 season in Italy. He had made his thoughts known to Matt Busby when playing at Old Trafford, representing the Italian League against the Football League in November 1961. Busby had given Law, then a Huddersfield player, his international debut in his brief spell as Scotland manager in 1958, ironically alongside another debutant, David Herd.

When Law and Busby next met, at Hampden Park in April 1962– following Scotland's victory over England – Law made it clear that he would love to return home. The circumspect Busby would only say that if Law became available, then United would be interested in signing him.

Law returned to Italy and demanded a transfer. Torino were displeased, but eventually became resigned to losing their leading scorer. United paid a British record fee of £115,000 to land their prey, and over the next eleven years 'the King', as he became known, would repay every penny as United scaled the dizzy heights once again.

Law was the only signing in the summer of 1962, but his arrival had some pundits once again tipping the Reds for the title. The early signs were not promising, with seven out of the first eleven games lost. These included three home defeats, including one to neighbours City, and an embarrassing loss at newly promoted Leyton Orient. Managed by Johnny Carey, Orient were destined to be the division's whipping boys.

As for Law, he started with a bang – scoring seven minutes into his debut – but managed only three more in the next thirteen games. Busby uncharacteristically lost patience: 'I am not prepared for players to find their form in the first team – there are reserves who deserve promotion.' He shuffled the team, introducing Nicholson, Lawton, Chisnall, Moir and McMillan, but to little effect. The absence of Charlton, recovering from a hernia operation, was also a major influence on the team's results.

The early front runners were big-spending Everton. Harry Catterick had taken over as manager from Johnny Carey and moulded a shrewd mix of expensive internationals (Alex Young, Roy Vernon, Billy Bingham) and home-grown talent (Brian Labone, Johnny Morrissey and Brian Harris). The Toffees defeated United home and away early in the season and would take some beating.

Two disastrous losses in mid-October – 0-3 at home to Blackburn and 2-6 at Tottenham – forced Busby into more changes. Charlton returned, as did Cantwell, Setters and Quixall. Dunne, Nicholson and young Sammy McMillan dropped out. Law and Herd suddenly hit form and the side went seven games without defeat. One of these was a 5-3 win at defending champions Ipswich, whose tactics had been rumbled and who were on a dramatic slide. Johnny Giles and Charlton were creating chances from the flanks and, although the defence was all too fragile, the attack was for the moment more than compensating. Quixall, dropped twice, had almost signed for Second Division Stoke weeks earlier, with his United career seemingly over.

Another facet of United's performances was a cause for concern – the players' indiscipline. Maurice Setters had never taken prisoners but he also had a fondness for arguing with referees. By December he had collected four bookings, a rare feat in an era when you had step seriously out of line to earn a caution, let alone a dismissal. Setters had missed most of the autumn with appendix problems, and was soon missing again, this time suspended for fourteen days. Law also upset referees with his petulant streak, and at West Brom in December he was so annoyed by the man in black that he complained to the authorities. They backed the player and censured the official, Gilbert Pullin, who promptly hung up his whistle. Problems resurfaced at Anfield in April, when Nobby Stiles gave a two-fingered salute to the Kop. Law and his Scotland teammate Ian St John squared up and were lucky not to be given their marching orders.

Neither Gaskell nor Gregg looked totally at ease in goal, and it was rumoured that Busby coveted Leicester and England Under-23 custodian Gordon Banks, but Busby denied the whispers and persevered with his flawed but loyal custodians.

The winter of 1962-63 was the worst in recent memory. The ice and snow meant there was very little football played between Christmas and the end of February. Week after week the football programme was cancelled. With the Football Pools seriously affected, a Pools Panel, comprised of former players, sat each Saturday to decide on the day's results for the benefit of punters.

When the thaw finally arrived, clubs faced a massive fixture backlog, not least in the FA Cup. United played eight games in March, four of them FA Cup-ties. Of these, the first three were at home and United safely circumnavigated Huddersfield, Aston Villa and Second Division leaders Chelsea to earn a quarter-final tie at giant-killers Coventry City from the Third Division. The Sky Blues, rejuvenated by the arrival of a new manager – former PFA chairman Jimmy Hill – shocked United by going ahead, but United recovered to win 3-1. This was just as well, for they had failed to win any of five league games since the thaw, or any since early December.

The long enforced break enabled Busby to assess matters and do some transfer business. Stoke wanted Mark Pearson, and although United agreed a £20,000 fee for the forward, 'Pancho' didn't want to drop a division, even though the Potteries club, inspired by Stanley Matthews and Dennis Viollet, were favourites for promotion.

Busby headed to Scotland for his latest acquisition. He had his eye on two wing-halves, Rangers' Jim Baxter, a prodigious ball-juggler, and Celtic's Pat Crerand, a non-stop midfield dynamo. Busby could only afford one or the other. According to Law in his book *The Lawman*, Busby asked Denis for his opinion. Law's view was that while Baxter was more skilful and would provide greater entertainment, Crerand would fit in better at Old Trafford and be a better long-term investment. Busby signed Crerand for £40,000 and United got eight years' excellent service. Baxter, who would give dazzling performances against England in 1963 and 1967, suffered several injuries and by 1969 his meteoric career had fizzled out.

Crerand's arrival in February meant that Nobby Lawton was also squeezed out, and he moved to Second Division Preston in March. A year later he would be a driving force behind Preston's FA Cup run to the final. Chelsea manager Tommy Docherty hoped to buy both Jimmy Nicholson and Nobby Stiles. Busby said no, despite Nicholson not featuring in the first team for some time.

On the field, matters did not improve during April, with only six points gained from seven games, and United slipped closer and closer to the trap door. United overcame Second Division Southampton in a tedious FA Cup semi-final at Villa Park, but were looking at a unique, unwanted double, relegation and the FA Cup trophy in the same season. Instead of spending the weeks between the semi-final and the final preparing for Wembley and giving games to reserves, United had to focus on avoiding the drop for the first time since the early 1930s. Leyton Orient were already down, and with four league games remaining United were eighteenth, just one point ahead of twentieth-placed Birmingham City and two points better off than Manchester City.

With only two teams relegated, United's future would rely on crucial games against three sides below them. Defeat at Birmingham set alarm bells ringing and set up arguably the most important derby game ever. The locked gates were broken down by fans desperate to see a game which could decide which of the Manchester clubs would be relegated, and thousands watched the game for free. United kicked off one point better off, and the outcome hinged on a controversial penalty. City had led 1-0 from the early minutes and looked certain of two vital points until a sloppy back-pass saw Law and City goal-keeper Harry Dowd chase the loose ball. Although Dowd appeared to win the race, Law tumbled in the penalty area. The referee awarded a penalty and Quixall levelled the scores.

Three days later United beat doomed Leyton to record their first home win since December, while City collapsed 1-6 at West Ham and were relegated. United's nervous last month had not been the best preparation for the Cup final seven days hence, and for the first time in a post-War final the Reds would start as underdogs.

The First Division title went to Everton for the first time since 1939, with Tottenham six points behind in second place, despite scoring 111 goals, of which the division's leading scorer Jimmy Greaves scored 37.

Match of the Season 1962-63

United 3 Leicester 1

FA Cup final, 25 May 1963

Preparation for England's hosting of the 1966 World Cup had already commenced, and Wembley Stadium had been given a major facelift. £500,000 had been spent on the 40-year-old stadium, re-roofing the stands and covering both ends for the first time. The translucent fibre-glass roof meant that all 100,000 spectators would now be covered. The 1963 final was therefore the first in the modernised arena, and also commemorated the centenary of the Football Association.

DID YOU KNOW?

Between 1909 and 1957, only once did Manchester United achieve the league 'double' over neighbours Manchester City – in 1949-50.

Opponents Leicester started as favourites, having just completed their most successful season ever, finishing fourth. At one stage a League and Cup double had looked a possibility. The two teams had recently met in the League, and City's 4-3 win at Filbert Street on Easter Tuesday had sent them to the top of the table, but four defeats in their last five games had shattered their title hopes. Manager Matt Gillies had retained an unchanged side throughout the Cup run that had seen them beat Grimsby, Ipswich, Leyton Orient and Norwich, before a Mike Stringfellow goal saw off Liverpool at Hillsborough to send Leicester to Wembley for the second time in three years.

They were a team of few stars. Goalkeeper Gordon Banks had just won his first England cap, and Frank McLintock and Davie Gibson were on the verge of full caps for Scotland. Their secret weapon was centre-forward Ken Keyworth, a converted wing-half, who had netted a six-minute hat-trick against United in City's 4-3 Easter victory.

On the day, Leicester froze, whilst United – many believe – came of age. Leicester, though, playing in all white, might have scored when Cantwell almost headed Stringfellow's shot into his own net. Then, after half an hour, United went ahead, Law swivelling on Crerand's square pass for his sixth goal in the competition.

David Herd, whose father had played for Manchester City in the 1933 and 1934 finals, scored United's second early in the second half when Banks failed to hold Charlton's shot. Keyworth reduced the arrears with a diving header, only for Banks to err again, leaving Herd to bundle the ball into the net.

United had many stars on the day, but the Scots – Crerand and Law – came of age on the big stage. Crerand, who had failed to live up to his reputation since his transfer, caught the eye throughout, and the extrovert Law was a thorn in Leicester's side with his superb heading and nifty footwork. He would have bagged a hat-trick had his header not hit a post, or his dribble not been cleared off the line.

At the final whistle the Queen presented the trophy to skipper Noel Cantwell. The United players went on a lap of honour to receive the applause due to a team that had found itself at last. The misery of the winter months was forgotten and a new dawn was breaking for Britain's most famous club.

CHAPTER SIX

THE GLORY YEARS – II (1963-68)

LEAGUE DIVISION 1	**1963-64**
Division 1	Runners-Up
FA Cup	Semi-finals
League Cup	Did not enter
European Cup-Winners' Cup	Quarter-finals

Despite finishing nineteenth in Division One, United's FA Cup victory gave reason for optimism. Behind the scenes, however, there was unrest about money. The players had been promised a bonus for winning the Cup but not told how much. Newspaper speculation had led the players to believe that a figure of £2,000-per-man was on the cards. Leicester had reputedly been set to receive a similar figure had they won, and the previous season Burnley had received £1,000 per man for losing. Whilst in Italy on a post-season tour, Busby informed the players that they would receive just £20 each for winning the trophy, leaving them stunned. Several took their grievances to Busby personally, but to no avail. By all accounts, Busby and chairman Harold Hardman had been loath to ask the board for a larger sum in light of the dreadful league season. It was also apparent at this time that, despite United's high profile, their players generally were amongst the lowest paid in the top division.

Back in 1948, Busby had resented the outspoken criticism of one player, Johnny Morris. In 1963 it appears that David Herd and Johnny Giles were the instigators of the players' dissatisfaction. When the new season kicked off with a humbling 0-4 defeat at Everton in the Charity Shield, Busby acted swiftly. Cup final heroes Herd, Giles and Quixall were dropped, and replaced by Ian Moir, Phil Chisnall and the little-known David Sadler. The manager's actions were vindicated as the team enjoyed their best start since 1956-57 – remaining unbeaten after seven games. The fine start included a revenge win over Everton, 5-1 at Old Trafford, and a 7-2 win at Ipswich, who were doomed to a quick return to Division Two.

Giles' career at Old Trafford was over, and within weeks Busby accepted a £34,000 bid from Leeds. Busby lived to regret the departure as Giles, and Leeds, came to haunt United over the coming years.

DID YOU KNOW?

When Johnny Carey lifted the FA Cup in 1948 he was the first Southern Irishman ever to do so.

Giles had started out as an inside-forward, but after the FA Cup semi-final defeat by Tottenham in 1962 – when he had been indisposed with a viral infection – Busby switched him to the right wing and gave him few opportunities in his favourite role. At Leeds, Don Revie played him at inside-forward and Giles became one of the best midfield schemers in the country.

Herd was recalled after United's first defeat, at Blackpool, and showed that Busby's motives may have been just right. The Scot now enjoyed his best season at United, scoring 27 goals.

David Sadler's rise was meteoric. The Kent-born 17-year-old had only signed as a professional in January 1963, after he had won England Amateur international caps. His first-team call-up came after just one Central League game, but he did not look out of place in the first team. As a striker, however, Sadler would be a fringe player. He only became a regular later, in 1966, when he switched to central defence, a position in which he won four England caps and fended off all competition at United until 1973.

On 14 September, a spindly 17-year-old from Belfast was given a first-team debut at home to West Brom, in place of the injured Ian Moir. George Best had shown enormous talent in the youth team but many inside the club had doubts over his application. It was immediately obvious that his was a remarkable and precocious talent and he gave West Brom's experienced full-back Graham Williams a chasing as United won 1-0. The following week Best was back to the reserves, but his time was coming.

The 1963-64 season belonged to Denis Law. He scored 30 league goals in 30 games and another sixteen in cup competitions. He was untouchable amongst goalscorers in the English game and, but for his disciplinary and injury problems, United might have won the championship. Law's reflexes were at their sharpest this season and he was deadly on the ground and in the air.

Law faced some of the hardest men in football history. Players like Liverpool's Tommy Smith, Chelsea's Ron 'Chopper' Harris and Tottenham's Dave Mackay were among the most intimidating of a new breed of defenders who – unlike their muscle-bound post-War counterparts – were as quick as the forwards they ruthlessly pursued.

Not only did Law pick up injuries from their bone-crushing challenges, he also often retaliated. By November he had been warned by the FA, following a glut of bookings. Then, at Villa Park, he lashed out at Alan Deakin in frustration at his own ill-treatment. Law was sent off and, in view of his poor disciplinary record, was suspended for a punitive 28 days. In those days, suspensions were not imposed for so many matches, but for a period of time. Law was banned from early December, therefore missing the glut of Christmas fixtures.

His absence coincided with United's worst spell of the season – three defeats in four league games. Law had been in dazzling form in his last game, hitting four goals against Stoke as the newly promoted Potters were demolished 5-2. Ironically, a week before Law's expulsion at Villa, Busby – unconvinced about Chisnall's suitability – had splashed out £35,000 on Chelsea's Welsh international forward Graham Moore. The skilful, burly Moore had an exciting debut in the 4-1 win over Spurs, but rarely impressed thereafter and has to go down as one of Busby's transfer mistakes. In the short term, however, Moore filled Law's shoes.

Christmas thrashings were endured at Everton (0-4) and Burnley (1-6), prompting Busby to change the front line. He had his mind on George Best, but the young Irishman had been given permission to go back to Belfast for Christmas. Best was located and flown back to Manchester where he played a sensational game at outside-left and scored his first goal in a 5-1 win over Burnley. Charlton moved to centre-forward to accommodate the precocious imp, a switch which soon became permanent and ushered in a new era for the popular England international who would win his 50th cap in April.

Another young winger, Willie Anderson, debuted against Burnley. With Sadler, Anderson and Best in the youth team, United harboured their best crop of youngsters since pre-Munich, and lifted the FA Youth Cup for the first time since 1957 by beating Bert Head's Swindon babes. Anderson would later struggle to make an impact at Old Trafford, and in 1967 joined Aston Villa, whom he helped knock United out of the League Cup in 1970.

The heavy defeats did not persuade Busby to ring the changes in defence. Dave Gaskell had returned to duty in late-November, after Gregg broke his collar-bone against Liverpool, otherwise the defence picked itself. Tony Dunne had seized the right-back place from Brennan, and Cantwell was first choice at left-back. Crerand, Foulkes and Setters constituted a virtually ever-present half-back line.

As Cup holders, everyone wanted to topple United. Second Division Southampton took a two-goal lead at the Dell in the third round and looked set to avenge the semi-final defeat of the previous season. But Best and Anderson sparked a 3-2 win. After victories over Bristol Rovers, Barnsley and Sunderland (after a struggle), United faced West Ham at Hillsborough in the semi-final.

Despite West Ham's stylish football and commitment to attack, Busby's team were favourites. They had lost only twice in fourteen games since Best's return against Burnley, and defeated the Hammers 2-0 at Upton Park the week before the semi-final. The Reds fielded their strongest team, but could not master the quagmire conditions, nor 22-year-old Bobby Moore, who was a Trojan in defence. West Ham deservedly won and progressed to beat Second Division Preston in the final. Crestfallen United flew off to Lisbon for a crucial European tie on the Wednesday night.

United's progress in the Cup-Winners' Cup had seen Dutch amateurs Willem II defeated in round one, before two gripping encounters with the holders, Tottenham, in round two. United lost the away leg 0-2 but bounced back to win the return 4-1, with Bobby Charlton scoring the deciding goal in the 89th minute. Tottenham had lost Dave Mackay with a broken leg early in the game and their ten men failed to contain United. After this comeback, the prospect of Sporting Lisbon in the quarter-finals was hardly daunting. When United took a 4-1 lead in the first leg a place in the last four of the competition looked a formality.

Instead, the hoop-shirted Portuguese inflicted a 5-0 whitewash on United, with Osvaldo netting three. Setters and Chisnall were probably no worse than anyone else, but neither would feature regularly for United again. According to insiders, Setters was a barrack-room lawyer type and Busby had lost patience and wanted him out. Fortunately, in Nobby Stiles he had the perfect replacement. Within twelve months Stiles would be part of the England squad.

After the exciting spring, when United had looked capable of lifting two, if not three trophies, the two Cup defeats in four days were a massive blow. Leaders Liverpool looked unlikely to loosen their grip and confirmed their superiority with a 3-0 Anfield win in early April. Liverpool's final margin, however, was only four points – which they had gained in the two games between the clubs.

One negative aspect of United's season had been the growth in hooliganism. The media reported on various negative aspects of the club's 'supporters'. There was serious crowd trouble at Aston Villa, and at Old Trafford for the visit of Birmingham. Fans were criticised for their vulgar chants, the throwing of toilet rolls at Nottingham, and most seriously the wrecking of a British Rail train returning from the Cup game at Southampton.

Football hooliganism was a relatively new phenomenon and a big club like United were sure to attract their share of yobs and thugs. The United away following had been growing for some time as fewer people worked on a Saturday and were free to travel. Sociologists made tenuous links between the players' unruly behaviour and that of the fans, and in United's case there might have been a correlation. United had become known as a dirty side and were regularly in trouble with referees. In addition to Law, Cantwell was warned about his behaviour after several bookings, Crerand was sent off at Burnley for elbowing an opponent, and David Herd got his marching orders at Willem. Setters and Stiles were hard and, some might say, dirty players, not really in the tradition of United's whiter than white stars. Busby, by not clamping down on the players' behaviour – especially Law's – seemed to condone the indiscipline.

Match of the Season 1963-64

United 5 Sunderland 1

FA Cup, quarter-final, 2nd replay, 9 March 1964

The FA Cup quarter-final draw paired United with Sunderland, who had been out of the top division for six years and were on the verge of a triumphal return. Managed by former Burnley hard-man Alan Brown, the Wearsiders were unbeaten since before Christmas and topped Division Two from Don Revie's Leeds. Roker Park's attendance of 62,000 against Everton in the fifth round illustrated the club's potential.

Sunderland's side was virtually unchanged all season. A solid defence built around Irish international and Wearside legend Charlie Hurley also included goalkeeper Jim Montgomery and wing-halves Martin Harvey and Jimmy McNab. In attack, the club boasted heavy scorers in Johnny Crossan and Nick Sharkey, who were served by skilful wingers Brian Usher and Scot George Mulhall.

The first game, at Old Trafford, belonged to Sunderland who, with five minutes remaining, led 3-1. Mulhall had headed them ahead after

Gaskell failed to catch a cross, and Crossan, with a dazzling run from the halfway line, made it 2-0 by lobbing Gaskell. Hurley headed Crerand's lob past Montgomery before Shay Brennan brought Crossan down for a penalty which the Irishman converted himself. Sunderland, in their change sky blue shirts, defended in depth, but Bobby Charlton scored with a rare header and almost at once Stiles crossed from the right, allowing Best to steer the ball through a forest of legs for a barely deserved equaliser.

Sunderland had the advantage of a home replay, but psychologically United's late goals may have swung the tie in Manchester's direction. At Roker Park four days later the locked gates were broken down, whereupon approximately 25,000 gained illegal admittance. Eye-witnesses estimated the crowd at 70,000, with another 30,000 outside. Those inside saw United again saved at the bell. Sunderland led through Sharkey's volley, but were pegged back when Montgomery miscued a goal-kick straight to Law. In extra-time Sunderland regained the lead when Setters, trying to clear, headed a George Herd cross past Gaskell. With two minutes remaining, Charlton headed home to save United's bacon.

In view of the crowd problems at Roker, the third game – at Huddersfield – was made a 55,000 all-ticket tie. Sharkey yet again put Sunderland ahead, just after half-time but it was not long before United were level through Law. Thirty seconds later, Chisnall netted from the edge of the box and United were ahead for the first time in 260 minutes of struggle. Almost immediately Hurley up-ended David Herd and Law scored from the spot. Four goals in five minutes and Sunderland were destroyed. Law and Herd added further goals as United's torrent swept over the last remains of wretched Sunderland.

LEAGUE DIVISION 1	**1964-65**
Division 1	Champions
FA Cup	Semi-finals
League Cup	Did not enter
Inter-Cities Fairs Cup	Semi-finals

Eight years after their last championship, Manchester United reclaimed the First Division title in 1964-65. The margin over second-placed Leeds was not points but goal-average. It was the closest finish since 1953 and only the fourth time since the Football League commenced in 1888 that the title had been decided by this method.

For most of the season the race was contested by three teams, Chelsea being the third member of the trio – and all three also reached the FA Cup semi-finals. Each of the three clubs coveted hopes of a League and Cup double, but at the final reckoning Leeds and Chelsea were left as bridesmaids, with United the champions and Liverpool winning the FA Cup.

For United, two matches against Don Revie's Leeds ultimately decided their rival's fate in the two domestic competitions. Busby's men lost the FA Cup semi-final replay at Nottingham at the end of March, but won the crucial league game at Elland Road two weeks later. The Reds went on to win three games in a row to clinch the title. Leeds marched on to Wembley but were destined to be bridesmaids in the Cup too, a role they would become accustomed to over the next decade. Bill Shankly's Liverpool followed up their League title of 1964 by winning the Cup 2-1 after extra-time.

In the summer of 1964, Busby had entered the transfer market. The press speculated about big names like Blackburn's Welsh centre-half Mike England, Blackpool's England international full-back Jimmy Armfield, and Rangers' willowy midfielder Jim Baxter. But Busby's requirements were more specific and his sights set on less high-profile players who would cost less. Since Giles' departure, he had experimented with Ian Moir, Albert Quixall and David Herd in the outside-right position. He now signed Burnley's John Connelly, who had been a regular thorn in United's side over a number of seasons. Connelly, a key member of Burnley's 1960 championship side, cost £60,000 and would prove an inspired signing.

Busby also wanted a goalkeeper and paid £10,500 for Shamrock Rovers' Pat Dunne. After a handful of reserve games, Dunne was given his first-team chance after Gaskell's nightmare at Fulham.

Dunne's arrival sparked a remarkable unbeaten run, which saw United win thirteen league games out of fifteen. Dunne, however, was to prove just the latest in the bizarre tradition of Busby goalkeepers; occasionally inspired, often competent, never completely reassuring. As it turned out, he was a one-season wonder, replaced by Gregg early the following season – but what a season!

After United's dodgy start – one win in the first six games – Busby settled on his preferred line-up and the team remained virtually unchanged throughout a momentous season. Herd was back at centre-forward, with Charlton at inside-right. Stiles had finally seen off the challenge of Maurice Setters. Setters was one of several fringe players sold during the season, as Busby put it, 'to relieve the bottleneck in the reserves.' Whilst the United production line was not as prolific as it had been, it was still unearthing some gems. In addition to Best, Sadler and Anderson, there was a gritty Scot named John Fitzpatrick, winger John Aston (son of the former United full-back), full-back Bobby Noble, and forward Jimmy Ryan. All these would be blooded over the next two seasons.

Setters transferred to Stoke in the autumn and on his return to Old Trafford with the Potters received a standing ovation. Jimmy Nicholson moved to Second Division Huddersfield, Phil Chisnall to Liverpool, Albert Quixall to Third Division Oldham, and Ian Moir to Blackpool. None raised large sums, but the total proceeds probably helped balance the books.

The unbeaten run hoisted United to the top of the League. The results included a 7-0 thumping of Aston Villa, a first win at Stoke for 30 years, a 2-0 win at high-flying Chelsea, and a 2-0 triumph at champions Liverpool. United remained unbeaten until the December visit of newly promoted Leeds. Don Revie's team were hard and ugly. Lacking the talent at Busby's disposal, they cynically set out to stop their opponents playing.

Revie was a paradox: as a player he had not been ruthless. Indeed, he is fondly remembered as the innovative, deep-lying centre-forward in the mid-1950s Manchester City team. As a manager, however, he changed his spots: he appeared to encourage foul play, the excesses of professionalism, and even blatant cheating. With iron men like Norman Hunter, Jack Charlton (brother of Bobby), Bobby Collins and even Johnny Giles, Revie had a rogues' gallery on his playing staff which would keep Leeds at or near the top of British and European football for a decade.

DID YOU KNOW?

Against Bolton in January 1955 the referee blew for time four minutes early. By the time he realised his blunder several Bolton players had to be got out of the bath.

Now, in a fog-affected game, Leeds snatched a goal and defended using all their strength, gamesmanship and guile.

In the meantime, Law was in trouble again, sent off for swearing at referee Peter Rhodes at Blackpool. Law argued that he was swearing at teammate Crerand, but the disciplinary panel sided with the referee's version, despite Rhodes selling his story to a Sunday newspaper. Law received another 28-day ban, but this time missed only three games, so was barely missed. During his absence he learned that he had been voted European Footballer of the Year, the ultimate accolade, chosen by Europe's top sportswriters. Law was only the second British player to win the coveted prize (Stanley Matthews had been the inaugural winner in 1956).

Following the defeat by Leeds, United drew five of the next six league games and were deposed at the top by Tommy Docherty's Chelsea. Three of those draws were at home to strugglers. Defeats at Tottenham and Sunderland demonstrated the toll taken from competing in three competitions, for they left United three points adrift of Chelsea and Leeds.

After a gruelling seven games in February, United had reached the last eight of the FA Cup and Inter-Cities Fairs Cup – forerunner of the UEFA Cup. Early wins over Djurdardens (Sweden) and Borussia Dortmund (West Germany) – the latter performance described by Busby as 'our greatest show in Europe for many years' – had set up an all-English tie, for the second season running, with Everton. Although Everton were favourites, by virtue of a 1-1 draw at Old Trafford, United won it with a Herd goal.

For Busby, the team and supporters, however, the biggest prize was the League championship. Mid-March brought a crunch clash with Chelsea at Old Trafford. Defeat would have left United seven points adrift. The gates were locked an hour before the kick-off and those outside missed seeing United win 4-0. Two days later United won their game in hand against Fulham and now trailed Chelsea and Leeds by just one point. All three leaders had played 33 games.

United still faced banana skins. A 0-1 defeat at Sheffield Wednesday, a week before the Cup semi-final at the same ground, handed the title advantage to Leeds. The heavy Hillsborough pitch had not suited

United's free-flowing football and many feared the worst against Leeds. Revie's team were spiteful and malicious and bent on intimidation. United were no angels either, and the game degenerated into a brawl. There were no winners and, amazingly, no one was sent off. Four days later in the replay at Nottingham's City Ground, United were thwarted by Leeds goalkeeper Gary Sprake and the woodwork. With extra-time looming, a Johnny Giles' free-kick bounced off the back of Billy Bremner's head and Leeds were through.

United looked gutted – the defeat not only gave Leeds a Wembley place but also ensured their psychological advantage in the League. With the whole season at stake, United bounced back with Bobby Charlton's hat-trick inspiring a 5-0 away win at Blackburn.

Easter would prove to be significant. On Easter Saturday, the two fierce rivals met again at Elland Road in a vital league match. Connelly – so impressive that he had won a recall to the England squad – handed Busby's men an early lead which was bravely defended. At the final whistle, although United were still third in the table, they had knocked Leeds off their perch. Chelsea were now top, with United a point behind.

On Easter Monday, with Leeds and Chelsea losing, the division saw its third different leaders in four days as United came from behind to win 4-2 at St Andrews, a result which condemned Birmingham to relegation. Five days later another hurdle was removed from United's path when Liverpool were beaten 3-0. For the first time, the title looked within United's grasp.

Chelsea, meanwhile, were racked by disciplinary problems. Eight first-team players broke manager Docherty's curfew in Blackpool before a crucial game and were sent home in disgrace. A makeshift Chelsea side lost badly at Burnley the following day. On the Monday evening, Arsenal were the visitors to an electrified Old Trafford. With Chelsea out of contention and Leeds having an inferior goal-average, the fans knew a United win would clinch the title – provided Leeds did not win at Birmingham, in which case United would have to gain a point in their final game at Aston Villa.

George Best gave United a first-half lead. News filtered through that Leeds were losing 0-3 at St Andrews and the celebrations started, albeit prematurely. Leeds pulled level in the second half, but United won 3-1. The title was secure, barring a 0-16 defeat at Villa.

There was still the Fairs Cup to chase. Two weeks after the domestic season ended, United overcame Strasbourg in the two-legged quarter-final. The second leg at Old Trafford was the occasion when the League championship trophy was presented.

The semi-final was against Ferencvaros, the star-studded Hungarians. United looked jaded in a niggly three-game series which extended to a play-off in Budapest which United lost 1-2 on 16 June – making it the longest season in the club's history. Ferencvaros went on to beat Juventus in the final, held over until the following season.

The defeat, however, did not detract from United's achievements. The team had conceded only 39 league goals – the lowest by any Division One team since 1949-50 – with a club record sixteen clean sheets. In a season of heavy defence, United – who were generally not renowned for their defensive resilience – had proved as mean as any. Crucially, they also had the forward talent to score goals. For the first time, United fielded a side of eleven internationals. Best, at eighteen, was already a Northern Ireland regular, and Stiles completed the set by winning his first England cap against Scotland in April.

Seven years after Munich, United had regained their position as the best club side in England and could now restart their quest for the biggest prize, the European Cup.

Match of the Season 1964-65

Wolverhampton 3 United 5

FA Cup, quarter-final, 10 March 1965

Notwithstanding his disciplinary problems, Denis Law was again a massive influence. He netted 39 goals in all competitions and was only pipped, by one goal, as Division One's top scorer by Tottenham's Greaves and Blackburn's McEvoy.

Double-chasing United had again made hard work of reaching the last eight. They had to come from behind to beat Fourth Division Chester, then struggled to overcome Stoke after a replay. Burnley looked set to win in the fifth round before a boot-less George Best set up a bicycle kick for Law. Crerand clinched victory a minute later.

Wolves's golden days under Stan Cullis were a distant memory. The team that had led England's assault on Europe in the 1950s had broken up. Key players such as Billy Wright, Bill Slater, Jimmy Mullen and Jimmy Murray had not been replaced. A disastrous start to 1964-65 had resulted in Cullis being unceremoniously sacked, after a 30-year career as Wolves player and manager.

DID YOU KNOW?

Between 1953 and 1955 United went 68 games without being awarded a penalty before Roger Byrne netted from the spot at Preston in March 1955.

Cullis's replacement Andy Beattie, the former Huddersfield and Forest manager, had struggled to revive the famous old club. The team were still at the foot of the table and only two weeks previously had lost 0-3 at Old Trafford. Beattie had blooded a number of youngsters, including inside-forward Peter Knowles, and recruited experienced pros like Hugh McIlmoyle. McIlmoyle had been the hat-trick hero of their fifth round victory over Aston Villa but had scored only once in twelve league outings. At least Wolves still had evergreen Ron Flowers, a hard-tackling defender, who had shone at Old Trafford when keeping Law shackled.

The game, postponed from the Saturday because of heavy snow, went ahead under floodlights. Wolves were ahead in three minutes. A long throw by Bobby Woodruff provoked a melee in which McIlmoyle lashed the ball home. The match programme had urged Wolves fans to roar on their heroes with cheers of 1950 proportions, and the din was deafening twelve minutes later when McIlmoyle seized on Foulkes' error to make it 2-0.

Just before half-time Law, previously subdued by Flowers, headed in a deflected cross. Within minutes the Scot had missed an easy chance but as the teams came out for the second half his jaunty trot was back. It spelled trouble for Wolves.

Within six minutes Law created the equaliser for Herd, and Best soon made it 3-2 direct from a corner. Crerand scored a fourth, and Law rounded things off with a disguised free-kick. It seemed almost an idle flick, but keeper Davies hardly moved.

Wolves looked shattered. Knowles scored a late consolation but the home fans cheers had by now been drowned by the Red Army's victory chants.

United thus went through to their fourth FA Cup semi-final appearance in a row. Wolves won their next three league games but at the final reckoning were relegated with 30 points.

LEAGUE DIVISION 1	**1965-66**
Division 1	Fourth
FA Cup	Semi-finals
League Cup	Did not enter
European Cup	Semi-finals

League champions rarely start the defence of their title convincingly, and Manchester United, as in 1952-53, were no exceptions. By the time they clicked into gear, Liverpool were well out in front. Although United crept into second place by February, the strain of tough European Cup and FA Cup campaigns took their toll. United finished well back in fourth position in the league and failed at the semi-final stages in the two cup competitions.

For the season's opener against Liverpool in the Charity Shield, the new United Road stand was mostly open. Seating 10,000, the stand – which had been commissioned with the 1966 World Cup finals in mind – was something of a trendsetter. It was the country's second cantilever stand (Hillsborough's North Stand had been the first), which meant no pillars obscured the view of spectators. It was also the first British ground to incorporate glass-fronted private boxes. The new stand, which was finally completely opened for the European Cup-tie with Helsinki in October, cost £350,000, £40,000 of which had been funded by the Football Association. United now had the beginnings of a super stadium to match their super team.

A 1-0 home win over Sheffield Wednesday constituted their first opening-day league win for seven years, but only one further victory came in the next seven games. This dismal run saw three home draws and heavy defeats at Nottingham Forest and Burnley. Once again, the goalkeeping position was causing Busby headaches. Pat Dunne, so solid in the previous campaign, had a nightmare at Forest and was dropped. For the umpteenth time, Dave Gaskell came in, but not for long. United's upturn in November coincided with the return of Harry Gregg, who did not take long to blot his copybook. He kicked Blackburn's centre-half Mike England and was ordered off. His stand-in, David Herd, was beaten twice in the last seven minutes to give Blackburn a point.

Other factors were responsible for the poor start. After three dazzling seasons Denis Law was off-colour. The press were critical of him, and George Best, for not releasing the ball quickly enough and for being too greedy. Best had started the season at inside-left, with young John Aston wide on the left. Aston's directness contrasted with Best's wide repertoire, but after a number of lacklustre performances Best was axed for the visit of Chelsea. Law probably only avoided a similar fate by scoring a hat-trick in that 4-1 win, but three weeks later he was out of the side for different reasons. Playing for Scotland against Poland he injured a knee and, contravening the club's rules, he failed to report it to the club doctor. The following Saturday at Tottenham he lasted less than an hour and became the first United player to be substituted in a league game, John Fitzpatrick replacing him and becoming the first United substitute. Subsequent knee problems would blight Law's career.

United's biggest problem was inconsistency, especially away from home. Two results in October summed up the enigma. Liverpool were beaten 2-0 at Old Trafford. A week later, in a 1-5 defeat at Tottenham before BBC's Match of the Day cameras, United's defence was ripped apart. Jimmy Greaves scored a wonder goal which the BBC would rerun *ad nauseam* for years.

A twelve-game unbeaten run restored confidence and included an avenging 5-1 defeat of Spurs at Old Trafford. Progress had been made in the European Cup, where the Finns from Helsinki and East German army team ASK Vorwarts had been comfortably defeated. A New Year's Day trip to Anfield would prove to be the defining point of the championship. United played well enough, but despite resolutely defending of Law's early goal they were beaten by a late strike. The result left United seven points behind Bill Shankly's team, although United had two games in hand.

All over the country, it seemed, football fans wanted to see United play. At virtually every First Division ground Busby's team would attract the biggest crowd of the season. There were two main reasons for this: first, the club's following was now national, if not global. Large contingents of fans in every part of the country would turn out when United came to town. Second, neutral fans wanted to see United's star names – Charlton, Law and Best. Televised highlights of soccer was relatively new – BBC's Match of the Day had only started the previous season (on the minority channel BBC2 and watched initially by only a few thousand viewers). Fans living any distance from Old Trafford had only limited opportunities to see the Reds in action, and that was in live games. At Newcastle, Highbury, White Hart Lane, Anfield, Everton and Chelsea, the attendances for the visit of United exceeded 50,000, with 60,000 attending the Stamford Bridge game. At Old Trafford, however, gates were down. Despite the new stand and extra seating, the average fell from 46,000 to 38,000. Pundits believed that United's fans were spoilt by success.

Goalkeeper apart, the defence was settled. Crerand, Foulkes and Stiles were virtual ever-presents. Although Manchester-born Shay Brennan, by now the club's fourth Eire international – following the two Dunnes and Noel Cantwell – was injured for four months, his stand-in Cantwell was an effective replacement. Foulkes missed one game, through injury, in November but was adequately replaced by David Sadler, converted to central defence. The switch was the making of Sadler, who went on to be capped by England in that position.

Best and Law recovered their form, although Law had his poorest scoring season since joining United with only eighteen league goals. Herd usurped Law as leading scorer, netting 24 league goals and a further eight in cup games.

Anfield would be United's only defeat in 25 competitive games. By mid-March, they had progressed to the semi-final of the European Cup and the quarter-final of the FA Cup, where they had been paired with Second Division sides in all four rounds. Derby had been slammed 5-2 but Rotherham held United 0-0 at Old Trafford and lost unluckily in the replay. For the second season running, United recovered from two down to beat Wolves at Molineux and set up a quarter-final tie with Preston.

The quest for European glory continued with a quarter-final clash with Benfica. The success in Lisbon (see Match of the Season) saw United, now the favourites, join Real Madrid, Inter-Milan and the Yugoslav champions Partizan Belgrade in the semi-finals. United got the tie they wanted, Partizan, avoiding the holders Inter and Real, champions in the first five years of the trophy.

Fate, however, saw Best suffer a cartilage injury in his right knee during the FA Cup-tie with Preston. Surgery was needed but Busby asked Best to continue playing for as long as United remained in the European Cup. Best was rested for a league game but returned for the first leg in Belgrade, taking the field heavily strapped up. The gamble failed. Best missed an early chance and Law hit the bar, but soon afterwards Best felt a stab of pain in his knee and from then on was a virtual passenger. United conceded two second-half goals and failed to make any impression on the tight home defence. On the team's return, Best entered hospital for surgery and from that point it seemed that the magic went out of the team.

DID YOU KNOW?

During United's 1956-57 championship season, they achieved the double over 11 of their 21 league opponents.

Partizan defended ruthlessly in a bruising second leg. Although United won 1-0 on the night, Partizan went through 2-1 on aggregate, becoming the first Yugoslav club to reach the European Cup final. To compound matters, Pat Crerand was sent off for trading punches with an opponent. Partizan went on to lose the final to Real Madrid, who exposed the Slavs' weaknesses.

Busby was devastated. He knew his team had peaked and that, having finished only fourth in the League, he would have to wait at least another two years before a further crack at the main prize. He told Crerand, 'We'll never win the European Cup now.'

Later, Harry Gregg criticised Busby's tactics in away European ties: 'Our team talk in Belgrade was the usual, "go out and enjoy yourselves, play it as it comes." That's what we had always done. We made no adjustments, which you have to do in the away leg of a European tie.' Busby had made the same error as in Lisbon two years previously. Time, however, would show that he had learned his lesson in Belgrade.

On the Saturday following the Partizan defeat United lost again, to Everton in the FA Cup semi-final at Bolton. It was a repeat of 1964 when they had lost two semi-finals in four days. United's trophy ambitions were in tatters.

The run-in saw United lose only one game in seven, but it was academic. Liverpool won the title by six points from Leeds and Burnley, with United ten points adrift. Busby took the opportunity to rest England squad members Charlton, Stiles and Connelly, and give games to youngsters like full-back Bobby Noble, winger Jimmy Ryan and David Sadler, who reverted to centre-forward. Connelly, however, not an England regular, was miffed at losing his place to Ryan, and his days at Old Trafford were numbered. The consistent Charlton, a key member of United and England's team, was voted Footballer of the Year by the Football Writers Association, the first United player to win it since Johnny Carey in 1949.

Whilst the three England men prepared for the World Cup finals, Law was grabbing the close season headlines. His contract expired in June and Law asked for a substantial pay-rise. Remarkably, five years after the abolition of the maximum wage, no United player came close to earning the magic £100 per week that former England captain Johnny Haynes earned at Fulham. Despite the club's renewed pre-eminence, the going-rate at Old Trafford was half that amount. Law had netted 138 goals in four seasons and was not called 'The King' by the Stretford End for nothing.

Law eventually got half the rise he sought, but not before Busby informed the press that Law was transfer-listed and ordered him back to Manchester like a naughty schoolboy. Then he made Law apologise in public for the trouble he had caused, making him keep the details of his rise a secret from other players. Busby thereby ensured that other potential rebels sensed that no player was indispensable.

Match of the Season 1965-66

Benfica 1 United 5

European Cup, quarter-final, 2nd leg, 9 March 1966

Manchester United emulated the 1957 and 1958 achievements in reaching the last four of the European Cup. This time they did so with arguably their finest European performance. Benfica, champions of Portugal, had lifted the trophy in 1961 and 1962 and been beaten finalists in 1963 and 1965. In a total of nineteen home ties they had won eighteen and drawn one, scoring 78 goals. Their ace player, Eusebio, was on the verge of taking Pele's crown as the top player in the world. He was a deadly striker and a lover of the spectacular. The Portugal national side, which would reach the semi-finals of the World Cup four months later, was composed mainly of Benfica players – Coluna, Augusto, Torres, Simoes, Eusebio.

A crowd of 64,000, paying record receipts of £30,000, had watched the first leg at Old Trafford, United winning 3-2. Charlton had matched Eusebio for skill, although the Portuguese striker had created both away goals. In the cold light of day, however, a one-goal lead was a fragile advantage to take to Portugal, scene of United's 0-5 hiding at Sporting Lisbon two years earlier.

75,000 packed into Lisbon's Stadium of Light. Before the kick-off the crowd rose to applaud Eusebio being presented with his European Footballer of the Year trophy. Sixteen minutes later he should have handed it to George Best. By then the Belfast genius had scored United's first two goals and set up Connelly for the third.

DID YOU KNOW?

When Duncan Edwards won his first England cap at the age of 18 years 183 days, he was the youngest England player of the century until Michael Owen.

United were 3-0 ahead on the night, four overall, and thoughts that they would try and defend their precarious lead were dismissed. Best headed his first goal from Tony Dunne's free-kick, and his second came from Harry Gregg's mammoth punt downfield. Herd headed down and Best raced through the home defence to slam a right-foot shot past goalkeeper Pereira. Law was architect of number three, slipping the ball through to Best, who crossed for Connelly. In a one-sided first half, United even had two efforts disallowed.

Benfica pulled a goal back early in the second half, courtesy of Shay Brennan's slice into his own net. In the last ten minutes, with the Portuguese champions still shell-shocked from the opening salvo, Crerand and Charlton scored a goal apiece. Benfica's unbeaten home record in Europe had been smashed.

Best became a world star overnight. The Portuguese press christened him 'El Beatle' – the British pop group were at the height of their popularity at the time – and life for the slight, quiet lad from Belfast would never quite be the same again. Busby later admitted that Best had ignored his instructions to 'keep it tight for the first twenty minutes' but how could he be angry with him. 'The boy's a genius.'

United were installed as the favourites to win the competition but they came a cropper in Belgrade and lost over two legs to Partizan.

LEAGUE DIVISION 1	**1966-67**
Division 1	Champions
FA Cup	Fourth round
League Cup	Second round

By finishing fourth in the League, United failed to qualify for European competition for 1966-67. Whilst seen as a failure at the time, in retrospect it enabled the club to focus on their most important objective – to qualify again for the European Cup by winning the championship. United would exit both domestic cups with tame defeats.

Most pundits expected the League to be dominated by north-west giants – champions Liverpool and United. Everton, strengthened by the £110,000 signing from Blackpool of World Cup hero Alan Ball, were also expected to offer a stern challenge. Don Revie's Leeds could not be ruled out, and Burnley, who kept on churning out quality home-grown teams, were outsiders for the title.

United's pre-season warm-ups did not augur well. Games against Celtic, Bayern Munich and FK Austria were all lost and thirteen goals conceded. Although Dave Gaskell started the season in the green jersey, behind the scenes a new signing was planned. Busby had claimed to be happy with his squad, but at one stage he competed with Everton for Ball's signature and was linked to Blackburn's centre-half Mike England, who signed for Tottenham.

Law had resolved his wage issues, whilst Bobby Charlton, Nobby Stiles and John Connelly returned in triumph from the World Cup. Charlton and Stiles had enhanced their reputations, with many experts naming Charlton in their team of the tournament. Stiles, after much criticism for some nasty tackles against France, had blossomed in the later stages and in the semi-final had completely blotted out Portugal's Eusebio, the tournament's leading scorer. Another member of the United staff, Wilf McGuinness, had also been part of Alf Ramsey's team – in a back-room coaching role which taught him a lot about tactics and the handling of players.

The World Cup heroes received a standing ovation at Old Trafford before the opening-day victory over West Brom – United scored five goals in the first 22 minutes and ran out 5-3 winners. Jimmy Murphy, celebrating twenty years as assistant manager, was also given a moving reception by the shirt-sleeved crowd.

The inconsistency prevalent in the previous season was evident in the first ten games, four of which were lost. In the space of seven days in early September Busby threw out three goalkeepers. Harry Gregg, still suffering with his shoulder, had been at fault for several goals during pre-season, and was dropped after a 0-3 defeat at Stoke. Three days later Dave Gaskell was recalled at Tottenham, but another defeat, 1-2, proved to be his swansong. Then Pat Dunne was summoned for the League Cup-tie at Blackpool. On a miserably wet night, Dunne was just one of several players to have a stinker in the 1-5 reverse, but his time was also up. The following day Chelsea's England Under-23 goalkeeper Alex Stepney was signed for £55,000, a world record fee for a goalkeeper. Chelsea boss Tommy Docherty had signed Stepney from Millwall just three months earlier – despite having England's number two Peter Bonetti already on his staff. Stepney had appeared only once for Chelsea, but following his move would go on to make over 500 appearances for the Reds.

Stepney went straight into the team for the Manchester derby. City, managed by Joe Mercer and Malcolm Allison, were back in the top flight for the first time since 1963. The new keeper kept a clean sheet in the one-goal victory and United – as when signing Pat Dunne in 1964 – rarely looked back.

With Busby given little in the way of funds to strengthen the team, he raised most of the Stepney fee by selling Connelly to Second Division Blackburn. Connelly had done his job in 1964-65 but Busby felt the time was right to cash in. John Aston was champing at the bit and Busby switched Best to the right wing to accommodate him.

A 1-4 defeat at Nottingham Forest, who – managed by Johnny Carey – would emerge as the season's dark horses, prompted a further defensive change. Local-born full-back Bobby Noble's performances in the reserves had convinced Busby that he should be given a chance, and Shay Brennan had to make way.

Noble grabbed his chance and was ever-present until a car accident in April 1967 left him with serious chest and head injuries and effectively ended his brief career. The inclusion of Noble at Brennan's expense was significant. Brennan was a footballing full-back in the traditional Busby style, whilst Noble was a tough-tackling defender, fast but with fire in his belly. It showed that Busby's views were changing – that previously his team had sometimes been a soft touch, especially away from home. Noble's promotion emphasised Busby's desire to get meaner.

Following the defeat at Forest, United lay eighth, four points behind leaders Chelsea, whom they faced twice the following month.

Stoke, Burnley and Tottenham were also amongst the early pacesetters. United's away form had to improve if they were to be serious title challengers. October and November were crucial months, and seven wins out of eight, including four successive away wins, pushed United into top position.

Alex Stepney quickly settled in and appeared to give the rest of the defence much-needed confidence. The attack saw David Herd playing on the right wing for several games, David Sadler at centre-forward, and Aston back on the bench as substitute. In mid-November injuries to Bill Foulkes and his deputy Noel Cantwell meant that Sadler, the object of interest from Bolton weeks earlier, reverted to centre-half. Herd celebrated his return to an inside role by scoring four in the 5-0 thumping of Sunderland. United were in imperious form, never more so than at Chelsea where they destroyed the leaders with the injured Law's stand-in, Aston, scoring twice.

England's World Cup victory had generated massive interest in football generally, and this was reflected in increased attendances in all four divisions. United were averaging over 50,000 at Old Trafford and it seemed that every away ground was overflowing when United visited. Fulham and West Ham recorded their biggest crowds since the War for United's visit, and 91,000 watched the Friday night game at Arsenal – 63,000 inside Highbury and 28,000 watching a relayed live broadcast on giant screens at Old Trafford.

In December, United stuttered, losing at Aston Villa and Sheffield United and drawing at home to Liverpool, who were strong challengers, but United stayed top. Herd hit another hat-trick as West Brom were beaten 4-3 away. Stiles was absent for five games, suspended after five bookings, but this marked the end of United's disciplinary concerns for the season – no United player was booked from Christmas until the end of March.

December saw two departures. After nine years at Old Trafford Harry Gregg joined Stoke on a free transfer but played only two games for the Potters before his longstanding shoulder injury forced him into retirement. He went on to become a respected manager at Swansea and Shrewsbury before returning to Old Trafford in 1978 as a goalkeeping coach, a position he held until 1981. Winger Willie Anderson was sold to Aston Villa for £20,000. He was unable to save Villa from relegation but played a key part in their 1970s resurgence.

From Boxing Day until the end of the season United lost only one competitive game – to Second Division Norwich in the FA Cup. Tony

Waddington's Stoke, full of veterans, had given United a tough game in the third round, and Dennis Viollet and Maurice Setters were applauded as returning heroes. Second Division strugglers Norwich inflicted United's earliest exit from the competition since 1961, repeating their 1959 victory and becoming the first lower division side to win a Cup-tie at Old Trafford since Hull in 1952. United's record of five successive semi-finals was over. Both Stoke and Norwich brought massive followings (it was estimated that 21,000 Stoke fans travelled) and both games attracted over 63,000, testimony to the Cup's allure.

In the league, United were invincible. It is popular wisdom that to win a championship you have to win home games and draw away. That is exactly what United did from New Year's Day until the end of April. Eight home wins, eight away draws, with only eleven goals conceded. The side was virtually unchanged during the run as they reclaimed the leadership from Liverpool, then saw off a challenge from Forest who – with a run of 28 games with only one defeat – looked capable of winning the double. Ultimately they would finish four points behind United and lose in the Cup semi-final to the eventual winners Tottenham.

In March, Herd broke his leg against Leicester, and with Law struggling for fitness, the goalscoring duties fell to Best, Sadler and Charlton. A goalless draw at Anfield protected United's two-point advantage. Forest climbed to second and got within one point before the pressures of going for two trophies caught up with them. When United arrived at West Ham on 6 May for their penultimate game they required just a draw to clinch their fifth post-War title and their seventh overall, equalling the record of Liverpool and Arsenal.

The crushing win at Upton Park was, curiously, United's first away from home since December. A week later against Stoke the trophy was presented to skipper Law and a lap of honour was taken. Stage one, the League championship was complete; now stage two, the European Cup was ready to be challenged for again.

Match of the Season 1966-67

West Ham 1 United 6

Division One, 6 May 1967

The signing of Alex Stepney had been vital to United's title challenge. A string of away draws had taken the team to the verge of success.

DID YOU KNOW?

During the 1955-56 season, Manchester United came from behind eight times to win games that might otherwise have been lost.

Despite having three World Cup stars (Moore, Peters and Hurst), West Ham had struggled. The problem was clear: while only United had bettered West Ham's 80 goals, only Aston Villa and Southampton – both to be relegated – had conceded more than the Hammers' 84. West Ham fans had not seen a 0-0 draw all season.

Despite West Ham's lowly position of sixteenth, World Cup hat-trick hero Geoff Hurst had scored 29 league goals (only bettered by Southampton's Ron Davies) and a further twelve in cup-ties. Martin Peters had added sixteen from midfield. Bobby Moore somehow avoided criticism for the team's defensive disasters – they were normally blamed on goalkeeper Jim Standen. But on this day Standen was injured, and reserve Colin Mackleworth stood in.

The occasion was marred by some of the worst violence ever seen inside an English football ground. United's fans had been involved in various acts of hooliganism throughout the season, smashing Norwich's team-coach windows after the FA Cup-tie and clashing with opposing fans at away games. At Upton Park, pre-match scuffles became full-scale terrace battles, with youngsters led away with blood pouring from head wounds from bottle throwing.

The game started in sunshine and within ten minutes the ball had hit the home net three times – first, Charlton with a thunderbolt, then Crerand with a header from Aston's cross, and finally a thumping Foulkes header. After 25 minutes it was 4-0. Stiles set up Best who bamboozled full-back John Charles.

Charles atoned by scoring from 30 yards, but then pushed Law in the box after being slapped. Law scored from the spot, and then made it six near the end. At the final whistle United fans invaded the pitch to cheer their heroes, provoking more trouble on the terraces.

Afterwards Busby admitted that the old United credo had been modified: 'ability is no longer enough, although there is still no real substitute for it. You need a combination of ability plus work-rate.'

Critics said Busby's third great team had been bought. His first (1948-52), it was argued, had been inherited; his second (1956-58) was home-grown. But Best, Charlton, Stiles, Foulkes, Aston and Sadler were products of United's youth policy. Although Law, Crerand and Stepney had cost big money, it was the mix that had brought success.

LEAGUE DIVISION 1	**1967-68**
Division 1	Runners-Up
FA Cup	Third round
League Cup	Did not enter
European Cup	Winners

United's preparation for the coming season was far from perfect. A seven-week summer tour of USA, Australia and New Zealand was probably unwise. It reduced the close season to just a few weeks, but on the positive side it enabled Brian Kidd, an 18-year-old striker to blossom and stake a claim for a first-team place. For the traditional Charity Shield fixture between the League champions and the FA Cup winners, United faced Tottenham and Kidd was handed the No 8 shirt. In a 3-3 draw, Kidd set up Charlton's stunning second goal and gave former United target Mike England a hard time.

Collyhurst-born Kidd was the automatic replacement for David Herd, still recovering from his broken leg. By November, Kidd was in England's Under-23 team, along with David Sadler. Although not a prolific scorer, Kidd added much to United's attack and his dramatic arrival convinced Sadler that his move to defence should be permanent. Once again the United youth machine had produced another gem and soon there were others. An 18-year-old Scottish left-back, Francis Burns, was blooded at West Ham in September after only four reserve games and immediately became first choice. Dunne switched to right-back and Shay Brennan was again in the cold. Frank Kopel made a couple of appearances at full-back and Manchester University student Alan Gowling scored goals for fun in the reserves. United's long-term future looked assured.

The press had speculated about summer signings. The League's two top scorers, Ron Davies and Geoff Hurst, were both rumoured to be signing for the Reds. In truth, only Sheffield Wednesday's Jimmy McCalliog was ever close to joining United that summer. Chelsea's Bobby Tambling, long admired by Busby, was allegedly set to sign in October but Tommy Docherty's sudden departure from Chelsea put paid to any deal. Kidd's emergence effectively ended any interest Busby had in the transfer market. In the New Year, when Southampton's Martin Chivers became available at £125,000, Busby remarked, 'why do I need Chivers when I have Kidd?'

The opening-day defeat at Everton ended United's twenty-game unbeaten run, but it was followed by an eleven-game undefeated sequence which took them to second place behind Liverpool. Off the field, however, United were in trouble. Their fans seemed to be in the news every week, provoking trouble at Hillsborough, Upton Park and Maine Road. The latest fads included wrecking trains to away games, a habit United's so-called supporters carried out with brutal efficiency on the trip to Chelsea in November.

Against Arsenal in early October Denis Law saw red again. He had been in trouble on the Australian leg of the summer tour, fined and suspended for bad language and the target of hate mail after breaking an opponent's jaw. This time he clashed with another Scottish fire-brand, Ian Ure, fists flew and both players were sent off. In the light of both players' previous records the FA banned them both for six weeks. For the third time since joining United, Law faced a lengthy suspension, missed nine games, and Busby was thought to be losing patience with his fiery genius.

Law and Best were marked men for the assassins, without whom no First Division team felt properly equipped to counter the great attacking players of the era. Best, however, did not get into the same scrapes as Law, and in the Scot's absence Best blossomed in an inside-forward role, scoring both goals at Anfield as United knocked Liver-pool off the top. Best was confirming that he was perhaps the greatest player post-War British player. He scored 28 league goals and made as many for others. Despite being pursued by the media, his football was at this stage unaffected.

Law had another problem. Although it was not yet apparent, he would miss most of United's critical games with knee trouble that was defying diagnosis. He scored only seven league goals and would spend the night of European triumph in hospital. Another injury victim was Nobby Stiles, who needed a cartilage operation in October and missed seventeen games. In his absence, Sadler and Foulkes performed so well that Sadler was awarded his first England cap, against Northern Ireland.

Apart from losses at Nottingham Forest and Leeds, United were unbeatable until late-January. In the European Cup. Maltese part-timers Hibernians were overcome in the first round, but Yugoslav champions Sarajevo were a tougher nut. Busby described their first-leg tactics as 'the most disgraceful tackling I have ever seen'. At Old Trafford festering feuds boiled over, one Sarajevo player was ordered off and fists flew in the tunnel after the final whistle. United won 2-1 to progress to a quarter-final against the Poles from Gornik Zabrze.

DID YOU KNOW?

Although Jeff Whitefoot – 16 years, 105 days –is United's youngest League debutant, Dave Gaskell was only 16 years, 19 days when playing in the 1956 Charity Shield.

United and Tottenham were undoubtedly the English glamour sides of the 1960s, and whenever the two clubs met the media interest was enormous. The games, too, were usually rip-roaringly entertaining. Spurs – with Jimmy Greaves, Dave Mackay, Cliff Jones, Alan Mullery – could always be relied upon to play attacking soccer. United seemed to save some of their best, and worst, performances for White Hart Lane. The clubs had already had two thrillers this season – the 3-3 draw in the Charity Shield and United's 3-1 home league victory in September. When the clubs were paired in the third round of the FA Cup, no other tie received comparable attention. Between the draw and the game, Spurs' manager Bill Nicholson paid a British record £125,000 for Martin Chivers, and the tall target man scored twice, the second a minute from time, to earn a draw at Old Trafford. In the replay, the two teams battered each other into submission, literally in Kidd and Joe Kinnear's case – they were sent off for fighting – but Spurs grabbed the winner in extra-time.

Busby was disappointed, but three days later his team returned to White Hart Lane and won 2-1 in the league. Suddenly United were three points ahead of second-placed Leeds, with a game in hand. With Stiles and Herd returning from injury, few would back against another League title for the Reds.

United lost at Burnley before warming up for the first leg with Gornik by winning 2-0 at Arsenal. An Old Trafford full-house saw United struggle to break down the Gornik defence and it looked as though they would have to travel to Poland with just a one-goal lead until Kidd's last-minute goal doubled the advantage.

In Poland, United were greeted by a severe freeze. Busby considered seeking a postponement but the referee could not be found until it was too late. On a snow-covered pitch in a blizzard, United held out until twenty minutes from time before the Poles, roared on by 100,000 supporters, halved the deficit. A brave rearguard action orchestrated by the superb Stiles and Fitzpatrick saw United hang on to go through to the semi-finals.

League form stuttered in March, with games lost on the Saturdays following both Gornik ties. United had the look of a European hangover, judging by the way Chelsea – inflicting United's first home defeat for two years – and Coventry, struggling to avoid the drop, stole the points. Coventry, managed by Noel Cantwell and captained by Maurice Setters, won 2-0 to knock United off the top, replaced by Manchester City on goal-average.

Eleven days later, in the crucial league game with Manchester City, United lost at home again. The two Manchester clubs and Leeds were all level on points, with United having the worst goal-average. United faced a further six league games before the semi-final, first leg, with Real Madrid. Although they suffered a third home reverse – Liverpool winning 2-1 – United hit the top again by winning seven points out of eight. Their chief rivals were also stuttering in the final furlong, with Leeds still involved in the League, the FA Cup and the Fairs Cup. On the eve of the home leg against Real Madrid, United led the table by one point from Leeds, with their Moss-side rivals four points behind, with a game in hand. Joe Mercer's City, however, had no distractions.

A George Best goal was all United had to show for their Herculean efforts in the first leg against Madrid and their supporters feared the worst for the visit to the Bernabeu Stadium three weeks later. Meanwhile, the destination of the League title had to be decided and United once again suffered a European hangover, this time at West Brom, who trounced them 6-3. It was a crucial day in the race, as Manchester City's defeat of Everton took them ahead of United on goal-average. City's last two games were away and tough, at Tottenham and Newcastle, whilst United had what appeared to be easier home games against Newcastle and Sunderland.

City, however, true to the positive principles of their co-managers Mercer and Allison, attacked in both games and won both – 3-1 at Tottenham and 4-3 at Newcastle. United, despite hammering Newcastle 6-0, fell apart on the final day, losing 1-2 to lowly Sunderland. The championship trophy would move across Manchester and sit in the Maine Road boardroom for the first time since 1937. The final league game attracted almost 63,000 to Old Trafford – the twelfth 60,000-plus crowd of the season – and took United's average league attendance to a new English record of 57,552, surpassing Newcastle United's 1947-48 average of 56,283.

Attention now focused on the final against Benfica. 100,000 spectators, the majority supporting United, were present at 'neutral' Wembley to see the first English team in a European Cup final. With both clubs having red as their first-choice colours, United switched to an all-blue kit, whilst Benfica, Portugal's Red Devils, played in all white.

The game was no classic and the first half was memorable for two misses. Eusebio hit the bar and Sadler missed a chance that the injured Law would have scored in his sleep. Eight minutes into the second half Charlton scored with a rare header that looped over the keeper. In the last twenty minutes United faded and let Benfica in for an equaliser. In the final minute Eusebio escaped Stiles' clutches, but Stepney's save ensured extra-time.

Busby's instructions for the extra half-hour were simple: 'Just don't give the ball away. When you make a pass, make sure it reaches your teammate.' Kidd, celebrating his nineteenth birthday, has probably never enjoyed a better one. He created the second goal, Best slaloming through a square defence before foxing the goalkeeper, and headed the third at the second attempt after his first effort hit the bar. At 3-1 he veered to the right, held his marker at bay and waited for Charlton to arrive. The balding Munich survivor hit Kidd's subtle pass with his right foot for goal number four. United were Champions of Europe.

Match of the Season 1967-68

Real Madrid 3 United 3

European Cup, semi-final, 2nd leg, 15 May 1968

Standing between Manchester United and their first European Cup final were their old foes Real Madrid – winners of the first five European finals between 1956 and 1960, and United's nemesis in 1957, when players like Di Stefano and Gento had ripped the pre-Munich Busby Babes apart. A great sporting friendship had developed between the two clubs, with Real having waived their normal match fee to play a friendly to ease the financial strain at Old Trafford in the period after the crash.

The first leg, at Old Trafford, in front of a full house, had seen United do most of the attacking. At the end of 90 minutes, however, they only had a single goal to show. That goal, just before half-time, was created by Kidd, who sent John Aston away down the left wing. Aston's pull-back was met with a thunderous left-footer from George Best. There were few other chances in a nerve-tingling game, with Real keeping a tight rein on United's stars.

In Madrid, United – scarred by losing their championship crown four days earlier – had to make changes. Law's knee required an operation, and Sadler switched to the forward line. The old guard,

Foulkes and Brennan, were recalled, the latter replacing the inexperienced Burns. Real recalled local hero Amancio, suspended for the first leg, and with six of the Spanish national side in their ranks were confident of overhauling the one-goal deficit.

By half-time their confidence seemed justified, as Real left the field 3-1 ahead. Although the Reds had held out for half an hour, the roof had then caved in. Pirri headed Real in front from Amancio's bending free-kick, and ten minutes later Gento – the only Spanish survivor from the 1957 tie – hit a scorcher from a narrow angle. Within a minute United got a lifeline when Zoco panicked under pressure from Kidd and turned the ball into his own net. Almost at once Amancio made it 3-1 with a shot on the turn. Few in the Bernabeu Stadium gave United much hope of recovering.

Busby's half-time words were simple: 'I reminded them that we were only 3-2 down on aggregate and to go out and play.' United attacked from the whistle and the new Spanish champions crumbled. Sadler, previously an extra defender, abandoned his defensive duties and moved forward with telling effect. In the 75th minute he was on hand to score, following Crerand's free-kick. Three minutes later United scored from an unlikely source. For some unknown reason Foulkes joined the attack as George Best jinked down the right wing. As Best delivered his cross he saw Big Bill on the end of it and anticipated a ballooned shot into the sky. To everyone's astonishment the finish was sweet and perfect and the ball was nestling in the back of the Spanish net. Foulkes later described scoring the goal as 'my most precious moment in football'.

United played out the remaining minutes before a stunned Spanish crowd and celebrated joyously at the final whistle. At the fourth attempt at the semi-final stage, United had reached their pinnacle and more old foes, Benfica, awaited in the final at Wembley.

CHAPTER SEVEN

AFTER THE BALL – (1969-71)

LEAGUE DIVISION 1	**1968-69**
Division 1	Eleventh
FA Cup	Quarter-finals
League Cup	Did not enter
European Cup	Semi-finals

The season following victory in the European Cup was a major anti-climax. The warning signs had been present the previous campaign – a number of players were past their best, but the quality of the youngsters coming through was not up to past standards. Injuries would also affect the team during Busby's final season.

In June, Busby was knighted for his services to football (only the second football man to be honoured, after Alf Ramsey in 1966). This was a deserved reward for leading the club to victory in the European Cup, ten years after losing the heart of his team at Munich. He would turn 60 in May 1969, and the effort of restoring the glory to the club after the disaster had taken its toll.

In the aftermath of the Wembley triumph he warned: 'This is not the end of something, it is just the beginning.' He was both right and wrong. He was right in a sense that the club was becoming world-famous, ideally placed to take advantage of the burgeoning global nature of the game. He was wrong in the short-term, however. Busby had fulfilled his dream and completed the massive task of restoring Manchester United to the pinnacle. The club would never be the quite the same again and he would hand over the reins to others with unfortunate consequences.

He knew the day would not be far away when he would have to break up the side that had won two championships and seized the biggest prize. Several of his ageing stars were close to the point where they could no longer meet Busby's exacting standards, and the drop in quality of the home-grown players would force United to break with Busby's tradition. The club would have to resort to the transfer market to bolster an ageing side. The club's European triumph had generated profits of £250,000, but with Busby reluctant to sign tax-deductible players, the club had paid out large sums in Corporation

Tax. Remarkably, they were the only Division One club not to spend money in the transfer market during the 1967-68 season.

The early season form was poor. Law was back from surgery but was missing an extra gear. John Aston broke his leg at Maine Road in the third game of the season, and Brennan and Foulkes both had nightmare games early in the season. Busby recalled Francis Burns to replace Brennan, Sadler came in for Foulkes, and £95,000 captured Burnley's Scottish winger Willie Morgan to replace Aston. Aston in time recovered his place, but would never be the same player again and would join Luton three years later.

The European campaign started with a 10-2 aggregate thrashing of Irish club Waterford, with Law netting seven goals in the two games. Any dreams of an all-Manchester final were dashed when Mercer and Allison's City went out to Turkish champions Fenerbahce.

However, United's visit to Argentina in the World Club Championship in October affected players' minds. After the hot-tempered first game, United lost to Liverpool and failed to beat Arsenal and Spurs. The prospect of the return leg in the middle of the month hung over the team like a cloud. Suddenly they were struggling to score, with Kidd netting only one goal in 29 league appearances. He lost his place first to Sadler, then later John Fitzpatrick, but returned after Christmas to play a key role in the team's revival.

Between late-September and mid-March, United won only four league games out of 21, and one of those was against the First Division whipping boys Queen's Park Rangers. In that period United scored only twenty goals, almost all from Law and Best. When United faced QPR again at Old Trafford in March, Busby's team had slipped to seventeenth, and were under serious threat of being dragged into a relegation battle. Willie Morgan finally came good, and with Best also in superb form Rangers were thumped 8-1, United's biggest win for 70 years. After that, United romped through their final eleven games and were beaten only twice.

United's cup form was, thankfully, more imposing. After the defeat of Waterford, Law scored twice in a 3-0 home win over Belgian foes Anderlecht. In Brussels, United lived dangerously but squeezed through 4-3 on aggregate. Another 3-0 home win over Rapid Vienna paved the way for a fifth semi-final appearance.

In the FA Cup, Law netted seven goals in three rounds as three lower division clubs were eliminated. However, at the first sign of First Division opposition – Everton – United fell by the wayside.

DID YOU KNOW?

In October 1958, United were involved in the first League game played on a Saturday evening under floodlights when they lost 0-4 at Wolves.

Willie Morgan had initially been disappointing. In December he was dropped in favour of young Carlo Sartori – another Collyhurst lad following in the footsteps of Stiles, McGuinness and Kidd. The centre-half position was giving cause for concern and United were strongly linked with Derby's up-and-coming star Roy McFarland, Sunderland's Dave Watson, and Arsenal's tough-guy Ian Ure. Busby pondered the situation, then promoted Wolverhampton-born Steve James in place of Sadler, upon which the defence assumed a more solid look. Injuries to key players took their toll. Burns, a revelation the previous season, needed three cartilage operations within a year, Kidd twisted an ankle and missed two months, Charlton missed nine weeks with knee ligament problems, and Stiles also had an on-going knee injury.

On 14 January, three days after a defeat at champions-elect Leeds, the players were summoned to be informed that Sir Matt would be retiring as team manager at the end of the season. He would still be around – as general manager dealing with administration – but no longer involved with the first team, or so he said. The club did not name his successor and the football grapevine buzzed with speculation for three months about the identity of the new 'boss'. Amongst the names mentioned were Leeds' Don Revie, Celtic's Jock Stein, well-respected Burnley coach Jimmy Adamson, and the shrewd young Chelsea boss Dave Sexton, feted for his tactical wisdom. For various reasons, none of these were serious candidates. Revie was ruled out on the grounds that Leeds were the antithesis of everything Busby stood for; Sexton was not interested – he was a family man and would not uproot to move north. Ultimately, though, it was Busby's decision and he did not trust anyone outside Old Trafford.

Surprisingly, Busby's assistant Jimmy Murphy was not considered, probably because at the age of 59 he was reckoned to be too old. In retrospect, many thought Murphy, a mentor of McGuinness in Wilf's playing days, might have made an excellent sidekick for the new coach. He was a wily old fox who knew how to get the best out of young talent and would have helped McGuinness in his new role. Busby, though, did not appear to consider Murphy in the equation and instead focused on two former United players. Noel Cantwell had turned down an Old Trafford coaching role eighteen months earlier to follow Jimmy Hill as manager of Coventry City, and had impressed many with his ability to motivate players. McGuinness had coached United's youth team with success and although he had only won the Youth Cup once, in 1964, he had kept the production line of young stars going.

Despite McGuinness's dreadful injuries incurred in 1959 – he ran with a tortured limp afterwards – he had vainly attempted a comeback in 1966, playing 30 reserve games and sitting on the bench for a first-team game at Leicester.

In April, with United out of contention for prizes – the earliest this had happened for seven years – Busby announced that McGuinness was the appointee: it later transpired that he had always been first choice. It is a mystery why Busby failed to keep McGuinness informed of developments. The new man was not, however, given the title of team manager: instead he was titled chief coach with responsibility for team selection, coaching, training and tactics. Busby became general manager with, ominously, responsibility for all other matters affecting the club and its players, as well as club spokesman. McGuinness was given a three-year contract and at 31 became one of the youngest 'managers' ever in the First Division.

Before Busby's farewell, however, there was unfinished business to be attended to. In the European Cup semi-final United pulled the short straw in the shape of AC Milan, the strongest of the opposition, when they would have preferred Ajax Amsterdam or Czech champions Spartak Trnava. Milan had knocked out Jock Stein's Celtic in the previous round – wrecking another dream tie – and were renowned for their defensive strength. The first leg was in Milan, and United transmitted the game on huge screens at Old Trafford. Over 23,000 fans cheered the black and white images as if watching a live game. They chanted and booed as though the players, hundreds of miles away in Italy, could hear them.

Milan scored a controversial first goal and stand-in goalkeeper Jimmy Rimmer, replacing the injured Stepney, could do little to stop the second goal. Tempers frayed and John Fitzpatrick was sent off for kicking Kurt Hamrin, Milan's Swedish international winger. As in 1957, 1966, and 1968, United were left facing a two-goal deficit to recoup in the second leg. At Old Trafford, Milan's strong *catenaccio* defensive trap kept United at bay for 70 minutes before a Bobby Charlton goal gave the team and fans some hope. With time running out, Law thought he had scored a second, which would have forced a third game in neutral Brussels. The French referee, however, ruled that Law's shot had not crossed the line. To this day Law and Morgan, who was following up, insist that the ball was in. Milan won 2-1 on aggregate and went on to beat Ajax 4-1 in a thrilling final.

Busby's personal grand finale was against Leicester, in a match delayed until four weeks after the end of the League season on account of City's fixture backlog, caused by an icy winter and a protracted FA Cup run. Leicester, who had lost the FA Cup final to Manchester City, arrived at Old Trafford needing to win to avoid relegation and send Coventry down.

United's players had a double motivation: it was Busby's final game in charge, but also they were determined to assist their former popular colleague Cantwell and his gritty Coventry team. Despite Leicester taking an early lead, they could not cope with the pressure and United ran out 3-2 winners. Relegated Leicester's manager, Frank O'Farrell, was one of the first to shake Matt Busby's hand at the final whistle. Busby returned the applause of the adoring supporters before turning to walk down the tunnel one last time. His face would be seen around Old Trafford for many years to come but there was no denying that this was the end of an era.

Match of the Season 1968-69

United 1 Estudiantes 1 (aggregate 1-2)

World Club Championship, 2nd leg, 16 October 1968

As European champions, United qualified to play the South American champions over two legs for the World Club Championship. The previous year Celtic had experienced a nightmare tie against Racing Club of Buenos Aires, and their manager Jock Stein vowed never to play in the competition again. For a time, United also seemed reluctant to participate in a potentially explosive tie against another Argentinian club, Estudiantes de la Plata. Busby, however, had the final word and decided that the chances were slim of the games being as volatile as those experienced by Celtic.

Argentina had felt insulted by Alf Ramsey during the 1966 World Cup, when he had derided their players as animals, following England's 1-0 quarter-final victory, which had seen the Argentine captain Antonio Rattin sent off.

DID YOU KNOW?

In March 1958, Alex Dawson, at the age of 18 years, 33 days, became the youngest post-War scorer of a hat-trick in the English domestic game.

As a member of that England side, Nobby Stiles was an obvious focus of hatred for the Estudiantes fans and players. He was head-butted early on by future Argentine manager Carlos Bilardo and kicked and spat at throughout. Stiles did not retaliate but, with ten minutes remaining, gestured with his arm after one of many dubious refereeing decisions and was sent off for dissent by the Paraguayan official. At the time, United were losing to a single goal by Togneri. Bobby Charlton needed stitches in a shin wound and the Argentinians did everything legal or illegal they could do to stop United playing. The referee turned a blind eye to their antics and also upset United by ruling out what looked like a good goal from Sadler before half-time.

The English press vilified the South Americans. *The Daily Mirror* screamed: 'The night they spat on sportsmanship.' In the circumstances, United counted themselves fortunate to escape with a narrow defeat and fancied their chances in the second leg at Old Trafford.

Stiles' expulsion meant he had to sit out the return game. Sadler moved back to defence with Kidd starting up front. The game was only five minutes old when Estudiantes scored. Ramon Veron, father of Juan Sebastian – who would later play for United – headed in Madero's free-kick. United were further hampered when Law had to leave the pitch with a gashed leg. The visitors were less cynical than in the first match, but that did not stop the Stretford End baiting them with chants of 'animals'.

With fifteen minutes left, Best, frustrated by the illegal attentions of Medina, floored his tormentor with a punch. Both players were ordered off. With three minutes left, Willie Morgan fired an equaliser from Crerand's free-kick. In a final fling, Brian Kidd lashed home a Morgan cross, but the Yugoslav referee had blown for time moments before the ball hit the net.

Despite United's sour experiences, Busby remained upbeat, insisting that he would not hesitate to re-enter if the club won the European Cup again. Just like in the 1950s, when he ignored those who questioned the rationale of entering the European Cup, he could see the benefits of pitting his team against the world's best. Whether his views changed a year later, when three Estudiantes' players ended up in a Milan jail after another brutal match, is unknown.

THE AFTERMATH

The day-to-day presence of Sir Matt Busby – he even retained his office, with McGuinness having to make use a smaller and less salubrious one – made it virtually impossible for the new man to operate properly. Busby apparently limited his influence over team selection, training and coaching, but he still held sway over players' contracts and transfers. In the summer of 1969 Busby revealed a list of players' salaries and McGuinness saw that several earned more than him.

On the training pitch, McGuinness ensured that his players were fit, but his methods caused resentment. He wanted to change United's traditional 4-2-4 system to a 4-3-3 style adopted by many English club sides following Alf Ramsey's success in the 1966 World Cup.

The start of 1969-70 saw the first two home games lost and United were soon struggling. There were no external distractions for the team, and the fans had expected a title challenge. McGuinness realised that the old core of the 1968 side would have to go. Foulkes and Brennan – best man at McGuinness's wedding – were the first victims. Stiles had not recovered from his knee problems, whilst Crerand was dropped, too slow for the rigours of top-flight football.

Arsenal's centre-half Ian Ure was bought for £80,000. McGuinness later admitted that this was Busby's initiative, and he had had little say. Ure's arrival helped the team to their first good run in the League Cup, until they lost a two-legged semi-final to Manchester City. A combination of City's FA Cup victory the previous season, and European and domestic trophies in the current campaign, meant they would overtake United as the top team in Manchester.

Following a third home defeat, by Chelsea, in December, Crerand and Willie Morgan were recalled for the visit to Anfield. United's 4-1 win sparked a seventeen-match unbeaten run which lifted the team above halfway and into the FA Cup semi-finals. The two Scottish players were close to Busby and it is likely he influenced their recall. Best was banned for a month after knocking the ball out of the referee's hands in a League Cup-tie with Manchester City, but returned for the fifth-round tie at Northampton where he scored six goals as United won 8-2.

Despite the resurgence, McGuinness knew the side needed reinforcements just to tread water in an increasingly competitive league. Two players he identified – Malcolm Macdonald and Colin Todd –

never arrived. McGuinness told Busby of his interest in Macdonald, a prolific scorer with Luton, but Busby replied that Liverpool had first option on the player. Within weeks Macdonald joined Newcastle.

Colin Todd was a bright young defender, but his team, Sunderland, were slipping into Division Two. McGuinness saw him as the man around whom to build a new defence, but Busby refused to meet the asking price. It was the same with another future England man, Ipswich's Mick Mills. Later McGuinness admitted that he should have tried to be firmer with Busby regarding transfers.

In the dressing room, players moaned about McGuinness's complicated team-talks and blackboards explaining tactics.

Wembley briefly beckoned, but Leeds were ultimately too good for United, winning a second FA Cup replay. An incident at a Birmingham hotel before the first replay soured relations between McGuinness and Best. According to several accounts, McGuinness caught Best *in flagrante* with a young lady hours before the game. That left enough time for Busby to intervene. Best played, but missed a golden chance to win the tie.

United finished the 1969-70 season eighth, but McGuinness survived only until the following Christmas. Successive home defeats by Manchester City and Arsenal – the latter watched by only 31,000 – and a League Cup semi-final defeat by Third Division Aston Villa, sealed his fate. United lay eighteenth and a relegation battle loomed. McGuinness was offered his old job as reserve-team coach. It was a massive blow to him at a time when his wife was pregnant and his father-in-law dying of cancer.

When the players were informed that Busby was temporarily back, Brian Kidd – a Collyhurst lad like McGuinness, and not afraid to express his views – turned to the senior pros and said: 'You lousy bastards, you've let him [McGuinness] down.' Within months McGuinness had left Old Trafford and become manager of Greek club Aris Salonika. In Greece his hair fell out and he became bald at the age of 33. The doctor said it was delayed shock.

Results improved under Busby's caretaker control and United recovered to finish eighth again. Best, who had netted just four goals before McGuinness's departure, scored fourteen afterwards, whilst Law also enjoyed a purple patch and finished second top scorer with fifteen. It was always clear that Busby's second stint would only be temporary – until the end of the current 1970-71 season – and he led the search for another successor.

Celtic manager Jock Stein was top of the list. But among other things his wife did not want to leave Scotland. Then Chelsea manager Dave Sexton rejected United's overtures for a second time. The eventual choice was Leicester boss Frank O'Farrell. O'Farrell was an experienced football manager who had just led his team out of Division Two. He had a reputation for high principles and Busby was impressed by what he knew of the man and his ways. O'Farrell had heard all about Sir Matt inhibiting McGuinness, and Busby assured him that as he was becoming a director he would no longer be involved in team affairs. Busby also accepted that the rebuilding of the club would take time and that the directors should be patient.

O'Farrell took the job. On his first day at the club he made it clear that he wanted Busby's office. Busby agreed, but eyebrows were raised at this statement of intent – the confident Irishman was going to do things his own way. On the field, things went well and United were top of the league by Christmas, mainly down to George Best, who scored fourteen goals by the end of November. Law also hit a golden vein and chipped in with twelve goals. The good form masked a multitude of problems, however, not least in the dressing room. Players like Law, Morgan, Stepney and Crerand still socialised with Busby. On the pitch, the goals dried up and United's championship challenge petered out to an eighth place finish.

The following season, 1972-73, United had a dreadful start, failing to win any of their first ten games and by Christmas O'Farrell was out. He was scapegoated for the team's poor form and also for the declining state of affairs with George Best. In truth, he had inherited a club in terminal decline run by a dictatorial Busby who just could not hand over the reins. By all accounts, Busby meddled in team matters via the cabal of players he socialised with.

Somehow, new manager Tommy Docherty kept United in the First Division, but the following season the chickens came home to roost and United were relegated for the first time in 37 years. When the trap door finally opened, only Stepney and Morgan remained from the team that Busby had bequeathed to McGuinness. Bobby Charlton, Foulkes, Brennan and Crerand had all retired, Dunne, Kidd, Sadler and Law sold – the latter to Manchester City for whom he uncomfortably scored the goal which sealed United's fate – and Best was jettisoned by Docherty after numerous scrapes.

Five years after being crowned kings of Europe, Manchester United were no longer good enough to dine at the top table.

Matt Busby – A Retrospective

In February 1969 a poll undertaken by the Gallup organisation placed Matt Busby as the seventh most popular man in Britain. His inclusion in the top ten was achieved despite his never having appeared on a television chat-show nor even profiled in any depth in print. Very few people knew the man behind the legend. Those voting for him were voting for an image, one built upon the football played by his superb Manchester United teams who had won the hearts and minds of many who knew little or nothing about football but had been seduced by either the Busby Babes or the swashbuckling side of the 1960s. That image was one of a courageous, gracious man, an avuncular character who had gained the nation's sympathy when he hobbled into Wembley Stadium just months after his young team had been destroyed at Munich. His aura was that of a nobleman from the world of professional football where such are rarely found.

Busby carefully cultivated this image, rarely letting his guard down, and never letting the media get to know the real man. He built a myth around Manchester United and himself, but beneath that myth was a single-minded man who built three great teams by being tough, focused, and totally in control of everything about the club. He did not tolerate dissent, and there are several examples of players who thought they could take on Matt Busby but found to their cost that they could not. In 1948 Johnny Morris was the ringleader of the revolt following the club's first post-War success – he was unceremoniously shown the door, despite the fact that he was one of the best inside-forwards in the country.

In 1963 Johnny Giles went the same way. Giles was not a barrack-room lawyer like Morris, but a thoughtful, erudite and eloquent but not disloyal young man who had views on the game. Giles probably intimidated Busby, who was used to players showing their loyalty by trusting him to guard their interests, on or off the field. Busby repaid loyalty handsomely but at a cost of toeing the line and not voicing dissent. Those that persisted would apparently see a glint of steel in his eye. No raised voices, no tantrums, no tea-cups thrown across the room. Just a clear indication that the 'rebel' was letting the club down and, if he persisted, he would be shown the door.

There is clear evidence that once a player fell out with Busby he was soon on his way. In addition to Morris and Giles, other, less high-profile and not necessarily dissenting players were frozen out. Dennis Viollet went from hero to zero in a few months, whilst Stan Crowther and Maurice Setters were, in Busby's eyes, rabble-rousers who were eased out when the manager had had enough. Some of the Munich survivors and families of the players killed in the crash were critical of the club and of Busby in subsequent years, arguing that Busby could have done more for them.

Busby did, however, enjoy the total respect of most of his players, and some of the best post-War British players adored the man. Johnny Carey, Bobby Charlton, Denis Law, George Best all, apparently, craved his affection and attention. One period when he faced internal opposition and discord was in the barren years from 1958 to 1963. Against his better judgement, Busby had no option but to buy players after the seemingly endless production line of young talent coming through dried up. Some of those signed in those years lacked respect for the manager. Busby did not have the luxury of jettisoning them, but, as soon as he found the opportunity he did so, never afraid of making tough decisions for the good of the club. From the outset, Busby knew that the best way to build a successful and contented club was to unearth the best young talent and mould them in their teens when they were at their most malleable. It would also save the club a fortune in outgoing transfer fees.

Busby's other key relationship was with the directors. In his playing career he had experienced directors who thought they could pick the team and reduce the manager to glorified errand boy. Busby believed that a football club should be like a family, with a manager at its head. He must have ultimate power and run the club as he sees fit, and live or die on results. Soon after arriving as manager he reacted to overhearing a director's criticism by putting an item, 'Interference by Directors', on the agenda of the next board meeting. He knew that to turn a blind eye would only make things worse. He was helped by a chairman, James Gibson, who realised the need for a professional to manage his club and accordingly gave Busby a relatively free hand. Gibson's successor, Harold Hardman, was a tougher chairman who would have liked greater control. Although the two men enjoyed mutual respect, Hardman was not Busby's lap-dog.

In 1962, when a board vacancy arose, Busby manipulated things so that Louis Edwards – a wealthy butcher and friend – was appointed. Within eighteen months, Edwards had acquired sufficient shares to take control the club. Busby's reward for his support was an almost total free rein. Edwards admired Busby and it appears to have been a near-perfect manager-director relationship.

Many players have talked about going to see 'the Boss' about some issue or another, normally money, and going up the stairs ready to give Busby a piece of their mind. They would emerge sheepishly some time later having been won over by Busby's style. He would always mention the club's finances, which were rarely a problem, and team spirit. Players talk about his 'presence'. He was never confrontational, always charming, listening to the players' concerns but keen that they understand the club's interests as well as their own. More often than not they fell under his charismatic spell. As the players descended the stairs they tried to work out what had happened and how they would explain it to their teammates.

Before the maximum wage was abolished in 1961, all clubs paid their top players the same amount. Some clubs evaded this restriction by making under-the table payments to avoid the gaze of the taxman. Busby always refused to tread that path, and as a result United's players were generally worse off than others. According to many ex-United players, Busby would insist that Football League regulations prohibited the club from breaking the rules. Several clubs, including Manchester City and Sunderland, fell foul of the regulations in the 1950s and paid a price. Whilst it suited Busby to use the regulations to avoid paying his players more – he wanted United to be whiter than white and would instead give them perks like golf club memberships and regular 'breaks' in Blackpool.

Matt Busby's record of building three teams, each of which won the Football League Championship, was an extraordinary feat when there was far greater parity between teams than in the present day. In the 21 seasons following World War II, United won the League five times while *nine* other clubs lifted the title – a spread that would be impossible to imagine in the modern game. The wise but miserly Busby spent very little money until the Munich disaster demanded it. Of the 1948 team, only Delaney and Rowley had cost fees. The 1957 championship side had eight home-grown players, with only Wood, Taylor and Berry being bought. When Busby did spend, it was only to compliment the home-grown talent. His 1967 team had only four 'big' signings – Law, Stepney, Crerand and Herd. At the height of Busby's powers in the early 1950s the club spent nothing between March 1953 and December 1957. In that time United went from being a team of ageing champions to arguably the finest ever British club side.

Portsmouth v United. United's goalkeeper Jack Crompton tips Peter Harris's shot over the bar at Fratton Park (December 1947)

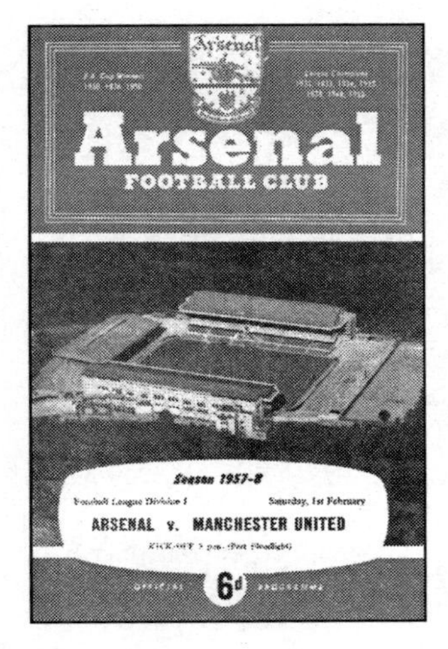

This match between Arsenal and United at Highbury on 1 February 1958 turned out to be United's last game in England before the fatal air crash at Munich

(Below) Coventry City v United. Denis Law throws his arms high after Bobby Charlton scores at Highfield Road (March 1963)

Hull City v United. Allenby Chilton moves in for a shoulder-charge on Hull's centre-forward (February 1949)

Luton Town v United. Luton's forwards put United under pressure (December 1957)

(Below) Busby gives a team talk in 1957. Viollet is behind him; Byrne leans on railings

The United squad in their momentous 1967-68 European Cup-winning season

England's golden boy of the late-1950s, Bobby Charlton signs autographs outside Old Trafford

(Below) An image of domestic bliss for David Herd and family

Luton Town v United. Goodwin and Greaves defend stoutly on a snow-bound Kenilworth Road pitch (February 1956)

This is what bomb-damaged Old Trafford looked like in 1945 – a far cry from today's superb stadium. Jimmy Murphy shows sports-writer Bill Bowes the extent of the damage

United v Portsmouth.
Pearson challenges goalkeeper Thompson as Cockburn closes in (April 1950)

Burnley goalkeeper Strong is beaten by Manchester United's No 11 Mitten, who cleverly back-heels a goal

Duncan Edwards clears against Scotland at Wembley in April 1957. England won 2-1

Bolton's Nat Lofthouse charges Harry Gregg and the ball into the net during the 1958 FA Cup final. Bolton won 2-0

Luton Town v United. Goalkeeeper Ron Bainham is beaten by Charlton's shot (November 1958)

Busby trains with (left to right) Byrne, Webster, Whelan, Bent

Bolton's Nat Lofthouse beats United's centre-half Cope to get in a shot in the 1958 FA Cup final

Hull City v United. Jack Crompton dives at the feet of a home forward (February 1949)

Luton Town v United. Mark Jones wins an aerial duel (December 1957)

Tommy Taylor scores against Aston Villa in the 1957 FA Cup final,
but the goal comes too late. United lost 1-2

United goalkeeper Jack Crompton saves this effort from Portsmouth's Ike Clark
at Fratton Park (December 1948)

The match programme for what was the greatest night in United's history. Ten years after the plane crash that destroyed the Busby Babes, United won the European Cup against Benfica at Wembley in 1968

United's Quixall (8) and Herd celebrate Quixall's third goal at Coventry (March 1963)

Johnny Carey in one of the high-kicking staged photographic poses typical of the time

Luton Town v United. Foulkes heads clear from strong Luton pressure (April 1959)

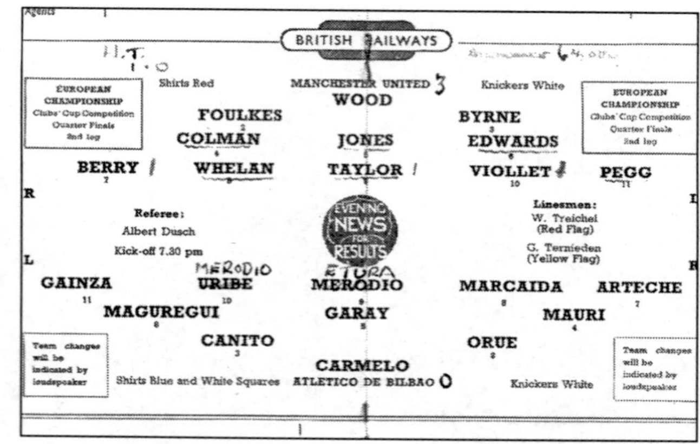

BRITISH RAILWAYS

EUROPEAN CHAMPIONSHIP
Clubs' Cup Competition
Quarter Finals
2nd leg

Shirts Red — MANCHESTER UNITED — Knickers White

WOOD

FOULKES 2 — BYRNE 3

COLMAN 4 — JONES 5 — EDWARDS 6

BERRY 7 — WHELAN 8 — TAYLOR 9 — VIOLLET 10 — PEGG 11

Referee:
Albert Dusch
Kick-off 7.30 pm

EVENING NEWS FOR RESULTS

Linesmen:
W. Treichel (Red Flag)
G. Ternieden (Yellow Flag)

GAINZA 11 — URIBE 10 — MERODIO 9 — MARCAIDA 8 — ARTECHE 7

MAGUREGUI 6 — GARAY 5 — MAURI 4

CANITO 3 — ORUE 2

CARMELO

Shirts Blue and White Squares — ATLETICO DE BILBAO — Knickers White

Team changes will be indicated by loudspeaker

It was customary for the two teams to be laid out like this across the centre pages of the match programme. This one is from 16 January 1957

Watford v United. Watford claimed that this corner-kick had crossed the goal-line, but the referee ruled that full-back Aston had headed clear. United goalkeeper Lancaster is stranded at his near post (January 1950)

GUIDE TO SEASONAL SUMMARIES

Col 1: Match number (for league fixtures); Round (for cup-ties).
e.g. 2:1 means 'Second round; first leg.'
e.g. 4R means 'Fourth round replay.'

Col 2: Date of the fixture and whether Home (H), Away (A), or Neutral (N).

Col 3: Opposition.

Col 4: Attendances. Home gates appear in roman; Away gates in *italics*.
Figures in **bold** indicate the largest and smallest gates, at home and away.
Average home and away attendances appear after the final league match.

Col 5: Respective league positions of United and their opponents after the match.
United's position appears on the top line in roman.
Their opponents' position appears on the second line in *italics*.
For cup-ties, the division and position of opponents is provided.
e.g. *2:12* means the opposition are twelfth in Division 2.

Col 6: The top line shows the result: W(in), D(raw), or L(ose).
The second line shows United's cumulative points total.

Col 7: The match score, United's given first.
Scores in **bold** indicate United's biggest league win and heaviest defeat.

Col 8: The half-time score, United's given first.

Col 9: The top line shows United's scorers and times of goals in roman.
The second line shows opponents' scorers and times of goals in *italics*.
A 'p' after the time of a goal denotes a penalty; 'og' an own-goal.
The third line gives the name of the match referee.

Team line-ups: United line-ups appear on the top line, irrespective of whether they are home or away. Opposition teams appear on the second line in *italics*.
Players of either side who are sent off are marked !
United players making their league debuts are displayed in **bold**.

N.B. For clarity, all information appearing in *italics* relates to opposing teams.

LEAGUE DIVISION 1   Manager: Matt Busby   SEASON 1946-47

No	Date		Att	Pos	Pt	F-A	H-T	Scorers, Times, and Referees	1	2	3	4	5	6	7	8	9	10	11
1	H	GRIMSBY			W	2-1	1-0	Mitten 33, Rowley 66	**Crompton**	Carey	**McGlen**	Warner	Chilton	**Cockburn**	**Delaney**	Pearson	Hanlon	Rowley	**Mitten**
	31/8		41,025		2			*McGowan 51*	*Tweedy*	*Vincent*	*Hodgson JV*	*Hodgson S*	*Charlesworth*	*Reeve*	*Johnson Jack*	*Clifton*	*Johnson Jim*	*McGowan*	*Wardle*
								Ref: G Appleyard	Grimsby are poor but the Reds don't make their superiority count, and when Jack Johnson hits the post two minutes from time there are hearts in mouths. Young Walton is injured, so the versatile Carey moves back from wing-half. Good debut from the ex-Blyth Spartan Billy McGlen.										
2	A	CHELSEA			W	3-0	2-0	Rowley 12, Pearson 44, Mitten 75	Crompton	Carey	McGlen	Warner	Chilton	Cockburn	Delaney	Pearson	Hanlon	Rowley	Mitten
	4/9		*27,750*		4				*Robertson*	*Winter*	*Lewis*	*Williams*	*Harris*	*Foss*	*Spencer*	*Galloway*	*Lawton*	*Goulden*	*Bain*
								Ref: T Smith	United are in Berkshire on a golfing break and travel in to demolish Chelsea. Tommy Lawton misses a penalty in front of England boss Walter Winterbottom who must be impressed by Rowley and Cockburn. Stan Pearson's header is a peach of a goal and United are rarely troubled.										
3	A	CHARLTON		1	W	3-1	2-0	Rowley 22, Johnson 29 (og), Hanlon 65	Crompton	Carey	McGlen	Warner	Chilton	Cockburn	Delaney	Pearson	Hanlon	Rowley	Mitten
	7/9		*44,088*	*11*	6			*Fell 50*	*Bartram*	*Turner*	*Shreeve*	*Dawson*	*Phipps*	*Johnson*	*Fell*	*Robinson G*	*Robinson W*	*Welsh*	*Duffy*
								Ref: F Green	Cockburn is again awesome and Jimmy Seed's Charlton are put to the sword. Crompton saves Welsh's penalty before Johnny Hanlon's header clinches the points. Sam Bartram knows little about late shots from Rowley and Pearson that would have given an embarrassing scoreline.										
4	H	LIVERPOOL		1	W	5-0	3-0	Pearson 10, 15, 87, Rowley 36, [Mitten 49]	Crompton	Carey	McGlen	Warner	Chilton	Cockburn	Delaney	Pearson	Hanlon	Rowley	Mitten
	11/9		40,874	*12*	8				*Sidlow*	*Lambert*	*Ramsden*	*Taylor*	*Hughes*	*Paisley*	*Nieuwenhuys*	*Balmer*	*Jones*	*Fagan*	*Priday*
								Ref: R Overden	Liverpool are on the verge of paying a record £13,000 for centre-forward Albert Stubbins and it is obvious why. United's five forwards are dazzling. For the first 20 minutes it is a ceaseless bombardment of the visitors' goal and Cyril Sidlow keeps the score from cricket proportions.										
5	H	MIDDLESBROUGH		1	W	1-0	1-0	Rowley 40	Crompton	Carey	McGlen	Warner	Chilton	Cockburn	Delaney	Pearson	Hanlon	Rowley	Mitten
	14/9		65,279	*7*	10				*Cumming*	*Robinson*	*Stuart*	*Bell*	*Hardwick*	*Gordon*	*Spuhler*	*Mannion*	*Fenton*	*Murphy*	*Walker*
								Ref: A Ellis	Boro lose their 100% record in an enthralling game, won by Jack Rowley's shot which is fumbled by Cumming. It's United's best start since 1908. Jack Warner's cut eyebrow needs stitches, whilst England captain George Hardwick, with the Hollywood looks, plays at centre-half.										
6	H	CHELSEA		1	D	1-1	0-1	Chilton 78	Crompton	Carey	Chilton	Warner	Whalley	Cockburn	Delaney	**Aston**	Hanlon	Pearson	Mitten
	18/9		30,275	*11*	11			*Machin 40*	*Robertson*	*Winter*	*White*	*Williams*	*Harris*	*Foss*	*Spencer*	*Walker*	*Machin*	*Goulden*	*Dolding*
								Ref: T Smith	Continuous rain before the 6pm kick-off leaves the pitch sodden and the crowd well down. Chelsea's new Scottish inside-forward Tommy Walker masters the conditions and sets up the goal with Chilton out of position. Allenby redeems himself and preserves the unbeaten run.										
7	A	STOKE		1	L	2-3	0-1	Hanlon 72, Delaney 77	Crompton	Carey	McGlen	Warner	Chilton	Cockburn	Delaney	Pearson	Hanlon	Rowley	Mitten
	21/9		41,966	*10*	11			*Antonio 20, Steele 57, 58*	*Jepson*	*Brigham*	*McCue*	*Mountford*	*Franklin*	*Kirton*	*Matthews*	*Antonio*	*Steele*	*Baker*	*Ormston*
								Ref: R Greenwood	After being 0-3 down, the Reds almost grab a point which their defensive play did not deserve. Antonio looks offside for the first but Steele is deadly. Stanley Matthews returns from injury but is limping after 30 minutes. Henry Cockburn, a mill-fitter in Oldham, is picked for England.										
8	H	ARSENAL		2	W	5-2	2-1	Hanlon 30,39, Wrig'70p, Row' 77, 89	Crompton	**Walton**	McGlen	Warner	Chilton	Aston	Delaney	Pearson	Hanlon	Rowley	Wrigglesworth
	28/9		62,905	*18*	13			*Lewis 25, McPherson 57*	*Swindin*	*Male*	*Joy*	*Bastin*	*Compton L*	*Logie*	*McPherson*	*Sloan*	*Lewis*	*Jones*	*Nelson*
								Ref: G Blackhall	George Allison's Arsenal are having a miserable time and get thumped. Time has caught up with Cliff Bastin and this is his last game for the Gunners. The speedy Hanlon gives Compton a torrid time in the scorching heat and veteran Male thumps out Pearson's header for the penalty.										
9	H	PRESTON		2	D	1-1	0-1	Wrigglesworth 60	Crompton	Carey	McGlen	Warner	Chilton	Cockburn	Delaney	Pearson	Hanlon	Rowley	Wrigglesworth
	5/10		55,562	*14*	14			*McIntosh 25*	*Fairbrother*	*Beattie A*	*Scott*	*Shankly*	*Williams*	*Hamilton*	*Finney*	*Horton*	*McIntosh*	*Beattie R*	*Wharton*
								Ref: F Wort	Cockburn and Carey return from international duty but can't do enough to get both points against tricky Preston in a poor match. Busby is absent looking for a new keeper and Jimmy Murphy is in charge. Jack Fairbrother is outstanding in goal for the visitors but can't stop the goal.										
10	A	SHEFFIELD UTD		2	D	2-2	1-0	Rowley 32, 74	Crompton	Walton	McGlen	Warner	Chilton	Carey	Delaney	Pearson	Hanlon	Rowley	Wrigglesworth
	12/10		*35,620*	*10*	15			*Forbes 70, Thompson 83*	*Smith*	*Shimwell*	*Cox*	*Machent*	*Latham*	*Forbes*	*Nightingale*	*Brook*	*Thompson*	*Hagan*	*Collindridge*
								Ref: A Meadows	The rain is drizzling on a wretched Sheffield day and with rumours of a new keeper growing - Frank Swift is mentioned - Jack Crompton saves Hagan's 57th-minute penalty. He is unsighted for Forbes' free-kick but Rowley comes up trumps with two thunderous drives for a vital point.										

No	Venue	Opponent / Date	Att	Pos	Res / Pts	FT	HT	Scorers, Times, and Referees	1	2	3	4	5	6	7	8	9	10	11
11	A	BLACKPOOL		2	L	1-3	0-2	Delaney 85	Crompton	Walton	McGlen	Carey	Chilton	Cockburn	Delaney	Pearson	Hanlon	Rowley	Wrigglesworth
		19/10	*26,307*	*1*	15			*Farrow 2, Mortensen 3, Dick 64*	*Wallace*	*Sibley*	*Lewis*	*Farrow*	*Suart*	*Johnston*	*Munro*	*Dick*	*Mortensen*	*Eastham*	*McIntosh*
								Ref: J Brown	The leaders give United a going-over. Farrow, in his first game of the season, hits a thumping free-kick after McGlen fouls Mortensen. Morty's header makes it two before Wrigglesworth hits the bar from a penalty. Johnny Hanlon is off concussed and unconscious for the second half.										
12	H	SUNDERLAND		5	L	0-3	0-1		Crompton	Walton	McGlen	Warner	Chilton	Cockburn	Delaney	**Morris**	**Burke**	Pearson	Rowley
		26/10	48,566	*4*	15			*Whitelum 5, 47, 75*	*Mapson*	*Stelling*	*Jones*	*Willingham*	*Hall*	*Housam*	*Duns*	*Lloyd*	*Whitelum*	*Watson*	*Burbanks*
								Ref: H Moore	United's patchy form is punished by a smooth Sunderland on a greasy pitch. Ronnie Burke and Johnny Morris miss a host of chances on their debuts, Chilton and Cockburn are off colour, and captain Carey is injured. Morris is back from Army service and looks an outstanding player.										
13	A	ASTON VILLA		5	D	0-0	0-0		**Collinson**	Walton	McGlen	Warner	Chilton	Cockburn	Delaney	Morris	Rowley	Pearson	Mitten
		2/11	*53,668*	*8*	16				*Rutherford*	*Potts*	*Cummings*	*Iverson*	*Moss F*	*Lowe*	*Dixon*	*Martin*	*Edwards*	*Dorsett*	*Smith*
								Ref: B Flanagan	Cliff Collinson makes his debut in place of Jack Crompton who has a sprained ankle and makes two great saves. Chilton is a rock against Villa's strong attack. 33-year-old Billy Wrigglesworth, dropped after two goals in four games, asks for a transfer and could move to Bolton.										
14	H	DERBY		4	W	4-1	3-1	Pearson 19, 24, Mitten 32, Rowley 55	Collinson	Walton	McGlen	Warner	Chilton	Cockburn	Delaney	Morris	Rowley	Pearson	Mitten
		9/11	57,517	*17*	18			*Carter 15*	*Woodley*	*Mozley*	*Parr*	*Ward*	*Leuty*	*Howe*	*Harrison*	*Carter*	*Broome*	*Doherty*	*Stamps*
								Ref: G Clark	The star-studded FA Cup holders are woeful but take the lead with a comic goal. Cockburn's poor back-pass beats Collinson, hits the bar and with Collinson slipping up Raich Carter nips in. Starman Peter Doherty is kept quiet by Warner and Jimmy Delaney has a hand in all the goals.										
15	A	EVERTON		4	D	2-2	2-2	Pearson 3, Rowley 5	Collinson	Walton	McGlen	Warner	Chilton	Cockburn	Delaney	Morris	Rowley	Pearson	Mitten
		16/11	*45,932*	*17*	19			*Dodds 4, 14*	*Sagar*	*Humphreys*	*Greenhalgh*	*Bentham*	*Jones*	*Watson*	*McIlhatton*	*Wainwright*	*Dodds*	*Stevenson*	*Eglington*
								Ref: E Smith	A thrilling start to an exciting game which the Reds would have won but for wayward shooting. The first stunning goal involves Rowley and Delaney, and Sagar can't hold the latter's shot and Pearson scores. 14-stone Jock Dodds makes it four in three since his move from Blackpool.										
16	H	HUDDERSFIELD		3	W	5-2	2-1	Mitten 1,81, Rowley 15, Morris 71, 80	Collinson	Walton	McGlen	Carey	Chilton	Cockburn	Delaney	Morris	Rowley	Pearson	Mitten
		23/11	39,200	22	21			*Thompson 16, Glazzard 46*	*Hesford*	*Bailey*	*Barker*	*Smith*	*Briggs*	*Boot*	*Poole*	*Glazzard*	*Rodgers*	*Thompson*	*Metcalfe*
								Ref: A Denham	It's the coldest day of the year but United warm their fans with an easy win which, but for Hesford, would have been much bigger. Carey is fit again and as solid as ever but Morris is the star with two excellent goals set up by Rowley and Delaney. Rowley runs from halfway to score.										
17	A	WOLVERHAMPTON		4	L	2-3	1-1	Delaney 29, Hanlon 65	Collinson	**Worrall**	McGlen	Carey	Chilton	Cockburn	Delaney	Morris	Hanlon	Pearson	Mitten
		30/11	*46,704*	2	21			*Westcott 34, 77, Hancocks 85*	*Williams*	*McLean*	*Crook*	*Galley*	*Cullis*	*Wright*	*Hancocks*	*Pye*	*Westcott*	*Forbes*	*Mullen*
								Ref: J Parker	The rain is so heavy that Wolves don't have to water the pitch. Hanlon deputises for Rowley who was injured in training and scores a good goal. Wolves are saved by Bert Williams but in the last quarter they step up the tempo. Williams' makes a great late save from Jimmy Delaney.										
18	H	BRENTFORD		3	W	4-1	1-0	Rowley 2, 47, 68, Smith G 70 (og)	Collinson	Carey	McGlen	Warner	Chilton	Cockburn	Hanlon	Morris	Rowley	Pearson	Mitten
		7/12	31,956	*18*	23			*Macauley 52*	*Crozier*	*Gorman*	*Munro*	*Wilkins*	*Smith G*	*Paterson*	*Hopkins*	*Macauley*	*Townsend*	*MacDonald*	*Smith A*
								Ref: T Smith	United slip and slide through the mud for a comfortable win over the Bees. Jack Rowley's first skids past the otherwise solid Crozier but Macauley's goal sets the alarm bells ringing. Rowley is in stunning form and is tipped for international caps. Delaney is out with tonsillitis.										
19	A	BLACKBURN		5	L	1-2	0-2	Morris 80	Collinson	Carey	McGlen	Warner	Chilton	Cockburn	Hanlon	Morris	Rowley	Pearson	Mitten
		14/12	*21,455*	*12*	23			*Smith 22, 44*	*Hayhurst*	*Cook*	*Bell*	*Stephan*	*Pryde*	*Wightman*	*Baldwin*	*Guest*	*Smith*	*Campbell*	*Langton*
								Ref: W Martin	The away form is hampering the championship challenge and Utd are beaten by Eddie Hapgood's Rovers. Former Red Jack Smith is the hero, despite United's territorial advantage. Hayhurst's debut is a memorable one whilst Cliff Collinson's first-team career is over after seven games.										
20	A	BOLTON		8	D	2-2	2-0	Rowley 10, 20	Crompton	Carey	McGlen	Warner	Chilton	Cockburn	Delaney	Morris	Rowley	Pearson	Mitten
		25/12	*30,511*	*13*	24			*Lofthouse 62, Woodward 70*	*Hanson*	*Hamlett*	*Hubbick*	*Gillies*	*Atkinson*	*Forrest*	*Woodward*	*Roberts*	*Lofthouse*	*Moir*	*Westwood*
								Ref: W Evans	Full-strength United's first-half bombardment of a lethargic Bolton looks set to end the poor away run with Rowley taking advantage of slow defenders. Wanderers step it up after the break and throw everything at the Reds. Stan Pearson misses a golden chance to win it near the end.										
21	H	BOLTON		7	W	1-0	1-0	Pearson 2	Crompton	Carey	McGlen	Warner	Chilton	Cockburn	Delaney	Morris	Rowley	Pearson	Mitten
		26/12	57,446	*15*	26				*Hanson*	*Hamlett*	*Hubbick*	*Gillies*	*Atkinson*	*Forrest*	*Woodward*	*Roberts*	*Lofthouse*	*Moir*	*Westwood*
								Ref: W Evans	The early goal raises expectations but a miserable first half is followed by a marginally better second period. The goal comes after several United players had chances to score but missed. Jack Crompton comes to the rescue with great saves from Westwood and Nat Lofthouse.										

LEAGUE DIVISION 1 — Manager: Matt Busby — SEASON 1946-47

No	Date		Att	Pos	Pt	F-A	H-T	Scorers, Times, and Referees	1	2	3	4	5	6	7	8	9	10	11
22	A	GRIMSBY		6	D	0-0	0-0		Crompton	Whalley	Aston	Warner	Chilton	Cockburn	Delaney	Morris	Rowley	Pearson	Mitten
	28/12		*17,183*	*11*	27				*Tweedy*	*Vincent*	*Fisher*	*Hall*	*Betmead*	*Reeve F*	*Johnson Jack*	*Clifton*	*Blenkinsop*	*Cairns*	*Wardle*
								Ref: G Appleyard	Injuries mean 34-year-old Bert Whalley and John Aston are emergency full-backs and ex-commando Aston looks a natural. There are more missed chances with Rowley the main culprit. Morris hits the bar and courageous Tweedy is a star. Vincent's late free-kick is inches too high.										
23	H	CHARLTON		6	W	4-1	2-0	Burke 17, 37, Pearson 46, Buckle 89p	Crompton	Aston	McGlen	Warner	Chilton	Cockburn	Delaney	Morris	Burke	Pearson	**Buckle**
	4/1		*43,658*	*18*	29			*Duffy 80*	*Hobbins*	*Croker P*	*Lock*	*Dawson*	*Phipps*	*Revell*	*Hurst*	*Johnson*	*Robinson W*	*Purves*	*Duffy*
								Ref: F Green	Reserves Ronnie Burke and Ted Buckle, in for the injured Rowley and Mitten, score in this easy victory. It's a bitterly cold afternoon and Charlton show little interest once the first goal goes in. Harold Phipps handles for the late penalty and ex-Navy man Buckle gets a debut goal.										
24	A	MIDDLESBROUGH		3	W	4-2	0-1	Pearson 52, 75, Buckle 64, Morris 72	Crompton	Aston	McGlen	Warner	Chilton	Carey	Delaney	Morris	Rowley	Pearson	Buckle
	18/1		*37,556*	*4*	31			*Fenton 43, Mannion 80*	*Cumming*	*Robinson*	*Stuart*	*Bell*	*Hardwick*	*Gordon*	*Spuhler*	*Murphy*	*Fenton*	*Mannion*	*Walker*
								Ref: A Ellis	The first away win since early September as the chances start flying in. United are the only team in the top eight to win and title dreams are in the air. Boro captain Hardwick says United are the best side they have met this season - his own side are poor with Wilf Mannion invisible.										
25	A	ARSENAL		7	L	**2-6**	2-2	P'son 10, Morris 43 *[Rooke 70, 72, 75]*	**Fielding**	Aston	McGlen	Warner	Chilton	Cockburn	Delaney	Morris	Hanlon	Pearson	Buckle
	1/2		*29,415*	*15*	31			*Rudkin 20, Logie 28, McPherson 48,*	*Swindin*	*Male*	*Barnes*	*Sloan*	*Compton L*	*Mercer*	*McPherson*	*Logie*	*Rooke*	*Jones B*	*Rudkin*
								Ref: G Blackhall	United have a Cup hangover at snowbound Highbury but the defeat is largely down to Chilton's groin injury at 2-2. The recent signings of Joe Mercer and Ronnie Rooke have saved Arsenal's season and they are pulling away from the drop zone. McPherson on the wing is devastating.										
26	H	STOKE		5	D	1-1	1-0	Buckle 44p	Fielding	Aston	Walton	Warner	Chilton	Cockburn	Delaney	Morris	Hanlon	Pearson	Buckle
	5/2		**8,456**	6	32			*Ormston 50p*	*Jepson*	*Mould*	*McCue*	*Sellars*	*Franklin*	*Wordley*	*Mountford*	*Peppit*	*Jackson*	*Mitchell*	*Ormston*
								Ref: R Greenwood	A midweek afternoon game on a frostbound pitch is watched by the smallest home crowd for 12 years and is strewn with errors. Stoke have a Cup-tie in three days and field five reserves. Buckle misses a penalty but nets after Mould's handball, and Ormston after a foul on Mountford.										
27	H	BLACKPOOL		7	W	3-0	1-0	Hanlon 40, Rowley 87p, 88	Fielding	Aston	Walton	Warner	Chilton	Carey	Delaney	Morris	Hanlon	Pearson	Rowley
	22/2		30,823	*6*	34				*Wallace*	*Shimwell*	*Lewis*	*Farrow*	*Hayward*	*Johnston*	*Nelson*	*Munro*	*Mortensen*	*Dick*	*Blair*
								Ref: J Brown	Title rivals are beaten on a frosty pitch in bitterly cold weather. Munro runs the game for twenty minutes but Blackpool are unable to capitalise. Wallace parries Rowley's stinging shot and Hanlon scores. Later, Jack scores a model penalty and then runs from the halfway line to score.										
28	A	SUNDERLAND		7	D	1-1	0-0	Delaney 80	Fielding	Aston	Walton	Warner	Chilton	Cockburn	Delaney	Morris	Hanlon	Pearson	Rowley
	1/3		*25,038*	*12*	35			*Robinson 78*	*Mapson*	*Stelling*	*Hudgell*	*Scotson*	*Walsh*	*Wright*	*Duns*	*Robinson*	*Whitelum*	*Watson*	*Burbanks*
								Ref: W Martin	The cold weather won't lift but the two teams warm the small crowd with a thrilling match. Sunderland-born Allenby Chilton is like a rock but can do nothing when Walton's miskick lets in Robinson. Almost immediately Mapson can't hold Rowley's corker and Delaney pops the ball in.										
29	H	ASTON VILLA		5	W	2-1	0-1	Burke 61, Pearson 63	Fielding	Aston	Walton	Warner	Chilton	Carey	Delaney	Morris	Burke	Pearson	Rowley
	8/3		37,555	*8*	37			*Dorsett 36*	*Rutherford*	*Potts*	*Cummings*	*Iverson*	*Moss F*	*Lowe*	*Edwards*	*Martin*	*Graham*	*Dorsett*	*Smith*
								Ref: B Flanagan	Treacherous conditions are more conducive to skating, and Villa are well in charge up to half-time with Aston twice heading clear from under the bar. After the break United find their feet and the pressure pays off with Burke scoring his third in three games, but Villa are unlucky.										
30	A	DERBY		5	L	3-4	3-2	Burke 19, 43, Pearson 25	Fielding	Walton	McGlen	Warner	Chilton	Carey	Delaney	Morris	Burke	Pearson	Rowley
	15/3		*19,679*	*11*	37			*Antonio 9, Carter 27, Broome 49, 77*	*Woodley*	*Nicholas*	*Howe*	*Ward*	*Leuty*	*Musson*	*Harrison*	*Carter*	*Stamps*	*Antonio*	*Broome*
								Ref: G Clark	A blizzard rages after half-time and the Rams, inspired by Raich Carter, come from behind to win. Fielding doesn't inspire confidence in goal and this is his final game. Debutant Antonio, recently signed from Stoke, scores against United again, whilst veteran Frank Broome is the hero.										
31	H	EVERTON		4	W	3-0	1-0	Delaney 28, Burke 57, Warner 86	Crompton	Carey	McGlen	Warner	Chilton	Cockburn	Delaney	Morris	Burke	Pearson	Rowley
	22/3		44,297	*12*	39				*Sagar*	*Jackson*	*Greenhalgh*	*Bentham*	*Humphreys*	*Farrell*	*McIlhatton*	*Stevenson*	*Wainwright*	*Fielding*	*Eglington*
								Ref: H Berry	The scoreline doesn't tell the story. Eglington hits the bar twice and forces Crompton to make a stunning save. Delaney controversially charges Ted Sagar into the net for the first goal. The injured Warner spends the second half limping out on the wing but pops up to score the third goal.										

No	H/A	Opponent	Pos	Res	F-A	H-T	Scorers, Times, and Referees	1	2	3	4	5	6	7	8	9	10	11
32	A	HUDDERSFIELD	4	D	2-2	1-1	Delaney 1, Pearson 67	Crompton	Carey	Aston	Cockburn	Chilton	McGlen	Delaney	Hanlon	Burke	Pearson	Rowley
29/3		*18,509*	*20*	40			*Whittingham 38, Doherty 87*	*Hesford*	*Bailey*	*Hayes*	*Barker*	*Hepplewhite*	*Boot*	*Bateman*	*Thompson*	*Whittingham*	*Doherty*	*Metcalfe*
							Ref: A Denham	Recent signing Peter Doherty, playing against doctor's orders with a strapped wrist, grabs a late equaliser after Pearson's header looked enough to win. Hesford slips in the mud for the first and Town are lucky to win a point in their relegation struggle. Aston looks assured at left-back.										
33	H	WOLVERHAMPTON	4	W	3-1	1-0	Hanlon 24, Rowley 55, 67	Crompton	Carey	Aston	Cockburn	Chilton	McGlen	Delaney	Hanlon	Burke	Pearson	Rowley
5/4		**67,204**	*2*	42			*Westcott 53*	*Williams*	*McLean*	*Crook*	*Galley*	*Cullis*	*Wright*	*Hancocks*	*Pye*	*Westcott*	*Ramscar*	*Mullen*
							Ref: J Parker	United are back in the race after a deserved win over the leaders in the wet and wind. The gates are shut before the kick-off with thousands locked out. In a fast game Carey nullifies the speedy Mullen and Chilton bosses 31-goal Dennis Westcott. Jack Rowley's precise shots win it.										
34	H	LEEDS	5	W	3-1	1-1	Burke 2, 75, Delaney 51	Crompton	Carey	Aston	Cockburn	Chilton	McGlen	Delaney	Hanlon	Burke	Pearson	Rowley
7/4		41,912	*22*	44			*Cochrane 13*	*Hodgson*	*Milburn*	*Bannister*	*Willingham*	*Holley*	*Henry*	*Cochrane*	*Ainsley*	*Clarke*	*Hindle*	*Heaton*
							Ref: H Holt	Leeds have only one away point all season and should have been 0-3 down after five minutes. They have lost seven of the last eight and their goal is a freak - Cochrane's shot is caught in a gust of wind. 35-year-old former England star Ken Willingham can't even raise Leeds' game.										
35	A	LEEDS	3	W	2-0	1-0	Burke 30, McGlen 70	Crompton	Carey	Aston	Cockburn	Chilton	McGlen	Delaney	Hanlon	Burke	Pearson	Rowley
8/4		***15,528***	*22*	46				*Twomey*	*Milburn*	*Bannister*	*Willingham*	*Holley*	*Henry*	*Cochrane*	*Ainsley*	*Clarke*	*Hindle*	*Heaton*
							Ref: H Holt	It's an Easter Tuesday cake-walk in front of Leeds' lowest crowd of the season. The wind and the cloying mud spoil it as a spectacle and Crompton is a virtual spectator. The injured McGlen moves to the left-wing and scores with his bad leg. Twomey prevents a heavier defeat.										
36	A	BRENTFORD	2	D	0-0	0-0		Crompton	Carey	Aston	Warner	Chilton	Cockburn	Rowley	Hanlon	Burke	Pearson	Mitten
12/4		*22,035*	*21*	47				*Crozier*	*Munro*	*Oliver*	*Toulouse*	*Smith G*	*Paterson*	*Hopkins*	*MacDonald*	*Townsend*	*Naylor*	*Girling*
							Ref: T Smith	United are a point behind Wolves after a poor game against relegation certainties Bees. Delaney is playing at Wembley for Scotland. Chances galore are missed and Carey loses the ball on the main stand roof with a clearance. How Brentford did the double over Wolves is a mystery.										
37	H	BLACKBURN	2	W	4-0	3-0	Pearson 5, 20, Rowley 25, [Higgins 74 (og)]	Crompton	Carey	Aston	Warner	Whalley	Cockburn	Delaney	Morris	Hanlon	Pearson	Rowley
19/4		46,390	*18*	49				*Marks*	*Cook*	*Higgins*	*Rogers*	*Pryde*	*Bell*	*Oakes*	*Venters*	*Godwin*	*McClelland*	*Langton*
							Ref: W Martin	Chilton misses his first game of the season with an injury but Whalley deputises. United are superior thanks to a stunning first half-hour. Rovers, manager-less since Hapgood's exit in February, are poor and Rogers' woeful back-pass, which hands Rowley the third, sums them up.										
38	A	PORTSMOUTH	2	W	1-0	0-0	Delaney 47	Crompton	Carey	Aston	Cockburn	Chilton	McGlen	Delaney	Hanlon	Burke	Pearson	Rowley
26/4		*30,623*	*13*	51				*Butler*	*Rookes*	*Ferrier*	*Scoular*	*McCoy*	*Dickinson*	*Froggatt*	*McAlinden*	*Reid*	*Barlow*	*Parker*
							Ref: G Clark	United keep the pressure on Wolves with their first win at Fratton Park for 40 years on FA Cup final day. Butler drops McGlen's shot and Delaney is on hand to hammer it home. It's only Pompey's second defeat in 16 games and Chilton is back to shackle hot-shot Duggie Reid.										
39	A	LIVERPOOL	3	L	0-1	0-1		Crompton	Carey	Aston	Warner	Chilton	McGlen	Delaney	Hanlon	Burke	Pearson	Rowley
3/5		*48,800*	*4*	51			*Stubbins 10*	*Sidlow*	*Lambert*	*Spicer*	*Jones*	*Hughes*	*Paisley*	*Polk*	*Balmer*	*Stubbins*	*Watkinson*	*Liddell*
							Ref: R Duerden	Liverpool are only a point behind with a game in hand after this fortunate win continues their title charge. United spurn chances but Liddell gives Carey an uncomfortable time and sets up the over-rated Stubbins' goal. Now any of five can win the title but Wolves still look favourites.										
40	A	PRESTON	3	D	1-1	1-0	Pearson 10	Crompton	Walton	Aston	Warner	Chilton	McGlen	Delaney	Morris	Burke	Pearson	Rowley
10/5		*23,278*	*6*	52			*McLaren 60*	*Fairbrother*	*Watson*	*Scott*	*Shankly*	*Williams*	*Hamilton*	*Finney*	*McLaren*	*McIntosh*	*Beattie R*	*Wilson*
							Ref: F Wort	Heavy rain leaves the surface greasy and the superlative Finney is the master. Preston deserve a point from a hard-fought game and United will rue this result. Wolves lose but Liverpool and Stoke are lurking ominously. Carey is absent playing for Britain against the Rest of Europe.										
41	H	PORTSMOUTH	2	W	3-0	1-0	Morris 10, Mitten 53, Rowley 84	Crompton	Walton	Aston	Warner	Chilton	Carey	Buckle	Morris	Rowley	Pearson	Mitten
17/5		37,746	*15*	54				*Butler*	*Rookes*	*Ferrier*	*Scoular*	*McCoy*	*Dickinson*	*Froggatt*	*McAlinden*	*Reid*	*Barlow*	*Parker*
							Ref: G Clark	Morris is in scintillating form, hitting the post before his goal. United fritter chances again on a hard ground in broiling sunshine. Carey returns to set up Mitten with a shrewd pass. Delaney is on international duty. Wolves drop a home point and lead on goal-average with two games left.										
42	H	SHEFFIELD UTD	2	W	6-2	3-2	Pear' 2, Row' 8,14, 64, Morris 61,65	Crompton	Carey	Aston	Warner	Chilton	McGlen	Hanlon	Morris	Rowley	Pearson	Mitten
26/5		34,209	*8*	56			*Collindridge 19, Nightingale 39*	*Smith*	*Furniss*	*Cox*	*Jackson*	*Latham*	*Young*	*Rickett*	*Nightingale*	*Thompson*	*Machent*	*Collindridge*
Average	Home 43,945	Away 31,507					Ref: A Meadows	United round off the long season with their eighth straight home win. The Blades are overrun by United's attacking power but Crompton has to save a penalty. The title is between Wolves and Liverpool who meet next week in the final game. Jack Rowley sets a new club scoring record.										

FA Cup

Rd	H/A	Opponent / Date / Att	Pos	Res	F-A	H-T	Scorers / Ref	1	2	3	4	5	6	7	8	9	10	11
3	A	BRADFORD PA	6	W	3-0	2-0	Buckle 11, Rowley 43, 85	Crompton	Aston	McGlen	Warner	Chilton	Carey	Delaney	Morris	Rowley	Pearson	Buckle
	11/1	*24,270 2:17*						*Farr*	*Stephen*	*Farrell*	*White*	*Danskin*	*Greenwood*	*Smith*	*Horsman*	*McIlvenny*	*Gibbons*	*Donaldson*
							Ref: P Stevens	Torrential rain has made the pitch like a gluepot but any Bradford hopes that it will be a leveller are dispelled by slick United, who are stronger in all departments. Amateur Harold McIlvenny makes his debut whilst Ron Greenwood is at centre-half. John Aston is outstanding at the back.										
4	H	NOTT'M FOREST	3	L	0-2	0-1		Fielding	Aston	McGlen	Warner	Chilton	Carey	Delaney	Morris	Rowley	Pearson	Buckle
	25/1	58,641 *2:10*					*Barks 31, Lyman 68*	*Platts*	*Brigham*	*McCall*	*Pritty*	*Blagg*	*Knight*	*Scott*	*Brown*	*Barks*	*Edwards*	*Lyman*
							Ref: G Blackhall	Shock defeat to a workmanlike Forest team for whom Sailor Brown and Platts, who served at Tobruk, are heroes. Fielding, on his debut for the injured Crompton, is not at fault for the goals but both Buckle and Rowley hit the post at 0-0. Dropped Mitten has a transfer request rejected.										

	P	Home W	D	L	F	A	Away W	D	L	F	A	Pts
1 Liverpool	42	13	3	5	42	24	12	4	5	42	28	57
2 MAN UNITED	42	17	3	1	61	19	5	9	7	34	35	56
3 Wolves	42	15	1	5	66	31	10	5	6	32	25	56
4 Stoke	42	14	5	2	52	21	10	2	9	38	32	55
5 Blackpool	42	14	1	6	38	32	8	5	8	33	38	50
6 Sheffield Utd	42	12	4	5	51	32	9	3	9	38	43	49
7 Preston	42	10	7	4	45	27	8	4	9	31	47	47
8 Aston Villa	42	9	6	6	39	24	9	3	9	28	29	45
9 Sunderland	42	11	3	7	33	27	7	5	9	32	39	44
10 Everton	42	13	5	3	40	24	4	4	13	22	43	43
11 Middlesbro	42	11	3	7	46	32	6	5	10	27	36	42
12 Portsmouth	42	11	3	7	42	27	5	6	10	24	33	41
13 Arsenal	42	9	5	7	43	33	7	4	10	29	37	41
14 Derby	42	13	2	6	44	28	5	3	13	29	51	41
15 Chelsea	42	9	3	9	33	39	7	4	10	36	45	39
16 Grimsby	42	9	6	6	37	35	4	6	11	24	47	38
17 Blackburn	42	6	5	10	23	27	8	3	10	22	26	36
18 Bolton	42	8	5	8	30	28	5	3	13	27	41	34
19 Charlton	42	6	6	9	34	32	5	6	10	23	39	34
20 Huddersfield	42	11	4	6	34	24	2	3	16	19	55	33
21 Brentford	42	5	5	11	19	35	4	2	15	26	53	25
22 Leeds	42	6	5	10	30	30	0	1	20	15	60	18
	924	232	90	140	882	631	140	90	232	631	882	924

Odds & ends

Double wins: (4) Charlton, Middlesbrough, Leeds, Portsmouth.
Double losses: (0).

Won from behind: (4) Arsenal (h), Derby (h), Middlesbrough (a), Villa (h).
Lost from in front: (3) Wolves (a), Arsenal (a), Derby (a).

High spots: Five-win start to the season.
Home win over the champions.
Goalscoring form of Jack Rowley.
Home win over Wolves.

Low spots: Poor away form.
FA Cup exit to Forest.
Defeat at Anfield in what turned out to be a title decider.

Red cards: United (0).
Red cards: Opponents (0).

Ever-presents: (1) Pearson.
Hat-tricks: (3) Rowley (2), Pearson (1).
Opposing hat-tricks: (2) Whitelum (Sunderland), Rooke (Arsenal).
Leading scorer: (28) Rowley.

	Appearances Lge	FAC	Goals Lge	FAC	Tot
Aston, John	**21**	2			
Buckle, Ted	**5**	2	**3**	1	**4**
Burke, Ronnie	**13**		**9**		**9**
Carey, Johnny	**31**	2			
Chilton, Allenby	**41**	2	**1**		**1**
Cockburn, Henry	**32**				
Collinson, Cliff	**7**				
Crompton, Jack	**29**	1			
Delaney, Jimmy	**37**	2	**8**		**8**
Fielding, Bill	**6**	1			
Hanlon, Johnny	**27**		**7**		**7**
McGlen, Billy	**33**	2	**1**		**1**
Mitten, Charlie	**20**		**7**		**7**
Morris, Johnny	**24**	2	**8**		**8**
Pearson, Stan	**42**	2	**19**		**19**
Rowley, Jack	**37**	2	**26**	2	**28**
Walton, Joe	**15**				
Warner, Jack	**34**	2	**1**		**1**
Whalley, Bert	**3**				
Worrall, Harry	**1**				
Wrigglesworth, Billy	**4**		**2**		**2**
(own-goals)			**3**		**3**
21 players used	**462**	**22**	**95**	**3**	**98**

No	Date	Att	Pos	Pt	F-A	H-T	Scorers, Times, and Referees	1	2	3	4	5	6	7	8	9	10	11
1	A MIDDLESBROUGH			D	2-2	0-2	Rowley 64, 75	Crompton	Carey	Aston	Warner	Chilton	McGlen	Delaney	Morris	Rowley	Pearson	Mitten
	23/8	*39,554*		1			*Fenton 16, 19*	*Goodfellow*	*Robinson*	*Hardwick*	*Bell*	*Whitaker*	*Gordon*	*McCormack*	*Dews*	*Fenton*	*Mannion*	*Dicks*
							Ref: H Berry	Rowley's two headers, one from Delaney's centre, the other from Mitten's cross, bring United back into a game they should have won in a canter. There are no newcomers and the old failings are still there. David Jack's team will struggle and but for Mannion would be a poor team.										
2	H LIVERPOOL			W	2-0	1-0	Morris 26, Pearson 69	Crompton	Carey	Aston	Warner	Chilton	McGlen	Delaney	Morris	Rowley	Pearson	Mitten
	27/8	53,610		3				*Sidlow*	*Harley*	*Lambert*	*Taylor*	*Hughes*	*Paisley*	*Watkinson*	*Balmer*	*Stubbins*	*Polk*	*Liddell*
							Ref: H Hartley	The champions are defeated but neither side look likely champions in an early evening midweek game. For the second year running veteran Scots full-back Jim Harley is injured and is a passenger on the wing for an hour. Jack Rowley looks offside for the first goal but it is allowed.										
3	H CHARLTON	2		W	6-2	4-1	Morris 10p, Pearson 16,	Crompton	Carey	Aston	Warner	Chilton	McGlen	Delaney	Morris	Rowley	Pearson	Mitten
	30/8	53,833	*17*	5			*V'an 41, 70* [Rowley 22, 38, 68, 82]	*Bartram*	*Croker P*	*Shreeve*	*Johnson*	*Phipps*	*Hobbis*	*Hurst*	*Purves*	*Vaughan*	*McCrae*	*Duffy*
							Ref: F Green	On a sweltering afternoon the FA Cup winners are put to the sword with a thrilling display. The woodwork is struck on five occasions. Charlton somehow score twice but Jimmy Seed's boys are never in the game. Stan Pearson scores a scorcher from 25 yards. Rowley tipped for England.										
4	A LIVERPOOL	5		D	2-2	2-0	Mitten 2, Pearson 15	Crompton	Carey	Aston	Warner	Chilton	McGlen	Delaney	Morris	Rowley	Pearson	Mitten
	3/9	*48,081*	*7*	6			*Stubbins 48, Balmer 68p*	*Sidlow*	*Jones*	*Lambert*	*Taylor*	*Hughes*	*Paisley*	*Watkinson*	*Balmer*	*Stubbins*	*Polk*	*Liddell*
							Ref: J Tregellas	For once Carey masters Billy Liddell and United are too strong for Pool in the first half, with Rowley even missing a penalty. After the break the home side drag themselves back into the game but the reason for the penalty is a mystery, yet Balmer rarely misses. Morris is the star man.										
5	A ARSENAL	6		L	1-2	1-1	Morris 43	Crompton	Carey	Aston	Warner	Chilton	McGlen	Delaney	Morris	Rowley	Pearson	Mitten
	6/9	*64,905*	*1*	6			*Rooke 25, Lewis 65*	*Swindin*	*Scott*	*Barnes*	*Macauley*	*Fields*	*Mercer*	*Roper*	*Logie*	*Lewis*	*Rooke*	*McPherson*
							Ref: T Smith	Arsenal maintain their 100% record under new manager Tom Whittaker but United are unlucky to lose. Goal-machine Jack Rowley is well controlled by Fields. Ronnie Rooke scores from 25 yards and Reg Lewis wins it with a diving header. Veteran Joe Mercer is immaculate.										
6	A BURNLEY	5		D	0-0	0-0		Crompton	Carey	Aston	Warner	Chilton	McGlen	Delaney	Morris	Rowley	Pearson	Mitten
	8/9	*38,517*	*7*	7				*Strong*	*Woodruff*	*Mather*	*Attwell*	*Brown*	*Bray*	*Chew*	*Morris*	*Billingham*	*Potts*	*Hays*
							Ref: G Salmon	Losing FA Cup finalists Burnley are newly promoted and a tough nut at home. Manager Cliff Britton's 'Iron Curtain' defence is effective and a draw is a fair result. Burnley have more chances and John Billingham misses the best of them after four minutes by shooting wide of goal.										
7	H SHEFFIELD UTD	8		L	0-1	0-1		Crompton	Carey	Aston	Warner	Chilton	McGlen	Delaney	Morris	Burke	Pearson	Rowley
	13/9	50,979	*11*	7			*Brook 11*	*Smith*	*Young*	*Cox*	*Jackson*	*Latham*	*Forbes*	*Thompson*	*Brook*	*Rickett*	*Hagan*	*Collindridge*
							Ref: A Ellis	The run of sixteen unbeaten home games is ended by a spiky Blades team marshalled by Alex Forbes. The injured Mitten's stand-in, Burke, misses several good chances and Delaney does not impress the Scottish selectors. Brook catches Carey and Chilton sleeping for the winner.										
8	A MANCHESTER C	12		D	0-0	0-0		Crompton	Carey	Aston	Warner	Chilton	McGlen	Delaney	Morris	Rowley	Pearson	Mitten
	20/9	***71,364***	*8*	8				*Thurlow*	*Sproston*	*Westwood*	*Walsh*	*Fagan*	*Emptage*	*Wharton*	*Smith*	*McMorran*	*Capel*	*Clarke*
							Ref: C Fletcher	Newly promoted City have made a good start under new boss John Thomson. They have reserve Thurlow in goal for Swift who is on England duty. Several thousand tickets are left with the touts. This first post-war derby is poor fare. Carey is injured and a passenger on the right wing.										
9	A PRESTON	14		L	1-2	0-1	Morris 61	Crompton	Aston	McGlen	Warner	Chilton	Cockburn	**Dale**	Morris	Hanlon	Pearson	Rowley
	27/9	*34,372*	*2*	8			*Beattie 10, McLaren 66*	*Gooch*	*Gray*	*Scott*	*Shankly*	*Williams*	*Horton*	*Finney*	*McLaren*	*McIntosh*	*Beattie*	*Calverley*
							Ref: F Milner	Mitten and Delaney are rested to give Joe Dale a debut and he hits the bar. Chilton's back-pass creates Beattie's goal but Gooch's fine saves keep United at bay. McLaren's header from Bill Shankly's free-kick wins it for Preston, for whom Finney is irresistible. Stan Pearson shines.										
10	H STOKE	14		D	1-1	1-1	Hanlon 15	Crompton	Aston	McGlen	Warner	Chilton	Cockburn	Dale	Morris	Hanlon	Pearson	Rowley
	4/10	46,942	*20*	9			*Kiernan 8*	*Herod*	*Mould*	*McCue*	*Sellars*	*Franklin*	*Kirton*	*Mountford G*	*Kiernan*	*Mountford F*	*McAlinden*	*Ormston*
							Ref: E Plinston	Tom Kiernan, Stoke's £8,500 record signing from Celtic, scores in his second game but United should have won handsomely. Delaney is on Scotland duty and the subject of transfer rumours. Johnny Hanlon scores with a diving header after Stan Pearson's header beats Dennis Herod.										

No / Date	Venue	Opponent / Att	Pos	Res / Pts	F-A	H-T	Scorers, Times, and Referees	1	2	3	4	5	6	7	8	9	10	11
11	H	GRIMSBY	17	L	3-4	0-3	Mitten 55, Rowley 60, Morris 76	Crompton	Aston	McGlen	Warner	Chilton	Pearson	Delaney	Morris	Hanlon	Rowley	Mitten
11/10		41,202	*21*	9			*Cairns 14, 23, 40, Blenkinsopp 86*	*Tweedy*	*Fisher*	*Hodgson J*	*Penrose*	*Taylor*	*Reeve*	*Wilson*	*McGowan*	*Blenkinsopp*	*Cairns*	*Wardle*
							Ref: G Sunderland	The veteran Cairns is the Mariners' hero with a first-half hat-trick against a hesitant home defence, making him Div 1's leading scorer. Roared on by a vociferous crowd, United score three in 11 minutes but lose when wing-half Blenkinsopp, playing at centre-forward, grabs the winner.										
12	A	SUNDERLAND	18	L	0-1	0-0		Crompton	Walton	Aston	Carey	Chilton	McGlen	Delaney	Pearson	Hanlon	Rowley	Mitten
18/10		*37,148*	*17*	9			*Duns 80*	*Mapson*	*Stelling*	*Hudgell*	*McLain*	*Hall*	*Wright*	*Duns*	*Lloyd*	*Davis*	*Watson*	*Reynolds*
							Ref: H Moore	With Hanlon a passenger on the wing and Walton stretchered off, 10-man United can't hang on for a point. Duns' goal looks offside and Jimmy Delaney, in a rare attack, has his shot cleared off the line. It is Sunderland's first home win since August and they will struggle to stay up.										
13	H	ASTON VILLA	17	W	2-0	0-0	Rowley 57, Delaney 82	Crompton	Aston	Worrall	Carey	Chilton	Cockburn	Delaney	Morris	Rowley	Pearson	Mitten
25/10		48,264	*14*	11				*Rutherford*	*Potts*	*Guttridge*	*Dorsett*	*Moss F*	*Parkes*	*Edwards*	*Martin*	*Ford*	*Brown*	*Smith*
							Ref: G Appleyard	At last United get some luck in front of goal and a plucky Villa side are swept aside for United's first win for two months. Both goals are the fruit of unstoppable shots. Fulham's offer for Ronnie Burke is rejected and United are strongly linked with Liverpool stopper Tommy Jones.										
14	A	WOLVERHAMPTON	15	W	6-2	4-1	Pear' 8, 17, Morris 15, 30, Mitten 54	Crompton	Aston	Worrall	Carey	Chilton	Cockburn	Delaney	Morris	Rowley	Pearson	Mitten
1/11		*44,309*	*6*	13			*Dunn 7, Hancocks 70p* [Delaney 85]	*Williams*	*McLean*	*Pritchard*	*Forbes*	*Shorthouse*	*Wright*	*Hancocks*	*Dunn*	*Westcott*	*Smyth*	*Mullen*
							Ref: J Parker	Cullis has retired and Wolves are in transition but it's their first home defeat of the season and their biggest home reverse for 13 years. Delaney and Rowley are unstoppable as United make scoring look frighteningly easy with their first away win. The wobbly Bill Shorthouse is at all sea.										
15	H	HUDDERSFIELD	15	D	4-4	3-1	Rowley 13, 18, 39, 66 *[Bateman 76]*	Crompton	Aston	Worrall	Carey	Chilton	Cockburn	Delaney	Morris	Rowley	Pearson	Mitten
8/11		60,180	*18*	14			*Glazzard 32, Doherty 60, 70p,*	*Hesford*	*Hayes*	*Barker*	*Smith L*	*Hepplewhite*	*Boot*	*Bateman*	*Glazzard*	*Whittingham*	*Doherty*	*Metcalfe*
							Ref: A Denham	United are coasting at half-time and if Rowley's fifth goal had not been disallowed it would have been all over. Then veteran Peter Doherty takes over and mesmerises the home defence with a goal, then a penalty after Chilton's unnecessary lunge, and a set up for Bateman's equaliser.										
16	A	DERBY	13	D	1-1	1-0	Carey 42	**Pegg**	Aston	Worrall	Carey	Chilton	Cockburn	Delaney	Morris	Rowley	Pearson	Mitten
15/11		*32,990*	*6*	15			*Harrison 86*	*Townsend*	*Mozley*	*Howe*	*Ward*	*Leuty*	*Musson*	*Harrison*	*Carter*	*Morrison*	*Steel*	*Oliver*
							Ref: C Fletcher	£15,000 Billy Steel, the most expensive player in Britain, can't score and is outshone by the skilful Morris. The newly signed Ken Pegg, in for the injured Crompton, lets Harrison's tame shot through his hands. Johnny Carey's goal is direct from a free-kick through a crowd of players.										
17	H	EVERTON	15	D	2-2	0-1	Morris 57, Cockburn 78	Pegg	Aston	Worrall	Carey	Chilton	Cockburn	Delaney	Morris	Rowley	Pearson	Mitten
22/11		**36,715**	*13*	16			*Fielding 29, Dodds 77*	*Sagar*	*Saunders*	*Dugdale*	*Farrell*	*Jones*	*Watson*	*Johnson*	*Wainwright*	*Dodds*	*Fielding*	*Eglington*
							Ref: H Wright	United's defence, with Pegg playing his second and final game, is suspect, with the reliable Aston boobing for the first. Morris is again classy and nets when Sagar hesitates. The injured Dodds is limping on the wing but pops up to score. Pearson misses a sitter three minutes from time.										
18	A	CHELSEA	11	W	4-0	1-0	Morris 13, 60, 79, Rowley 85	Crompton	Aston	Walton	Carey	Chilton	Cockburn	Delaney	Morris	Rowley	Pearson	Mitten
29/11		*43,617*	*16*	18				*Medhurst*	*Winter*	*Bathgate*	*Goddard*	*Harris*	*Machin*	*Campbell*	*Walker*	*Armstrong*	*Goulden*	*Jones*
							Ref: W Dixon	Chelsea's unbeaten home record is smashed and manager Billy Birrell is bemused. Johnny Morris presses his case for an England cap with a brilliant display and United's forwards leave the home defenders bewildered. But for the solid John Harris, United would have won by more.										
19	H	BLACKPOOL	11	D	1-1	1-0	Pearson 29	Crompton	Walton	Aston	Carey	Chilton	Cockburn	Delaney	Morris	Rowley	Pearson	Mitten
6/12		64,852	*4*	19			*Mortensen 52*	*Wallace*	*Shimwell*	*Suart*	*Kelly*	*Hayward*	*Johnston*	*Matthews*	*McKnight*	*Mortensen*	*Buchan*	*McIntosh*
							Ref: F Thurman	A hard-fought game against one of the division's top sides. Blackpool play a canny offside game which United struggle to master. Carey's run through the middle sets up Pearson and Mortensen capitalises on Chilton's miscue. Matthews, well held by Aston, almost wins it near the end.										
20	A	BLACKBURN	11	D	1-1	0-0	Morris 60	Crompton	Walton	Aston	Carey	Chilton	Cockburn	Delaney	Morris	Rowley	Pearson	Mitten
13/12		*22,784*	*20*	20			*Weir 70*	*Marks*	*Cook*	*Tomlinson*	*Baldwin*	*Pryde*	*Miller*	*Weir*	*Graham*	*Webber*	*Stephan*	*Oakes*
							Ref: E Plinston	Rovers are still smarting from a 1-7 defeat to Boro in their last home game and a new manager, Bruton, will be named next week. United's exciting start is unrewarded but, with Cook on the wing injured, Morris nets from Pearson's cross. Weir, moved to centre-forward, grabs a goal.										
21	H	MIDDLESBROUGH	10	W	2-1	1-1	Pearson 32, 72	Crompton	Walton	Aston	**Anderson**	Chilton	Cockburn	Delaney	Morris	Rowley	Pearson	Mitten
20/12		47,879	*6*	22			*Fenton 35*	*Goodfellow*	*Robinson*	*Hardwick*	*Bell*	*Whitaker*	*Gordon*	*Spuhler*	*McCormack*	*Fenton*	*Mannion*	*Walker*
							Ref: H Berry	Stan Pearson is skipper as Carey is ruled out with a stomach problem and scores from Rowley's free-kick. Div 1 top scorer Micky Fenton equalises from Chilton's miscued header. The unknown John Anderson looks useful. Delaney's cross sets up the deserved winner for Stan.										

No		Date	Att	Pos	Pt	F-A	H-T	Scorers, Times, and Referees	1	2	3	4	5	6	7	8	9	10	11
22	H	PORTSMOUTH		10	W	3-2	1-1	Rowley 23, Morris 47, 88	Crompton	Walton	Aston	Carey	Chilton	Cockburn	Delaney	Morris	Rowley	Pearson	Mitten
		25/12	44,007	*18*	24			*Froggatt 35, Brown 65*	*Butler*	*Rookes*	*Ferrier*	*Scoular*	*Flewin*	*Dickinson*	*Harris*	*Brown*	*Reid*	*Barlow*	*Froggatt*
								Ref: P Stevens	Pompey's side is taking shape under Bob Jackson with a virtually unchanged team and two superb wing-halves in the two Jimmy's, Scoular and Dickinson. United's late winner from Morris is deserved but Pompey rattle the Reds. Carey is back but Anderson will soon get his chance.										
23	A	PORTSMOUTH		6	W	3-1	1-1	Morris 40, 75, Delaney 89	Crompton	Carey	Aston	Anderson	Chilton	Cockburn	Delaney	Morris	Rowley	Pearson	Mitten
		27/12	*27,674*	*19*	26			*Reid 20*	*Butler*	*Rookes*	*Ferrier*	*Scoular*	*Flewin*	*Dickinson*	*Harris*	*Brown*	*Reid*	*Barlow*	*Froggatt*
								Ref: P Stevens	Pompey are too good to go down but they lack punch up front and the signing of Ike Clarke will help. Reid's glancing header gives them hope but once Morris takes control on a churned up surface there is only one winner. 1939 Cup final hero Barlow is carried off with a twisted knee.										
24	H	BURNLEY		5	W	**5-0**	3-0	Mitten 10, 62, Rowley 21, 43, 72	Crompton	Carey	Aston	Anderson	Chilton	Cockburn	Delaney	Morris	Rowley	Pearson	Mitten
		1/1	61,100	*2*	28				*Strong*	*Woodruff*	*Mather*	*Attwell*	*Brown*	*Bray*	*Chew*	*Potts*	*Billingham*	*Knight*	*Hays*
								Ref: G Salmon	Burnley have lost only one in 14 but this is their biggest loss since 1937. Torrential rain has left a large pool down the middle of the pitch and Burnley's passes get bogged down. The second best defence in Div 1 is swamped after Crompton saves Potts' penalty for Chilton's foul at 2-0.										
25	A	CHARLTON		4	W	2-1	1-1	Morris 9, Pearson 80	Crompton	Carey	Aston	Warner	Chilton	**Lynn**	Delaney	Morris	Rowley	Pearson	Mitten
		3/1	*40,484*	*9*	30			*McCrae 7*	*Bartram*	*Campbell*	*Lock*	*Revell*	*Phipps*	*Hobbis*	*Robinson W*	*O'Linn*	*Vaughan*	*McCrae*	*Duffy*
								Ref: F Green	With Delaney carrying a bandaged wrist, Morris a strapped thigh and Cockburn out injured, Charlton fancy their chances. United are superior all round and come through a stern test for their fifth win in a row. Robinson misses two openings at 1-1. The pundits tip United for the Cup.										
26	H	ARSENAL		5	D	1-1	1-1	Rowley 27	Crompton	Carey	Aston	Anderson	Chilton	Cockburn	Delaney	Morris	Rowley	Pearson	Mitten
		17/1	**83,260**	1	31			*Lewis 18*	*Swindin*	*Scott*	*Barnes*	*Macauley*	*Compton L*	*Mercer*	*Roper*	*Logie*	*Lewis*	*Rooke*	*McPherson*
								Ref: T Smith	Arsenal lost to Bradford in the FA Cup a week earlier but have only lost two league games all season. An English record league crowd see Arsenal stifle the game, although United hit wood three times and Reg Lewis's late shot rattles the post. Compton deflects Rowley's shot in.										
27	A	SHEFFIELD UTD		5	L	1-2	1-2	Rowley 11	**Brown**	Carey	Aston	Anderson	Chilton	Cockburn	Delaney	Morris	Rowley	Pearson	Mitten
		31/1	*45,125*	*12*	31			*Jones 15, 27*	*Smith*	*Furniss*	*Cox*	*Jackson*	*Young*	*Brook*	*Thompson*	*Nightingale*	*Whitelum*	*Collindridge*	*Jones*
								Ref: A Ellis	The Blades rebound from a Cup exit at Crewe to end the 16-game unbeaten run. Sheffield keeper Jack Smith is carried off after seven minutes and Collindridge goes between the posts. Jones equalises Jack's goal and then heads the Blades' winner before Ernie Jackson misses a penalty.										
28	H	PRESTON		7	D	1-1	0-1	Delaney 87	Crompton	Carey	Aston	Warner	Chilton	Cockburn	Delaney	Morris	Rowley	Pearson	Mitten
		14/2	64,902	*4*	32			*McLaren 25*	*Gooch*	*Gray*	*Scott*	*Shankly*	*Waters*	*Horton*	*Anders*	*Beattie*	*McIntosh*	*McLaren*	*Jackson*
								Ref: F Milner	Preston keeper Gooch makes five super saves to almost earn a win before Delaney's late header from Rowley's cross. Carey had been pushed forward. The teams will meet again in the Cup in two weeks. Rowley is marked superbly by young Waters, and Morris is denied by Gooch.										
29	A	STOKE		5	W	2-0	1-0	Buckle 35p, Pearson 52	Crompton	Carey	Aston	Anderson	Chilton	Cockburn	Delaney	Morris	Rowley	Pearson	Buckle
		21/2	*44,115*	*18*	34				*Jepson*	*Meakin*	*McCue*	*Mountford F*	*Franklin*	*Giblin*	*Sellars*	*Bowyer*	*Steele*	*Baker*	*Ormston*
								Ref: E Plinston	45,000 tickets are sold but cold weather keeps the crowd down. Stoke haven't scored in five games and even miss a penalty, Bowyer shooting wide. Buckle makes no mistake after Mountford handles. Cricketer Arthur Jepson plays his final game whilst it is Giblin's one and only game.										
30	H	SUNDERLAND		4	W	3-1	1-0	Mitten 29p, Delaney 70, Rowley 73	Crompton	Carey	Aston	Anderson	Chilton	Cockburn	Delaney	Morris	Rowley	Pearson	Mitten
		6/3	56,384	*15*	36			*Reynolds 81*	*Mapson*	*Stelling*	*Hudgell*	*McLain*	*Hall*	*Scotson*	*Burbanks*	*Bee*	*Turnbull*	*Shackleton*	*Reynolds*
								Ref: H Moore	It is one-way traffic and Mitten, in goal for 35 mins for the injured Crompton, has little to do. Only sloppy finishing keeps the score down. Hall handles for the penalty, Delaney heads home and Jack's rocket makes it 3-0. Len Shackleton, a £20,000 signing from Newcastle is subdued.										
31	A	GRIMSBY		4	D	1-1	0-1	Rowley 80	Crompton	Carey	Aston	Anderson	Chilton	Cockburn	Delaney	Hanlon	Rowley	Pearson	Mitten
		17/3	***12,284***	*22*	37			*McGowan 36*	*Tweedy*	*Moody*	*Fisher*	*Whitfield*	*Galley*	*Blenkinsopp*	*Wilson*	*Briggs*	*Armitage*	*McGowan*	*Pearson*
								Ref: G Sunderland	United are almost beaten by a Grimsby team who are seven points adrift. In this midweek game Morris is absent, playing for the Football League, and is missed. Town, with seven reserves, are ten games without a win and down to ten, with Armitage injured. Rowley's header saves the day.										

No	Venue	Opponent	Pos	Res	FT	HT	Scorers, Times, and Referees	1	2	3	4	5	6	7	8	9	10	11
32	H	WOLVERHAMPTON	4	W	3·2	0·1	Mitten 52, Morris 69, Delaney 74	Crompton	Carey	Aston	Warner	Chilton	Anderson	Delaney	Morris	Rowley	Pearson	Mitten
20/3		51,849	*6*	39			*Dunn 27, Smyth 56*	*Williams*	*Kelly*	*Springthorpe*	*Crook*	*Shorthouse*	*Wright*	*Dunn*	*Pye*	*Westcott*	*Smyth*	*Hancocks*
							Ref: J Parker	United have a hangover from the semi-final and Cockburn is out with flu. Billy Wright-inspired Wolves are on top for 40 minutes, then United throw off the lethargy and rip into them. Delaney's winner is a superb individual goal: three men are beaten before he shoots into an empty net.										
33	A	ASTON VILLA	3	W	1·0	1·0	Pearson 15	Crompton	Carey	Aston	Anderson	Chilton	Lynn	Delaney	Morris	Rowley	Pearson	Mitten
22/3		*52,368*	*10*	41				*Jones*	*Moss F*	*Cummings*	*Dorsett*	*Parkes*	*Lowe*	*Edwards*	*Dixon*	*Ford*	*Brown*	*Smith*
							Ref: G Appleyard	A Monday evening return to the scene of Utd's cup triumph should have been won more easily. Chances galore are spurned on a hard pitch with a high bouncing ball. Villa are poor and lose at home for only the second time since August. Morris misses a glorious chance to make it 2-0.										
34	H	BOLTON	4	L	**0·2**	0·1		Crompton	Carey	Aston	Anderson	Chilton	Lynn	Delaney	Morris	Rowley	Pearson	Mitten
26/3		72,840	*17*	41			*Woodward 32, Barrass 65*	*Hanson*	*Roberts*	*Banks*	*Howe*	*Gillies*	*Murphy*	*Woodward*	*Barrass*	*Lofthouse*	*Bradley*	*Moir*
							Ref: W Evans	Bolton, with their eighth win in nine games, jump four places out of the relegation zone with a fighting display. United miss two good chances but Bolton deserve their win. Bradley sets up Woodward with a superb pass and Barrass's fierce drive after a one-two with Moir seals the win.										
35	A	HUDDERSFIELD	3	W	2·0	1·0	Pearson 32, Burke 63	Brown	Carey	Aston	Warner	McGlen	Cockburn	Delaney	Morris	Burke	Pearson	Mitten
27/3		*38,266*	*18*	43				*Mills*	*Hayes*	*Barker*	*Whittingham*	*Hepplewhite*	*Boot*	*Bateman*	*Nightingale*	*Glazzard*	*Doherty*	*Metcalfe*
							Ref: A Denham	A stroll in the sun on Easter Saturday sees the struggling Terriers slide closer to relegation. Delaney pulls a muscle, Warner breaks his nose, and Crompton and Chilton are rested but it doesn't stop an easy win for the Reds. Enormous demand for the club's 18,000 Wembley tickets.										
36	A	BOLTON	2	W	1·0	0·0	Anderson 88	Brown	Carey	Aston	Anderson	Chilton	Cockburn	Hanlon	Morris	Burke	Pearson	Mitten
29/3		*46,322*	*19*	45				*Hanson*	*Roberts*	*Banks*	*Howe*	*Gillies*	*Murphy*	*Moir*	*Barrass*	*Lofthouse*	*Bradley*	*McShane*
							Ref: W Evans	The Good Friday defeat is avenged in a scrappy game. Anderson's first goal is a lob over Hanson. Berry Brown makes a sensational save from Bradley and Lofthouse is unlucky not to equalise at the death when he hits the underside of the bar. Star man Bradley limps out on the wing.										
37	H	DERBY	2	W	1·0	0·0	Pearson 76	Crompton	Carey	Aston	Anderson	Chilton	Cockburn	Delaney	Morris	Rowley	Pearson	Mitten
1/4		50,700	*5*	47				*Wallace*	*Mozley*	*Howe*	*Ward*	*Leuty*	*Musson*	*Harrison*	*Steel*	*Morrison*	*Stamps*	*Broome*
							Ref: C Fletcher	The Rams had lost only two in 16 before today and fail to avenge their semi-final defeat. Raich Carter has joined Hull as player-manager and the reshuffle doesn't work. Pearson celebrates his England call-up with the only goal and many are coasting with internationals next week.										
38	H	MANCHESTER C	2	D	1·1	1·1	Rowley 31	Crompton	Carey	Aston	Anderson	Chilton	**Lowrie**	Hanlon	Morris	Burke	Rowley	Mitten
7/4		73,114	*6*	48			*Linacre 16*	*Thurlow*	*Sproston*	*Westwood*	*Murray*	*Fagan*	*Walsh*	*Munro*	*Black*	*Linacre*	*Emptage*	*Clarke*
							Ref: C Fletcher	In an electric atmosphere a pulsating draw is fair. Clarke's cross sets up Linacre and joke defending gifts Rowley a goal. Frank Swift is on England duty, allowing Thurlow a rare game in goal. For United, Burke and 19-year-old Lowrie stand in for England's Pearson and Cockburn.										
39	A	EVERTON	2	L	**0·2**	0·0		Crompton	**Ball**	Aston	Anderson	Chilton	Lowrie	Buckle	Morris	Burke	**Cassidy**	Mitten
10/4		*44,098*	*13*	48			*Dodds 53, Stevenson 82*	*Sagar*	*Saunders*	*Hedley*	*Lindley*	*Jones*	*Farrell*	*Grant*	*Fielding*	*Dodds*	*Stevenson*	*Higgins*
							Ref: H Wright	With Wembley looming, new signing from Wigan, John Ball, gets a chance, as does 25-year-old schoolteacher Laurie Cassidy, and neither disappoint. Chilton is superb but United are undone by the winger Jackie Grant who makes both goals. Arsenal clinch the title at Huddersfield.										
40	H	CHELSEA	2	W	**5·0**	2·0	Mitten 11p, Delaney 43, Rowley 48, [Pearson 83, 89]	Crompton	Carey	Aston	Anderson	Chilton	Cockburn	Delaney	Morris	Rowley	Pearson	Mitten
17/4		44,366	*15*	50				*Medhurst*	*Lewis*	*Bathgate*	*Armstrong*	*Harris*	*Macauley*	*Jones*	*Bentley*	*Billingham*	*Walker*	*Campbell*
							Ref: W Dixon	The Cup final team are on show but Rowley limps off with a groin strain. United never need to exceed a canter, and play with a confidence that makes Wembley defeat unthinkable. All change at Chelsea: £11,000 Roy Bentley looks over-rated, but he will save them from relegation.										
41	A	BLACKPOOL	2	L	0·1	0·1		Crompton	Carey	Aston	Anderson	Chilton	Cockburn	Buckle	Hanlon	Rowley	Pearson	Mitten
28/4		*32,236*	*9*	50			*Mortensen 10*	*Robinson*	*Shimwell*	*Crosland*	*Johnston*	*Hayward*	*Kelly*	*Matthews*	*Mortensen*	*McIntosh*	*McCall*	*Rickett*
							Ref: F Thurman	Four days after the final a full-house sees Blackpool regain some pride. Mortensen scores, then is taken to hospital after colliding with Jack Crompton, who plays outfield for the second half. Hanlon goes closest with a header that hits the post. John Aston again masters Matthews.										
42	H	BLACKBURN	2	W	4·1	2·0	Delaney 35, Pearson 42, 78, 83	Crompton	Carey	Aston	Anderson	Chilton	Cockburn	Delaney	Burke	Rowley	Pearson	Mitten
1/5		45,711	22	52			*Murphy 50*	*Marks*	*Holliday*	*Eckersley*	*Baldwin*	*Pryde*	*Horton*	*Campbell*	*Graham*	*McClelland*	*Murphy*	*Langton*
Average	Home 54,890	Away 40,982					Ref: E Plinston	The FA Cup is on display and Rovers are already relegated. At 0-0 Rovers spurn two golden chances, and this awakens United. The heat is swiftly turned up, with player of the season Pearson peerless. He twice repeats his Wembley goal with diagonal runs through Rovers' defence.										

FA Cup					F-A	H-T	Scorers, Times, and Referees	1	2	3	4	5	6	7	8	9	10	11
3	A	ASTON VILLA	4	W	6-4	5-1	R' 8, Mor' 17, 31, P'son 29,88, Del' 43	Crompton	Carey	Aston	Anderson	Chilton	Cockburn	Delaney	Morris	Rowley	Pearson	Mitten
	10/1	*58,683*	*8*				*Edw' 1, 46, Smith 70, Dorsett 81p*	*Jones*	*Potts*	*Parkes*	*Dorsett*	*Moss F*	*Lowe*	*Edwards*	*Martin*	*Ford*	*Brown*	*Smith*
							Ref: H Berry	It's the game of the century as Edwards scores after 13½ seconds before a Red has touched the ball. Four goals in 22 minutes and then another before half-time give United a seemingly unassailable lead. The fans roar on Villa's fight-back in this thriller before Pearson's late clincher.										
4	H	LIVERPOOL	5	W	3-0	3-0	Rowley 30, Morris 35, Mitten 37	Crompton	Carey	Aston	Anderson	Chilton	Cockburn	Delaney	Morris	Rowley	Pearson	Mitten
	24/1	74,721	*16*					*Minshull*	*Jones*	*Lambert*	*Taylor*	*Hughes*	*Paisley*	*Liddell*	*Balmer*	*Stubbins*	*Done*	*Priday*
		(at Goodison Pk)					Ref: J Wiltshire	With Man City also drawn at home, Busby shrewdly switches the tie to Everton. 10,000 are locked out but the record crowd inside sees another United supershow. The turning point comes at 0-0 when Chilton clears off the line and Done shoots wide. Within ten minutes the game is over.										
5	H	CHARLTON	5	W	2-0	1-0	Warner 24, Mitten 85	Crompton	Carey	Aston	Warner	Chilton	Cockburn	Delaney	Morris	Rowley	Pearson	Mitten
	7/2	33,312	*13*					*Bartram*	*Campbell*	*Lock*	*Johnson*	*Bicknell*	*Revell*	*Hurst*	*Fenton*	*Vaughan*	*McCrae*	*Duffy*
		(at Huddersfield)					Ref: J Barrick	The Cup holders are outclassed at Leeds Road and their keeper Sam Bartram is chaired off the pitch for keeping the score down. Jack Warner returns to score from 20 yards with a deflection from Bicknell. Charlie Mitten hits the post then scores with a header from Delaney's cross.										
QF	H	PRESTON	5	W	4-1	2-1	Mitten 23, Pearson 33, 77, Rowley 84	Crompton	Carey	Aston	Anderson	Chilton	Cockburn	Delaney	Morris	Rowley	Pearson	Mitten
	28/2	74,213	*4*				*McIntosh 43*	*Hindle*	*Gray*	*Scott*	*Shankly*	*Waters*	*Horton*	*Finney*	*Beattie*	*McIntosh*	*McLaren*	*Anders*
							Ref: T Smith	United are mesmeric, apart from a brief period at 2-1.Goalie Jack Hindle, making his debut for the injured Gooch, cannot be blamed. The limpet-like Waters keeps Rowley quiet but the other United forwards are rampant. Tom Finney flashes spasmodically and the Reds march on.										
SF	N	DERBY	4	W	3-1	2-1	Pearson 30, 32, 55	Crompton	Carey	Aston	Anderson	Chilton	Cockburn	Delaney	Morris	Rowley	Pearson	Mitten
	13/3	62,250	*5*				*Steel 44*	*Wallace*	*Mozley*	*Howe*	*Ward*	*Leuty*	*Musson*	*Harrison*	*Carter*	*Stamps*	*Steel*	*Morrison*
		(at Hillsborough)					Ref: T Smith	Pearson is heading for an England cap after a stunning performance. The first comes after Rowley's overhead kick, the second a header after Wallace's poor punch, and Mitten sets up the third. Raich Carter has a stinker and despite Steel's drive Derby can't compete in a poor game.										
F	N	BLACKPOOL	2	W	4-2	1-2	Rowley 30, 69, P'son 79, And'son 85	Crompton	Carey	Aston	Anderson	Chilton	Cockburn	Delaney	Morris	Rowley	Pearson	Mitten
	24/4	*99,000*	10				*Shimwell 15p, Mortensen 35*	*Robinson*	*Shimwell*	*Crosland*	*Johnston*	*Hayward*	*Kelly*	*Matthews*	*Munro*	*Mortensen*	*Dick*	*Rickett*
		(at Wembley)					Ref: J Barrick	It's the final of the century with thrills aplenty. Chilton fouls Mortensen for the early penalty and the same man puts Blackpool ahead again. Just when it seems that Matthews will get his medal United hit top gear and deservedly win. Carey is the first southern Irishman to lift the Cup.										

		Home					Away					
	P	W	D	L	F	A	W	D	L	F	A	Pts
1 Arsenal	42	15	3	3	56	15	8	10	3	25	17	59
2 MAN UNITED	42	11	7	3	50	27	8	7	6	31	21	52
3 Burnley	42	12	5	4	31	12	8	7	6	25	31	52
4 Derby	42	11	6	4	38	24	8	6	7	39	33	50
5 Wolves	42	12	4	5	45	29	7	5	9	38	41	47
6 Aston Villa	42	13	5	3	42	22	6	4	11	23	35	47
7 Preston	42	13	4	4	43	35	7	3	11	24	33	47
8 Portsmouth	42	13	5	3	44	17	6	2	13	24	33	45
9 Blackpool	42	13	4	4	37	14	4	6	11	20	27	44
10 Manchester C	42	13	3	5	37	22	2	9	10	15	25	42
11 Liverpool	42	9	8	4	39	23	7	2	12	26	38	42
12 Sheffield Utd	42	13	4	4	44	24	3	6	12	21	46	42
13 Charlton	42	8	4	9	33	29	9	2	10	24	37	40
14 Everton	42	10	2	9	30	26	7	4	10	22	40	40
15 Stoke	42	9	5	7	29	23	5	5	11	12	32	38
16 Middlesbro	42	8	7	6	37	27	6	2	13	34	46	37
17 Bolton	42	11	2	8	29	25	5	3	13	17	33	37
18 Chelsea	42	11	6	4	38	27	3	3	15	15	44	37
19 Huddersfield	42	7	6	8	25	24	5	6	10	26	36	36
20 Sunderland	42	11	4	6	33	18	2	6	13	23	49	36
21 Blackburn	42	8	5	8	35	30	3	5	13	19	42	32
22 Grimsby	42	5	5	11	20	35	3	1	17	25	76	22
	924	236	104	122	815	528	122	104	236	528	815	924

Odds & ends

Double wins: (5) Wolves, Chelsea, Portsmouth, Charlton, Aston Villa.
Double losses: (0)

Won from behind: (6) Wolves (a), Portsm'th (a), Charlton (a), Wolves (h), Aston Villa FAC (a), Blackpool FAC (n)
Lost from in front: (1) Sheffield United (a).

High spots: 16-match unbeaten run from October to January.
Wembley triumph over Blackpool.
Good form of Morris, Pearson and Aston earning representative honours.
Stunning victories at Wolves and Aston Villa.

Low spots: Nine-game run without a win in early season.

Red cards: (United)- none.
Red cards: (Opponents)- none.

Ever-presents: (1) John Aston.
Hat-tricks: (6) Jack Rowley (3), Stan Pearson (2), Johnny Morris (1).
Opposing hat-tricks: (1) Cairns (Grimsby).
Leading scorer: (28) Jack Rowley.

	Appearances		Goals		
	Lge	FAC	Lge	FAC	Tot
Anderson, John	**18**	5	**1**	1	**2**
Aston, John	**42**	6			
Ball, John	**1**				
Brown, Berry	**3**				
Buckle, Ted	**3**		**1**		**1**
Burke, Ronnie	**6**		**1**		**1**
Carey, Johnny	**37**	6	**1**		**1**
Cassidy, Laurie	**1**				
Chilton, Allenby	**41**	6			
Cockburn, Henry	**26**	6	**1**		**1**
Crompton, Jack	**37**	6			
Dale, Joe	**2**				
Delaney, Jimmy	**36**	6	**8**	1	**9**
Hanlon, Johnny	**8**		**1**		**1**
Lowrie, Tommy	**2**				
Lynn, Sammy	**3**				
McGlen, Billy	**13**				
Mitten, Charlie	**38**	6	**8**	3	**11**
Morris, Johnny	**38**	6	**18**	3	**21**
Pearson, Stan	**40**	6	**18**	8	**26**
Pegg, Ken	**2**				
Rowley, Jack	**39**	6	**23**	5	**28**
Walton, Joe	**6**				
Warner, Jack	**15**	1		1	**1**
Worrall, Harry	**5**				
25 players used	**462**	**66**	**81**	**22**	**103**

No	Date	Att	Pos	Pt	F-A	H-T	Scorers, Times, and Referees	1	2	3	4	5	6	7	8	9	10	11
1	H DERBY			L	1-2	0-0	Pearson 85	Crompton	Carey	Aston	Anderson	Chilton	Cockburn	Delaney	Morris	Rowley	Pearson	Mitten
	21/8	52,922		0			*Broome 75, Harrison 79*	*Townsend*	*Mozley*	*Howe*	*Ward*	*Leuty*	*Musson*	*Harrison*	*Stamps*	*Thompson*	*Steel*	*Broome*
							Ref: B Flanagan	The Rams achieve their first win at United since 1928, thanks to keeper Townsend, making his first appearance since January. Derby have recovered from having to sell Carter and Doherty and their defence is superb. United, fielding their Cup final team, make a late rally in vain.										
2	A BLACKPOOL			W	3-0	0-0	Mitten 51, 84, Pearson 87	Crompton	Ball	Carey	Anderson	Chilton	McGlen	Delaney	Morris	Rowley	Pearson	Mitten
	23/8	*31,996*		2				*Robinson*	*Shimwell*	*Stuart*	*Johnston*	*Hayward*	*Kelly*	*Matthews*	*Munro*	*Mortensen*	*McCall*	*Rickett*
							Ref: W Evans	The score flatters an average United team. A full house sees Joe Smith's Pool side struggle, with Stan Matthews quiet under the cool control of Aston and Chilton. Mitten scores two headers, both created by Jack Rowley. Hanlon misses a good chance and has a goal ruled out for offside.										
3	A ARSENAL		4	W	1-0	0-0	Mitten 48	Crompton	Carey	Aston	Anderson	Chilton	Cockburn	Delaney	Morris	Rowley	Pearson	Mitten
	28/8	*64,150*	8	4				*Swindin*	*Barnes*	*Smith*	*Macaulay*	*Compton L*	*Mercer*	*Roper*	*Logie*	*Rooke*	*Forbes*	*McPherson*
							Ref: F Milner	A superb match between the champions and the Cup winners. United win a high speed, skilful game with Mitten's header from Delaney's fast cross. United defend well and Arsenal, despite the magnificence of Archie Macaulay and the hard work of 38-year-old Ron Rooke, are beaten.										
4	H BLACKPOOL		9	L	3-4	1-1	Delaney 43, Mitten 55p, Morris 67	Brown	Carey	Aston	Anderson	Chilton	Cockburn	Delaney	Morris	Rowley	Pearson	Mitten
	1/9	54,046	12	4			*Rickett 33, Mc'sh W 51, 90, Kelly 81*	*Robinson*	*Shimwell*	*Suart*	*Johnston*	*Hayward*	*Kelly*	*Rickett*	*Mortensen*	*McIntosh W*	*McCall*	*Wardle*
							Ref: W Evans	A see-saw thriller is won in the last minute, when stand-in keeper Brown punches Wardle's cross on to McIntosh's head. Ten minutes earlier Pearson blew a chance to make it 4-2, after United had found their goal hunger. Rowley has still to score but is fouled by Shimwell for the pen.										
5	H HUDDERSFIELD		5	W	4-1	3-0	Mitten 1p, Pearson 32, 74, Delaney 35	Crompton	Carey	Aston	Anderson	Chilton	McGlen	Delaney	Morris	Rowley	Pearson	Mitten
	4/9	60,561	21	6			*Doherty 78*	*Mills*	*Hayes*	*Whittingham*	*Hunter*	*Hepplewhite*	*Boot*	*McKenna*	*Smith EC*	*Glazzard*	*Doherty*	*Metcalfe*
							Ref: A Denham	Huddersfield have used 18 players in five games and only Doherty and Metcalf, who skins Carey, look Div 1 material. United win easily but are not hitting the heights of last year. Hunter handles for the penalty and Delaney breasts a lob from McGlen, in for the injured Cockburn.										
6	A WOLVERHAMPTON		10	L	2-3	1-1	Morris 6, Rowley 53	Crompton	Carey	Aston	Anderson	Chilton	McGlen	Delaney	Morris	Rowley	Pearson	Mitten
	8/9	*42,617*	7	6			*Hancocks 9, 75p, Smyth 76*	*Williams*	*McLean*	*Springthorpe*	*Crook W*	*Shorthouse*	*Wright*	*Hancocks*	*Dunn*	*Pye*	*Smyth*	*Mullen*
							Ref: F Overton	On a surface slippery after rain, Wolves are in their element. With Stan Cullis their new manager, they come from behind twice. Wolves are on top in the first half but are mesmerised after the break. The wingers Hancocks and Jimmy Mullen are irrepressible. It's United's first away loss.										
7	A MANCHESTER C		11	D	0-0	0-0		Crompton	Carey	Aston	Cockburn	Chilton	McGlen	Delaney	Morris	Rowley	Pearson	Mitten
	11/9	*67,616*	8	7				*Swift*	*Williams*	*Westwood*	*Fagan*	*McDowall*	*Walsh*	*Oakes*	*Black*	*Godwin*	*Linacre*	*Clarke*
							Ref: A Ellis	Another indifferent United display in a quiet derby. City's Bert Sproston is injured but United's half-backs are all fit and Cup final hero John Anderson is left out. Morris has a shot hit the post and Mitten's header rattles the angle. For City, Oakes has two shots well saved by Crompton.										
8	H WOLVERHAMPTON		7	W	2-0	2-0	Pearson 16, Buckle 17	Crompton	Carey	Aston	Cockburn	Chilton	McGlen	Buckle	Morris	Rowley	Pearson	Mitten
	15/9	36,690	8	9				*Williams*	*McLean*	*Springthorpe*	*Crook W*	*Shorthouse*	*Wright*	*Hancocks*	*Dunn*	*Pye*	*Smyth*	*Mullen*
							Ref: F Overton	Wolves play their part in a thriller and lose their first away game. Bert 'The Cat' Williams saves brilliantly from Rowley and then Mitten, but Pearson follows up to score. Buckle heads in Mitten's cross. Aston has Hancocks in his pocket and although Pye hits the bar it's United's day.										
9	A SHEFFIELD UTD		9	D	2-2	0-2	Buckle 71, Pearson 73	Crompton	Carey	Aston	Cockburn	Chilton	McGlen	Buckle	Morris	Rowley	Pearson	Mitten
	18/9	*36,755*	19	10			*Collindridge 20, Jones 24*	*Smith J*	*Furniss*	*Parkin*	*Jackson*	*Latham*	*Young*	*Thompson*	*Brook*	*Collindridge*	*Hagan*	*Jones*
							Ref: J South	The Blades have started badly and are eight games without a win. United should have won with ease but Jack Smith makes some good saves and chances are missed before they get a shock. After Pearson's equaliser, an away win looks certain. Jimmy Hagan celebrates England recall.										
10	H ASTON VILLA		7	W	3-1	2-1	Mitten 20p, Rowley 34, 87	Crompton	Ball	Carey	Anderson	Chilton	McGlen	Delaney	Morris	Rowley	Pearson	Mitten
	25/9	53,820	22	12			*Edwards 3*	*Jones*	*Ashton*	*Cummings*	*Dorsett*	*Parkes*	*Lowe*	*Mulraney*	*Graham*	*Ford*	*Edwards*	*Smith L*
							Ref: L Thompson	The referee is too soft in an ill-tempered match. Parkes handles for a controversial penalty and Villa, now nine games without a win, harass the ref after Rowley's second. Ford is booked for petulance and Villa only shine for 20 mins. Aston and Cockburn are in Denmark with England.										

No	Date	H/A	Opponent	Att	Pos	Res	Pts	F-A	H-T	Scorers, Times, and Referees	1	2	3	4	5	6	7	8	9	10	11
11		A	SUNDERLAND		9	L		1-2	0-1	Rowley 86	Crompton	Carey	Aston	Cockburn	Chilton	McGlen	Delaney	Buckle	Rowley	Pearson	Mitten
	2/10			*54,419*	*5*		12			*Davis 2, Reynolds 58*	*Mapson*	*Stelling*	*Hudgell*	*Watson*	*Hall*	*Wright A*	*Turnbull*	*Robinson J*	*Davis*	*Shackleton*	*Reynolds*
										Ref: C Warburton	Sunderland are unbeaten at home and win with comfort, with Reynolds missing a penalty after McGlen was penalised. Davis nets after Jackie Robinson hits the post, then Reynolds scores from an acute angle. Yorkshire cricketer Willie Watson is switched to wing-half to great effect.										
12		H	CHARLTON		9	D		1-1	1-1	Burke 9	Crompton	Ball	Aston	Anderson	Chilton	Warner	Delaney	Morris	Burke	Rowley	Mitten
	9/10			49,822	*4*		13			*Vaughan 44*	*Bartram*	*Shreeve*	*Lock*	*Fenton*	*Phipps*	*Revell*	*Hurst*	*O'Linn*	*Vaughan*	*McCrae*	*Duffy*
										Ref: R Leafe	International calls rob United of three players but one stand-in, John Ball, is superb against the elusive Chris Duffy. It's a game of misplaced passes and unbelievable misses. Burke plays well and Sam Bartram can't hold his shot for the goal. McCrae's jinking run sets up Vaughan.										
13		A	STOKE		11	L		1-2	1-1	Morris 42	Crompton	Carey	Aston	Anderson	Chilton	Cockburn	Delaney	Morris	Rowley	Pearson	Mitten
	16/10			*43,916*	*8*		13			*Steele 6, Mountford G 60*	*Herod*	*Mould*	*McCue*	*Mountford F*	*Franklin*	*Sellars*	*Mountford G*	*Bowyer*	*Steele*	*Baker*	*Ormston*
										Ref: S Roberts	United's away form is better but lucky Stoke hang on to win despite Delaney being rugby tackled two minutes from time. Baker is carried off with a broken leg with 15 minutes left. Herod is Stoke's saviour, saving from Pearson and Rowley. Crompton misjudges a cross for the winner.										
14		H	BURNLEY		12	D		1-1	0-0	Mitten 84	Crompton	Carey	Aston	Anderson	Chilton	Cockburn	Delaney	Morris	Rowley	Pearson	Mitten
	23/10			49,919	*17*		14			*Billingham 85*	*Strong*	*Loughran*	*Mather*	*Attwell*	*Woodruff*	*Bray*	*Chew*	*Knight*	*Billingham*	*Haigh*	*Wilson*
										Ref: F Gerrard	Frank Hill's first game as Burnley boss, following Britton's move to Everton, earns a good result through negativity and time-wasting. Mather is brutal with Delaney. Mitten's volley looks to have sealed the points but Carey immediately heads Attwell's free-kick straight to Billingham.										
15		A	PRESTON		10	W		**6-1**	3-1	Pear' 8, 37, Mit'n 32, 51, Morris 82, [Rowley 89]	Crompton	Carey	Aston	Warner	Chilton	Cockburn	Delaney	Morris	Rowley	Pearson	Mitten
	30/10			*37,372*	*18*		16			*Beattie 3*	*Newlands*	*Brown W*	*Scott*	*Shankly*	*Corbett*	*Horton*	*Bogan*	*McLaren*	*McIntosh*	*Beattie*	*Langton*
										Ref: W Evans	At last United come good and relentlessly demolish North End who fight hard but are let down by silly errors. Beattie's volley sparks the Reds into action but only Bogan and Langton are effective for Proud. Morris and Pearson are back to their best and the recalled Jack Warner is solid.										
16		H	EVERTON		7	W		2-0	1-0	Delaney 18, Morris 85	Crompton	Carey	Aston	Warner	Chilton	Cockburn	Delaney	Morris	Rowley	Pearson	Mitten
	6/11			45,636	*22*		18				*Sagar*	*Saunders*	*Hedley*	*Bentham*	*Jones*	*Farrell*	*Higgins*	*Stevenson*	*Catterick*	*Juliussen*	*Eglington*
										Ref: H Wright	Everton have lost eleven out of 16 and Cliff Britton is their new boss. Warner's recall has inspired United, and Mitten crosses for Delaney and Morris, with a header, to score. Veteran keeper Ted Sagar (38) is brilliant as exciting United threaten to sink the Toffees without trace early on.										
17		A	CHELSEA		6	D		1-1	1-0	Rowley 22	Crompton	Carey	Aston	Anderson	Chilton	Cockburn	Delaney	Morris	Rowley	Pearson	Mitten
	13/11			*62,542*	*15*		19			*Bentley 55*	*Pickering*	*Bathgate*	*Hughes*	*Goulden*	*Harris*	*Macaulay*	*Campbell*	*Williams*	*Bentley*	*Bowie*	*McInnes*
										Ref: T Rand	Chelsea are pulling in massive crowds with their attractive football and Bowie is the star today. The result is fair but United argue that Roy Bentley's goal was not over the line when it cannoned down from the crossbar. John Aston is immaculate and praises his mentor Johnny Carey.										
18		H	BIRMINGHAM		5	W		3-0	3-0	Pearson 22, Rowley 33, Morris 44	Crompton	Carey	Aston	Cockburn	Chilton	McGlen	Delaney	Morris	Rowley	Pearson	Mitten
	20/11			48,325	*12*		21				*Merrick*	*Green*	*Jennings*	*Harris*	*McDonnell*	*Mitchell*	*Stewart*	*McKee*	*Garrett*	*Bodle*	*Laing*
										Ref: J Williams	Birmingham have injury problems and, but for Merrick, it would have been a bigger defeat. Four successive losses, after only one in 11, have marred Blues' good start. Rowley scores from 30 yards and Morris heads a third. Blues boss Storer will resign this week to return to Coventry.										
19		A	MIDDLESBROUGH		4	W		4-1	1-0	Rowley 12, 60, 69, Delaney 73	Crompton	Carey	Aston	Cockburn	Chilton	McGlen	Delaney	Morris	Rowley	Pearson	Mitten
	27/11			*31,435*	*17*		23			*McCrae 88*	*Ugolini*	*Robinson*	*Hardwick*	*Blenkinsopp*	*Whittaker*	*Gordon*	*Reagan*	*Spuhler*	*Fenton*	*McCrae*	*Walker*
										Ref: R Mortimer	Boro fans applaud United as they approach last season's form. Rowley, with nine goals in ten games, puts pressure on England selectors to pick him for England. It is a great team effort and United are five points behind the leaders Derby. Boro look doomed, with Fenton held by Chilton.										
20		H	NEWCASTLE		4	D		1-1	0-0	Mitten 88	Crompton	Carey	Aston	Cockburn	Chilton	McGlen	Delaney	Morris	Rowley	Pearson	Mitten
	4/12			**73,632**	*3*		24			*Stobbart 81*	*Fairbrother*	*Cowell*	*Batty*	*Harvey*	*Brennan*	*Dodgin*	*Stobbart*	*Gibson*	*Donaldson*	*Taylor*	*Hair*
										Ref: H Jackson	Newly promoted Newcastle are going like a train, but with Jackie Milburn out injured they rely on Fairbrother to keep them in the game. Jack Rowley made a strong debut for England and is in superb form but can't score. Lucky Magpies almost snatch it but Mitten squares things.										
21		A	PORTSMOUTH		4	D		2-2	1-0	Mitten 45p, McGlen 88	Crompton	Carey	Aston	Cockburn	Chilton	McGlen	Delaney	Morris	Rowley	Pearson	Mitten
	11/12			29,966	*3*		25			*Froggatt 60, Clarke 63*	*Butler*	*Rookes*	*Ferrier*	*Scoular*	*Flewin*	*Dickinson*	*Harris*	*Barlow*	*Clarke*	*Phillips*	*Froggatt*
										Ref: H Pearce	United are only the third side to get a point at Fratton Park, where Pompey are unbeaten. Mitten hits his fourth penalty of the season after Reg Flewin upends him. Rowley's piledriver leaves Butler groggy, before McGlen gets a black eye heading a late goal from one of many corners.										

No		Date	Att	Pos	Pt	F-A	H-T	Scorers, Times, and Referees	1	2	3	4	5	6	7	8	9	10	11
22	A	DERBY		4	W	3-1	2-1	Burke 19, 27, Pearson 60	Crompton	Carey	Aston	Cockburn	Chilton	McGlen	Delaney	Pearson	Burke	Rowley	Mitten
		18/12	*31,498*	*3*	27			*Mozley 35*	*Townsend*	*Mozley*	*Parr*	*Ward*	*Leuty*	*Musson*	*Harrison*	*Powell*	*Stamps*	*Steel*	*Broome*
								Ref: B Flanagan	United are definitely back in business, knocking the Rams off top spot. It's their first home defeat and fourth defeat in six. Burke upsets Leon Leuty with his physical approach and sets up Pearson with a strong run. Bert Mozley is injured on the wing when he lobs the dodgy Crompton.										
23	H	LIVERPOOL		4	D	0-0	0-0		Crompton	Carey	Aston	Cockburn	Chilton	McGlen	Delaney	Pearson	Burke	Rowley	Mitten
		25/12	50,649	*13*	28				*Minshull*	*Shepherd*	*Lambert*	*Taylor*	*Jones*	*Paisley*	*Payne*	*Balmer*	*Done*	*McLeod*	*Brierley*
								Ref: E Varney	A dull game for Christmas revellers, with Liverpool grateful that United's forwards are goal-shy. Cyril Done and Tom McLeod are inadequate Liverpool replacements for Stubbins, and Billy Liddell is missed. Bill Jones is on the verge of the England team and keeps Rowley in check.										
24	A	LIVERPOOL		4	W	2-0	0-0	Burke 54, Pearson 57	Crompton	Carey	Aston	Cockburn	Chilton	McGlen	Buckle	Pearson	Burke	Rowley	Mitten
		27/12	*53,273*	*13*	30				*Minshull*	*Shepherd*	*Lambert*	*Taylor*	*Jones*	*Paisley*	*Payne*	*Balmer*	*Done*	*McLeod*	*Liddell*
								Ref: E Varney	Liddell is back but Liverpool are clumsy and floundering, whilst United are effortless. Both goals are from defensive lapses with Ray Minshull failing to stop an easy Pearson shot. Jim Payne is dangerous early on but Crompton is in good form. Liverpool are seven games without a win.										
25	H	ARSENAL		4	W	2-0	1-0	Mitten 10, Burke 84	Crompton	Carey	Aston	Cockburn	Chilton	McGlen	Delaney	Morris	Burke	Pearson	Mitten
		1/1	61,527	*9*	32				*Swindin*	*Barnes*	*Smith*	*Macaulay*	*Compton L*	*Mercer*	*Roper*	*Lewis*	*Rooke*	*Lishman*	*McPherson*
								Ref: F Milner	With all three sides above them losing, United are only two points behind Pompey. Burke continues his scoring run with a shot from a difficult angle to clinch the points. Arsenal, not the force of last year, are linked with the unhappy Wilf Mannion of Boro. Johnny Morris looks unfit.										
26	H	MANCHESTER C		3	D	0-0	0-0		Crompton	Carey	Aston	Cockburn	Chilton	McGlen	Delaney	Morris	Rowley	Pearson	Mitten
		22/1	69,191	9	33				*Swift*	*Sproston*	*Westwood*	*Walsh*	*Fagan*	*Emptage*	*Linacre*	*Hart*	*Black*	*Smith*	*Clarke*
								Ref: A Ellis	City manager Jock Thomson's tactics are spot on and his team, whilst inferior in quality, more than match the Reds for guts. United's forwards adopt their switching tactics but City's wing-halves are superb. Rumours of Johnny Morris' unrest grow. Keeper Berry Brown joins Doncaster.										
27	A	ASTON VILLA		5	L	1-2	0-0	Rowley 81	Crompton	Carey	Aston	Cockburn	Chilton	McGlen	Delaney	Pearson	Burke	Rowley	Mitten
		19/2	***68,354***	*19*	33			*Dixon 49, Ford 80*	*Rutherford*	*Parkes*	*Cummings*	*Powell*	*Martin C*	*Moss*	*Gibson*	*Dixon*	*Ford*	*Dorsett*	*Smith L*
								Ref: L Thompson	After only one league game in six weeks, United have lost ground on Pompey and their 18-match unbeaten run comes to an end. Villa's fourth win in five is in front of Villa's record league crowd. Dixon races through for the first and Trevor Ford's guile unnerves Chilton for a second.										
28	A	CHARLTON		5	W	3-2	1-0	Pearson 4, 62, Downie 52	Crompton	Carey	Aston	Cockburn	Chilton	McGlen	Delaney	**Downie**	Rowley	Pearson	Mitten
		5/3	*55,291*	*7*	35			*O'Linn 51, Vaughan 88*	*Bartram*	*Campbell*	*Lock*	*Johnson*	*Phipps*	*Revell*	*Hurst*	*O'Linn*	*Vaughan*	*Purves*	*Fenton*
								Ref: R Leafe	Seed missed second half to see reserves at Millwall. Busby says 'Charlton let you play'. Attractive Charlton are averaging over 40,000 but are mesmerised. New £18,000-man Downie looks at home, whilst Johnny Morris looks set to go to Liverpool. Sid O'Linn's cross-shot is stunning.										
29	H	STOKE		4	W	3-0	1-0	Rowley 45, Downie 57, Mitten 71	Crompton	Carey	Aston	Cockburn	Chilton	McGlen	Delaney	Downie	Rowley	Pearson	Mitten
		12/3	58,804	*9*	37				*Herod*	*Watkin*	*McCue*	*Mountford F*	*Franklin*	*Sellars*	*Mountford G*	*Bowyer*	*Steele*	*Baker*	*Ormston*
								Ref: S Roberts	Morris joins Derby for a world record £24,500 and his replacement John Downie scores a slick goal from an acute angle and makes Mitten's. The beleaguered Dennis Herod and Neil Franklin are superb for the Potters but in reality it should have been 6-0 with Crompton a spectator.										
30	A	BIRMINGHAM		4	L	0-1	0-0		Crompton	Carey	Aston	Cockburn	Chilton	McGlen	Delaney	Anderson	Rowley	Pearson	Mitten
		19/3	*46,819*	*12*	37			*Boyd 49*	*Merrick*	*Badham*	*Green*	*Boyd*	*McDonnell*	*Ferris*	*Stewart*	*Jordan*	*Slater*	*Harris*	*Roberts*
								Ref: J Williams	Defeat at St Andrews leaves United nine points adrift of Pompey and the title bid looks over. New boss Bob Brocklebank gains a vital win with newcomer from Juventus, Jordan, looking good. With the semi-final looming and Downie cup-tied, John Anderson gets a surprise run-out.										
31	A	HUDDERSFIELD		7	L	1-2	0-1	Rowley 75	Crompton	Carey	Ball	Anderson	Chilton	McGlen	Delaney	Downie	Burke	Rowley	Mitten
		6/4	***17,368***	*21*	37			*Doherty 31p, Metcalfe 55*	*Mills*	*Hayes*	*Stewart H*	*Whittaker*	*Hepplewhite*	*Boot*	*McKenna*	*Hansen*	*Rodgers*	*Doherty*	*Metcalfe*
								Ref: A Denham	United are uncertain all over the muddy pitch and Town climb off the foot of the table. McKenna is fouled for Doherty's spot-kick and Metcalfe scores after Carey's mistake. Mitten misses his first senior penalty after Delaney was fouled, and Jack Rowley's stunning free-kick is too late.										

No	H/A	Opponent / Date	Att	Pos	Res / Pts	F-A	H-T	Scorers, Times, Referees	1	2	3	4	5	6	7	8	9	10	11
32	H	CHELSEA		7	D	1-1	0-0	Mitten 80p	Crompton	Carey	Ball	Anderson	Chilton	McGlen	Buckle	Downie	Burke	Rowley	Mitten
		9/4	30,123	*13*	38			*McInnes 74*	*Medhurst*	*Winter*	*Hughes*	*Dickson*	*Warren*	*Mitchell*	*Campbell*	*McInnes*	*Billington*	*Goulden*	*Jones*
								Ref: T Rand	United have three on England duty against Scotland and Delaney is injured. Chelsea have injuries, notably Harris, so Warren makes his only appearance. Things only warm up when Carey is pushed forward with 15 minutes left. Winter's handball has Chelsea appealing to no avail.										
33	A	BOLTON		5	W	1-0	1-0	Carey 32	Crompton	Ball	Aston	Lowrie	Chilton	Cockburn	Downie	Carey	Rowley	Pearson	Mitten
		15/4	47,157	*16*	40				*Elvy*	*Roberts*	*Banks R*	*Howe*	*Aspinall*	*Barrass*	*Westwood*	*Moir*	*Lofthouse*	*Bradley*	*Hernon*
								Ref: A Denham	Carey, playing at inside-forward, celebrates being named Footballer of the Year with a rare goal after Pearson's shot rebounded out of Elvey's reach. But for poor finishing, the margin would have been greater in front of Bolton's biggest crowd of the season, but Barrass hits a goal-post.										
34	A	BURNLEY		4	W	2-0	0-0	Rowley 55, 72	Crompton	Ball	Aston	Lowrie	Chilton	Cockburn	Downie	Carey	Rowley	Pearson	Mitten
		16/4	*38,682*	*10*	42				*Strong*	*Loughran*	*Mather*	*Attwell*	*Cummings*	*Bray*	*Chew*	*Morris*	*Harrison*	*Potts*	*Hays*
								Ref: F Gerrard	Easter Saturday sees a full house at Turf Moor stunned into silence by slick United. Burnley's cultured wing-half, Reg Attwell, twists an ankle just before half-time and does not return. Tommy Lowrie impresses again at right-half, while Carey, the ultimate utility player, is awesome.										
35	H	BOLTON		3	W	3-0	1-0	Rowley 14, 68, Mitten 75	Crompton	Ball	Aston	Lowrie	Chilton	Cockburn	Delaney	Carey	Rowley	Pearson	Mitten
		18/4	50,504	*17*	44				*Elvy*	*Roberts*	*Banks R*	*Howe*	*Aspinall*	*Barrass*	*Lofthouse*	*Moir*	*Dillon*	*Bradley*	*McShane*
								Ref: A Denham	The officials get some stick after Rowley has three goals disallowed and Bolton persist in offside tactics. Jack scores two and makes Mitten's in a supreme individual performance. The second is hilarious as Elvey dashes out and completely misses the ball. Bolton barely muster a shot.										
36	H	SUNDERLAND		3	L	1-2	1-2	Mitten 22p	Crompton	Ball	Aston	Lowrie	Chilton	Cockburn	Delaney	Carey	Rowley	Pearson	Mitten
		21/4	33,437	*10*	44			*Broadis 19, Robinson J 40*	*Robinson R*	*Stelling*	*Hudgell*	*Watson*	*Hall*	*Wright A*	*Wright T*	*Robinson J*	*Broadis*	*Shackleton*	*Reynolds*
								Ref: C Warburton	Sunderland have recovered from their Cup defeat at Yeovil. They are the first side to do the double over United since the war. New signing Ivor Broadis scores and makes the second, and combines with Len Shackleton in a silky display. Two clear Sunderland handballs are rejected.										
37	H	PRESTON		4	D	2-2	1-1	Downie 39, 80	Crompton	Carey	Aston	Lowrie	Chilton	Cockburn	Delaney	Downie	Rowley	Pearson	Mitten
		23/4	46,086	*20*	45			*Finney 6, Brown E 65*	*Gooch*	*Brown W*	*Walton*	*Robertson*	*Waters*	*Dougall*	*Anders*	*Beattie*	*Brown E*	*Finney*	*Langton*
								Ref: W Evans	Preston have drafted in new faces in the fight to avoid the drop. Three wins in five have given them hope. Joe Walton has an impressive return, whilst Finney's header and Brown, from Chilton's back-pass, earn a deserved point. Carey rushes off to Dublin afterwards for an Eire game.										
38	A	EVERTON		4	L	0-2	0-2		Crompton	Carey	Aston	Lowrie	Chilton	Cockburn	Delaney	Downie	Cassidy	Pearson	Mitten
		27/4	*39,106*	*17*	45			*Wainwright 19, McIntosh 31*	*Sagar*	*Saunders*	*Dugdale*	*Farrell*	*Jones*	*Lello*	*Powell*	*Wainwright*	*McIntosh*	*Fielding*	*Eglington*
								Ref: H Wright	After eight games without a win, Everton earn a vital two points in the relegation battle. Eglington is a fast winger and sets up Wainwright's superb header. Cassidy cuts his eye after five minutes and struggles. United unlikely to finish second after fourth defeat in seven away games.										
39	A	NEWCASTLE		4	W	1-0	0-0	Burke 84	Crompton	Carey	Aston	Lowrie	Chilton	Cockburn	Delaney	Downie	Burke	Pearson	Mitten
		30/4	*38,266*	*2*	47				*Fairbrother*	*Cowell*	*Graham*	*Houghton*	*Brennan*	*Dodgin*	*Walker*	*Robledo*	*Milburn*	*Thompson*	*Mitchell*
								Ref: H Jackson	Portsmouth clinch the title on FA Cup final day and a weary United grab a late winner. Stand-in Ronnie Burke never lets the side down and despite being well shepherded by Brennan he pops up to grab the goal. Like most of the players, England star Jackie Milburn is off-colour.										
40	H	MIDDLESBROUGH		3	W	1-0	0-0	Rowley 63	Crompton	Carey	Aston	Lowrie	Chilton	Cockburn	Delaney	Downie	Rowley	Pearson	Mitten
		2/5	**22,889**	*19*	49				*Ugolini*	*Robinson*	*Hardwick*	*Bell*	*Blenkinsopp*	*Gordon*	*Reagan*	*Mannion*	*Donaldson*	*McCrae*	*Hartnett*
								Ref: W Evans	Boro have only one away win all season and even with Mannion back in favour they are poor and not safe. Rowley is tamed in the air by Tom Blenkinsopp but escapes his clutches to score from Downie's pass as Ugolini falls over. Donaldson is foiled by Crompton when clean through.										
41	H	SHEFFIELD UTD		2	W	3-2	0-2	Mitten 47, Pearson 67, Downie 83	Crompton	Carey	Aston	Cockburn	Chilton	McGlen	Delaney	Downie	Rowley	Pearson	Mitten
		4/5	23,725	*20*	51			*Jones 15, Thompson 16*	*Smith J*	*Bailey*	*Furniss*	*Hitchin*	*Chisholm*	*Shaw*	*Thompson*	*Hagan*	*Jones*	*Whitelum*	*Hutchinson*
								Ref: J South	A midweek defeat leaves the Blades needing to win their final game to stay up. They throw away a two-goal lead, the first coming after Jack Crompton's mistake. Stan Pearson's header is adjudged to be over the line for his first goal in 15 games but the Blades players are very angry.										
42	H	PORTSMOUTH		2	W	3-2	2-2	Rowley 10, 54, Mitten 44p	Crompton	Carey	Aston	Anderson	Chilton	Cockburn	Delaney	Downie	Rowley	Pearson	Mitten
		7/5	52,661	*1*	53			*Reid 25, Harris 35*	*Butler*	*Hindmarsh*	*Yeuell*	*Scoular*	*Thompson*	*Dickinson*	*Harris*	*Reid*	*Clarke*	*Phillips*	*Froggatt*
		Home	Away					Ref: H Pearce	Ten-man Pompey - Harris hobbled off in the second half - should have had a point, but Reid sees his late penalty saved after a handball. An all-action first half saw Reid's back-heel and Harris' header cancel out Rowley's drive, but Mitten levels from the spot after Yeuell fouled him.										
		Average 48,808	44,695																

FA Charity Shield			F-A	H-T	Scorers, Times, and Referees	1	2	3	4	5	6	7	8	9	10	11
A ARSENAL	9	L	3-4	2-4	Rowley 12, Burke 42, Smith 60 (og)	Crompton	Carey	Aston	Anderson	Chilton	Warner	Delaney	Morris	Burke	Rowley	Mitten
6/10 *31,000*	7				*Jones 2, Lewis 3, 34, Rooke 6*	*Swindin*	*Barnes*	*Smith*	*Macaulay*	*Compton L*	*Mercer*	*Roper*	*Logie*	*Lewis*	*Rooke*	*Jones B*
					Ref: R Burgess	The game starts five minutes early to allow United to catch a train home. After six minutes Arsenal are 3-0 up, including a Rooke thunderbolt. Reg Lewis's swerver is the best of the seven goals in a football feast. Veterans Ronnie Rooke (38) and Bryn Jones (37) are in amazing form.										

FA Cup			F-A	H-T	Scorers, Times, and Referees	1	2	3	4	5	6	7	8	9	10	11
3 H BOURNEMOUTH	4	W	6-0	2-0	Burke 27, 51, Pearson 33,	Crompton	Carey	Aston	Cockburn	Chilton	McGlen	Delaney	Pearson	Burke	Rowley	Mitten
8/1 55,012	*3S:3*				[Rowley 49, 77, Mitten 52]	*Bird*	*Cunningham*	*Sanaghan*	*Woodward*	*Stirling*	*Percival*	*Rampling*	*Blair*	*McGibbon*	*Bennett*	*Cheney*
					Ref: F Overton	It is 26 minutes before the avalanche and Bournemouth have a good penalty appeal turned down. Saves by the flying Bird keep them in the game. Henry Cockburn and McGlen are superb as probing wing-halves and it is all over by half-time against opposition who quickly wilt.										
4 H BRADFORD PA	3	D	1-1	0-1	Mitten 53	Crompton	Carey	Aston	Cockburn	Chilton	McGlen	Delaney	Morris	Rowley	Pearson	Mitten
29/1 82,771	*2:7*		*aet*		*Henry 29*	*Farr*	*Stephen*	*Farrell*	*White*	*Horsman*	*Elliott*	*Glover*	*Henry*	*McIlvenny*	*Downie*	*Deplidge*
					Ref: A Blythe	A record FA Cup crowd, outside of a final, sees plucky Bradford, victors over Newcastle, earn a replay. Henry scores from a Deplidge corner and Mitten levels with a header. In extra-time a hobbling Pearson and Downie have goals disallowed. The latter shoots wide with the last kick.										
4R A BRADFORD PA	4	D	1-1	1-1	Mitten 31	Crompton	Carey	Aston	Cockburn	Chilton	McGlen	Buckle	Pearson	Burke	Rowley	Mitten
5/2 *30,000*	*2:9*		*aet*		*Farrell 33p*	*Farr*	*Stephen*	*Farrell*	*White*	*Horsman*	*Elliott*	*Glover*	*Henry*	*McIlvenny*	*Downie*	*Deplidge*
					Ref: A Blythe	Mitten's lead lasts two minutes before Chilton handles. Crowds line the touchline at fog-shrouded Park Avenue. United are slick on the icy surface but the game deteriorates after half-time. Mitten and Glover kick each other and McIlvenny breaks a leg in extra-time. Farr is the hero.										
4R H BRADFORD PA	4	W	5-0	1-0	Burke 25, 65, Rowley 55,57,	Crompton	Carey	Aston	Cockburn	Chilton	McGlen	Buckle	Pearson	Burke	Rowley	Mitten
7/2 70,434	*2:9*				[Pearson 75]	*Farr*	*Stephen*	*Farrell*	*White*	*Horsman*	*Elliott*	*Glover*	*Henry*	*Ainsley*	*Downie*	*Deplidge*
					Ref: A Blythe	Over 70,000 pay on a Monday afternoon and many more climb walls and gates. A minute's silence for League president Will Cuff is followed by a lecture for all 22 players from the ref. Burke rips Avenue apart and United are made Cup favourites as Bradford's defence finally caves in.										
5 H YEOVIL	4	W	8-0	4-0	Rowley 6,12, 22, 65, 88,	Crompton	Carey	Aston	Cockburn	Chilton	McGlen	Delaney	Pearson	Burke	Rowley	Mitten
12/2 81,565	*SL:18*				[Burke 44 ,47, Mitten 72]	*Hall*	*Hickman*	*Davis*	*Keeton*	*Blizzard*	*Collins*	*Hamilton*	*Stock*	*Bryant*	*Wright*	*Roy*
					Ref: A Bond	Player-manager Alec Stock has no special plan and his conquerors of Sunderland are put to the sword. Rowley is the first United man to score five in a game but is helped by an injury to keeper Hall after 20 mins. Yeovil, who have earned £5,000 from their cup jaunt, have a party later.										
QF A HULL	4	W	1-0	0-0	Pearson 75	Crompton	Ball	Aston	Cockburn	Chilton	McGlen	Delaney	Pearson	Burke	Rowley	Mitten
26/2 *55,000*	*3N:2*					*Bly*	*Taylor*	*Berry*	*Greenhalgh*	*Meens*	*Mellor*	*Harrison*	*Jensen*	*Moore*	*Buchan*	*Carter*
					Ref: R Leafe	Everyone in Hull wants to see this and a record crowd ensues, with thousands of forgeries. Hull fail to become the first Div 3 North team to reach the semi-final in a poor game on a hard pitch. Ball clears off the line and United roar down the pitch and Pearson taps in Delaney's cross.										
SF N WOLVERHAMPTON	4	D	1-1	1-1	Mitten 24	Crompton	Carey	Aston	Cockburn	Chilton	McGlen	Delaney	Anderson	Rowley	Pearson	Mitten
26/3 *62,250*	*9*		*aet*		*Smyth 12*	*Williams*	*Kelly*	*Pritchard*	*Crook W*	*Shorthouse*	*Wright*	*Hancocks*	*Smyth*	*Pye*	*Dunn*	*Mullen*
(at Hillsborough)					Ref: J Parker	An ill-tempered match starts well but fizzles out. Kelly and Pritchard take bad knocks and are virtual passengers, whilst Cockburn is concussed and Rowley needs head stitches. The Anderson gamble fails but United deserve to win. Chilton's back-pass lets in Smyth and Mitten lobs in.										
SF N WOLVERHAMPTON	5	L	0-1	0-0		Crompton	Carey	Aston	Cockburn	Chilton	McGlen	Delaney	Rowley	Burke	Pearson	Mitten
R 2/4 *72,631*	*9*				*Smyth 85*	*Williams*	*Crook A*	*Springthorpe*	*Crook W*	*Shorthouse*	*Wright*	*Hancocks*	*Smyth*	*Pye*	*Dunn*	*Mullen*
(at Goodison Pk)					Ref: J Parker	United get no reward for a constant barrage on the awesome Bert Williams' goal. Wolves' team effort is rewarded when Pye, looking offside, breaks clear and his cross bounces off Crompton for Smyth to head home. Alf Crook, brother of Walter, comes in for his second and last game.										

		Home						Away					
		P	W	D	L	F	A	W	D	L	F	A	Pts
1	Portsmouth	42	18	3	0	52	12	7	5	9	32	30	58
2	MAN UNITED	42	11	7	3	40	20	10	4	7	37	24	53
3	Derby	42	17	2	2	48	22	5	7	9	26	33	53
4	Newcastle	42	12	5	4	35	29	8	7	6	35	27	52
5	Arsenal	42	13	5	3	51	18	5	8	8	23	26	49
6	Wolves	42	13	5	3	48	19	4	7	10	31	47	46
7	Manchester C	42	10	8	3	28	21	5	7	9	19	30	45
8	Sunderland	42	8	10	3	27	19	5	7	9	22	39	43
9	Charlton	42	10	5	6	38	31	5	7	9	25	36	42
10	Aston Villa	42	10	6	5	40	36	6	4	11	20	40	42
11	Stoke	42	14	3	4	43	24	2	6	13	23	44	41
12	Liverpool	42	5	10	6	25	18	8	4	9	28	25	40
13	Chelsea	42	10	6	5	43	27	2	8	11	26	41	38
14	Bolton	42	10	4	7	43	32	4	6	11	16	36	38
15	Burnley	42	10	6	5	27	19	2	8	11	16	31	38
16	Blackpool	42	8	8	5	24	25	3	8	10	30	42	38
17	Birmingham	42	9	7	5	19	10	2	8	11	17	28	37
18	Everton	42	12	5	4	33	25	1	6	14	8	38	37
19	Middlesbro	42	10	6	5	37	23	1	6	14	9	34	34
20	Huddersfield	42	6	7	8	19	24	6	3	12	21	45	34
21	Preston	42	8	6	7	36	36	3	5	13	26	39	33
22	Sheffield Utd	42	8	9	4	32	25	3	2	16	25	53	33
		924	232	133	97	788	515	97	133	232	515	788	924

Odds & ends

Double wins: (3) Arsenal, Middlesboro, Bolton.
Double losses: (1) Sunderland.

Won from behind: (4) A Villa (h), Preston (a), Sheff U (h), Portsmouth (h).
Lost from in front: (2) Blackpool (h), Wolves (a).

High spots: Winning early season games at Arsenal and Blackpool.
13-game unbeaten league run from October to January.
Ten away victories – the best since 1905-06.
The big FA Cup wins over Bournemouth, Bradford and Yeovil.

Low spots: The poor home form – only 11 wins.
Cup defeat in the semi final.
Too many defeats against mediocre opposition.

Red cards: (United) none.
Red cards: (Opponents) none.

Hat-tricks: (2) Rowley.
Ever-presents: (2) Chilton and Mitten.
Leading scorer: Rowley (29).

	Appearances		Goals		
	Lge	FAC	Lge	FAC	Tot
Anderson, John	**15**	1			
Aston, John	**38**	8			
Ball, John	**9**	1			
Brown, Berry	**1**				
Buckle, Ted	**5**	2	**2**		**2**
Burke, Ronnie	**9**	6	**6**	6	**12**
Carey, Johnny	**41**	7	**1**		**1**
Cassidy, Laurie	**1**				
Chilton, Allenby	**42**	8			
Cockburn, Henry	**35**	8			
Crompton, Jack	**41**	8			
Delaney, Jimmy	**36**	6	**4**		**4**
Downie, Johnny	**12**		**5**		**5**
Lowrie, Tommy	**8**				
McGlen, Billy	**24**	8	**1**		**1**
Morris, Johnny	**22**	1	**6**		**6**
Mitten, Charlie	**42**	8	**18**	5	**23**
Pearson, Stan	**39**	8	**14**	3	**17**
Rowley, Jack	**39**	8	**20**	9	**29**
Warner, Jack	**3**				
21 players used	**462**	**88**	**77**	**23**	**100**

No	Date	Att	Pos	Pt	F-A	H-T	Scorers, Times, and Referees	1	2	3	4	5	6	7	8	9	10	11
1	A DERBY			W	1-0	1-0	Rowley 5	Crompton	Carey	Aston	Warner	Lynn	Cockburn	Delaney	Pearson	Rowley	**Birch**	Mitten
	20/8	*35,787*		2				*Webster*	*Mozley*	*Howe*	*Ward*	*Leuty*	*Musson*	*Harrison*	*Morris*	*Stamps*	*Steel*	*Broome*
							Ref: B Flanagan	Johnny Morris is captain for the day against his old club but Rowley's drive spoils his day. 17-year old Salford youngster Brian Birch plays for the injured Downie and dazzles with his footwork. Derby's other big money signing Billy Steel misses two chances but United deserve to win.										
2	H BOLTON			W	3-0	1-0	Gillies 40 (og), Mitten 66p, Rowley 80	Crompton	Carey	Aston	Warner	Lynn	Cockburn	Delaney	Downie	Rowley	Pearson	Mitten
	24/8	42,515		4				*Elvey*	*Roberts*	*Kinnell*	*Howe*	*Gillies*	*Barrass*	*Woodward*	*Moir*	*Lofthouse*	*Bradley*	*McShane*
							Ref: T Rand	The return to Old Trafford brings pre-match traffic and spectator congestion and a fan runs on the pitch. United win in a canter as Rowley goes down like a sack of potatoes for the spot-kick and is then unmarked to nod home Carey's free-kick. Crompton is lucky after flooring Moir.										
3	H WEST BROM		2	D	1-1	0-1	Pearson 89	Crompton	Carey	Aston	Warner	Lynn	Cockburn	Delaney	Downie	Rowley	Pearson	Mitten
	27/8	46,407	*9*	5			*Williams 38*	*Sanders*	*Pemberton*	*Millard*	*Kennedy*	*Vernon*	*Hood*	*Elliott*	*Williams*	*Walsh*	*Haines*	*Lee*
							Ref: R Leafe	Stan Pearson's late header saves United's blushes. Jack Crompton fails to hold Walsh's shot and Cyril Williams nips in to score. Billy Elliott misses two golden chances to seal victory. Jack Smith's newly promoted Albion team look capable of staying clear of relegation trouble.										
4	A BOLTON		2	W	2-1	1-0	Mitten 28, Pearson 76	Crompton	Carey	Aston	Warner	Lynn	Cockburn	Delaney	Pearson	Rowley	Buckle	Mitten
	31/8	*39,226*	*18*	7			*McShane 84*	*Hanson*	*Roberts*	*Kinnell*	*Howe*	*Gillies*	*Barrass*	*Woodward*	*Moir*	*Lofthouse*	*Hernon*	*McShane*
							Ref: T Rand	Mitten atones for his earlier penalty miss, after Roberts fouled Rowley, by netting. Aggrieved Bolton argue the ball is not over the line. Moir is a passenger for the second half and Rowley sets up Pearson. Bolton's revival sees star man McShane score and force Crompton to save well.										
5	H MANCHESTER C		2	W	2-1	0-1	Williams 74 (og), Pearson 78	Crompton	Carey	Aston	Warner	Lynn	Cockburn!	Delaney	Pearson	Rowley	Buckle	Mitten
	3/9	51,108	*17*	9			*Munro 30*	*Swift*	*Williams*	*Westwood*	*Walsh*	*Fagan*	*Emptage*	*Linacre!*	*Munro*	*Smith*	*Black*	*Oakes*
							Ref: A Ellis	Linacre and Cockburn are ordered off for fisticuffs but it is not a dirty derby. Frank Swift makes his penultimate appearance before retiring and fumes about the equaliser. He claims Pearson handled beforehand. 29-year old Sammy Lynn is a more than adequate replacement for Chilton.										
6	A LIVERPOOL		1	D	1-1	1-0	Mitten 43	Crompton	Carey	Aston	Lowrie	Lynn	Chilton	Delaney	Pearson	Rowley	Buckle	Mitten
	7/9	*51,857*	*4*	10			*Stubbins 76*	*Sidlow*	*Lambert*	*Spicer*	*Taylor*	*Hughes*	*Paisley*	*Payne*	*Baron*	*Stubbins*	*Fagan*	*Liddell*
							Ref: J Houston	Both teams remain unbeaten after this exciting tussle. Billy Liddell creates Stubbins' goal with a fine run and cross. Earlier Mitten headed in Rowley's cross. Chilton only plays because Cockburn is suspended. Lynn doesn't give Stubbins an inch. United top for first time since 1946.										
7	A CHELSEA		2	D	1-1	0-0	Rowley 70	Crompton	Carey	Aston	Lowrie	Lynn	Chilton	Delaney	Pearson	Rowley	Buckle	Mitten
	10/9	*61,357*	*5*	11			*Bentley 85*	*Medhurst*	*Winter*	*Willemse*	*Armstrong*	*Harris*	*Mitchell*	*Campbell*	*Billington*	*Bentley*	*Williams*	*Gray*
							Ref: R Wood	The temperature is over 70 degrees and the pitch bone hard and United throw it away. Young winger Gray gives Carey a hard time for 25 mins before Carey gets his act together. Harris marshals Chelsea well but can't stop Rowley netting. United look an average team and lack sparkle.										
8	H STOKE		2	D	2-2	1-1	Rowley 10, 57	Crompton	Carey	Aston	Chilton	Lynn	Cockburn	Delaney	Pearson	Rowley	Buckle	Mitten
	17/9	45,325	*12*	12			*Godwin 39, Mountford F 49p*	*Wilkinson*	*Watkin*	*McCue*	*Mountford F*	*Franklin*	*Kirton*	*Mountford G*	*Bowyer*	*Godwin*	*Caton*	*Baker*
							Ref: J Pickles	Rowley is dropped by England but scores two unstoppable goals against the reserve Wilkinson. United concede two for the first time but Stoke don't deserve a point. Lynn's innocuous handball gives Stoke a penalty and it's a mystery why Pearson's shoulder-charged goal is disallowed.										
9	A BURNLEY		3	L	0-1	0-1		Crompton	Carey	Aston	Chilton	Lynn	Cockburn	Delaney	Pearson	Rowley	Buckle	Mitten
	24/9	*41,262*	*4*	12			*Spencer 7*	*Strong*	*Woodruff*	*Mather*	*Attwell*	*Cummings*	*Bray*	*Morris*	*Spencer*	*Clarke*	*Potts*	*Hays*
							Ref: W Evans	Lucky Burnley are less skilful but faster to the ball with Potts and Hays making Chilton look clumsy. Jack Spencer's home debut goal ends United's 12-game unbeaten run. Reg Attwell is Burnley's star man. Carey returns from captaining Eire to victory over England at Goodison.										
10	H SUNDERLAND		5	L	**1-3**	0-3	Pearson 57	Crompton	Carey	Aston	Lowrie	Chilton	Cockburn	Delaney	Pearson	Rowley	Buckle	Mitten
	1/10	51,240	*11*	12			*Carey 9 (og), Davis 16, Shackleton 38*	*Mapson*	*Stelling*	*Hudgell*	*Watson*	*Hall*	*Wright A*	*Wright T*	*Broadis*	*Davis*	*Shackleton*	*Reynolds*
							Ref: H Williams	For once United are outwitted - by England reject Len Shackleton and Ivor Broadis. Shack makes the first as Dickie Davis's shot deflects off Carey and is set up by Broadis for the third. It is Sunderland's third successive win over the Reds and Stan Pearson's header is no consolation.										

No	Venue	Opponent	Pos	Res	Score	HT	Scorers	1	2	3	4	5	6	7	8	9	10	11
11	H	CHARLTON	3	W	3-2	2-0	Mitten 15p, 39, Rowley 68	Crompton	Ball	Aston	Warner	Chilton	McGlen	Delaney	**Bogan**	Rowley	Pearson	Mitten
	8/10	43,809	*17*	14			*Vaughan 55, Purves 88*	*Bartram*	*Campbell*	*Shreeve*	*Forbes*	*Phipps*	*Revell*	*Hurst*	*O'Linn*	*Vaughan*	*Purves*	*Brown*
							Ref: C Jacobs	Crompton is married in the morning and Carey is in Finland with Eire. 38-year-old Warner is recalled and Bogan, signed from Preston, enjoys a good debut. Charlie Mitten is fouled by Campbell for the penalty and his 30-yard free-kick goes in off the post, as do both of Charlton's goals.										
12	A	ASTON VILLA	3	W	4-0	3-0	Rowley 1, Bogan 13, Mitten 31, 80p	Crompton	Ball	Carey	Warner	Lynn	Cockburn	Delaney	Bogan	Rowley	Pearson	Mitten
	15/10	*47,483*	*15*	16				*Jones*	*Parkes*	*Dorsett*	*Powell*	*Martin*	*Moss F*	*Craddock*	*Dixon*	*Howarth*	*Lowe*	*Goffin*
							Ref: R Lloyd	Villa's unbeaten home record is smashed as United hit top form at last. Rowley's header sets the tone after 45 seconds and Jack breasts down for Bogan. Mitten races clear for the third and is brought down by Jones for the spot-kick. Tommy Bogan and Delaney are almost telepathic.										
13	H	WOLVERHAMPTON	3	W	3-0	1-0	Pearson 31, 59, Bogan 78	Crompton	Carey	Aston	Warner	Chilton	Cockburn	Delaney	Bogan	Rowley	Pearson	Mitten
	22/10	53,269	*1*	18				*Parsons*	*Kelly*	*Springthorpe*	*Russell*	*Chatham*	*Crook W*	*Hancocks*	*Smyth*	*Pye*	*Dunn*	*Mullen*
							Ref: A Murdoch	Wright and Williams are sorely missed by Cullis's Wolves and their unbeaten league record goes in a flawless United display. Mitten's crosses make the first two goals and the third is a brilliant solo effort; Bogan dribbles from the halfway line before scoring. Pye well held by Chilton.										
14	A	PORTSMOUTH	3	D	0-0	0-0		Crompton	Carey	Aston	Warner	Chilton	Cockburn	Delaney	Bogan	Rowley	Pearson	Mitten
	29/10	40,586	*5*	19				*Butler*	*Hindmarsh*	*Ferrier*	*Scoular*	*Spence*	*Dickinson*	*Harris*	*Pickett*	*Clarke*	*Phillips*	*Froggatt*
							Ref: W Ling	Pompey draft in reserve Spence for his debut. In the first half Phillips goes close, firing wide, but after the break Pompey are lucky to survive some goalmouth scrambles. Aston and Cockburn are in international form and both sides get a standing ovation at the end for a thrilling game.										
15	H	HUDDERSFIELD	3	W	6-0	2-0	Rowley 6, 47, Pearson 39, 75, [Delaney 87, Mitten 89]	**Feehan**	Carey	Aston	Cockburn	Chilton	McGlen	Delaney	Bogan	Rowley	Pearson	Mitten
	5/11	41,157	*16*	21				*Hesford*	*Hayes*	*Howe*	*Whittaker*	*Heppelwhite*	*Boot*	*McKenna*	*Glazzard*	*McEvoy*	*Nightingale*	*Metcalfe*
							Ref: T Rand	Town manager George Stephenson may struggle to perform his Houdini act this season as his team are woeful. It is a busy final game for 33-year-old Bob Hesford and a quiet debut for 'Sonny' Feehan, in because of Crompton's broken wrist. Mitten even misses a twice-taken penalty.										
16	A	EVERTON	4	D	0-0	0-0		Crompton	Carey	Aston	Warner	Chilton	Cockburn	Delaney	Bogan	Rowley	Pearson	Mitten
	12/11	*46,672*	*20*	22				*Sagar*	*Saunders*	*Dugdale*	*Farrell*	*Humphreys*	*Lello*	*Higgins*	*Wainwright*	*McIntosh*	*Powell*	*Buckle*
							Ref: R Hartley	Struggling Everton put on one of their best shows for the Reds and ex-Red debutant Ted Buckle gives Carey a roasting, but shoots wide from a good position. On a blustery day it's not pretty. Cliff Britton's men deserve a point but Stan Pearson should have buried a sitter near the end.										
17	H	MIDDLESBROUGH	2	W	2-0	0-0	Pearson 52, Rowley 65	Crompton	Carey	Aston	Cockburn	Chilton	McGlen	Delaney	Bogan	Rowley	Pearson	Mitten
	19/11	44,646	*16*	24				*Ugolini*	*Robinson*	*Dicks*	*Bell*	*Blenkinsopp*	*Gordon*	*Linacre*	*Mannion*	*McKenna*	*McCrae*	*Walker*
							Ref: J Topliss	Rowley and Pearson carry on their good work in England's midweek 9-2 win over Ireland. Their one-two sets up Pearson, then Rowley rifles home to add to his four for England. Boro are excellent in the first half but Robinson limps off injured after an hour. Six clean sheets in a row.										
18	A	BLACKPOOL	2	D	3-3	2-0	Bogan 1, Pearson 25, 60	Feehan	Carey	Aston	Cockburn	Chilton	McGlen	Delaney	Bogan	Rowley	Pearson	Mitten
	26/11	***27,742***	*6*	25			*Shim'l 70p, Mc'tosh 74, Johnson 90*	*Farm*	*Shimwell*	*Garrett*	*Johnson*	*Hayward*	*Kelly*	*Matthews*	*McCall*	*Mortensen*	*McIntosh*	*Wardle*
							Ref: F Walton	With Chilton and Aston controlling the two Stans, United look to be coasting with 20 minutes left. Pearson is sublime. He hits a post for Bogan to tap in, looks offside for the second, but finishes coolly for the third. Cockburn handles as Liverpool besiege United and Johnston heads home.										
19	H	NEWCASTLE	2	D	1-1	1-1	Mitten 37	**Wood**	Carey	Aston	Cockburn	Chilton	McGlen	Delaney	Downie	Bogan	Pearson	Mitten
	3/12	31,793	*10*	26			*Walker 17*	*Garbutt*	*Graham*	*Batty*	*Dodgin*	*Brennan*	*Crowe*	*Walker*	*Houghton*	*Milburn*	*Robledo*	*Mitchell*
							Ref: A Blythe	18-year-old Ray Wood is signed before this game, played in miserably wet and windy conditions. George Martin's Magpies are on top and Walker has a good goal ruled out before he scores from Aston's slip. Mitten chips over the wall for the undeserved equaliser. Milburn tamed.										
20	A	FULHAM	2	L	0-1	0-1		Feehan	Carey	Aston	Cockburn	Chilton	McGlen	Delaney	Bogan	Rowley	Pearson	Mitten
	10/12	*35,362*	*14*	26			*Jezzard 7*	*Kelly*	*Freeman*	*Bacuzzi*	*Quested*	*Taylor*	*Beasley*	*Stevens*	*Thomas R*	*Rowley*	*Jezzard*	*McDonald*
							Ref: F Chadwick	Bill Dodgin's Fulham are in their first season in Division 1 and throw United out of their stride with some quick tackling. 14-stone Arthur Rowley, brother of Jack, sets up Jezzard's headed goal. In a second-half blitz Feehan is the star and saves at full stretch from Arthur Stevens.										
21	H	DERBY	3	L	0-1	0-0		Feehan	Carey	Aston	Cockburn	Chilton	McGlen	Delaney	Bogan	Rowley	Pearson	Mitten
	17/12	35,203	*9*	26			*Stamps 81*	*Townsend*	*Mozley*	*Parr*	*Ward*	*Oliver*	*Musson*	*Powell*	*Morris*	*Stamps*	*Steel*	*McLaren*
							Ref: B Flanagan	United's goal-shy forwards are out of touch and lack the vision to break down Derby's frustrating offside tactics. Johnny Morris misses a good early chance on his return to his home. The conditions are wintry and the wind howls. Jack Stamps' half-hit shot fools Feehan and creeps in.										

No	Date		Att	Pos	Pt	F-A	H-T	Scorers, Times, and Referees	1	2	3	4	5	6	7	8	9	10	11
22	A	WEST BROM		2	W	2-1	2-0	Bogan 8, Rowley 38	Feehan	Carey	Aston	Cockburn	Chilton	McGlen	Delaney	Bogan	Rowley	Pearson	Mitten
	24/12		*46,973*	*11*	28			*Walsh 68*	*Sanders*	*Pemberton*	*Millard*	*Kennedy*	*Vernon*	*Ryan*	*Elliott*	*Williams*	*Walsh*	*Barlow*	*Lee*
								Ref: R Leafe	Jack Smith's Albion push hard for an equaliser after the hard-working Dave Walsh pulls a goal back set up by Lee. United are well in charge in the first half with Bogan fed by Cockburn and Rowley on target. Billy Elliott carried off after half an hour with Achilles tendon problems.										
23	H	ARSENAL		2	W	2-0	2-0	Pearson 2, 30	Feehan	Carey	Aston	Warner	Chilton	McGlen	Delaney	Bogan	Rowley	Pearson	Mitten
	26/12		**55,757**	*4*	30				*Platt*	*Barnes*	*Smith*	*Forbes*	*Compton L*	*Mercer*	*Cox*	*Macaulay*	*Goring*	*Lewis*	*McPherson*
								Ref: G Iliffe	United win the top of the table clash with two gems from Pearson. Arsenal's Christmas Eve 5-0 thrashing of Sunderland is forgotten as United win easily. Arsenal's Leslie Compton, brother of Dennis, is in top form and just capped by England, aged 38, but 35-year old Mercer is slow.										
24	A	ARSENAL		2	D	0-0	0-0		Feehan	Carey	Aston	Warner	Chilton	McGlen	Delaney	Bogan	Rowley	Pearson	Mitten
	27/12		***65,133***	*5*	31				*Swindin*	*Scott*	*Barnes*	*Macaulay*	*Compton L*	*Forbes*	*Cox*	*Logie*	*Goring*	*Lewis*	*McPherson*
								Ref: G Iliffe	George Swindin's return in goal is one of four changes for Tom Whittaker's side. There is no lack of thrills and Pearson should have clinched both points. Twice Swindin saves well and Stan's best effort hits George's body. Peter Goring misses two inviting chances for the Gunners.										
25	A	MANCHESTER C		2	W	2-1	0-1	Delaney 55, Pearson 75	Feehan	Carey	Aston	Warner	Chilton	McGlen	Delaney	Bogan	Rowley	Pearson	Mitten
	31/12		*63,593*	*21*	33			*Black 10*	*Trautmann*	*Phillips*	*Westwood*	*Gill*	*Fagan*	*Walsh*	*Munro*	*Black*	*Turnbull*	*Alison*	*Clarke*
								Ref: A Ellis	In the 50th derby fixture United do the double for the first time since 1909. City are not overawed. Black nods home Clarke's cross and has another inexplicably ruled out. Rowley sets up Delaney. Then new keeper, the German Trautmann, lets slip Delaney's shot and Stan wins it.										
26	H	CHELSEA		1	W	1-0	0-0	Mitten 53	**Lancaster**	Carey	Aston	Cockburn	Chilton	McGlen	Delaney	Downie	Rowley	Pearson	Mitten
	14/1		48,466	*10*	35				*Medhurst*	*Winter*	*Willemse*	*Armstrong*	*Harris*	*Mitchell*	*Gray*	*Bowie*	*Bentley*	*Billington*	*Campbell*
								Ref: R Wood	With Liverpool losing, United go top but only impress in the last 20 minutes. With the World Cup in mind, the press compare Rowley with Roy Bentley, and prefer Jack. 19-year-old Joe Lancaster has a quiet game. Harry Medhurst punches straight to Mitten, who blasts the winner.										
27	A	STOKE		2	L	**1-3**	0-1	Mitten 81	Feehan	Carey	Aston	Cockburn	Chilton	McGlen	Delaney	Bogan	Rowley	Pearson	Mitten
	21/1		*38,951*	*16*	35			*Mountford G 10, 75, Bowyer 76*	*Wilkinson*	*Watkin*	*McCue*	*Mountford F*	*Franklin*	*Sellars*	*Malkin*	*Bowyer*	*Mountford G*	*Johnston*	*Oscroft*
								Ref: J Pickles	Manager McGrory is pulling Stoke away from the drop zone and they outclass United. Oscroft, signed from Mansfield, gives Carey a skinning on his home debut. Injuries hit the Reds, with McGlen limping on the wing and Rowley off near the end. Mountford's second looks offside.										
28	H	BURNLEY		2	W	3-2	0-0	Mitten 48, Rowley 64, 70	Lancaster	Carey	Aston	Warner	Chilton	Cockburn	Delaney	Bogan	Rowley	Pearson	Mitten
	4/2		48,528	*8*	37			*Potts 58, Carey 87 (og)*	*Strong*	*Woodruff*	*Kirkham*	*Attwell*	*Cummings*	*Bray*	*Chew*	*Morris*	*Spencer*	*Potts*	*Wilson*
								Ref: W Evans	United are in their best form for weeks but take their foot off the gas. Slick Burnley go close in the first half before Rowley chips for man-of-the-match Mitten. Charlie later repays the compliment. Potts' volley is helped in by Joe Lancaster. Carey nets trying to protect the new keeper.										
29	A	SUNDERLAND		2	D	2-2	1-1	Rowley 24, Chilton 80	Feehan	Carey	Aston	Warner	Chilton	Cockburn	Delaney	**Clempson**	Rowley	Downie	Mitten
	18/2		*63,251*	*4*	38			*Davis 27, Reynolds 73*	*Mapson*	*Stelling*	*Hudgell*	*Watson*	*Walsh*	*Wright A*	*Wright T*	*Broadis*	*Davis*	*Shackleton*	*Reynolds*
								Ref: H Williams	Without a win at Roker Park for 20 years, United face a wind at the start. Rowley's goal is their only shot, and the league's top scorer, Davis, soon replies. Reynolds nets after Feehan misses Broadis' cross, but Chilton's thunderous header nicks a point. Debutant Clempson hits a post.										
30	A	CHARLTON		1	W	2-1	0-1	Rowley 73, Carey 76	Crompton	Ball	Aston	Carey	Chilton	Cockburn	Delaney	Downie	Rowley	Pearson	Mitten
	25/2		*44,920*	*20*	40			*Hurst 36*	*Bartram*	*Croker P*	*Shreeve*	*Revell*	*Phipps*	*Ufton*	*Hurst*	*Cullum*	*Vaughan*	*Purves*	*Kiernan*
								Ref: C Jacobs	Watching Chelsea boss Birrell sees evidence of anxiety in United's defence. United struggle to turn supremacy into goals against a mediocre team. Crompton fails to clear Kiernan's corner and Hurst scores. Rowley, with an individual goal, and Carey, with a cool finish, clinch the win.										
31	H	ASTON VILLA		1	W	**7-0**	1-0	Mitten 40p, 47p, 48, 88p, Rowley 68, [Downie 69, 75]	Crompton	Ball	Aston	Warner	Carey	Cockburn	Delaney	Downie	Rowley	Pearson	Mitten
	8/3		24,072	*14*	42				*Rutherford*	*Parkes*	*Dorsett*	*Powell*	*Moss A*	*Moss F*	*Dixon*	*Gibson*	*Harrison*	*Goffin*	*Smith L*
								Ref: R Lloyd	Villa's Martin and Ford are on international duty. England's selectors can't ignore Mitten – the Prince of wingers – for much longer. Jack's penalty save from Goffin atones for Chelsea. All Charlie's penalties aim right of the keeper and into the roof. Villa's worst defeat since 1890.										

No	Venue / Date	Opponent	Att	Pos	Res / Pts	F-A	H-T	Scorers, Times, and Referees	1	2	3	4	5	6	7	8	9	10	11
32	A	MIDDLESBROUGH		1	W	3-2	0-1	Downie 53, 85, Rowley 78	Crompton	Ball	Aston	Warner	Chilton	Carey	Delaney	Downie	Rowley	Pearson	Mitten
	11/3		*46,702*	*8*	44			*Walker 28, Woodward 52*	*Ugolini*	*Robinson*	*Blenkinsopp*	*Bell*	*Whittaker*	*Gordon*	*Woodward*	*Mannion*	*McKenna*	*McCrae*	*Walker*
								Ref: J Toplis	Carey's appearance at centre-half means he has played in four different positions in four games and he nullifies Wilf Mannion. Boro's run of nine home wins is ended by some calculated moves and deadly finishing. Walker's goal looks like handball and Woodward's nothing but a gift.										
33	H	LIVERPOOL		1	D	0-0	0-0		Crompton	Carey	Aston	Warner	Chilton	Cockburn	Delaney	Downie	Rowley	Pearson	Mitten
	15/3		45,283	*2*	45				*Sidlow*	*Lambert*	*Spicer*	*Taylor*	*Jones*	*Paisley*	*Payne*	*Baron*	*Stubbins*	*Christie*	*Liddell*
								Ref: J Houston	With Liverpool in the FA Cup semi-final, the Kop are dreaming of the double, but they are outplayed. United have sixteen corners and Welsh keeper Sidlow is brilliant as United throw ten players into attack at the finish. Liverpool, with Christie debuting, are lucky but hard-working.										
34	H	BLACKPOOL		1	L	1-2	1-1	Delaney 35	Crompton	Carey	Aston	Warner	Chilton	Cockburn	Bogan	Downie	Delaney	Pearson	Mitten
	18/3		55,517	*2*	45			*Mortensen 21, 50p*	*Farm*	*Shimwell*	*Wright*	*McKnight*	*Johnston*	*Kelly*	*Hobson*	*Mortensen*	*Mudie*	*Slater*	*Perry*
								Ref: F Walton	Blackpool, with their youngest ever front line, are now three points behind with two games in hand. Aston misjudges South African debutant Perry's lob for the first and concedes the penalty for hands. Farm carries Delaney's cross into the net under pressure from Downie and Bogan.										
35	A	HUDDERSFIELD		1	L	**1-3**	1-0	Downie 24	Crompton	Ball	Aston	Warner	Chilton	Cockburn	Delaney	Downie	Carey	Pearson	Mitten
	25/3		*34,348*	*16*	45			*Crompton 47 (og), Metcalfe 65, 89p*	*Mills*	*Gallogly*	*Howe*	*Battye*	*Hepplewhite*	*Boot*	*McKenna*	*Smith WC*	*Taylor JN*	*Nightingale*	*Metcalfe*
								Ref: T Rand	On a bare pitch United are stunned by Town's long-ball game. Crompton blames the sun for fisting in McKenna's corner and for missing Vic Metcalfe's lob. Henry Cockburn, with a bandaged head, concedes the penalty. Mills is in great form for Town but United don't deserve a thing.										
36	H	EVERTON		1	D	1-1	0-0	Delaney 58	Feehan	Ball	Aston	Carey	Chilton	Cockburn	Delaney	Downie	Rowley	Pearson	Mitten
	1/4		37,166	*19*	46			*Grant 82*	*Burnett*	*Moore*	*Hedley*	*Grant*	*Falder*	*Lindley*	*Powell*	*Wainwright*	*Catterick*	*Farrell*	*Buckle*
								Ref: R Hartley	Another disastrous result means that three points cover the top six and Blackpool are title favourites. Against the losing FA Cup semi-finalists the fire is missing and United look stale. Rowley rarely troubles Falder and Pearson is off the pace. A vital point for Everton who may stay up.										
37	H	BIRMINGHAM		2	L	0-2	0-1		Feehan	Ball	Aston	Carey	Chilton	Cockburn	Delaney	Pearson	Rowley	Downie	Mitten
	7/4		48,991	*21*	46			*Stewart 30, Berry 70*	*Merrick*	*Badham*	*Jennings*	*Boyd*	*Atkins*	*Ferris*	*Stewart*	*Brennan*	*Trigg*	*Evans*	*Berry*
								Ref: R Wood	The fans are mystified as Birmingham win away for the first time in 16 months. Both sides have two men injured at the end, with Jack Rowley concussed. Berry crosses for Stewart to nod in and bemuses Aston and Chilton to score a brilliant individual goal. United miss chances galore.										
38	A	WOLVERHAMPTON		2	D	1-1	0-0	Rowley 50	Crompton	Ball	Aston	Carey	Chilton	Cockburn	Delaney	Pearson	Rowley	Downie	Mitten
	8/4		*54,296*	*6*	47			*Walker 85*	*Williams*	*McLean*	*Kelly*	*Crook W*	*Shorthouse*	*Wright*	*Hancocks*	*Walker*	*Swinbourne*	*Pye*	*Mullen*
								Ref: A Murdoch	The rain pours and the wind blows but it is a wonderful advert for the game. United recapture their old form and Wolves match them. Williams hesitates and Rowley heads in before Crompton fails to hold Pye's shot and Walker pounces. Johnny Hancocks is electric and roasts Aston.										
39	A	BIRMINGHAM		1	D	0-0	0-0		Crompton	Ball	Aston	Carey	Chilton	Cockburn	Delaney	Pearson	Rowley	Downie	Mitten
	10/4		*35,868*	*21*	48				*Merrick*	*Duckhouse*	*Jennings*	*Boyd*	*Atkins*	*Ferris*	*Berry*	*Brennan*	*Trigg*	*Evans*	*Warhurst*
								Ref: R Wood	With Sunderland not playing, United go top but the fans aren't fooled in a wind-spoiled game. The old forward failings are there again and it is now seven without a win. Carey, limping out on the right, almost heads the winner but relegation haunted Blues' solid defence deserve a point.										
40	H	PORTSMOUTH		2	L	0-2	0-0		Crompton	**McNulty**	Ball	**Whitefoot**	Chilton	Cockburn	Delaney	Pearson	Rowley	Downie	Mitten
	15/4		46,709	*1*	48			*Reid 84, Froggatt 89*	*Butler*	*Hindmarsh*	*Ferrier*	*Scoular*	*Spence*	*Thompson*	*Harris*	*Reid*	*Clarke*	*Phillips*	*Froggatt*
								Ref: W Ling	The reigning champions go top with late goals that will ultimately clinch the title. Reid feeds off McNulty's error, then Jack Froggatt nods in Scoular's cross. International calls see debuts for McNulty and Jeff Whitefoot, at 16 years 105 days, the youngest player in the club's history.										
41	A	NEWCASTLE		4	L	1-2	0-0	Downie 66	Crompton	Ball	Aston	Warner	Chilton	Cockburn	Delaney	Pearson	Rowley	Downie	Mitten
	22/4		*52,203*	*7*	48			*Mitchell 58, Walker 72*	*Lowery*	*Cowell*	*Corbett*	*Harvey*	*Brennan*	*Houghton*	*Walker*	*Taylor*	*Milburn*	*Hannah*	*Mitchell*
								Ref: A Blythe	The title hopes are dashed with a ninth game without a win - equalling the worst run since the war. In Jack Warner's final game the forwards are woeful and Pearson has not scored in 13 games. Aston and Cockburn will go to Brazil for the World Cup – but Rowley and Pearson miss out.										
42	H	FULHAM		4	W	3-0	1-0	Cockburn 6, Rowley 47, 78	Crompton	McNulty	Ball	Aston	Chilton	Cockburn	Delaney	Pearson	Rowley	Downie	Mitten
	29/4		**11,968**	*17*	50				*Kelly*	*Freeman*	*Pavitt*	*Quested*	*Taylor*	*Beasley*	*Stevens*	*Thomas R*	*Rowley*	*Jezzard*	*McDonald*
		Home	Away					Ref: G Iliffe	Bill Dodgin's Fulham have gone 12 games without a win and United finally end their dreadful run. It's a mudlark against the ragged Cottagers. Cockburn bosses the midfield and scores after Downie's shot rebounds off the post. Jack hits a trademark 25-yarder and scores with a rebound.										
	Average	43,282	46,361																

FA Cup					F-A	H-T	Scorers, Times, and Referees	1	2	3	4	5	6	7	8	9	10	11
3	H	WEYMOUTH	2	W	4-0	2-0	Rowley 32, 89, Pearson 35,	Feehan	Carey	Aston	Cockburn	Chilton	McGlen	Delaney	Bogan	Rowley	Pearson	Mitten
	7/1	38,284	*SL:1*				[Delaney 51]	*Lucas*	*Marsden*	*Ranson*	*Grant*	*Brawley*	*Lawes*	*McGowan*	*Haynes*	*Johnston*	*Gallacher*	*Jones*
							Ref: G Salmon	Plucky Southern League Weymouth suffer their first defeat in 24 games but hold the Reds for half an hour. Keeper Lucas has a bandaged thumb and misses Delaney's corner for the third. No 1 was Jack Rowley's overhead kick, but Pearson's is the pick, a wonderful solo effort.										
4	A	WATFORD	2	W	1-0	0-0	Rowley 89	Lancaster	Carey	Aston	Warner	Chilton	Cockburn	Delaney	Bogan	Rowley	Pearson	Mitten
	28/1	*32,384*	*3:10*					*Morton*	*Eggleston*	*Harper*	*Paton*	*Oliver*	*Fisher*	*Worthington*	*Brown*	*Thomas*	*Cumner*	*Davies*
							Ref: B Griffiths	A record crowd watches United beat gallant Watford. On a frost-bound pitch a shock looks on but Rowley and Pearson play a delightful one-two for the goal. Earlier Mitten, in rubber soles, fired a penalty over after Eggleston handled. Manager Hapgood is in dispute and will soon go.										
5	H	PORTSMOUTH	2	D	3-3	2-0	Mitten 24, 51p, Pearson 40	Lancaster	Carey	Aston	Warner	Chilton	Cockburn	Delaney	Bogan	Rowley	Pearson	Mitten
	11/2	53,688	*4*				*Clarke 48, Parker 49, Ferrier 68p*	*Butler*	*Hindmarsh*	*Ferrier*	*Scoular*	*Flewin*	*Dickinson*	*Harris*	*Clarke*	*Froggatt*	*Phillips*	*Parker*
							Ref: R Leafe	United streak ahead - but not before Phillips hit a post – through Mitten's header and Pearson's shot. Clarke scores from close in. 36-year-old Cliff Parker, who played at Wembley in 1939 levels from Harris' cross. Ferrier atones for his handball by keeping cool after Chilton handles.										
5R	A	PORTSMOUTH	2	W	3-1	2-1	Mitten 11, Downie 24, Delaney 46	Feehan	Carey	Aston	Warner	Chilton	Cockburn	Delaney	Bogan	Rowley	Downie	Mitten
	15/2	*49,962*	*4*				*Harris 42*	*Butler*	*Hindmarsh*	*Ferrier*	*Scoular*	*Flewin*	*Dickinson*	*Harris*	*Clarke*	*Froggatt*	*Phillips*	*Parker*
							Ref: R Leafe	The recalled Downie is the mainspring and sets up Mitten, then his own drive nearly bursts the net. Harris' run and shot gives Pompey hope, but a minute after the restart Delaney puts United through and inflicts only Pompey's second home defeat in two years. A flawless performance.										
QF	A	CHELSEA	1	L	0-2	0-1		Crompton	Carey	Aston	Warner	Chilton	Cockburn	Delaney	Downie	Rowley	Pearson	Mitten
	4/3	*70,362*	*10*				*Campbell 6, Bentley 70*	*Medhurst*	*Winter*	*Hughes*	*Armstrong*	*Harris*	*Mitchell*	*Gray*	*Williams*	*Bentley*	*Billington*	*Campbell*
							Ref: H Beacock	United's double hopes are shattered by a useful and prepared Chelsea team. Campbell's weak shot slides under Crompton and Gray's darting run and back-heel sets up Bentley's whipped goal. Ken Armstrong is the hero, marking Pearson well. Chelsea play Arsenal in the semi-final.										

	Home						Away					
	P	W	D	L	F	A	W	D	L	F	A	Pts
1 Portsmouth	42	12	7	2	44	15	10	2	9	30	23	53
2 Wolves	42	11	8	2	47	21	9	5	7	29	28	53
3 Sunderland	42	14	6	1	50	23	7	4	10	33	39	52
4 MAN UNITED	42	11	5	5	42	20	7	9	5	27	24	50
5 Newcastle	42	14	4	3	49	23	5	8	8	28	32	50
6 Arsenal	42	12	4	5	48	24	7	7	7	31	31	49
7 Blackpool	42	10	8	3	29	14	7	7	7	17	21	49
8 Liverpool	42	10	7	4	37	23	7	7	7	27	31	48
9 Middlesbro	42	14	2	5	37	18	6	5	10	22	30	47
10 Burnley	42	9	7	5	23	17	7	6	8	17	23	45
11 Derby	42	11	5	5	46	26	6	5	10	23	35	44
12 Aston Villa	42	10	7	4	31	19	5	5	11	30	42	42
13 Chelsea	42	7	7	7	31	30	5	9	7	27	35	40
14 West Brom	42	9	7	5	28	16	5	5	11	19	37	40
15 Huddersfield	42	11	4	6	34	22	3	5	13	18	51	37
16 Bolton	42	10	5	6	34	22	0	9	12	11	37	34
17 Fulham	42	8	6	7	24	19	2	8	11	17	35	34
18 Everton	42	6	8	7	24	20	4	6	11	18	46	34
19 Stoke	42	10	4	7	27	28	1	8	12	18	47	34
20 Charlton	42	7	5	9	33	35	6	1	14	20	30	32
21 Manchester C	42	7	8	6	27	24	1	5	15	9	44	29
22 Birmingham	42	6	8	7	19	24	1	6	14	12	43	28
	924	219	132	111	764	483	111	132	219	483	764	924

Odds & ends

Double wins: (5) Bolton, Aston Villa, Man City, Charlton, Middlesbrough.
Double losses: (0).

Won from behind: (4) Man City (h) & (a), Charlton (a), Middlesbrough (a).
Lost from in front: (1) Huddersfield (a).

High Spots: Six successive clean sheets in the autumn.
High scoring home games with Huddersfield and Aston Villa.
Wins at Molineux and Fratton Park (FA Cup).
Good form of Mitten and Cockburn.

Low spots: Home lapses especially to Birmingham and Pompey.
FA Cup exit at Chelsea.
Run of nine games without a win in March and April.

Sent off: United – Cockburn (Man City h).
Sent off: Opponents – Linacre (Man City a).

Ever-presents: (2) Delaney and Mitten.
Hat-tricks: (1) Mitten.
Opposing hat-tricks: (0).
Leading scorer: Rowley (23).

	Appearances		Goals		
	Lge	FAC	Lge	FAC	Tot
Aston, John	**40**	5			
Ball, John	**13**				
Birch, Brian	**1**				
Bogan, Tommy	**18**	4	**4**		**4**
Buckle, Ted	**7**				
Carey, Johnny	**38**	5	**1**		**1**
Chilton, Allenby	**35**	5	**1**		**1**
Clempson, Frank	**1**				
Cockburn, Henry	**35**	5	**1**		**1**
Crompton, Jack	**27**	1			
Delaney, Jimmy	**42**	5	**4**	2	**6**
Downie, Johnny	**18**	2	**6**	1	**7**
Feehan, John	**12**	2			
Lancaster, Joe	**2**	2			
Lowrie, Tommy	**3**				
Lynn, Sammy	**10**				
McGlen, Billy	**13**	1			
McNulty, Tommy	**2**				
Mitten, Charlie	**42**	5	**16**	3	**19**
Pearson, Stan	**41**	4	**14**	2	**16**
Rowley, Jack	**39**	5	**20**	3	**23**
Warner, Jack	**21**	4			
Whitefoot, Jeff	**1**				
Wood, Ray	**1**				
(own-goals)			**2**		**2**
24 players used	**462**	**55**	**69**	**11**	**80**

LEAGUE DIVISION 1   Manager: Matt Busby   SEASON 1950-51

No	Date		Att	Pos	Pt	F-A	H-T	Scorers, Times, and Referees	1	2	3	4	5	6	7	8	9	10	11
1	H	FULHAM			W	1-0	0-0	Pearson 63	**Allen**	Carey	Aston	**McIlvenney**	Chilton	Cockburn	Delaney	Downie	Rowley	Pearson	McGlen
	19/8		45,857		2				*Black*	*Freeman*	*Bacuzzi*	*Macaulay*	*Taylor*	*Lowe E*	*Stevens*	*Quested*	*Jezzard*	*Brennan*	*McDonald*
								Ref: M Griffiths	Debutant Reg Allen has little to do and US star McIlvenney looks unready for Division 1. McGlen replaces Mitten who has absconded to Bogota. Fulham have four new signings in an effort to avoid another dog-fight, including Archie Macaulay and Eddie Lowe, but are wasteful.										
2	A	LIVERPOOL			L	1-2	1-2	Rowley 30	Allen	Carey	Aston	McIlvenney	Chilton	Cockburn	Delaney	Downie	Rowley	Pearson	McGlen
	23/8		*30,211*		2			*Liddell 12, Allen 38 (og)*	*Sidlow*	*Shepherd*	*Spicer*	*Jones*	*Hughes*	*Paisley*	*Payne*	*Taylor*	*Done*	*Balmer*	*Liddell*
								Ref: C Fletcher	The beaten cup finalists are too good in a fast exciting game. In poor light the referee takes the teams off at one stage. Stand-in McGlen crosses for Rowley's goal. Allen takes his eye off Done's cross and punches into his net. Billy Liddell, who also hits the bar, gives Carey a roasting.										
3	A	BOLTON		15	L	0-1	0-0		Allen	Carey	Aston	**Gibson**	Chilton	Cockburn	Delaney	Downie	Rowley	Pearson	McGlen
	26/8		*40,759*	*16*	2			*Lofthouse 78*	*Hanson*	*Banks R*	*Banks T*	*Barrass*	*Gillies*	*Howe*	*McShane*	*Moir*	*Lofthouse*	*Hernon*	*Langton*
								Ref: E Plinston	Walter Rowley's team deserve their win, courtesy of Nat Lofthouse's finish from Langton's nod-on. McShane causes flutters with two long shots. Hanson saves well from Pearson and Rowley. United's wingers are out of touch and Delaney has lost his fire. Don Gibson looks a bit raw.										
4	H	LIVERPOOL		14	W	1-0	1-0	Downie 23	Allen	Carey	Aston	Gibson	Chilton	Cockburn	Bogan	Downie	Rowley	Pearson	McGlen
	30/8		36,654	*11*	4				*Sidlow*	*Shepherd*	*Spicer*	*Jones*	*Hughes*	*Paisley*	*Payne*	*Taylor*	*Done*	*Fagan*	*Brierley*
								Ref: C Fletcher	Johnny Carey is relieved that Liddell is injured, for he masters Brierley. George Kay's Liverpool, who put four past high-flying Sunderland on Saturday, are rarely threatening after Reg Allen's fine save from Cyril Done. Johnnie Downie is left unmarked to head in Aston's deep cross.										
5	H	BLACKPOOL		7	W	1-0	1-0	Bogan 8	Allen	Carey	Aston	Gibson	Chilton	Cockburn	Bogan	Downie	Rowley	Pearson	McGlen
	2/9		**55,090**	*14*	6				*Farm*	*Shimwell*	*Wright*	*Johnston*	*Hayward*	*Kelly*	*Matthews*	*Mudie*	*McIntosh*	*Slater*	*Wardle*
								Ref: G Black	Blackpool miss the injured Mortensen and have McIntosh hobbling on the left wing for the second half. The capacity crowd is there to see Stan Matthews and his duel with Aston is enthralling. He twice beats Aston but nothing comes of it. Hayward hits his own post and Farm tips over.										
6	A	ASTON VILLA		4	W	3-1	1-0	Rowley 14, 65 Pearson 61	Allen	Carey	Aston	Gibson	Chilton	Cockburn	Bogan	Downie	Rowley	Pearson	McGlen
	4/9		*42,724*	*10*	8			*Ford 80*	*Jones*	*Parkes*	*Dorsett*	*Powell*	*Martin*	*Moss F*	*Edwards*	*Gibson*	*Ford*	*Craddock*	*Goffin*
								Ref: B Flanagan	United, showing flashes of their old brilliance, get a deserved win, although Allen has to save well from Goffin, Edwards and Gibson. At 3-0 Villa are inexplicably given a penalty but Allen saves from Dorsett. Billy McGlen is enthusiastic but Busby is looking for a new left-winger.										
7	A	TOTTENHAM		8	L	0-1	0-1		Allen	Carey	Aston	Gibson	Chilton	Cockburn	Bogan	Downie	Rowley	Pearson	McGlen
	9/9		*60,621*	*9*	8			*Walters 44*	*Ditchburn*	*Ramsey*	*Willis*	*Nicholson*	*Clarke*	*Burgess*	*Walters*	*Bennett*	*Duquemin*	*Baily*	*Murphy*
								Ref: T Glendenning	Arthur Rowe's newly promoted Spurs have only one player who cost a fee but have started the season promisingly. A throw by Allen, watched by the England selectors, fails to reach McGlen and Walters' shot is deflected past him. But for the rock-like Chilton the loss would be greater.										
8	H	ASTON VILLA		7	D	0-0	0-0		Allen	Carey	Aston	Gibson	Chilton	Cockburn	Delaney	Bogan	Rowley	Cassidy	**McShane**
	13/9		34,824	*14*	9				*Hindle*	*Parkes*	*Dorsett*	*Canning*	*Martin*	*Moss F*	*Gibson*	*Powell*	*Ford*	*Dixon*	*Goffin*
								Ref: B Flanagan	Harry McShane has arrived from Bolton in exchange for Ball, but sees little of the ball in a woeful game. Debutant Hindle saves well from Rowley in the first minute and Delaney fluffs a shot when through. Cassidy is a poor stand-in for the injured Pearson. Villa have few ideas.										
9	H	CHARLTON		4	W	3-0	2-0	Rowley 10, Pearson 44, Delaney 77	Allen	Carey	Aston	Gibson	Chilton	Cockburn	Delaney	Downie	Rowley	Pearson	McShane
	16/9		37,976	*10*	11				*Bartram*	*Shreeve*	*Lock*	*Fenton*	*Phipps*	*Forbes*	*Hurst*	*Cullum*	*Vaughan*	*Lumley*	*Kiernan*
								Ref: J Topliss	Allen has kept five successive clean sheets at home and Charlton, for all their possession, want too many passes and rarely threaten. Rowley pulls a muscle and plays on the wing, whilst the returning Downie looks fresher. Chilton's form looks good enough for an England call-up.										
10	A	MIDDLESBROUGH		2	W	2-1	1-1	Pearson 13, 58	Allen	Carey	Aston	Gibson	Chilton	Cockburn	Delaney	Downie	Rowley	Pearson	McShane
	23/9		*48,051*	*4*	13			*Delapenha 41*	*Ugolini*	*Robinson*	*Dicks*	*Bell*	*Whitaker*	*Gordon*	*Delapenha*	*Mannion*	*Spuhler*	*McCrae*	*Walker*
								Ref: A Luty	England rejects Cockburn and Pearson are in top form and Henry marks Mannion out of the game as Boro's unbeaten home record goes. Pearson sweeps home Rowley's cross and is on hand when McShane's free-kick thumps the bar. Delapenha scores after Allen's weak punch.										

No	Venue	Opponent	Pos	Res	F-A	H-T	Scorers, Times, and Referees	1	2	3	4	5	6	7	8	9	10	11
11	A	WOLVERHAMPTON	4	D	0-0	0-0		Allen	Carey	Aston	Gibson	Chilton	Cockburn	Delaney	Downie	Rowley	Pearson	McShane
	30/9	45,898	5	14				Williams	McLean	Shorthouse	Crook	Chatham	Wright	Hancocks	Dunn	Swinbourne	Pye	Mullen
							Ref: J Platt	United's defence looks mean, while keeper Reg Allen is superb and tipped for an England cap. The game is spoilt by petty fouls and bickering but 5ft 4in Johnny Hancocks is magical. Wolves' Jimmy Mullen, on the other hand, is impetuous and wastes a glorious chance created by Pye.										
12	H	SHEFFIELD WED	3	W	3-1	3-0	Downie 7, McShane 31, Rowley 37	Allen	Carey	**Redman**	Gibson	**Jones**	McGlen	Delaney	Downie	Rowley	Pearson	McShane
	7/10	42,444	21	16			McJarrow 89	McIntosh	Bannister	Swift	Gannon	Packard	Witcomb	Marriott	Jordan J	McJarrow	Froggatt	Tomlinson
							Ref: H Jackson	International games for Aston and 32-year-old Chilton mean debuts for 22-year-old Redman and 17-year-old Jones. Newcomers Owls work hard but are no match. Downie nets from McGlen's long pass. The second provokes a row with McShane's shot over the line before it is cleared.										
13	A	ARSENAL	4	L	0-3	0-1	[Goring 71]	Allen	Carey	Aston	Gibson	Chilton	Cockburn	Delaney	Downie	Rowley	Pearson	McShane
	14/10	66,157	1	16			Cockburn 16 (og), Lishman 60,	Swindin	Barnes	Smith	Forbes	Compton L	Mercer	McPherson	Logie	Goring	Lishman	Roper
							Ref: R Wood	The Cup holders have lost only one in 13 and are too good for goal-shy United. McPherson, fed by the immaculate Jimmy Logie, torments Aston and his cross is turned in by Chilton. Peter Goring sets up Lishman and Allen stops Goring's volley but the ball dribbles over the line.										
14	H	PORTSMOUTH	5	D	0-0	0-0		Allen	Carey	Aston	Gibson	Chilton	McGlen	Delaney	Downie	Rowley	Pearson	McShane
	21/10	43,595	10	17				Butler	Earl	Ferrier	Scoular	Flewin	Dickinson	Harris	Reid	Clarke	Phillips	Froggatt
							Ref: G Clark	The champions are stuttering and rampant United could have scored seven but are still goal-shy. Near the end Harris misses a good chance after Chilton and Aston left the ball to each other. Allen played for the Football League in midweek but Gibson and McShane are today's heroes.										
15	A	EVERTON	4	W	4-1	1-0	Rowley 40, 62, Pearson 75, Aston 86	Crompton	Carey	Aston	Gibson	Jones	Cockburn	Delaney	Bogan	Rowley	Pearson	McShane
	28/10	51,142	21	19			McIntosh 46	Burnett	Clinton	Moore	Grant	Jones TE	Farrell	Buckle	Fielding	McIntosh	Potts	Eglington
							Ref: J Houston	Neither £20,000 signing Harry Potts nor ex-Red Buckle can stop United who run riot in the last quarter. Everton had fifteen minutes on top and McIntosh headed in Buckle's cross. Jack Rowley's cannonball knocks out Moore and goes in. Aston's 35-yarder passes through Delaney's legs.										
16	H	BURNLEY	5	D	1-1	0-1	McShane 60	Allen	Carey	Aston	Gibson	Chilton	Cockburn	Delaney	Bogan	Rowley	Pearson	McShane
	4/11	41,244	8	20			Holden 35	Strong	Woodruff	Mather	Attwell	Cummings	Bray	Chew	Morris	Holden	McIlroy	Hays
							Ref: R Mortimer	Frank Hill's Burnley celebrate Jimmy Strong's 199th successive game with a fine display in an entertaining match. Young Holden drifts out on the wing, bemuses Aston, and scores from an acute angle. Rowley and Pearson look jaded, but 30-year-old Harry McShane is looking the part.										
17	A	CHELSEA	5	L	0-1	0-0		Allen	Carey	Aston	Gibson	Chilton	Cockburn	Delaney	Pearson	Rowley	Downie	McShane
	11/11	51,882	19	20			Billington 59	Pickering	Bathgate	Hughes	Armstrong	Harris	Mitchell	Dyke	Campbell	Billington	Bentley	Gray
							Ref: G Iliffe	A sloppy display against a Chelsea team who have won three in a row. Billington pounces on the out-of-form Cockburn's woeful back-pass and later forces a stunning save from Allen. United switch Rowley and Delaney and it almost works. Chilton and Aston dropped by England.										
18	H	STOKE	5	D	0-0	0-0		Allen	Carey	Aston	Gibson	Chilton	Cockburn	Bogan	Pearson	Rowley	Birch	McShane
	18/11	31,880	9	21				Herod	Mould	McCue	Sellars	Mountford F	Kirton	Ormston	Bowyer	Brown	Johnston	Oscroft
							Ref: H Wright	Delaney has gone to Aberdeen whilst Stoke's Neil Franklin and George Mountford are earning big money in Bogota. Stoke have drawn six out of nine aways and United have four blanks in six. Rowley is fouled by Sellars for the 60th-minute penalty but McShane's effort is easily saved.										
19	A	WEST BROM	5	W	1-0	0-0	Birch 60	Allen	McNulty	Aston	Gibson	Chilton	Cockburn	Bogan	Pearson	Rowley	Birch	McShane
	25/11	28,146	16	23				Heath	Rickaby	Millard	Dudley	Vernon	Barlow	Allen	Gordon	Richardson	Ryan	Lee
							Ref: R Leafe	Albion's home form is woeful and United inflict their fifth defeat. Birch's header from Pearson's nod-on is his first goal. Both Pearson and Bogan miss good chances. Reg Allen rebuff's Albion's late rally and saves twice from Ronnie Allen. Carey is away winning his 25th Eire cap.										
20	H	NEWCASTLE	6	L	1-2	1-0	Birch 39	Allen	Carey	Aston	Gibson	Chilton	Cockburn	**Birkett**	Pearson	Rowley	Birch	McShane
	2/12	36,300	3	23			Hannah 64, Walker 86	Fairbrother	Cowell	McMichael	Harvey	Brennan	Crowe	Walker	Taylor	Robledo	Hannah	Corbett
							Ref: A Holland	The Magpies recover from a 0-7 mauling at Spurs and notch their fifth away win. Busby is relying on youth, but Birkett and Birch look raw in another indifferent display. Hannah turns in Corbett's cross, and Walker's speculative shot dips and goes in off the crossbar with Allen static.										
21	A	HUDDERSFIELD	5	W	3-2	1-2	Aston 13, 75, Birkett 56	Allen	McNulty	McGlen	Gibson	Chilton	Cockburn	Birkett	Pearson	Aston	Birch	McShane
	9/12	26,845	16	25			Metcalfe 32p, Taylor 42	Wheeler	Gallogly	Kelly	Battye	Hepplewhite	Boot	McKenna	Nightingale	Taylor J	Hassall	Metcalfe
							Ref: S Law	The lack of goals and Rowley's flu forces Busby to switch Aston to centre-forward and he heads two, from McShane and Birkett's crosses. Birkett's pile-driver is the best, though. Chilton handles for the penalty and Taylor's goal looks like handball. Tempers frayed in the gloom.										

LEAGUE DIVISION 1

Manager: Matt Busby

SEASON 1950-51

No Date	Att	Pos	Pt	F-A	H-T	Scorers, Times, and Referees	1	2	3	4	5	6	7	8	9	10	11
22 A FULHAM		6	D	2-2	0-2	Pearson 52, 62	Allen	McNulty	McGlen	Gibson	Chilton	Cockburn	Birkett	Pearson	Aston	Downie	McShane
16/12	***19,649***	*13*	26			*Stevens 10, 27p*	*Black*	*Bacuzzi*	*Lowe R*	*Quested*	*Taylor*	*Lowe E*	*Stevens*	*Macaulay*	*Thomas*	*Brennan*	*Jezzard*
						Ref: M Griffiths	Reg Allen returns to his childhood haunts and is masterly but can't stop Stevens' goals. On a snowbound pitch United finally find their feet and are well worth a point. The Lowe brothers, Eddie and Reg, are immaculate whilst Cliff Birkett is beginning to fulfil his schoolboy promise.										
23 H BOLTON		7	L	2-3	1-2	Pearson 11, Aston 49	Allen	Carey	McGlen	Gibson	Chilton	Cockburn	Birkett	Pearson	Aston	Downie	McShane
23/12	37,235	*8*	26			*Webster 2, Lofthouse 38, 62*	*Hanson*	*Ball*	*Kennedy*	*Howe*	*Barrass*	*Edwards*	*Hughes*	*Moir*	*Lofthouse*	*Webster*	*Langton*
						Ref: E Plinston	Aston and McShane are both suffering from boils, but are able to play, the latter against his old club. Nat Lofthouse is just about the best line leader in the country and punishes Chilton with his speed on the slippery surface. Hanson fails to hold a cross and Pearson scores in vain.										
24 A SUNDERLAND		8	L	1-2	1-1	Aston 2	Allen	Carey	McGlen	Gibson	Chilton	Cockburn	Birkett	Pearson	Aston	Birch	Rowley
25/12	*41,215*	*16*	26			*Wright T 5, 62*	*Mapson*	*Hedley*	*Hudgell*	*McLain*	*Walsh*	*Wright A*	*Wright T*	*Kirtley*	*Ford*	*Davis*	*Watson*
						Ref: R Mortimer	On a bone hard pitch Sunderland win successive games for the first time this season. Aston's opportunist effort is cancelled out as Wright's direct free-kick bamboozles Allen. Wright's winner comes as Allen fails to hold Davis' vicious shot. Mapson saves well from Gibson & Aston.										
25 H SUNDERLAND		9	L	**3-5**	2-4	Aston 2, Bogan 44, 75 *[Davis 61]*	Allen	Carey	McGlen	Gibson	Chilton	Cockburn	McShane	Bogan	Aston	Pearson	Rowley
26/12	37,024	*15*	26			*Bingham 3, Broadis 29, 30, 40,*	*Mapson*	*Hedley*	*Hudgell*	*McLain*	*Walsh*	*Wright A*	*Bingham*	*Wright T*	*Davis*	*Broadis*	*Watson*
						Ref: R Mortimer	The Sunderland bogey continues, one win in 10 games since the War, even though Shackleton and Ford are missing. This is the biggest home defeat since 1936 and Ivor Broadis, over his flu, is the star. Rowley misses a penalty and Billy McGlen is roasted by young Billy Bingham.										
26 H TOTTENHAM		9	W	2-1	1-1	Birch 15, Rowley 50	Allen	Carey	Redman	Gibson	Chilton	Cockburn	Birkett	Pearson	Aston	Birch	Rowley
13/1	45,104	1	28			*Baily 7*	*Ditchburn*	*Ramsey*	*Willis*	*Brittan*	*Clarke*	*Nicholson*	*Walters*	*Murphy*	*McLellan*	*Baily*	*Medley*
						Ref: T Glendenning	The contrasting styles of the teams make a thrilling contest. The unsighted Allen lets Eddie Baily's shot under his body. Birch bundles the ball and Ditchburn into the net for a disputed equaliser. Rowley wins it with an electric run and stirring shot. Rowe's team look good for the title.										
27 A CHARLTON		7	W	2-1	0-1	Birkett 46, Aston 59	Crompton	Carey	Redman	Gibson	Chilton	Cockburn	Birkett	Pearson	Aston	Birch	Rowley
20/1	*31,978*	*21*	30			*Hurst 10*	*Bartram*	*Croker P*	*Lock*	*Fenton*	*Phipps*	*Forbes*	*Hurst*	*Johnson*	*Jeppson*	*Cullum*	*Kiernan*
						Ref: J Topliss	Swedish international Hans Jeppson, in only his second game, sets up Hurst before two Sam Bartram blunders leave Charlton in deep trouble. Birkett's sliced cross goes through his legs. Bartram is slow to come for Carey's harmless looking lob and Aston's back header wins the game.										
28 H MIDDLESBROUGH		6	W	1-0	1-0	Pearson 37	Allen	Carey	Redman	Gibson	Chilton	Cockburn	Birkett	Bogan	Aston	Pearson	Rowley
3/2	46,454	*2*	32				*Ugolini*	*Dicks*	*Hepple*	*Bell*	*Whitaker*	*Gordon*	*Woodward*	*Delapenha*	*Robinson*	*Mannion*	*Walker*
						Ref: A Luty	A rare defeat for high-flying Boro, who miss injured leading scorer Alex McCrae. United have got the Arsenal cup-tie on their minds and ease off, but Carey is sublime. Stan Pearson is buzzing after his Cup hat-trick and toe-ends the ball past Ugolini when it seemed he had over-run it.										
29 H WOLVERHAMPTON		6	W	2-1	0-1	Rowley 46, Birch 54	Allen	McNulty	Carey	Gibson	Chilton	Cockburn	Birkett	Pearson	Aston	Birch	Rowley
17/2	43,941	*7*	34			*Wilshaw 9*	*Williams*	*Short*	*Pritchard*	*McLean*	*Shorthouse*	*Wright*	*Hancocks*	*Pye*	*Wilshaw*	*Walker*	*Mullen*
						Ref: J Platt	Both sides have the Cup in mind and United are the better side once they have the wind at their backs. Allen saves well from Wright but Wilshaw follows up to score. Birkett centres for Rowley, and Birch's header deflects off Wright's shoulder. Williams saves Rowley's penalty.										
30 A SHEFFIELD WED		4	W	4-0	2-0	Pearson 3, Downie 36, Rowley 55, [McShane 70]	Allen	Carey	McGlen	Gibson	Jones	Cockburn	McShane	Pearson	Aston	Downie	Rowley
26/2	*25,767*	*22*	36				*Morton*	*Swift*	*Curtis*	*Gannon*	*Packard*	*Witcomb*	*Finney*	*Quixall*	*McJarrow*	*Froggatt*	*Woodhead*
						Ref: H Jackson	United bounce back from Cup trauma to find their shooting boots against doomed Owls. Alan Finney and Albert Quixall play their second game whilst Busby rests Birch and Birkett. Downie's move to Burnley is off and he enjoys a stormer. McShane scores one and makes Pearson's goal.										
31 H ARSENAL		3	W	3-1	3-1	Downie 14, Aston 16, 32	Allen	Carey	Redman	Whitefoot	Jones	Cockburn	McShane	Pearson	Aston	Downie	Rowley
3/3	48,025	*5*	38			*Holton 39*	*Kelsey*	*Scott*	*Barnes*	*Mercer*	*Compton L*	*Forbes*	*McPherson*	*Logie*	*Holton*	*Goring*	*Marden*
						Ref: R Wood	Arsenal's transition has started with Marden's debut and Holton and Kelsey playing their second game. It is one-way traffic until half-time. Downie nets and Aston - who exposes Compton - taps in after Kelsey's fumble. Six wins in a row, but still five points behind leaders Spurs.										

No	H/A	Opponent / Date	Att	Pos	Pts	Res	FT	HT	Scorers, Times, Referees	1	2	3	4	5	6	7	8	9	10	11
32	A	PORTSMOUTH		4		D	0-0	0-0		Allen	Carey	Redman	Whitefoot	Chilton	McGlen	McShane	Pearson	Aston	Downie	Rowley
		10/3	*33,148*	*13*	39					*Butler*	*Stephen*	*Ferrier*	*Scoular*	*Froggatt*	*Dickinson*	*Harris*	*Reid*	*Mundy*	*Phillips*	*Gaillard*
									Ref: G Clark	United maintain their unbeaten record at Fratton since the War in a poor game spoiled by a sticky pitch which is impossible to dribble on. Ex-Gosport debutant Mundy gets no change out of the rock-like Chilton. Pompey's Jack Froggatt has been successfully converted to centre-half.										
33	H	EVERTON		2		W	3-0	3-0	Aston 1, Downie 11, Pearson 37	Allen	Carey	Redman	Gibson	Chilton	McGlen	McShane	Pearson	Aston	Downie	Rowley
		17/3	31,108	*17*	41					*Sagar*	*Moore*	*Lindsay*	*Grant*	*Jones TE*	*Farrell*	*Buckle*	*Hold*	*Catterick*	*Potts*	*McIntosh*
									Ref: J Houston	With the rain pouring down, the pitch is heavy and United have it won by half-time. Aston nets in 25 seconds after slick inter-passing and Stan nets with a neat hook. Sagar's saves keep the score down but Everton's February revival is over. Rowley misses his third penalty of the season.										
34	H	DERBY		2		W	2-0	1-0	Downie 40, Aston 68	Allen	Carey	Redman	Gibson	Chilton	McGlen	McShane	Clempson	Aston	Downie	Rowley
		23/3	43,802	*12*	43					*Webster*	*Mozley*	*Revell*	*Mays*	*Oliver*	*Musson*	*Harrison*	*Stamps*	*Lee*	*Morris*	*McLaren*
									Ref: C Fletcher	Derby's early domination peters out before half-time and United's gear shift on the mud heap wins the points. Frank Clempson, in for the injured Pearson, helps Aston set up Downie for his fourth goal in five games. Aston clinches it with a bullet-like header from Rowley's corner.										
35	A	BURNLEY		2		W	2-1	1-1	McShane 18, Aston 60	Allen	Carey	Redman	Gibson	Chilton	McGlen	McShane	Clempson	Aston	Downie	Rowley
		24/3	*36,656*	*9*	45				*Stephenson 21*	*McNulty*	*Woodruff*	*Mather*	*Adamson*	*Cummings*	*Bray*	*Stephenson*	*Morris*	*Holden*	*McIlroy*	*Lyons*
									Ref: R Mortimer	A strong wind prevents a classic but it is exciting fare. Strong is out after 220 games in a row and his stand-in, McNulty, watches as the wind curls McShane's centre into the net. Stephenson quickly levels but the Reds win it as Rowley centres for Aston to net his fifth in five games.										
36	A	DERBY		2		W	4-2	3-2	Pearson 20, Downie 40, Rowley 44, [Aston 84]	Allen	Carey	Redman	Cockburn	Chilton	McGlen	McShane	Pearson	Aston	Downie	Rowley
		26/3	*25,861*	*14*	47				*Stamps 26, Harrison 36*	*Webster*	*Bell*	*Revell*	*Mays*	*Oliver*	*Musson*	*Harrison*	*Stamps*	*Lee*	*Morris*	*McLaren*
									Ref: C Fletcher	The Baseball Ground is the worst pitch in the league when it rains, but United master the atrocious conditions and the mud. Cockburn returns after flu and leads the fightback, whilst ex-Red Johnny Morris is off-colour. Aston is unstoppable in the mud but his lobbed goal looks offside.										
37	H	CHELSEA		2		W	4-1	3-1	Pearson 28, 33, 75, McShane 38	Allen	Carey	Redman	Cockburn	Chilton	McGlen	McShane	Pearson	Aston	Downie	Rowley
		31/3	**25,779**	*21*	49				*Willemse 13*	*Pickering*	*Bathgate*	*Hughes*	*Armstrong*	*Harris*	*Dickson*	*Hinshelwood*	*Campbell*	*Williams*	*Gray*	*Willemse*
									Ref: G Iliffe	The pitch is a morass after rain and hail and United adapt far better than the supine Chelsea, who have gone eleven games without a win and look certs for the drop. McShane's flying header and Pearson's third from an acute angle are the best goals. Pearson tipped for England recall.										
38	A	STOKE		2		L	0-2	0-2		Allen	Carey	Redman	Cockburn	Chilton	McGlen	McShane	Pearson	Aston	Downie	Rowley
		7/4	*25,700*	*11*	49				*Oscroft 27, Mullard 42*	*Herod*	*Watkin*	*McCue*	*Sellars*	*Mountford F*	*Kirton*	*Ormston*	*Bowyer*	*Mullard*	*Johnston*	*Oscroft*
									Ref: H Wright	Goals from Albert Mullard - his first senior goal - and hump-backed Oscroft end United's 12-match unbeaten run. Stoke are very much a bogey side and it's three years since United beat them. The Reds are six points behind Spurs and the title is surely headed for White Hart Lane.										
39	H	WEST BROM		2		W	3-0	1-0	Rowley 27, Pearson 84, Downie 85	Allen	Carey	Redman	Gibson	Chilton	McGlen	McShane	Pearson	Aston	Downie	Rowley
		14/4	26,523	*16*	51					*Sanders*	*Rickaby*	*Millard*	*Kennedy*	*Vernon*	*Ryan*	*Elliott*	*Allen*	*Barlow*	*McCall*	*Lee*
									Ref: T Rand	The April weather is bitterly cold and the fans have little to keep them warm until the last ten minutes. Aston sets up Rowley before Pearson nets from close range. Downie's goal is outstanding and raises the roof. Albion had won three out of four before today and are almost safe.										
40	A	NEWCASTLE		2		W	2-0	2-0	Rowley 7, Pearson 35	Allen	Carey	Redman	Cockburn	Chilton	McGlen	McShane	Pearson	Aston	Downie	Rowley
		21/4	*45,209*	*6*	53					*Fairbrother*	*Cowell*	*Corbett*	*Harvey*	*Brennan*	*Crowe*	*Walker*	*Taylor*	*Milburn*	*Robledo*	*Mitchell*
									Ref: A Holland	Newcastle have one eye on the Cup final next week but put out their Wembley team. They don't look a good bet and have won only once at home in eight games. England forward Jackie Milburn is quiet and Stan and Gunner set up goals for each other. Pearson's back-heel is superb.										
41	H	HUDDERSFIELD		2		W	**6-0**	3-0	McShane 6, 67 Rowley 25p, [Aston 40, 65, Downie 50]	Allen	Carey	Redman	Cockburn	Chilton	McGlen	McShane	Pearson	Aston	Downie	Rowley
		28/4	28,310	*18*	55					*Wheeler*	*Gallogly*	*Kelly*	*McGarry*	*McEvoy*	*Boot*	*Gunn*	*Glazzard*	*Taylor J*	*Hassall*	*Metcalfe*
									Ref: S Law	Busby uses sprinklers on the dry pitch and the surface is in deluxe condition. Rowley and Cockburn are back to their best, although Jack has to take a penalty twice. Huddersfield had won six out of eight to pull themselves clear of the drop zone. United's ninth successive home win.										
42	A	BLACKPOOL		2		D	1-1	1-0	Downie 32	Allen	Carey	Redman	Cockburn	Chilton	McGlen	McShane	Pearson	Aston	Downie	Rowley
		5/5	*22,864*	*3*	56				*Perry 60*	*Farm*	*Shimwell*	*Garrett*	*Johnston*	*Hayward*	*Kelly*	*Adams*	*Mudie*	*Mortensen*	*Withers*	*Perry*
		Home	Away						Ref: G Black	A week after losing against the odds to Newcastle in the Cup final, Blackpool look tired and jaded. South African Bill Perry gives Carey the runaround and left-back Garrett is superb against Harry McShane. Downie's excellent shot on the turn is cancelled out by Perry's late goal.										
Average		39,008	38,118																	

FA Cup					F-A	H-T	Scorers, Times, and Referees	1	2	3	4	5	6	7	8	9	10	11
3	H 6/1	OLDHAM 37,161	11 *3N:23*	W	4-1	2-1	Pearson 28, Aston 42, Whyte 49 (og), [Birch 73] *Smith 43* Ref: R Leafe	Allen *Ogden*	Carey *Naylor*	McGlen *Bell*	Lowrie *Smith*	Chilton *Whyte*	Cockburn *Goodfellow*	Birkett *McIlvenney*	Pearson *Munro*	Aston *Gemmell*	Birch *Hardwick*	McShane *Jessop*
								With George Hardwick up front, both sides have an England left-back in the forward line. Oldham are not disgraced. Birkett crosses for Stan Pearson and Aston to head in, before Smith's 25-yarder deflects off Chilton. Whyte turns in Birkett's cross and Pearson's lob sets up Birch.										
4	H 27/1	LEEDS 55,434	7 *2:10*	W	4-0	4-0	Pearson 7, 25, 30, Rowley 24 Ref: R Wood	Allen *Searson*	Carey *Dunn*	Redman *Milburn*	Gibson *McCabe*	Chilton *Charles*	Cockburn *Burden*	Birkett *Harrison*	Pearson *Iggleden*	Aston *Browning*	Birch *Dudley*	Rowley *Williams*
								The gates are locked before kick-off with 7,000 Leeds fans in. United hit top form and blow Major Frank Buckley's team away. Leeds' tonic injections are no use as Pearson hooks in from a narrow angle, heads a second, and nods on Aston's header. Buckley has the flu and misses out.										
5	H 10/2	ARSENAL 55,058	6 *3*	W	1-0	1-0	Pearson 17 Ref: M Griffiths	Allen *Platt*	Carey *Barnes*	Redman *Smith*	Gibson *Forbes*	Chilton *Compton L*	Cockburn *Mercer*	Birkett *McPherson*	Pearson *Logie*	Aston *Goring*	Birch *Lewis*	Rowley *Roper*
								United knock the holders out in the tie of the round. Age is creeping up on certain Gunners and 38-year-old Les Compton, harassed by Aston, nods to Pearson's feet and his 20-yard shot wins it. 13,000 fans and Joe Mercer urge the Gunners on in vain. Birkett faints at the final whistle.										
QF	A 24/2	BIRMINGHAM *50,000*	6 *2:7*	L	0-1	0-1	*Higgins 1* Ref: A Blythe	Allen *Merrick*	McNulty *Badham*	Carey *Green*	Gibson *Boyd*	Chilton *Atkins*	Cockburn *Ferris*	Birkett *Stewart*	Pearson *Higgins*	Aston *Trigg*	Birch *Smith*	Rowley *Berry*
								Higgins' 21-second volley from Stewart's cross ends United's run. Manager Brocklebank's homework is spot on, and Busby is criticised for playing 'too many kids'. Only in the last 20 minutes, as Matt shuffles things, do United threaten. Birmingham ban the newsreels from the game.										

		Home						Away					
		P	W	D	L	F	A	W	D	L	F	A	Pts
1	Tottenham	42	17	2	2	54	21	8	8	5	28	23	60
2	MAN UNITED	42	14	4	3	42	16	10	4	7	32	24	56
3	Blackpool	42	12	6	3	43	19	8	4	9	36	34	50
4	Newcastle	42	10	6	5	36	22	8	7	6	26	31	49
5	Arsenal	42	11	5	5	47	28	8	4	9	26	28	47
6	Middlesbro	42	12	7	2	51	25	6	4	11	25	40	47
7	Portsmouth	42	8	10	3	39	30	8	5	8	32	38	47
8	Bolton	42	11	2	8	31	20	8	5	8	33	41	45
9	Liverpool	42	11	5	5	28	25	5	6	10	25	34	43
10	Burnley	42	9	7	5	27	16	5	7	9	21	27	42
11	Derby	42	10	5	6	53	33	6	3	12	28	42	40
12	Sunderland	42	8	9	4	30	21	4	7	10	33	52	40
13	Stoke	42	10	5	6	28	19	3	9	9	22	40	40
14	Wolves	42	9	3	9	44	30	6	5	10	30	31	38
15	Aston Villa	42	9	6	6	39	29	3	7	11	27	39	37
16	West Brom	42	7	4	10	30	27	6	7	8	23	34	37
17	Charlton	42	9	4	8	35	31	5	5	11	28	49	37
18	Fulham	42	8	5	8	35	37	5	6	10	17	31	37
19	Huddersfield	42	8	4	9	40	40	7	2	12	24	52	36
20	Chelsea	42	9	4	8	31	25	3	4	14	22	40	32
21	Sheff Wed	42	9	6	6	43	32	3	2	16	21	51	32
22	Everton	42	7	5	9	26	35	5	3	13	22	51	32
		924	218	114	130	832	581	130	114	218	581	832	924

Odds & ends

Double wins: (7) Middlesbrough, Everton, West Brom, Huddersfield, Charlton, Sheff Wed, Derby.
Double losses: (2) Bolton, Sunderland.

Won from behind: (6) Huddersfield (a), Tottenham (h), Charlton (a), Wolves (h), Derby (a), Chelsea (h).
Lost from in front: (3) Newcastle (h), Sunderland (a) & (h).

High spots: 12 match unbeaten run in League including 11 wins.
Excellent away form.
Highest number of wins (24) in a season since 1906.
Conversion of Aston to centre-forward.

Low spots: Poor scoring record of Rowley.
FA Cup exit at Second Division Birmingham.
Miserable December with four defeats in six games, three at home.

Sent off: United - none.
Sent off: Opponents - none.

Ever-presents: (0).
Hat-tricks: (2) Pearson.
Opposing hat-tricks: (1) Broadis (Sunderland)
Leading scorer: Pearson (23).

	Appearances		Goals		
	Lge	FAC	Lge	FAC	Tot
Allen, Reg	**40**	4			
Aston, John	**41**	4	**15**	1	**16**
Birch, Brian	**8**	4	**4**	1	**5**
Birkett, Cliff	**9**	4	**2**		**2**
Bogan, Tommy	**11**		**3**		**3**
Carey, Johnny	**39**	4			
Cassidy, Laurie	**1**				
Chilton, Allenby	**38**	4			
Clempson, Frank	**2**				
Cockburn, Henry	**35**	4			
Crompton, Jack	**2**				
Delaney, Jimmy	**13**		**1**		**1**
Downie, Johnny	**29**		**10**		**10**
Gibson, Don	**32**	3			
Jones, Mark	**4**				
Lowrie, Tommy		1			
McGlen, Billy	**26**	1			
McIlvenney, Eddie	**2**				
McNulty, Tommy	**4**	1			
McShane, Harry	**30**	1	**7**		**7**
Pearson, Stan	**39**	4	**18**	5	**23**
Redman, Billy	**16**	2			
Rowley, Jack	**39**	3	**14**	**1**	**15**
Whitefoot, Jeff	**2**				
(own-goals)				**1**	**1**
24 players used	**158**	**11**	**74**	**9**	**83**

LEAGUE DIVISION 1

Manager: Matt Busby

SEASON 1951-52

No	Date		Att	Pos	Pt	F-A	H-T	Scorers, Times, and Referees	1	2	3	4	5	6	7	8	9	10	11
1	A	WEST BROM			D	3-3	1-1	Rowley 9, 69, 79	Allen	Carey	Redman	Cockburn	Chilton	McGlen	McShane	Pearson	Rowley	Downie	**Bond**
	18/8		*29,769*		1			*Allen 19, Smith 62, 67*	*Sanders*	*Rickaby*	*Millard*	*Dudley*	*Vernon*	*Ryan*	*Allen*	*Smith*	*Richardson*	*McCall*	*Lee*
								Ref: C Fletcher	A late rally sees United draw and Bond missed a great chance to win the game. United's shaky defence is unhinged by the pacy Lee and the prodigious Ronnie Allen. Smith kicks one out of Reg Allen's hands and hits a 30-yard swerver. Jack Rowley defies the critics with a hat-trick.										
2	H	MIDDLESBROUGH			W	4-2	2-0	Rowley 10, 46, 72, Pearson 14	Allen	Carey	Redman	Gibson	Chilton	Cockburn	McShane	Pearson	Rowley	Downie	Bond
	22/8		39,176		3			*Mochan 77, 90*	*Ugolini*	*Robinson*	*Dicks*	*Bell*	*Blenkinsopp*	*Gordon*	*Linacre*	*Delapenha*	*Mochan*	*Mannion*	*Walker*
								Ref: H Jackson	With Blenkinsopp limping out wide for the second half, Jack has a field day – scoring three, hitting the post and having two other shots saved. Gibson overshadows Wilf Mannion and United are in a different class. Ugolini is a revelation and Mochan's first ever goals are a consolation.										
3	H	NEWCASTLE		2	W	2-1	0-1	Rowley 49, Downie 59	Allen	Carey	Redman	Gibson	Chilton	Cockburn	McShane	Pearson	Rowley	Downie	Bond
	25/8		53,673	*9*	5			*Robledo 18*	*Fairbrother*	*Cowell*	*Corbett*	*Harvey*	*Brennan*	*Crowe*	*Walker*	*Taylor*	*Robledo G*	*Hannah*	*Mitchell*
								Ref: T Seymour	The FA Cup winners are beaten in a fascinating game. At 1-1 Fairbrother is caught by Cowell's knee and fractures a collar bone. The Chilean Robledo goes in goal but can't prevent Downie'shot in off the post. 10-men Magpies are sterner than Boro. Joe Harvey and Brennan look good.										
4	A	MIDDLESBROUGH		2	W	4-1	1-0	Pearson 25, 66, Rowley 58, 90	Allen	Carey	Redman	Gibson	Chilton	Cockburn	McShane	Pearson	Rowley	Downie	Bond
	29/8		*44,434*	*14*	7			*Delapenha 85p*	*Ugolini*	*Robinson*	*Dicks*	*Bell*	*Whitaker*	*Gordon*	*Linacre*	*Delapenha*	*Mochan*	*Mannion*	*Walker*
								Ref: H Jackson (sub J Bruce)	Boro are baffled as United make it eleven wins out of 12 against them since the War. Pearson and Rowley are back to international form and United's half-back line looks awesome. Gibson fouls Mannion for the consolation penalty. The referee, Jackson, limps off with a knee injury.										
5	A	BOLTON		4	L	0-1	0-0		Allen	Carey	Redman	Gibson	Chilton	Cockburn	**Berry**	Pearson	Rowley	Downie	Bond
	1/9		55,477	*1*	7			*Lofthouse 52*	*Hanson*	*Ball*	*Higgins*	*Wheeler*	*Barrass*	*Edwards*	*Codd*	*Moir*	*Lofthouse*	*Webster*	*Langton*
								Ref: E Hill	Bill Ridding's Wanderers win the clash of the unbeaten with a controversial Nat Lofthouse diving header that looks offside. When Pearson's 75th-minute effort is ruled out for offside, United's players are livid. Bolton's tough-tackling defence are unbreachable, with Barrass superb.										
6	H	CHARLTON		3	W	3-2	1-1	Rowley 23, 87, Downie 90	Allen	Carey	Redman	Gibson	Chilton	Cockburn	Berry	Pearson	Rowley	Downie	Bond
	5/9		28,627	*15*	9			*Kiernan 40, Vaughan 50*	*Gill*	*Hewie*	*Lock*	*Fenton*	*Ufton*	*Johnson*	*Hurst*	*Evans*	*Vaughan*	*Kiernan*	*Duffy*
								Ref: R Wood	Ken Gill makes his only appearance, in for the injured Bartram, but is at fault for the first, then Ufton slips and Rowley scores. In the gloom of injury-time Downie bundles Gill with the ball over the line to save the day. Charlton come close to ending the 15-game winning home streak.										
7	H	STOKE		3	W	4-0	1-0	Rowley 7, 69, 79, Pearson 86	Allen	Carey	Redman	Gibson	Chilton	Cockburn	Berry	Pearson	Rowley	Downie	McShane
	8/9		45,494	22	11				*Herod*	*Watkin*	*McCue*	*Brown*	*Mountford F*	*Kirton*	*Malkin*	*Mullard*	*Mountford G*	*Ormston*	*Oscroft*
								Ref: L Peake	Stoke's sixth defeat in seven increases the pressure on 57-year-old boss Bob McGrory. United coast to their 16th successive home win and Jack Rowley sets a record with his third hat-trick of the season, two bullet shots and a header where he collides with a post. Berry plays well.										
8	A	CHARLTON		1	D	2-2	1-1	Downie 14, 65	Allen	Carey	Redman	Gibson	Chilton	Cockburn	Berry	Pearson	Rowley	Downie	McShane
	12/9		*27,048*	*11*	12			*Kiernan 29, Hurst 82*	*Bartram*	*Hewie*	*Lock*	*Fenton*	*Ufton*	*Johnson*	*Hurst*	*Evans*	*Vaughan*	*Kiernan*	*Duffy*
								Ref: R Wood	United start like world beaters but end hanging on for a point. The outstanding Downie misses two before his first. Vaughan's cross is half-volleyed by Kiernan, then Duffy sets up Hurst. Football-writer Charles Buchan predicts a big future for young Hewie, who sews up McShane.										
9	A	MANCHESTER C		1	W	2-1	1-0	Berry 8, McShane 88	Allen	Carey	Redman	Gibson	Chilton	Cockburn	Berry	Pearson	Cassidy	Downie	McShane
	15/9		*52,520*	*17*	14			*Hart 63*	*Trautmann*	*Phillips*	*Hannaway*	*Paul*	*Rigby*	*McCourt*	*Meadows*	*Hart*	*Williamson*	*Westcott*	*Clarke*
								Ref: J Clough	Under Les McDowall, newly promoted City are ambitious and are close to buying Ivor Broadis. United have the luck as Trautmann is wrong-footed by Berry and Cassidy's dummy makes the winner. City, with their best player Hart hobbling, pile on the pressure but Allen defies them.										
10	A	TOTTENHAM		3	L	0-2	0-1		Allen	Carey	Redman	Gibson	Chilton	Cockburn	Berry	Pearson	Rowley	Downie	McShane
	22/9		***70,882***	*4*	14			*Medley 44, Walters 64*	*Ditchburn*	*Ramsey*	*Willis*	*Nicholson*	*Clarke*	*Burgess*	*Walters*	*Bennett*	*McLellan*	*Harmer*	*Medley*
								Ref: T Rand	Arthur Rowe's champions won 6-1 at Stoke last week and keep up their good run with some cultured play. Allen saves Alf Ramsey's penalty but Les Medley's goal is against the run of play. England selectors watch a quiet Rowley who has a jaw injury. Tiny Tommy Harmer is a gem.										

No Date	H/A	Opponent Att	Pos	Res Pts	F-A	H-T	Scorers, Times, and Referees	1	2	3	4	5	6	7	8	9	10	11
11	H	PRESTON	6	L	1-2	1-1	Aston 2	Allen	Carey	Redman	Gibson	Chilton	Cockburn	Berry	Walton	Aston	Pearson	Rowley
29/9		55,267	*5*	14			*Quigley 10, Wayman 78*	*Gooch*	*Cunningham*	*Scott*	*Docherty*	*Marston*	*Forbes*	*Finney*	*Beattie*	*Wayman*	*Quigley*	*Morrison*
							Ref: A Ellis	Preston, under Will Scott, deservedly end the great home run. Aston, recovered from his op, looks unfit and, though Redman tames Finney, Morrison causes trouble. Amateur Johnny Walton impressed in a 6-0 friendly win over Hapoel but struggles. Two points separate the top six.										
12	H	DERBY	3	W	2-1	1-1	Pearson 38, Berry 87	Allen	Carey	Redman	Gibson	Chilton	Cockburn	Berry	Walton	Rowley	Pearson	McShane
6/10		41,563	*21*	16			*Stamps 34*	*Middleton*	*Mozley*	*Barrowcliff*	*McLachlan*	*Oliver*	*Bell*	*Harrison*	*Morris*	*Stamps*	*Parry*	*McLaren*
							Ref: J Bell	Chilton and Cockburn are in the England team and Allen in the Football League XI. Morris lobs Chilton to set up Stamps. Pearson's low shot levels matters before Berry's late prod after Pearson nodded down Walton's cross. A poor game between two average sides. Carey limps off.										
13	A	ASTON VILLA	1	W	5-2	1-2	Pears'n 8, 54, Rowley 53, 59, Bond 57	Allen	McNulty	Redman	Gibson	Chilton	Cockburn	Berry	Pearson	Rowley	Downie	Bond
13/10		*47,765*	*9*	18			*Goffin 4, Smith 44*	*Rutherford*	*Parkes*	*Aldis*	*Blanchflower*	*Moss F*	*Canning*	*Smith H*	*Thompson*	*Dixon*	*Dorsett*	*Goffin*
							Ref: H Bearcock	Villa's good start is petering out, but on a rain-sodden surface they are well in control at half-time. Four goals in six minutes leave them shell-shocked, with Berry skinning Aldis. New England man Tommy Thompson looks average. Mitten is training at Old Trafford but looks heavy.										
14	H	SUNDERLAND	3	L	0-1	0-0		Allen	Carey	Redman	Gibson	Chilton	McGlen	Berry	Downie	Rowley	Pearson	McShane
20/10		42,707	*17*	18			*Davis 70*	*Mapson*	*Stelling*	*Hudgell*	*Watson*	*Hall*	*Wright A*	*Bingham*	*Kirtley*	*Davis*	*Shackleton*	*McSeveney*
							Ref: P Rhodes	Sunderland's Indian sign continues with a harsh win. Davis handled before he scores. £30,000 Trevor Ford is absent with Wales and Cockburn is England's reserve. Berry's offside 'goal' looked good, and Downie was blatantly fouled when shooting. The robust visitors spoil the game.										
15	A	WOLVES	3	W	2-0	1-0	Pearson 7, Rowley 77	Allen	Carey	Redman	Gibson	Chilton	Cockburn	McShane	Pearson	Rowley	Birch	Bond
27/10		*46,167*	*10*	20				*Williams*	*Short*	*Pritchard*	*Crook*	*Chatham*	*Wright*	*Hancocks*	*Dunn*	*Wilshaw*	*Pye*	*Mullen*
							Ref: T Seymour	A tactical success for Busby over Cullis as the Reds soak up Wolves pressure and catch them on the break. Pearson is at the heart of everything scoring from an acute angle and setting up Rowley. Wolves' long-ball game does not work and it's a rare home defeat. Everton eye McGlen.										
16	H	HUDDERSFIELD	2	D	1-1	0-0	Pearson 77	Allen	Carey	Redman	Gibson	Chilton	Cockburn	McShane	Pearson	Rowley	Birch	Bond
3/11		**27,420**	*21*	21			*Metcalfe 81p*	*Wheeler*	*Gallogly*	*Boot*	*McGarry*	*McEvoy*	*Quested*	*McKenna*	*Hassall*	*Burke*	*Metcalfe*	*Gunn*
							Ref: R Wood	After five successive relegation battles, time is running out for George Stephenson's team, but they snatch their third away point on a sticky pitch. New signing from Fulham Quested looks good and Metcalfe nets his 13th successive penalty when Allen fouled ex-Red Ronnie Burke.										
17	A	CHELSEA	5	L	**2-4**	2-2	Pearson 8, Rowley 17	Allen	Carey	Redman	Gibson	Chilton	Cockburn	Berry	Pearson	Aston	Downie	Rowley
10/11		*48,960*	*17*	21			*D'Arcy 18, 75, Bentley 33, Smith 70*	*Robertson*	*Bathgate*	*Tickridge*	*Armstrong*	*Harris*	*Dickson*	*Gray*	*D'Arcy*	*Smith R*	*Bentley*	*Campbell*
							Ref: R Leafe	United are stuttering badly and despite being in charge for 20 minutes are blown away. D'Arcy and Bobby Smith's goals are both headers, whilst Roy Bentley's cannonball takes the cake. Irish international Dickson is outstanding. Rowley's cross cum shot sails into an empty net.										
18	H	PORTSMOUTH	7	L	1-3	0-2	Downie 49 *[Cockburn 52 (og)]*	Allen	Carey	Redman	Gibson	Chilton	Cockburn	Berry	Pearson	Aston	Downie	Rowley
17/11		37,703	*1*	21			*Henderson 17, Gaillard 27,*	*Butler*	*Gunter*	*Ferrier*	*Beale*	*Froggatt*	*Dickinson*	*Harris*	*Reid*	*Henderson*	*Mundy*	*Gaillard*
							Ref: R Hall	With their fourth win in a row, Pompey go top of the table. Gaillard crosses for 19-year-old Henderson to nod in, and he drives in the second. Downie's nod from Berry's cross gives hope before Cockburn hooks in Harris's teasing cross. Froggatt will replace Chilton in England team.										
19	A	LIVERPOOL	7	D	0-0	0-0		Crompton	Carey	**Byrne**	**Blanchflow'r**	Chilton	Cockburn	Berry	Pearson	Rowley	Downie	Bond
24/11		*42,378*	*9*	22				*Ashcroft*	*Jones W*	*Lambert*	*Heydon*	*Hughes*	*Paisley*	*Jackson*	*Baron*	*Smith*	*Payne*	*Liddell*
							Ref: F Gerrard	Redman and Gibson are dropped in favour of home-grown kids and McGlen is transfer listed. Byrne is good but Blanchflower has two stitches over his eye. Crompton is the hero, saving Liddell's point-blank shot. Rowley and Bond miss chances but a win would have been undeserved.										
20	H	BLACKPOOL	6	W	3-1	2-1	Rowley 14, Downie 20, 72	Crompton	McNulty	Byrne	Carey	Chilton	Cockburn	Berry	Pearson	Rowley	Downie	Bond
1/12		35,977	*12*	24			*Perry 44*	*Farm*	*Shimwell*	*Garrett*	*Johnston*	*Hayward*	*Fenton*	*Hobson*	*Taylor*	*Slater*	*Brown*	*Perry*
							Ref: T Glendenning	Scottish keeper Farm keeps United's back-to-form forwards at bay, otherwise it could have been seven. Stanley's Matthews and Mortensen are injured and Harry Johnston can't plug the gaps. There are appeals for hands as Rowley scores and Farm dives over Downie's shot for the third.										
21	A	ARSENAL	3	W	3-1	2-0	Rowley 11, Pearson 30, Daniel 77 (og)	Crompton	McNulty	Byrne	Carey	Chilton	Cockburn	Berry	Pearson	Rowley	Downie	Bond
8/12		*53,451*	*2*	26			*Logie 85*	*Swindin*	*Barnes*	*Smith*	*Forbes*	*Daniel*	*Mercer*	*Milton*	*Logie*	*Holton*	*Lishman*	*Roper*
							Ref: S Law (sub R Tarrett)	Arsenal's first home defeat is evidence that United are title contenders. In atrocious wet conditions the Reds turn to the long ball. Berry sets up Rowley, Swindin drops a corner for Stan, and Ray Daniel can't avoid Berry's hard cross. Referee Law is injured in a clash with Doug Lishman.										

No	Date		Att	Pos	Pt	F-A	H-T	Scorers, Times, and Referees	1	2		4	5	6	7	8	9	10	11
22	H	WEST BROM		2	W	5-1	0-1	Berry 46, Pearson 48, 85,	Allen	McNulty	Byrne	Carey	Chilton	Cockburn	Berry	Pearson	Rowley	Downie	Bond
	15/12		29,402	*17*	28			*Allen 1* [Downie 69, 71]	*Sanders*	*Rickaby*	*Millard*	*Kennedy*	*Vernon*	*Dudley*	*Griffin*	*McCall*	*Allen*	*Ryan*	*Lee*
								Ref: C Fletcher	Ronnie Allen nets his 17th of the season in 12 seconds, after Lee had hit the bar. The turning point is Allen's great save from Lee. Berry nods in Bond's cross. The impressive Downie bags two, including one from Vernon's back-pass. Johnny Berry looks world-class and is cheered off.										
23	A	NEWCASTLE		2	D	2-2	2-2	Cockburn 13, Bond 39	Allen	McNulty	Byrne	Carey	Chilton	Cockburn	Berry	Pearson	Rowley	Downie	Bond
	22/12		*45,414*	*6*	29			*Foulkes 19, Milburn 21*	*Simpson*	*Cowell*	*McMichael*	*Harvey*	*Brennan*	*Robledo E*	*Walker*	*Foulkes*	*Milburn*	*Robledo G*	*Mitchell*
								Ref: T Seymour	A thrilling match sees the return of local hero Milburn after injury. He scores one, makes the other, and is robbed of a third by Allen. Cockburn scores the 50th goal of the season and United, despite hanging on at the end, deserve to win. League leading scorer George Robledo is quiet.										
24	H	FULHAM		2	W	3-2	0-0	Berry, Bond, Rowley	Allen	McNulty	Byrne	Chilton	Jones	Cockburn	Berry	Pearson	Rowley	Downie	Bond
	25/12		35,697	*21*	31			*Thomas 2*	*Black*	*Bacuzzi*	*Dodgin*	*Macaulay*	*Taylor Jim*	*Lowe E*	*Campbell*	*Thomas*	*Jezzard*	*Taylor Jeff*	*Robson*
								Ref: W Barnes	Mark Jones gets a rare start in place of injured Carey. Fulham put up stubborn resistance but are beaten by the perennial Rowley. Bob Thomas's casual shot from 40 yards sails under the crossbar for the freak goal of the season. With one win in thirteen Fulham look doomed.										
25	A	FULHAM		2	D	3-3	1-1	Rowley 12, Pearson 49, Bond 51	Allen	McNulty	Byrne	Chilton	Jones	Cockburn	Berry	Pearson	Rowley	Downie	Bond
	26/12		*32,671*	*21*	32			*Lowe 16, 89, Stevens 75*	*Black*	*Bacuzzi*	*Dodgin*	*Macaulay*	*Taylor Jim*	*Lowe E*	*Stevens*	*Thomas*	*Jezzard*	*Taylor Jeff*	*Campbell*
								Ref: W Barnes	United get casual and throw the win away. Fulham with only two home wins are plucky but are heading for the drop. The limping Eddie Lowe is a hero, scoring twice, the first direct from a corner. Unmarked Rowley scores before Byrne sets up Pearson and Ernie Bond's stunning drive.										
26	H	BOLTON		1	W	1-0	1-0	Pearson 26	Allen	McNulty	Byrne	Chilton	Jones	Cockburn	Berry	Pearson	Rowley	Downie	Bond
	29/12		55,073	7	34				*Hanson*	*Ball*	*Higgins*	*Wheeler*	*Gillies*	*Edwards*	*Holden*	*Moir*	*Lofthouse*	*Howe*	*Langton*
								Ref: E Hill	With Arsenal losing at Roker, the Reds go top. Bolton turn up the heat in the second half but with the youngsters looking assured at the back Pearson's header is sufficient - he is knocked out in the process. McNulty controls England winger Bobby Langton well in the dreadful mud.										
27	A	STOKE		2	D	0-0	0-0		Allen	McNulty	Byrne	Carey	Chilton	Cockburn	Berry	Pearson	Rowley	Downie	Bond
	5/1		*36,389*	*19*	35				*Herod*	*Mould*	*McCue*	*Martin*	*Mountford F*	*Kirton*	*Malkin*	*Bowyer*	*Sellars*	*Smyth*	*Oscroft*
								Ref: L Peake	Sammy Smyth has revitalised Stoke since signing from Wolves but fails to keep up his goal-a-game record. Thick mud dulls the game as Stoke pull away from the drop zone. With ten minutes left a lighter white ball is introduced and Stan Pearson balloons it high over from Berry's cross.										
28	H	MANCHESTER C		2	D	1-1	0-0	Carey 60	Allen	McNulty	Byrne	Carey	Chilton	Cockburn	Berry	Pearson	Aston	Downie	Rowley
	19/1		**56,122**	*8*	36			*McCourt 49*	*Trautmann*	*Branagan*	*Hannaway*	*Spurdle*	*Rigby*	*McCourt*	*Hart*	*Revie*	*Meadows*	*Broadis*	*Clarke*
								Ref: J Clough	Confidence is unaffected by the club's exit from the FA Cup and this is a thriller on an icy pitch where standing up is hard. Manager McDowall has invested shrewdly in Broadis and Revie but Roy Paul is out. Trautmann is in top form and United have three shots headed off the goal-line.										
29	H	TOTTENHAM		1	W	2-0	0-0	Ramsey 55 (og), Pearson 87	Allen	McNulty	Byrne	Carey	Chilton	Cockburn	Berry	Clempson	Aston	Pearson	Rowley
	26/1		42,668	*6*	38				*Ditchburn*	*Ramsey*	*Withers*	*Nicholson*	*Clarke*	*Burgess*	*Walters*	*Baily*	*Duquemin*	*Harmer*	*Medley*
								Ref: T Rand	Spurs' find of the season, Harmer, doesn't get a look in as Chilton is back to his best. The second half defies the icy conditions and is a credit to both sides. Frank Clempson, getting a rare game, misses under the bar but Ramsey can't evade the rebound. Spurs rally but Pearson wraps it up.										
30	A	PRESTON		1	W	2-1	1-1	Aston 4, Berry 57	Allen	McNulty	Byrne	Carey	Chilton	Cockburn	Berry	Clempson	Aston	Pearson	Rowley
	9/2		*38,792*	*6*	40			*Wayman 30*	*Gooch*	*Cunningham*	*Scott*	*Docherty*	*Marston*	*Dunn*	*Finney*	*Foster*	*Wayman*	*Beattie*	*Morrison*
								Ref: A Ellis	Dunn plays for the injured Forbes as PNE make their first defensive change for 45 games. Byrne is tipped as a future England full-back after mastering Finney. Aston hits a stunner and Berry's shot deflects in off Docherty's knee. Allen leaves Wayman's half-hit shot, but it sneaks in.										
31	A	DERBY		1	W	3-0	1-0	Pearson 26, Rowley 69, Aston 88	Crompton	McNulty	Byrne	Carey	Chilton	Cockburn	Berry	Clempson	Aston	Pearson	Rowley
	16/2		*27,693*	*15*	42				*Middleton*	*Mozley*	*Parr*	*McLachlan*	*Oliver*	*Bell*	*Harrison*	*Morris*	*Wilkins*	*Stamps*	*Powell*
								Ref: J Bell	The daring Ray Middleton saves Stewart McMillan's struggling Rams from a heavy defeat and he is not to blame for the goals. Big Jack Lee is missed by Derby, who are not the force they were. There are seven Manchester-born players in United's team and they put on a fine exhibition.										

No	Venue	Opponent / Date	Att	Pos	Pts	Res	F-A	H-T	Scorers, Times, Referees	1	2	3	4	5	6	7	8	9	10	11
32	H	ASTON VILLA		1		D	1-1	1-1	Berry 30	Crompton	McNulty	Byrne	Carey	Chilton	Cockburn	Berry	Clempson	Aston	Pearson	Rowley
		1/3	41,717	*7*	43				*Dixon 28*	*Jones*	*Lynn*	*Parkes*	*Blanchflower*	*Moss F*	*Dorsett*	*Gibson*	*Thompson*	*Walsh*	*Dixon*	*Goffin*
									Ref: H Beacock	Villa for once perform at Old Trafford and deserve a point. The two-week break has not helped United who look rusty and lacklustre. Berry is the best player on show and is impressing selectors. Dixon's unstoppable shot is cancelled out immediately by Berry after a barrage of shots.										
33	A	SUNDERLAND		1		W	2-1	0-1	Rowley 88, Cockburn 90	Crompton	McNulty	Byrne	Carey	Chilton	Cockburn	Berry	Clempson	Aston	Pearson	Rowley
		8/3	*48,078*	*15*	45				*Ford 14p*	*Mapson*	*Stelling*	*Hedley*	*Aitken*	*Hall*	*Wright A*	*Bingham*	*Kirtley*	*Ford*	*Shackleton*	*Watson*
									Ref: P Rhodes	An amazing finish ends the bogey. Ford needs two chances to score after Byrne handles. After Rowley equalises, Willie Watson hits the bar and the ball is transferred up the pitch, United win a corner and Cockburn smacks in the winner with the last kick. Tireless Carey is superb.										
34	H	WOLVES		1		W	2-0	1-0	Clempson 26, Aston 85	Crompton	McNulty	Byrne	Carey	Chilton	Cockburn	Berry	Clempson	Aston	Pearson	Rowley
		15/3	46,933	*8*	47					*Williams*	*Shorthouse*	*Gibbons*	*Wright*	*Chatham*	*Crook*	*Smith*	*Broadbent*	*Swinbourne*	*Wilshaw*	*Hancocks*
									Ref: J Topliss	Spring has arrived in Manchester and the fans see a thrilling match with end-to-end action. Wolves, without Pye, Mullen and Dunn are just not good enough. Pearson and Berry set up Clempson and John Aston blasts home after tricking Billy Wright. The title looks there for the taking.										
35	A	HUDDERSFIELD		1		L	2-3	1-2	Clempson 22, Pearson 62	Crompton	McNulty	Byrne	Carey	Chilton	Cockburn	Berry	Clempson	Aston	Pearson	Rowley
		22/3	*30,316*	*22*	47				*Glazzard 19, 87, Metcalfe 44p*	*Mills*	*Gallogly*	*Kelly*	*McGarry*	*McEvoy*	*Quested*	*Gunn*	*Boot*	*Glazzard*	*Davie*	*Metcalfe*
									Ref: R Wood	United, unchanged for a fifth, lose as managerless Town keep their faint survival hopes alive by ending the 16-match unbeaten run. Glazzard gives the injured Chilton the runaround and is fouled by Byrne for the penalty. Metcalfe scores his fourth penalty in five games with United.										
36	A	PORTSMOUTH		1		L	0-1	0-0		Crompton	McNulty	Byrne	Carey	Chilton	Whitefoot	Berry	Clempson	Aston	Downie	Bond
		5/4	***25,522***	*3*	47				*Reid 76*	*Dore*	*Stephen*	*Ferrier*	*Beale*	*Flewin*	*Thompson*	*Harris*	*Reid*	*Henderson*	*Phillips*	*Dale*
									Ref: R Hall	Both sides are under strength because of internationals but Pompey cope better. Clempson blasts United's best chance high into the terraces. Reid scores from Gordon Dale's cross. The Reds' first defeat at Fratton since 1936. Three points separate the top four teams - United are shaky.										
37	A	BURNLEY		1		D	1-1	1-0	Byrne 15	Allen	McNulty	Aston	Carey	Chilton	Cockburn	Berry	Downie	Rowley	Pearson	Byrne
		11/4	*38,907*	*11*	48				*Shannon 87*	*McNulty*	*Aird*	*Mather*	*Adamson*	*Cummings*	*Attwell*	*Chew*	*Morris*	*Shannon*	*McIlroy*	*Cheesebrough*
									Ref: A Ellis	Arsenal are level on points with a game in hand and Pompey also have 48 points. Byrne's looping header seems to have won the points until Burnley's rally, when debutant Albert Cheesebrough rattles the bar and Shannon earns a point. Burnley's McNulty makes three fine saves.										
38	H	LIVERPOOL		1		W	4-0	1-0	Byrne 26p, 53, Downie 51, Rowley 59	Allen	McNulty	Aston	Carey	Chilton	Whitefoot	Berry	Downie	Rowley	Pearson	Byrne
		12/4	44,899	*7*	50					*Ashcroft*	*Lambert*	*Parr*	*Jones W*	*Heydon*	*Paisley*	*Jackson*	*Baron*	*Smith*	*Payne*	*Liddell*
									Ref: F Gerrard	After having won at Maine Road the previous day, Liverpool are outclassed. John Aston and Jeff Whitefoot are superb and Byrne a revelation on the left wing. Liverpool battle hard but have no answers to Downie's magical footwork. Arsenal lose, opening a gap of two points at the top.										
39	H	BURNLEY		1		W	**6-1**	0-0	Rowley 49, Pearson 50, Downie 56,	Allen	McNulty	Aston	Carey	Chilton	Whitefoot	Berry	Downie	Rowley	Pearson	Byrne
		14/4	46,339	*14*	52				*Corr 85* [Byrne 61, 89, Carey 90]	*McNulty*	*Aird*	*Mather*	*Adamson*	*Cummings*	*Attwell*	*Cheesebrough*	*Morris*	*Corr*	*McIlroy*	*Elliott*
									Ref: A Ellis	The well-watered pitch suits United's style. Chances go begging before the break but then Frank Hill's Burnley are blitzed. Rowley's 26th goal equals his own record and Pearson's header is carried over the line. All the goals are stunning. Burnley's Pat Corr plays his one and only game.										
40	A	BLACKPOOL		1		D	2-2	1-2	Byrne 12, Rowley 53	Allen	McNulty	Aston	Carey	Chilton	Cockburn	Berry	Downie	Rowley	Pearson	Byrne
		19/4	*29,118*	*7*	53				*Mudie 19, 31*	*Farm*	*Shimwell*	*Garrett*	*Johnston*	*Hayward*	*Kelly*	*Hobson*	*Taylor*	*Mudie*	*Brown*	*Withers*
									Ref: T Glendenning	Matthews, Mortensen and Perry are injured and Blackpool try to sit on a lead against the top scorers in the division. Farm only partially clears Carey's centre and Byrne scores his sixth goal in four. Ernie Taylor and Allan Brown set up Mudie's goals. Arsenal are level on points again.										
41	H	CHELSEA		1		W	3-0	2-0	Pear' 23, Carey 44, McKnight 48 (og)	Allen	McNulty	Aston	Carey	Chilton	Cockburn	Berry	Downie	Rowley	Pearson	Byrne
		21/4	39,272	*18*	55					*Robertson*	*Tickridge*	*Willemse*	*McKnight*	*Harris*	*Dickson*	*Gray*	*Campbell*	*D'Arcy*	*Bentley*	*Smith J*
									Ref: R Leafe	With news that Arsenal are losing at West Brom, Carey's left-footer from 25 yards brings the house down. Losing Cup semi-finalists Chelsea are never in the game and Cockburn's fierce drive bounces off McKnight's head before Byrne misses a penalty for a foul by Bill Robertson.										
42	H	ARSENAL		1		W	**6-1**	3-0	Rowley 8, 74, 82, Pearson 40, 89,	Allen	McNulty	Aston	Carey	Chilton	Cockburn	Berry	Downie	Rowley	Pearson	Byrne
		26/4	55,516	*3*	57				*Cox 76* [Byrne 44]	*Swindin*	*Barnes*	*Smith*	*Forbes*	*Shaw*	*Mercer*	*Cox*	*Goring*	*Holton*	*Lewis*	*Roper*
		Home	Away						Ref: S Law	Arsenal need to win 7-0 to take the title and the celebrations start early. It is a handsome victory over 10-man Arsenal - Shaw goes off injured - and a sad farewell for Reg Lewis. The crowd invade the pitch at the end and Johnny Carey is chaired off. Jack reaches a club record 30 goals.										
Average		42,916	41,512																	

LEAGUE DIVISION 1 (CUP-TIES) Manager: Matt Busby SEASON 1951-52

FA Cup			Att			F-A	H-T	Scorers, Times, and Referees	1	2	3	4	5	6	7	8	9	10	11
3	H	HULL		2	L	0-2	0-2		Allen	McNulty	Byrne	Carey	Chilton	Cockburn	Berry	Pearson	Rowley	Downie	Bond
	12/1		43,517	*2:21*				*Gerrie 16, Harrison 43*	*Robinson*	*Hassall*	*Jensen*	*Harris*	*Berry*	*Durham*	*Harrison*	*Carter*	*Gerrie*	*Todd*	*Burbanks*
								Ref: R Leafe	Hull pull off the shock of the day. Ex-manager Raich Carter has returned as a player and Jack Hill is caretaker. Carter mesmerises United, who are warned when Harrison blazes wide after 10 minutes. Jack misses a penalty when Durham fouls Bond but United's rally comes too late.										

		Home					Away					
	P	W	D	L	F	A	W	D	L	F	A	Pts
1 MAN UNITED	42	15	3	3	55	21	8	8	5	40	31	57
2 Tottenham	42	16	1	4	45	20	6	8	7	31	31	53
3 Arsenal	42	13	7	1	54	30	8	4	9	26	31	53
4 Portsmouth	42	13	3	5	42	25	7	5	9	26	33	48
5 Bolton	42	11	7	3	35	26	8	3	10	30	35	48
6 Aston Villa	42	13	3	5	49	28	6	6	9	30	42	47
7 Preston	42	10	5	6	39	22	7	7	7	35	32	46
8 Newcastle	42	12	4	5	62	28	6	5	10	36	45	45
9 Blackpool	42	12	5	4	40	27	6	4	11	24	37	45
10 Charlton	42	12	5	4	41	24	5	5	11	27	39	44
11 Liverpool	42	6	11	4	31	25	6	8	7	26	36	43
12 Sunderland	42	8	6	7	41	28	7	6	8	29	33	42
13 West Brom	42	8	9	4	38	29	6	4	11	36	48	41
14 Burnley	42	9	6	6	32	19	6	4	11	24	44	40
15 Man City	42	7	5	9	29	28	6	8	7	29	33	39
16 Wolves	42	8	6	7	40	33	4	8	9	33	40	38
17 Derby	42	10	4	7	43	37	5	3	13	20	43	37
18 Middlesbro	42	12	4	5	37	25	3	2	16	27	63	36
19 Chelsea	42	10	3	8	31	29	4	5	12	21	43	36
20 Stoke	42	8	6	7	34	32	4	1	16	15	56	31
21 Huddersfield	42	9	3	9	32	35	1	5	15	17	47	28
22 Fulham	42	5	7	9	38	31	3	4	14	20	46	27
	924	227	113	122	888	602	122	113	227	602	888	924

Odds & ends
Double wins: (4) Middlesbro, Wolves, Arsenal, Derby.
Double losses: (1) Portsmouth.
Won from behind: (6) Newcastle (h), Charlton (h), Derby (h), A Villa (a), West Brom (h), Sunderland (a).
Lost from in front: (2) Preston (h), Chelsea (a).
High spots: 16-match unbeaten run.
Goalscoring and good form of Rowley and Pearson.
Emergence of youngsters Byrne, Whitefoot and McNulty.
The away wins at Arsenal and Aston Villa.
Low spots: Dreadful November when United did not win a game.
The late season slips at Huddersfield and Portsmouth.
FA Cup exit versus Hull.
Sent off: United – (0).
Sent off: Opponents – (0).
Ever-presents: (1) Chilton.
Hat-tricks: (4) Rowley.
Opposing hat-tricks: (0).
Leading scorer: Rowley (30).

	Appearances		Goals		
	Lge	FAC	Lge	FAC	Tot
Allen, Reg	33	1			
Aston, John	18		4		4
Berry, Johnny	36	1	6		6
Birch, Brian	2				
Blanchflower, Jackie	1				
Bond, Ernie	19	1	4		4
Byrne, Roger	24	1	7		7
Carey, Johnny	38	1	3		3
Cassidy, Laurie	1				
Chilton, Allenby	42	1			
Clempson, Frank	8		2		2
Cockburn, Henry	38	1	2		2
Crompton, Jack	9				
Downie, Johnny	31	1	11		11
Gibson, Don	17				
Jones, Mark	3				
McGlen, Billy	2				
McNulty, Tommy	24	1			
McShane, Harry	12		1		1
Pearson, Stan	41	1	22		22
Redman, Billy	18				
Rowley, Jack	40	1	30		30
Walton, Johnny	2				
Whitefoot, Jeff	3				
(own-goals)			3		3
24 players used	**462**	**11**	**95**		**95**

No	Date	Att	Pos	Pt	F-A	H-T	Scorers, Times, and Referees	1	2	3	4	5	6	7	8	9	10	11
1	H CHELSEA			W	2-0	0-0	Downie 63, Berry 80	Wood	McNulty	Aston	Carey	Chilton	Gibson	Berry	Downie	Rowley	Pearson	Byrne
	23/8	43,629		2				*Robertson*	*Tickridge*	*Willemse*	*Armstrong*	*Harris*	*Dickson*	*Parsons*	*McNichol*	*D'Arcy*	*Bentley*	*Gray*
							Ref: M Griffiths	Ted Drake's impressive Chelsea more than hold their own until the first goal. Downie, sporting a crew-cut from the US tour, heads in Carey's free-kick. Bill Robertson saves Byrne's penalty but Berry's goal seals the points for the champions against ten men, with Tickridge off injured.										
2	A ARSENAL			L	1-2	0-1	Rowley 62	Crompton	McNulty	Aston	Carey	Chilton	Cockburn	Berry	Downie	Rowley	Pearson	Byrne
	27/8	***57,831***		2			*Cox 13, Goring 82*	*Swindin*	*Wade*	*Smith*	*Shaw*	*Daniel*	*Mercer*	*Cox*	*Oakes*	*Goring*	*Lishman*	*Roper*
							Ref: J Williams	United are lucky not to get a point against the Cup finalists who have 38-year old Joe Mercer still going strong. Wood can't get RAF leave, so Crompton is recalled and Cockburn is over his cold. Rowley casually side-foots Berry's pass in, but Goring scores from one of many chances.										
3	A MANCHESTER C		14	L	1-2	0-0	Downie 79	Crompton	McNulty	Aston	Carey	Chilton	Cockburn	Berry	Downie	Rowley	Pearson	Byrne
	30/8	*56,240*	*17*	2			*Clarke 50, Broadis 69*	*Trautmann*	*Branagan*	*Westwood*	*Paul*	*Rigby*	*Spurdle*	*Meadows*	*Revie*	*Sowden*	*Broadis*	*Clarke*
							Ref: E Plinston	City gain their first post-war victory over the Reds at the ninth attempt, despite dropping Fred Smith in favour of the young Bill Sowden. Roy Clarke sprints past McNulty and hits a left-footer; then Broadis slams a second after a one-two with Don Revie. Spurdle's slip lets in Downie.										
4	H ARSENAL		13	D	0-0	0-0		Crompton	Carey	Byrne	Gibson	Chilton	Cockburn	Berry	Clempson	Aston	Pearson	Bond
	3/9	39,193	*5*	3				*Swindin*	*Chenhall*	*Smith*	*Shaw*	*Daniel*	*Bowen*	*Cox*	*Goring*	*Holton*	*Lishman*	*Roper*
							Ref: J Williams	37-year-old George Swindin has turned down the Bradford City manager's job and is the star in the Gunners' draw. One double save from Frank Clempson and Ernie Bond brings the house down. United's established stars are not performing, and the axed Downie wants a transfer.										
5	A PORTSMOUTH		19	L	0-2	0-0		Crompton	McNulty	Byrne	Gibson	Chilton	Cockburn	Berry	Clempson	Aston	Pearson	Rowley
	6/9	*37,278*	*16*	3			*Harris 63, Gordon 78*	*Butler*	*Stephen*	*Thompson*	*Scoular*	*Froggatt*	*Dickinson*	*Harris*	*Gordon*	*Mundy*	*Phillips*	*Gaillard*
							Ref: A Bond	A sorry Reds' display as struggling Pompey notch their first win. The attack is completely out of touch and Busby's patience is wearing thin. Peter Harris is the best winger in the land and his speedy run ends with a shot from an acute angle. 21-year-old Johnny Gordon nets a second.										
6	A DERBY		13	W	3-2	1-0	Pearson 30, 83, 84	Crompton	McNulty	Aston	Carey	Chilton	Gibson	Berry	Downie	Rowley	Pearson	Byrne
	10/9	***20,226***	*20*	5			*Harrison 50, Hazledine 55*	*Middleton*	*Parr*	*Bell*	*Morris*	*Nielson*	*Mays*	*Harrison*	*Hazledine*	*Straw*	*Lee*	*Williams*
							Ref: P Power	In a frantic finish, United – or rather Stan Pearson – gets it right. Downie's transfer request has been rejected and he dazzles the Rams. Byrne's pass sets up the first before Harrison's direct free-kick. Rowley sets up the second and Berry obliges for the winner. Crompton breaks a finger.										
7	H BOLTON		11	W	1-0	0-0	Berry 56	Allen	McNulty	Aston	Carey	Chilton	Gibson	Berry	Downie	Rowley	Pearson	Byrne
	13/9	42,370	*16*	7				*Hanson*	*Ball*	*Higgins*	*Wheeler*	*Barrass*	*Edwards*	*Holden*	*Bell*	*Lofthouse*	*Moir*	*Parry*
							Ref: H Jackson	The winner comes after Hanson's wild punch goes to Berry, who nets with ease. Allen gets a rare game but a Lofthouse rocket opens an old hand wound and Rowley has to go between the sticks. 16-year-old Ray Parry – in for the transfer-listed Bobby Langton – looks a fine prospect.										
8	A ASTON VILLA		12	D	3-3	1-1	Downie 33, Rowley 71p, 73p	Wood	McNulty	Aston	Carey	Chilton	Gibson	Berry	Downie	Rowley	Pearson	Byrne
	20/9	*43,490*	*19*	8			*Lockhart 26, Pace 49, Roberts 54*	*Cordell*	*Lynn*	*Parkes*	*Blanchflower*	*Martin*	*Dorsett*	*Goffin*	*Gibson*	*Pace*	*Roberts*	*Lockhart*
							Ref: A Holland	Without touching their heights, United come back from 1-3 down to earn a point in a poor game. Villa end a run of four defeats as Irish cap Lockhart nets on his debut and 20-year-old Doc Pace scores. Dorsett and Martin handle goalbound shots and Rowley is deadly from the spot.										
9	H SUNDERLAND		15	L	0-1	0-1		Wood	McNulty	Aston	Chilton	Jones	Gibson	Berry	Downie	Clempson	Pearson	Byrne
	27/9	30,771	*8*	8			*Ford 23*	*Threadgold*	*Stelling*	*Hedley*	*Watson*	*Hall*	*Wright A*	*Wright T*	*Kirtley*	*Ford*	*Shackleton*	*Reynolds*
							Ref: J Pickles	The old timers are outclassed by their bogey team, who beat United at home for the sixth time in seven years. Welsh leader Trevor Ford is too good for Mark Jones and nods in Tommy Wright's super cross. Shackleton is a wizard and the defence is solid. Cockburn out with bronchitis.										
10	A WOLVERHAMPTON		17	L	2-6	2-2	Rowley 19, 20 *[Mullen 46]*	Allen	McNulty	Aston	Carey	Chilton	Gibson	Berry	Downie	Rowley	Pearson	**Scott**
	4/10	*39,667*	*2*	8			*Wilshaw 25, 54, Swinb' 40, 55, 88,*	*Williams*	*Short*	*Pritchard*	*Flowers*	*Shorthouse*	*Slater*	*Smith*	*Broadbent*	*Swinbourne*	*Wilshaw*	*Mullen*
							Ref: B Flanagan	Belfast-born John Scott has a nightmare debut but sets up the goals. Poor Reg Allen has to take the blame with three goals down to him. Billy Wright is on England duty but debutant Bill Slater is a great stand-in. Swinbourne heads the scoring list and an England call-up is on the cards.										

No	Venue	Opponent	Pos	Res	F-A	H-T	Scorers, Times, and Referees	1	2	3	4	5	6	7	8	9	10	11
11	H	STOKE	21	L	0-2	0-0		Wood	McNulty	Aston	Carey	Chilton	Gibson	Scott	Clempson	Rowley	Downie	Berry
11/10		30,818	*18*	8			*Siddall 63, Finney 77*	*Robertson*	*Bourne*	*McCue*	*Martin*	*Thomson*	*Sellars*	*Siddall*	*McClelland*	*Finney*	*Smyth*	*Oscroft*
							Ref: T Seymour	Frank Taylor's lowly Stoke grab a first away win since February and United's fans are streaming out well before the end. Stoke's Bill Finney makes a dream debut and United are embarrassed in every position. Roger Byrne wants away after being axed and Pearson asks to be rested.										
12	A	PRESTON	17	W	**5-0**	5-0	Pearson 4, 37, Aston 12, 15, [Rowley 21]	Crompton	Carey	Byrne	Whitefoot	Chilton	Gibson	Berry	Downie	Aston	Pearson	Rowley
18/10		*33,502*	*14*	10				*Newlands*	*Cunningham*	*Walton*	*Docherty*	*Marston*	*Dunn*	*Finney*	*Beattie*	*Wayman*	*Baxter*	*Morrison*
							Ref: R Hartley	Preston have been plagued with a virus and United's nine changes pay off. Byrne comes off the transfer list and bosses England star Finney; but the fans don't like Aston up front despite his two goals. Johnny Berry murders ex-Red Walton and Chilton keeps tabs on the wily Wayman.										
13	H	BURNLEY	19	L	1-3	1-2	Aston 3	Crompton	Carey	Byrne	Whitefoot	Chilton	Gibson	Berry	Downie	Aston	Pearson	Rowley
25/10		38,754	*7*	10			*McIlroy 25, 36, Holden 80*	*Strong*	*Aird*	*Mather*	*Adamson*	*Cummings*	*Attwell*	*Chew*	*McIlroy*	*Holden*	*Shannon*	*Elliott*
							Ref: A Luty	Burnley end a run of seven games without win despite United's bright start. Irish star Jimmy McIlroy scores two and makes Holden's but Carey boobs for the first and Crompton spills the ball for the second. United resort to long-ball tactics which Burnley's tall defence relish.										
14	A	TOTTENHAM	18	W	2-1	1-1	Berry 38, 74	Crompton	McNulty	Byrne	Whitefoot	Chilton	Gibson	Berry	Downie	Aston	Pearson	McShane
1/11		*44,285*	*15*	12			*Walters 5*	*Ditchburn*	*Ramsey*	*Willis*	*Nicholson*	*Clarke*	*Burgess*	*Walters*	*Uphill*	*Duquemin*	*Bailey*	*Medley*
							Ref: E Vickery	Spurs' first-half domination spearheaded by England man Eddie Baily is countered by United's stylish comeback. First Berry's shot flies of the outstanding Ron Burgess's shoulder; then his speed fools the Spurs defence. Ramsey's pinpoint crosses create chances for Baily and Medley.										
15	H	SHEFFIELD WED	19	D	1-1	0-1	Pearson 88	Crompton	McNulty	Byrne	Whitefoot	Chilton	Gibson	Berry	Downie	Aston	Pearson	McShane
8/11		50,426	*9*	13			*Dooley 30*	*Capewell*	*Jackson*	*Curtis*	*Witcomb*	*Turton*	*Davies*	*Quixall*	*Sewell*	*Dooley*	*Froggatt*	*Woodhead*
							Ref: H Deacock	Dooley, last season's 46-goal man, is stuttering in Div 1 but follows up to score after heading onto the bar. Pearson's header from McShane's centre saves more blushes but the boo boys are loud. Britian's costliest player Sewell is recalled after a month out. Wednesday unbeaten in ten.										
16	A	CARDIFF	15	W	2-1	2-1	Aston 37, Pearson 42	Crompton	McNulty	Byrne	Cockburn	Chilton	Gibson	Berry	Downie	Aston	Pearson	McShane
15/11		*40,096*	*19*	15			*Chisholm 44*	*Howells*	*Stitfall*	*Sherwood*	*Baker*	*Montgomery*	*Blair*	*Tiddy*	*Sullivan*	*Northcutt*	*Chisholm*	*Edwards*
							Ref: R Leafe	Cockburn's return from illness sparks United and Carey, on Eire duty, is not missed. Newly promoted Cardiff, managed by Cyril Spiers, are in Div 1 after a gap of 23 years. They do most attacking, but Ken Chisholm's header is poor reward. Defensive errors hand United both goals.										
17	H	NEWCASTLE	15	D	2-2	0-1	Pearson 67, Aston 74	Crompton	McNulty	Byrne	Cockburn	Chilton	Gibson	Berry	Downie	Aston	Pearson	McShane
22/11		35,380	*10*	16			*Keeble 26, Robledo 85*	*Simpson*	*Cowell*	*McMichael*	*Stokoe*	*Brennan*	*Casey*	*Walker*	*Mulgrew*	*Robledo G*	*Keeble*	*Mitchell*
							Ref: J Williams	It's over two months since a home win and a draw is fair. McShane is the creator with Pearson heading in a corner and his pass perfect for Aston, but Chilean Robledo's late header grabs a point. Downie treads on the ball when it is easier to score and veteran Simpson is a saviour.										
18	A	WEST BROM	16	L	1-3	1-0	Lewis 8	Crompton	McNulty	Byrne	Gibson	Chilton	Cockburn	Berry	Downie	**Lewis**	Pearson	McShane
29/11		*23,499*	*4*	16			*Allen 51, Lee 68, Griffin 75*	*Heath*	*Rickaby*	*Millard*	*Dudley*	*Kennedy*	*Barlow*	*Griffin*	*Nicholls*	*Allen*	*Ryan*	*Lee*
							Ref: L Howarth	17-year-old Eddie Lewis has a dream start as Heath spills McShane's shot on the snow-covered pitch. The playing conditions are farcical as a snowstorm obliterates the markings. All the goals come from errors. Jesse Carver's team's long ball splits United's back line like an ice floe.										
19	H	MIDDLESBROUGH	15	W	3-2	3-2	Pearson 7, 32, Aston 23	Crompton	McNulty	Byrne	Carey	Chilton	Cockburn	Berry	**Doherty**	Aston	Pearson	**Pegg**
6/12		29,619	*13*	18			*Mannion 35, Delapenha 42p*	*Ugolini*	*Bilcliff*	*Corbett*	*Bell*	*Aitken*	*Russell*	*Lawrie*	*Delapenha*	*Norris*	*Mannion*	*Fitzsimmons*
							Ref: G Black	Two more teenage debutants acquit themselves well but the old-stagers star. Pearson nets a left-footer after a one-two with Aston; and Doherty crosses for Aston to nod in before Cockburn makes a third. Wilf Mannion's thunderbolt and a spot-kick after Chilton handled gives Boro hope.										
20	A	LIVERPOOL	11	W	2-1	0-1	Aston 50, Pearson 80	Crompton	**Foulkes**	Byrne	Carey	Chilton	Cockburn	Berry	Doherty	Aston	Pearson	Pegg
13/12		*34,450*	*12*	20			*Liddell 10*	*Ashcroft*	*Taylor*	*Moran*	*Heydon*	*Jones*	*Paisley*	*Payne*	*Baron*	*Stubbins*	*Smith*	*Liddell*
							Ref: J Houston	St Helens miner Foulkes looks mature in a baptism of fire against Scottish legend Liddell, whose shot flies off Chilton's chest. The elusive Berry is too much for young Ronnie Moran. Pegg's cross nodded down by Pearson for Aston, and Stan grabs a soft second as Pool capitulate.										
21	A	CHELSEA	8	W	3-2	3-0	Doherty 11, 29, Aston 23	Crompton	Foulkes	Byrne	Carey	Chilton	Cockburn	Berry	Doherty	Aston	Pearson	Pegg
20/12		*23,261*	*20*	22			*Dickson 55, Smith 74*	*Robertson*	*Tickridge*	*Willemse*	*Armstrong*	*Saunders*	*Dickson*	*Gray*	*Bentley*	*Smith R*	*McNichol*	*Campbell*
							Ref: M Griffiths	Ted Drake is under pressure after a seventh defeat in a row. It looks over at half-time as Doherty, with a slick left foot and a tap-in after Pearson hits the bar, shines. Crompton breaks a cheekbone in a clash with Bentley. Deputy Carey is covered in mud and glory in frantic finale.										

No	Date	Att	Pos	Pt	F-A	H-T	Scorers, Times, and Referees	1	2	3	4	5	6	7	8	9	10	11
22	A BLACKPOOL		9	D	0-0	0-0		Wood	McNulty	Byrne	Carey	Chilton	Cockburn	Berry	Doherty	Aston	Pearson	Pegg
	25/12	*27,778*	*5*	23				*Farm*	*Shimwell*	*Garrett*	*Johnston*	*Crosland*	*Fenton*	*Wright*	*Taylor*	*Mortensen*	*Brown*	*Perry*
							Ref: J Williams	Ray Wood, home on leave from the RAF, has a solid game. Doherty gets a bump on the head which slows him down. Few teams come away from Blackpool with a point. Blackpool's early season form has slipped due to the absence of Stanley Matthews but he is almost fit to resume.										
23	H BLACKPOOL		8	W	2-1	1-1	Carey 40, Lewis 80	Wood	McNulty	Byrne	Carey	Chilton	Cockburn	Berry	Lewis	Aston	Pearson	Pegg
	26/12	49,934	*5*	25			*Mortensen 10*	*Farm*	*Shimwell*	*Garrett*	*Johnston*	*Crosland*	*Fenton*	*Wright*	*Taylor*	*Mortensen*	*Brown*	*Perry*
							Ref: J Williams	With Britain's fastest winger Perry going past McNulty at will Blackpool are in charge and Morty scores a goal out of nothing. Lewis looks here to stay after his second in two games. The absent Stan Matthews wants to return to Stoke. United are only five points behind the leaders.										
24	H DERBY		8	W	1-0	1-0	Lewis 8	Wood	Redman	Byrne	Carey	Chilton	Cockburn	Berry	Aston	Lewis	Pearson	Pegg
	1/1	36,649	*17*	27				*Middleton*	*Mozley*	*Barrowcliffe*	*Bell*	*Oliver*	*Musson*	*Powell*	*Hazledine*	*Lee*	*Stamps*	*McLaren*
							Ref: P Power	United's defence looks jittery, with Redman especially vulnerable. The attack struggle, too, with the fans on Aston's back again. Wonder-boy Lewis is the hero again. 32-year-old Jack Rowley rumoured to have broken down in training. Stuart McMillan's Rams look relegation fodder.										
25	H MANCHESTER C		7	D	1-1	1-0	Pearson 11	Wood	Aston	Byrne	Carey	Chilton	Whitefoot	Berry	Doherty	Lewis	Pearson	Pegg
	3/1	49,738	*22*	28			*Broadis 59*	*Trautmann*	*Branagan*	*Westwood*	*Revie*	*Ewing*	*Paul*	*Meadows*	*Hart*	*Williamson*	*Broadis*	*Cunliffe*
							Ref: E Plinston	Aston becomes the third right-back in three games, and the defence looks tighter. Ivor Broadis brightens a poor Derby game but looks offside when scoring after Ray Wood spilled Meadows' shot. Lewis has a fine tussle with debutant Dave Ewing. City grab only their third away point.										
26	H PORTSMOUTH		6	W	1-0	0-0	Lewis 60	Wood	Aston	Byrne	Carey	Chilton	Cockburn	Berry	Downie	Lewis	Pearson	Pegg
	17/1	34,173	*18*	30				*Uprichard*	*Gunter*	*Wilson*	*Scoular*	*Froggatt*	*Dickinson*	*Harris*	*Gordon*	*Henderson*	*Mundy*	*Reagan*
							Ref: A Bond	The Reds are at their best in their fourth home game in a row and tear Pompey apart. Uprichard saves everything thrown at him and is finally beaten by Lewis's mis-hit shot. England players Froggatt and Dickinson are poor but Jimmy Scoular is a rock. Pompey's glory days look over.										
27	A BOLTON		7	L	1-2	0-1	Lewis 75	Wood	Aston	Byrne	Carey	Chilton	Cockburn	Berry	Downie	Lewis	Pearson	Pegg
	24/1	*46,818*	*13*	30			*Moir 40, 52*	*Hanson*	*Hartle*	*Higgins*	*Wheeler*	*Barrass*	*Bell*	*Holden*	*Moir*	*Lofthouse*	*Hassall*	*Langton*
							Ref: H Jackson	The 3 pm kick-off is a farce with the second half played in almost darkness on a mud-heap. United pay for a profligate first half but deserve a point. Wood spills Hassall's shot and Moir nets. Lofthouse fools the square defence and crosses for Moir. Berry and Pegg hit the woodwork.										
28	H ASTON VILLA		7	W	3-1	2-1	Rowley 28, 48 Lewis 44	Wood	Aston	Byrne	Carey	Chilton	Cockburn	Berry	Lewis	Rowley	Pearson	Pegg
	7/2	36,134	*16*	32			*Walsh 32*	*Parsons*	*Aldis*	*Parkes*	*Blanchflower*	*Moss F*	*Dorsett*	*Gibson*	*Thompson*	*Walsh*	*Dixon*	*Lockhart*
							Ref: A Holland	Rowley scores his first home goals of the season on a hard, icy pitch – the first a diving header from Byrne's free-kick, the second a trademark cannonball. Berry sets up Lewis, and Chilton and Wood boob for Dave Walsh's goal. United rarely hit the heights but are too good for Villa.										
29	A SUNDERLAND		7	D	2-2	1-0	Pegg 39, Lewis 56	Carey	Aston	Byrne	Gibson	Chilton	Cockburn	Berry	Lewis	Rowley	Pearson	Pegg
	18/2	*24,263*	*6*	33			*Chilton 84 (og), Watson 90*	*Threadgold*	*Stelling*	*Hudgell*	*Watson*	*Hall*	*Aitken*	*Bingham*	*Shackleton*	*Davis*	*Wright A*	*Wright T*
							Ref: J Pickles	With Wood with RAF and Crompton taken ill in the morning Carey gets the jersey and plays a blinder. Pegg scores and lays on Lewis's goal. Willie Watson moves to the wing and the barrage begins. His shot glances off Chilton's head and in injury time he lobs into an untended net.										
30	H WOLVERHAMPTON		8	L	0-3	0-1		Wood	Aston	Byrne	Carey	Chilton	Cockburn	Berry	Lewis	Rowley	Pearson	Pegg
	21/2	40,078	*2*	33			*Wilshaw 25, Mullen 60, 88*	*Sims*	*Short*	*Pritchard*	*Flowers*	*Shorthouse*	*Slater*	*Hancocks*	*Stockin*	*Swinbourne*	*Wilshaw*	*Mullen*
							Ref: B Flanagan	Lingering title hopes are dashed by Wright-less Wolves, who with their long-ball game win easily. Cockburn and Lewis have head knocks and the old 'uns are off colour. Mullen takes advantage of Wood's mistakes and the fleet of foot Denis Wilshaw is too quick for a slow defence.										
31	A STOKE		9	L	1-3	1-2	Berry 22	Crompton	McNulty	Byrne	Chilton	Jones	Gibson	Berry	Aston	Rowley	Downie	Pegg
	28/2	*30,227*	*17*	33			*Brown 31, 43, Martin 57*	*Elliott*	*Bourne*	*McCue*	*Mountford F*	*Thomson*	*Sellars*	*Malkin*	*Bowyer*	*Brown*	*Martin*	*Oscroft*
							Ref: T Seymour	Carey and Pearson are rested and Wood has fractured a wrist. The seven changes don't work on the hard dry ground. It is a vital win for drop-fighting Stoke and Rowley's offside goal looks fine. Jones collides with Gibson and limps on the wing. United eye Barnsley's Tommy Taylor.										

No		Opponent	Att	Pos	Res	Pts	Score	HT	Scorers, times and referees	1	2	3	4	5	6	7	8	9	10	11
32	H	PRESTON		9	W		5-2	3-1	Taylor 17, 88, Pegg 36, 40, Row' 48	Crompton	Aston	Byrne	Carey	Chilton	Cockburn	Berry	Rowley	**Taylor**	Pearson	Pegg
7/3			**54,397**	*3*		35			*Wayman 28, 66*	*Thompson*	*Cunningham*	*Scott*	*Docherty*	*Marston*	*Forbes*	*Finney*	*Lewis*	*Wayman*	*Baxter*	*Morrison*
									Ref: R Hartley	Preston have lost once in fourteen but are thumped with £29,999 Tommy Taylor starring. Rowley crosses for his header and Pearson sets up an easy second. Pegg scores at his second bite and lobs his other. Byrne is in the England 'B' team and Downie turns down Cardiff and Man City.										
33	A	BURNLEY		9	L		1-2	0-0	Byrne 80p	Crompton	Aston	Byrne	Carey	Chilton	Cockburn	Berry	Rowley	Taylor	Pearson	Pegg
14/3			*45,422*	*1*		35			*Chew70, Holden 72*	*Thompson*	*Aird*	*Mather*	*Adamson*	*Cummings*	*Attwell*	*Chew*	*McIlroy*	*Holden*	*Shannon*	*Elliott*
									Ref: A Luty	Burnley are in the title hunt and have lost one in fourteen but are lucky to survive United's pressure. On a rock-hard pitch the wind causes havoc and blows Pearson's shot wide. Cummings handles and Byrne nets. Elliott's cross falls at Chew's feet and Holden powers in the winner.										
34	H	TOTTENHAM		8	W		3-2	1-1	Pegg 11, Pearson 49, 60	Crompton	Aston	Byrne	Gibson	Chilton	Cockburn	Berry	Rowley	Taylor	Pearson	Pegg
25/3			**20,215**	*10*		37			*McClellan 37, Walters 51*	*Ditchburn*	*Ramsey*	*Withers*	*Nicholson*	*King*	*Burgess*	*Walters*	*McClellan*	*Duquemin*	*Bailey*	*Robb*
									Ref: E Vickery	Mid-table mediocrity and Spurs have a Cup hangover after semi final defeat to Blackpool . United cannot match Spurs' artistry and the highlight is David Pegg's duel with Alf Ramsey. Spurs have impressive amateur George Robb on the wing. Rowley's dummy sets up Pegg.										
35	A	SHEFFIELD WED		8	D		0-0	0-0		Crompton	Aston	Byrne	Carey	Chilton	Cockburn	Berry	Rowley	Taylor	Pearson	Pegg
28/3			*36,509*	*16*		38				*McIntosh*	*Kenny*	*Curtis*	*Witcomb*	*Turton*	*Davies*	*Marriott*	*Sewell*	*Codd*	*Froggatt*	*Woodhead*
									Ref: H Beacock	An instantly forgettable match. Wednesday are shell-shocked after Derek Dooley's tragic injury results in him losing a leg but he will survive. England's selectors come to see Jackie Sewell and Redfearn Froggatt, but leave impressed with Berry, Taylor and youth-teamer Pegg.										
36	A	CHARLTON		8	D		2-2	1-2	Taylor 30, Berry 86	Crompton	Aston	Byrne	Carey	Chilton	Blanchflower	Berry	Rowley	Taylor	Pearson	Pegg
¾			*41,814*	*2*		39			*Hurst 13, Leary 37*	*Bartram*	*Campbell*	*Hewie*	*Fenton*	*Ufton*	*Hammond*	*Hurst*	*O'Linn*	*Leary*	*Firmani*	*Kiernan*
									Ref: J Topliss	Charlton's unbeaten home record is intact on Good Friday morning but they fail to go top. Their South African inside-forward trio are superb and batter United's goal. Charlton's first post-war win over United looks on until Berry's goal but Jack saves from Firmani in the last minute.										
37	H	CARDIFF		8	L		1-4	0-2	Byrne 86p	Crompton	Aston	Byrne	Gibson	Chilton	**Edwards**	Berry	Rowley	Taylor	Pearson	Pegg
4/4			38,987	*12*		39			*Grant 11, 75, Chisholm 15, Tiddy 60*	*Howells*	*Sherwood*	*Mansell*	*Hollyman*	*Montgomery*	*Blair*	*Tiddy*	*Williams R*	*Grant*	*Chisholm*	*Northcutt*
									Ref: R Leafe	16-year-old Duncan Edwards is United's greatest prospect and can't be faulted for this defeat. Crompton presents Cardiff with three Easter gifts in their first visit to Old Trafford since 1928. They are a speedy team with good positional sense and a number of experienced players.										
38	H	CHARLTON		8	W		3-2	1-1	Taylor 10, 73, Rowley 47	Crompton	McNulty	Byrne	Carey	Chilton	Whitefoot	Berry	Lewis	Taylor	Pearson	Rowley
6/4			31,914	*5*		41			*O'Linn 44, Firmani 50*	*Bartram*	*Campbell*	*Lock*	*Fenton*	*Ufton*	*Hammond*	*O'Linn*	*Evans*	*Leary*	*Hewie*	*Firmani*
									Ref: J Topliss	This defeat ends Charlton's title hopes on a rain-drenched pitch. United make five changes and Carey restores stability in defence. Tommy Taylor looks the part and wins the game with a fierce drive from Berry's cross after Eddie Firmani's volley seems to have gained a point.										
39	A	NEWCASTLE		8	W		2-1	1-1	Taylor 7, 58	**Olive**	McNulty	Byrne	Carey	Chilton	Whitefoot	**Viollet**	Pearson	Aston	Taylor	Rowley
11/4			*39,078*	*15*		43			*Mitchell 18*	*Simpson*	*Cowell*	*McMichael*	*Harvey*	*Brennan*	*Crowe*	*Walker*	*Mulgrew*	*Milburn*	*Hannah*	*Mitchell*
									Ref: J Williams	Jackie Milburn returns from injury to face two more United debutants. Assistant Secretary and amateur Les Olive plays because of injuries and saves well from Mitchell. 19-year-old Dennis Viollet has enormous potential. Taylor's winner comes when Simpson can't hold Aston's shot.										
40	H	WEST BROM		8	D		2-2	2-1	Pearson 8, Violett 27	Olive	McNulty	Byrne	Carey	Chilton	Whitefoot	Viollet	Pearson	Aston	Taylor	Rowley
18/4			33,161	*6*		44			*Hodgkisson 3, Ryan 71*	*Sanders*	*Rickaby*	*Millard*	*Dudley*	*Dugdale*	*Barlow*	*Nicholls*	*Hodgkisson*	*Allen*	*Ryan*	*Lee*
									Ref: L Howarth	United are lucky to get a point against superior Albion. Berry is on England duty as a reserve but his deputy – Viollet's –clinical finish reminds fans of Pearson at his peak. Hodgkisson catches Olive off his line and the elegant Ray Barlow shows why he is in the England tour party.										
41	H	LIVERPOOL		6	W		3-1	2-0	Pearson 6, Rowley 9, Berry 80	Crompton	Aston	Byrne	Carey	Chilton	Whitefoot	Berry	Downie	Taylor	Pearson	Rowley
20/4			22,645	*18*		46			*Smyth 88*	*Ashcroft*	*Jones*	*Lamb*	*Williams*	*Taylor*	*Maloney*	*Payne*	*Smyth*	*Bimpson*	*Rowley*	*Liddell*
									Ref: J Houston	United coast home against a poor Liverpool. Three points separate seven teams at the foot of the table and Pool look vulnerable. The early goals make for a dull second half. Pearson limps off near the end before Berry races half the pitch and beats Charlie Ashcroft from 20 yards.										
42	A	MIDDLESBROUGH		8	L		**0-5**	0-2	*[Spuhler 75, Fitzsimmons 81]*	Crompton	McNulty	Byrne	Carey	Chilton	Whitefoot	Berry	Viollet	Aston	Taylor	Rowley
25/4			*34,344*	*15*		46			*Mannion 35, 42, Delapenha 47,*	*Ugolini*	*Bilcliff*	*Corbett*	*Bell*	*Dicks*	*Mulholland*	*Delapenha*	*Mannion*	*Spuhler*	*Fitzsimmons*	*Walker G*
		Home	Away						Ref: G Black	Middlesbrough end a run of 13 matches against United without a win and inflict the Reds biggest defeat since 1939. Wilf Mannion is in superb form but is not in the England tour party. Crompton should have prevented two on the hard bumpy surface but United's finishing is woeful.										
Average		37,570	37,146																	

LEAGUE DIVISION 1 (CUP-TIES) Manager: Matt Busby SEASON 1952-53

Charity Shield			F-A	H-T	Scorers, Times, and Referees	1	2	3	4	5	6	7	8	9	10	11
H NEWCASTLE	12	W	4-2	0-1	Rowley 48, 53, Byrne 63, Downie 75	Wood	McNulty	Aston	Carey	Chilton	Gibson	Berry	Downie	Rowley	Pearson	Byrne
24/9	11,381 *15*				*Keeble 35, 69*	*Simpson*	*Cowell*	*Batty*	*Robledo E*	*Stokoe*	*Casey*	*Walker*	*Robledo G*	*Keeble*	*Black*	*Mitchell*
					Ref: A Luty	The attendance is badly affected by the midweek afternoon kick-off and the televising of the second half. Viewers marvel at a thriller with spectacular goals. The Cup winners field several reserves and miss Jackie Milburn but the defence caves in under waves of United pressure.										

FA Cup			F-A	H-T	Scorers, Times, and Referees	1	2	3	4	5	6	7	8	9	10	11
3 A MILLWALL	7	W	1-0	0-0	Pearson 86	Wood	Aston	Byrne	Carey	Chilton	Cockburn	Berry	Downie	Lewis	Pearson	Rowley
10/1	*35,652 3S:5*					*Finlayson*	*Jardine*	*Fisher*	*Short*	*Bowler*	*Saward*	*Neary*	*Stobbart*	*Shepherd*	*Morgan*	*Hartburn*
					Ref: W Ratcliffe	United, with Aston and Chilton supreme, survive a bombardment in docklands thanks to Pearson's late header after Finlayson misses a cross. Lions boss Charlie Hewitt can't believe the result and rues John Shepherd's open-goal miss. Millwall's run of five wins comes to an end.										
4 H WALTHAMSTOW	7	D	1-1	1-0	Lewis 39	Wood	Aston	Byrne	Carey	Chilton	Cockburn	Berry	Downie	Lewis	Pearson	Rowley
31/1	34,748 *Ist:1*				*Lewis 75*	*Gerula*	*Young*	*Stratton*	*Harper*	*Saunders*	*Hall*	*Bailey*	*Lucas*	*Lewis*	*Fielder*	*Camis*
					Ref: P Rhodes	The Isthmian League side put on a brave rearguard action and keeper Gerula is chaired off by the 1,000 Walthamstow Avenue fans. In truth he has few shots to save from a woeful attack. England cricketer Trevor Bailey plays for the amateurs and England amateur cap Jim Lewis scores.										
4R A WALTHAMSTOW	7	W	5-2	4-1	Pearson 15, Lewis 17, Row' 21, 85,	Wood	Aston	Byrne	Carey	Chilton	Cockburn	Berry	Lewis	Rowley	Pearson	Pegg
5/2	*49,119 Ist:1*				*Lewis 43p, 60* [Byrne 30p]	*Gerula*	*Young*	*Stratton*	*Harper*	*Saunders*	*Hall*	*Bailey*	*Lucas*	*Lewis*	*Fielder*	*Camis*
(at Highbury)					Ref: P Rhodes	30,000 fans pass through the turnstiles after the kick-off and many miss four goals. The valiant amateurs in their blue and white hooped shirts are given massive support at 2-4. Stan Pearson nods in Rowley's cross, Eddie Lewis blasts home and Stratton nudges Pearson for the penalty.										
5 A EVERTON	7	L	1-2	1-1	Rowley 27	Wood	Aston	Byrne	Carey	Chilton	Cockburn	Berry	Lewis	Rowley	Pearson	Pegg
14/2	*77,920 2:13*				*Eglington 32, Hickson 64*	*O'Neill*	*Clinton*	*Lindsay*	*Farrell*	*Jones*	*Lello*	*Buckle*	*Cummins*	*Hickson*	*Parker*	*Eglington*
					Ref: H Beacock	United fan Dave Hickson gives Chilton a hard time and knocks United out despite a badly cut eye. The Second Division side are too good as too many Reds have an off-day. The experiment of playing Lewis and Rowley as dual centre-forwards fails as Jack does nothing but score.										

		Home					Away					
	P	W	D	L	F	A	W	D	L	F	A	Pts
1 Arsenal	42	15	3	3	60	30	6	9	6	37	34	54
2 Preston	42	15	3	3	46	25	6	9	6	39	35	54
3 Wolves	42	13	5	3	54	27	6	8	7	32	36	51
4 West Brom	42	13	3	5	35	19	8	5	8	31	41	50
5 Charlton	42	12	8	1	47	22	7	3	11	30	41	49
6 Burnley	42	11	6	4	36	20	7	6	8	31	32	48
7 Blackpool	42	13	5	3	45	22	6	4	11	26	48	47
8 MAN UNITED	42	11	5	5	35	30	7	5	9	34	42	46
9 Sunderland	42	11	9	1	42	27	4	4	13	26	55	43
10 Tottenham	42	11	6	4	55	37	4	5	12	23	32	41
11 Aston Villa	42	9	7	5	36	23	5	6	10	27	38	41
12 Cardiff	42	7	8	6	32	17	7	4	10	22	29	40
13 Middlesboro	42	12	5	4	46	27	2	6	13	24	50	39
14 Bolton	42	9	4	8	39	35	6	5	10	22	34	39
15 Portsmouth	42	10	6	5	44	34	4	4	13	30	49	38
16 Newcastle	42	9	5	7	34	33	5	4	12	25	37	37
17 Liverpool	42	10	6	5	36	28	4	2	15	25	54	36
18 Sheff Wed	42	8	6	7	35	32	4	5	12	27	40	35
19 Chelsea	42	10	4	7	35	24	2	7	12	21	42	35
20 Man City	42	12	2	7	45	28	2	5	14	27	59	35
21 Stoke	42	10	4	7	35	26	2	6	13	18	40	34
22 Derby	42	9	6	6	41	29	2	4	15	18	45	32
	924	240	116	106	913	595	106	116	240	595	913	924

Odds & ends

Double wins: (5) Derby, Preston, Tottenham, Liverpool, Chelsea.
Double losses: (3) Stoke, Burnley, Wolves.

Won from behind: (5) Derby (a), Tottenham (a), Liverpool (a), Blackpool (h), Newcastle (h) CS.
Lost from in front: (5) Wolves (a), Burnley (h), West Brom (a), Stoke (a), Everton (a) FAC.

High spots: Emergence of more youngsters.
Inaugural winners of FA Youth Cup.
Double over league runners-up Preston.
Form of Berry, Byrne and Pegg.

Low spots: Three successive autumn home defeats.
Heavy defeats at Wolves and Middlesbrough.
FA Cup exit at second division Everton.
Goalkeeping calamities.

Sent off: United- none.
Sent off: Opponents- none.

Ever-presents: (1) Chilton.
Hat-tricks: (1) Pearson.
Opposing hat-tricks: (1) Swinbourne (Wolves).
Leading scorer: Pearson (18).

	Appearances		Goals		
	Lge	FAC	Lge	FAC	Tot
Allen, Reg	2				
Aston, John	40	4	8		8
Berry, Johnny	40	4	7		7
Blanchflower, Jackie	1				
Bond, Ernie	1				
Byrne, Roger	40	4	2	1	3
Carey, Johnny	32	4	1		1
Chilton, Allenby	42	4			
Clempson, Frank	4				
Cockburn, Henry	22	4			
Crompton, Jack	25				
Doherty, John	5		2		2
Downie, Johnny	20	2	3		3
Edwards, Duncan	1				
Foulkes, Bill	2				
Gibson, Don	20				
Jones, Mark	2				
Lewis, Eddie	10	4	7	2	9
McNulty, Tom	23				
McShane, Harry	5				
Olive, Les	2				
Pearson, Stan	39	4	16	2	18
Pegg, David	19	2	4		4
Redman, Billy	1				
Rowley, Jack	26	4	11	3	14
Scott, Jackie	2				
Taylor, Tommy	11		7		7
Viollet, Dennis	3		1		1
Whitefoot, Jeff	10				
Wood, Ray	12	4			
30 players used	**462**	**44**	**69**	**8**	**77**

LEAGUE DIVISION 1

Manager: Matt Busby

SEASON 1953-54

No	Date	Att	Pos	Pt	F-A	H-T	Scorers, Times, and Referees	1	2	3	4	5	6	7	8	9	10	11
1	H CHELSEA			D	1-1	0-1	Pearson 61	Crompton	Aston	Byrne	Gibson	Chilton	Cockburn	Berry	Rowley	Taylor	Pearson	Pegg
	19/8	30,759		1			*McNichol 39*	*Robertson*	*Sillett P*	*Willemse*	*Armstrong*	*Greenwood*	*McKnight*	*Bentley*	*Smith R*	*Lewis*	*McNichol*	*Blunstone*
							Ref: J Topliss	A midweek start to the season sees Taylor miss a penalty after Greenwood handles. Captain Pearson's shot is deflected in by Greenwood to equalise the Blues' Blunstone-made goal. Chelsea show more attacking flair on the day England win the Ashes. Willemse tackles Berry rashly.										
2	A LIVERPOOL			D	4-4	1-2	Row' 9, Byrne 49p, Lewis 60, Tay' 84	Crompton	Aston	Byrne	Gibson	Chilton	Cockburn	Berry	Rowley	Taylor	Lewis	Pegg
	22/8	*46,725*		2			*Lid' 20, Jones 44, Bimp' 54, Byrne58(og)*	*Ashcroft*	*Lambert*	*Spicer*	*Taylor*	*Hughes*	*Paisley*	*Payne*	*Baron*	*Bimpson*	*Jones W*	*Liddell*
							Ref: G Black	A thrilling match with lots of close shaves but United are lucky. Liverpool are unhappy with Taylor bundling Charlie Ashcroft into the net for the fourth. Three goals are lapses by Crompton but the fearless Bimpson's header is a stunner. Byrne's penalty after Tommy Taylor is fouled.										
3	H WEST BROM		18	L	1-3	1-1	Taylor 21	Crompton	Aston	Byrne	Gibson	Chilton	Cockburn	Berry	Rowley	Taylor	Lewis	Pegg
	26/8	33,652	*2*	2			*Dudley 28, Nicholls 66, Lee 74*	*Heath*	*Rickaby*	*Millard*	*Dudley*	*Dugdale*	*Barlow*	*Griffin*	*Hodgkisson*	*Allen*	*Nicholls*	*Lee*
							Ref: P Power	After a bright start United lose to a useful Albion side who, in wingers Griffin and Lee, have the best players on the park. Taylor misses two gifts and United lack guile with David Pegg off-colour. Dudley's shot hits both posts and bounces out to Crompton but the ref gives a goal.										
4	H NEWCASTLE		19	D	1-1	0-1	Chilton 62	Wood	McNulty	Aston	Whitefoot	Chilton	Cockburn	Berry	Byrne	Taylor	Lewis	Rowley
	29/8	29,676	*10*	3			*Hannah 30*	*Simpson*	*Cowell*	*Batty*	*Stokoe*	*Brennan*	*Crowe*	*Milburn*	*Davies*	*Keeble*	*Hannah*	*Mitchell*
							Ref: H Davis	Stan Seymour's men are good value for the point but Milburn looks odd on the wing. John Aston is barracked unnecessarily but heads off the line. Lewis lacks a yard of pace and has lost his shock factor and Byrne is uncomfortable up front. Chilton nods in from Rowley's corner.										
5	A WEST BROM		19	L	0-2	0-1		Wood	Aston	Byrne	Whitefoot	Chilton	Cockburn	Berry	Lewis	Taylor	Viollet	Rowley
	2/9	*28,892*	*1*	3			*Allen 35, Hodgkisson 87*	*Heath*	*Rickaby*	*Millard*	*Dudley*	*Dugdale*	*Barlow*	*Griffin*	*Hodgkisson*	*Allen*	*Nicholls*	*Lee*
							Ref: P Power	Albion have only dropped one point but United let them off the hook with poor finishing. Taylor, released from National Service, has little support. Wood rashly comes out of his goal after a poor punch and is beaten by Allen, but redeems later. Lee's cross is nodded in for a second.										
6	A MANCHESTER C		20	L	0-2	0-0		Wood	Aston	Byrne	Whitefoot	Chilton	Cockburn	Berry	Viollet	Taylor	Pearson	Rowley
	5/9	*53,097*	*18*	3			*Hart 50, Revie 65*	*Trautmann*	*Branagan*	*Little*	*Revie*	*Ewing*	*Paul*	*Anders*	*Hart*	*Whitfield*	*Spurdle*	*Clarke*
							Ref: R Hartley	Few thrills in a poor derby with Viollet looking out of touch. Aston's wayward pass sets up Hart. The tricky Clarke beats Aston to set up Revie for a cool finish. Only Taylor causes German Bert Trautmann any concern with his shooting. Busby is not panicking but the poor run goes on.										
7	H MIDDLESBROUGH		19	D	2-2	2-0	Rowley 16, 33	Wood	McNulty	Byrne	Whitefoot	Chilton	Cockburn	Berry	Lewis	Rowley	Pearson	McShane
	9/9	**19,893**	*20*	4			*Fitzsimmons 54, Delapenha 65*	*Ugolini*	*Bilcliff*	*Corbett*	*Bell*	*Dicks*	*Mulholland*	*Delapenha*	*Mannion*	*Spuhler*	*Fitzsimmons*	*Walker*
							Ref: J Pickles	McShane returns to set up Rowley's second, a diving header as United look set to win. Ray Wood's bungled clearance is snapped up by Arthur Fitzsimmons and Boro gain their first point at Old Trafford since the war. Pearson is being written off by the fans, whilst Mannion is superb.										
8	A BOLTON		19	D	0-0	0-0		Wood	McNulty	Byrne	Whitefoot	Chilton	Cockburn	Berry	Taylor	Rowley	Pearson	McShane
	12/9	*48,591*	*4*	5				*Hanson*	*Ball*	*Banks T*	*Wheeler*	*Barrass*	*Bell*	*Holden*	*Moir*	*Lofthouse*	*Hassall*	*Parry*
							Ref: H Jackson	Wanderers drop their first home point despite the first appearance of Lofthouse after injury. Chilton masters Nat but Harold Hassall looks good enough for an England recall. Young Ray Parry gives McNulty plenty to think about and looks a star of the future. Taylor ill at ease at inside.										
9	A MIDDLESBROUGH		16	W	4-1	1-1	Byrne 23p, Taylor 49, 85, Rowley 87	Wood	McNulty	Byrne	Whitefoot	Chilton	Cockburn	Berry	Taylor	Rowley	Pearson	McShane
	16/9	*23,791*	*21*	7			*Delapenha 35p*	*Ugolini*	*Bicliff*	*Corbett*	*Bell*	*Robinson*	*Mulholland*	*Delapenha*	*Mannion*	*McPherson*	*Fitzsimmons*	*Walker*
							Ref: J Pickles	Struggling Boro are still shell-shocked after losing 1-8 at Charlton four days previously, and United get their first win. Boro are on top until half-time with Robinson and McNulty handling for the penalties. The unmarked Tommy Taylor heads in and the late goals flatter the scoreline.										
10	H PRESTON		13	W	1-0	1-0	Byrne 40p	Wood	Foulkes	Byrne	Whitefoot	Chilton	Cockburn	Berry	Taylor	Rowley	Pearson	McShane
	19/9	43,003	*11*	9				*Thompson*	*Cunningham*	*Walton*	*Mattinson*	*Marston*	*Dunn*	*Finney*	*Hatsell*	*Wayman*	*Baxter*	*Foster*
							Ref: J Bell	A disputed penalty given when Marston holds down Taylor is enough for the first home win over Scot Symon's team in a poor game. Wayman misses two sitters and debutant Hatsell misses a good chance. England star Tom Finney is lively and hits a post but Berry and Taylor are poor.										

No	Venue	Opponent / Date	Att	Pos	Res / Pts	F-A	H-T	Scorers, Times, and Referees	1	2	3	4	5	6	7	8	9	10	11
11	A	TOTTENHAM		12	D	1-1	1-0	Rowley 34	Wood	Foulkes	Byrne	Whitefoot	Chilton	Cockburn	Berry	Taylor	Rowley	Pearson	McShane
		26/9	*52,837*	*6*	10			*Duquemin 88*	*Ditchburn*	*Ramsey*	*Withers*	*Nicholson*	*Clarke*	*Burgess*	*Hutchinson*	*Bennett*	*Duquemin*	*Baily*	*Robb*
								Ref: M Griffiths	England boss Winterbottom watches a drab game which United almost undeservedly win. Rowley scores a classic when Pearson heads back McShane's cross. Foulkes trips over the ball leaving 'The Duke' to equalise. Wood enhances his England chances but 'old' Chilton is the hero.										
12	H	BURNLEY		13	L	1-2	1-2	Pearson 43	Wood	Foulkes	Byrne	Whitefoot	Chilton	Cockburn	Berry	Taylor	Rowley	Pearson	McShane
		3/10	39,550	*6*	10			*Stephenson 12, Gray 35*	*Thompson*	*Aird*	*Mather*	*Seith*	*Cummings*	*Adamson*	*Gray*	*Stephenson*	*Holden*	*Chew*	*Pilkington*
								Ref: L Richardson	A laboured performance against a swift and tight-marking Burnley. Holden's blind-side pass sets up Stephenson who, deputising for McIlroy on international duty, is the star player. Ex-Chelsea winger Gray again gives United a hard time. Duncan Edwards has signed pro forms.										
13	H	SUNDERLAND		12	W	1-0	0-0	Rowley 60	Wood	Aston	Byrne	Whitefoot	Chilton	Cockburn	Berry	Taylor	Rowley	Pearson	McShane
		10/10	36,482	*20*	12				*Cowan*	*Stelling*	*Hudgell*	*Anderson*	*Aitken*	*Snell*	*Bingham*	*Shackleton*	*Wright T*	*Watson*	*Elliott*
								Ref: H Webb	Aston, back after a spell in the reserves, breaks a bone in his arm but is still too good for Elliott. Trevor Ford is on Wales duty and Shackleton over-elaborates. Pearson sets up Rowley and ends Sunderland's run of five wins at Old Trafford. Scottish international Cowan is excellent.										
14	A	WOLVERHAMPTON		13	L	1-3	1-2	Taylor 30 *[Swinbourne 72]*	Wood	Foulkes	Byrne	Whitefoot	Chilton	Cockburn	Berry	Pearson	Taylor	Rowley	McShane
		17/10	*40,084*	*2*	12			*Hancocks 15p, Broadbent 42,*	*Williams*	*Short*	*Guttridge*	*Slater*	*Shorthouse*	*Wright*	*Hancocks*	*Broadbent*	*Swinbourne*	*Wilshaw*	*Mullen*
								Ref: A Brown	Wolves are unbeaten in 11 games and United can't dent their 100% home record. After Byrne's handball a Guttridge error lets in Taylor, as the Reds match the Wolves. Broadbent scores from Hancocks' corner and Slater's through ball sets up Swinbourne as Wolves rip United apart.										
15	H	ASTON VILLA		13	W	1-0	0-0	Berry 70	Wood	Foulkes	Byrne	Whitefoot	Chilton	Cockburn	Berry	Pearson	Taylor	Rowley	McShane
		24/10	32,106	*12*	14				*Parsons*	*Parkes*	*Aldis*	*Blanchflower*	*Moss F*	*Moss A*	*Gibson*	*Thompson*	*Walsh*	*Pace*	*Lockhart*
								Ref: A Holland	Villa's fourth defeat in a row and new boss Eric Houghton has a big job to do. A dire match with little constructive play and Berry shoots in off a post from Harry McShane's cross. Villa are a shadow of their great teams. United are off to Scotland for a break and changes are expected.										
16	A	HUDDERSFIELD		14	D	0-0	0-0		Wood	Foulkes	Byrne	Whitefoot	Chilton	Edwards	Berry	Blanchflower	Taylor	Viollet	Rowley
		31/10	*34,175*	*3*	15				*Mills*	*Staniforth*	*Howe*	*McGarry*	*McEvoy*	*Quested*	*Gunn*	*Watson*	*Glazzard*	*Davie*	*Metcalfe*
								Ref: R Wood	Newly promoted Town have lost only one in 10 and Busby rings the changes to good effect. Leading scorer Jimmy Glazzard is given few chances by Chilton in an entertaining match. United's best chance comes when Berry sets up Viollet but the shot hits Mills and goes wide.										
17	H	ARSENAL		12	D	2-2	2-0	Rowley 3, Blanchflower 44	Wood	Foulkes	Byrne	Whitefoot	Chilton	Edwards	Berry	Blanchflower	Taylor	Viollet	Rowley
		7/11	29,914	*11*	16			*Holton 68, Roper 87*	*Kelsey*	*Wills*	*Barnes*	*Dickson*	*Dodgin*	*Forbes*	*Roper*	*Logie*	*Holton*	*Lishman*	*Marden*
								Ref: F Overton	Arsenal have lost one in nine but are lucky to draw. Rowley nets when Kelsey drops the ball and Blanchflower profits from Forbes' back-pass. After the break Rowley has five super shots on target but Welsh keeper Kelsey tips four over and saves the other. Roper beats Wood in the air.										
18	A	CARDIFF		9	W	**6-1**	2-1	Viol' 3, 80, Row' 4, Berry 48, Tay' 52,	Wood	Foulkes	Byrne	Whitefoot	Chilton	Edwards	Berry	Blanchflower	Taylor	Viollet	Rowley
		14/11	*26,844*	*8*	18			*Chisholm 30* [Blanchflower 87]	*Howells*	*Rutter*	*Mansell*	*Baker W*	*Montgomery*	*Sullivan*	*Grant*	*Northcott*	*Dudley*	*Chisholm*	*Edwards*
								Ref: R Hall	Only three of the United team played at Cardiff last year and seven of the team are 21 or under. The kids run riot with the biggest away win for five years. Cyril Spiers' Cardiff are left dizzy with the high-speed passing and can do little to stem the second-half tide as United run riot.										
19	H	BLACKPOOL		8	W	4-1	3-1	Taylor 28, 42, 52, Viollet 40	Wood	Foulkes	Byrne	Whitefoot	Chilton	Edwards	Berry	Blanchflower	Taylor	Viollet	Rowley
		21/11	**51,688**	*6*	20			*Perry 22*	*Farm*	*Shimwell*	*Garrett*	*Fenton*	*Johnston*	*Kelly*	*Hobson*	*Taylor*	*Mortensen*	*Brown*	*Perry*
								Ref: J McCann	The best performance of the season sees the FA Cup holders, minus Matthews, thumped. Tommy Taylor is magnificent and outshines Morty. Not far behind are Whitefoot and Edwards. The latter gives new England man Ernie Taylor no scope. The passing and the skill are stunning.										
20	A	PORTSMOUTH		8	D	1-1	0-1	Taylor 70	Wood	Foulkes	Byrne	Whitefoot	Chilton	Edwards	**Webster**	Blanchflower	Taylor	Viollet	Rowley
		28/11	*29,236*	*19*	21			*Froggatt 40*	*Platt*	*Gunter*	*Mansell*	*Phillips*	*Reid*	*Dickinson*	*Harris*	*Gordon*	*Froggatt*	*Hunt*	*Henderson*
								Ref: W Clapton	Pompey have won only once in ten and Dickinson is shell-shocked from England's 6-3 defeat by Hungary. Harris sets up Froggatt and Taylor - in pain with toothache - scrambles a goal. Fighting Portsmouth are good value in the brilliant sunshine. Mansell marks debutant Webster well.										
21	H	SHEFFIELD UTD		7	D	2-2	1-0	Blanchflower 30, 67	Wood	Foulkes	Byrne	Whitefoot	Chilton	Edwards	Berry	Blanchflower	Taylor	Viollet	Rowley
		5/12	33,524	*16*	22			*Toner 46, Hawkesworth 65*	*Burgin*	*Coldwell*	*Ridge*	*Shaw J*	*Johnson*	*Rawson*	*Ringstead*	*Wragg*	*Toner*	*Brook*	*Hawksworth*
								Ref: F Read	Reg Freeman's Blades hit Spurs for five last week but are over physical. Berry and Taylor end up limping and Edwards and Wragg mix things. Hawksworth looks England class and roasts Foulkes, sets up Toner's goal and hits a flashing drive. Rowley's 45-yard effort is inches wide.										

No	Date	Opponent	Att	Pos	Pt	F-A	H-T	Scorers, Times, and Referees	1	2	3	4	5	6	7	8	9	10	11
22	A	CHELSEA		9	L	1-3	0-1	Berry 76	Wood	Foulkes	Byrne	Whitefoot	Chilton	Edwards	Berry	Blanchflower	Taylor	Violett	Rowley
	12/12		*37,153*	*16*	22			*McNichol 30, 55, Parsons 62*	*Robertson*	*Harris*	*Willemse*	*Armstrong*	*Greenwood*	*Saunders*	*Parsons*	*McNichol*	*Bentley*	*Stubbs*	*Blunstone*
								Ref: J Topliss	Berry has two black eyes from the Blades battle. The kids lose their calm but Jimmy Murphy tells Matt to keep the faith. Chelsea look very good despite their league position. McNichol heads in Bentley's cross and Parsons heads in from Blunstone. Chilton is magnificent as captain.										
23	H	LIVERPOOL		7	W	5-1	4-0	Taylor 14, 36, Blanchflower 34, 79,	Wood	Foulkes	Byrne	Whitefoot	Chilton	Edwards	Berry	Blanchflower	Taylor	Viollet	Rowley
	19/12		27,916	*22*	24			*Bimpson 58* [Viollet 44]	*Underwood*	*Lambert*	*Spicer*	*Saunders*	*Wilkinson*	*Twentyman*	*Jackson*	*Baron*	*Bimpson*	*Smyth*	*Liddell*
								Ref: G Black	Despite a spending spree Don Welsh's Pool are in trouble with 39 goals conceded in eleven away defeats. Spicer breaks an ankle in clash with debutant Underwood and with Liddell at left-back the game is as good as over. Whitefoot and Edwards are awesome on the slippery pitch.										
24	H	SHEFFIELD WED		5	W	5-2	1-1	Taylor 3, Viollet, Blanchflower	Wood	Foulkes	Byrne	Whitefoot	Chilton	Edwards	Berry	Blanchflower	Taylor	Viollet	Rowley
	25/12		28,953	*17*	26			*Gannon, Woodhead*	*Ryalls*	*Kenny*	*Curtis*	*McAnearney T*	*Turton*	*Gannon*	*Finney*	*Quixall*	*Froggatt*	*Sewell*	*Woodhead*
								Ref: A Ellis	Wednesday have the worst defence in Div 1 with 59 goals against. Taylor heads one from a free-kick, then is set up by Blanchflower, who later scores with a classy diving header. Edwards' silky pass puts in Viollet and the Reds are unstoppable. Albert Quixall is elegant but can't shoot.										
25	A	SHEFFIELD WED		5	W	1-0	0-0	Viollet 65	Wood	Foulkes	Byrne	Whitefoot	Chilton	Edwards	Berry	Blanchflower	Taylor	Viollet	Rowley
	26/12		*43,526*	*17*	28				*Ryalls*	*Kenny*	*Curtis*	*Gannon*	*Turton*	*Seemly*	*Finney*	*Quixall*	*Woodhead*	*Sewell*	*Marriott*
								Ref: A Ellis	Eric Taylor's Wednesday's lack of a marksman is obvious but United's defence is solid and secure. Ryalls spills the livewire Taylor's shot and Dennis Viollet pounces to make up for two bad misses. 33-year-old Jack Rowley is a shadow of his former self but is mentoring Taylor well.										
26	A	NEWCASTLE		6	W	2-1	2-0	Foulkes 17, Blanchflower 31	Wood	Foulkes	Byrne	Whitefoot	Chilton	Edwards	Berry	Blanchflower	Taylor	Viollet	Rowley
	2/1		***56,034***	*14*	30			*Broadis 62*	*Simpson*	*Cowell*	*McMichael*	*Scoular*	*Brennan*	*Stokoe*	*Foulkes*	*Broadis*	*Milburn*	*Hannah*	*Mitchell*
								Ref: H Davis	Newcastle are breathless at the break but regain their cool to almost snatch a draw. Foulkes' freak 40-yard lob beats Simpson but old adversary Ivor Broadis revives the Magpies. Ex-Pompey man Scoular is industrious and Brennan masters Taylor. Edwards has two shots well saved.										
27	H	MANCHESTER C		6	D	1-1	1-0	Berry 37	Wood	Foulkes	Byrne	Whitefoot	Chilton	Edwards	Berry	Blanchflower	Taylor	Viollet	Pegg
	16/1		48,216	*18*	31			*McAdams 81*	*Trautmann*	*Branagan*	*Meadows*	*McTavish*	*Ewing*	*Paul*	*Fagan*	*Hart*	*McAdams*	*Revie*	*Clarke*
								Ref: R Hartley	Heavy morning rain keeps the derby crowd down and the players plough through the cloying mud. United deserve to win but Taylor lacks support. Clarke sets up McAdams for his fifth in three games to snatch a point. The German keeper Trautmann saves Taylor's diving header										
28	H	BOLTON		6	L	**1-5**	0-4	Taylor 80	Wood	Foulkes	Byrne	Whitefoot	Chilton	Edwards	Berry	Blanchflower	Taylor	Viollet	Pegg
	23/1		48,505	*5*	31			*Loft'se 2, 24, Parry 36, 43, Moir 72*	*Hanson*	*Ball*	*Banks T*	*Wheeler*	*Barrass*	*Bell*	*Holden*	*Moir*	*Lofthouse*	*Stevens*	*Parry*
								Ref: H Jackson	Bolton's forwards are in stunning form and could have scored eight. Wood, Edwards and Whitefoot have been in Italy with England Under 23s and look weary. Cockburn, resigned to not displacing Edwards, asks for a move, as do McShane and McNulty. 17-year-old Ray Parry stars.										
29	A	PRESTON		6	W	3-1	3-0	Blanchflow' 1, Rowley 15, Taylor 24	Crompton	Foulkes	Byrne	Whitefoot	Chilton	Edwards	Berry	Blanchflower	Taylor	Viollet	Rowley
	6/2		*30,064*	*8*	33			*Baxter 60p*	*Thompson*	*Cunningham*	*Walton*	*Docherty*	*Marston*	*Forbes*	*Finney*	*Foster*	*Wayman*	*Baxter*	*Morrison*
								Ref: J Bell	On a bone-hard surface, United have it won by half-time. Rowley replaces Pegg and looks sharper, and it's United's fourth win in a row at Deepdale. A debatable penalty sparks a brief rally from physical North End but, with Byrne in control of Tom Finney, there is little danger.										
30	H	TOTTENHAM		6	W	2-0	1-0	Rowley 39, Taylor 77	Crompton	Foulkes	Byrne	Whitefoot	Chilton	Edwards	**McFarlane**	Blanchflower	Taylor	Viollet	Rowley
	13/2		37,289	*12*	35				*Ditchburn*	*Ramsey*	*Willis*	*Nicholson*	*Clarke*	*Wetton*	*Walters*	*Bennett*	*Duquemin*	*Baily*	*Robb*
								Ref: M Griffiths	Noel McFarlane, playing for Berry, injured playing for the Football League, is out of his depth despite forcing a fine save from Ditchburn. The speedy Robb is fouled by Foulkes but Ramsey misses the penalty. Defences are on top with England man Clarke a rock. Pearson joins Bury.										
31	A	BURNLEY		6	L	0-2	0-1		Crompton	Foulkes	Byrne	Whitefoot	Chilton	Edwards	Berry	Blanchflower	Taylor	Viollet	Pegg
	20/2		*31,402*	*4*	35			*Gray 12, 89*	*Thompson*	*Aird*	*Mather*	*Seith*	*Cummings*	*Attwell*	*Gray*	*McIlroy*	*Holden*	*Shannon*	*Pilkington*
								Ref: L Richardson	Burnley repeat the Cup win and have more guile and speed than the Reds. Bill Holden, rumoured to be unhappy, has the sign over Chilton who struggles to control him. Crompton has no chance against the ubiquitous Billy Gray. McShane joins Oldham and McNulty joins Liverpool.										

No	Venue / Date	Opponent / Att	Pos	Res / Pts	F-A	H-T	Scorers, Times, and Referees	1	2	3	4	5	6	7	8	9	10	11
32	A	SUNDERLAND	6	W	2-0	1-0	Taylor 7, Blanchflower 77	Wood	Foulkes	Byrne	Whitefoot	Chilton	Edwards	Berry	Blanchflower	Taylor	Viollet	Rowley
	27/2	*38,400*	*19*	37				*Cowan*	*Hedley*	*Hudgell*	*Anderson*	*Hall*	*Wright A*	*Bingham*	*Shackleton*	*Purdon*	*Chisholm*	*Elliott*
							Ref: H Webb	Sunderland are the longest serving Div 1 club never to be relegated, but things are looking bleak. Their stars never twinkle and the great Len Shackleton is booed as Edwards shines. On a snow-covered pitch, Jackie Blanchflower ends a superb five-man movement with a special goal.										
33	H	WOLVERHAMPTON	5	W	1-0	0-0	Berry 85	Wood	Foulkes	Byrne	Whitefoot	Chilton	Edwards	Berry	Blanchflower	Taylor	Viollet	Rowley
	6/3	40,774	*2*	39				*Williams*	*Stuart*	*Shorthouse*	*Slater*	*Wright*	*Clamp*	*Hancocks*	*Broadbent*	*Flowers*	*Wilshaw*	*Mullen*
							Ref: A Brown	Wolves and West Brom are in a two-horse race for the title and United help Albion by beating negative Wolves. The offside trap is sprung as Blanchflower's ball finds Berry and the linesman starts to raise a flag then drops it. The fans boo the ref and England captain Billy Wright.										
34	A	ASTON VILLA	5	D	2-2	2-1	Taylor 4, 41	Crompton	Foulkes	Byrne	Whitefoot	Chilton	Cockburn	Berry	Blanchflower	Taylor	Viollet	Rowley
	13/3	*26,023*	*14*	40			*Thompson 23, Baxter 75*	*Jones*	*Parkes*	*Aldis*	*Blanchflower*	*Moss F*	*Baxter*	*Roberts KO*	*Dixon*	*Walsh*	*Thompson*	*McParland*
							Ref: A Holland	United have lost only once at Villa Park since the war but are hanging on at the end as Villa rally. Blanchflower plays against brother Danny and creates both for Taylor. With Edwards on Youth Cup duty, Cockburn plays but is off the pace. Johnny Berry leads Aldis a merry dance.										
35	H	HUDDERSFIELD	5	W	3-1	1-0	Rowley 6, Viollet 61, Blanchflow' 83	Crompton	Foulkes	Byrne	Whitefoot	Chilton	Edwards	Berry	Blanchflower	Taylor	Viollet	Rowley
	20/3	43,015	*3*	42			*Metcalfe 76p*	*Wheeler*	*Staniforth*	*Kelly*	*McGarry*	*Taylor*	*Watson*	*Burrell*	*Frear*	*Glazzard*	*Cavanagh*	*Metcalfe*
							Ref: R Wood	McGarry and Staniforth have England call-ups as reward for Town's best season for years, but United are too good. Taylor gives 18-year-old Ken Taylor a torrid time and tees up Blanchflower's stunner. Byrne fouls Glazzard for a penalty. Unhappy fans chant, 'oh my, what a referee'.										
36	A	ARSENAL	6	L	1-3	1-0	Taylor 2	Crompton	Foulkes	Byrne	Gibson	Chilton	Edwards	Berry	Blanchflower	Taylor	Viollet	Rowley
	27/3	*42,735*	*11*	42			*Logie 53, 80, Holton 65*	*Kelsey*	*Wills*	*Smith*	*Dickson*	*Dodgin*	*Forbes*	*Walsh*	*Logie*	*Holton*	*Goring*	*Roper*
							Ref: F Overton	United fail to take advantage of sluggish Arsenal who have won only four home games all season. Jeff Whitefoot can't get leave from the RAF and Edwards has his first poor game as England selectors watch. Blanchflower is in Irish squad and Byrne and Edwards in England 'B' team.										
37	H	CARDIFF	6	L	2-3	1-0	Viollet 30, Rowley 75	Crompton	Foulkes	Redman	Whitefoot	Chilton	Edwards	Berry	Blanchflower	Lewis	Viollet	Rowley
	3/4	24,616	*10*	42			*Grant 77, 87, Sullivan 79*	*Howells*	*Stitfall*	*Sherwood*	*Baker W*	*Montgomery*	*Rutter*	*Tiddy*	*Nugent*	*Grant*	*Sullivan*	*Edwards*
							Ref: R Hall	Cardiff make it six wins in seven with a late smash-and-grab as United go to sleep. Rowley's 30-yard free-kick looks to have won the points, but the menacing Tiddy and Grant's heading are key. Byrne wins his first cap v Scotland and Taylor has an ankle injury. Whole team off form.										
38	A	BLACKPOOL	6	L	0-2	0-1		Crompton	Foulkes	Byrne	Whitefoot	Chilton	Edwards	Berry	Blanchflower	Aston	Viollet	Rowley
	10/4	*25,996*	*8*	42			*Mortensen 21, Perry 57*	*Farm*	*Gratrix*	*Wright*	*Fenton*	*Johnston*	*Kelly*	*Matthews*	*Taylor*	*Mortensen*	*Brown*	*Perry*
							Ref: J McCann	Blackpool, with veteran Matthews back on form, have lost only once in nine. 33-year-old Mortensen is going strong and scores from an acute angle. Aston is a poor stand-in for Taylor who is sorely missed. Ernie Taylor is a box of tricks and the Babes' heads drop after the second goal.										
39	H	CHARLTON	5	W	2-0	0-0	Viollet 61, Aston 70	Crompton	Foulkes	Byrne	Whitefoot	Chilton	Edwards	Gibson	Blanchflower	Aston	Viollet	Pegg
	16/4	33,663	*7*	44				*Bartram*	*Campbell*	*Ellis*	*Fenton*	*Ufton*	*Hammond*	*Hurst*	*Ayre*	*Terry*	*Firmani*	*Kiernan*
							Ref: E Vickery	Sam Bartram's 501st league match is a dire, guileless game. Eddie Firmani misses a penalty. Chilton plays his 134th successive league game and still performs with panache. Pegg gives prospective Scottish cap Campbell a rough ride. Aston makes the first and nets from Pegg's cross.										
40	H	PORTSMOUTH	5	W	2-0	0-0	Blanchflower 48, Viollet 77	Crompton	Foulkes	Byrne	Whitefoot	Chilton	Edwards	Gibson	Blanchflower	Aston	Viollet	Pegg
	17/4	31,426	*16*	46				*Dore*	*Wilson*	*Mansell*	*Gunter*	*Rutter*	*Dickinson*	*Harris*	*Gordon*	*Ames*	*Barnard*	*Dale*
							Ref: W Clapton	Eddie Leavers is rebuilding Pompey but his young team lacks experience. Edwards compares well with England left-half Jimmy Dickinson. Gibson tries hard out of position on the wing and Aston helps his corner on for the first goal. Aston then sets up Dennis Viollet in an easy win.										
41	A	CHARLTON	5	L	0-1	0-0		Crompton	Foulkes	Byrne	Whitefoot	Chilton	Cockburn	Gibson	Blanchflower	Aston	Viollet	Pegg
	19/4	*19,111*	*8*	46			*Firmani 59*	*Bartram*	*Campbell*	*Firmani*	*Hewie*	*Ufton*	*Hammond*	*Hurst*	*Ayre*	*Leary*	*White*	*Kiernan*
							Ref: E Vickery	England manager Winterbottom is at the match and finalising his World Cup squad. Byrne and the absent Taylor will go to Switzerland whilst Chilton is a reserve. Firmani scores after switching to the left wing. Charlton are unbeaten at home since November thanks to a solid defence.										
42	A	SHEFFIELD UTD	4	W	3-1	2-1	Aston 21, Blanchflow' 34, Viollet 48	Crompton	Foulkes	Byrne	Whitefoot	Chilton	Cockburn	Berry	Blanchflower	Aston	Viollet	Rowley
	25/4	*29,189*	*20*	48			*Brook 22*	*Burgin*	*Coldwell*	*Shaw G*	*Shaw J*	*Toner*	*Rawson*	*Ringstead*	*Hoyland*	*Cross*	*Brook*	*Hawksworth*
	Home	Away					Ref: F Read	At the final whistle the dejected Blades think they are relegated but they are saved by Middlesbrough losing at Highbury. Cockburn, deputising for Edwards on Youth Cup duty, is sadly struggling. Crompton saves well twice and Chilton is awesome. Burgin is in the World Cup squad.										
Average	35,458	36,376																

FA Cup

No	Date	Opponents	Att	Pos	Res	F-A	H-T	Scorers, Times, and Referees	1	2	3	4	5	6	7	8	9	10	11
3	A	BURNLEY		6	L	3-5	2-3	Viollet 6, Blanch' 7, Tay' 51 *[Gray 70]*	Wood	Foulkes	Byrne	Whitefoot	Chilton	Edwards	Berry	Blanchflower	Taylor	Viollet	Rowley
	9/1		*52,847*	*5*				*Shannon 1, 18, Holden 5, McIlroy 67,*	*Thompson*	*Aird*	*Mather*	*Adamson*	*Cummings*	*Attwell*	*Gray*	*McIlroy*	*Holden*	*Shannon*	*Pilkington*
								Ref: A Luty	Shannon's 50-second goal sparks a goal-fest with four goals in seven minutes and the Reds come off second best. The fans are breathless after a super match: all the goals come from errors on the muddy pitch. 12,000 United fans see Holden and Pilkington inflict the main damage.										

		Home					Away					
	P	W	D	L	F	A	W	D	L	F	A	Pts
1 Wolves	42	16	1	4	61	25	9	6	6	35	31	57
2 West Brom	42	13	5	3	51	24	9	4	8	35	39	53
3 Huddersfield	42	13	6	2	45	24	7	5	9	33	37	51
4 MAN UNITED	42	11	6	4	41	27	7	6	8	32	31	48
5 Bolton	42	14	6	1	45	20	4	6	11	30	40	48
6 Blackpool	42	13	6	2	43	19	6	4	11	37	50	48
7 Burnley	42	16	2	3	51	23	5	2	14	27	44	46
8 Chelsea	42	12	3	6	45	26	4	9	8	29	42	44
9 Charlton	42	14	4	3	51	26	5	2	14	24	51	44
10 Cardiff	42	12	4	5	32	27	6	4	11	19	44	44
11 Preston	42	12	2	7	43	24	7	3	11	44	34	43
12 Arsenal	42	8	8	5	42	37	7	5	9	33	36	43
13 Aston Villa	42	12	5	4	50	28	4	4	13	20	40	41
14 Portsmouth	42	13	5	3	53	31	1	6	14	28	58	39
15 Newcastle	42	9	2	10	43	40	5	8	8	29	37	38
16 Tottenham	42	11	3	7	38	33	5	2	14	27	43	37
17 Manchester C	42	10	4	7	35	31	4	5	12	27	46	37
18 Sunderland	42	11	4	6	50	37	3	4	14	31	52	36
19 Sheffield Wed	42	12	4	5	43	30	3	2	16	27	61	36
20 Sheffield Utd	42	9	5	7	43	38	2	6	13	26	52	33
21 Middlesbro'	42	6	6	9	29	35	4	4	13	31	56	30
22 Liverpool	42	7	8	6	49	38	2	2	17	19	59	28
	924	254	99	109	983	643	109	99	254	643	983	924

Odds & ends

Double wins: (3) Preston, Sheff Wed, Sunderland.
Double losses: (2) West Brom, Burnley.

Won from behind: (1) Blackpool (h).
Lost from in front: (3) West Brom (a), Arsenal (a), Cardiff (h).

High Spots: The development of the youngsters.
Seven game unbeaten run in the autumn.
The five-goal thrashings of Liverpool and Sheff Wed at Christmas.
The international recognition.

Low spots: The terrible start – the worst since 1930.
The sloppy home defeats to Bolton and Cardiff.
The FA Cup exit at the third round stage.

Sent off: United (0).
Sent off: Opponents (0).

Ever-presents: (1) Chilton.
Hat-tricks: (2) Taylor.
Opposing hat-tricks: (0).
Leading scorer: Taylor (23)

	Appearances		Goals		
	Lge	FAC	Lge	FAC	Tot
Aston, John	12		2		2
Berry, Johnny	37	1	5		5
Blanchflower, Jackie	27	1	13	1	14
Byrne, Roger	41	1	3		3
Chilton, Allenby	42	1	1		1
Cockburn, Henry	18				
Crompton, Jack	15				
Edwards, Duncan	24	1			
Foulkes, Bill	32	1	1		1
Gibson, Don	7				
Lewis, Eddie	6		1		1
McFarlane, Noel	1				
McNulty, Tom	4				
McShane, Harry	9				
Pearson, Stan	11		2		2
Pegg, David	9				
Redman, Billy	1				
Rowley, Jack	36	1	12		12
Taylor, Tommy	35	1	22	1	23
Viollet, Dennis	29	1	11	1	12
Webster, Colin	1				
Whitefoot, Jeff	38	1			
Wood, Ray	27	1			
23 players used	**462**	**11**	**73**	**3**	**76**

No	Date		Att	Pos	Pt	F-A	H-T	Scorers, Times, and Referees	1	2	3	4	5	6	7	8	9	10	11
1	H	PORTSMOUTH			L	1-3	0-1	Rowley 64	Wood	Foulkes	Byrne	Whitefoot	Chilton	Edwards	Berry	Blanchflower	Webster	Viollet	Rowley
	21/8		39,985		0			*Dale 20, Chilton 50(og), Henderson 62*	*Uprichard*	*Wilson*	*Mansell*	*Phillips*	*Reid*	*Pickett*	*Harris*	*Gordon*	*Henderson*	*Barnard*	*Dale*
								Ref: B Buckle	Despite Dickinson's injury, Pompey have too much for United's kids who try to play football on a swamplike pitch caused by heavy thunderstorms. Dale is deadly, scoring off the upright and hitting the post for Henderson to follow-up. In between, Chilton slices in a corner.										
2	A	SHEFFIELD WED			W	4-2	2-1	Viollet 4, 9, Blanchflower 61, 84	Wood	Foulkes	Byrne	Whitefoot	Chilton	Edwards	Berry	Blanchflower	Webster	Viollet	Rowley
	23/8		*33,983*		2			*Shaw 30, Curtis 60p*	*Ryalls*	*Kenny*	*Curtis*	*Gannon*	*O'Donnell*	*Davies*	*Finney*	*Quixall*	*Shaw*	*Sewell*	*Marriott*
								Ref: W Heselton	The early lead is wiped out by gritty Wednesday, until Blanchflower takes over. He is unmarked for a header and hits a 40-yarder that Ryalls is at fault for. A sloppy defence is at sea for a spell and Edwards fouls Albert Quixall for the penalty. Berry is deadly and Curtis can't handle him.										
3	A	BLACKPOOL		8	W	4-2	4-1	Webster 16, 33 Blanch' 18, Viollet 26	Wood	Foulkes	Byrne	Whitefoot	Chilton	Edwards	Berry	Blanchflower	Webster	Viollet	Rowley
	28/8		*31,855*	*15*	4			*Mortensen 20, Fenton 64*	*Farm*	*Shimwell*	*Garrett*	*Fenton*	*Johnston*	*Kelly H*	*Matthews*	*Taylor*	*Mortensen*	*Brown*	*Withers*
								Ref: A Jones	A large holiday crowd in sunny weather watches United dazzle in the first half. Matthews leads a Pool revival in vain, but Fenton's 30-yarder is a stunner. Harry Johnston and Co don't know who to mark as the Reds come at them from all angles. The injured Taylor is not missed.										
4	H	SHEFFIELD WED		5	W	2-0	2-0	Viollet 8, 26	Wood	Foulkes	Byrne	Whitefoot	Chilton	Edwards	Berry	Blanchflower	Webster	Viollet	Rowley
	1/9		31,371	*16*	6				*McIntosh*	*Conwell*	*Curtis*	*Gannon*	*O'Donnell*	*Davies*	*Finney*	*Quixall*	*Shaw*	*Sewell*	*Froggatt*
								Ref: W Heselton	McIntosh replaces Ryalls and plays well on a sweltering evening. Dennis Viollet's work-rate is rewarded with two rebounds and he is well supported by Rowley. United take their foot off the pedal and Wednesday look dangerous for a time but United's half-back line is superb.										
5	H	CHARLTON		3	W	3-1	1-0	Rowley 15, 83, Taylor 53	Wood	Foulkes	Byrne	Whitefoot	Chilton	Edwards	Berry	Blanchflower	Taylor	Viollet	Rowley
	4/9		39,968	*14*	8			*Fenton 89*	*Bartram*	*Townsend*	*Firmani*	*Fenton*	*Chamberlain*	*Hammond*	*Hurst*	*O'Linn*	*Leary*	*White*	*Kiernan*
								Ref: R Leafe	No London club has won at Old Trafford since the war and Charlton never look like stopping United going joint top. Sam Bartram, in his 20th season is the hero and gets a standing ovation. Taylor tires on his return but when his shot is saved by Bartram Gunner Jack whacks in his first.										
6	A	TOTTENHAM		1	W	2-0	1-0	Berry 5, Webster 57	Wood	Foulkes	Byrne	Whitefoot	Chilton	Edwards	Berry	Blanchflower	Webster	Viollet	Rowley
	8/9		*35,162*	*16*	10				*Ditchburn*	*Ramsey*	*Hopkins*	*Woods*	*Clarke*	*Brittan*	*Walters*	*Harmer*	*Dunmore*	*Baily*	*Robb*
								Ref: R Smith	The London scribes get their first glimpse of the Reds and are impressed. Chelsea boss Ted Drake describes them as a 'great side'. Spurs boss Arthur Rowe commends their 'delightful football'. It is a slick display and several Reds, including the sturdy Edwards, are tipped for England.										
7	A	BOLTON		2	D	1-1	0-0	Webster 88	Wood	Foulkes	Byrne	Whitefoot	Chilton	Edwards	Berry	Blanchflower	Webster	Viollet	Rowley
	11/9		*50,708*	*8*	11			*Lofthouse 85*	*Hanson*	*Ball*	*Banks T*	*Wheeler*	*Barrass*	*Edwards*	*Holden*	*Moir*	*Lofthouse*	*Hassall*	*Webster*
								Ref: A Webb	Chilton is 36 next week but is so good he is tipped for England again! He tears down the middle and sets up Colin Webster's goal that cancels out Nat Lofthouse's header. Otherwise it's a disappointing game after a lot of hype, with only Doug Holden of Bolton's star front-line on form.										
8	H	TOTTENHAM		1	W	2-1	2-1	Rowley 5, Viollet 18	Wood	Foulkes	Byrne	Whitefoot	Chilton	Edwards	Berry	Blanchflower	Taylor	Viollet	Rowley
	15/9		31,041	*18*	13			*McClellan 14*	*Ditchburn*	*Ramsey*	*Hopkins*	*Woods*	*King*	*Brittan*	*McClellan*	*Harmer*	*Duquemin*	*Baily*	*Robb*
								Ref: R Smith	Arthur Rowe is under pressure as Spurs make it six without a win. United don't seem to click but Edwards is sublime, defending like a demon and creating openings for his forwards. Foulkes is also in form and Taylor comes through without any problems. Many late fans miss the goals.										
9	H	HUDDERSFIELD		1	D	1-1	1-0	Viollet 44	Wood	Foulkes	Byrne	Whitefoot	Chilton	Edwards	Berry	Blanchflower	Taylor	Viollet	Rowley
	18/9		47,496	*13*	14			*Cavanagh 71*	*Wheeler*	*Staniforth*	*Kelly*	*McGarry*	*Taylor*	*Quested*	*Burrell*	*Watson*	*Glazzard*	*Cavanagh*	*Metcalfe*
								Ref: H Beacock	England's selectors are unimpressed by the Reds' worst performance of the season against a rough Town. United miss three good chances in the first ten minutes and rely on Viollet again. England full-back Ron Staniforth has Rowley in his pocket and Tommy Taylor looks rusty.										
10	A	MANCHESTER C		3	L	2-3	1-2	Taylor 28, Blanchflower 86	Wood	Foulkes	Byrne	Gibson	Chilton	Edwards	Berry	Blanchflower	Taylor	Viollet	Rowley
	25/9		*54,105*	*5*	14			*McAdams 9, Fagan 21, Hart 83*	*Trautmann*	*Meadows*	*Little*	*Barnes*	*Ewing*	*Paul*	*Fagan*	*McAdams*	*Revie*	*Hart*	*Clarke*
								Ref: G Black	Two points separate the top seven teams and City, unusually, are up there. They deservedly win and the Revie plan, with Don in a deep-lying role, is the key. McAdams heads in Johnny Hart's lob after a glorious move. United, pushing up for an equaliser, are caught out for the third.										

No	Venue	Opponent	Pos	Res	F-A	H-T	Scorers, Times, and Referees	1	2	3	4	5	6	7	8	9	10	11
11	A	WOLVERHAMPTON	7	L	2-4	1-0	Viollet 25, Rowley 73 [Cock' 87(og)]	Crompton	**Greaves**	**Kennedy**	Gibson	Chilton	Cockburn	Berry	Edwards	Taylor	Viollet	Rowley
	2/10	*39,617*	*6*	14			*Swinb' 70, Broad' 77, Hancocks 84,*	*Williams*	*Stuart*	*Shorthouse*	*Flowers*	*Russell*	*Clamp*	*Hancocks*	*Broadbent*	*Swinbourne*	*Deeley*	*Wilshaw*
							Ref: J Sherlock	Wood, Foulkes and Byrne are playing for England, as is Billy Wright, but Edwards is not ready yet. The stand-ins are exposed by Wolves' darting wingers and Chilton's knock hampers United, but the score is flattering to Wolves. Debutant Russell wins a sluggish Taylor over.										
12	H	CARDIFF	4	W	5-2	2-1	Taylor 30, 42, 59, 67, Viollet 60	Wood	Foulkes	Byrne	Gibson	Chilton	Edwards	Berry	Blanchflower	Taylor	Viollet	Rowley
	9/10	41,159	*13*	16			*Ford 10, Stockin 85*	*Howells*	*Stitfall*	*Sherwood*	*Harrington*	*Montgomery*	*Jones*	*Tiddy*	*Sullivan*	*Ford*	*Stockin*	*Nugent*
							Ref: F Stringer	Cardiff, unbeaten in seven, bring a large support, some of whom plant a leek on the centre-spot. After a bright Cardiff opening, Taylor hits top form as the free-roaming Berry and Rowley torture the visitors. Edwards is in a Football League XI. Bill Foulkes gives up his job as a miner.										
13	A	CHELSEA	1	W	6-5	3-2	Viol' 15,41,57, Tay' 38,47, Blanch' 63	Wood	Foulkes	Byrne	Gibson	Chilton	Edwards	Berry	Blanchflower	Taylor	Viollet	Rowley
	16/10	*55,966*	*11*	18			*O'Con' 20, 67, 76, Lewis 35, Arm' 61*	*Robertson*	*Harris*	*Willemse*	*Armstrong*	*Greenwood*	*Saunders*	*Parsons*	*McNichol*	*Bentley*	*O'Connell*	*Lewis*
							Ref: R Mann	United shade a wonderful action-packed game. Chelsea, with classy amateurs Jim Lewis and Seamus O'Connell, the latter scoring a debut hat-trick, are woeful in defence. United's back-line is little better, but Ray Wood's late save from Derek Saunders' free-kick partially redeems him.										
14	H	NEWCASTLE	1	D	2-2	0-1	Scoular 52 (og),Taylor 57	Wood	Foulkes	Byrne	Gibson	Chilton	Edwards	Berry	Blanchflower	Taylor	Viollet	Rowley
	23/10	31,071	*13*	19			*Broadis 17, Mitchell 75*	*Thompson*	*Cowell*	*McMichael*	*Scoular*	*Paterson*	*Crowe*	*Milburn*	*Broadis*	*White*	*Curry*	*Mitchell*
							Ref: E Oxley	Newcastle are without a win in six games but debutant third-choice keeper John Thompson makes three great saves. Bobby Mitchell destroys Bill Foulkes, sets up Broadis' header, and taps in after Scoular's freak shot hit the bar. Taylor's acute shot bounces off Scoular and Thompson.										
15	A	EVERTON	5	L	2-4	2-2	Rowley 10, Taylor 20	Wood	Foulkes	Byrne	Gibson	Chilton	Edwards	Berry	Blanchflower	Taylor	Viollet	Rowley
	30/10	***63,021***	*3*	19			*Hick' 11, Jones 30p, 85p, Egling' 65*	*O'Neill*	*Moore*	*Donovan*	*Farrell*	*Jones*	*Lello*	*McNamara*	*Wainwright*	*Hickson*	*Parker*	*Eglington*
							Ref: F Gerrard	Cliff Britton's side are having their best season since the war and United suffer their first defeat at Goodison since 1949. Edwards concedes two penalties, one for a foul, the other a handball. Eglington runs the length of the pitch for a brilliant goal. Henry Cockburn has gone to Bury.										
16	H	PRESTON	3	W	2-1	1-1	Viollet 44, 75	Wood	Foulkes	Byrne	Gibson	Chilton	Edwards	Berry	Blanchflower	Taylor	Viollet	Rowley
	6/11	31,902	*8*	21			*Baxter 10*	*Thompson*	*Wilson*	*Walton*	*Dunn*	*Marston*	*Forbes*	*Finney*	*Hatsell*	*Higham*	*Baxter*	*Morrison*
							Ref: T Seymour	Preston are fresh from a 6-0 thumping of Sheff Wednesday and are the classier team. United's passing is awry on a rain-drenched pitch but they still create and miss a ton of chances. Viollet makes it fourteen goals with a hook-shot over his shoulder and smacks home a loose ball.										
17	A	SHEFFIELD UTD	5	L	0-3	0-0		Wood	Foulkes	Byrne	Gibson	Chilton	Edwards	Berry	Blanchflower	Taylor	Viollet	Rowley
	13/11	*26,076*	*17*	21			*Grainger 70, Cross 75, Hagan 83*	*Burgin*	*Furniss*	*Shaw G*	*Hoyland*	*Shaw J*	*Fountain*	*Ringstead*	*Hagan*	*Cross*	*Waldock*	*Grainger*
							Ref: H Hawthorne	The Blades are unbeaten in six and Burgin is pressing for Wood's England place. The Reds try to walk the ball through the mud whilst the Blades hoof the ball. Long clearances catch Chilton and Co out of position for all three, with Hagan's delightful lob bringing the house down.										
18	H	ARSENAL	3	W	2-1	0-1	Taylor 60, Blanchflower 87	Wood	Foulkes	Byrne	Gibson	Chilton	**Goodwin**	Berry	Blanchflower	Taylor	Viollet	**Scanlon**
	20/11	35,230	*20*	23			*Tapscott 32*	*Kelsey*	*Wills*	*Wade*	*Goring*	*Fotheringham*	*Bowen*	*Milton*	*Logie*	*Tapscott*	*Lishman*	*Roper*
							Ref: H Beacock	Five defeats in six is unheard of for Arsenal, and they haven't won at United since the war. Edwards is on Youth international duty. The first half is dire but Busby gees them up with Gibson leading the charge in a storming finish. Taylor nods in and Gibson's centre creates the winner.										
19	A	WEST BROM	5	L	0-2	0-1		Wood	Foulkes	Byrne	Gibson	Chilton	Edwards	Berry	Blanchflower	Taylor	Viollet	Scanlon
	27/11	*33,095*	*9*	23			*Nicholls44, Allen 78p*	*Sanders*	*Rickaby*	*Millard*	*Dudley*	*Kennedy*	*Williams*	*Griffin*	*Ryan*	*Allen*	*Nicholls*	*Carter*
							Ref: R Wood	United fail to take advantage of the wind in the first half and are punished by the Cup holders with their long-ball game. Chilton's error lets in Johnny Nicholls and the unsighted Edwards handballs again. The Reds' critics argue that they can't play in the mud and the facts support them.										
20	H	LEICESTER	3	W	3-1	2-1	Webster 17, Rowley 42, Viollet 70	Wood	Foulkes	Byrne	Gibson	Chilton	Whitefoot	Berry	Blanchflower	Webster	Viollet	Rowley
	4/12	21,173	*20*	25			*Hines 20*	*Anderson*	*Milburn*	*Jackson*	*Baldwin*	*Froggatt*	*Russell*	*Griffiths*	*Morris*	*Hines*	*Rowley*	*Hogg*
							Ref: J Topliss	United master gale-force winds a glue-pot pitch to beat newly promoted Leicester. Norman Bullock's team are hampered by Hines' injury after his wonderful solo effort and poor displays from ex-Red Morris and Jack's brother Arthur. Duncan Edwards is out with a boil on his ankle.										
21	A	BURNLEY	3	W	4-2	0-1	Webster 47, 57, 84, Viollet 88	Wood	Foulkes	**Bent**	Gibson	Chilton	Whitefoot	Berry	Blanchflower	Webster	Viollet	Rowley
	11/12	*24,967*	*15*	27			*Holden 14, Gray 70*	*McDonald*	*Rudman*	*Winton*	*Seith*	*Cummings*	*Shannon*	*Gray*	*Cheesebrough*	*Holden*	*McIlroy*	*Pilkington*
							Ref: R Wood	Burnley's former player Alan Brown is now manager, overseeing a period of change. With the fog and failing light, few spectators see the last two goals as the home defence collapses. Byrne has carbuncles on his neck but his deputy Bent is cool. Wood and Foulkes are impressive too.										

No	Date	Opponent	Att	Pos	Pt	F-A	H-T	Scorers, Times, and Referees	1	2	3	4	5	6	7	8	9	10	11
22	A	PORTSMOUTH		3	D	0-0	0-0		Wood	Foulkes	Byrne	Gibson	Chilton	Edwards	Berry	Blanchflower	Webster	Viollet	Rowley
	18/12		26,020	7	28				Uprichard	McGhee	Mansell	Phillips	Reid	Pickett	Harris	Gordon	Henderson	Barnard	Dale
								Ref: B Buckle	The fog clears to leave perfect sunshine, but England boss Winterbottom is unimpressed. Pompey, as ever, are hard to beat at home and United haven't won there since 1947. Reid pockets Webster, who misses his only chance. At the death Dale is through but shoots straight at Wood.										
23	H	ASTON VILLA		7	L	0-1	0-1		Wood	Foulkes	Byrne	Gibson	Chilton	Edwards	Berry	Blanchflower	Webster	Viollet	Rowley
	27/12		50,941	20	28			Dixon 20	Jones	Lynn	Aldis	Moss A	Moss F	Crowe	Southren	Thompson	Dixon	Follan	Lockhart
								Ref: J Sherlock	Villa are the Christmas Scrooges with their first win at Old Trafford since 1930. United's attack is woeful and Johnny Dixon scores off the post when Wood drops Lockhart's corner. Southren, signed from West Ham, is impressive for Eric Houghton's team. Taylor sorely missed.										
24	A	ASTON VILLA		7	L	1-2	0-1	Taylor 70	Wood	Foulkes	Byrne	Gibson	Chilton	Edwards	Berry	Webster	Taylor	Viollet	Pegg
	28/12		48,718	17	28			Dixon 25, Lockhart 80	Jones	Lynn	Aldis	Moss A	Martin	Crowe	Southren	Thompson	Dixon	Follan	Lockhart
								Ref: J Sherlock	The first reverse at Villa since 1949 and undeserved. All the play is in Villa's half but the finishing is poor. Dixon latches onto Foulkes' back-pass and then superbly dummies for the second. Taylor, back from a worrying ankle injury, heads a wonderful equaliser. Rowley dropped.										
25	H	BLACKPOOL		5	W	4-1	2-0	Blanch' 20, 89, Viollet 34, Edwards 78	Wood	Foulkes	Byrne	Gibson	Chilton	Edwards	Berry	Blanchflower	Taylor	Viollet	Pegg
	1/1		54,774	20	30			Perry 80	Farm	Armfield	Gratrix	Fenton	Johnston	Kelly H	Matthews	Taylor	Mortensen	Mudie	Perry
								Ref: A Jones	A white ball is in use for the poor light, but it is one of the best displays of the season. Blackpool, with Matthews playing at Old Trafford for the first time since 1950, fade after a promising start. Edwards finally gets his first goal, a cannonball from 25 yards which raises the roof.										
26	H	BOLTON		3	D	1-1	0-0	Taylor 47	Wood	Foulkes	Byrne	Gibson	Chilton	Edwards	Berry	Blanchflower	Taylor	Viollet	Rowley
	22/1		41,719	17	31			Stevens 57	Hanson	Ball	Edwards	Wheeler	Barrass	Bell	Holden	Moir	Lofthouse	Stevens	Parry
								Ref: H Webb	The two candidates for the England No 9 shirt are both impressive until Taylor limps off near the end with a muscle strain. The pitch and the tackling is heavy and the ref blunders by blowing four minutes early. Several Bolton players are getting in the bath before they are recalled.										
27	A	HUDDERSFIELD		3	W	3-1	3-0	Pegg 15, Edwards 35, Berry 40	Wood	Foulkes	Byrne	Gibson	Chilton	Whitefoot	Berry	Blanchflower	Webster	Edwards	Pegg
	5/2		31,408	9	33			Glazzard 90	Wheeler	Staniforth	Quested	McGarry	Taylor	Connor	Hobson	Watson	Glazzard	Cavanagh	Metcalfe
								Ref: H Beacock	After four draws in a row Town are mesmerised by United's eight home-grown players. The left wing pairing inflict the early damage, with Pegg's ground shot and Edwards' cannonball. United sit back later and soak up minimal Town pressure. Jack Rowley is set to join Plymouth.										
28	H	MANCHESTER C		6	L	**0-5**	0-1		Wood	Foulkes	Byrne	Gibson	Chilton	Whitefoot	Berry	Blanchflower	Webster	Edwards	Pegg
	12/2		49,733	4	33			Hart 15, Fagan 58, 89, Hayes 62, 69	Trautmann	Meadows	Little	Barnes	Ewing	Paul	Fagan	Hayes	Revie	Hart	Clarke
								Ref: G Black	City are in dazzling form and with three points separating the top six they look worth a flutter for the League and Cup double. Hart's goal, following a six-man move, is exquisite, but United are on top until the break. Revie's plan works as Joe Hayes scores his seventh in six games.										
29	H	WOLVERHAMPTON		6	L	2-4	2-1	Taylor 36, Edwards 38 [Wilshaw 82]	Wood	Foulkes	Byrne	Gibson	Chilton	Whitefoot	Webster	Viollet	Taylor	Edwards	Pegg
	23/2		**17,534**	1	33			Flowers 17, Smith 48, Hancocks 73,	Sims	Stuart	Shorthouse	Flowers	Wright	Clamp	Hancocks	Broadbent	Swinbourne	Wilshaw	Smith
								Ref: A Ellis	The midweek afternoon kick-off and the bitter cold means the gate is the lowest since 1950. The snow-covered pitch has red markings and United are on top until Taylor and Edwards are injured and the defence is wide open. The hungry Wolves go for the jugular and win with style.										
30	A	CARDIFF		8	L	0-3	0-1		Wood	Foulkes	Byrne	Gibson	Jones	Whitefoot	Webster	Viollet	Taylor	Edwards	Pegg
	26/2		16,329	15	33			Stockin 30, 60, Nutt 73	Howells	Rutter	Gale	Harrington	Montgomery	Sullivan	Nutt	Williams	Ford	Stockin	Northcott
								Ref: F Stringer	After 175 successive games, Chilton asks to be rested. His deputy, Mark Jones, is given a rough ride by Welsh striker Trevor Ford, who has a hand in all three goals. Byrne and Wood both make boobs and Ron Stockin's goal looks offside, but under-strength Cardiff deserve the win.										
31	H	BURNLEY		7	W	1-0	0-0	Edwards 66	Wood	Foulkes	Byrne	Gibson	Jones	Whitefoot	Berry	Taylor	Webster	Edwards	Scanlon
	5/3		33,577	9	35				McDonald	Rudman	Winton	Adamson	Cummings	Shannon	Gray	McIlroy	Holden	Walton	Scott
								Ref: E Hill	With an average age of 21½, it is United's youngest ever team. Colin McDonald saves three certain goals in the first ten minutes and, whilst Burnley miss chances, a draw would have been an injustice. United's defence looks more solid and keeps a clean sheet for the first game in 12.										

32	H	EVERTON		9	L	1·2	1·1	Scanlon 14	Wood	Foulkes	Byrne	Gibson	Jones	Whitefoot	Berry	Taylor	Webster	Edwards	Scanlon
	19/3		34,152	*6*	35			*Parker 40, Eglington 50*	*O'Neill*	*Moore*	*Donovan*	*Farrell*	*Jones*	*Lello*	*McNamara*	*Fielding*	*Hickson*	*Parker*	*Eglington*
								Ref: F Gerrard	Everton have lost once in nine and win at United for the first time since 1939. Eglington again torments Foulkes and United in general and his shot nutmegs Wood. Fielding's glorious pass sets up Parker. Scanlon's first ever goal is off a post. Chilton moves to Grimsby as player-boss.										
33	A	PRESTON		8	W	2·0	1·0	Scanlon 14, Byrne 60p	Wood	Foulkes	Byrne	Gibson	Jones	Whitefoot	Berry	**Whelan**	Taylor	Edwards	Scanlon
	26/3		*13,328*	*11*	37				*Thompson*	*Cunningham*	*Walton*	*Docherty*	*Marston*	*Forbes*	*Campbell*	*Foster*	*Evans*	*Baxter*	*Morrison*
								Ref: T Seymour	Edwards is back from England 'B' duty and praying for a full call-up. He and Scanlon are outstanding, whilst Billy Whelan has a good debut. United's first penalty for 68 games is slotted home by new captain, Byrne. Finney is injured and his 18-year-old deputy, Les Campbell, tires.										
34	H	SHEFFIELD UTD		4	W	**5·0**	1·0	Taylor 17, 65, Berry 66, Viollet 73, [Whelan 86]	Wood	Foulkes	Bent	Gibson	Jones	Whitefoot	Berry	Whelan	Taylor	Viollet	Scanlon
	2/4		22,952	*16*	39				*Burgin*	*Coldwell*	*Shaw G*	*Fountain*	*Johnson*	*Iley*	*Cross*	*Hoyland*	*Hawksworth*	*Hagan*	*Grainger*
								Ref: H Hawthorne	Edwards is at Wembley against Scotland, the youngest England player of the century, and not missed. On a pitch like a paddy-field, Tommy Taylor is back to his best and supported confidently by Whelan. It is men against boys, with the superb Eddie Burgin keeping the score down.										
35	A	SUNDERLAND		6	L	3·4	2·1	Edwards 16, 52, Scanlon 44	Wood	Foulkes	Byrne	Gibson	Jones	Whitefoot	Berry	Whelan	Taylor	Edwards	Scanlon
	8/4		*43,882*	*5*	39			*Chisholm 26, 49, 51, Anderson 86*	*Fraser*	*Hedley*	*McDonald*	*Anderson*	*Daniel*	*Aitken*	*Bingham*	*Shackleton*	*Purdon*	*Chisholm*	*Elliott*
								Ref: F Coultas	Sunderland bounce back from their Cup semi-final defeat to win a classic, their first home win for 18 weeks. Ken Chisholm scores three headers and also hits the bar. Elliott and Bingham provide the crosses. Anderson misses a penalty after he is fouled, but atones with the winner.										
36	A	LEICESTER		8	L	0·1	0·1		Crompton	Foulkes	Byrne	Gibson	Jones	Whitefoot	Berry	Whelan	Taylor	Edwards	Scanlon
	9/4		*34,634*	*21*	39			*Froggatt 30*	*Anderson*	*Milburn*	*Cunningham*	*Baldwin*	*Fincham*	*Russell*	*Hogg*	*Morris*	*Hines*	*Graver*	*Froggatt*
								Ref: J Topliss	A sunny Easter Saturday sees a capacity crowd and relegation-haunted City grab a vital win. Edwards is targeted with some vicious tackles. Wood is axed in favour of 34-year-old Crompton. Arthur Rowley misses his first game for three years and expensive flop Andy Graver plays.										
37	H	SUNDERLAND		7	D	2·2	1·2	Taylor 2, Byrne 80p	Crompton	Foulkes	Byrne	Gibson	Jones	Whitefoot	Berry	Whelan	Taylor	Edwards	Scanlon
	11/4		43,882	*6*	40			*Chisholm 20, Bingham 43*	*Fraser*	*Hedley*	*McDonald*	*Anderson*	*Daniel*	*Aitken*	*Bingham*	*Shackleton*	*Fleming*	*Chisholm*	*Elliott*
								Ref: F Coultas	In a wind-spoilt game, United grab their only Easter point with Byrne's penalty after Welsh international Ray Daniel, back after injury, fouled Taylor. Taylor had headed in Scanlon's corner before Len Shackleton's magic set up Chisholm. This is Sunderland's 18th draw of the season.										
38	H	WEST BROM		6	W	3·0	1·0	Taylor 43, 85, Viollet 82	Crompton	Foulkes	Byrne	Goodwin	Jones	Whitefoot	Berry	Whelan	Taylor	Viollet	Scanlon
	16/4		26,568	*12*	42				*Sanders*	*Williams*	*Millard*	*Dudley*	*Kennedy*	*Brookes*	*Griffin*	*Carter*	*Allen*	*Barlow*	*Lee*
								Ref: R Wood	Duncan Edwards is helping win the Youth Cup again, and Gibson is injured. Freddie Goodwin and Dennis Viollet step in with no effect on United's slick form. Albion are not the power they were last season, but two goals flatter the Reds. Tommy Taylor is back in England form.										
39	A	NEWCASTLE		7	L	0·2	0·0		Crompton	Foulkes	Byrne	Gibson	Jones	Whitefoot	Berry	Whelan	Taylor	Viollet	Scanlon
	18/4		*35,569*	*11*	42			*Hannah 52, White 69*	*Simpson*	*Cowell*	*Batty*	*Scoular*	*Stokoe*	*Crowe*	*White*	*Davies*	*Keeble*	*Hannah*	*Mitchell*
								Ref: E Oxley	Newcastle will play Man City at Wembley in two weeks and are sharp on a heavily watered pitch. Gibson is on the transfer list after becoming engaged to Busby's daughter. Mitchell is the star. Hannah's near-post header from his free-kick and White's shot from his corner are enough.										
40	A	ARSENAL		6	W	3·2	2·2	Blanchflower 6, 60, Goring 30 (og)	Wood	Foulkes	Byrne	Gibson	Jones	Goodwin	Berry	Blanchflower	Taylor	Viollet	Scanlon
	23/4		*42,751*	*7*	44			*Lishman 3, 9*	*Kelsey*	*Wills*	*Evans*	*Goring*	*Fotheringham*	*Oakes*	*Clapton*	*Tapscott*	*Roper*	*Lishman*	*Bloomfield*
								Ref: H Beacock	Seven straight wins have got Whittaker's Arsenal out of trouble and they start like a train. On the day Chelsea clinch the title, United are still fighting for top-four talent money. Goring's driven back-pass goes in. The recalled Blanchflower is deadly, but Tapscott almost grabs a point.										
41	A	CHARLTON		6	D	1·1	1·1	Viollet 4	Wood	Foulkes	Byrne	Gibson	Jones	Goodwin	Berry	Blanchflower	Taylor	Viollet	Scanlon
	26/4		***13,139***	*13*	45			*O'Linn 34*	*Bartram*	*Campbell*	*Townsend*	*Hewie*	*Ufton*	*Pembery*	*Hurst*	*O'Linn*	*Leary*	*Firmani*	*Kiernan*
								Ref: R Leafe	The rearranged game has a Tuesday afternoon kick-off, thus the low gate. Charlton have gone twelve without a win and never look like ending the run. A bone-hard pitch ruins the game but Taylor and Berry come closest to winning it. Jones and Fred Goodwin look solid in defence.										
42	H	CHELSEA		5	W	2·1	1·0	Scanlon 34, Taylor 85	Wood	Foulkes	Byrne	Gibson	Jones	Goodwin	Berry	Blanchflower	Taylor	Viollet	Scanlon
	30/4		34,933	*1*	47			*Bentley 82*	*Thomson*	*Sillett P*	*Willemse*	*Armstrong*	*Wicks*	*Saunders*	*Parsons*	*McNichol*	*Bentley*	*O'Connell*	*Blunstone*
		Home	Away					Ref: R Mann	The champions are given a guard of honour and a noisy acclaim but their 10-match unbeaten run ends in a tea-party atmosphere. Scanlon's run and shot hits the angle and goes in. Bentley nods in England winger Blunstone's cross. Viollet's delicious pass sets up Taylor for a just result.										
Average		35,960	35,921																

FA Cup																			
3	A	READING		5	D	1-1	0-1	Webster 85	Wood	Foulkes	Byrne	Gibson	Chilton	Edwards	Berry	Blanchflower	Webster	Viollet	Rowley
	8/1		26,500	*3S:20*				*Chilton 22 (og)*	*Meeson*	*Penford*	*Leach*	*Davis*	*Livingstone*	*McLaren*	*Simpson*	*Hinshelwood*	*Campbell*	*Uphill*	*Mansell*
								Ref: F Coultas	Reading have lost four games since the draw, but give the Reds a massive shock. With Campbell and Mansell to the fore, United's defence are forced into blunders and Chilton nets trying to clear from Uphill. Hinshelwood misses three good chances before Webster rescues lucky Reds.										
3R	H	READING		5	W	4-1	1-0	Webster 36, 62, Viollet 53, Rowley 64	Wood	Foulkes	Byrne	Gibson	Chilton	Edwards	Berry	Blanchflower	Webster	Viollet	Rowley
	12/1		24,578	*3S:20*				*Uphill 84p*	*Meeson*	*Penford*	*Leach*	*Davis*	*Livingstone*	*McLaren*	*Simpson*	*Hinshelwood*	*Campbell*	*Uphill*	*Mansell*
								Ref: F Coultas	United master the ice-rink conditions better than Arthur Smith's Reading and it's all over soon after the break. Many away fans arrive at half-time after train delays and many United fans leave in the second half as a snowstorm descends. Veteran Jack Rowley shows he can still shoot.										
4	A	MANCHESTER C		3	L	0-2	0-0		Wood	Foulkes	Byrne	Gibson	Chilton !	Edwards	Berry	Blanchflower	Taylor	Viollet	Rowley
	29/1		74,723	*8*				*Hayes 65, Revie 89*	*Trautmann*	*Meadows*	*Little*	*Barnes*	*Ewing*	*Paul*	*Fagan*	*Hayes*	*Revie*	*Hart*	*Clarke*
								Ref: E Oxley	The interest in the match is phenomenal and it is the largest Manchester derby gate ever. City bamboozle United again with Hart's jinking run setting up Hayes and Clarke's dummy leaving Revie to ram home. Chilton falls on Hart and his dismissal, United's first since 1949, is baffling.										

		Home					Away					
	P	W	D	L	F	A	W	D	L	F	A	Pts
1 Chelsea	42	11	5	5	43	29	9	7	5	38	28	52
2 Wolves	42	13	5	3	58	30	6	5	10	31	40	48
3 Portsmouth	42	13	5	3	44	21	5	7	9	30	41	48
4 Sunderland	42	8	11	2	39	27	7	7	7	25	27	48
5 MAN UNITED	42	12	4	5	44	30	8	3	10	40	44	47
6 Aston Villa	42	11	3	7	38	31	9	4	8	34	42	47
7 Manchester C	42	11	5	5	45	36	7	5	9	31	33	46
8 Newcastle	42	12	5	4	53	27	5	4	12	36	50	43
9 Arsenal	42	12	3	6	44	25	5	6	10	25	38	43
10 Burnley	42	11	3	7	29	19	6	6	9	22	29	43
11 Everton	42	9	6	6	32	24	7	4	10	30	44	42
12 Huddersfield	42	10	4	7	28	23	4	9	8	35	45	41
13 Sheffield Utd	42	10	3	8	41	34	7	4	10	29	52	41
14 Preston	42	8	5	8	47	33	8	3	10	36	31	40
15 Charlton	42	8	6	7	43	34	7	4	10	33	41	40
16 Tottenham	42	9	4	8	42	35	7	4	10	30	38	40
17 West Brom	42	11	5	5	44	33	5	3	13	32	63	40
18 Bolton	42	11	6	4	45	29	2	7	12	17	40	39
19 Blackpool	42	8	6	7	33	26	6	4	11	27	38	38
20 Cardiff	42	9	4	8	41	38	4	7	10	21	38	37
21 Leicester	42	9	6	6	43	32	3	5	13	31	54	35
22 Sheffield Wed	42	7	7	7	42	38	1	3	17	21	62	26
	924	223	111	128	918	654	128	111	223	654	918	924

Odds & ends

Double wins: (7) Sheff Wed, Blackpool, Tottenham, Chelsea, Burnley, Preston, Arsenal.
Double losses: (4) Aston Villa, Man City, Wolves, Everton.

Won from behind: (6) Cardiff (h), Chelsea (a), Preston (h), Arsenal (h), Burnley (a), Arsenal (a).
Lost from in front: (4) Wolves (a), Everton (a), Wolves (h), Everton (h), Sunderland (a).

High spots: Double win over the eventual champions, Chelsea.
Eight game unbeaten run at start of the season.
Dazzling form of Duncan Edwards.
Six more youth players blooded.

Low spots: Home hammering and Cup exit to Man City.
Suspect form on heavy pitches.

Sent off: United (1) Chilton (Man City FAC a).
Sent off: Opponents (0).

Ever-presents: (0).
Hat-tricks: (3) Taylor, Viollet & Webster.
Opposing hat-tricks: (2) O'Connell (Chelsea) & Chisholm (Sunderland).
Leading scorer: Taylor (22).

	Appearances		Goals		
	Lge	FAC	Lge	FAC	Tot
Bent, Geoff	**2**				
Berry, Johnny	**40**	3	**3**		**3**
Blanchflower, Jackie	**29**	3	**10**		**10**
Byrne, Roger	**39**	3	**2**		**2**
Chilton, Allenby	**29**	3			
Cockburn, Henry	**1**				
Crompton, Jack	**5**				
Edwards, Duncan	**33**	3	**6**		**6**
Foulkes, Bill	**41**	3			
Gibson, Don	**32**	3			
Goodwin, Freddie	**5**				
Greaves, Ian	**1**				
Jones, Mark	**13**				
Kennedy, Paddy	**1**				
Pegg, David	**6**		**1**		**1**
Rowley, Jack	**22**	3	**7**	1	**8**
Scanlon, Albert	**14**		**4**		**4**
Taylor, Tommy	**30**	1	**20**		**20**
Viollet, Dennis	**34**	3	**20**	1	**21**
Webster, Colin	**17**	2	**8**	3	**11**
Whelan, Billy	**7**		**1**		**1**
Whitefoot, Jeff	**24**				
Wood, Ray	**37**	3			
(own-goals)			**2**		**2**
23 players used	**462**	**33**	**84**	**5**	**89**

No	Date		Att	Pos	Pt	F-A	H-T	Scorers, Times, and Referees	1	2	3	4	5	6	7	8	9	10	11
1	A	BIRMINGHAM			D	2-2	1-0	Viollet 31, 82	Wood	Foulkes	Byrne	Whitefoot	Jones	Edwards	Webster	Blanchflower	Taylor	Viollet	Scanlon
	20/8		*37,612*		1			*Kinsey 63, Astall 84*	*Merrick*	*Hall*	*Green*	*Boyd*	*Smith*	*Warhurst*	*Astall*	*Kinsey*	*Brown*	*Murphy*	*Govan*
								Ref: A Holland	United wear their new lightweight kit in glorious weather. Newly promoted Blues under Arthur Turner give United a tough first twenty minutes before Viollet poaches a goal. Astall sets up Kinsey's header and nods in Govan's cross. Berry cries off and Taylor's muscle is pulled.										
2	H	TOTTENHAM			D	2-2	1-1	Webster 21, Berry 65	Wood	Foulkes	Byrne	Whitefoot	Jones	Edwards	Berry	Blanchflower	Webster	Viollet	Scanlon
	24/8		28,713		2			*Gavin 31p, Stokes 49*	*Ditchburn*	*Withers*	*Hopkins*	*Blanchflower*	*Clarke*	*Marchi*	*Gavin*	*Brooks*	*Stokes*	*Baily*	*Robb*
								Ref: K Howley	Jimmy Anderson is the new Spurs boss and his side give an outstanding display in wilting heat. A draw is an injustice to two excellent sides. Albert Scanlon is off-form but United's goals are excellent with the classy Viollet the star. Alfie Stokes, in his third game, is a constant threat.										
3	H	WEST BROM		6	W	3-1	1-0	Lewis 38, Viollet 50, Scanlon 75	Wood	Foulkes	Byrne	Whitefoot	Jones	Edwards	Webster	Blanchflower	Lewis	Viollet	Scanlon
	27/8		32,267	*13*	4			*Kevan 52*	*Sanders*	*Howe*	*Millard*	*Dudley*	*Kennedy*	*Barlow*	*Griffin*	*Carter*	*Kevan*	*Nicholls*	*Lee*
								Ref: T Jepson	There is barely a weak link as United have Albion chasing shadows in the sun. Lewis, playing his first game for 16 months, takes advantage of slack defending – Viollet from Edwards' sublime pass and Scanlon in off the post. Derek Kevan scores his third goal in only his second game.										
4	A	TOTTENHAM		5	W	2-1	2-0	Edwards 3, 41	Wood	Foulkes	Byrne	Whitefoot	Jones	Edwards	Webster	Blanchflower	Lewis	Viollet	Scanlon
	31/8		*27,453*	*21*	6			*Clarke 87*	*Ditchburn*	*Withers*	*Hopkins*	*Walley*	*Clarke*	*Marchi*	*Walters*	*Blanchflower*	*Stokes*	*Duquemin*	*Robb*
								Ref: K Howley	Edwards scores two awesome goals to despatch Spurs. Both are thunderous left-footers from outside the area, the first after a swashbuckling run, the second from Lewis's pass. Viollet's injury causes a reshuffle and a rearguard action. The smooth machine is looking a shade rusty.										
5	A	MANCHESTER C		7	L	0-1	0-1		Wood	Foulkes	Byrne	Whitefoot	Jones	Goodwin	Webster	Blanchflower	Lewis	Edwards	Scanlon
	3/9		***59,192***	*14*	6			*Hayes 28*	*Trautmann*	*Branagan*	*Little*	*Barnes*	*Ewing*	*Paul*	*Spurdle*	*Hayes*	*Revie*	*Johnstone*	*Fagan*
								Ref: R Hartley	Footballer of the Year Revie may be out of touch, but Scots' schemer Bobby Johnstone is superb and robs Byrne to set up Hayes. The FA Cup finalists gain in confidence and win an end-to-end game with both keepers overworked. Edwards lacks the finesse of the injured Viollet.										
6	H	EVERTON		4	W	2-1	0-1	Edwards 60, Blanchflower 85	Wood	Foulkes	Byrne	Whitefoot	Jones	Goodwin	Webster	Blanchflower	Lewis	Edwards	Scanlon
	7/9		35,238	*18*	8			*Wainwright 31*	*O'Neill*	*Moore*	*Tansey*	*Farrell*	*Jones*	*Lello*	*Wainwright*	*Fielding*	*Harris J*	*Parker*	*Eglington*
								Ref: R Windle	A controversial equaliser as Edwards heads against the underside of the bar and O'Neill punches out. Farrell is certain it doesn't cross the line. A labouring United are poor in a scrambled victory but Goodwin and Edwards stand out. The winner creeps through hero O'Neill's legs.										
7	A	SHEFFIELD UTD		7	L	0-1	0-0		Wood	Foulkes	Byrne	Whitefoot	Jones	Goodwin	Berry	Whelan	Webster	Blanchflower	Pegg
	10/9		*28,027*	*17*	8			*Jones 85 (og)*	*Burgin*	*Coldwell*	*Shaw G*	*Hoyland*	*Shaw J*	*Rawson*	*Ringstead*	*Hagan*	*Wragg*	*Howitt*	*Grainger*
								Ref: R Wood	Edwards joins the injured list but Berry returns and is the best forward against Joe Mercer's team. Jones's lob over Wood is immaculate but United go down fighting. Colin Grainger is an exciting prospect and skins Foulkes. 37-year old Jimmy Hagan goes on and on and shines today.										
8	A	EVERTON		7	L	2-4	2-1	Webster 14, Blanchflower 43	Wood	Foulkes	Byrne	**Whitehurst**	Jones	Goodwin	Webster	Whelan	Blanchflower	Doherty	Berry
	14/9		*35,238*	*9*	8			*Parker 12, 47, Wainwr't 64, Egl'n 82*	*O'Neill*	*Moore*	*Tansey*	*Farrell*	*Jones*	*Lello*	*Wainwright*	*Fielding*	*Harris J*	*Parker*	*Eglington*
								Ref: R Windle	Whitehurst, a pro only two weeks, comes in for the axed Whitefoot, but struggles after setting up Webster. Doherty returns after over two years of cartilage problems. Wood and Byrne are off-form and the defence, for once, lets the side down. Edwards is in hospital with a bad chill.										
9	H	PRESTON		6	W	3-2	1-2	Pegg 2, Taylor 54, Viollet 73	Wood	Foulkes	Byrne	Whitefoot	Jones	Goodwin	Webster	Blanchflower	Taylor	Viollet	Pegg
	17/9		33,362	*9*	10			*Baxter 15, Taylor 44*	*Thompson G*	*Wilson*	*Walton*	*Docherty*	*Mattinson*	*Forbes*	*Taylor S*	*Thompson T*	*Waterhouse*	*Baxter*	*Morrison*
								Ref: J Mitchell	Taylor and Viollet finally return and make a difference in a hectic game. United's defence is still wobbly but the goals come on demand with Pegg and Taylor scoring with headers and Viollet from Taylor's nod down. Tommy Thompson PNE's £27,500 signing from Villa is classy.										
10	A	BURNLEY		6	D	0-0	0-0		Wood	Foulkes	Byrne	Whitefoot	Jones	Goodwin	Webster	Blanchflower	Taylor	Viollet	Pegg
	24/9		*26,723*	*15*	11				*McDonald*	*Rudman*	*Winton*	*Seith*	*Cummings*	*Shannon*	*Gray*	*Burke*	*McIlroy*	*Cheesebrough*	*Pilkington*
								Ref: T Seymour	Two strong defences have the upper hand and neither keeper is really stretched. Brian Pilkington's early miss from Foulkes' woeful back-pass is the closest to a goal. An instantly forgettable game with Viollet limping again and Taylor looking rusty. Whitefoot accused of rough play.										

No	Venue	Opponent / Date	Att	Pos	Res / Pts	F-A	H-T	Scorers, Times, and Referees	1	2	3	4	5	6	7	8	9	10	11
11	H	LUTON		4	W	3-1	0-1	Webster 52, Taylor 64, 65	Wood	Foulkes	Bent	Whitefoot	Jones	Goodwin	Berry	Blanchflower	Taylor	Webster	Pegg
		1/10	34,661	*14*	13			*Cummins 20p*	*Streten*	*Dunne*	*Aherne*	*Morton*	*Owen*	*Shanks*	*Cullen*	*Groves*	*MacEwan*	*Cummins*	*Adam*
								Ref: W Heselton	Newly promoted Luton make their first trip to Old Trafford since 1938 and give the Reds a shock. Keeper Ron Baynham is on England duty with Byrne. Webster almost flunks his goal from Whitefoot's free-kick and Taylor makes sure with a tap-in and a header from Berry's cross.										
12	H	WOLVERHAMPTON		4	W	4-3	1-0	Pegg 42, Taylor 71, 88, Doherty 84	Wood	Byrne	Bent	Whitefoot	Jones	**McGuinness**	Berry	Doherty	Taylor	Webster	Pegg
		8/10	48,890	*11*	15			*Slater 61, Swinbourne 68, 74*	*Williams*	*Showell*	*Shorthouse*	*Slater*	*Wright*	*Clamp*	*Hancocks*	*Broadbent*	*Swinbourne*	*Wilshaw*	*Mullen*
								Ref: L Richardson	For the fourth home game running, United come from behind to win. Wolves trail at half-time despite dominating the game and are deadly on the break. The second half is a flurry of goals and Swinbourne makes it 16 in ten games. Bill Slater is awesome but the Reds win through.										
13	A	ASTON VILLA		3	D	4-4	3-2	Blanch' 25, Webster 35, Pegg 42, 50	Wood	Foulkes	Byrne	Whitefoot	Jones	McGuinness	Berry	Blanchflower	Taylor	Webster	Pegg
		15/10	*29,478*	*18*	16			*Dixon 16, 21, Hick'n 61, Saward 65*	*Jones*	*Lynn*	*Aldis*	*Crowe*	*Moss A*	*Baxter*	*Southren*	*Dixon*	*Hickson*	*Saward*	*McParland*
								Ref: G McCabe	'The best match for years' say Villa fans and no one argues. At 2-4, Villa look dead but Dave Hickson's first goal in 8 games since a big move and Pat Saward's debut goal earn a point. Either side could have won it in a frantic last fifteen minutes but Villa have only one win in thirteen.										
14	H	HUDDERSFIELD		2	W	3-0	1-0	Berry 40, Taylor 47, Pegg 89	Crompton	Foulkes	Bent	Whitefoot	Jones	Edwards	Berry	Blanchflower	Taylor	Viollet	Pegg
		22/10	34,201	*21*	18				*Wheeler*	*Conwell*	*Wilson*	*Coddington*	*Taylor*	*Quested*	*Burrell*	*Frear*	*Watson*	*Cavanagh*	*Metcalfe*
								Ref: R Langdale	Bill McGarry and Roger Byrne are playing for England, Wood has the flu but Edwards and Viollet is fit again. 20-year-old Ray Wilson's debut is tough. Pegg creates two and scores the third against struggling Town, with only two wins, who tackle strongly and adopt spoiling tactics.										
15	A	CARDIFF		1	W	1-0	1-0	Taylor 43	Wood	Foulkes	Byrne	Whitefoot	Jones	Edwards	Berry	Blanchflower	Taylor	Viollet	Pegg
		29/10	*27,795*	*20*	20				*Howells*	*Stitfall*	*Sherwood*	*Rutter*	*Sullivan*	*Harrington*	*Walsh*	*Kirtley*	*Ford*	*Stockin*	*McSeveney*
								Ref: E Abbott	Welsh striker Trevor Ford is at his belligerent best but misses two sitters. Cardiff's offside tactics catch United 20 times but Taylor is onside as Blanchflower and Viollet's headers set him up. Hero Wood makes a great late save from Stockin. Whitefoot and Edwards are in fine form.										
16	H	ARSENAL		1	D	1-1	0-0	Taylor 70	Wood	Foulkes	Byrne	Whitefoot	Jones	Edwards	Berry	Blanchflower	Taylor	Viollet	Pegg
		5/11	41,836	*18*	21			*Lishman 60*	*Kelsey*	*Wills*	*Evans*	*Goring*	*Fotheringham*	*Holton*	*Clapton*	*Tapscott*	*Roper*	*Lishman*	*Tiddy*
								Ref: H Broadhurst	Arsenal are struggling and haven't won away, but catch a cocky United cold. Clapton and Tapscott go close before Lishman lashes home after Jones and Wood, playing his 100th game, miss a corner. The scrambled equaliser is lucky and Whitefoot is foiled by Jack Kelsey near the end.										
17	A	BOLTON		3	L	1-3	1-2	Taylor 3	Wood	Foulkes	Byrne	**Colman**	Jones	Edwards	Berry	Blanchflower	Taylor	Webster	Pegg
		12/11	*41,829*	*8*	21			*Lofthouse 26, 39, Parry 89*	*Grieves*	*Hartle*	*Banks T*	*Wheeler*	*Barrass*	*Edwards*	*Holden*	*Stevens*	*Lofthouse*	*Parry*	*Gubbins*
								Ref: G Black	Lofthouse pushes his claims for an England recall with a virtuoso performance, running rings around Mark Jones. Ralph Gubbins is the provider. A hard game but United lack finishing power and it's the first defeat in nine. Another local boy Colman looks a star in the making.										
18	H	CHELSEA		2	W	3-0	0-0	Byrne 46p, Taylor 50, 68	Wood	Foulkes	Byrne	Colman	Jones	Edwards	Berry	Doherty	Taylor	Viollet	Pegg
		19/11	**22,365**	*15*	23				*Robertson*	*Sillett P*	*Willemse*	*Armstrong*	*Wicks*	*Saunders*	*Parsons*	*Brabrook*	*Tindall*	*Bentley*	*Blunstone*
								Ref: J Gardner	More sides are using physical means to stop United but Chelsea's attempts fail. Willemse handles Berry's cross and Taylor's speed and skill make his two goals; he is recalled by England after 11 goals in ten games. The fog is so thick that many believe the game will not start.										
19	A	BLACKPOOL		2	D	0-0	0-0		Wood	Greaves	Byrne	Colman	Jones	Edwards	Berry	Doherty	Taylor	Viollet	Pegg
		26/11	*26,240*	*1*	24				*Farm*	*Armfield*	*Wright*	*Fenton*	*Gratrix*	*Kelly H*	*Matthews*	*Taylor*	*Mudie*	*Brown*	*Perry*
								Ref: F Gerrard	Stan Mortensen has gone to Hull and Pool want to sign United's Eddie Lewis. On a bone-hard pitch United look the more likely to break the stalemate but a draw is fair. Foulkes is on Army duty and 'swivel-hips' Colman looks a fixture. Young Jimmy Armfield finds Pegg hard work.										
20	H	SUNDERLAND		1	W	2-1	0-0	Doherty 60, Viollet 86	Wood	Foulkes	Byrne	Colman	Jones	Edwards	Berry	Doherty	Taylor	Viollet	Pegg
		3/12	40,150	*5*	26			*Purdon 56*	*Dodds*	*Hedley*	*McDonald*	*Anderson*	*Daniel*	*Aitken*	*Bingham*	*Fleming*	*Purdon*	*Chisholm*	*Elliott*
								Ref: L Howarth	Bill Murray's expensive Sunderland team have lost 2-8 at Luton and 3-7 at Blackpool but are on top after Purdon's shock goal from Bingham's header. United bombard them for 45 minutes and Taylor's through ball makes the late winner for Viollet. Ken Chisholm is quiet this year.										
21	A	PORTSMOUTH		2	L	2-3	1-0	Taylor 37, Pegg 66 *[Jones 90 (og)]*	Wood	Foulkes	Byrne	Colman	Jones	Edwards	Berry	Doherty	Taylor	Viollet	Pegg
		10/12	*24,186*	*15*	26			*Henderson 63, Dickinson 89,*	*Uprichard*	*McGhee*	*Mansell*	*Gunter*	*Reid*	*Dickinson*	*Harris*	*Gordon*	*Rees*	*Barnard*	*Henderson*
								Ref: R Smith	The poor away form is worrying – only one win in nine – but this game should not have been lost. Two goals in the last ninety seconds after Taylor's simple miss ends Pompey's four game goal-less run. Dickinson's shot goes in off two players and Jones deflects in Henderson's shot.										

LEAGUE DIVISION 1

Manager: Matt Busby

SEASON 1955-56

No	Date		Att	Pos	Pt	F-A	H-T	Scorers, Times, and Referees	1	2	3	4	5	6	7	8	9	10	11
22	H	BIRMINGHAM		1	W	2-1	1-0	Viollet 29, Jones 76	Wood	Foulkes	Byrne	Colman	Jones	Edwards	Berry	Doherty	Taylor	Viollet	Pegg
	17/12		27,936	*10*	28			*Brown 70*	*Schofield*	*Hall*	*Martin*	*Watts*	*Smith*	*Warhurst*	*Astall*	*Kinsey*	*Brown*	*Murphy*	*Hill*
								Ref: A Holland	Manager Turner makes four changes from the team that lost 0-6 at Bolton and they give United a good game. The dodgy ref rules out a good Blues goal and strong United penalty claims then gives the visitors a late penalty which Wood turns over the bar. Jones bullet header seals win.										
23	A	WEST BROM		1	W	4-1	3-0	Viollet 25, 32, 82, Taylor 44	Wood	Foulkes	Byrne	Colman	Jones	Edwards	Berry	Doherty	Taylor	Viollet	Pegg
	24/12		*25,168*	*14*	30			*Lee 58*	*Sanders*	*Williams S*	*Millard*	*Dudley*	*Kennedy*	*Summers*	*Crowshaw*	*Barlow*	*Carter*	*Allen*	*Lee*
								Ref: T Jepson	Byrne's early saved penalty is quickly forgotten as WBA's resistance is broken with three in 16 minutes. A dazzling display and supported by strong defence as Albion later rally. Sanders saves Vic Buckingham's team from a heavy drubbing. Dennis Viollet tipped for an England cap.										
24	H	CHARLTON		1	W	**5-1**	2-1	Viollet 2, Byrne p, Doherty, Taylor	Wood	Foulkes	Byrne	Colman	Jones	Edwards	Berry	Doherty	Taylor	Viollet	Pegg
	26/12		44,838	*5*	32			*Kiernan*	*Bartram*	*Campbell*	*Ellis*	*O'Linn*	*Chamberlain*	*Pembery*	*Ayre*	*Ryan*	*Leary*	*White*	*Kiernan*
								Ref: F Overton	Charlton rest five men, hoping to win the return at the Valley. Taylor is the decoy as Viollet scores another brace, with Doherty the provider. Byrne's model penalty after O'Linn fouls Taylor and Taylor's cunning free-kick complete the rout. Wood misses a long centre for the reply.										
25	A	CHARLTON		1	L	**0-3**	0-0		Wood	Foulkes	Byrne	Colman	Jones	Edwards	Berry	Doherty	Taylor	Viollet	Pegg
	27/12		*41,340*	*4*	32			*Gauld 47, Jones 72 (og), Ryan 82*	*Bartram*	*Campbell*	*Townsend*	*Hewie*	*Ufton*	*Hammond*	*Ayre*	*Gauld*	*Leary*	*Ryan*	*Kiernan*
								Ref: F Overton	Charlton's manager Jimmy Seed's greatest moment. Leary and Gauld are superb, and lead United a merry dance. Jimmy Gauld harasses Jones for the second and sets up No 3. United, who rarely threaten the veteran Sam Bartram, suffer their first defeat in London for almost two years.										
26	H	MANCHESTER C		1	W	2-1	0-1	Taylor 56, Viollet 66	Wood	Foulkes	Byrne	Colman	Jones	Edwards	Berry	Doherty	Taylor	Viollet	Pegg
	31/12		61,194	15	34			*Dyson 26*	*Trautmann*	*Leivers*	*Little*	*Barnes*	*Ewing*	*Paul*	*Spurdle*	*Hayes*	*Johnstone*	*Dyson*	*Clarke*
								Ref: R Hartley	United break the hoodoo after nine derby games without a win. Taylor scores from Wood's enormous kick and Viollet's head glances in Pegg's corner, but Dyson almost grabs a late goal. The largest crowd at Old Trafford since 1936. Last year's hero Revie is on the transfer list.										
27	H	SHEFFIELD UTD		1	W	3-1	1-0	Taylor 2, Berry 55, Pegg 80	Wood	Foulkes	Byrne	Colman	Jones	Edwards	Berry	Whelan	Taylor	Viollet	Pegg
	14/1		30,388	*21*	36			*Hoyland 47*	*Burgin*	*Coldwell*	*Mason*	*Fountain*	*Johnson*	*Iley*	*Hawksworth*	*Hoyland*	*Howitt*	*Wragg*	*Grainger*
								Ref: R Wood	The goal-glut anticipated after Taylor headed in Pegg's cross never materialises. The waterlogged pitch dries out quickly and Grainger's cross finds Hoyland unmarked to nod in. Pegg's 20-yard screamer seals the win and he is tipped for international honours. Blades look doomed.										
28	A	PRESTON		1	L	1-3	1-1	Whelan 11	Wood	Foulkes	Byrne	Colman	Jones	Edwards	Scott	Whelan	Webster	Viollet	Pegg
	21/1		*28,047*	*15*	36			*Lewis 9, Thompson T 47, Foster 85*	*Thompson G*	*Cunningham*	*Walton*	*Docherty*	*Dunn*	*Evans*	*Finney*	*Thompson T*	*Lewis*	*Baxter*	*Foster*
								Ref: J Mitchell	Another away blip as Preston celebrate Finney's 300th league game on a greasy pitch. Wood is at fault as ex-Red Lewis scores his first goal for Preston and he also drops Cunningham's free-kick for the third. A run of five wins at Deepdale is over. John Scott returns after three years.										
29	H	BURNLEY		1	W	2-0	0-0	Taylor 46, Viollet 65	Wood	Greaves	Byrne	Colman	Jones	Edwards	Berry	Whelan	Taylor	Viollet	Pegg
	4/2		27,542	*5*	38				*McDonald*	*Cummings*	*Winton*	*Seith*	*Adamson*	*Miller*	*Gray*	*Burke*	*McKay*	*Walton*	*Cargill*
								Ref: T Seymour	Most of the league programme is off due to snow and the bone-hard pitch makes conditions dire. Burnley are in the throes of a five-game FA Cup-tie with Chelsea. They hold out until Taylor's individual effort and Viollet, back to his best adds another as United keep their feet in style.										
30	A	LUTON		1	W	2-0	1-0	Viollet 7, Whelan 84	Wood	Greaves	Byrne	Goodwin	Jones	Blanchflower	Berry	Whelan	Taylor	Viollet	Pegg
	11/2		***16,368***	*15*	40				*Baynham*	*Dunne*	*Jones*	*Pemberton*	*Kelly*	*Shanks*	*Pearce*	*Turner*	*Morton*	*Groves*	*Cullen*
								Ref: W Heselton	Dally Duncan's team lose their fourth game in a row, against a weakened United team. Edwards, Colman and Foulkes are in Belgium playing for the British Army. Luton's defensive errors are punished on the icy surface in a fast-moving game with the sure-footed Taylor dazzling.										
31	A	WOLVERHAMPTON		1	W	2-0	1-0	Taylor 30, 71	Wood	Greaves	Byrne	Colman	Jones	Edwards	Berry	Whelan	Taylor	Viollet	Pegg
	18/2		*40,014*	*3*	42				*Sims*	*Stuart*	*Shorthouse*	*Flowers*	*Wright*	*Clamp*	*Hancocks*	*Broadbent*	*Murray*	*Booth*	*Wilshaw*
								Ref: L Richardson	A vital win over a close rival on another snowy pitch with the defence superb. Greaves is preferred to Foulkes. Edwards handles for a penalty but Hancocks blazes over. Early season sensation Roy Swinbourne is forced to retire with injury. A rare Wright error is punished by Taylor.										

32	H	ASTON VILLA	1	W	1-0	0-0	Whelan 54	Wood	Greaves	Byrne	Colman	Jones	Edwards	Berry	Whelan	Taylor	Viollet	Pegg
25/2		36,476	*22*	44				*Jones*	*Lynn*	*Aldis*	*Baxter*	*Dugdale*	*Crowe*	*Smith*	*Sewell*	*Pace*	*Dixon*	*McParland*
							Ref: G McCabe	Villa have won one in ten and are in serious trouble but United are strangely off-colour on another snow-covered pitch. The win means they are six points clear at the top and the title is in sight. Whelan's speculative shot is the difference but Nigel Sims makes three superb saves.										
33	A	CHELSEA	1	W	4-2	1-2	Pegg 26, Viollet 60, 69, Taylor 89	Wood	Greaves	Byrne	Colman	Jones	Edwards	Berry	Whelan	Taylor	Viollet	Pegg
3/3		*32,050*	*13*	46			*Parsons 21, Bentley 22*	*Robertson*	*Sillett P*	*Willemse*	*Nicholas*	*Wicks*	*Saunders*	*Parsons*	*Brabrook*	*Bentley*	*Tindall*	*Blunstone*
							Ref: J Gardner	Ted Drake is following Busby's lead and has three under-20s in his team. They take a 2-0 lead but United respond in classical style to destroy the reigning champions. Berry and Pegg murder their full-backs and Colman is exquisite in midfield as United take a step towards the title.										
34	H	CARDIFF	1	D	1-1	0-0	Byrne 49p	Wood	Greaves	Byrne	Colman	Jones	Edwards	Berry	Whelan	Taylor	Viollet	Pegg
10/3		44,914	*12*	47			*Hitchens 77*	*Vearncombe*	*Stitfall*	*Sullivan*	*Harrington*	*Malloy*	*Baker*	*Walsh*	*Kirtley*	*Ford*	*Hitchens*	*McSeveney*
							Ref: E Abbott	Cardiff are unbeaten in six and deserve a point against a casual United. Danny Malloy, signed from Dundee, tightens the Welsh defence and it needs a penalty after Viollet is hacked down. Edwards is in top form and set for an England recall. Colman's back-pass sets up Hitchens' goal.										
35	A	ARSENAL	1	D	1-1	0-0	Viollet 54	Wood	Greaves	Byrne	Colman	Jones	Edwards	Berry	Whelan	Taylor	Viollet	Pegg
17/3		*50,758*	*16*	48			*Holton 76*	*Kelsey*	*Charlton*	*Evans*	*Goring*	*Dodgin*	*Bowen*	*Clapton*	*Tapscott*	*Holton*	*Bloomfield*	*Haverty*
							Ref: H Broadhurst	Arsenal are still smarting from their Cup exit to Birmingham and struggling in the league. A scrappy game watched by top Soviet politician Malenkov is not helped by poor refereeing. Roger Byrne scoops an early penalty over the bar. Pegg, Taylor and Edwards in England 'B' team.										
36	H	BOLTON	1	W	1-0	1-0	Taylor 30	Wood	Greaves	Byrne	Colman	Jones	Edwards	Berry	Whelan	Taylor	Viollet	Pegg
24/3		46,346	*3*	50				*Grieves*	*Hartle*	*Banks T*	*Wheeler*	*Barrass*	*Edwards*	*Holden*	*Stevens*	*Lofthouse*	*Gubbins*	*Birch*
							Ref: G Black	Every game is a Cup-tie now and the renowned Bolton defence is giving nothing away. Whelan hobbles on the wing and Taylor outshines Lofthouse, who is well held by Jones. Two hard-earned points. Bolton hard-man Barrass misjudges a bouncing ball and Tommy pounces.										
37	H	NEWCASTLE	1	W	5-2	1-1	Pegg 6, Taylor 47, Viollet 69, 75,	Wood	Greaves	Byrne	Colman	Jones	Edwards	Berry	Doherty	Taylor	Viollet	Pegg
30/3		58,994	*5*	52			*Keeble 33, Stokoe 86* [Doherty 78]	*Simpson*	*Lackenby*	*McMichael*	*Stokoe*	*Paterson*	*Casey*	*Milburn*	*Davies*	*Keeble*	*Hannah*	*Mitchell*
							Ref: A Holland	Since FA Cup-winning manager Livingstone went to Fulham, Newcastle are without a manager. They give United a good game until half-time but collapse after the break with Jimmy Scoular badly missed. Byrne is outstanding and John Doherty's brilliant goal is given long applause.										
38	A	HUDDERSFIELD	1	W	2-0	1-0	Taylor 20, 74	Wood	Greaves	Byrne	Colman	Jones	Edwards	Berry	Doherty	Taylor	Viollet	Pegg
31/3		*37,780*	*22*	54				*Fearnley*	*Gibson*	*Kelly*	*McGarry*	*Taylor*	*Quested*	*Marriott*	*Cavanagh*	*Hickson*	*Davie*	*Simpson*
							Ref: R Langdale	Dave Hickson plays his third game against United with three different clubs. Brave Town, in dire straits in the drop zone, go close to scoring early on, but can't stop Tommy Taylor notching his 99th and 100th league goals. United move seven points clear of second-placed Blackpool.										
39	A	NEWCASTLE	1	D	0-0	0-0		Wood	Greaves	Byrne	Colman	Jones	Edwards	Berry	Doherty	Taylor	Viollet	Pegg
2/4		*37,395*	*9*	55				*Simpson*	*Lackenby*	*Batty*	*Scoular*	*Stokoe*	*Crowe*	*Taylor J*	*Milburn*	*Keeble*	*Hannah*	*Mitchell*
							Ref: A Holland	The tension is showing in a tough battle, with United's defence working hard to stem the black and white tide. The champagne stays on ice as Blackpool win at Bolton. The United players are tired after a hard Easter programme and Newcastle's run of eight without a win almost ends.										
40	H	BLACKPOOL	1	W	2-1	0-1	Berry 60p, Taylor 80	Wood	Greaves	Byrne	Colman	Jones	Edwards	Berry	Doherty	Taylor	Viollet	Pegg
7/4		**62,522**	*2*	57			*Durie 2*	*Farm*	*Frith*	*Wright*	*Kelly J*	*Gratrix*	*Kelly H*	*Matthews*	*Taylor*	*Mudie*	*Durie*	*Perry*
							Ref: F Gerrard	The title is clinched as United come from behind for the eighth time this season. Despite the heavy showers, 14,000 Pool fans are amongst the biggest post-war crowd at the ground. Durie's early stunner is cancelled out after Doherty is felled by Farm. Taylor prods in the winner.										
41	A	SUNDERLAND	1	D	2-2		McGuinness 26, Whelan 62	Wood	Greaves	Bent	Colman	Jones	McGuinness	Berry	Whelan	Blanchflower	Viollet	Pegg
14/4		*19,855*	*14*	58			*Anderson 27p, Elliott 38*	*Fraser*	*Stelling*	*McDonald*	*Anderson*	*Bone*	*Aitken*	*Kemp*	*Fleming*	*Holden*	*Elliott*	*Shackleton*
							Ref: L Howarth	Sunderland's Cup semi-final loss has hit them hard. Byrne, Edwards and Taylor are at Hampden with England, and Berry captains the team. Stand-in McGuinness in his third game scores a beauty, then handballs for the penalty. United's defence holds out under heavy pressure.										
42	H	PORTSMOUTH	1	W	1-0	1-0	Viollet 19	Wood	Greaves	Byrne	Colman	Jones	Edwards	Berry	Doherty	Taylor	Viollet	Pegg
21/4		38,672	*12*	60				*Uprichard*	*McGhee*	*Mansell*	*Gunter*	*Rutter*	*Dickinson*	*Harris*	*Rees*	*Robertson*	*Barnard*	*Penk*
Average	Home 39,254	Away 32,978					Ref: R Smith	A half-hearted game sees the unbeaten home record maintained, thanks to Viollet's slick goal. Duggie Reid plays his 327th and penultimate game but few are here for that. The pitch is invaded two minutes from time and again at the end. The league trophy is presented to Byrne.										

LEAGUE DIVISION 1 (CUP-TIES) Manager: Matt Busby SEASON 1955-56

FA Cup					F-A	H-T	Scorers, Times, and Referees	1	2	3	4	5	6	7	8	9	10	11
3	A	BRISTOL ROV	1	L	0-4	0-2		Wood	Foulkes	Byrne	Colman	Jones	Whitefoot	Berry	Docherty	Taylor	Viollet	Pegg
		35,872 2:6					*Biggs 11, 60, Meyer 44, Brad'rd 83p*	*Nicholls*	*Bamford*	*Allcock*	*Pitt*	*Hale*	*Simpson*	*Petherbridge*	*Biggs*	*Bradford*	*Meyer*	*Hooper*
							Ref: K Aston	Smog shrouds Manchester, but Bristol is clear and Rovers pull off the shock of the day. United are outfought on the churned up pitch where Rovers have lost only two games. England man Geoff Bradford and Alfie Biggs are the architects. Duncan Edwards has a boil on his knee.										

		Home						Away					
		P	W	D	L	F	A	W	D	L	F	A	Pts
1	MAN UNITED	42	18	3	0	51	20	7	7	7	32	31	60
2	Blackpool	42	13	4	4	56	27	7	5	9	30	35	49
3	Wolves	42	15	2	4	51	27	5	7	9	38	38	49
4	Manchester C	42	11	5	5	40	27	7	5	9	42	42	46
5	Arsenal	42	13	4	4	38	22	5	6	10	22	39	46
6	Birmingham	42	12	4	5	51	26	6	5	10	24	31	45
7	Burnley	42	11	3	7	37	20	7	5	9	27	34	44
8	Bolton	42	13	3	5	50	24	5	4	12	21	34	43
9	Sunderland	42	10	8	3	44	36	7	1	13	36	59	43
10	Luton	42	12	4	5	44	27	5	4	12	22	37	42
11	Newcastle	42	12	4	5	49	24	5	3	13	36	46	41
12	Portsmouth	42	9	8	4	46	38	7	1	13	32	47	41
13	West Brom	42	13	3	5	37	25	5	2	14	21	45	41
14	Charlton	42	13	2	6	47	26	4	4	13	28	55	40
15	Everton	42	11	5	5	37	29	4	5	12	18	40	40
16	Chelsea	42	10	4	7	32	26	4	7	10	32	51	39
17	Cardiff	42	11	4	6	36	32	4	5	12	19	37	39
18	Tottenham	42	9	4	8	37	33	6	3	12	24	38	37
19	Preston	42	6	5	10	32	36	8	3	10	41	36	36
20	Aston Villa	42	9	6	6	32	29	2	7	12	20	40	35
21	Huddersfield	42	9	4	8	32	30	5	3	13	22	53	35
22	Sheffield Utd	42	8	6	7	31	35	4	3	14	32	42	33
		924	248	95	119	910	619	119	95	248	619	910	924

Odds & ends

Double wins: (5) West Brom, Luton, Wolves, Chelsea, Huddersfield.
Double losses: (0).

Won from behind: (8) Everton (h), Preston (h), Luton (h), Wolves (h), Sunderland (h), Man City (h), Chelsea (a), Blackpool (h).

Lost from in front: (3) Everton (a), Bolton (a), Portsmouth (a).

High spots: 14-game unbeaten run-in.
Taylor and Viollet's partnership.
Emergence of Eddie Colman.
Unbeaten at home for the first time since 1897.

Low spots: Cup defeat at Bristol Rovers.
More distress with Bolton.

Sent off: United (0).
Sent off: Opponents (0).

Ever-presents: (1) Jones.
Hat-tricks: (1) Viollet.
Opposing hat-tricks: (0).
Leading scorer: Taylor (25).

	Appearances		Goals		
	Lge	FAC	Lge	FAC	Tot
Bent, Geoff	4				
Berry, Johnny	34	1	4		4
Blanchflower, Jackie	18		3		3
Byrne, Roger	39	1	3		3
Colman, Eddie	25	1			
Crompton, Jack	1				
Doherty, John	16	1	4		4
Edwards, Duncan	33		3		3
Foulkes, Bill	26	1			
Goodwin, Freddie	8				
Greaves, Ian	15				
Jones, Mark	42	1	1		1
Lewis, Eddie	4		1		1
McGuinness, Wilf	3		1		1
Pegg, David	35	1	9		9
Scanlon, Albert	6		1		1
Scott, John	1				
Taylor, Tommy	33	1	25		25
Viollet, Dennis	34	1	20		20
Webster, Colin	15		4		4
Whelan, Billy	13		4		4
Whitefoot, Jeff	15	1			
Whitehurst, Walter	1				
Wood, Ray	41	1			
24 players used	**462**	11	**83**		**83**

No	Date		Att	Pos	Pt	F-A	H-T	Scorers, Times, and Referees	1	2	3	4	5	6	7	8	9	10	11
1	H	BIRMINGHAM			D	2-2	1-0	Viollet 30, 80	Wood	Foulkes	Byrne	Colman	Jones	Edwards	Berry	Whelan	Taylor	Viollet	Pegg
	18/8		32,958		1			*Jones 67 (og), Govan 70*	*Merrick*	*Hall*	*Green*	*Linnecor*	*Smith*	*Warhurst*	*Astall*	*Kinsey*	*Brown*	*Murphy*	*Govan*
								Ref: M Griffiths	In torrential rain the Blues almost cause an upset. United rely on Merrick's only error when he drops a back-pass and Dennis nets. The visitors' tactics are more suited to the wet than United's fancy play. England winger Astall's shot hits Jones' ankle and his cross is nodded in by Govan.										
2	A	PRESTON			W	3-1	1-1	Taylor 12, 77, Whelan 67	Wood	Foulkes	Byrne	Colman	Jones	Edwards	Berry	Whelan	Taylor	Viollet	Pegg
	20/8		*32,569*		3			*Waterhouse 44*	*Else*	*Cunningham*	*Walton*	*Docherty*	*Dunn*	*Mattinson*	*Finney*	*Waterhouse*	*Hatsell*	*Baxter*	*Taylor*
								Ref: R Hartley	The sixth win in seven visits to Deepdale, thanks to two Pegg-created Taylor headers and Viollet profiting from Fred Else's dropped ball. Preston rely to much on Tom Finney, who is well held by Byrne. Waterhouse's header causes a temporary panic to a casual United defence.										
3	A	WEST BROM		1	W	3-2	1-0	Taylor13, Viollet 74, Whelan 82	Wood	Foulkes	Byrne	Colman	Jones	Edwards	Berry	Whelan	Taylor	Viollet	Pegg
	25/8		*26,387*	*17*	5			*Allen 47, Lee 72*	*Sanders*	*Howe*	*Williams S*	*Dudley*	*Kennedy*	*Barlow*	*Griffin*	*Robson*	*Allen*	*Whitehouse*	*Lee*
								Ref: T Jepson	Berry celebrates his 200th game for United and, despite Whelan limping, United find it easy. Byrne and Wood's poor clearances are punished. Bobby Robson (future England boss), Albion's £20,000 signing from Fulham, looks good. In pouring rain Taylor's flying header is crucial.										
4	H	PRESTON		1	W	3-2	2-2	Viollet 14, 37, 65	Wood	Foulkes	Byrne	Colman	Jones	Edwards	Berry	Whelan	Taylor	Viollet	Pegg
	29/8		32,515	*20*	7			*Taylor 34, Finney 44p*	*Else*	*Cunningham*	*Walton*	*Docherty*	*Dunn*	*Mattinson*	*Campbell*	*Thompson*	*Finney*	*Baxter*	*Taylor*
								Ref: R Hartley	Cliff Britton is the new manager of Preston and they are a different proposition than a week ago. Finney plays centre-forward for the first time and North End are unlucky to lose. Viollet is exquisite and wins the game by intercepting Walton's back-header. Coleman is back to his best.										
5	H	PORTSMOUTH		1	W	3-0	2-0	Berry 26, Violett 33, Pegg 74	Wood	Foulkes	Byrne	Colman	Jones	Edwards	Berry	Whelan	Taylor	Viollet	Pegg
	1/9		40,595	*19*	9				*Uprichard*	*McGhee*	*Gunter*	*Pickett*	*Rutter*	*Dickinson*	*Harris*	*Gordon*	*Henderson*	*Rees*	*Dale*
								Ref: G Pullen	Eddie Lever's Portsmouth's dismal start continues as United hit championship form for the first time. Pompey play well but lack finishing power. Billy Whelan sets up Viollet and looks set for an Eire cap. Taylor's cheeky back-heel makes Berry's goal. Pegg's speed earns the third.										
6	A	CHELSEA		1	W	2-1	1-1	Taylor 39, Whelan 86	Wood	Foulkes	Byrne	Colman	Jones	Edwards	Berry	Whelan	Taylor	Viollet	Pegg
	5/9		*29,082*	*18*	11			*Blunstone 35*	*Robertson*	*MacFarlane*	*Whittaker*	*Armstrong*	*Wicks*	*Saunders*	*Lewis*	*Brabrook*	*Tindall*	*Nicholas A*	*Blunstone*
								Ref: J Williams	Walter Winterbottom watches Edwards give another gigantic display as United come from behind to snatch a win. They are unchanged for the sixth time and are looking invincible. On a wet, muggy night, Pegg is irrepressible and the first goal sees Taylor's header end a stunning move.										
7	A	NEWCASTLE		1	D	1-1	0-0	Whelan 65	Wood	Foulkes	Byrne	Colman	Jones	Edwards	Berry	Whelan	Taylor	Viollet	Pegg
	8/9		*50,133*	*13*	12			*Milburn 85*	*Simpson*	*Keith*	*Batty*	*Keery*	*Stokoe*	*Crowe*	*Hughes*	*Davies*	*Milburn*	*Hannah*	*Prior*
								Ref: P Power	Newcastle have lost 1-6 at Birmingham and Scoular is dropped, but they run United close. Whelan taps in after Simpson hesitates, but Milburn grabs a point. The defence is solid but the attack has an off-day. Byrne's 200th match for the Reds as the unbeaten run is extended to 21 games.										
8	H	SHEFFIELD WED		1	W	4-1	3-0	Viollet 5, Whelan 19, Berry 32, [Taylor 75]	Wood	Foulkes	Byrne	Colman	Jones	Edwards	Berry	Whelan	Taylor	Viollet	Pegg
	15/9		48,306	*9*	14			*Quixall 55*	*McIntosh*	*Staniforth*	*Curtis*	*McAnearney T*	*Swan*	*O'Donnell*	*Finney*	*Quixall*	*Shiner*	*Froggatt*	*Wilkinson*
								Ref: R Langdale	United's teamwork and superior fitness is too much for newly promoted Wednesday, who are unchanged for the 21st game. The much-vaunted Finney-Quixall wing are kept quiet and Coleman is inspirational. Berry's diving header is the best of the four. Viollet in Football League side.										
9	H	MANCHESTER C		1	W	2-0	1-0	Viollet 37, Whelan 70	Wood	Foulkes	Byrne	Colman	Jones	Edwards	Berry	Whelan	Taylor	Viollet	Pegg
	22/9		53,751	*19*	16				*Savage*	*Leivers*	*Hannaway*	*Barnes*	*Ewing*	*Paul*	*Spurdle*	*McAdams*	*Revie*	*Dyson*	*Clarke*
								Ref: J Clough	The classy Don Revie has an early shot tipped onto the bar by Wood, but is subsequently shackled by Colman. Tommy Taylor has trouble with City's offside tactics but Berry's pass sets up Viollet. Whelan scores from Viollet's cross and a poor City are lucky to keep the score down.										
10	A	ARSENAL		1	W	2-1	2-0	Whelan 10, Berry 35p	Wood	Foulkes	Byrne	Colman	**Cope**	Edwards	Berry	Whelan	Taylor	Viollet	Pegg
	29/9		*62,479*	*14*	18			*Evans 65p*	*Kelsey*	*Charlton*	*Evans*	*Goring*	*Dodgin*	*Bowen*	*Clapton*	*Tapscott*	*Groves*	*Bloomfield*	*Tiddy*
								Ref: F Coultas	Highbury's biggest league gate for two years sees Whelan score for the fifth game in a row. Bill Dodgin fouled Taylor for a penalty. Bill Foulkes obstructs Tapscott, Arsenal get a dubious penalty, but United cling on. The injured Mark Jones is missing after 64 games in a row.										

No	Venue	Opponent	Att	Pos	Res	FT	HT	Scorers	1	2	3	4	5	6	7	8	9	10	11
11	H	CHARLTON		1	W	4·2	3·2	Berry 25, Charlton 32, 37, Whelan 65	Wood	Foulkes	Bent	Colman	Jones	McGuinness	Berry	Whelan	**Charlton**	Viollet	Pegg
		6/10	41,698	*22*	20			*Lucas 24, Ayre 40*	*Marsh*	*Campbell*	*Ellis*	*O'Linn*	*Hewie*	*Hammond*	*Ayre*	*Gauld*	*Leary*	*Lucas*	*White*
								Ref: K Stokes	After Charlton's disastrous start, Jimmy Seed is replaced by England trainer Jimmy Trotter. United with four on international duty win easily. Bobby Charlton's debut is memorable but he misses an easy chance for a hat-trick. Campbell is off injured as Billy Whelan scores the fourth.										
12	A	SUNDERLAND		1	W	3·1	1·1	Viollet 19, Whelan 49, Morrison 73(og)	Wood	Foulkes	Byrne	Colman	Jones	Edwards	Berry	Whelan	Taylor	Viollet	Pegg
		13/10	*49,487*	*19*	22			*Purdon 20*	*Bollands*	*Hedley*	*McDonald*	*Morrison*	*Daniel*	*Aitken*	*Bingham*	*Shackleton*	*Purdon*	*Fleming*	*Hannigan*
								Ref: P Rhodes	Despite Sunderland losing four in a row, they give United their hardest 45 minutes of the season, with Purdon on top of Jones and their whole team scrapping for every ball. The second goal kills them off however, but the tackles are still robust. Dennis Viollet looks offside for his goal.										
13	H	EVERTON		1	L	**2·5**	1·3	Charl' 10, Whelan 52 *[McNamara 90]*	Wood	Foulkes	Byrne	Colman	Jones	Edwards	Berry	Whelan	Taylor	Charlton	Pegg
		20/10	43,677	*18*	22			*Donovan 17, Kirby 38, 76, Egling' 44,*	*Dunlop*	*Donovan*	*Tansey*	*Birch*	*Jones*	*Farrell*	*McNamara*	*Gauld*	*Kirby*	*Fielding*	*Eglington*
								Ref: H Haworth	The biggest shock of the season as the Reds' 31-match unbeaten home run goes, as well as being their first defeat for 26 matches. Dunlop and Gauld make impressive debuts and the win is deserved despite a United barrage. Viollet is injured and they all look tired after the midweek tie.										
14	A	BLACKPOOL		1	D	2·2	1·1	Taylor 25, 90	**Hawksworth**	Foulkes	Byrne	Colman	Jones	Edwards	Berry	Whelan	Taylor	Viollet	Pegg
		27/10	*32,632*	*3*	23			*Durie 23, Mudie 55*	*Farm*	*Armfield*	*Wright*	*Kelly J*	*Gratrix*	*Fenton*	*Matthews*	*Taylor*	*Mudie*	*Durie*	*Perry*
								Ref: J Clough	Wood fails a fitness test and 18-year-old Tony Hawksworth makes a solid debut after only three reserve games. Blackpool, unbeaten in six, are robbed by Taylor's last-minute header. Matthews is irresistible and sets up the second goal. England winger Bill Perry is under Foulkes' spell.										
15	H	WOLVERHAMPTON		1	W	3·0	2·0	Whelan 2, Pegg 20, Taylor 80	Wood	Foulkes	Byrne	Colman	Jones	Edwards	Berry	Whelan	Taylor	Charlton	Pegg
		3/11	55,071	*8*	25				*Finlayson*	*Stuart*	*Harris*	*Slater*	*Wright*	*Flowers*	*Hooper*	*Booth*	*Wilshaw*	*Murray*	*Mullen*
								Ref: J Powell	United defy their critics with a dazzling win which leaves Billy Wright speechless, and ends Wolves' six-game unbeaten run. Despite missing a penalty, Berry is magical and Taylor scores his seventh successive headed goal. 11 England internationals on show, and Whelan is the star.										
16	A	BOLTON		2	L	0·2	0·1		Wood	Foulkes	Byrne	Colman	Jones	Edwards	Berry	Whelan	Taylor	Charlton	Pegg
		10/11	*39,922*	*5*	25			*Holden 11, Allcock 63*	*Hopkinson*	*Hartle*	*Banks*	*Hennin*	*Higgins*	*Edwards*	*Holden*	*Stevens*	*Allcock*	*Parry*	*Gubbins*
								Ref: E Oxley	With black clouds looming, the ref kicks off five minutes early. Complacent United find Bolton's rearguard immovable and their attacks lack guile. Terry Allcock, deputising for Lofthouse, scores from Stevens' deft flick. Ray Parry hits the bar and has a shot well saved by Wood.										
17	H	LEEDS		1	W	3·2	1·1	Whelan 19, 64, Charlton 57	Wood	Foulkes	Byrne	Colman	Jones	McGuinness	Berry	Whelan	Taylor	Charlton	Pegg
		17/11	52,402	*4*	27			*McKenna 26, Charles 66p*	*Wood*	*Dunn*	*Hair*	*Gibson*	*Charlton*	*Kerfoot*	*Meek*	*Charles*	*McKenna*	*Forrest*	*Overfield*
								Ref: R Windle	Raich Carter's newly promoted Leeds have the Welsh gentle giant John Charles in top form and he almost saves a point in the failing light. United's giant, Edwards, has an ankle injury and is missed. Ray Wood is at fault for the first but United deserve to go top of the table again.										
18	A	TOTTENHAM		1	D	2·2	0·2	Berry 47, Colman 88	Wood	Foulkes	Byrne	Colman	Blanchflower	McGuinness	Berry	Whelan	Taylor	Edwards	Pegg
		24/11	*57,724*	*2*	28			*Harmer 3p, Robb 7*	*Ditchburn*	*Baker*	*Hopkins*	*Blanchflower*	*Clarke*	*Marchi*	*Medwin*	*Harmer*	*Smith*	*Brooks*	*Robb*
								Ref: L Callaghan	Spurs start like world beaters but United, despite their trip to Germany, finish like champions and deserve a point. Harmer and Brooks are superb as Spurs threaten to win by a mile; then McGuinness sets up Berry and Edwards' run and cross makes Eddie Coleman's equaliser.										
19	H	LUTON		1	W	3·1	1·0	Edwards 4, Taylor 63, Pegg 79	Wood	Foulkes	Byrne	Colman	Jones	McGuinness	Berry	Whelan	Taylor	Edwards	Pegg
		1/12	34,954	*12*	30			*Gregory 87*	*Baynham*	*Dunne*	*Aherne*	*Pemberton*	*Kelly*	*Shanks*	*Davies*	*Turner*	*Morton*	*Cummins*	*Gregory*
								Ref: P Brandwood	Despite Viollet's absence through injury and Taylor and Whelan being quiet United win with ease. Duncan Edwards' thunderbolt and Taylor's header set the Reds up, but too many chances are missed against a woeful Luton team who, without captain Syd Owen, will surely struggle.										
20	A	ASTON VILLA		1	W	3·1	1·0	Taylor 42, 49, Viollet 73	Wood	Foulkes	Bent	Colman	Jones	Edwards	Berry	Whelan	Taylor	Viollet	Pegg
		8/12	*42,530*	*13*	32			*Saward 78*	*Sims*	*Lynn*	*Aldis*	*Crowe*	*Dugdale*	*Saward*	*Smith*	*Sewell*	*Dixon*	*Roberts KO*	*McParland*
								Ref: T Blenkinsopp	Viollet returns and United are well in control. Nigel Sims keeps the score respectable with several good saves. Berry captains the team in Byrne's absence and leads Villa a merry dance. Tommy Taylor in top form and scores two with his feet. United four points clear of Spurs.										
21	A	BIRMINGHAM		1	L	1·3	0·3	Whelan 60	Wood	Foulkes	Bent	Colman	Jones	Edwards	Berry	Whelan	Taylor	Viollet	Pegg
		15/12	*36,146*	*5*	32			*Orritt 4, Brown 23, 30*	*Merrick*	*Hall*	*Green*	*Linnecor*	*Smith*	*Warhurst*	*Astall*	*Orritt*	*Brown*	*Murphy*	*Govan*
								Ref: M Griffiths	Blues maintain their unbeaten home record against a strangely lacklustre United, who nevertheless miss five close-range chances in the first half. Gordon Astall troubles stand-in Bent and Brown upstages Jones again. Wood is at fault for the first and Jones misjudges for the second.										

No	Date		Att	Pos	Pt	F-A	H-T	Scorers, Times, and Referees	1	2	3	4	5	6	7	8	9	10	11
22	H	CARDIFF		1	W	3-1	1-1	Taylor 19, Viollet 53, Whelan 70	Wood	Foulkes	Byrne	Colman	Jones	Edwards	Berry	Whelan	Taylor	Viollet	Pegg
	26/12		28,810	*19*	34			*Malloy 2p*	*Vearncombe*	*Stitfall*	*Sullivan*	*Harrington*	*Malloy*	*Baker*	*Walsh*	*Reynolds*	*Hitchens*	*Stockin*	*Nugent*
								Ref: D Howell	Snow on an icy pitch makes it a nightmare for defenders. Jones' handball gives Cardiff a spot-kick but the visitor's long train journey has left them weary. Viollet scores from a defensive mix-up and Whelan's vicious shot wraps it up in poor light after Foulkes' 35-yard shot is parried.										
23	A	PORTSMOUTH		1	W	3-1	0-1	Pegg 48, Edwards 52, Viollet 69	Wood	Foulkes	Byrne	Colman	Jones	McGuinness	Berry	Whelan	Edwards	Viollet	Pegg
	29/12		*32,052*	*21*	36			*Henderson 32*	*Uprichard*	*McGhee*	*Mansell*	*Phillips*	*Gunter*	*Dickinson*	*Harris*	*McClellan*	*Henderson*	*Gordon*	*Dale*
								Ref: G Pullen	United's first win at Fratton since 1947 and Pompey have not won at home since October. Wood seems to dive over Henderson's shot but the Reds bounce back with Edwards, deputising for the injured Taylor thumping a glorious goal. By the end Pompey are grateful that it is only 3-1.										
24	H	CHELSEA		1	W	3-0	3-0	Taylor 17, 49, Whelan 43	Wood	Foulkes	Byrne	Colman	Jones	Edwards	Berry	Whelan	Taylor	Viollet	Pegg
	1/1		42,282	*14*	38				*Matthews*	*Sillett J*	*Sillett P*	*Mortimore*	*Livingstone*	*Saunders*	*Brabrook*	*Gibbs*	*Tindall*	*Nicholas A*	*Blunstone*
								Ref: J Williams	David Pegg wins the plaudits for making all three goals and destroying 19-year-old John Sillett. Drakes Ducklings, average age 21, are outclassed on the icy surface. Taylor is unmarked for the first goal and Whelan scores the best of the game before United ease off the pedal.										
25	H	NEWCASTLE		1	W	**6-1**	3-0	Pegg 5, 43, Whelan 21, 82,	Wood	Foulkes	Byrne	Colman	Jones	Edwards	Berry	Whelan	Taylor	Viollet	Pegg
	12/1		45,132	*12*	40			*Milburn 89* [Viollet 61, 70]	*Simpson*	*Keith*	*Batty*	*Scoular*	*Scott*	*Crowe*	*White*	*Milburn*	*Curry*	*Eastham*	*Mitchell*
								Ref: P Power	Newcastle are tired from their midweek FA Cup replay win over Man City and capitulate without a fight. A great warm-up for the trip to Spain with Berry leading the charge with a textbook display. United look champions already and but for Ronnie Simpson would have scored ten.										
26	A	SHEFFIELD WED		1	L	1-2	0-1	Taylor 81	Wood	Foulkes	Byrne	Colman	Jones	Edwards	Berry	Whelan	Taylor	Viollet	Pegg
	19/1		*49,398*	14	40			*Shiner 16, Quixall 48*	*McIntosh*	*Staniforth*	*Curtis*	*McAnearney T*	*McEvoy*	*O'Donnell*	*Finney*	*Quixall*	*Shiner*	*McAnearney J*	*Broadbent*
								Ref: R Langdale	Everyone wants to see United and the biggest league crowd at Hillsborough for four years roars the Owls to their first post-war win over United, who look tired after the Spain trip. Byrne's error lets in Shiner and a jittery defence is undone by Quixall, who scores from a rebound.										
27	A	MANCHESTER C		1	W	4-2	3-1	Whelan 3, Taylor 30, Viollet 31,	Wood	Foulkes	Byrne	Colman	Jones	Edwards	Berry	Whelan	Taylor	Viollet	Pegg
	2/2		***63,872***	*17*	42			*Clarke 12, Hayes 75* [Edwards 80]	*Trautmann*	*Leivers*	*Little*	*Barnes*	*Ewing*	*Paul*	*Fagan*	*Hayes*	*Johnstone*	*Dyson*	*Clarke*
								Ref: A Murdoch	The biggest derby crowd at Maine Road since 1948 sees City continue their poor league form. Their offside trap does not always work on the puddle-covered surface, and Taylor and Viollet are both unmarked for their goals. Edwards' power shot leaves Bert Trautmann speechless.										
28	H	ARSENAL		1	W	6-2	3-2	Whelan 16, 80, Berry 25,49p, Edw' 35,	Wood	Foulkes	Byrne	Colman	Jones	Edwards	Berry	Whelan	Taylor	Viollet	Pegg
	9/2		**61,628**	*6*	44			*Herd 2, 43* [Taylor 60]	*Sullivan*	*Charlton*	*Evans*	*Holton*	*Dodgin*	*Bowen*	*Clapton*	*Swallow*	*Herd*	*Bloomfield*	*Haverty*
								Ref: F Coultas	Arsenal have lost only once in twelve since Jack Crayston took over as manager, but are annihilated by a wonder show. Sullivan saves Arsenal from a massive defeat and Berry misses a late penalty. Whelan is the ringmaster and a wizard to boot. Taylor's thumping header is the best.										
29	A	CHARLTON		1	W	5-1	3-0	Taylor 12, 26, Charlton 42, 46, 59	Wood	Byrne	Bent	Colman	Jones	McGuinness	Berry	Whelan	Taylor	Charlton	Pegg
	18/2		***16,408***	*22*	46			*Ayre 86*	*Duff*	*Edwards*	*Townsend*	*Hewie*	*Jago*	*Cox*	*Lawrie*	*Ayre*	*Leary*	*White*	*Kiernan*
								Ref: K Stokes	Charlton are five points adrift and have conceded 96 goals. Their defence, with debutant Trevor Edwards, caves in to a slick United attack with young Charlton deadly with his shooting. Despite fine weather, the midweek afternoon kick-off means that big areas of the Valley are deserted.										
30	H	BLACKPOOL		1	L	0-2	0-0		Wood	Foulkes	Byrne	Colman	Jones	Edwards	Berry	Whelan	Taylor	Charlton	Pegg
	23/2		42,707	*5*	46			*Perry 60, Durie 84*	*Farm*	*Armfield*	*Garrett*	*Kelly J*	*Gratrix*	*Fenton*	*Matthews*	*Taylor*	*Hepton*	*Durie*	*Perry*
								Ref: J Clough	Blackpool shoot United down in a mudbath and make it four away wins in a row. Tommy Taylor is limping early on and Pegg and Charlton are off colour. Tiny Ernie Taylor has a hand in both goals – Perry scoring from a rebound and Durie's deadly shooting. The lead is four points.										
31	A	EVERTON		1	W	2-1	1-0	Webster 30, 75	Wood	Byrne	Bent	Goodwin	Blanchflower	McGuinness	Berry	Whelan	Webster	Doherty	Pegg
	6/3		*34,029*	*11*	48			*Fielding 54*	*Dunlop*	*Donovan*	*Tansey*	*Farrell*	*Jones*	*Rea*	*Harris*	*Thomas*	*Gauld*	*Fielding*	*Eglington*
								Ref: H Howarth	Six of the Bournemouth Cup heroes are rested as United comfortably avenge the home defeat. Billy Whelan's ball work is amazing. Webster scores off the post and Fielding heads a leveller. The European Cup draw pairs the Reds, now 5-1 for the treble, with the mighty Real Madrid.										

No	H/A	Opponent	Pos	Res	F-A	H-T	Scorers, Times, and Referees	1	2	3	4	5	6	7	8	9	10	11
32	H	ASTON VILLA	1	D	1-1	1-0	Charlton 15	Wood	Foulkes	Byrne	Goodwin	Blanchflower	McGuinness	Berry	Whelan	Edwards	Charlton	Pegg
	9/3	55,686	*15*	49			*Dixon 60*	*Sims*	*Lynn*	*Aldis*	*Crowther*	*Dugdale*	*Saward*	*Smith*	*Sewell*	*Myerscough*	*Dixon*	*McParland*
							Ref: T Blenkinsopp	Villa have drawn five in a row and deserve a point. United run them off their feet for 45 minutes and lead through Charlton's crackerjack goal. Dogged Villa fight back and, when Billy Myerscough's header bounces down off the crossbar, their claims look justified but are rejected.										
33	A	WOLVERHAMPTON	1	D	1-1	1-1	Charlton 35	**Clayton**	Foulkes	Byrne	Coleman	Blanchflower	Edwards	Berry	Whelan	Webster	Charlton	Pegg
	16/3	*53,238*	*5*	50			*Broadbent 17*	*Williams*	*Stuart*	*Harris*	*Clamp*	*Wright*	*Flowers*	*Hooper*	*Murray*	*Wilshaw*	*Broadbent*	*Deeley*
							Ref: J Powell	An under-strength side grinds out a courageous result after soaking up strong Wolves pressure. Gordon Clayton's debut is solid – he can do little about Broadbent's header from Wilshaw's cross. Clamp hesitates and Charlton scores with a half-hit shot. Home fans jeer 'lucky' Reds.										
34	H	BOLTON	1	L	0-2	0-1		Wood	Foulkes	Byrne	Coleman	Blanchflower	McGuinness	Berry	Whelan	Edwards	Charlton	Pegg
	25/3	61,101	*8*	50			*Parry 30, Foulkes 49(og)*	*Hopkinson*	*Hartle*	*Banks*	*Hennin*	*Higgins*	*Edwards*	*Holden*	*Stevens*	*Allcock*	*Parry*	*Gubbins*
							Ref: E Oxley	The floodlights are used for the first time and United play in all red. The party is spoiled by Parry's murderous shot and Hartle's shot that flies off Foulkes' head. Edwards, for once, labours up front and Taylor is missed. Gubbins spurns two good chances but Bolton deserve the win.										
35	A	LEEDS	1	W	2-1	1-1	Berry 34, Charlton 88	Wood	Foulkes	Byrne	Coleman	Blanchflower	Edwards	Berry	Whelan	Webster	Charlton	Pegg
	30/3	*47,216*	*7*	52			*Charles 42*	*Wood*	*Dunn*	*Hair*	*Gibson*	*Charlton*	*Kerfoot*	*Meek*	*Crowe*	*Charles*	*O'Brien*	*Overfield*
							Ref: R Windle	Elland Road's biggest crowd of season sees the Reds almost clinch the title with Charlton's late close-range goal after Royden Wood fails to hold Whelan's shot. Leeds players claim Bobby handled. Preston and Spurs slip up. Blanchflower keeps close tabs on Juventus-bound Charles.										
36	H	TOTTENHAM	1	D	0-0	0-0		Wood	Foulkes	Bent	Coleman	Blanchflower	McGuinness	Berry	Whelan	Taylor	Viollet	Scanlon
	6/4	60,583	*3*	53				*Reynolds*	*Baker*	*Hopkins*	*Blanchflower*	*Norman*	*Marchi*	*Medwin*	*Harmer*	*Dunmore*	*Brooks*	*Dyson*
							Ref: L Callaghan	Byrne and Edwards are playing for England v Scotland, David Pegg has a sore throat, but Taylor returns. Spurs defend stoutly with strong-arm tactics at times. Dennis Viollet is off colour and there are few chances. The players' minds may be on the Madrid first leg on Thursday night.										
37	A	LUTON	1	W	2-0	0-0	Taylor 52, 76	Wood	Foulkes	Byrne	Goodwin	Blanchflower	Edwards	Berry	Viollet	Taylor	Charlton	Scanlon
	13/4	*21,244*	*17*	55				*Baynham*	*McNally*	*Jones*	*Morton*	*Kelly*	*Pearce*	*Cullen*	*Turner*	*Davies*	*Brown*	*Adam*
							Ref: P Brandwood	Less than forty-eight hours after Madrid, a very tired looking United have scarcely a shot on target in the first half. A poor Luton side are struggling and have gone five games without goal. Edwards sets up the first for Tommy before Berry's free-kick is headed in by the assassin.										
38	A	BURNLEY	1	W	3-1	2-1	Whelan 17, 44, 65	Wood	Foulkes	Byrne	Goodwin	Blanchflower	Edwards	Berry	Whelan	Taylor	Charlton	Pegg
	19/4	*37,823*	*7*	57			*McIlroy 36*	*McDonald*	*Angus*	*Winton*	*Seith*	*Adamson*	*Miller*	*Newlands*	*McIlroy*	*Shackleton*	*Cheesebrough*	*Pilkington*
							Ref: A Ellis	Billy Whelan had gone twelve games without a goal, but smashes Burnley's year-long unbeaten home record. At 1-2, Burnley miss a penalty after Foulkes punched out a shot. Taylor is immaculate and has a hand in all three and Charlton hit the post. Brave Burnley go down fighting.										
39	H	SUNDERLAND	1	W	4-0	1-0	Whelan 12, 74, Edwards 81, Taylor 89	Wood	Foulkes	Byrne	Colman	Blanchflower	Edwards	Berry	Whelan	Taylor	Charlton	Pegg
	20/4	58,725	*19*	59				*Bollands*	*Hedley*	*McDonald*	*Revie*	*Aitken*	*Elliott*	*Bingham*	*Anderson*	*Fleming*	*Shackleton*	*Grainger*
							Ref: P Rhodes	United are champions after a one-sided match. Sunderland are safe from relegation but lose keeper Bollands just after half-time. Fleming deputises and can't be faulted and earns a standing ovation. 35-year-old Len Shackleton is magical, but the day belongs to the rampant babes.										
40	H	BURNLEY	1	W	2-0	0-0	Dawson 65, Webster 88	Wood	Foulkes	Greaves	Goodwin	Cope	McGuinness	Webster	Doherty	**Dawson**	Viollet	Scanlon
	22/4	41,540	*8*	61				*McDonald*	*Angus*	*Winton*	*Seith*	*Adamson*	*Miller*	*Newlands*	*McIlroy*	*Lawson*	*Cheesebrough*	*Pilkington*
							Ref: A Ellis	Busby rests nine players ahead of the Real second leg and they are still too good for Burnley in an anticlimactic game. Dawson has a heap of chances before he heads in and United's reserves should have scored more. Six-footer, 18-year-old Ian Lawson gives the defence a few scares.										
41	A	CARDIFF	1	W	3-2	1-0	Scanlon 43, 90p, Dawson 86	Wood	Foulkes	Greaves	Coleman	Blanchflower	McGuinness	Webster	Whelan	Dawson	Viollet	Scanlon
	27/4	*17,708*	*21*	63			*Hitchens 47, 52*	*Vearncombe*	*Rutter*	*Stitfall*	*Harrington*	*Malloy*	*Baker*	*Walsh*	*McSeveney*	*Hitchens*	*Jones*	*Tucker*
							Ref: D Howell	Blanchflower captains an under-strength team in the Wembley kit. Doomed Cardiff look set to win until Dawson's shot flies in off McSeveney and Scanlon nets late winner after Webster was fouled. Scanlon's earlier volley is the club's 100th league goal and it's the record 11th double.										
42	H	WEST BROM	1	D	1-1	1-0	Dawson 24	Clayton	Greaves	Byrne	Goodwin	Jones	McGuinness	Berry	Doherty	Dawson	Viollet	Scanlon
	29/4	**20,976**	*11*	64			*Millard 90p*	*Sanders*	*Howe*	*Millard*	*Williams S*	*Barlow*	*Setters*	*Griffin*	*Robson*	*Allen*	*Kevan*	*Horobin*
	Home	Away					Ref: T Jepson	The curtain comes down on a Monday evening with Clayton deputising for the injured Wood. It is virtually a reserve team that has a win snatched from its grasp by a last-minute penalty after a late pitch invasion. Berry misses a penalty as United coast in the last twenty minutes.										
Average	45,481	39,623																

LEAGUE DIVISION 1 (CUP-TIES)

Manager: Matt Busby

SEASON 1956-57

Charity Shield			F-A	H-T	Scorers, Times, and Referees	1	2	3	4	5	6	7	8	9	10	11
A MANCHESTER C	1	W	1-0	0-0	Viollet 75	Wood	Foulkes	Byrne	Colman	Jones	Edwards	Berry	Whelan	Taylor	Viollet	Pegg
24/10 30,495 20						*Savage*	*Leivers*	*Little*	*Revie*	*Ewing*	*Paul*	*Fagan*	*Hayes*	*Johnstone*	*Dyson*	*Clarke*
					Ref: J Clough	The game is played under floodlights and televised live. An injury to Wood allows 16-year-old Dave Gaskell to become the youngest debutant and he performs well. United are in command but over-elaborate. A one-two between Whelan and Berry allows Viollet to lash in the winner.										

European Cup			F-A	H-T	Scorers, Times, and Referees	1	2	3	4	5	6	7	8	9	10	11
1:1 A ANDERLECHT	1	W	2-0	1-0	Viollet 20, Taylor 70	Wood	Foulkes	Byrne	Colman	Jones	Blanchflower	Berry	Whelan	Taylor	Viollet	Pegg
12/9 (Belgium) *35,000*						*Week*	*Matthys*	*Culot*	*Lippens*	*De Koster*	*Vanderwilt*	*DeDryver*	*Jurion*	*Dewael*	*Mermans*	*Vandenbosch*
					Ref: L Horn (Holland)	Edwards misses the European debut under the Parc Astrid lights with a chipped toe. Ex-Blackburn keeper Bill Gormlie's team of part-time Belgian internationals, including 57-cap Jeff Mermans, pile the pressure on. The brave Wood saves a penalty after the excellent Jones handled.										
1:2 H ANDERLECHT	1	W	10-0	5-0	Taylor 9, 21, 48, Viollet 27, 34, 40, 75, Whelan 64, 87, Berry 85	Wood	Foulkes	Byrne	Colman	Jones	Edwards	Berry	Whelan	Taylor	Viollet	Pegg
26/9 43,635 (At Maine Road)						*Week*	*Gettemans*	*Culot*	*Hanon*	*De Koster*	*Vanderwilt*	*DeDryver*	*Vandenbosche*	*Mermans*	*Dewael*	*Jurion*
					Ref: M Griffiths (Wales) (United win 12-0 on aggregate)	In heavy rain and on a muddy Maine Road pitch, the Babes are awesome. Anderlecht are ripped apart with Pegg, despite not scoring, creating havoc in the first half. Referee Griffths says, 'they couldn't pick an England team to beat this United team'. The Belgians get a super ovation.										
2:1 H BORUSSIA DORT	1	W	3-2	3-0	Viollet 11, 26, Pegg 34 *Kapitulski 68, Preissler 78*	Wood	Foulkes	Byrne	Colman	Jones	Edwards	Berry	Whelan	Taylor	Viollet	Pegg
17/10 (W Germ) 75,598 (At Maine Road)						*Kwiatkowski*	*Burgsmuller*	*Sandmann*	*Schlebrowski*	*Michallek*	*Bracht*	*Peters*	*Preissler*	*Kelbassa*	*Schmidt*	*Kapitulski*
					Ref: L Horn (Holland)	In an atmosphere of white heat, United flag after a breathless first half that could have had six goals. The skilful German part-timers fight back and sloppy defending leaves the tie finely balanced. Viollet is in dazzling form. The press think United and Edwards especially are too cocky.										
2:2 A BORUSSIA DORT	1	D	0-0	0-0		Wood	Foulkes	Byrne	Colman	Jones	McGuinness	Berry	Whelan	Taylor	Edwards	Pegg
21/11 *44,570*						*Kwiatkowski*	*Burgsmuller*	*Sandmann*	*Schlebrowski*	*Michallek*	*Bracht*	*Peters*	*Preissler*	*Kelbassa*	*Schmidt*	*Niepieklo*
					Ref: J Martens (Holland) (United win 3-2 on aggregate)	United have to play on the bone-hard icy Rote Erde pitch without rubber studs. It is a plucky display and they are cheered on by hundreds of British soldiers stationed in Germany, many perched up trees. Wood, Byrne and Jones get the plaudits for a brave display under floodlights.										
3:1 A ATHLETIC BILBAO	1	L	3-5	0-3	Taylor 49, Viollet 54, Whelan 85 *Uribe 2, 20, Marc' 44, 72, Arteche 79*	Wood	Foulkes	Byrne	Colman	Jones	Edwards	Berry	Whelan	Taylor	Viollet	Pegg
16/1 (Spain) *45,000*						*Carmelo*	*Orue*	*Canito*	*Mauri*	*Garay*	*Etura*	*Arteche*	*Marcaida*	*Merodio*	*Uribe*	*Gainza*
					Ref: A Dusch (W Germany)	After 48 hours of rain before the match, snow falls from the start, turning the pitch into a morass. Mark Jones slips in the mud for the first and poor marking at set pieces is punished by the Basques. A vociferous crowd is stunned by United's reposte, and Whelan's late goal is a lifeline.										
3:2 H ATHLETIC BILBAO	1	W	3-0	1-0	Viollet 43, Taylor 72, Berry 84	Wood	Foulkes	Byrne	Colman	Jones	Edwards	Berry	Whelan	Taylor	Viollet	Pegg
6/2 70,000						*Carmelo*	*Orue*	*Canito*	*Mauri*	*Garay*	*Maguregui*	*Arteche*	*Marcaida*	*Etura*	*Merodio*	*Gainza*
					Ref: A Dusch (W Germany) (United win 6-5 on aggregate)	United go through after a dramatic pulse-stirring game. 7s 6d seats are going for £11 and Bilbao are on £200 to win. Patient United have to wait for Edwards' vicious shot to bounce off Garay for Viollet to net. Two offside goals are disallowed before Taylor makes Berry's late goal.										
SF 1 A REAL MADRID	1	L	1-3	0-0	Taylor 82 *Rial 60, Di Stefano 75, Mateos 85*	Wood	Foulkes	Byrne	Colman	Blanchflower	Edwards	Berry	Whelan	Taylor	Viollet	Pegg
11/4 *(Spain) 130,000*						*Alonso*	*Becceril*	*Lesmes*	*Munoz*	*Marquitos*	*Zarraga*	*Kopa*	*Mateos*	*Di Stefano*	*Rial*	*Gento*
					Ref: L Horn (Holland)	Real are held for an hour and get the breaks. Foulkes fouls the speedy Gento but the ref plays advantage and Rial nets. Di Stefano lobs Wood, then Gento and Rial set up Mateos. Di Stefano lashes out at his marker Eddie Colman and is lucky to stay on. Real are on £350 per man to win.										
SF 2 H REAL MADRID	1	D	2-2	0-2	Taylor 61, Charlton 85 *Kopa 24, Rial 32*	Wood	Foulkes	Byrne	Colman	Jones	Edwards	Berry	Whelan	Taylor	Charlton	Pegg
25/4 61,676						*Alonso*	*Torres*	*Lesmes*	*Munoz*	*Marquitos*	*Zarraga*	*Kopa*	*Mateos*	*Di Stefano*	*Rial*	*Gento*
					Ref: M Lequesne (France) (United lose 3-5 on aggregate)	Becceril, fleeced by Pegg in Madrid is controversially replaced by on-loan Torres. Real commit 29 fouls in a bruising match and are booed off. The awesome Di Stefano sets up Kopa before Wood parried Gento's shot straight to Rial. United's goals set the crowd alight but are too late.										

FA Cup			F-A	H-T	Scorers, Times, and Referees	1	2	3	4	5	6	7	8	9	10	11
3 A HARTLEPOOLS	1	W	4-3	3-1	Whelan 9, 79, Berry 10, Taylor 30 *Stamper 35, Johnson 53, Newton 65*	Wood	Foulkes	Byrne	Colman	Jones	Edwards	Berry	Whelan	Taylor	Viollet	Pegg
5/1 *17,426 3N:4*						*Guthrie*	*Cameron*	*Thompson*	*Newton*	*Moore*	*Anderson*	*Robinson*	*Stamper*	*Johnson*	*McGuigan*	*Luke*
					Ref: J Sherlock	In front of a record crowd, big-hearted Pool stage a thrilling recovery and pull level after looking dead. Hartlepool have lost only once at home and their mudheap of a pitch is to their advantage. There are 11 heroes, but Guthrie makes some wonder saves and the limping Johnson scores.										
4 A WREXHAM	1	W	5-0	3-0	Whelan 7, 47, Byrne 16p, Taylor 39, 59	Wood	Foulkes	Byrne	Colman	Jones	Edwards	Webster	Whelan	Taylor	Viollet	Pegg
26/1 *34,445 3N:7*						*Waters*	*McGowan*	*Parker*	*Green*	*Fox*	*Davies*	*Jones G*	*Hewitt*	*Thompson*	*Anderson*	*Jones D*
					Ref: J Swain	For seven minutes United look jittery, but once in the lead they never look like repeating the Hartlepool showing and are rarely extended. The										

Rd		Opponents		Res	F-A	H-T	Scorers, Times, and Referees											
5	H	EVERTON	1	W	1-0	0-0	Edwards 68	Wood	Foulkes	Byrne	Colman	Jones	Edwards	Berry	Whelan	Taylor	Viollet	Pegg
	16/2	61,803 *11*						*Dunlop*	*Donovan*	*Tansey*	*Farrell*	*Jones*	*Rea*	*Payne*	*Gauld*	*Harris J*	*Fielding*	*Eglington*
							Ref: H Webb	After a bright opening from the visitors, United have the Everton goal under siege with 12 shots in thirty minutes before Edwards scores from 18 yards. This is revenge for the league defeat, but 10 minutes from time Gauld intercepts Byrne's back-pass. Wood somehow saves the day.										
6	A	BOURNEMOUTH	1	W	2-1	0-1	Berry 60, 65p	Wood	Foulkes	Byrne	Colman	Jones	McGuinness	Berry	Whelan	Edwards	Viollet	Pegg
	2/3	*28,799 3S:8*					*Bedford 25*	*Godwin*	*Lyons*	*Woollard*	*Clayton*	*Hughes*	*Brown*	*Stiffle*	*Newsham*	*Bedford*	*Norris*	*Cutler*
							Ref: F Coultas	Edwards, deputising for the injured Taylor, is switched to the back when Jones was carried off after 11 minutes. Giant-killers Bournemouth have beaten Spurs and Wolves and it looks ominous when Bedford nets. Berry breaks the offside trap to score. Whelan's header is palmed out.										
SF	N	BIRMINGHAM	1	W	2-0	2-0	Berry 12, Charlton 13	Wood	Foulkes	Byrne	Colman	Blanchflower	Edwards	Berry	Whelan	Viollet	Charlton	Pegg
	23/3	*65,107 12*						*Merrick*	*Hall*	*Green*	*Watts*	*Smith*	*Warhurst*	*Astall*	*Kinsey*	*Brown*	*Murphy*	*Govan*
		(at Hillsborough)					Ref: J Sherlock	Without hitting the heights, United are too good for a poor Blues team. It is all over quickly. First Berry beats Green for speed and hits a left foot shot past Merrick. Then Pegg roars away and crosses for a Charlton special. Taylor is injured but United are on course for the double.										
F	N	ASTON VILLA	1	L	1-2	0-0	Taylor 83	Wood	Foulkes	Byrne	Colman	Blanchflower	Edwards	Berry	Whelan	Taylor	Charlton	Pegg
	4/5	*99,225 10*					*McParland 67, 71*	*Sims*	*Lynn*	*Aldis*	*Crowther*	*Dugdale*	*Saward*	*Smith*	*Sewell*	*Myerscough*	*Dixon*	*McParland*
		(at Wembley)					Ref: F Coultas	The game is marred by McParland's reckless challenge on Wood after six minutes. Blanchflower stars in goal as ten-men United are denied the double by the villains. The concussed Wood returns to limp on the wing and Taylor heads a goal in vain. Villa win the Cup after 37 years.										

			Home					Away					
	P	W	D	L	F	A	W	D	L	F	A	Pts
1 MAN UNITED	42	14	4	3	55	25	14	4	3	48	29	64
2 Tottenham	42	15	4	2	70	24	7	8	6	34	32	56
3 Preston	42	15	4	2	50	19	8	6	7	34	37	56
4 Blackpool	42	14	3	4	55	26	8	6	7	38	39	53
5 Arsenal	42	12	5	4	45	21	9	3	9	40	48	50
6 Wolves	42	17	2	2	70	29	3	6	12	24	41	48
7 Burnley	42	14	5	2	41	21	4	5	12	15	29	46
8 Leeds	42	10	8	3	42	18	5	6	10	30	45	44
9 Bolton	42	13	6	2	42	23	3	6	12	23	42	44
10 Aston Villa	42	10	8	3	45	25	4	7	10	20	30	43
11 West Brom	42	8	8	5	31	25	6	6	9	28	36	42
12 Birmingham	42	12	5	4	52	25	3	4	14	17	44	39
12 Chelsea	42	7	8	6	43	36	6	5	10	30	37	39
14 Sheffield W	42	14	3	4	55	29	2	3	16	27	59	38
15 Everton	42	10	5	6	34	28	4	5	12	27	51	38
16 Luton	42	10	4	7	32	26	4	5	12	26	50	37
17 Newcastle	42	10	5	6	43	31	4	3	14	24	56	36
18 Manchester C	42	10	2	9	48	42	3	7	11	30	46	35
19 Portsmouth	42	8	6	7	37	35	2	7	12	25	57	33
20 Sunderland	42	9	5	7	40	30	3	3	15	27	58	32
21 Cardiff	42	7	6	8	35	34	3	3	15	18	54	29
22 Charlton	42	7	3	11	31	44	2	1	18	31	76	22
	924	246	109	107	996	616	107	109	246	616	996	924

Odds & ends

Double wins: (11) Preston, Portsmouth, Chelsea, Man City, Arsenal, Charlton, Leeds, Luton, Sunderland, Burnley, Cardiff.
Double losses: (1) Bolton.

Won from behind: (8) West Brom (a), Chelsea (a), Charlton (h), Cardiff (h), Portsm'th (a), Arsenal (h), Cardiff (a), Bournem'th FAC (a).
Lost from in front: (1) Everton (h).

High spots: Retaining the title.
The great European nights at Maine Road.
The first Wembley appearance since 1948.
The international recognition of the players.

Low spots: Defeat at Wembley.
Defeat to Real Madrid in the European Cup semi-final.

Sent off: United (0).
Sent off: Opponents (0).

Ever-presents: (0).
Hat-tricks: (5) Viollet (2), Charlton, Whelan, Taylor.
Opposing hat-tricks: (0).
Leading scorer: Whelan (26).

	Appearances			Goals			
	Lge	FAC	Eur	Lge	FAC	Eur	Tot
Bent, Geoff	**6**						
Berry, Johnny	**40**	5	8	**8**	4	2	**14**
Blanchflower, Jackie	**11**	2	2				
Byrne, Roger	**36**	6	8		1		**1**
Charlton, Bobby	**14**	2	1	**10**	1	1	**12**
Clayton, Gordon	**2**						
Colman, Eddie	**36**	6	8	**1**			**1**
Cope, Ronnie	**2**						
Dawson, Alex	**3**			**3**			**3**
Doherty, John	**3**						
Edwards, Duncan	**34**	6	7	**5**	1		**6**
Foulkes, Bill	**39**	6	8				
Goodwin, Freddie	**6**						
Greaves, Ian	**3**						
Hawksworth, Tony	**1**						
Jones, Mark	**29**	4	7				
McGuinness, Wilf	**13**	1	1				
Pegg, David	**37**	6	8	**6**		1	**7**
Scanlon, Albert	**5**			**2**			**2**
Taylor, Tommy	**32**	4	8	**22**	4	8	**34**
Viollet, Dennis	**27**	5	6	**16**		9	**25**
Webster, Colin	**5**	1		**3**			**3**
Whelan, Billy	**39**	6	8	**26**	4	3	**33**
Wood, Ray	**39**	6	8				
(own-goals)				**1**			**1**
24 players used	**462**	**66**	**88**	**103**	**15**	**24**	**142**

LEAGUE DIVISION 1

Manager: Matt Busby

SEASON 1957-58

No	Date	Opponent	Att	Pos	Pt	F-A	H-T	Scorers, Times, and Referees	1	2	3	4	5	6	7	8	9	10	11
1	A	LEICESTER			W	3-0	0-0	Whelan 71, 75, 79	Wood	Foulkes	Byrne	Colman	Blanchflower	Edwards	Berry	Whelan	Taylor T	Viollet	Pegg
	24/8		*40,214*		2				*Maclaren*	*Milburn*	*Ogilvie*	*Morris*	*Froggatt*	*O'Neill*	*McDonald*	*McNeill*	*Hines*	*Rowley*	*Hogg*
								Ref: A Bond	Leicester's return to the top flight is spoiled by Whelan's hat-trick in eight minutes after Maclaren had kept the home side in the game. 44-goal Arthur Rowley and ex-Red Johnny Morris, now 33 and sent off in a trial match last week, are quiet. Edwards' silky passing catches the eye.										
2	H	EVERTON			W	3-0	1-0	Taylor T 44, Jones 54 (og), Viollet 60	Wood	Foulkes	Byrne	Colman	Blanchflower	Edwards	Berry	Whelan	Taylor T	Viollet	Pegg
	28/8		59,343		4				*Dunlop*	*Donovan*	*Tansey*	*Birch*	*Jones*	*Meagan*	*Harris J*	*Temple*	*Hickson*	*Fielding*	*Williams*
								Ref: E Oxley	Last season's defeat is avenged in style. United turn up the heat and win with ease. Taylor heads in Viollet's cross and Viollet scores through Dunlop's legs. Everton, managed by Ian Buchan keep trying but make no impression. Dave Hickson is back at Goodison after two years away.										
3	H	MANCHESTER C		1	W	4-1	2-0	Edwards 15, Berry 20, Viollet 65,	Wood	Foulkes	Byrne	Colman	Blanchflower	Edwards	Berry	Whelan	Taylor T	Viollet	Pegg
	31/8		63,347	*17*	6			*Barnes 59* [Taylor T 86]	*Trautmann*	*Leivers*	*Little*	*Barnes*	*Ewing*	*Warhurst*	*Barlow*	*Hayes*	*Johnstone*	*McAdams*	*Clarke*
								Ref: F Coultas	A stroll in the sun for the Reds as they cut repeatedly through City's disorganised defence. City fight but have no answer to United's skill. Edwards' shot crashes in after a one-two with Whelan, Berry nods in, Viollet waltzes through, and Taylor taps in after Pegg's shot is parried.										
4	A	EVERTON		1	D	3-3	3-1	Viollet 12, Berry 30, Whelan 39	Wood	Foulkes	Byrne	Colman	Blanchflower	Edwards	Berry	Whelan	Taylor T	Viollet	Pegg
	4/9		***71,868***	*8*	7			*Temple 37, 77, Harris J 57*	*Dunlop*	*Donovan*	*Tansey*	*Birch*	*Jones*	*Meagan*	*Harris J*	*Temple*	*Hickson*	*Fielding*	*Harris B*
								Ref: A Westwood	A record away league attendance for United as everyone wants to see the Reds. Blanchflower's facial injury upsets the rhythm with Edwards switched to centre-half. Everton's fitness enables them to get back into a classic match. Dave Hickson upsets United and makes two goals.										
5	H	LEEDS		1	W	5-0	1-0	Berry 44, 65, Viollet 60, [Taylor T 62, 69]	Wood	Foulkes	Byrne	Colman	Blanchflower	Edwards	Berry	Whelan	Taylor T	Viollet	Pegg
	7/9		50,842	*15*	9				*Wood*	*Dunn*	*Hair*	*Ripley*	*Marsden*	*Kerfoot*	*Meek*	*O'Brien*	*Baird*	*Brook*	*Overfield*
								Ref: H Husband	Leeds are rudderless after John Charles' move to Italy. Hair is stretchered off after a clash with Berry and Leeds rarely get out of their half again. Four goals in nine minutes leave Leeds shell-shocked and only the brilliance of Royden Wood keeps the score down. Colman superb.										
6	A	BLACKPOOL		1	W	4-1	2-0	Whelan 8, 60, Viollet 12, 75	Wood	Foulkes	Byrne	Colman	Blanchflower	Edwards	Berry	Whelan	Taylor T	Viollet	Pegg
	9/9		*34,181*	*15*	11			*Mudie 87*	*Farm*	*Armfield*	*Garrett*	*Kelly J*	*Gratrix*	*Fenton*	*Matthews*	*Taylor*	*Mudie*	*Peterson*	*Perry*
								Ref: A Ellis	Blackpool, fielding 42-year-old Stanley Matthews, set a fierce pace and Edwards twice clears off the line. United step up a gear and demolish the Seasiders. Matthews is superbly handled by Byrne and Whelan and Viollet snatch the goals. Pool manager Joe Smith's reign nears its end.										
7	A	BOLTON		1	L	0-4	0-1	*[Lofthouse 85]*	Wood	Foulkes	Byrne	Colman	Blanchflower	Edwards	Berry	Whelan	Taylor T	Viollet	Pegg
	14/9		*48,003*	*9*	11			*Stevens 6, Birch 52, Parry 72p,*	*Hopkinson*	*Ball*	*Edwards*	*Hennin*	*Higgins*	*Bell*	*Birch*	*Stevens*	*Lofthouse*	*Parry*	*Holden*
								Ref: E Jennings	The pundits who say it's a one-horse race are quiet after Bolton's blitz of a slack United. The nippy home forwards run amok and, although Whelan hits the bar, chances are few. Even Ball's injury fails to stop Bill Ridding's Trotters, who have not lost at home to United since 1949.										
8	H	BLACKPOOL		2	L	1-2	0-2	Edwards 86	Wood	Foulkes	Byrne	Colman	Blanchflower	Edwards	Berry	Whelan	Taylor T	Viollet	Pegg
	18/9		41,003	*16*	11			*Mudie 1, 31*	*Farm*	*Garrett*	*Wright*	*Kelly J*	*Gratrix*	*Kelly H*	*Harris*	*Taylor*	*Mudie*	*Peterson*	*Perry*
								Ref: J Powell	Matthews is injured and one of six Blackpool changes after five defeats in seven. Blackpool defend like demons with Farm and Gratrix superb. Little Ernie Taylor is at the heart of everything and Scottish striker Jackie Mudie gives Blanchflower a rough time. Berry's 250th game in red.										
9	H	ARSENAL		2	W	4-2	3-2	Taylor T 10, Whelan 22, 43, Pegg 82	Wood	Foulkes	Byrne	Colman	Blanchflower	Edwards	Berry	Whelan	Taylor T	Viollet	Pegg
	21/9		47,389	*9*	13			*Tiddy 38, Herd 39*	*Sullivan*	*Charlton*	*Evans*	*Holton*	*Dodgin*	*Bowen*	*Clapton*	*Herd*	*Groves*	*Bloomfield*	*Tiddy*
								Ref: R Mann	United start like a train and deserve the early lead but Arsenal are given two goals on a plate. Chances galore are missed by United's forwards, but Wood is flailing at crosses begging to be put in the net. Berry destroys Evans, and the brilliant Colman sets up Pegg to clinch the points.										
10	A	WOLVERHAMPTON		4	L	1-3	0-0	Doherty 89	Wood	Foulkes	McGuinness	Goodwin	Blanchflower	Edwards	Berry	Doherty	Taylor T	Charlton	Pegg
	28/9		*48,825*	*2*	13			*Deeley 63, 68, Wilshaw 70*	*Finlayson*	*Showell*	*Harris*	*Clamp*	*Wright*	*Flowers*	*Deeley*	*Broadbent*	*Murray*	*Wilshaw*	*Mullen*
								Ref: M Griffiths	The flu epidemic hits United badly. Four players are missing and Berry and Taylor are weak. They hold out for an hour before the ubiquitous Norman Deeley takes over. The 5ft 4in winger heads in from Murray's cross and makes the third with Wilf McGuinness trailing in his wake.										

11	H	ASTON VILLA		4	W	4-1	2-0	Taylor T 15, 68, Dugdale 32(og),	Wood	Foulkes	Byrne	Colman	Jones M	McGuinness	Berry	Whelan	Taylor T	Charlton	Pegg
	5/10		43,332	*18*	15			*Pace 55* [Pegg 62]	Sims	Lynn	Aldis	Crowther	Dugdale	Saward	Hinchcliffe	Sewell	Pace	Crowe	Myerscough
								Ref: E Hill	The Wembley defeat is avenged but it's little consolation. Eric Houghton's injury-hit Villa lack punch and their defence is all at sea. Taylor is excellent and scores two with his feet. Jimmy Dugdale turns Berry's cross in and Pegg rams home a fourth after half a dozen shots are blocked.										
12	A	NOTT'M FOREST		3	W	2-1	1-0	Whelan 3, Viollet 59	Wood	Foulkes	Byrne	Colman	Blanchflower	Edwards	Berry	Whelan	Taylor T	Viollet	Pegg
	12/10		*47,804*	*4*	17			*Imlach 47*	*Thomson*	*Whare*	*Thomas*	*Morley*	*Watson*	*Burkitt*	*Gray*	*Quigley*	*Wilson*	*Baily*	*Imlach*
								Ref: L Howarth	Forest are back in the top flight after 32 years and have started well under veteran Billy Walker. A ground record crowd watch a breathtaking game with United needing to be in top form to win. Whelan's toe-end could have gone anywhere, and Viollet looks offside. Wood is brilliant.										
13	H	PORTSMOUTH		4	L	0-3	0-3		Wood	Foulkes	**Jones P**	Colman	Blanchflower	McGuinness	Berry	Whelan	Dawson	Viollet	Pegg
	19/10		39,423	*17*	17			*Henderson 6, Newman 43, Harris 44*	*Uprichard*	*Gunter*	*Wilson*	*Albury*	*Rutter*	*Dickinson*	*Harris*	*Gordon*	*Dougan*	*Henderson*	*Newman*
								Ref: J Topliss	United's grip on the title is slipping – they are five points behind leaders Wolves. Pompey are without a win in seven but tackle like demons and United miss their England stars. Foulkes miskicks for the first, Newman hooks in a corner, and debut boy Dougan sends Harris through.										
14	A	WEST BROM		5	L	3-4	2-3	Taylor T 7, 22, Whelan 76	Wood	Foulkes	Byrne	Goodwin	Blanchflower	Edwards	Berry	Whelan	Taylor T	Charlton	Pegg
	26/10		*52,664*	*2*	17			*Robson 16, 27, Kevan 41, Allen 62*	*Sanders*	*Howe*	*Setters*	*Dudley*	*Kennedy*	*Barlow*	*Griffin*	*Robson*	*Allen*	*Kevan*	*Horobin*
								Ref: J Baxter	The away crowds are phenomenal –everyone wants to see the Babes. Black Country rivals Wolves and Albion are roaring away. The pace of the game is breathtaking and Albion sneak it after United twice lead. Sanders saves Berry's penalty and new England cap Don Howe is superb.										
15	H	BURNLEY		4	W	1-0	0-0	Taylor T 52	Wood	Foulkes	Byrne	Goodwin	Blanchflower	Edwards	Berry	Whelan	Taylor T	Webster	Pegg
	2/11		49,689	*13*	19				*McDonald*	*Smith*	*Winton*	*Seith*	*Adamson*	*Shannon*	*Newlands*	*McIlroy*	*Pointer*	*Cheesebrough*	*Pilkington*
								Ref: A Holland	Billy Dougall has had a tough baptism as Burnley manager. In a fast and furious game Burnley soak up strong United pressure but lack any punch up front. Edwards is everywhere and Berry and Pegg threaten constantly. Pilkington almost saves a point but Wood saves brilliantly.										
16	A	PRESTON		3	D	1-1	0-0	Whelan 84	Wood	Foulkes	Byrne	Goodwin	Blanchflower	Edwards	Berry	Whelan	Taylor T	Webster	Pegg
	9/11		*39,066*	*4*	20			*Finney 71*	*Else*	*Cunningham*	*Walton*	*Docherty*	*Dunn*	*O'Farrell*	*Mayers*	*Thompson*	*Finney*	*Baxter*	*Taylor*
								Ref: A Luty	Preston are unbeaten at home since August 1956 and deserve a point in a thriller. Tom Finney misses a penalty when Edwards handles but later atones with a header. Edwards' goal is disallowed but, as United heap the pressure on, Billy Whelan is on the end of Taylor's powerful header.										
17	H	SHEFFIELD WED		4	W	2-1	2-1	Webster 6, 26	Wood	Foulkes	Byrne	Colman	Blanchflower	Edwards	Berry	Whelan	Taylor T	Webster	Pegg
	16/11		41,066	*21*	22			*Finney 10*	*Pllu*	*Martin*	*Curtis*	*McAnearney T*	*O'Donnell*	*Hill*	*Wilkinson*	*McAnearney J*	*Shiner*	*Froggatt*	*Finney*
								Ref: L Callaghan	Wednesday's league position is false – United are never in command. Webster's shot from a six-yard indirect free-kick spins through Charles Pllu's hands. Eric Taylor's team argue the ball did not cross the line but it stands. Webster nods in a second and Pllu saves a Berry penalty.										
18	A	NEWCASTLE		4	W	2-1	0-1	Edwards 85, Taylor T 88	Wood	Foulkes	Byrne	Colman	Blanchflower	Edwards	Scanlon	Whelan	Taylor T	Webster	Pegg
	23/11		*53,950*	*18*	24			*Mitchell 28*	*Simpson*	*Keith*	*McMichael*	*Scoular*	*Stokoe*	*Franks*	*Hughes*	*Eastham*	*White*	*Bell*	*Mitchell*
								Ref: A Holland	Newcastle's home form is dire – they have lost five – but United struggle to win. Edwards raced onto Taylor's pass and thunders home. Scanlon's superb hook is nodded in by Taylor. Scanlon also hits a post. Young George Eastham and Len White impress for the Magpies.										
19	H	TOTTENHAM		4	L	3-4	1-4	Pegg 17, 62, Whelan 67	**Gaskell**	Foulkes	Byrne	Colman	Blanchflower	Edwards	Scanlon	Whelan	Webster	Charlton	Pegg
	30/11		43,307	*11*	24			*Smith 22, 25, 44, Blanchfl' 35(og)*	*Ditchburn*	*Baker*	*Hopkins*	*Blanchflower*	*Norman*	*Ryden*	*Medwin*	*Brooks*	*Smith*	*Harmer*	*Robb*
								Ref: K Howley	The 47 game, 20 season unbeaten run at home to London clubs is ended by a sloppy display from the defence. Blanchflower is at fault for three goals as Bobby Smith has a field day. Young Gaskell is excused. Even so a minute from time Ditchburn pulls off a great save to deny Webster.										
20	A	BIRMINGHAM		4	D	3-3	2-3	Viollet 14, 46, Taylor T 18	Wood	Foulkes	Byrne	Colman	Jones M	Edwards	Berry	Whelan	Taylor T	Viollet	Pegg
	7/12		*35,191*	*15*	25			*Murphy 15, Astall 16, Kinsey 36*	*Merrick*	*Hall*	*Farmer*	*Larkin*	*Smith*	*Neal*	*Hooper*	*Kinsey*	*Brown*	*Murphy*	*Astall*
								Ref: L Howarth	United haven't won at St Andrews since 1929 and the Babes, looking weary from their Prague trip, are lucky to get a point from an all action game. Viollet's return peps the attack but Gordon Astall takes the honours, with one goal and two assists. England full-back Hall is cool.										
21	H	CHELSEA		4	L	0-1	0-0		Wood	Foulkes	Byrne	Colman	Jones M	Edwards	Berry	Whelan	Taylor T	Viollet	Pegg
	14/12		37,073	*10*	25			*Tindall 84*	*Matthews*	*Sillett P*	*Bellett*	*Casey*	*Mortimore*	*Saunders*	*Brabrook*	*McNichol*	*Tindall*	*Stubbs*	*Lewis*
								Ref: R Smith	Scoring sensation Jimmy Greaves has been rested, but Chelsea's first win at Old Trafford since 1920 is deserved. Woeful finishing by Viollet, Berry and Taylor leave United ten points adrift of Wolves. Taylor is well held by Mortimore and Brabrook's quick throw-ins faze United.										

No	Date	Att	Pos	Pt	F-A	H-T	Scorers, Times, and Referees	1	2	3	4	5	6	7	8	9	10	11
22	H LEICESTER		4	W	4-0	1-0	Scanlon 13, Charlt' 51, Viollet 65, 89	**Gregg**	Foulkes	Byrne	Colman	Jones M	Edwards	**Morgans**	Charlton	Taylor T	Viollet	Scanlon
	21/12	41,860	*22*	27				*Maclaren*	*Cunningham*	*Baillie*	*Morris*	*Newman*	*Walker*	*McDonald*	*Doherty*	*Gardiner*	*Rowley*	*Hogg*
							Ref: P Rhodes	Leicester just won 4-1 at Spurs for their first away win, but they are demolished as United find their shooting boots. Berry, Pegg and Wood are dropped. £23,000 keeper Harry Gregg has little to do and nippy Welsh winger Morgans looks good. Doherty's 11th City game since his move.										
23	H LUTON		2	W	3-0	2-0	Edwards 19p, Taylor T 31, Charlt' 70	Gregg	Foulkes	Byrne	Colman	Jones M	Edwards	Morgans	Charlton	Taylor T	Viollet	Scanlon
	25/12	*39,594*	*7*	29				*Baynham*	*Dunne*	*Hawkes*	*Pacey*	*Kelly*	*Pearce*	*Adam*	*Gregory*	*Brown*	*Groves*	*McLeod*
							Ref: R Hartley	Former England goalie Ron Baynham performs miracles, but is beaten three times. He fails to see Edwards' fierce penalty kick. He is on the ground as Taylor's shot goes in and Bobby Charlton's shot is diverted past him. The enthusiastic Charlton is the star and the crowd love him.										
24	A LUTON		3	D	2-2	2-0	Scanlon 28, Taylor T 43	Gregg	Foulkes	Byrne	Colman	Jones M	Edwards	Berry	Charlton	Taylor T	Viollet	Scanlon
	26/12	*26,478*	*6*	30			*Groves 50, Brown 89*	*Marsh*	*Dunne*	*Hawkes*	*Pacey*	*Kelly*	*Pearce*	*Adam*	*Groves*	*Brown*	*Cullen*	*McLeod*
							Ref: K Aston	Former Charlton reserve goalkeeper Eddie Marsh makes the first of only two appearances for Luton. The injury-crippled Hatters fight back to get a deserved point. Home debutant Dave Pacey has a cut forehead and needs treatment. Luton are in the highest position in their history.										
25	A MANCHESTER C		4	D	2-2	2-1	Viollet 7, Charlton 15	Gregg	Foulkes	Byrne	Colman	Jones M	Edwards	Morgans	Charlton	Webster	Viollet	Scanlon
	28/12	*70,483*	*5*	31			*Hayes 8, Foulkes 64(og)*	*Trautmann*	*Leivers*	*Little*	*Barnes*	*Ewing*	*Warhurst*	*Barlow*	*Kirkman*	*Johnstone*	*Hayes*	*Fagan*
							Ref: F Coultas	The highest derby crowd since 1947 see an enthralling match. Gregg is at fault for both goals and Foulkes nets when Harry misses a cross. Viollet is on-song, creating Charlton's goal and scoring a stunning goal – back-flicking the ball over his head and lobbing Bert Trautmann.										
26	A LEEDS		4	D	1-1	1-0	Viollet 37	Gregg	Foulkes	Byrne	Colman	Jones M	Edwards	Morgans	Charlton	Taylor T	Viollet	Scanlon
	11/1	*39,401*	20	32			*Baird 55*	*Wood*	*Dunn*	*Hair*	*Gibson*	*Charlton*	*Kerfoot*	*Meek*	*Cush*	*Baird*	*Forrest*	*Overfield*
							Ref: R Wood	Raich Carter's Leeds are struggling but put up a valiant show to earn a point. Jack Charlton is in fine form and overshadows his brother, who shoots wide twice and hits the bar. Viollet's header from Morgans' cross is cancelled out by Baird, when Gregg failed to hold a Meek shot.										
27	H BOLTON		4	W	**7-2**	4-1	Charl' 3,29,57, Viollet 30,65, Scan' 38, [Edwards 87p]	Gregg	Foulkes	Byrne	Colman	Jones M	Edwards	Morgans	Charlton	Taylor T	Viollet	Scanlon
	18/1	41,360	*13*	34			*Stevens 20, Loft' 64*	*Hopkinson*	*Hartle*	*Banks*	*Hennin*	*Higgins*	*Edwards B*	*Birch*	*Stevens*	*Lofthouse*	*Parry*	*Riley*
							Ref: J Topliss	England's keeper Eddie Hopkinson is blitzed by United at their best. Bolton lose the toss and face a strong wind and are outclassed. Charlton's opening goal is a gem as he beats three in a dribble before slamming home. Hoppie's only error is for Scanlon's goal. A perfect performance.										
28	A ARSENAL		3	W	5-4	3-0	Ed' 10, Charl' 34, Tay' T 43,72, Viol' 65	Gregg	Foulkes	Byrne	Colman	Jones M	Edwards	Morgans	Charlton	Taylor T	Viollet	Scanlon
	1/2	*63,578*	*12*	36			*Herd 58, Bloom' 60, 61, Tapsc't 77*	*Kelsey*	*Charlton*	*Evans*	*Ward*	*Fotheringham*	*Bowen*	*Groves*	*Tapscott*	*Herd*	*Bloomfield*	*Nutt*
							Ref: G Pullen	Arsenal, humbled in the FA Cup at Northampton, look set for a drubbing, but the Reds take their foot off the pedal and get blitzed. Classy United are six points behind the leaders. Scanlon's 70-yard run sets up Charlton's second and Taylor's winner is from an impossible angle.										
29	H NOTT'M FOREST		5	D	1-1	0-1	Dawson 75	Gregg	Foulkes	Greaves	Goodwin	Cope	**Crowther**	Webster	**Taylor E**	Dawson	**Pearson**	**Brennan**
	22/2	**66,346**	*6*	37			*Imlach 31*	*Thomson*	*Whare*	*Thomas*	*Morley*	*McKinlay*	*Burkitt*	*Gray*	*Quigley*	*Wilson*	*Joyce*	*Imlach*
							Ref: L Howarth	The gates are locked and, roared on by an emotional crowd, the biggest at the ground since 1920, United deserve a point. Imlach's brilliant strike is cancelled out by Dawson's header from a Pearson corner. The fans are openly weeping at the news that Duncan Edwards has died.										
30	H WEST BROM		6	L	**0-4**	0-2	*[Kevan 65]*	Gregg	Foulkes	Greaves	Goodwin	Cope	**Harrop**	Webster	Taylor E	Dawson	Pearson	Charlton
	8/3	63,479	*3*	37			*Allen 8, 81, Greaves 35(og),*	*Sanders*	*Howe*	*Williams S*	*Dudley*	*Kennedy*	*Barlow*	*Whitehouse*	*Robson*	*Allen*	*Kevan*	*Horobin*
							Ref: M Griffiths	Albion win the third game between the clubs in a week as the gates are locked again. Busby's voice from his Munich bed is emotionally relayed over the tannoy. United's tired defence is cut to shreds in a blizzard with Allen and Kevan, Taylor's England replacement to the fore.										
31	A BURNLEY		6	L	0-3	0-0	*[Cheesebrough 71]*	Gregg	Foulkes	Greaves	Goodwin	Cope	Crowther	Webster	Harrop	Dawson	Pearson!	Charlton
	15/3	*37,447*	*10*	37			*McIlroy 48, Shackleton 70,*	*McDonald*	*Smith*	*Winton*	*Shannon*	*Adamson*	*Miller*	*Newlands*	*McIlroy*	*Shackleton*	*Cheesebrough*	*Pilkington*
							Ref: E Oxley	Frayed tempers at Turf Moor as Harry Gregg and Shackleton clash. Pancho Pearson is ordered off for striking Les Shannon and Burnley take advantage with Pilkington in top form. Taylor has a pulled muscle and is missed. The emotion of it all is getting to some United players.										

No	H/A	Opponent	Pos	Res	F-A	HT	Scorers, Times, Referees	1	2	3	4	5	6	7	8	9	10	11
32	A	SHEFFIELD WED	8	L	0·1	0·1		Gregg	Foulkes	Cope	Goodwin	Harrop	Crowther	Webster	Taylor E	Dawson	Charlton	Brennan
29/3		*34,806*	*22*	37			*Shiner 40*	*Springett*	*Staniforth*	*Curtis*	*McAnearney T*	*Swan*	*O'Donnell*	*Wilkinson*	*Quixall*	*Shiner*	*Froggatt*	*Finney*
							Ref: J Topliss	The first of 11 games in 29 days. Wednesday are heading for the drop but grab a vital win. Harry Gregg is superb but has no chance as Shiner scores at the second attempt from Albert Quixall's slick pass. Quixall has a goal disallowed when the ref finds a gaping hole in the goal net.										
33	A	ASTON VILLA	8	L	2·3	1·1	Webster 13, Dawson 75	Gregg	Foulkes	Cope	Goodwin	Harrop	Crowther	Webster	Pearson	Dawson	Charlton	Brennan
31/3		***16,631***	*17*	37			*Myersc' 35, Hitchens 65, Sewell 90*	Sims	Lynn	Jones	Crowe	Dugdale	Saward	Smith	Hitchens	Sewell	Myerscough	McParland
							Ref: J Williams	A Monday afternoon means a small gate and the ground is half empty when the winner is scored. Charlton is in super form with his body swerves and change of pace bemusing Villa's leaden-footed backs. New signing Hitchens from Cardiff is helping to pull Villa out of trouble.										
34	H	SUNDERLAND	8	D	2·2	1·1	Charlton 7, Dawson 88	Gregg	Foulkes	Greaves	Goodwin	Cope	Crowther	Webster	Taylor E	Dawson	Charlton	Brennan
4/4		47,421	*19*	38			*Revie 43, O'Neill 60*	*Fraser*	*Hedley*	*Elliott*	*Anderson*	*Aitken*	*Pearce*	*Fogarty*	*Revie*	*Kitchenbrand*	*O'Neill*	*Grainger*
							Ref: M McCoy	Sunderland are unbeaten in five games as they fight to survive and they almost win against a United side preoccupied with Cup thoughts. Don Revie inspires Sunderland, who resort to time-wasting tactics. Bobby Charlton's left-footer swerves in the wind and goes in off the post.										
35	H	PRESTON	8	D	0·0	0·0		Gregg	Foulkes	Greaves	Goodwin	Cope	Crowther	Morgans	Taylor E	Webster	Charlton	**Heron**
5/4		48,413	*2*	39				*Else*	*Cunningham*	*Walton*	*Docherty*	*Dunn*	*O'Farrell*	*Mayers*	*Thompson*	*Finney*	*Farrall*	*Taylor*
							Ref: A Murdoch	Preston have lost one game in 16 and are chasing Wolves for the title. Tom Finney, on his 36th birthday, inspires them to a draw and, but for bad misses by Farrall and Thompson, would have won. Cup hero Dawson is axed and Irish hopeful Tom Heron shows a good turn of speed.										
36	A	SUNDERLAND	7	W	2·1	1·1	Webster 41, 65	Gregg	Foulkes	Greaves	Goodwin	Harrop	McGuinness	Morgans	Taylor E	Webster	Charlton	Pearson
7/4		*51,382*	*20*	41			*Fogarty 17*	*Fraser*	*Hedley*	*Elliott*	*Anderson*	*Aitken*	*Pearce*	*Fogarty*	*Revie*	*Kitchenbrand*	*O'Neill*	*Goodchild*
							Ref: L Howarth	The first win since the crash makes relegation a probability for the Roker men. Harry Gregg is hit by a stone and Ian Greaves by a bottle top in disgraceful crowd scenes. Taylor makes both goals and Wilf McGuinness makes a quick but welcome return after his cartilage operation.										
37	A	TOTTENHAM	9	L	0·1	0·1		Gregg	Foulkes	Greaves	Goodwin	Cope	Crowther	Morgans	Taylor E	Webster	Charlton	Pearson
12/4		*59,836*	*4*	41			*Harmer 42p*	*Reynolds*	*Hills*	*Henry*	*Blanchflower*	*Norman*	*Iley*	*Medwin*	*Harmer*	*Smith*	*Clayton*	*Jones*
							Ref: K Howley	A poor game is decided by a harsh penalty as Crowther is adjudged to have handled a high bouncing ball on a hard pitch. Spurs' new signing, Welsh winger Cliff Jones, looks useful. Cope is excellent against Bobby Smith but United for all their good moves rarely look like scoring.										
38	A	PORTSMOUTH	9	D	3·3	2·0	Webster 19, Taylor E 20, Dawson 84	Gaskell	Foulkes	Greaves	Crowther	Cope	McGuinness	Dawson	Taylor E	Webster	Pearson	Morgans
16/4		*39,975*	*18*	42			*Govan 61, Dougan 70, Harris 90*	*Uprichard*	*McGhee*	*Wilson*	*Phillips*	*Gunter*	*Dickinson*	*Harris*	*Govan*	*Dougan*	*Barnard*	*Crawford*
							Ref: R Warnke	Pompey grab a vital point in their relegation fight with a last-minute effort after bombarding United throughout the second half. Kenny Morgans, recovered from his Munich injuries makes all three goals. Gregg and Charlton are on international duty, Bobby winning his first cap.										
39	H	BIRMINGHAM	9	L	0·2	0·2		Gregg	Foulkes	Greaves	Goodwin	Cope	Crowther	Dawson	Taylor E	Webster	Pearson	Morgans
19/4		39,215	*13*	42			*Hooper 2, Green 26*	*Schofield*	*Hall*	*Green*	*Larkin*	*Sissons*	*Neal*	*Hooper*	*Jones*	*Orritt*	*Murphy*	*Astall*
							Ref: A Sparling	Pat Beasley's Blues are safe from relegation and comfortably beat a tired United side. England 'B' man Harry Hooper is in form and dribbles past five Reds before scoring from 15 yards. A keen breeze and a hard pitch make good football difficult. Cup final places still up for grabs.										
40	H	WOLVERHAMPTON	9	L	**0·4**	0·1	*[Broadbent 67p]*	Gaskell	Foulkes	Greaves	Goodwin	Cope	McGuinness	Dawson	Brennan	Webster	Viollet	Morgans
21/4		35,467	*1*	42			*Flowers 34, Clamp 60, Deeley 63,*	*Dwyer*	*Stuart*	*Jones*	*Clamp*	*Wright*	*Flowers*	*Deeley*	*Broadbent*	*Murray*	*Booth*	*Mullen*
							Ref: A Ellis	United give the league champions a guard of honour and allow themselves to be steamrollered by Cullis's worthy team. Dennis Viollet returns from his crash injuries, plays well and could get a game at Wembley. Wolves have lost only twice since September and have scored 112 goals.										
41	H	NEWCASTLE	9	D	1·1	1·0	Dawson 11	Gregg	Foulkes	Greaves	Crowther	Cope	McGuinness	Dawson	Taylor E	Webster	Charlton	Morgans
23/4		**28,573**	*18*	43			*White 86*	*Simpson*	*Keith*	*McMichael*	*Scoular*	*Stokoe*	*Franks*	*Hughes*	*Davies*	*White*	*Eastham*	*Mitchell*
							Ref: A Holland	Newcastle get the point they need for safety, with Len White's deserved late goal after Mitchell hit the post. Scoular and Eastham are too good to be relegated. United's play is pretty but lacks punch. Matt Busby returns for the first time since the crash and is given a hero's welcome.										
42	A	CHELSEA	9	L	1·2	1·2	Taylor E 15	Gregg	Foulkes	Greaves	Goodwin	Cope	Crowther	Dawson	Taylor E	Charlton	Viollet	Webster
26/4		*45,011*	*10*	43			*Cliss 13, Allen 24*	*Matthews*	*Sillett P*	*Sillett J*	*Mortimore*	*Scott*	*Casey*	*Brabrook*	*Cliss*	*Allen*	*Greaves*	*Harrison*
Home		Away					Ref: M Griffiths	Jimmy Murphy shuffles the side further, trying Webster on the left wing with success. Les Allen is Chelsea's oldest forward at 20, the rest are all teenagers, including Greaves, who spreads alarm every time he gets the ball. Chelsea's shoot-on-sight tactics pay off against a slack United.										
Average 46,073		45,562																

Charity Shield			F-A	H-T	Scorers, Times, and Referees	1	2	3	4	5	6	7	8	9	10	11
H ASTON VILLA	5	W	4-0	0-0	Taylor T 50, 54, 70, Berry 87p	Wood	Foulkes	Byrne	Goodwin	Blanchflower	Edwards	Berry	Whelan	Taylor T	Viollet	Pegg
22/10 27,923	*18*					Sims	Lynn	Aldis	Crowther	Dugdale	Saward	Smith	Sewell	Pace	Myerscough	McParland
					Ref: K Howley	In an effort to bury the memories of the Cup final, Wood and McParland shake hands as captains. The night belongs to Taylor. He is the first to react to Pegg's shot, taps in a second and scores from a rebound when Sims saves Berry's fierce shot. Wood is a spectator in a one-sided game.										

European Cup																			
P:1	A	SHAMROCK ROV		2	W	6-0	1-0	Taylor T 36, 70, Whelan 50, 53,	Wood	Foulkes	Byrne	Goodwin	Blanchflower	Edwards	Berry	Whelan	Taylor T	Viollet	Pegg
25/9		*(Eire)*	*46,000*					[Berry 84, Pegg 87]	*Darcy*	*Burke*	*Mackey*	*Nolan*	*Keogh*	*Hennessey*	*Peyton*	*Ambrose*	*Hamilton*	*Coad*	*Tuohy*
								Ref: L Van Nuffel (Belgium)	A full house at Dalymount Park have their hearts broken by a virtuoso performance from their countryman Billy Whelan. The game is even until Tommy Taylor's first goal but after the break United run riot against the green-hooped shirts. Tickets are selling for five times face value.										
P:2	H	SHAMROCK ROV		4	W	3-2	2-0	Viollet 5, 60, Pegg 22	Wood	Foulkes	Byrne	Colman	Jones M	McGuinness	Berry	Webster	Taylor T	Viollet	Pegg
2/10			33,754					*Peyton 55, Hamilton 68*	*Darcy*	*Burke*	*Mackey*	*Nolan*	*Keogh*	*Coad*	*McCann*	*Peyton*	*Ambrose*	*Hamilton*	*Tuohy*
								Ref: A Alsteen (Belgium) (United win 9-2 on aggregate)	How Rovers avoid a thrashing is a mystery as the shots rain in on Darcy, who is given a standing ovation. The Irish team's carefree attitude wins them many friends in a sporting encounter. Their second-half rally stuns the Reds, and Ray Wood has to save a late shot from Hamilton.										
1:1	H	DUKLA PRAGUE		4	W	3-0	0-0	Webster 72, Taylor T 76, Pegg 83	Wood	Foulkes	Byrne	Colman	Blanchflower	Edwards	Berry	Whelan	Taylor T	Webster	Pegg
20/11		(Czech)	62,000						*Pavlis*	*Jecny*	*Cadek*	*Novak*	*Pluskal*	*Masopust*	*Vacenovsky*	*Dvorak*	*Borovicka*	*Safranek*	*Dobai*
								Ref: W Treichel (Germany)	The skilful Czechs play some great football but lack punch near goal. They defend well and United have to be patient. Webster finally breaks the deadlock before Taylor's header and Pegg's vicious finish from Whelan's set-up. Masopust and Edwards enjoy a titanic duel in midfield.										
1:2	A	DUKLA PRAGUE		4	L	0-1	0-1		Wood	Foulkes	Byrne	Colman	Jones M	Edwards	Scanlon	Whelan	Taylor T	Webster	Pegg
4/12			*35,000*					*Dvorak 22*	*Pavlis*	*Jecny*	*Cadek*	*Novak*	*Pluskal*	*Masopust*	*Safranek*	*Dvorak*	*Urban*	*Borovicka*	*Vacenovsky*
								Ref: W Treichel (Germany) (United win 3-1 on aggregate)	A thawing pitch at Prague's Army Stadium quickly becomes a morass of mud. Without the injured Berry and Viollet, United are nervous after the early goal but the defence, with Edwards and Jones rocks, hold out to go through. Tommy Taylor has a 'good' goal disallowed for offside.										
2:1	H	RED STAR BELGR		4	W	2-1	0-1	Charlton 65, Colman 85	Gregg	Foulkes	Byrne	Colman	Jones M	Edwards	Morgans	Charlton	Taylor T	Viollet	Scanlon
14/1		(Yugoslavia)	60,000					*Tasic 35*	*Beara*	*Tomic*	*Zekovic*	*Mitic*	*Spajic*	*Popovic*	*Borozan*	*Sekularac*	*Toplak*	*Tasic*	*Kostic*
								Ref: M Lequesne (France)	On a memorable foggy night, United's patience pays off for a vital win. Heavy rain makes a slippery surface which United master after the break. Beara saves five certain goals before Charlton gleefully hooks in Scanlon's cross and Colman side-foots home from Viollet's pass.										
2:2	A	RED STAR BELGR		4	D	3-3	3-0	Viollet 2, Charlton 30, 32	Gregg	Foulkes	Byrne	Colman	Jones M	Edwards	Morgans	Charlton	Taylor T	Viollet	Scanlon
5/2			*52,000*					*Kostic 47, 86, Tasic 55p*	*Beara*	*Tomic*	*Zekovic*	*Mitic*	*Spajic*	*Popovic*	*Borozan*	*Sekularac*	*Tasic*	*Kostic*	*Gokic*
								Ref: K Kainer (Austria) (United win 5-4 on aggregate)	United are left hanging on at the end despite their exhilarating first half, which seemed to have finished the tie. United possibly eased off as they looked forward to Saturday's big match with Wolves. Bill Foulkes concedes a penalty and Gregg handles outside the area and is punished.										
SF 1	H	AC MILAN		9	W	2-1	1-1	Viollet 39, Taylor E 88p	Gregg	Foulkes	Greaves	Goodwin	Cope	Crowther	Morgans	Taylor E	Webster	Viollet	Pearson
8/5		(Italy)	44,880					*Bredesen 23*	*Buffon*	*Fontana*	*Beraldo*	*Bergamaschi*	*Maldini*	*Radice*	*Mariani*	*Bredesen*	*Schiaffino*	*Liedholm*	*Cucchiaroni*
								Ref: L Helge (Denmark)	A tired United, without Charlton, who is on tour with England, go behind when Crowther miskicks. Stan atones with a great run and shot from which Viollet levels. The crowd roar United on for the winner, which arrives courtesy of a disputed penalty after Cesare Maldini holds Viollet.										
SF 2	A	AC MILAN		9	L	0-4	0-1	*[Danova 68]*	Gregg	Foulkes	Greaves	Goodwin	Cope	Crowther	Morgans	Taylor E	Webster	Viollet	Pearson
14/5			*100,000*					*Schiffiano 3, 75, Liedholm 50p,*	*Buffon*	*Fontana*	*Beraldo*	*Bergamaschi*	*Zannier*	*Radice*	*Danova*	*Bredesen*	*Schiaffino*	*Liedholm*	*Cucchiaroni*
								Ref: A Dusch (Germany) (United lose 2-5 on aggregate)	The team travel by train, leaving the recuperating Busby at home. The much-vaunted Milan forward line clicks after United's brave resistance collapses. The noisy San Siro boos the Reds for their alleged rough tactics in the first leg. The Uruguayan Juan Schiffiano ends the dreams.										

LEAGUE DIVISION 1 (CUP-TIES)   Manager: Matt Busby   SEASON 1957-58

FA Cup	F-A	H-T	Scorers, Times, and Referees	1	2	3	4	5	6	7	8	9	10	11
3 A WORKINGTON 4 W	3-1	0-1	Viollet 54, 56, 62	Gregg	Foulkes	Byrne	Colman	Jones M	Edwards	Morgans	Charlton	Taylor T	Viollet	Scanlon
4/1 *21,500 3N:21*			*Colbridge 5*	*Newlands*	*Brown*	*Rollo*	*Bertolini*	*Aitken*	*Burkinshaw*	*Mitchell*	*Robson*	*Purdon*	*Chisholm*	*Colbridge*
			Ref: J Sherlock	A shock looks on for 45 minutes, as Joe Harvey's team harry the life out of United and Clive Colbridge scores a rebound off Gregg's legs. Viollet takes centre-stage and scores three from close range and Tommy Taylor misses two good chances near the end as Workington tire.										
4 H IPSWICH 4 W	2-0	1-0	Charlton 40, 75	Gregg	Foulkes	Byrne	Colman	Jones M	Edwards	Morgans	Charlton	Taylor T	Viollet	Scanlon
25/1 53,550 *2:7*				*Bailey*	*Acres*	*Malcolm*	*Pickett*	*Rees D*	*Elsworthy*	*Reed*	*Rees DW*	*Garneys*	*Millward*	*Leadbetter*
			Ref: L Callaghan	Alf Ramsey's Ipswich are under constant siege, and Roy Bailey brilliantly defies United. It is Town's first season in Division 2 and they create few chances. Charlton hits another stunning goal, from Morgans' pass. Colman fizzles out after a good start but Edwards is a man-mountain.										
5 H SHEFFIELD WED 4 W	3-0	1-0	Brennan 27, 70, Dawson 85	Gregg	Foulkes	Greaves	Goodwin	Cope	Crowther	Webster	Taylor E	Dawson	Pearson	Brennan
19/2 59,848 *22*				*Ryalls*	*Martin*	*Curtis*	*Kay*	*Swan*	*O'Donnell*	*Wilkinson*	*Quixall*	*Johnson*	*Froggatt*	*Cargill*
			Ref: A Bond	The FA bend the rules to allow cup-tied Crowther and Taylor to play and both are superb. The noise from the highly emotional crowd is deafening and the Owls stand no chance. Debutant Shay Brennan is one of seven reserves and scores direct from a corner and adds a second.										
QF A WEST BROM 5 D	2-2	2-1	Taylor E 6, Dawson 44	Gregg	Foulkes	Greaves	Goodwin	Cope	Crowther	Webster	Taylor E	Dawson	Pearson	Charlton
1/3 *57,574 3*			*Allen 12, Horobin 86*	*Sanders*	*Howe*	*Williams S*	*Dudley*	*Kennedy*	*Barlow*	*Whitehouse*	*Robson*	*Allen*	*Kevan*	*Horobin*
			Ref: K Howley	Brave United are robbed in a thrilling match when Gregg paws the ball on the line but the ref controversially gives a goal. Taylor is superb again and his wicked shot hits the bar and Dawson nods home. Albion almost seem guilty for forcing a replay with the team that won't die.										
QF H WEST BROM 5 W	1-0	0-0	Webster 89	Gregg	Foulkes	Greaves	Goodwin	Cope	Harrop	Webster	Taylor E	Dawson	Pearson	Charlton
R 5/3 60,523 *3*				*Sanders*	*Howe*	*Williams S*	*Dudley*	*Kennedy*	*Barlow*	*Whitehouse*	*Robson*	*Allen*	*Kevan*	*Horobin*
			Ref: K Howley	30,000 try to gatecrash to see the new Babes win a game that could have gone either way. Charlton, aided by a referee who plays advantage, races down the right and crosses for Webster to score. The joy is unrestrained and Albion are shattered after playing a big part in a classic.										
SF N FULHAM 6 D	2-2	2-2	Charlton 11, 43	Gregg	Foulkes	Greaves	Goodwin	Cope	Crowther	Webster	Taylor E	Dawson	Pearson	Charlton
22/3 *69,745 2:4*			*Stevens 13, Hill 38*	*Macedo*	*Cohen*	*Langley*	*Bentley*	*Stapleton*	*Lawler*	*Dwight*	*Hill*	*Stevens*	*Haynes*	*Chamberlain*
(at Villa Park)			Ref: C Kingston	Four days in Blackpool have rested the players. Second division Fulham start the stronger but United finish on top with Charlton hitting the bar near the end. Earlier he scored with a 20-yard half-volley and a rebound. Langley and Taylor are limping on the wing well before the finish.										
SF N FULHAM 6 W	5-3	3-2	Daw' 14, 33, 65, Bren' 44, Charl' 90	Gregg	Foulkes	Greaves	Goodwin	Cope	Crowther	Webster	Taylor E	Dawson	Charlton	Brennan
R 26/3 *32,800 2:4*			*Stevens 27, Cham'lain 38, Dwight 72*	*Macedo*	*Cohen*	*Langley*	*Bentley*	*Stapleton*	*Lawler*	*Dwight*	*Hill*	*Stevens*	*Haynes*	*Chamberlain*
(at Highbury)			Ref: C Kingston	Live TV coverage spoils the gate and the touts are left with a loss for this midweek afternoon replay. United dominate from the start and Dawson's flying header starts the rout. Macedo's two boobs on the wet ground are crucial. Few United fans see the Wembley dream fulfilled.										
F N BOLTON 9 L	0-2	0-1		Gregg	Foulkes	Greaves	Goodwin	Cope	Crowther	Dawson	Taylor E	Charlton	Viollet	Webster
3/5 *100,000 15*			*Lofthouse 3, 55*	*Hopkinson*	*Hartle*	*Banks*	*Hennin*	*Higgins*	*Edwards*	*Birch*	*Stevens*	*Lofthouse*	*Parry*	*Holden*
(at Wembley)			Ref: J Sherlock	Despite universal support, United's brave makeshift team are beaten by the opportunism of Nat Lofthouse. Jimmy Murphy leads the team out whilst a pale Busby sits on the bench. Nat bundles Gregg and the ball into the net for the second, controversial goal. Bolton have no sympathy.										

		Home					Away					
	P	W	D	L	F	A	W	D	L	F	A	Pts
1 Wolves	42	17	3	1	60	21	11	5	5	43	26	64
2 Preston	42	18	2	1	63	14	8	5	8	37	37	59
3 Tottenham	42	13	4	4	58	33	8	5	8	35	44	51
4 West Brom	42	14	4	3	59	29	4	10	7	33	41	50
5 Manchester C	42	14	4	3	58	33	8	1	12	46	67	49
6 Burnley	42	16	2	3	52	21	5	3	13	28	53	47
7 Blackpool	42	11	2	8	47	35	8	4	9	33	32	44
8 Luton	42	13	3	5	45	22	6	3	12	24	41	44
9 MAN UNITED	42	10	4	7	45	31	6	7	8	40	44	43
10 Nott'm Forest	42	10	4	7	41	27	6	6	9	28	36	42
11 Chelsea	42	10	5	6	47	34	5	7	9	36	45	42
12 Arsenal	42	10	4	7	48	39	6	3	12	25	46	39
13 Birmingham	42	8	6	7	43	37	6	5	10	33	52	39
14 Aston Villa	42	12	4	5	46	26	4	3	14	27	60	39
15 Bolton	42	9	5	7	38	35	5	5	11	27	52	38
16 Everton	42	5	9	7	34	35	8	2	11	31	40	37
17 Leeds	42	10	6	5	33	23	4	3	14	18	40	37
18 Leicester	42	11	4	6	59	41	3	1	17	32	71	33
19 Newcastle	42	6	4	11	38	42	6	4	11	35	39	32
20 Portsmouth	42	10	6	5	45	34	2	2	17	28	54	32
21 Sunderland	42	7	7	7	32	33	3	5	13	22	64	32
22 Sheffield Wed	42	12	2	7	45	40	0	5	16	24	52	31
	924	246	94	122	1036	685	122	94	246	685	1036	924

Odds & ends

Double wins: (2) Leicester, Arsenal.
Double losses: (4) West Brom, Wolves, Tottenham, Chelsea.

Won from behind: (5) Newcastle (a), Sunderland (a), Workington FAC (a). Red Star EC (h), AC Milan EC (h).
Lost from in front: (3) West Brom (a), Tottenham (h), Aston Villa (a).

High spots: Excellent start to the season.
Exciting post-Christmas form.
Post-Munich FA Cup form and phenomenal support.

Low spots: The Munich crash.
The poor pre-Christmas home form.
Losing at Wembley for the second year running.

Red cards (United): (1) Pearson.
Red cards (Opponents):
Ever-presents: (1) Foulkes.
Hat-tricks: (4) Whelan, Charlton, Viollet, Dawson.
Opposing hat-tricks: Smith (Tottenham).
Leading scorer: (23) Viollet.

	Appearances			Goals			
	Lge	FAC	E-ur	**Lge**	FAC	Eur	**Tot**
Berry, Johnny	**20**		3	**4**		1	**5**
Blanchflower, Jackie	**18**		2				
Brennan, Shay	**5**	2			3		**3**
Byrne, Roger	**26**	2	6				
Charlton, Bobby	**21**	7	2	**8**	5	3	**16**
Colman, Eddie	**24**	2	5			1	**1**
Cope, Ronnie	**13**	6	2				
Crowther, Stan	**11**	5	2				
Dawson, Alex	**12**	6		**5**	5		**10**
Doherty, John	**1**			**1**			**1**
Edwards, Duncan	**26**	2	5	**6**			**6**
Foulkes, Bill	**42**	8	8				
Gaskell, Dave	**3**						
Goodwin, Freddie	**16**	6	3				
Greaves, Ian	**12**	6	2				
Gregg, Harry	**19**	8	4				
Harrop, Bobby	**5**	1					
Heron, Tommy	**1**						
Jones, Mark	**10**	2	4				
Jones, Peter	**1**						
McGuinness, Wilf	**7**		1				
Morgans, Kenny	**13**	2	4				
Pearson, Mark	**8**	4	2				
Pegg, David	**21**		4	**4**		3	**7**
Scanlon, Albert	**9**	2	3	**3**			**3**
Taylor, Ernie	**11**	6	2	**2**	1	1	**4**
Taylor, Tommy	**25**	2	6	**16**		3	**19**
Viollet, Dennis	**22**	3	6	**16**	3	4	**23**
Webster, Colin	**20**	6	5	**6**	1	1	**8**
Whelan, Billy	**20**		3	**12**		2	**14**
Wood, Ray	**20**		4				
(own-goals)				**2**			**2**
31 players used	**462**	**88**	**88**	**85**	**18**	**19**	**122**

LEAGUE DIVISION 1 — Manager: Matt Busby — SEASON 1958-59

No	Date	Att	Pos	Pt	F-A	H-T	Scorers, Times, and Referees	1	2	3	4	5	6	7	8	9	10	11
1	H CHELSEA			W	5-2	2-1	Charlton 6, 27, 52, Dawson 70, 85	Gregg	Foulkes	Greaves	Goodwin	Cope	McGuinness	Dawson	Taylor	Viollet	Charlton	Scanlon
	23/8	52,382		2			*Greaves 41, 77*	*Matthews*	*Sillett P*	*Sillett J*	*Mortimore*	*Scott*	*Saunders*	*Brabrook*	*Greaves*	*Allen*	*Nicholas A*	*Block*
							Ref: L Howarth	United are tipped by many to struggle and the expectations on Charlton are enormous. Apart from a slight blip when Jimmy Greaves whips in a great shot it is all United and but for Reg Matthews it would have been ten. Scanlon's massive injuries are repaired and he is back to his best.										
2	A NOTT'M FOREST			W	3-0	3-0	Charlton 18, 23, Scanlon 20	Gregg	Foulkes	Greaves	Goodwin	Cope	McGuinness	Dawson	Taylor	Viollet	Charlton	Scanlon
	27/8	*44,971*		4				*Thomson*	*Whare*	*Thomas*	*Whitefoot*	*McKinlay*	*Burckitt*	*Gray*	*Dwight*	*Wilson*	*Baily*	*Imlach*
							Ref: A Bond	The game is over after three quick goals, with Charlton's deadly shooting crucial. Ironically, Billy Walker's Forest miss three good chances before that. The largest midweek crowd ever at Forest are silenced by Ernie Taylor's superb passes and Wilf McGuinness's surging runs.										
3	A BLACKPOOL		6	L	1-2	1-2	Viollet 9	Gregg	Foulkes	Greaves	Goodwin	Cope	McGuinness	Dawson	Taylor	Viollet	Charlton	Scanlon
	30/8	*36,719*	*3*	4			*Perry 35, Kelly H 43p*	*Farm*	*Garrett*	*Wright*	*Kelly J*	*Gratrix*	*Kelly H*	*Matthews*	*Mudie*	*Charnley*	*Durie*	*Perry*
							Ref: A Jobling	A bad day at the seaside after a promising start. United look well in control after captain-for-the-day Taylor sets up Viollet. Gregg fails to hold Perry's shot and then Cope handles Durie's cross for the penalty. Farm brings down Viollet but Charlton slams the penalty against the bar.										
4	H NOTT'M FOREST		6	D	1-1	1-0	Charlton 10	Gregg	Foulkes	Greaves	Goodwin	Cope	McGuinness	Dawson	Taylor	Viollet	Charlton	Scanlon
	3/9	51,880	*14*	5			*Wilson 60*	*Lightening*	*Whare*	*McDonald*	*Morley*	*McKinlay*	*Burckitt*	*Dwight*	*Quigley*	*Wilson*	*Gray*	*Imlach*
							Ref: R Smith	A swirling wind upsets United's rhythm after Freddie Goodwin's lob allows Charlton to net. A speedy Forest waste three chances at 0-0. With reserve keeper Arthur Lightening in great form they are well worth a point. United's passes are badly awry and their late barrage justly fails.										
5	H BLACKBURN		2	W	**6-1**	4-0	Charl' 15, 20, Viol'23, 55, Scan' 41, [Webster 80]	Gregg	Foulkes	Greaves	Goodwin	Cope	McGuinness	Webster	Taylor	Viollet	Charlton	Scanlon
	6/9	**65,187**	*4*	7			*Douglas 50*	*Leyland*	*Whelan*	*Eckersley*	*Clayton*	*Woods*	*McGrath*	*Douglas*	*Dobing*	*Johnston*	*Vernon*	*McLeod*
							Ref: K Howley	Johnny Carey returns with newly promoted Rovers, who have scored 16 goals in four games. United master the thunder, lightning and hail in a fierce first half and get all the breaks. Wilf McGuinness keeps England man Bryan Douglas quiet and Bobby Charlton can't stop scoring.										
6	A WEST HAM		3	L	2-3	0-2	Webster 66, McGuinness 84	Gregg	Foulkes	Greaves	Goodwin	Cope	McGuinness	Webster	Taylor	Viollet	Charlton	Scanlon
	8/9	*35,672*	*1*	7			*Dick 7, Smith 38, Musgrove 57*	*Gregory*	*Bond*	*Cantwell*	*Malcolm*	*Brown*	*Moore*	*Grice*	*Smith*	*Keeble*	*Dick*	*Musgrove*
							Ref: A Holland	An East End football lesson from the newly promoted Hammers, for whom youngster Bobby Moore makes a steady debut. McGuinness, limping with a pulled muscle, centres for Webster and smashes in the second. West Ham, with Andy Malcolm marking Charlton, hold out.										
7	A NEWCASTLE		7	D	1-1	1-1	Charlton 31	Gregg	Foulkes	Greaves	Goodwin	Cope	Crowther	Webster	Taylor	Dawson	Charlton	Scanlon
	13/9	*60,670*	*13*	8			*Davies 28*	*Mitchell*	*Keith*	*McMichael*	*Scoular*	*Stokoe*	*Bell*	*Hughes*	*White*	*Wright*	*Davies*	*Mitchell*
							Ref: P Rhodes	Cope is laid out twice and Viollet limping as Charlie Mitten's Newcastle look the better side. Charlton's special cancels out Davies' header. Two minutes from time Charlton almost sneaks an undeserved win. Webster's booking for persistent arguing displeases United's management.										
8	H WEST HAM		7	W	4-1	3-1	Webster 7, Scanlon 25, 37, 75	Gregg	Foulkes	Greaves	Goodwin	Cope	McGuinness	Webster	Taylor	Viollet	Charlton	Scanlon
	17/9	53,276	*11*	10			*Bond 35*	*Gregory*	*Bond*	*Cantwell*	*Malcolm*	*Brown*	*Landsdowne*	*Wragg*	*Smith*	*Keeble*	*Dick*	*Grice*
							Ref: A Holland	West Ham, in their white shirts with two claret hoops, are pulverised by Scanlon, whose dribble and shot for the third goal is special. Gregg is at his best and saves Bond's penalty only for the West Ham back to follow up. Wednesday's Albert Quixall all set to sign for a record £45,000.										
9	H TOTTENHAM		5	D	2-2	0-1	Webster 68, 77	Gregg	Foulkes	Greaves	Goodwin	Cope	McGuinness	Webster	**Quixall**	Dawson	Charlton	Scanlon
	20/9	62,277	*19*	11			*Smith 37, 61*	*Hollowbread*	*Baker*	*Hopkins*	*Blanchflower*	*Ryden*	*Iley*	*Medwin*	*Stokes*	*Smith*	*Clayton*	*Robb*
							Ref: J Williams	United give Spurs a two-goal lead in a poor game and Bobby Smith makes it five goals in two visits. An expectant crowd sees a quiet Quixall marked by three men. Scanlon and McGuinness are set for England call-ups. Spurs accuse Webster of handball as he equalises in a frantic end.										
10	A MANCHESTER C		6	D	1-1	1-1	Charlton 3p	Gregg	Foulkes	Greaves	Goodwin	Cope	McGuinness	Viollet	Quixall	Webster	Charlton	Scanlon
	27/9	*62,912*	*20*	12			*Hayes 37*	*Trautmann*	*Leivers*	*Sear*	*Cheetham*	*Ewing*	*Barnes*	*Fagan*	*Barlow*	*Hannah*	*Hayes*	*Sambrook*
							Ref: F Coultas	City have not won since the opening day, but make life difficult for the Reds. Cheetham fouls Charlton for the penalty but thereafter marks him out of the game. £18,000 George Hannah looks a snip, but flu-victim Sambrook misses a sitter. Gregg is superb and saves Barnes' late penalty.										

No	Venue	Opponent / Date	Att	Pos	Pts	Result	H-T	Scorers, Times, Referees	1	2	3	4	5	6	7	8	9	10	11
11	A	WOLVERHAMPTON		8	L	**0-4**	0-1		Wood	Foulkes	Greaves	Goodwin	Harrop	Crowther	Viollet	Quixall	Webster	Pearson	Scanlon
		4/10	*36,840*	*5*	12			*Mason 10, Murray 67, 89, Mullen 74*	*Finlayson*	*Stuart*	*Harris*	*Slater*	*Showell*	*Clamp*	*Deeley*	*Durandt*	*Murray*	*Mason*	*Mullen*
								Ref: A Bond	The country's first floodlit Saturday night game, and United are dazzled. With Gregg, Charlton and McGuinness on international duty, they are weak but Wolves get the breaks with three deflected goals. Wolves, missing Wright and Broadbent, give debut to South African Cliff Durandt.										
12	H	PRESTON		8	L	0-2	0-1		Gregg	Foulkes	Greaves	Goodwin	Cope	McGuinness	Dawson	Taylor	Viollet	Charlton	Scanlon
		8/10	46,163	*1*	12			*Thompson 38, Hatsell 59*	*Else*	*Cunningham*	*Walton*	*Milne*	*Dunn*	*O'Farrell*	*Mayers*	*Thompson*	*Hatsell*	*Baxter*	*Finney*
								Ref: A Ellis	Cliff Britton's boys go top of the league with a smash and grab display. Else is brilliant against United's heavy artillery and Preston hold out after Hatsell's goal from an oblique angle. Webster, dropped after dismissal in a friendly, may go to Swansea. Ray Wood may go to Coventry.										
13	H	ARSENAL		7	D	1-1	1-1	Viollet 15	Gregg	Foulkes	Greaves	Goodwin	Cope	McGuinness	Viollet	Quixall	Charlton	Taylor	Scanlon
		11/10	56,148	*3*	13			*Ward 23*	*Kelsey*	*Wills*	*Evans*	*Ward*	*Dodgin*	*Docherty*	*Clapton*	*Groves*	*Herd*	*Bloomfield*	*Henderson*
								Ref: R Windle	George Swindin has started well as Arsenal boss and deserves a point from an entertaining game. Charlton, on his 21st birthday, cannot find the net and is out of sorts. Busby must be pleased with the form of three Scots, Herd, Henderson and Docherty, who gives Quixall a rough ride.										
14	A	EVERTON		12	L	2-3	0-2	Cope 72, 82	Gregg	Foulkes	Greaves	Goodwin	Cope	McGuinness	Viollet	Quixall	Charlton	Taylor	Scanlon
		18/10	*64,079*	*18*	13			*Thomas 19, 37, Harris J 55*	*Dunlop*	*Sanders*	*Bramwell*	*King*	*Jones*	*Harris B*	*Harris J*	*Thomas*	*Hickson*	*Ashworth*	*O'Hara*
								Ref: P Smyth	Johnny Carey is set to take over as boss after Everton's 4-10 defeat at Spurs last week. United have Jack Crompton in charge with Busby and Murphy head-to-head in Cardiff for Wales v Scotland. Eddie Thomas heads in and nets a rebound. Limping Ronnie Cope on the wing nets two.										
15	H	WEST BROM		14	L	1-2	0-1	Goodwin 55	Gregg	Foulkes	Greaves	Goodwin	Harrop	McGuinness	Viollet	Quixall	Dawson	Charlton	Scanlon
		25/10	51,721	*5*	13			*Robson 41, Kevan 75*	*Potter*	*Howe*	*Williams S*	*Setters*	*Barlow*	*Dudley*	*Campbell*	*Robson*	*Kevan*	*Burnside*	*Hogg*
								Ref: E Crawford	Seven games without a win and outclassed by classy Albion for whom England cap Derek Kevan nets a stunning winner. Quixall is kicked and obstructed at every turn and United have no one to score, with Viollet limping and Charlton, back from England duty versus Russia, off colour.										
16	A	LEEDS		12	W	2-1	0-1	Scanlon 67, Goodwin 73	Gregg	Foulkes	Greaves	Goodwin	Harrop	McGuinness	Morgans	Quixall	Dawson	Charlton	Scanlon
		1/11	*48,574*	*18*	15			*Shackleton 30*	*Wood*	*Ashall*	*Hair*	*Cush*	*Charlton*	*Gibson*	*Humphries*	*Crowe*	*Shackleton*	*O'Brien*	*Overfield*
								Ref: R Wood	Questions are being asked about Quixall after his failure to score in seven games, but he shines and hits the bar. Harrop's slip lets in £8,000 Shackleton to score on his debut. United fight back to end their poor run and inflict Leeds' first home defeat with the steady Goodwin scoring.										
17	H	BURNLEY		14	L	1-3	0-2	Quixall 87	Gregg	Foulkes	Greaves	Goodwin	Harrop	McGuinness	Morgans	Quixall	Dawson	Charlton	Scanlon
		8/11	48,509	*13*	15			*McIlroy 24p, Pointer 30, 70*	*McDonald*	*Smith*	*Winton*	*Seith*	*Cummings*	*Adamson*	*Connolly*	*McIlroy*	*Pointer*	*Robson*	*Pilkington*
								Ref: J Powell	Burnley boss Harry Potts is slowly making changes and his side are starting to look useful. United fizzle out after a good start and Quixall's welcome first goal is overshadowed by Pointer's dream second goal; a flick over the advancing Harrop and a stunning volley past Gregg.										
18	A	BOLTON		15	L	3-6	1-3	Dawson 35, 65, Charl' 50 *[Parry 70p]*	Gregg	Foulkes	Greaves	Goodwin	Cope	McGuinness	**Bradley**	Quixall	Dawson	Charlton	Scanlon
		15/11	*33,358*	*4*	15			*Edw' 6, Stev' 15, 43, Gub's 57, 80,*	*Hopkinson*	*Hartle*	*Banks*	*Hennin*	*Higgins*	*Edwards*	*Birch*	*Stevens*	*Gubbins*	*Parry*	*Holden*
								Ref: A Luty	The Burnden hoodoo continues; no win at Bolton since 1949 and the 4th successive defeat. The fog ensures the goals are unseen by many and the lights make things worse. Lofthouse's deputy Gubbins' sixth goal is a mystery to most spectators but the Reds' slow defence is all at sea.										
19	H	LUTON		12	W	2-1	2-1	Viollet 1, Charlton 11	Gregg	Foulkes	**Carolan**	Goodwin	Cope	McGuinness	Bradley	Quixall	Viollet	Charlton	Scanlon
		22/11	42,428	*7*	17			*Cummins 19*	*Baynham*	*Dunne*	*Hawkes K*	*Morton*	*Owen*	*Pacey*	*Bingham*	*Turner*	*Brown*	*Cummins*	*Adam*
								Ref: J Swain	An unconvincing win over ordinary Luton, disorganised by injuries. Twice 36-year-old Sid Owen fails to clear and is punished. Viollet heads home and United's best forward Warren Bradley stars on his home debut. Viollet's welcome return ensures a first home win for two months.										
20	A	BIRMINGHAM		10	W	4-0	3-0	Charlton 11, 75, Bradley 29, [Scanlon 42]	Gregg	Foulkes	Carolan	Goodwin	Cope	McGuinness	Bradley	Quixall	Viollet	Charlton	Scanlon
		29/11	*28,658*	*19*	19				*Schofield*	*Farmer*	*Allen*	*Watts*	*Smith*	*Neal*	*Hooper*	*Gordon*	*Brown*	*Larkin*	*Taylor*
								Ref: M Griffiths	In a fog-shrouded match, United coast to their first post-war win on the ground. Charlton is back to his best and scores with a dipping right foot shot and a low drive from an acute angle. Scanlon scores from a rebound and Bradley has all the time in the world. Pat Beasley's side are poor.										
21	H	LEICESTER		9	W	4-1	2-0	Scanlon 6, Viollet 44, Bradley 47, [Charlton 51]	Gregg	Foulkes	Carolan	Goodwin	Cope	McGuinness	Bradley	Quixall	Viollet	Charlton	Scanlon
		6/12	**38,482**	*21*	21			*Kelly 88*	*Maclaren*	*Cunningham*	*Baillie*	*Newman*	*King*	*Keyworth*	*Riley*	*Kelly*	*Hines*	*Walsh*	*Leek*
								Ref: G McCabe	No contest, with Gregg having only one shot to save. The fog can't hamper United, and Scanlon's header and Viollet's tap-in from Quixall's skill give them a half-time lead. Two quick goals finish City off and the soccer press are pushing Viollet and Bradley for international honours.										

No		Date	Att	Pos	Pt	F-A	H-T	Scorers, Times, and Referees	1	2	3	4	5	6	7	8	9	10	11
22	A	PRESTON		8	W	4-3	1-2	Bradley 22, Viollet 54, Scanlon 80,	Gregg	Foulkes	Carolan	Goodwin	Cope	McGuinness	Bradley	Quixall	Viollet	Charlton	Scanlon
		13/12	*26,290*	*5*	23			*Hat' 28, 36, Thom' 88* [Charlton 81]	*Else*	*Cunningham*	*Walton*	*O'Farrell*	*Dunn*	*Smith*	*Mayers*	*Thompson*	*Hatsell*	*Baxter*	*Taylor*
								Ref: K Howley	One of the best games at Deepdale for years as United defy their critics to make it four wins in a row. Tom Finney is injured but Hatsell is a handful for Cope and scores two good goals. Keeper Fred Else, the hero at Old Trafford, is helpless as the Red machine rips his defence apart.										
23	A	CHELSEA		7	W	3-2	2-1	Goodwin 22, Charlton 34, Scott 47(og)	Gregg	Foulkes	Carolan	Goodwin	Cope	McGuinness	Bradley	Quixall	Viollet	Charlton	Scanlon
		20/12	*48,550*	*16*	25			*Brabrook 6, Sillett P 49p*	*Matthews*	*Sillett J*	*Sillett P*	*Mortimore*	*Scott*	*Crowther*	*Brabrook*	*Greaves*	*Tindall*	*Nicholas A*	*Blunstone*
								Ref: H Horner	Stan Crowther has joined Chelsea but spoils his debut with a crude foul on Charlton who leaves the game with a gashed leg. 20-goal Greaves is kept off the score-sheet as United survive a battering to win the points. Both full-backs are superb against good wingers and Bradley is classy.										
24	H	ASTON VILLA		7	W	2-1	1-1	Quixall 20, Viollet 73	Gregg	Foulkes	Carolan	Goodwin	Cope	McGuinness	Bradley	Quixall	Viollet	Pearson	Scanlon
		26/12	63,098	*22*	27			*Myerscough 40*	*Sims*	*Lynn*	*Aldis*	*Dixon*	*Dugdale*	*Crowe*	*Smith*	*Sewell*	*Myerscough*	*Wylie*	*McParland*
								Ref: J Cook	Villa's new boss, Joe Mercer, hasn't stemmed the flood of goals being conceded. Bradley sets up Quixall, Myerscough lobs Harry Gregg from 30 yards and Viollet's magnificent run and feint wins the game. Joe Carolan and Bradley end the game limping on a misty Manchester day.										
25	A	ASTON VILLA		4	W	2-0	0-0	Viollet 72, Pearson 84	Gregg	Foulkes	Greaves	Goodwin	Cope	McGuinness	**Hunter**	Quixall	Viollet	Pearson	Scanlon
		27/12	*56,450*	*22*	29				*Sims*	*Jackson*	*Aldis*	*Dixon*	*Dugdale*	*Crowe*	*Smith*	*Wylie*	*Myerscough*	*Hitchens*	*McParland*
								Ref: D Blues	A seventh straight win leaves United three points behind leaders Wolves. Villa's desperate strong-arm tactics are effective until Sims dropped Scanlon's cross and Viollet nets. Pearson, deputising for Charlton, dribbles through the mud for a second and leaves Villa in deep trouble.										
26	H	BLACKPOOL		3	W	3-1	2-0	Viollet 7, Charlton 22, 85	Gregg	Foulkes	Carolan	Goodwin	Cope	McGuinness	Bradley	Quixall	Viollet	Charlton	Scanlon
		3/1	61,961	8	31			*Fenton 50p*	*Farm*	*Armfield*	*Wright*	*Hauser*	*Gratrix*	*Fenton*	*Matthews*	*Mudie*	*Charnley*	*Durie*	*Perry*
								Ref: W Clements	Charlton returns from injury and has goals laid on a plate by Viollet and Scanlon. Stan Matthews is unsportingly booed after Carolan had brought him down for the penalty but the abuse inspires him to a thrilling display. Albert Scanlon hits the bar and misses two good chances.										
27	H	NEWCASTLE		4	D	4-4	4-1	Charl' 5p, Quix' 22, Scan' 27, Viol' 30	Gregg	Foulkes	Carolan	Harrop	Goodwin	McGuinness	Bradley	Quixall	Viollet	Charlton	Scanlon
		31/1	49,008	*13*	32			*Allch' 25, White 68, 70, McGuig' 77*	*Harvey*	*Keith*	*McMichael*	*Scoular*	*Scott*	*Franks*	*Taylor*	*Allchurch*	*White*	*Davies*	*McGuigan*
								Ref: H Husband	The proverbial game of two halves. United, irrepressible before the interval, succumb to the silky skills of George Eastham and Ivor Allchurch and the poaching of Len White. Scoular plugs the gaps and rallies the troops for a deserved point. United's experimental defence is half asleep.										
28	A	TOTTENHAM		3	W	3-1	2-0	Charlton 15p, 25, Scanlon 47	Gregg	Greaves	Carolan	Goodwin	Cope	McGuinness	Bradley	Quixall	Viollet	Charlton	Scanlon
		7/2	*48,401*	*18*	34			*Norman 50*	*Hollowbread*	*Baker*	*Hopkins*	*Dodge*	*Norman*	*Iley*	*Brooks*	*Harmer*	*Smith*	*Dunmore*	*Jones*
								Ref: A Moore	There is a minute's silence for the Munich anniversary before slick United expose Billy Nicholson's Spurs' deficiencies. Spurs face Norwich in the Cup next week and the Canaries' scouts are relishing the challenge. Bobby Charlton's 25-yarder barely lifts off the turf for the second.										
29	H	MANCHESTER C		3	W	4-1	0-1	Goodwin 48, Bradley 52, 69,	Gregg	Greaves	Carolan	Goodwin	Cope	McGuinness	Bradley	Quixall	Viollet	Charlton	Scanlon
		16/2	59,846	*20*	36			*Johnstone 10* [Scanlon 61]	*Trautmann*	*Leivers*	*Branagan*	*Barnes*	*McTavish*	*Phoenix*	*Sambrook*	*Barlow*	*Johnstone*	*Hayes*	*Fidler*
								Ref: J Kelly	United's fancy play gets them nowhere in poor conditions and they revert to a long-ball game after the break and City fall apart with ease. Lanky Goodwin is the star and Bradley and Scanlon are the best wingers in England at the moment. The gap to Wolves is now two points.										
30	H	WOLVERHAMPTON		2	W	2-1	1-0	Viollet 40, Charlton 89	Gregg	Greaves	Carolan	Goodwin	Cope	McGuinness	Bradley	Quixall	Viollet	Charlton	Scanlon
		21/2	62,794	*1*	38			*Mason 65*	*Finlayson*	*Stuart*	*Harris*	*Clamp*	*Wright*	*Flowers*	*Lill*	*Mason*	*Murray*	*Broadbent*	*Deeley*
								Ref: R Wood	United pull level on points with Wolves with a last-minute winner, Charlton atoning for an earlier miss. United adapt better to the drizzle and slippery pitch. Viollet leads England captain Billy Wright a merry dance and scores a stunning half-volley. The title push is gathering pace.										
31	A	ARSENAL		3	L	2-3	1-3	Viollet 34, Bradley 89	Gregg	Greaves	Carolan	Goodwin	Cope	McGuinness	Bradley	Quixall	Viollet	Charlton	Scanlon
		28/2	***67,162***	*1*	38			*Herd 12, Barnwell 22, 28*	*Standen*	*Wills*	*Evans*	*Docherty*	*Dodgin*	*Bowen*	*Clapton*	*Ward*	*Herd*	*Barnwell*	*Haverty*
								Ref: A Starling	Wolves' two main challengers clash and United lose their 12-game unbeaten run. Arsenal have not lost in eight and the youngsters David Herd and John Barnwell are deadly finishers. Docherty and Bowen mark Quixall and Charlton superbly and United's defence is alarmingly suspect.										

32	A	BLACKBURN	3	W	3-1	3-1	Bradley 15, 30, Scanlon 39	Gregg	Greaves	Carolan	Goodwin	Cope	McGuinness	Bradley	Quixall	Viollet	Charlton	Scanlon
	2/3	*40,401*	*11*	40			*Dobing 3*	*Leyland*	*Taylor*	*Whelan*	*Clayton*	*Woods*	*McGrath*	*Douglas*	*Stephenson*	*Dobing*	*Vernon*	*McLeod*
							Ref: W Surtees	Dally Duncan has taken over from Carey as manager with moderate success. A tough game with United and Gregg in particular booed after his foul on Douglas. Bradley stars with a header and a shot and Scanlon robs Taylor to clinch the points. McGuinness crashes into the hoardings.										
33	H	EVERTON	2	W	2-1	1-0	Goodwin 23, Scanlon 62	Gregg	Greaves	Carolan	Goodwin	Cope	McGuinness	Bradley	Quixall	Viollet	Charlton	Scanlon
	7/3	51,254	*14*	42			*Cope 68(og)*	*Dunlop*	*Parker*	*Bramwell*	*Harris B*	*Jones*	*Meagan*	*Harris J*	*Thomas*	*Hickson*	*Collins*	*Laverick*
							Ref: F Coultas	Inconsistent Everton run United close in a strong wind that makes good football impossible. Both goals come from wing play with Scanlon's diving header special. Gregg pushes Jimmy Harris but saves Jones' spot-kick. Ronnie Cope slices a free-kick past Gregg but United hang on.										
34	A	WEST BROM	2	W	3-1	3-0	Viollet 4, Scanlon 14, Bradley 26	Gregg	Greaves	Carolan	Goodwin	Cope	McGuinness	Bradley	Quixall	Viollet	Charlton	Scanlon
	14/3	*35,463*	*7*	44			*Kevan 50*	*Potter*	*Howe*	*Williams S*	*Setters*	*Barlow*	*Kennedy*	*Allen*	*Robson*	*Kevan*	*Burnside*	*Hogg*
							Ref: P Smyth	Vic Buckingham's team are struggling to maintain their early season form and their defence is exposed by United's first-half display. England full-back Don Howe is shaky and miskicks for Scanlon to score. Bradley rounds off a brilliant five-man move and Kevan's goal is too late.										
35	H	LEEDS	2	W	4-0	1-0	Viollet 14, 60, 85, Charlton 53p	Gregg	Greaves	Carolan	Goodwin	Cope	McGuinness	Bradley	Quixall	Viollet	Charlton	Scanlon
	21/3	45,473	*16*	46				*Burgin*	*Dunn*	*Ashall*	*Revie*	*Charlton*	*Kerfoot*	*Meek*	*Crowe*	*Shackleton*	*Cush*	*Overfield*
							Ref: A Bond	After a poor game in Dublin for the Football League, Viollet is masterly against managerless Leeds. He swivels to score the first, latches onto Quixall's through ball, and feints sending Burgin the wrong way for his hat-trick. Ashall handles for a penalty. Wolves are one point ahead.										
36	H	PORTSMOUTH	1	W	**6-1**	3-0	Brad' 7, Charl' 21, 49p, Viol' 65, 82,	Gregg	Greaves	Carolan	Goodwin	Cope	McGuinness	Bradley	Quixall	Viollet	Charlton	Scanlon
	27/3	52,004	*22*	48			*Newman 60* [Hayward 40(og)]	*Uprichard*	*Rutter*	*Wilson*	*Howells*	*Hayward*	*Dickinson*	*Harris P*	*White*	*Saunders*	*Harris D*	*Newman*
							Ref: M Dixon	Pompey in their Diamond Jubilee year are without a win since November. They give a chance to sixteen-year old Jimmy White, but veteran Peter Harris causes United more trouble. It is a Good Friday stroll for United and shooting practice for England hopefuls Charlton and Viollet.										
37	A	BURNLEY	2	L	2-4	1-2	Goodwin 40, Viollet 90	Gregg	Greaves	Carolan	Goodwin	Cope	McGuinness	Bradley	Quixall	Viollet	Charlton	Scanlon
	28/3	*44,577*	*7*	48			*Pilkin'n 15, Seith 22, Pointer 80, 86*	*Blacklaw*	*Angus*	*Smith*	*Seith*	*Cummings*	*Miller*	*Connelly*	*McIlroy*	*Pointer*	*Robson*	*Pilkington*
							Ref: R Leafe	Harry Potts' Burnley complete the double and make it six wins in a row with a gutsy display. United are never allowed to settle and the defensive flaws are exposed. England hopeful Ray Pointer wraps up the points with late goals. Cope and Gregg are in a mess for the third goal.										
38	A	PORTSMOUTH	1	W	3-1	2-1	Charlton 16, 70, Bradley 42	Gregg	Greaves	Carolan	Goodwin	Foulkes	McGuinness	Bradley	Quixall	Viollet	Charlton	Scanlon
	30/3	*29,359*	22	50			*Harris P 30*	*Brown*	*Rutter*	*Gunter*	*Howells*	*Hayward*	*Dickinson*	*Harris P*	*White*	*Saunders*	*Harris H*	*Newman*
							Ref: E Jennings	Cope is dropped, allowing Foulkes to be tried at centre-half. Bill impresses as United notch a tenth away win. Charlton pleases the watching England boss Winterbottom. With Wolves continuing to win, the Burnley defeat was critical. Saunders' bad miss just after the break is crucial.										
39	H	BOLTON	2	W	3-0	2-0	Charlton 8, Scanlon 12, Viollet 88	Gregg	Greaves	Carolan	Goodwin	Foulkes	McGuinness	Bradley	Quixall	Viollet	Charlton	Scanlon
	4/4	61,528	*8*	52				*Hopkinson*	*Hartle*	*Banks*	*Hennin*	*Edwards G*	*Edwards B*	*Bannister*	*Stevens*	*Lofthouse*	*Parry*	*Holden*
							Ref: E Oxley	There is a minute's silence for the Birmingham and England full-back Jeff Hall, who died of polio. United wrap up the points after 12 minutes. Foulkes masters Lofty, and Winterbottom must have liked United's wingers and Quixall. United reach 100 goals for only the second time ever.										
40	A	LUTON	2	D	0-0	0-0		Gregg	Greaves	Carolan	Goodwin	Foulkes	McGuinness	Bradley	Quixall	Viollet	Pearson	Scanlon
	11/4	*27,025*	*17*	53				*Baynham*	*McNally*	*Hawkes*	*Groves*	*Kelly*	*Pacey*	*Bingham*	*Brown*	*Morton*	*Cummins*	*Hawkes B*
							Ref: G Brandwood	Managerless Luton are in the FA Cup final and will face Forest. This is a rough game, with McGuinness and Bingham booked and almost sent off. Charlton is scoring the winning goal for England and his deputy Mark Pearson misses a sitter. Gregg at his best to foil Luton's late flurry.										
41	H	BIRMINGHAM	2	W	1-0	0-0	Quixall 60p	Gregg	Greaves	Carolan	Goodwin	Foulkes	McGuinness	Bradley	Quixall	Viollet	Charlton	Scanlon
	18/4	43,006	*10*	55				*Merrick*	*Farmer*	*Allen*	*Watts*	*Smith*	*Neal*	*Astall*	*Gordon*	*Stubbs*	*Larkin*	*Hooper*
							Ref: E Hill	The title is going to Wolves but United plough on. Watts handles but Charlton gives up a chance to equal Rowley's 30-goal haul by giving the spot-kick to Quixall. 17-year-old Robin Stubbs has scored eight in eight but Bill Foulkes is in charge. Six Reds are on England's tour short-list.										
42	A	LEICESTER	2	L	1-2	0-1	Bradley 88	Gregg	Greaves	Carolan	Goodwin	Foulkes	Brennan	Bradley	Quixall	Viollet	Charlton	Scanlon
	25/4	*38,466*	*19*	55			*Walsh 19, Wills 68*	*Maclaren*	*Chalmers*	*Baillie*	*Newman*	*Knapp*	*Appleton*	*Stephenson*	*Keyworth*	*Walsh*	*Leek*	*Wills*
	Home	Away					Ref: D Blues	Leicester have pulled out of relegation trouble with nine points from six games, and you would think they had won the league as the supporters invade the mud-covered pitch at the end. The first goal looks offside but Wills' header completes a great move. The tired Reds need a rest.										
Average	53,258	43,552																

FA Cup			F-A	H-T	Scorers, Times, and Referees	1	2	3	4	5	6	7	8	9	10	11
3 A NORWICH	3	L	0-3	0-1		Gregg	Foulkes	Carolan	Goodwin	Cope	McGuinness	Bradley	Quixall	Viollet	Charlton	Scanlon
10/1	*38,000 3:17*				*Bly 32, 87, Crossan 61*	*Nethercott*	*Thurlow*	*Ashman*	*McCrohan*	*Butler*	*Crowe*	*Crossan*	*Allcock*	*Bly*	*Hill*	*Brennan*
					Ref: W Clements	Eight straight league wins count for nothing on a bone-hard Carrow Road pitch with a light covering of snow. Lacklustre United are run ragged by the enthusiastic Canaries, whose ace scorer Terry Bly is in devastating form. It is a massive Cup shock and the start of a glorious City run.										

		Home					Away					
	P	W	D	L	F	A	W	D	L	F	A	Pts
1 Wolves	42	15	3	3	68	19	13	2	6	42	30	61
2 MAN UNITED	42	14	4	3	58	27	10	3	8	45	39	55
3 Arsenal	42	14	3	4	53	29	7	5	9	35	39	50
4 Bolton	42	14	3	4	56	30	6	7	8	23	36	50
5 West Brom	42	8	7	6	41	33	10	6	5	47	35	49
6 West Ham	42	15	3	3	59	29	6	3	12	26	41	48
7 Burnley	42	11	4	6	41	29	8	6	7	40	41	48
8 Blackpool	42	12	7	2	39	13	6	4	11	27	36	47
9 Birmingham	42	14	1	6	54	35	6	5	10	30	33	46
10 Blackburn	42	12	3	6	48	28	5	7	9	28	42	44
11 Newcastle	42	11	3	7	40	29	6	4	11	40	51	41
12 Preston	42	9	3	9	40	39	8	4	9	30	38	41
13 Nott'm Forest	42	9	4	8	37	32	8	2	11	34	42	40
14 Chelsea	42	13	2	6	52	37	5	2	14	25	61	40
15 Leeds	42	8	7	6	28	27	7	2	12	29	47	39
16 Everton	42	11	3	7	39	38	6	1	14	32	49	38
17 Luton	42	11	6	4	50	26	1	7	13	18	45	37
18 Tottenham	42	10	3	8	56	42	3	7	11	29	53	36
19 Leicester	42	7	6	8	34	36	4	4	13	33	62	32
20 Manchester C	42	8	7	6	40	32	3	2	16	24	63	31
21 Aston Villa	42	8	5	8	31	33	3	3	15	27	54	30
22 Portsmouth	42	5	4	12	38	47	1	5	15	26	65	21
	924	239	91	132	1002	690	132	91	239	690	1002	924

Odds & ends

Double wins: (6) Leeds, Birmingham, Chelsea, Aston Villa, Blackburn, Portsmouth.
Double losses: (1) Burnley.

Won from behind: (5) Leeds (a), Preston (a), Chelsea (a), Man City (h), Blackburn (a).
Lost from in front: (1) Blackpool (a).

High spots: 12-match unbeaten run through winter.
8 successive victories.
Emergence of Bradley, McGuinness and Scanlon.
Victory over the champions Wolves.
Home attendances the highest ever at Old Trafford.

Low spots: Cup exit at Third Division Norwich.
Poor early season away form that ultimately lost the title.

Red cards (United): (0).
Red cards (Opponents): (0).
Ever-presents: (2) Goodwin, Scanlon.
Hat-tricks: (3) Charlton, Scanlon, Viollet.
Opposing hat-tricks: (0).
Leading scorer: (29) Charlton.

	Appearances				Goals		
	Lge	*Sub*	FAC	*Sub*	Lge	FAC	Tot
Bradley, Warren	**24**		1		**12**		**12**
Brennan, Shay	**1**						
Carolan, Joe	**23**		1				
Charlton, Bobby	**38**		1		**29**		**29**
Cope, Ronnie	**32**		1		**2**		**2**
Crowther, Stan	**2**						
Dawson, Alex	**11**				**4**		**4**
Foulkes, Bill	**32**		1				
Goodwin, Freddie	**42**		1		**6**		**6**
Greaves, Ian	**34**						
Gregg, Harry	**41**		1				
Harrop, Bobby	**5**						
Hunter, Reg	**1**						
McGuinness, Wilf	**39**		1		**1**		**1**
Morgans, Kenny	**2**						
Pearson, Mark	**4**				**1**		**1**
Quixall, Albert	**33**		1		**4**		**4**
Scanlon, Albert	**42**		1		**16**		**16**
Taylor, Ernie	**11**						
Viollet, Dennis	**37**		1		**21**		**21**
Webster, Colin	**7**				**5**		**5**
Wood, Ray	**1**						
(own-goals)					**2**		**2**
22 players used	**462**		**11**		**103**		**103**

LEAGUE DIVISION 1 — Manager: Matt Busby — SEASON 1959-60

No	Date		Att	Pos	Pt	F-A	H-T	Scorers, Times, and Referees	1	2	3	4	5	6	7	8	9	10	11
1	A	WEST BROM			L	2-3	1-2	Viollet 18, 72	Gregg	Greaves	Carolan	Goodwin	Foulkes	McGuinness	Bradley	Quixall	Viollet	Charlton	Scanlon
	22/8		*40,706*		0			*Burnside 24, 73, Foulkes 25 (og)*	*Potter*	*Howe*	*Williams S*	*Setters*	*Kennedy*	*Barlow*	*Allen*	*Burnside*	*Robson*	*Kevan*	*Dixon*
								Ref: A Ellis	Gordon Clark's spirited Albion side look potential title contenders and dictate the game. In a thrilling match United, in their new kit with white socks and short shorts, are exposed with Gregg possibly at fault for Burnside's goals. Viollet is left to do too much, but scores two good goals										
2	H	CHELSEA			L	0-1	0-1		Gregg	Greaves	Carolan	Goodwin	Foulkes	McGuinness	Bradley	Quixall	Dawson	Viollet	Charlton
	26/8		57,903		0			*Greaves 26*	*Matthews*	*Sillett P*	*Whittaker*	*Anderton*	*Mortimore*	*Compton*	*Brabrook*	*Greaves*	*Livesey*	*Nicholas*	*Blunstone*
								Ref: M Dixon	Jimmy Greaves started the season with a hat-trick and impudently scores from Nicholas after rounding Gregg. United, with Charlton tried on the wing, are ragged and Reg Matthews saves everything. Five minutes from time Alex Dawson collides with Matthews and is stretchered off.										
3	H	NEWCASTLE		16	W	3-2	3-1	Viollet 2, 13, Charlton 27	Gregg	Cope	Carolan	Brennan	Foulkes	McGuinness	Bradley	Quixall	Viollet	Charlton	Scanlon
	29/8		53,500	*22*	2			*Allchurch 25, White 66*	*Harvey*	*Keith*	*McMichael*	*Scoular*	*Stokoe*	*Bell*	*Taylor*	*Allchurch*	*White*	*Eastham*	*Scott*
								Ref: J Cook	United are well on top in an entertaining first half but miss chances galore. Charlton superbly scores from almost on the by-line. The defence is not convincing and Newcastle are denied good penalty claims when Gregg brings down White. A draw would have flattered Newcastle.										
4	A	CHELSEA		10	W	6-3	3-2	Quixall 28, Charlton 31, Brad' 34, 70,	Gregg	Cope	Carolan	Brennan	Foulkes	McGuinness	Bradley	Quixall	Viollet	Charlton	Scanlon
	2/9		***66,579***	*17*	4			*Greav' 25, Sil' 39, 85p* [Viol' 47, 80]	*Matthews*	*Sillett P*	*Whittaker*	*Anderton*	*Scott*	*Compton*	*Brabrook*	*Greaves*	*Livesey*	*Nicholas*	*Blunstone*
								Ref: R Mann	The biggest crowd at the Bridge for five years come to see the scoring sensation Greaves and witness a classic. Both keepers are dodgy with Matthews failing to cut out centres for the first three goals. Viollet outshines Greaves and bewilders Scott. Scanlon and Bradley are deadly.										
5	A	BIRMINGHAM		8	D	1-1	1-0	Quixall 42	Gregg	Cope	Carolan	Brennan	Foulkes	McGuinness	Bradley	Quixall	Viollet	Charlton	Scanlon
	5/9		*38,242*	*16*	5			*Watts 85*	*Schofield*	*Farmer*	*Allen*	*Watts*	*Smith*	*Neal*	*Hooper*	*Gordon*	*Stubbs*	*Larkin*	*Orritt*
								Ref: A Murdoch	A warm day and a dominant United fail to capitalise on their domination. Birmingham have a tough reputation but don't faze the Reds. Bill Foulkes outshines England stopper Trevor Smith but Harry Gregg is at fault for Watts' header. United's wingers are again in top form.										
6	H	LEEDS		6	W	**6-0**	3-0	Charlton 7, 70, Bradley 26, 35, [Viollet 85, Scanlon 89]	Gregg	Cope	Carolan	Brennan	Foulkes	McGuinness	Bradley	Quixall	Viollet	Charlton	Scanlon
	9/9		48,619	*18*	7				*Burgin*	*Ashall*	*Hair*	*Revie*	*Charlton*	*Cush*	*Francis*	*Meek*	*Cameron*	*Peyton*	*Overfield*
								Ref: J Williams	Despite an early injury to Quixall, United have no problems despatching a brave but outclassed Leeds. Bradley moves to centre-forward and can do no wrong. Francis is a Leeds passenger for the second half. The reserve team, watched by huge crowds, hit Leeds' reserves for eight.										
7	H	TOTTENHAM		9	L	1-5	1-3	Viollet 43 *[Mackay 89]*	Gregg	Cope	Carolan	Goodwin	Foulkes	McGuinness	Bradley	**Giles**	Viollet	Charlton	Scanlon
	12/9		55,641	*1*	7			*Dunmore 18, Smith 23, 87, Harmer 28,*	*Brown*	*Baker*	*Hopkins*	*Blanchflower*	*Norman*	*Mackay*	*Medwin*	*Harmer*	*Smith R*	*Dunmore*	*Jones*
								Ref: P Rhodes	Undefeated Spurs are the most expensive team in history, costing over £180,000. Latest recruit is the formidable Dave Mackay and he may be the last piece in the jigsaw for Nicholson. Jones fleeces Cope and the bustling Smith unnerves Foulkes. The Londoners' keep-ball is awesome.										
8	A	LEEDS		10	D	2-2	1-2	Charlton 29, Cush 67(og)	Gregg	Foulkes	Carolan	Brennan	Cope	McGuinness	Bradley	Quixall	Viollet	Charlton	Scanlon
	16/9		*34,048*	*13*	8			*Crowe 2, Cush 37*	*Burgin*	*Ashall*	*Kilford*	*Gibson*	*Charlton*	*Cush*	*Meek*	*Peyton*	*Revie*	*Crowe*	*Overfield*
								Ref: W Surtees	Leeds, fielding one of the smallest teams in the division, are well on top until the break but succumb to United's pressure. The equaliser is lucky. Jack Charlton's attempted clearance rebounds off Cush and into his own net. Cope and Foulkes, back in their old positions, look good.										
9	A	MANCHESTER C		13	L	0-3	0-2		Gregg	Foulkes	Carolan	Brennan	Cope	McGuinness	Bradley	Quixall	Viollet	Charlton	Scanlon
	19/9		*58,300*	*15*	8			*Hayes 9, 12, Hannah 75*	*Trautmann*	*Leivers*	*Sear*	*Cheetham*	*McTavish*	*Barnes*	*Barlow*	*Hannah*	*McAdams*	*Hayes*	*Colbridge*
								Ref: J Kelly	City win their first derby game for four years with a magnificent display against an anxious Reds defence who look vulnerable. Hayes makes it nine goals in 10 derbies with his deadly shooting and crosses for Hannah's goal. Scanlon and McGuinness fail to impress England's selectors.										
10	A	PRESTON		16	L	0-4	0-1		Gregg	Foulkes	Carolan	Viollet	Cope	McGuinness	Bradley	Quixall	Dawson	Charlton	Scanlon
	26/9		*35,016*	*7*	8			*Taylor 15, Finney 64p, 89, Sneddon 77*	*Else*	*Cunningham*	*Walton*	*Milne*	*Dunn*	*Smith*	*Mayers*	*Farrall*	*Finney*	*Sneddon*	*Taylor*
								Ref: R Windle	The wheels are in danger of coming off as a faster, slicker North End rip the defence apart. Viollet's experiment at right-half is not a success and the attack lacks bite. As Preston turn the screw, veteran Finney misses a sitter and Gordon Milne hits the bar. Busby looks for new players.										

No	Venue	Opponent / Date	Att	Pos	Res / Pts	F-A	H-T	Scorers, Times, and Referees	1	2	3	4	5	6	7	8	9	10	11
11	H	LEICESTER		13	W	4-1	3-0	Charlton 5, Viollet 17, 68, Quixall 22	Gaskell	Foulkes	Carolan	Goodwin	Cope	McGuinness	Bradley	Quixall	Viollet	Charlton	Scanlon
		3/10	41,637	*14*	10			*Hines 65*	*Maclaren*	*Chalmers*	*Baillie*	*McLintock*	*Knapp*	*Appleton*	*McDonald*	*Keyworth*	*Hines*	*Cheesebrough*	*Wills*
								Ref: L Howarth	Gregg is on Irish international duty and Busby eyes Tony Knapp of Leicester and Rangers' full-back Eric Caldow. A thrilling first half peters out as the effects of a 1-6 midweek friendly defeat against Real Madrid begin to tell. Warren Bradley back to his best but others still off-colour.										
12	H	ARSENAL		10	W	4-2	1-2	Dodgin 7(og), Quixall 60, Charlton 83, [Viollet 89]	Gregg	Foulkes	Carolan	Goodwin	Cope	McGuinness	Bradley	Quixall	Viollet	Charlton	Scanlon
		10/10	51,872	*7*	12			*Henderson 14, Herd 43*	*Standen*	*Wills*	*McCullough*	*Docherty*	*Dodgin*	*Groves*	*Clapton*	*Bloomfield*	*Herd*	*Henderson*	*Haverty*
								Ref: K Tuck	George Swindin's Arsenal have lost only twice but are beaten by a sprightlier United. An excellent comeback with late goals. Scanlon on top form, harassing Dodgin for the first and then crossing for Quixall's header. Two sloppy goals conceded. The Gunners, Herd apart, are average.										
13	A	WOLVERHAMPTON		12	L	2-3	0-0	Stuart 66(og), Viollet 78	Gregg	Foulkes	Carolan	Goodwin	Cope	McGuinness	Bradley	Giles	Viollet	Pearson	Scanlon
		17/10	*45,451*	*2*	12			*Murray 59, 71, Broadbent 62*	*Finlayson*	*Kelly*	*Harris*	*Slater*	*Stuart*	*Kirkham*	*Deeley*	*Durrandt*	*Murray*	*Broadbent*	*Horne*
								Ref: J Hunt	Billy Wright and Jimmy Mullen have retired but Wolves, with only two defeats, are as strong as ever. Charlton and Flowers are on England duty and reserves Pearson and Giles deputise well. United deserve a point and argue that Murray is offside for the first and handles the third.										
14	H	SHEFFIELD WED		12	W	3-1	1-1	Viollet 42, 51, Bradley 50	Gregg	Foulkes	Carolan	Goodwin	Cope	McGuinness	Bradley	Quixall	Viollet	Charlton	Scanlon
		24/10	39,723	*14*	14			*McAnearney 5*	*Springett*	*Johnson*	*Curtis*	*McAnearney T*	*Swan*	*Kay*	*Wilkinson*	*Young*	*Ellis*	*Fantham*	*Finney*
								Ref: A Robotham	Newly promoted Wednesday under Harry Catterick deserve a point at least. They never stop playing good football and are beaten by a freak, a gift and Viollet's stunning second. Harry Gregg is brilliant and the Owls also hit the post. Viollet's goals make it 119 in his 200th league game.										
15	A	BLACKBURN		12	D	1-1	1-0	Quixall 16	Gregg	Foulkes	Carolan	Goodwin	Cope	McGuinness	Bradley	Quixall	Viollet	Charlton	Scanlon
		31/10	*39,621*	*4*	15			*MacLeod 85*	*Leyland*	*Bray*	*Whelan*	*Clayton*	*Woods*	*McGrath*	*Isherwood*	*McEvoy*	*Dobing*	*Vernon*	*MacLeod*
								Ref: E Crawford	Rovers are a strong side and their second-half rally led by the skilful Peter Dobing deservedly wins them a point. New England captain Ronnie Clayton is superb and ably supported by the Welsh wizard Vernon. United ease up after a strong first hour. Viollet picked for Football League.										
16	H	FULHAM		11	D	3-3	1-2	Viollet 9, Scanlon 52, Charlton 83	Gregg	Foulkes	Carolan	Goodwin	Cope	McGuinness	Bradley	Quixall	Viollet	Charlton	Scanlon
		7/11	44,304	*6*	16			*Leggat 22, 28, 77*	*Macedo*	*Cohen*	*Langley*	*Mullery*	*Bentley*	*Lowe*	*Key*	*Hill*	*Leggat*	*Haynes*	*Chamberlain*
								Ref: D Martin	Stylish Fulham deserve a point in an enthralling match. Winger Leggat scores three in his first game at centre-forward assisted by Cope's boob for the second. The duel between Haynes and Charlton is inconclusive. No one can catch a boxer dog and play is held up for six minutes.										
17	A	BOLTON		10	D	1-1	0-0	Dawson 73	Gregg	Foulkes	Carolan	Goodwin	Cope	McGuinness	Dawson	Quixall	Viollet	Charlton	Bradley
		14/11	*37,892*	*9*	17			*Stevens 89*	*Hopkinson*	*Hartle*	*Farrimond*	*Stanley*	*Higgins*	*Edwards B*	*Birch*	*Hill*	*Stevens*	*Parry*	*Holden*
								Ref: A Luty	Freddie Hill's splendid dribble and cross sets up Stevens' late goal to deny United their first win at Bolton since 1949. Lofthouse has retired but Ray Parry, who plays for England next week, outshines a lethargic Charlton. United look weary after a 5-6 friendly defeat in Madrid.										
18	H	LUTON		8	W	4-1	1-0	Quixall 22, Viollet 68, 87, Goodwin 74	Gregg	Foulkes	Carolan	Goodwin	Cope	McGuinness	Bradley	Quixall	Viollet	Charlton	Scanlon
		21/11	40,807	*22*	19			*Kilgannon 50*	*Baynham*	*Dunne*	*Daniel*	*Groves*	*Kelly*	*Brown*	*Bingham*	*Kilgannon*	*Pacey*	*Cummins*	*Gregory*
								Ref: P Brandwood	Last year's Cup finalists are having a tough time and play as though expecting defeat. The Hatters' negative tactics are undone by a late Red's flurry led by the sterling Goodwin. Bobby Charlton, dropped by England, is out of sorts, but Dennis Viollet, as ever, is deadly in front of goal.										
19	A	EVERTON		11	L	1-2	1-2	Viollet 2	Gregg	Foulkes	Carolan	Goodwin	Cope	McGuinness	Bradley	Quixall	Viollet	Charlton	Scanlon
		28/11	*46,095*	*17*	19			*Thomas 24, Collins 39p*	*Dunlop*	*Parker*	*Jones*	*King*	*Labone*	*Harris B*	*Harris J*	*Thomas*	*Shackleton*	*Collins*	*Laverick*
								Ref: A Holland	Gregg has a bad day, failing to cut out a cross for the first and fouling Alan Shackleton for the penalty. United have not won away since 2 Sept but come close to a fortuitous draw near the end. Jimmy Harris masters the glue-pot pitch and Carey's team maintain their good home form.										
20	H	BLACKPOOL		9	W	3-1	1-0	Pearson 37, Viollet 49, 73	Gaskell	Foulkes	Carolan	Goodwin	Cope	Brennan	Dawson	Quixall	Viollet	Pearson	Scanlon
		5/12	45,795	*18*	21			*Kaye 47*	*Farm*	*Armfield*	*Martin*	*Hauser*	*Gratrix*	*Kelly J*	*Kaye*	*Peterson*	*Charnley*	*Durie*	*Perry*
								Ref: G McCabe	Busby wields the axe on Gregg, McGuinness, Charlton and Bradley after recent poor form and it pays off. Struggling Blackpool are easily beaten after Hauser goes off injured. Jimmy Armfield is a classy player but can do little to halt Viollet who reaches 20 goals for the season.										
21	A	NOTT'M FOREST		8	W	5-1	2-1	Dawson 26, Viollet 43, 75, 81, [Scanlon 72]	Gaskell	Foulkes	Carolan	Goodwin	Cope	Brennan	Dawson	Quixall	Viollet	Pearson	Scanlon
		12/12	*31,816*	*18*	23			*Wilson 12*	*Thomson*	*McDonald*	*Patrick*	*Whitefoot*	*McKinlay*	*Iley*	*Barton*	*Booth*	*Wilson*	*Gray*	*Imlach*
								Ref: E Jennings	The struggling FA Cup winners are put to the sword as the Reds finally click. Forest are one of only two Div 1 clubs without lights so the game kicks off at 2.15. Pearson's back-pass sets up Wilson but Viollet's sharpshooting clinches the points. McGuinness breaks a leg in the reserves.										

No	Date	Att	Pos	Pt	F-A	H-T	Scorers, Times, and Referees	1	2	3	4	5	6	7	8	9	10	11
22	H WEST BROM		9	L	2-3	1-1	Dawson 8, Quixall 66p	Gaskell	Foulkes	Carolan	Goodwin	Cope	Brennan	Dawson	Quixall	Viollet	Pearson	Scanlon
	19/12	**33,902**	*10*	23			*Hogg 39, Allen 57, Burnside 74*	*Wallace*	*Howe*	*Williams S*	*Drury*	*Kennedy*	*Robson*	*Aitken*	*Burnside*	*Allen*	*Kevan*	*Hogg*
							Ref: R Reddaway	A dodgy home defence hands Albion an early Christmas present, all three goals coming from miskicks. United are constantly caught offside by an Albion defence well marshalled by Joe Kennedy but missing the suspended Maurice Setters. Viollet is a superb leader but lacks support.										
23	H BURNLEY		10	L	1-2	0-2	Quixall 79	Gaskell	Foulkes	Carolan	Goodwin	Cope	Brennan	Dawson	Quixall	Viollet	Charlton	Scanlon
	26/12	**62,673**	*3*	23			*Robson 27, Lawson 43*	*Blacklaw*	*Angus*	*Elder*	*Seith*	*Miller*	*Adamson*	*Connelly*	*Lawson*	*Pointer*	*Robson*	*Pilkington*
							Ref: L Tirebuck	Harry Potts' team's best season for years and they look genuine title challengers. This is a scrappy game with Burnley, and Angus in particular, over physical. He constantly bodychecks Scanlon, United's best forward. Charlton only starts to sparkle near the end. Lawson's scoring debut.										
24	A BURNLEY		10	W	4-1	1-1	Viollet 16, 63, Scanlon 89, 90	Gaskell	Foulkes	Carolan	Goodwin	Cope	Brennan	Dawson	Quixall	Viollet	Charlton	Scanlon
	28/12	*47,696*	*3*	25			*Robson 22*	*Blacklaw*	*Angus*	*Elder*	*Seith*	*Miller*	*Adamson*	*Connelly*	*McIlroy*	*Pointer*	*Robson*	*Pilkington*
							Ref: T Reynolds	The Reds gain revenge in front of Burnley's biggest league crowd since 1950. Schemer McIlroy returns but does not look fit and Gaskell keeps Burnley at bay when the pressure is high. Scanlon's late goals give the scoreline a flattering look but Busby celebrates becoming a grandfather.										
25	A NEWCASTLE		11	L	**3-7**	1-3	Daw' 27, Qux' 61,80p, *[Bell 76, All' 86]*	Gaskell	Foulkes	Carolan	Goodwin	Cope	Brennan	Dawson	Quixall	Viollet	Charlton	Scanlon
	2/1	*57,200*	*12*	25			*Hughes 7, White 16, 44, 54, East' 66p,*	*Harvey*	*Keith*	*McMichael*	*Scoular*	*Stokoe*	*Bell*	*Hughes*	*Eastham*	*White*	*Allchurch*	*Luke*
							Ref: R Ryalls	United concede seven for the first time since 1939 and their defensive inadequacies are exposed once more. Winger Hughes' speed and skill bemuse the Reds. Whites' finishing is predatory. Despite Allchurch limping throughout, it is a trouncing. Busby ready to pounce for Setters.										
26	H BIRMINGHAM		11	W	2-1	1-0	Quixall 40p, Viollet 51	Gregg	Foulkes	Carolan	**Setters**	Cope	Brennan	Bradley	Quixall	Viollet	Charlton	Scanlon
	16/1	47,606	21	27			*Larkin 57*	*Schofield*	*Farmer*	*Allen*	*Watts*	*Smith*	*Neal*	*Astall*	*Larkin*	*Weston*	*Hume*	*Rudd*
							Ref: J Husband	On an icy pitch, the relegation-threatened Blues are unlucky not to get a point. Debut-boy Setters, a £35,000 signing from West Brom, is quiet but effective. The penalty for Neal's handball is harsh and Blues think Viollet is offside and stop dead. Weston and Rudd debuts augur well.										
27	A TOTTENHAM		11	L	1-2	0-2	Bradley 48	Gregg	Foulkes	Carolan	Setters	Cope	Brennan	Bradley	Quixall	Viollet	Charlton	Scanlon
	23/1	*62,602*	*1*	27			*Smith 8, 32*	*Brown*	*Baker*	*Henry*	*Blanchflower*	*Norman*	*Mackay*	*White*	*Harmer*	*Smith R*	*Allen*	*Jones*
							Ref: G McCabe	Spurs have won five out of six and are four points clear of second-placed Burnley. Bobby Smith, tipped for England honours, scores from Gregg's awry goal-kick and Cliff Jones's cross. Bradley's diving header from Scanlon's cross sparks a brief rally but Spurs are good value.										
28	H MANCHESTER C		11	D	0-0	0-0		Gregg	Foulkes	Carolan	Setters	Cope	Brennan	Bradley	Quixall	Viollet	Charlton	Scanlon
	6/2	59,450	*14*	28				*Trautmann*	*Branagan*	*Sear*	*Barnes*	*McTavish*	*Oakes*	*Sambrook*	*Hannah*	*McAdams*	*Hayes*	*Colbridge*
							Ref: M McCoy	An anxious and fraught derby game ends all square. Setters and Cope are booked but it is not a dirty game. Viollet and Hayes both miss three chances. Eight minutes from time Branagan heads off the line with Trautmann beaten. United seem to have one eye on the upcoming Cup-tie.										
29	H PRESTON		11	D	1-1	1-0	Viollet 5	Gregg	Foulkes	Carolan	Setters	Cope	Brennan	Bradley	Quixall	Viollet	Charlton	Scanlon
	13/2	44,014	*5*	29			*Finney 70*	*Else*	*Heyes*	*Walton*	*Milne*	*Dunn*	*Smith*	*Dagger*	*Thompson*	*Finney*	*Sneddon*	*Taylor*
							Ref: A Sparling	United's patchy home form continues and will have to improve to progress in the Cup. Tom Finney makes his last appearance at Old Trafford. Preston, without a league win in ten games, rely on Else's great saves to keep them in the game. Setters looks a great buy. Ken Heyes' debut.										
30	A LEICESTER		11	L	1-3	1-1	Scanlon 39 *[Wills 82]*	Gregg	Foulkes	Carolan	Setters	Cope	Brennan	Viollet	Quixall	Dawson	Charlton	Scanlon
	24/2	*33,191*	*15*	29			*McLintock 26, Cheesebrough 75,*	*Banks*	*Chalmers*	*Cunningham*	*McLintock*	*Knapp*	*Appleton*	*McDonald*	*Cheesebrough*	*Leek*	*Walsh*	*Wills*
							Ref: I Rosekilly	Leicester have lost only two games in thirteen and with youngsters Banks and McLintock starring are too good for United. Frank McLintock's cute lob is followed by Setters woeful back-pass before Wills' curler deceives Gregg. Matt Gillies' side is pulling well clear of relegation.										
31	A BLACKPOOL		9	W	**6-0**	1-0	Charlton 10, 54, 88, Viollet 50, 52, [Scanlon 74]	Gregg	Foulkes	Carolan	Setters	Cope	Brennan	Viollet	Quixall	Dawson	Charlton	Scanlon
	27/2	*23,966*	*17*	31				*Waiters*	*Armfield*	*Martin*	*Hauser*	*Gratrix*	*Kelly H*	*Matthews*	*Mudie*	*Charnley*	*Crawford*	*Perry*
							Ref: R Windle	The 45-year-old maestro, Stan Matthews, is just back from injury but can do little to stem the tide. United's biggest away win since 1937 is down to the dazzling Charlton, who toys with a fragile defence and shatters Pool with a hat-trick. Relegation is looming for the Tangerines.										

No	Venue	Opponent	Pos	Res	F-A	H-T	Scorers, Times, and Referees	1	2	3	4	5	6	7	8	9	10	11
32	H	WOLVERHAMPTON	12	L	0-2	0-0		Gregg	Foulkes	Carolan	Setters	Cope	Brennan	Viollet	Quixall	Dawson	Charlton	Scanlon
5/3		60,403	2	31			*Deeley 47, Stobart 85*	*Sidebottom*	*Showell*	*Harris*	*Clamp*	*Slater*	*Flowers*	*Mannion*	*Broadbent*	*Stobart*	*Mason*	*Deeley*
							Ref: W Surtees	Wolves are in a transition period and are blooding the kids – Mannion and Stobart make their debuts. They bounce back from a European Cup mauling in Barcelona and with Bill Slater awesome are now one point behind leaders Spurs. Setters and Foulkes are good but others lack fire.										
33	H	NOTT'M FOREST	12	W	3-1	1-0	Dawson 26, Charlton 47, 51	Gregg	Foulkes	Carolan	Setters	Cope	Brennan	Giles	Viollet	Dawson	Pearson	Charlton
19/3		35,269	*18*	33			*Brennan 49(og)*	*Armstrong*	*Thomas*	*McDonald*	*Whitefoot*	*McKinlay*	*Burkitt*	*Barton*	*Booth*	*Wilson*	*Gray*	*Imlach*
							Ref: H Webb	Bobby Charlton is switched to left wing and stars – scoring two and crossing for Dawson's headed goal. Forest miss good chances but their forwards fail to gel. 19-year-old starlet John Giles is lively on the right and Gregg dominates the air. Goodwin has gone to Leeds for £15,000.										
34	A	FULHAM	11	W	5-0	2-0	Viollet 19, 23, Giles 77, Pearson 82, [Dawson 88]	Gregg	Foulkes	Carolan	Setters	Cope	Brennan	Giles	Viollet	Dawson	Pearson	Charlton
26/3		*38,250*	*10*	35				*Macedo*	*Cohen*	*Lawler*	*Mullery*	*Lampe*	*Lowe*	*Leggat*	*Hill*	*Bentley*	*Haynes*	*Langley*
							Ref: R Jordan	Bedford Jezzard's side are reduced to nine by injury; Lampe is concussed and Hill's knee has gone. United upset the home fans with their mickey-taking and are booed off. Viollet equals Rowley's 30-goal record and Charlton's form on the wing will earn him an England recall.										
35	A	SHEFFIELD WED	11	L	2-4	0-1	Viollet 52, Charlton 89 *[Wilk'son 78]*	Gaskell	Foulkes	Heron	Setters	Cope	Brennan	Bradley	Viollet	Dawson	Pearson	Charlton
30/3		*26,022*	*4*	35			*Griffin 35, 88, Fantham 65,*	*Springett*	*Johnson*	*Megson*	*McAnearney T*	*Swan*	*Kay*	*Wilkinson*	*Craig*	*Ellis*	*Fantham*	*Griffin*
							Ref: R Langdale	Despite a Cup semi-final exit, Wednesday have lost only one home game and are heading for their best post-war finish. Young Billy Griffin has a dream game with a disallowed goal after three minutes and two that count. A full-blooded second half sees the Owls deservedly win.										
36	H	BOLTON	10	W	2-0	1-0	Charlton 42, 88	Gaskell	Foulkes	Carolan	Setters	Cope	Brennan	Bradley	Giles	Dawson	Pearson	Charlton
2/4		45,482	*7*	37				*Bollands*	*Hartle*	*Banks*	*Stanley*	*Oxtoby*	*Cunliffe*	*Bannister*	*Hill*	*Stevens*	*Parry*	*Holden*
							Ref: R Leafe	Two Charlton screamers are sufficient to win a hard-fought game. Johnnie Bollands – in for the broken leg victim Eddie Hopkinson – can only parry the second into Bobby's path. Setters is inspired against England schemer Ray Parry. Mark Pearson is limping with a damaged ankle.										
37	A	LUTON	8	W	3-2	3-1	Bradley 20, Dawson 30, 32	Gregg	Foulkes	Carolan	Setters	Cope	Brennan	Bradley	Giles	Dawson	**Lawton**	Scanlon
9/4		***21,242***	*22*	39			*Cummins 27, 54*	*Baynham*	*Dunne*	*Hawkes K*	*Morton*	*Pacey*	*Brown*	*Bingham*	*Turner*	*McBride*	*Cummins*	*Noake*
							Ref: R Mann	Even with a makeshift forward line United are too good for almost relegated Luton. The Hatters have no plan other than long hopeful balls and the game is over before half-time. 20-year-old Nobby Lawton has a promising debut and Albert Scanlon is recalled for England cap Charlton.										
38	A	WEST HAM	8	L	1-2	1-2	Dawson 25	Gregg	Foulkes	Carolan	Setters	Cope	Brennan	Bradley	Giles	Dawson	Lawton	Charlton
15/4		*34,969*	*12*	39			*Musgrove 6, Grice 8*	*Rhodes*	*Bond*	*Cantwell*	*Malcolm*	*Brown*	*Moore*	*Grice*	*Woosnam*	*Dunmore*	*Smillie*	*Musgrove*
							Ref: J Cooke	West Ham are a useful home side and the early goals shock United. Dawson's 30-yard shot reduces the lead and Lawton hits the post but it's in vain. Setters upsets the referee with his arguing and deliberate handball when danger threatens. Charlton is buzzing and too hot for John Bond.										
39	H	BLACKBURN	8	W	1-0	0-0	Dawson 89	Gregg	Foulkes	Carolan	Setters	Cope	Brennan	Bradley	Giles	Dawson	Lawton	Charlton
16/4		46,071	*17*	41				*Jones*	*Bray*	*Whelan*	*Clayton*	*Woods*	*McGrath*	*Bimpson*	*Thomas*	*Dobing*	*Douglas*	*MacLeod*
							Ref: A Luty	Blackburn's league form is dire – 2 wins since Xmas but they are at Wembley to face Wolves. Blackburn play the offside trap and it's a yawn. Setters looks more an England player than Ronnie Clayton. Bryan Douglas's dribbles are delightful. Charlton's run and cross make the winner.										
40	H	WEST HAM	8	W	5-3	2-3	Daw' 25, 62, Charl' 34, 49, Quix' 84	Gregg	Foulkes	Carolan	Setters	Cope	Brennan	Giles	Quixall	Dawson	Viollet	Charlton
18/4		34,505	*12*	43			*Dunmore 5, Cantwell 30p, Scott 37*	*Rhodes*	*Kirkup*	*Cantwell*	*Bovington*	*Moore*	*Smillie*	*Scott*	*Cartwright*	*Dunmore*	*Brett*	*Musgrove*
							Ref: L Howarth	An excellent advert for the sport with two skilful sides going all out to attack. Johnny Giles creates the last three goals and it is his best game so far. Charlton is impressive too. Dawson makes it eight in eight games with his powerful headers. Tony Scott's first ever goal looks offside.										
41	A	ARSENAL	8	L	2-5	2-2	Pearson 12, Giles 44 *[Ward 88]*	Gregg	Foulkes	Carolan	Setters	Cope	Brennan	Giles	Quixall	Dawson	Pearson	Charlton
23/4		*40,837*	*13*	43			*Clapton 7, Bloomfield 16, 67, 79,*	*Kelsey*	*Wills*	*McCullough*	*Ward*	*Docherty*	*Everitt*	*Clapton*	*Henderson*	*Groves*	*Bloomfield*	*Haverty*
							Ref: A Robottom	Arsenal's season has run out of steam but they are too good for a casual United side, who displease Busby. Danny Clapton is back from a cartilage operation whilst Jimmy Bloomfield's second goal looks offside but starts the rout. United's defence must improve on days like this.										
42	H	EVERTON	7	W	5-0	0-0	Dawson 67, 75, 89, Bradley 73, [Quixall 86]	Gregg	Foulkes	Carolan	Setters	Cope	Brennan	Bradley	Quixall	Dawson	Pearson	Charlton
30/4		43,878	*15*	45				*Dunlop*	*Parker*	*Jones*	*Gabriel*	*Labone*	*Harris B*	*Tyrer*	*Collins*	*Shackleton*	*Vernon*	*Ring*
Average	Home 47,288	Away 40,940					Ref: A Ellis	The arrival of Welsh international Roy Vernon has kept Everton up and their approach play is superb. They rue their missed chances and collapse under an unexpected goal glut. Bobby Collins hits a post with a penalty and the strong Dawson continues his impressive scoring run.										

LEAGUE DIVISION 1 (CUP-TIES)   Manager: Matt Busby   SEASON 1959-60

FA Cup					F-A	H-T	Scorers, Times, and Referees	1	2	3	4	5	6	7	8	9	10	11
3	A	DERBY	11	W	4-2	3-0	Barrow' 3(og), Scan' 24, Goodw' 33,	Gregg	Foulkes	Carolan	Goodwin	Cope	Brennan	Dawson	Quixall	Viollet	Charlton	Scanlon
	9/1	*33,297*	*2:19*				*Thom' 52, Barrow' 83p* [Charl' 47]	*Oxford*	*Barrowcliffe*	*Conwell*	*Upton*	*Young*	*Davies*	*Powell*	*Parry*	*Thompson*	*Brown*	*Hannigan*
							Ref: A Luty	Harry Storer's side are no pushover but the Rams make too many mistakes and are punished. Derby's biggest crowd for four years marvel at United's first-half display and although the home side fight hard they are out of their class. Scanlon is at his best, making the first and scoring.										
4	A	LIVERPOOL	11	W	3-1	2-1	Charlton 13, 44, Bradley 70	Gregg	Foulkes	Carolan	Setters	Cope	Brennan	Bradley	Quixall	Viollet	Charlton	Scanlon
	30/1	*56,736*	*2:7*				*Wheeler 36*	*Slater*	*Molyneux*	*Moran*	*Wheeler*	*White*	*Leishman*	*Melia*	*Hunt*	*Hickson*	*Harrower*	*A'Court*
							Ref: A Murdoch	Setters heads off the line from 21-year-old scoring sensation Roger Hunt in the first minute. Bill Shankly is proud of his team after they battled through wind and rain. Charlton is back on form and silences the Kop. Veteran Billy Liddell is injured and Cope marks Dave Hickson well.										
5	H	SHEFFIELD WED	11	L	0-1	0-0		Gregg	Foulkes	Carolan	Setters	Cope	Brennan	Bradley	Quixall	Viollet	Charlton	Scanlon
	20/2	66,350	*4*				*McAnearney 63p*	*Springett*	*Johnson*	*Megson*	*McAnearney T*	*Swan*	*Kay*	*Finney*	*Craig*	*Ellis*	*Fantham*	*Young*
							Ref: J Hunt	Wednesday's tight tactics and well-drilled defence are too good for a shot-shy home attack. Kay outshines Setters, and England hopefuls Springett and Swan are in superb form. The penalty is controversial as Setters is adjudged to have fouled Fantham and United rue their misses.										

		Home					Away					
	P	W	D	L	F	A	W	D	L	F	A	Pts
1 Burnley	42	15	2	4	52	28	9	5	7	33	33	55
2 Wolves	42	15	3	3	63	28	9	3	9	43	39	54
3 Tottenham	42	10	6	5	43	24	11	5	5	43	26	53
4 West Brom	42	12	4	5	48	25	7	7	7	35	32	49
5 Sheff Wed	42	12	7	2	48	20	7	4	10	32	39	49
6 Bolton	42	12	5	4	37	27	8	3	10	22	24	48
7 MAN UNITED	42	13	3	5	53	30	6	4	11	49	50	45
8 Newcastle	42	10	5	6	42	32	8	3	10	40	46	44
9 Preston	42	10	6	5	43	34	6	6	9	36	42	44
10 Fulham	42	12	4	5	42	28	5	6	10	31	52	44
11 Blackpool	42	9	6	6	32	32	6	4	11	27	39	40
12 Leicester	42	8	6	7	38	32	5	7	9	28	43	39
13 Arsenal	42	9	5	7	39	38	6	4	11	29	42	39
14 West Ham	42	12	3	6	47	33	4	3	14	28	58	38
15 Everton	42	13	3	5	50	20	0	8	13	23	58	37
16 Manchester C	42	11	2	8	47	34	6	1	14	31	50	37
17 Blackburn	42	12	3	6	38	29	4	2	15	22	41	37
18 Chelsea	42	7	5	9	44	50	7	4	10	32	41	37
19 Birmingham	42	9	5	7	37	36	4	5	12	26	44	36
20 Nott'm Forest	42	8	6	7	30	28	5	3	13	20	46	35
21 Leeds	42	7	5	9	37	46	5	5	11	28	46	34
22 Luton	42	6	5	10	25	29	3	7	11	25	44	30
	924	232	99	131	935	683	131	99	232	683	935	924

Odds & ends

Double wins: (3) Nott'm Forest, Blackpool, Luton.
Double losses: (3) West Brom, Tottenham, Wolves.

Won from behind: (5) Chelsea (a), Arsenal (h), Sheff Wed (h), Nott'm Forest (a), West Ham (h).
Lost from in front: (3) West Brom (a), Everton (a), West Brom (h).

High points: Big away wins at Chelsea, Blackpool, Fulham and Forest.
Dennis Viollet's record scoring form wins him international honours.
Beating champions elect Burnley at Turf Moor.

Low points: Inconsistent away form. Losses at Newcastle and Arsenal.
Shaky defensive form throughout.
FA Cup defeat to Sheffield Wednesday.
McGuinness's broken leg.

Red cards(United): (0).
Red cards (Opponents): (0).
Ever-presents: (1) Foulkes.
Hat-tricks: (3) Viollet, Charlton, Dawson.
Opposing hat-tricks: (3) Leggat (Fulham), White (Newcastle), and Bloomfield (Arsenal).
Leading scorer: (32) Viollet.

	Appearances		Goals		
	Lge	FAC	Lge	FAC	Tot
Brennan, Shay	**29**	3			
Bradley, Warren	**29**	2	**8**	1	**9**
Carolan, Joe	**41**	3			
Charlton, Bobby	**37**	3	**18**	3	**21**
Cope, Ronnie	**40**	3			
Dawson, Alex	**22**	1	**15**		**15**
Foulkes, Bill	**42**	3			
Gaskell, Dave	**9**				
Giles, Johnny	**10**		**2**		**2**
Goodwin, Freddie	**18**	1	**1**	1	**2**
Greaves, Ian	**2**				
Gregg, Harry	**33**	3			
Heron, Tommy	**1**				
Lawton, Nobby	**3**				
McGuinness, Wilf	**19**				
Pearson, Mark	**10**		**3**		**3**
Quixall, Albert	**33**	3	**13**		**13**
Scanlon, Albert	**31**	3	**7**	1	**8**
Setters, Maurice	**17**	2			
Viollet, Dennis	**36**	3	**32**		**32**
(own-goals)			**3**	1	**4**
20 players used	**462**	33	**102**	7	**109**

No	Date		Att	Pos	Pt	F-A	H-T	Scorers, Times, and Referees	1	2	3	4	5	6	7	8	9	10	11
1	H	BLACKBURN			L	1-3	0-1	Charlton 70	Gregg	Cope	Carolan	Setters	**Haydock**	Brennan	Giles	Quixall	Viollet	Charlton	Scanlon
	20/8		47,838		0			*Dougan 11, 74, 89*	*Jones*	*England*	*Eckersley*	*Clayton*	*Woods*	*McGrath*	*Douglas*	*Dobing*	*Dougan*	*Crowe*	*MacLeod*
								Ref: W Clements	Managerless Rovers sacked Dally Duncan after the Cup final. They gain their first win at United since 1931 thanks to Derek Dougan's hat-trick and a Matt Woods-marshalled defence. John Giles, a ray of hope in the gloom, fleeces Bill Eckersley but Viollet fluffs three sitters.										
2	A	EVERTON			L	0-4	0-1		Gregg	Brennan	Carolan	Setters	Haydock	**Nicholson**	Giles	Quixall	Viollet	Charlton	Scanlon
	24/8		*51,602*		0			*Lill 23, 86, Collins 68, 87*	*Dunlop*	*Parker*	*Jones*	*Gabriel*	*Labone*	*Meagan*	*Lill*	*Collins*	*Harris J*	*Vernon*	*Ring*
								Ref: J Taylor	The United attack is out of touch again and outclassed on a rain-drenched pitch by an Everton team that cost £150,000. Two late goals due to slapdash defending make it the worst defeat at Goodison since 1921. Brennan is good at full-back and 17-year-old Nicholson is a fine prospect.										
3	H	EVERTON		18	W	4-0	2-0	Charlton 11, Dawson 40, 86,	Gregg	Foulkes	Brennan	Setters	Haydock	Nicholson	Quixall	Giles	Dawson	Viollet	Charlton
	31/8		51,915	*11*	2			[Nicholson 89]	*Dunlop*	*Parker*	*Jones*	*Gabriel*	*Labone*	*Meagan*	*Temple*	*Collins*	*Harris J*	*Vernon*	*Ring*
								Ref: L Tirebuck	Busby rings the changes and Quixall's switch to the wing is inspired as he destroys the veteran Jones. The blistering pace recalls the old United and Bobby's 30-yarder sparks a revenge victory. Nicholson scores on his home debut and has the fans drooling. Busby eyes Ray Wilson.										
4	A	TOTTENHAM		20	L	1-4	1-2	Viollet 43	Gregg	Foulkes	Brennan	Setters	Haydock	Nicholson	Quixall	Giles	Dawson	Viollet	Charlton
	3/9		***55,442***	*1*	2			*Smith 6, 85, Allen 20, 65*	*Brown*	*Baker*	*Henry*	*Blanchflower*	*Norman*	*Mackay*	*Medwin*	*White*	*Smith R*	*Allen*	*Dyson*
								Ref: A Moore	Nicholson's entertaining team make it five straight wins and are in a different class to an average United. The Reds' brittle defence is in tatters with Haydock shell-shocked by the bustling Bobby Smith. Scanlon is unhappy at being dropped. United ready to sign Swansea's Mel Nurse.										
5	A	WEST HAM		21	L	1-2	1-1	Quixall 44	Gregg	Foulkes	Brennan	Setters	Cope	Nicholson	Quixall	Giles	Dawson	Viollet	Charlton
	5/9		*30,506*	*9*	2			*Brett 18, Musgrove 54*	*Shearing*	*Bond*	*Cantwell*	*Malcolm*	*Brown*	*Moore*	*Grice*	*Woosnam*	*Dunmore*	*Brett*	*Musgrove*
								Ref: L Callaghan	Reserve striker Brett is on target for the attractive Hammers but Musgrove's winner is soft. A skilful match is enhanced by United's second-half search for an equaliser with Viollet and Charlton going close. Cope and Brennan off-colour and Busby's bid for Nurse will see Cope out.										
6	H	LEICESTER		20	D	1-1	1-1	Giles 19	Gregg	Foulkes	Brennan	Setters	Cope	Nicholson	Quixall	Giles	Dawson	Viollet	Charlton
	10/9		35,516	*18*	3			*Walsh 44*	*Banks*	*King*	*Norman*	*McLintock*	*Knapp*	*Appleton*	*Riley*	*Walsh*	*Leek*	*Cheesebrough*	*Wills*
								Ref: T Reynolds	Matt Gillies' Leicester have started poorly but defend in depth. The fans start the slow handclap and pour out before the end as United struggle to break them down. Charlton and Giles combine for Johnny to net. McLintock's probing creates chances and Gregg saves United from defeat.										
7	H	WEST HAM		18	W	6-1	2-1	Viol' 19, 39, Charl' 46,60, Scan' 75,	Gregg	Foulkes	Brennan	Setters	Cope	Nicholson	Quixall	Giles	Viollet	Charlton	Scanlon
	14/9		33,288	*16*	5			*Brett 44* [Quixall 87p]	*Shearing*	*Bond*	*Cantwell*	*Malcolm*	*Brown*	*Moore*	*Woodley*	*Woosnam*	*Dunmore*	*Brett*	*Musgrove*
								Ref: R Leafe	Busby's tongue-lashing works and, although Ted Fenton's team never stop playing football, United's shoot on sight policy pays off. Quixall, in a free role bemuses the Hammers and Viollet is back to his best, scoring twice and winning a penalty. Charlton responds with two stunners.										
8	A	ASTON VILLA		18	L	1-3	0-1	Viollet 56	Gregg	Foulkes	Brennan	Setters	Cope	Nicholson	Giles	Quixall	Viollet	Charlton	Scanlon
	17/9		*43,593*	*8*	5			*Burrows 33, Thom' 53, MacEwan 69*	*Sims*	*Neal*	*Winton*	*Crowe*	*Morrall*	*Deakin*	*MacEwan*	*Thomson*	*Hitchens*	*Wylie*	*Burrows*
								Ref: R Smith	Newly promoted Villa make it eight home wins in a row against a cocky United. Villa easily outmuscle United who manage only five shots on target. Cope is hard pressed by Gerry Hitchens, whilst Nicholson looks out of his depth. Joe Mercer's quick-tackling team deserve the points.										
9	H	WOLVES		20	L	1-3	1-3	Charlton 8	Gregg	Foulkes	Brennan	Setters	Cope	Nicholson	Giles	Quixall	Viollet	Charlton	Scanlon
	24/9		44,708	*5*	5			*Horne 28, Farmer 34, 37*	*Sidebottom*	*Showell*	*Harris*	*Clamp*	*Stuart*	*Flowers*	*Deeley*	*Broadbent*	*Farmer*	*Mason*	*Horne*
								Ref: R Windle	Another defeat means it is the worst start since the war and the restless fans are getting critical of the team. Ted Farmer makes a dream debut with two goals and Wolves are more hungry than the Reds. Only Brennan, Setters and Gregg are above criticism. Viollet and Quixall are hurt.										
10	A	BOLTON		19	D	1-1	0-1	Giles 75	Gregg	Setters	Brennan	**Stiles**	Foulkes	Nicholson	**Moir**	Giles	Dawson	Charlton	Scanlon
	1/10		*39,197*	*20*	6			*McAdams 13*	*Hopkinson*	*Hartle*	*Farrimond*	*Stanley*	*Higgins*	*Edwards M*	*Holden*	*McAdams*	*Lofthouse*	*Hill*	*Parry*
								Ref: A Edge	United survive a first-half onslaught with 35-year-old Lofthouse playing his first game for eighteen months and proving he is not past it. Burly McAdams scores and is fouled for a penalty, from which Hartle hits the post. 18-year-old debutant Stiles sets up a super equaliser for Giles.										

No	Venue	Opponent / Date	Att	Pos	Pts	Res	H-T	Scorers, Times, and Referees	1	2	3	4	5	6	7	8	9	10	11
11	A	BURNLEY		20	L	3-5	2-3	Viollet 30, 40, 80 [McIlroy 84]	Gregg	Setters	**Dunne**	Stiles	Foulkes	Nicholson	Quixall	Giles	Viollett	Pearson	Charlton
		15/10	33,611	3	6			Pointer 10, Connolly 33, 48, Joyce 37,	Blacklaw	Angus	Elder	Joyce	Adamson	Miller	Connolly	McIlroy	Pointer	Robson	Pilkington
								Ref: J Hemingway	The champions are in great form and the watching Reims spies must be shuddering. Despite Pointer being offside, Burnley's experience is too much for United's young team. Newcomer Joyce looks classy and a dodgy defence is more than compensated by the goal-hungry forward line.										
12	H	NEWCASTLE		19	W	3-2	1-0	Dawson 10, Stiles 51, Setters 72	Gregg	Setters	Brennan	Stiles	Foulkes	Nicholson	Dawson	Giles	Viollett	Charlton	Scanlon
		22/10	37,596	16	8			Hughes 56, Stokoe 87p	Harvey	Keith	McMichael	Scoular	Stokoe	Neale	Hughes	Woods	White	Allchurch	Mitchell
								Ref: A Sparling	Charlton returns from England duty and is in top form. Stiles' goal from a brilliant run from his own half is the best. Viollet misses a penalty before Setters' header. Gregg saves superbly from Woods but can't stop Stokoe's penalty. Charlie Mitten's team look too good to struggle.										
13	H	NOTT'M FOREST		17	W	2-1	1-1	Viollet 44, 59	Gregg	Dunne	Brennan	Stiles	Foulkes	Nicholson	Dawson	Giles	Viollett	Pearson	Scanlon
		24/10	**23,188**	22	10			Booth 8	Thomson	Patrick	McDonald	Whitefoot	McKinlay	Iley	Gray	Booth	Julians	Quigley	Le Flem
								Ref: A Luty	Struggling Forest look impressive until Viollet's equaliser, then develop an air of desperation as they slump to their fifth defeat in a row. Only an agile Chick Thomson foils a Viollet hat-trick and a Forest hammering. Quigley is their best player and his corner lands on Booth's head.										
14	A	ARSENAL		19	L	1-2	1-2	Quixall 26	Gregg	Brennan	Heron	Stiles	Foulkes	Nicholson	Dawson	Giles	Viollett	Quixall	Charlton
		29/10	45,495	8	10			Barnwell 9, Herd 21	Kelsey	Wills	McCullough	Docherty	Sneddon	Groves	Strong	Barnwell	Charles	Herd	Henderson
								Ref: M Fussey	United struggle in the muddy conditions and Arsenal's two long-range goals win the day. Quixall's header offers some hope but, despite Stiles and Nicholson's Herculean efforts, Arsenal take the points. Nicholson, called up by Ireland, hits a post. George Eastham set to join Gunners.										
15	H	SHEFFIELD WED		17	D	0-0	0-0		Gregg	Setters	Brennan	Stiles	Foulkes	Nicholson	Dawson	Giles	Viollett	Quixall	Charlton
		5/11	37,055	2	11				McLaren	Johnson	Megson	McAnearney	Swan	Kay	Griffin	Craig	Ellis	Fantham	Finney
								Ref: C Kingston	The Owls, having their best start for years, have lost only once. England keeper Springett is injured. Quixall's 68th minute shot looks over the line before Swan hooks it out. Wednesday are the better side but Gregg and Foulkes are rock solid. Bill looks better than England man Swan.										
16	A	BIRMINGHAM		19	L	1-3	0-1	Charlton 81	Gregg	Setters	Brennan	Stiles	Foulkes	Nicholson	Dawson	Giles	Viollett	Pearson	Charlton
		12/11	31,564	14	11			Neal 13, Gordon 72, Taylor 75	Schofield	Farmer	Allen	Watts	Smith	Neal	Hellawell	Gordon	Orritt	Singer	Taylor
								Ref: G McCabe	Gil Merrick's hard team make it seven away defeats out of eight for United. The brave Blues pile on the pressure and easily subdue the Reds' poor attack. Schofield fractures his skull and Orritt is in goal for most of the second half. Johnny Giles breaks his leg in an innocent incident.										
17	H	WEST BROM		15	W	3-0	2-0	Dawson 20, Viollet 31, Quixall 77p	Gregg	Setters	Brennan	Stiles	Foulkes	Nicholson	Bradley	Quixall	Dawson	Viollet	Charlton
		19/11	32,834	19	13				Wallace	Howe	Williams G	Drury	Kennedy	Robson	Jackson	Burnside	Allen	Hope	Carter
								Ref: J Powell	Thankfully the home form is good. Dawson's good form makes Herd's signing strange. Noel Cantwell is set to sign for £29,000, despite Brennan's fine form. On a murky day Albion are a pale shadow and Quixall and Viollet have a field day. Scanlon joins Newcastle for £18,000.										
18	A	CARDIFF		17	L	0-3	0-2		Gregg	Brennan	**Cantwell**	Setters	Foulkes	Nicholson	Bradley	Quixall	Dawson	Viollet	Charlton
		26/11	21,122	15	13			Hogg 30, 59, Edgeley 43	Vearncombe	Harrington	Stitfall	Gammon	Malloy	Baker	Walsh	Edgeley	Tapscott	Watkins	Hogg
								Ref: H Horner	Cardiff back in Division 1 under Bill Jones, pile on the misery on a glue-pot pitch. United argue that Watkins handled for the second goal and that Hogg was offside for the third. Viollet fractures a collarbone colliding with Vearncombe and the ten men splutter despite the brave Gregg.										
19	H	PRESTON		15	W	1-0	0-0	Dawson 60	Gregg	Brennan	Cantwell	Setters	Foulkes	Nicholson	Bradley	Quixall	Dawson	Pearson	Charlton
		3/12	24,698	19	15				Else	Cunningham	O'Neill	Fullam	Singleton	Wylie	Mayers	Thompson T	Alston	Sneddon	Thompson P
								Ref: J Mitchell	The lowest Saturday crowd for five years sees another mudlark. Alex Dawson relishes the conditions against struggling Preston, for whom youth star Peter Thompson sparkles. Noel Cantwell adds stability at the back and Mark Pearson, the subject of transfer rumours, is recalled.										
20	A	FULHAM		15	D	4-4	2-3	Charlton, Quixall 2 (1p), Dawson	Gregg	Brennan	Cantwell	Setters	Foulkes	Nicholson	Bradley	Quixall	Dawson	Pearson	Charlton
		10/12	23,625	10	16			Brown 2, Mullery, O'Connell	Hewkins	Cohen	Langley	Mullery	Lampe	Edwards	Leggat	O'Connell	Brown R	Haynes	Key
								Ref: E Clarke	Fulham have conceded 55 goals already and Jezzard drops Macedo with little effect. A thrilling match goes to the wire. Charlton dazzles on the wing destroying Under-23 cap George Cohen with his blistering pace. Warren Bradley is stretchered off and Pearson booed by the home fans.										
21	A	BLACKBURN		15	W	2-1	2-1	Pearson 12, 23	Gregg	Brennan	Cantwell	Setters	Foulkes	Nicholson	Quixall	Stiles	Dawson	Pearson	Charlton
		17/12	**17,285**	9	18			MacLeod 35	Reeves	Taylor	Bray	McEvoy	Woods	Clayton	Crowe	Dobing	MacLeod	Douglas	Isherwood
								Ref: A Murdoch	Finally an away win at the eleventh try. Tempers flair in a physical game with Stiles accused of being the instigator. Captains Setters and Clayton are told to calm their men by the ref. Stiles and Dawson make Pancho's goals whilst Blackburn are livid at Crowe's disallowed effort.										

LEAGUE DIVISION 1

Manager: Matt Busby

SEASON 1960-61

No	Date	Att	Pos	Pt	F-A	H-T	Scorers, Times, and Referees	1	2	3	4	5	6	7	8	9	10	11
22	A CHELSEA		14	W	2-1	0-0	Dawson, Charlton	Gregg	Brennan	Cantwell	Setters	Foulkes	Nicholson	Quixall	Stiles	Dawson	Pearson	Charlton
	24/12	*37,601*	*11*	20			*Brabrook*	*Bonetti*	*Sillett P*	*Harris A*	*Anderton*	*Evans*	*Mortimore*	*Brabrook*	*Greaves*	*Tindall*	*Blunstone*	*Tambling*
							Ref: H Horner	Chelsea's dynamic young attack has scored 58 goals but Ted Drake's team are tamed by United's solid defence. Maurice Setters blots out 36-goal Greaves. Busby puts the Reds' revival down to playing Real Madrid in a friendly in October. Cantwell's presence is another key factor.										
23	H CHELSEA		10	W	**6-0**	3-0	Dawson 3, Nicholson 2, Charlton	Gregg	Brennan	Cantwell	Setters	Foulkes	Nicholson	Quixall	Stiles	Dawson	Pearson	Charlton
	26/12	50,164	*14*	22				*Bonetti*	*Sillett P*	*Harris A*	*Anderton*	*Evans*	*Mortimore*	*Brabrook*	*Greaves*	*Tindall*	*Blunstone*	*Tambling*
							Ref: K Howley	Dawson is out to prove that United don't need David Herd, with a 35-minute hat-trick. Setters again shackles leading scorer Greaves, who misses a penalty and Stiles is the star. Nicholson's thunderous shots recall Duncan Edwards' shooting and Bobby chips in with a cracker.										
24	H MANCHESTER C		8	W	5-1	3-1	Charlton 5, 48, Dawson 19, 44, 65	Gregg	Brennan	Cantwell	Setters	Foulkes	Nicholson	Quixall	Stiles	Dawson	Pearson	Charlton
	31/12	61,621	*15*	24			*Barlow 16*	*Trautmann*	*Betts*	*Sear*	*Barnes*	*Plenderleith*	*Shawcross*	*Barlow*	*Hannah*	*Baker*	*Law*	*Hayes*
							Ref: R Leafe	City's boss Les McDowall has been in charge for ten years. United are back to their best with Setters nullifying the goal-poacher Law and Dawson continuing his prolific scoring against an off-form Trautmann with two headers. United's biggest league win over City in 69 derbies.										
25	H TOTTENHAM		8	W	2-0	1-0	Stiles 14, Pearson 73	Gregg	Brennan	Cantwell	Setters	Foulkes	Nicholson	Quixall	Stiles	Dawson	Pearson	Charlton
	16/1	**65,535**	*1*	26				*Brown*	*Barton*	*Henry*	*Blanchflower*	*Norman*	*Mackay*	*Smith J*	*White*	*Smith R*	*Allen*	*Dyson*
							Ref: W Surtees	The good form continues as Spurs suffer only their second defeat in an electric atmosphere in front of a ground record floodlit crowd. Gregg injures a shoulder before half-time and Dawson dons the jersey to great effect. Gregg plays up front and lays on a goal. Standing ovation.										
26	A LEICESTER		8	L	**0-6**	0-2	*[Wills 76, Riley 85p]*	**Briggs**	Brennan	Cantwell	Setters	Foulkes	Nicholson	Quixall	Stiles	Dawson	Pearson	Charlton
	21/1	*31,308*	10	26			*Walsh 21, 51, Keyworth 31, 70,*	*Banks*	*Chalmers*	*Norman*	*McLintock*	*King*	*Appleton*	*Riley*	*Walsh*	*Leek*	*Keyworth*	*Wills*
							Ref: R Windle	17-year-old Ronnie Briggs has a nightmare debut as United are outplayed in all sectors. The youngster is barely at fault for the avalanche that is engineered by a shrewd McLintock. Pearson's first minute goal is ruled out and City take over. United's biggest margin of defeat since 1939.										
27	H ASTON VILLA		9	D	1-1	0-0	Charlton 85	**Pinner**	Brennan	Cantwell	Setters	Foulkes	Nicholson	Quixall	Stiles	Dawson	Pearson	Charlton
	4/2	33,484	*6*	27			*Thomson 47*	*Sims*	*Neal*	*Winton*	*Crowe*	*Dugdale*	*Thomson*	*MacEwan*	*O'Neill*	*Hitchens*	*Wylie*	*Adam*
							Ref: M Dixon	Villa's early season form is fading but they deserve a point in miserably wet conditions. British Olympic keeper Mike Pinner has been signed to cover the problems and wears a natty sky blue jersey. Foulkes has a stormer against the dangerous Gerry Hitchens and Brennan impresses.										
28	A WOLVES		12	L	1-2	0-1	Nicholson 68	Pinner	Brennan	Cantwell	Setters	Foulkes	Nicholson	Quixall	Stiles	Dawson	Pearson	Charlton
	11/2	*38,526*	*2*	27			*Deeley 8, Flowers 53*	*Brodie*	*Stuart*	*Showell*	*Clamp*	*Slater*	*Kirkham*	*Deeley*	*Flowers*	*Farmer*	*Broadbent*	*Durrandt*
							Ref: C Rogers	The two great rivals put on a poor display at Molineux, where only leaders Spurs have won. Both Wolves goals come from defensive boobs with Foulkes culpable. Ted Farmer has scored 21 goals in 19 games but is off-target today. Hard-man Eddie Clamp head-butts Noel Cantwell.										
29	H BOLTON		9	W	3-1	0-1	Dawson 58, 79, Quixall 70p	Pinner	Brennan	Cantwell	Stiles	Foulkes	Setters	Morgans	Quixall	Dawson	Pearson	Charlton
	18/2	38,146	*16*	29			*McAdams 18*	*Hopkinson*	*Hartle*	*Farrimond*	*Stanley*	*Edwards M*	*Rimmer*	*Birch*	*Stevens*	*McAdams*	*Deakin*	*Holden*
							Ref: A Jobling	With Busby in hospital, Jimmy Murphy takes charge and recalls Kenny Morgans after 2½ years in the shadows. The Welsh winger is the star, setting up Dawson's first and winning the penalty. Dawson lets fly from 30 yards for his second. Jimmy Nicholson plays in the FA Youth Cup.										
30	A NOTT'M FOREST		10	L	2-3	1-1	Charlton 10, Quixall 48	Gregg	Brennan	Cantwell	Setters	Foulkes	Nicholson	Morgans	Quixall	Dawson	Pearson	Charlton
	25/2	*26,850*	12	29			*Rowland 24, Booth 84, Addison 85*	*Grummitt*	*Gray*	*McDonald*	*Palmer*	*McKinlay*	*Burckitt*	*Rowland*	*Booth*	*Addison*	*Quigley*	*Le Flem*
							Ref: A Moore	Forest deservedly win with two late goals after Gregg had foiled them. New signing Colin Addison from York makes a big impression. Forest have lost just twice in 15 games. Stiles is dropped and Morgans struggles. Veteran winger Billy Gray switches to right-back to mark Charlton.										
31	A MANCHESTER C		10	W	3-1	2-0	Dawson 18, Charlton 28, Pearson 69	Gregg	Brennan	Cantwell	Setters	Foulkes	Stiles	Moir	Quixall	Dawson	Pearson	Charlton
	4/3	*50,479*	*19*	31			*Wagstaffe 62*	*Fleet*	*Leivers*	*Betts*	*Shawcross*	*Plenderleith*	*Oakes*	*Colbridge*	*Hannah*	*Barlow*	*Law*	*Wagstaffe*
							Ref: A Ellis	Gregg's return is halted with an injury to the same shoulder but United deserve their win over struggling City. Colbridge is in the news, winning a penalty that Betts misses and splitting his head open. Setters wins the battle with Law again. City feel Dawson punched his goal in.										

No	Venue	Opponent	Pos	Res	F-A	H-T	Scorers, Times, Referees	1	2	3	4	5	6	7	8	9	10	11
32	A	NEWCASTLE	10	D	1-1	1-1	Charlton 4	Pinner	Brennan	Cantwell	Setters	Foulkes	Stiles	Moir	Quixall	Lawton	Pearson	Charlton
11/3		28,867	20	32			*Scanlon 7*	*Mitchell S*	*McKinney*	*McMichael*	*Neale*	*McGrath*	*Bell*	*Hughes*	*Allchurch*	*White*	*McGuigan*	*Scanlon*
							Ref: J Powell	Charlie Mitten's hardline stance has not worked and Newcastle, with one win in 14, are in disarray. Charlton's 20-yarder should have been stopped and his miss near the end is one of few bright spots in a poor game. Strong penalty appeals are rejected when Setters appears to handle.										
33	H	ARSENAL	10	D	1-1	1-1	Moir 11	Gaskell	Brennan	Cantwell	Setters	Foulkes	Stiles	Moir	Quixall	Dawson	Pearson	Charlton
18/3		30,517	7	33			*Charles 17*	*Kelsey*	*Bacuzzi*	*McCullough*	*Charles*	*Snedden*	*Groves*	*Henderson*	*Eastham*	*Herd*	*Barnwell*	*Haverty*
							Ref: J Williams	Injuries mean Gaskell is rushed back from his broken hand and, apart from missing the corner from which Mel Charles scored, he plays well. Moir follows up to score after Charlton's fierce shot is saved. Herd wins the battle of the big men, whilst new signing George Eastham is class.										
34	A	SHEFFIELD WED	11	L	1-5	0-2	Charlton 89 *[Craig 72]*	Gaskell	Brennan	Cantwell	Setters	Foulkes	Stiles	Moir	Quixall	Dawson	Pearson	Charlton
25/3		32,953	2	33			*Cantwell 4 (og), Young 14, 52, 65,*	*Springett*	*Johnson*	*Megson*	*McAnearney*	*Swan*	*Kay*	*Finney*	*Craig*	*Young*	*Fantham*	*Wilkinson*
							Ref: K Howley	Stand-in striker Gerry Young ensures the Owls' 15-game unbeaten run is maintained. Spurs' lead is cut to three points. The best Wednesday team for years are too good for a mediocre United. Cantwell deflects in the first and Foulkes boobs for the last. Only Charlton puts up a fight.										
35	A	BLACKPOOL	11	L	0-2	0-1		Gaskell	Brennan	Cantwell	Setters	Foulkes	Stiles	Moir	Quixall	Dawson	Pearson	Charlton
31/3		30,835	19	33			*Peterson 32, Stiles 71(og)*	*West*	*Armfield*	*Martin*	*Hauser*	*Gratrix*	*Salt*	*Hill*	*Peterson*	*Charnley*	*Parry*	*Horne*
							Ref: K Seddon	Blackpool are fighting hard and in front of their biggest crowd of season they leapfrog out of the drop zone. Methodist teacher Durie refuses to play on Good Friday. United are criticised for their robust style and moaning. Stiles, under pressure, lobs Gaskell. Armfield blots out Charlton.										
36	H	FULHAM	11	W	3-1	1-1	Charlton, Quixall, Viollet	Gaskell	Brennan	Cantwell	Setters	Foulkes	Nicholson	Giles	Quixall	Viollet	Pearson	Charlton
1/4		24,937	17	35			*O'Connell*	*Macedo*	*Cohen*	*Langley*	*Lawler*	*Dodgin*	*Lowe*	*Watson*	*O'Connell*	*Cook*	*Haynes*	*Johnson*
							Ref: R Jordan	Giles and Viollet return after long lay-offs and impress. United tame Fulham's lively forwards and England captain Haynes and run out comfortable winners. Fulham's aging defence is struggling for pace although Cohen looks an exciting prospect. Nicholson is back to his best										
37	H	BLACKPOOL	9	W	2-0	2-0	Nicholson 1, Hauser 42 (og)	Gaskell	Brennan	Cantwell	Setters	Foulkes	Nicholson	Giles	Quixall	Viollet	Pearson	Charlton
3/4		39,169	22	37				*West*	*Armfield*	*Garrett*	*Hauser*	*Gratrix*	*Durie*	*Hill*	*Peterson*	*Charnley*	*Parry*	*Perry*
							Ref: P Rhodes	17-year-old Gordon West lets Nicholson's swerving shot through his hands and, with their rivals all drawing, Blackpool are back in trouble. Peter Hauser deflects Viollet's cross in when there is no danger. Veteran Bill Perry has recovered from a cartilage operation but looks rusty.										
38	A	WEST BROM	10	D	1-1	0-0	Pearson 48	Gaskell	Brennan	Cantwell	Setters	Foulkes	Nicholson	Giles	Quixall	Viollet	Pearson	Charlton
8/4		28,033	11	38			*Howe 79*	*Wallace*	*Howe*	*Williams G*	*Robson*	*Jones*	*Drury*	*Jackson*	*Burnside*	*Lovatt*	*Kevan*	*Clark*
							Ref: J Finney	Seven straight wins have lifted Gordon Clark's Albion out of the drop zone. Maurice Setters returns to the Hawthorns for the first time. The impressive Mark Pearson scores against the run of play and the brilliant Gaskell keeps the Baggies at bay until Don Howe's blasted shot.										
39	H	BURNLEY	9	W	**6-0**	2-0	Viollet 30, 55, 82, Quixall 43, 61, 75	Gaskell	Brennan	Cantwell	Setters	Foulkes	Stiles	Giles	Quixall	Viollet	Pearson	Moir
12/4		24,646	5	40				*Blacklaw*	*Smith*	*Angus*	*Joyce*	*Cummings*	*Scott*	*Meredith*	*Fenton*	*Lochhead*	*Harris*	*Connolly*
							Ref: A Holland	Burnley field seven reserves because of injuries and international games. Chairman Bob Lord is still booed over his 'United teddy boys' jibe in 1958. Burnley take 88 minutes to shoot at goal but never give up. Quixall and Viollet are exquisite. Yuri Gagarin is the first man in space.										
40	H	BIRMINGHAM	6	W	4-1	2-1	Pearson 16, 64, Quixall 25p, Viollet 58	Gaskell	Brennan	Cantwell	Setters	Foulkes	Stiles	Giles	Quixall	Viollet	Pearson	Moir
15/4		28,376	16	42			*Foulkes 4 (og)*	*Withers*	*Farmer*	*Allen*	*Hennessey*	*Smith*	*Neal*	*Hellawell*	*Orritt*	*Stubbs*	*Bloomfield*	*Taylor*
							Ref: A Hawcroft	Pearson is the star as the good run is extended. He is tripped by Hennessey for the penalty and scores two good goals. For his second he beats three men in a confined space with superb control and leaves Withers helpless. Blues have a Fairs Cup semi final with Inter Milan coming up.										
41	A	PRESTON	6	W	4-2	3-2	Charlton 18, 87, Setters 20,44	Gaskell	Dunne	Brennan	Setters	Foulkes	Stiles	Giles	Quixall	Viollet	Pearson	Charlton
22/4		21,256	22	44			*Thompson 28, Richardson 32*	*Else*	*Cunningham*	*O'Neill*	*Wylie*	*Singleton*	*O'Farrell*	*Alston*	*Thompson P*	*Richardson*	*Sneddon*	*Taylor*
							Ref: L Hamer	Sad Preston are relegated with this unlucky defeat. They recover from 0-2 to level, only to lose to two deflected goals after dominating the second half. Charlton screws the coffin lid down with his late effort. Cliff Britton will resign next week after five years in charge at Deepdale.										
42	H	CARDIFF	7	D	3-3	3-1	Charlton 19, 35, Setters 31	Gaskell	Brennan	Cantwell	Setters	Foulkes	Stiles	Giles	Quixall	Viollet	Pearson	Charlton
29/4		30,420	15	45			*Tapscott 29, Hogg 53p, 74*	*Vearncombe*	*Harrington*	*Milne*	*Hole*	*Malloy*	*Baker*	*Walsh*	*Tapscott*	*Moore*	*Ward*	*Hogg*
		Home / Away					Ref: R Mann	United miss out on sixth place with a sloppy finish. All their goals are deflections. Cantwell is harshly penalised for pushing Moore and Hogg scores from the spot. Hogg and Tapscott's long drives earn a point. Pearson stars again. United fly off to Malta and Italy for a playing break.										
Average		37,888 / 34,274																

LEAGUE DIVISION 1 (CUP-TIES)

Manager: Matt Busby

SEASON 1960-61

League Cup			F-A	H-T	Scorers, Times, and Referees	1	2	3	4	5	6	7	8	9	10	11
1 A EXETER	20	D	1-1		Dawson 78	Gregg	Setters	Brennan	Stiles	Foulkes	Nicholson	Dawson	Lawton	Viollet	Pearson	Scanlon
19/10	*14,494 4:20*				*Rees 15*	*Lobbett*	*Whitnall*	*MacDonald*	*Wilson*	*Harvey*	*Thompson*	*Welsh*	*Gordon*	*Donaldson*	*Rees*	*Harrison*
					Ref: S Yates	United's first ever League Cup-tie attracts one of the biggest post-war crowds to St James Park. A fiery home side throw United out of their stride with Rees giving Stiles a torrid time. Dawson has a header disallowed and a clear penalty turned down before his saver. Fixtures pile-up.										
1R H EXETER	17	W	4-1	3-1	Quixall 7, 85p, Giles 25, Pearson 31	Gaskell	Dunne	Carolan	Stiles	Cope	Nicholson	Dawson	Giles	Quixall	Pearson	Scanlon
26/10	15,662 *4:21*				*Thompson 14p*	*Lobbett*	*Whitnall*	*MacDonald*	*Wilson*	*Harvey*	*Thompson*	*Welsh*	*Gordon*	*Donaldson*	*Rees*	*Dale*
					Ref: A Holland	In their third game in five days, United have a stroll. Quixall, experimented at centre-forward flicks in Dawson's free-kick and Giles' shot goes through the keeper's legs. In-form Scanlon sets up Pearson before Dawson is felled by the keeper. United end with 10 men with Dunne hurt.										
2 A BRADFORD CITY	19	L	1-2	1-0	Viollet 25	Gregg	Setters	Brennan	**Bratt**	Foulkes	Nicholson	Dawson	Giles	Viollet	Pearson	Scanlon
2/11	*4,670 3:22*				*Smith 55, Webb 57*	*Downie*	*Flockett*	*Barnes*	*Jackson P*	*Lawlor*	*Roberts*	*Webb*	*Jackson D*	*Duncan*	*Reid*	*Smith*
					Ref: R Langdale	Injuries and internationals force Busby to play a weakened side and the result is a major shock. Two players who cost nothing send United out on a mudbath. Smith fleeces Setters for the first and Gregg fumbles the second. With no lights, there is an afternoon kick-off with a tiny crowd.										

FA Cup			F-A	H-T	Scorers, Times, and Referees	1	2	3	4	5	6	7	8	9	10	11
3 H MIDDLESBROUGH	8	W	3-0	1-0	Cantwell 25, Dawson 77, 84	Gregg	Brennan	Cantwell	Setters	Foulkes	Nicholson	Quixall	Stiles	Dawson	Pearson	Charlton
7/1	49,184 *2:5*					*Appleby*	*Stonehouse*	*McNeill*	*Yeoman*	*Thompson*	*Walker*	*Kaye*	*Waldock*	*Clough*	*Peacock*	*Burbeck*
					Ref: K Aston	The scoreline flatters United against Bob Dennison's Boro, who are fresh from a 4-3 win at Anfield. England caps Clough and Mick McNeill are classy. Cantwell's floated free-kick is delicious and Quixall and Pearson lay on Dawson's late goals. Boro's defence hacks Charlton to bits.										
4 A SHEFFIELD WED	10	D	1-1	1-1	Cantwell 43p	Briggs	Brennan	Cantwell	Setters	Foulkes	Nicholson	Viollet	Stiles	Dawson	Pearson	Charlton
28/1	*58,000 3*				*Wilkinson 14*	*Springett*	*Johnson*	*Megson*	*McAnearney*	*O'Donnell*	*Kay*	*Wilkinson*	*Quinn*	*Ellis*	*Fantham*	*Finney*
					Ref: P Brandwood	United's resurgence is put to the test in a rough game and they are lucky to survive. The Owls dominate and miss chances but United, with the feisty Stiles to the fore, make it a physical battle. The team coach is held up in Pennine blizzards and Ronnie Briggs gets a second chance.										
4R H SHEFFIELD WED	10	L	2-7	1-4	Pear'n 4, Daw' 60 *[Ellis 32, 38, 64]*	Briggs	Brennan	Cantwell	Setters	Foulkes	Nicholson	Quixall	Stiles	Dawson	Pearson	Charlton
1/2	65,243 *3*				*Fantham 2, 52, Finney 30, 80,*	*Springett*	*Johnson*	*Megson*	*McAnearney*	*O'Donnell*	*Kay*	*Wilkinson*	*Craig*	*Ellis*	*Fantham*	*Finney*
					Ref: P Brandwood	Poor Briggs is at fault for three goals after United dominate the first half-hour. Once in front, an impressive Wednesday look dangerous every time they attack and United's defence caves in to the lanky Keith Ellis. The fans are streaming out well before the end with United humiliated.										

		Home					Away					
	P	W	D	L	F	A	W	D	L	F	A	Pts
1 Tottenham	42	15	3	3	65	28	16	1	4	50	27	66
2 Sheffield Wed	42	15	4	2	45	17	8	8	5	33	30	58
3 Wolves	42	17	2	2	61	32	8	5	8	42	43	57
4 Burnley	42	11	4	6	58	40	11	3	7	44	37	51
5 Everton	42	13	4	4	47	23	9	2	10	40	46	50
6 Leicester	42	12	4	5	54	31	6	5	10	33	39	45
7 MAN UNITED	42	14	5	2	58	20	4	4	13	30	56	45
8 Blackburn	42	12	3	6	48	34	3	10	8	29	42	43
9 Aston Villa	42	13	3	5	48	28	4	6	11	30	49	43
10 West Brom	42	10	3	8	43	32	8	2	11	24	39	41
11 Arsenal	42	12	3	6	44	35	3	8	10	33	50	41
12 Chelsea	42	10	5	6	61	48	5	2	14	37	52	37
13 Manchester C	42	10	5	6	41	30	3	6	12	38	60	37
14 Nott'm Forest	42	8	7	6	34	33	6	2	13	28	45	37
15 Cardiff	42	11	5	5	34	26	2	6	13	26	59	37
16 West Ham	42	12	4	5	53	31	1	6	14	24	57	36
17 Fulham	42	8	8	5	39	39	6	0	15	33	56	36
18 Bolton	42	9	5	7	38	29	3	6	12	20	44	35
19 Birmingham	42	10	4	7	35	31	4	2	15	27	53	34
20 Blackpool	42	9	3	9	44	34	3	6	12	24	39	33
21 Newcastle	42	7	7	7	51	49	4	3	14	35	60	32
22 Preston	42	7	6	8	28	25	3	4	14	15	46	30
	924	245	97	120	1029	695	120	97	245	695	1029	924

Odds & ends

Double wins: (3) Chelsea, Manchester C, Preston.
Double losses: (1) Wolves.

Won from behind: (4) Nott'm Forest (h), Bolton (h), Fulham (h), Birmingham (h).
Lost from in front: (3) Wolves (h), Nott'm Forest (a), Bradford C LC (a).

High spots: Eight game unbeaten run after arrival of Cantwell.
Excellent home form.
Defeat of double winners Spurs.
Seven game unbeaten run to end the season.

Low spots: Woeful away form including the defeat at Leicester.
Bradford League Cup defeat.
Sheffield Wednesday debacle in the FA Cup.

Red cards (United): (0).
Red cards (Opponents): (0).
Ever-presents: (0).
Hat-tricks: (5) Viollet (2), Dawson (2), Quixall.
Opposing hat-tricks: (3) Dougan (Portsmouth), Young (Sheff Wed), and Ellis (Sheff Wed FAC).
Leading scorer: (21) Charlton.

	Appearances			Goals			
	Lge	LC	FAC	Lge	LC	FAC	Tot
Bradley, Warren	**4**						
Brennan, Shay	**41**	2	3				
Bratt, Harold		1					
Briggs, Ronnie	**1**		2				
Cantwell, Noel	**24**		3			2	**2**
Carolan, Joe	**2**	1					
Charlton, Bobby	**39**		3	**21**			**21**
Cope, Ronnie	**6**	1					
Dawson, Alex	**28**	3	3	**16**	1	3	**20**
Dunne, Tony	**3**	1					
Foulkes, Bill	**40**	2	3				
Gaskell, Dave	**10**	1					
Giles, Johnny	**23**	2		**2**	1		**3**
Gregg, Harry	**27**	2	1				
Haydock, Frank	**4**						
Heron, Tommy	**1**						
Lawton, Nobby	**1**	1					
Moir, Ian	**8**			**1**			**1**
Morgans, Kenny	**2**						
Nicholson, Jimmy	**31**	3	3	**5**			**5**
Pearson, Mark	**27**	3	3	**7**	1	1	**9**
Pinner, Mike	**4**						
Quixall, Albert	**38**	1	2	**13**	2		**15**
Scanlon, Albert	**8**	3		**1**			**1**
Setters, Maurice	**40**	2	3	**4**			**4**
Stiles, Nobby	**26**	2	3	**2**			**2**
Viollet, Dennis	**24**	2	1	**15**	1		**16**
(own-goals)				**1**			**1**
26 players used	**462**	**33**	**33**	**88**	**6**	**6**	**100**

No	Date		Att	Pos	Pt	F-A	H-T	Scorers, Times, and Referees	1	2	3	4	5	6	7	8	9	10	11
1	A	WEST HAM		-	D	1-1	1-1	Stiles 18	Gregg	Brennan	Cantwell	Stiles	Foulkes	Setters	Quixall	Viollet	**Herd**	Pearson	Charlton
	19/8		*32,628*	-	1			*Dick 37*	*Leslie*	*Kirkup*	*Bond*	*Malcolm*	*Brown*	*Moore*	*Scott*	*Woosnam*	*Sealey*	*Dick*	*Musgrove*
								Ref: M Dixon	West Ham's new boss Ron Greenwood misses the game with a head cold. Both sides entertain with fast, neat play. New man David Herd, a £30,000 signing from Arsenal has a quiet game. Viollet's lob is turned in by Stiles and Alan Sealey squares for Dick to tap in. Moore is classy.										
2	H	CHELSEA		-	W	3-2	2-0	Herd 14, Viollet 25, Pearson 75	Gregg	Brennan	Cantwell	Stiles	Foulkes	Setters	Quixall	Viollet	Herd	Pearson	Charlton
	23/8		45,847	-	3			*Tambling 67, 89*	*Bonetti*	*Sillett J*	*Sillett P*	*Venables*	*Scott*	*Upton*	*Brabrook*	*Cliss*	*Tindall*	*Tambling*	*Blunstone*
								Ref: K Howley	Despite Albert Quixall missing his first spot-kick in 34 attempts, United are well in control. Gregg saves a thrice-taken Bobby Tambling penalty, whilst Peter Bonetti saves eight certain goals. Pearson's goal is the best, a scorcher from 25 yards. Chelsea are in for a hard season.										
3	H	BLACKBURN		3	W	**6-1**	1-0	Charl' 3, Quix' 58p, 59, Herd 74, 78,	Gregg	Brennan	Cantwell	Stiles	Foulkes	Setters	Quixall	Viollet	Herd	Pearson	Charlton
	26/8		45,302	*22*	5			*Bray 48* [Setters 87]	*Else*	*Bray*	*Newton*	*McEvoy*	*Appleby*	*McGrath*	*Douglas*	*Crowe*	*Pickering*	*Thomas*	*Haverty*
								Ref: A Edge	A flattering result and not a good one for Rovers, who spent £55,000 in the summer. In bright sunshine Pearson is the best forward, creating chances galore. Charlton's early solo effort is the best goal and Quixall rediscovers his penalty form. Fred Pickering makes a bright debut.										
4	A	CHELSEA		7	L	0-2	0-1		Gregg	Brennan	Cantwell	Stiles	Foulkes	Setters	Quixall	Viollet	Herd	Pearson	Charlton
	30/8		*42,248*	*14*	5			*Tambling 38, Bridges 70*	*Bonetti*	*Sillett J*	*Harris A*	*Venables*	*Scott*	*Mortimore*	*Brabrook*	*Cliss*	*Bridges*	*Tambling*	*Harrison*
								Ref: D Howell	Chelsea boss Ted Drake is under pressure but his young home-grown team gain their first win of the season. United's full-backs are run ragged by Brabrook and Tambling. Disputed second goal as Cantwell kicks into touch to allow treatment of a player and Chelsea take a quick throw.										
5	A	BLACKPOOL		3	W	3-2	2-2	Viollet 3, 74, Charlton 22	Gregg	Brennan	Cantwell	Stiles	Foulkes	Setters	Bradley	Viollet	Herd	Pearson	Charlton
	2/9		*28,156*	*19*	7			*Charnley 26, 39p*	*West*	*Armfield*	*Martin*	*Hauser*	*Gratrix*	*Durie*	*Peterson*	*Green*	*Charnley*	*Parry*	*Horne*
								Ref: L Tirebuck	Seaside temperatures are in the 80s as United gain a scrappy win. Warren Bradley is back after a cartilage operation and he replaces Quixall. Busby is not happy with the blend and Gregg keeps the Blackpool forwards at bay in the second half, with Ray Charnley in stunning form.										
6	H	TOTTENHAM		4	W	1-0	0-0	Quixall 67	Gregg	Brennan	Cantwell	Stiles	Foulkes	Setters	Quixall	Viollet	Herd	Pearson	Charlton
	9/9		**57,135**	*6*	9				*Brown*	*Baker*	*Henry*	*Blanchflower*	*Norman*	*Marchi*	*Jones*	*White*	*Smith R*	*Allen*	*Dyson*
								Ref: A Sparling	United snatch victory over the double winners. The recalled Quixall nets from Viollet's cross to win a defence-dominated game. Jones and White hit the bar, but the Reds' defence is solid with Foulkes marking the dangerous Smith. Spurs start their European campaign this week.										
7	A	CARDIFF		3	W	2-1	1-1	Quixall 21p, Dawson 75	Gregg	Brennan	Cantwell	Stiles	Foulkes	Setters	Quixall	Viollet	Dawson	Pearson	Charlton
	16/9		*29,251*	*14*	11			*Ward 30*	*Vearncombe*	*Harrington*	*Milne*	*Hole*	*Rankmore*	*Baker*	*Tapscott*	*Ward*	*King J*	*Moore*	*Donnelly*
								Ref: H Horner	A hard, defence-dominated game, with Foulkes fouling King 10 times. United with Viollet playing deeper to counteract Cardiff's 4-2-4 system still don't click. Vearncombe is the villain, fouling Pearson for the penalty and fumbling a shot for the winner. Setters at fault for the goal.										
8	A	ASTON VILLA		3	D	1-1	1-1	Stiles 43	Gaskell	Brennan	Dunne	Stiles	Foulkes	Setters	Quixall	Viollet	Herd	Pearson	Charlton
	18/9		*38,837*	*18*	12			*McParland 36*	*Sidebottom*	*Neal*	*Aitken*	*Crowe*	*Sleeuwenh'k*	*Deakin*	*Ashe*	*Tindall*	*McParland*	*Wylie*	*Burrows*
								Ref: K Tuck	Injuries force Gregg and Cantwell out but United deserve their point against Joe Mercer's struggling young team. Tony Dunne is a classy deputy with excellent distribution. A quick throw in allows Stiles to crash home the equaliser after veteran McParland had foxed Foulkes.										
9	H	MANCHESTER C		2	W	3-2	2-2	Stiles 2, Viollet 14, Ewing 50(og)	Gregg	Brennan	Dunne	Stiles	Foulkes	Setters	Quixall	Viollet	Herd	Pearson	Charlton
	23/9		56,345	*5*	14			*Stiles 19(og), Kennedy 24*	*Trautmann*	*Betts*	*Sear*	*Kennedy*	*Ewing*	*Oakes*	*Sambrook*	*Dobing*	*Baker*	*Hayes*	*Wagstaffe*
								Ref: A Luty	City's best start for years has been sparked by the signings of Peter Dobing and Bobby Kennedy. United's speed and skill in the drizzle is too much but they are lucky to take both points. 18-year-old David Wagstaffe gives Shay Brennan a hard time and Baker misses a sitter at the end.										
10	H	WOLVERHAMPTON		3	L	0-2	0-1		Gregg	Brennan	Cantwell	Stiles	Foulkes	Lawton	Quixall	Giles	Dawson	Pearson	Charlton
	30/9		39,457	*15*	14			*Kirkham 41, Broadbent 50*	*Finlayson*	*Stuart*	*Harris*	*Clamp*	*Slater*	*Kirkham*	*Mason*	*Broadbent*	*Farmer*	*Murray*	*Deeley*
								Ref: E Crawford	Wolves' have had their worst start since the war but click to inflict United's first home defeat for a year. United's failings are exposed by their old enemy whose sturdy defence cannot be breached by the Reds' powder puff attack. Joyous Wolves fans sing their 'Happy Wanderer' song.										

11	A	WEST BROM	2	D	1-1	0-0	Dawson 74	Gaskell	Brennan	Cantwell	Stiles	Foulkes	Lawton	Moir	Quixall	Dawson	Giles	Charlton
7/10			*25,645*	*19*	15		*Kevan 87*	*Millington*	*Howe*	*Williams S*	*Robson*	*Jones*	*Drury*	*Jackson*	*Hope*	*Burnside*	*Kevan*	*Clark*
							Ref: G Pullin	A long injury list includes Setters, Pearson, Herd and Dennis Viollet, whose belated England debut was average. United dominate for long periods and have two strong penalty appeals rejected. Derek Kevan's late rocket grabs a point. Manager Gordon Clark resigns three days later.										
12	H	BIRMINGHAM	4	L	0-2	0-1		Gregg	Brennan	Cantwell	Stiles	Haydock	Lawton	Bradley	Giles	Dawson	Herd	Moir
14/10			30,674	*21*	15		*Orritt 26, Hellawell 87*	*Schofield*	*Farmer*	*Sissons*	*Hennessey*	*Foster*	*Beard*	*Hellawell*	*Bloomfield*	*Harris*	*Orritt*	*Auld*
							Ref: P Rhodes	Foulkes pulls out with a foot injury before the kick-off and Frank Haydock struggles. Giles' midfield promptings are wasted by the reshuffled attack and Herd especially is out-of-sorts. Blues claim their first away win courtesy of two sloppy defensive mistakes. The fans are restless.										
13	A	ARSENAL	8	L	**1-5**	0-1	Viollet 86 *[Skirton 65, 75]*	Gregg	Brennan	Cantwell	Nicholson	Foulkes	Lawton	Moir	Giles	Herd	Viollet	Charlton
21/10			*54,245*	*12*	15		*Ward 37, Barnwell 49, Eastham 60,*	*Kelsey*	*Bacuzzi*	*McCullough*	*Ward*	*Brown*	*Groves*	*MacLeod*	*Barnwell*	*Charles*	*Eastham*	*Skirton*
							Ref: S Yates	More changes after Stiles goes down with flu. The patched-up team match the Gunners until half-time with Giles and Viollet close to scoring. Then George Eastham takes over and makes four goals as Arsenal run riot. An unhappy return for Herd but Jack Kelsey plays his 300th game.										
14	H	BOLTON	10	L	0-3	0-2		Gregg	Brennan	Dunne	Nicholson	Foulkes	Setters	Moir	Quixall	Herd	Viollet	Charlton
28/10			31,442	*13*	15		*Pilkington 13, Hill 18, McAdams 63*	*Hopkinson*	*Hartle*	*Farrimond*	*Threlfall*	*Edwards*	*Rimmer*	*Holden*	*Stevens*	*McAdams*	*Hill*	*Pilkington*
							Ref: R Mann	Three home defeats in a row and Alex Dawson's surprise move to Preston has the fans up in arms. A middling performance is unable to stop the Trotters, inspired by the England possible Freddie Hill. Johnny Giles and Cantwell are away with Eire, with Noel the temporary manager.										
15	A	SHEFFIELD WED	14	L	1-3	1-2	Viollet 20	Gregg	Brennan	Cantwell	Stiles	Foulkes	Setters	Bradley	Giles	Viollet	Charlton	**McMillan**
4/11			*35,998*	*5*	15		*Fantham 9, Kay 14, Ellis 88*	*Springett*	*Johnson*	*Megson*	*McAnearney*	*Swan*	*Kay*	*Finney*	*Griffin*	*Ellis*	*Fantham*	*Dobson*
							Ref: W Clements	Another violent game between these two rivals. United are accused of rough-house tactics against the superior Owls. Quixall and Herd are dropped. The fiery Stiles is roundly booed by the home fans and Cantwell misses a penalty. Tony Kay and John Fantham look England class.										
16	H	LEICESTER	13	D	2-2	1-2	Giles 38, Viollet 65	Gaskell	Brennan	Dunne	Stiles	Foulkes	Setters	Bradley	Giles	Viollet	Charlton	McMillan
11/11			21,567	*11*	16		*McLintock 2, Appleton 35*	*Banks*	*Chalmers*	*Norman*	*McLintock*	*King*	*White*	*Riley*	*Keyworth*	*Wills*	*Appleton*	*Mitten*
							Ref: V James	United fans vote with their feet and it's the lowest Saturday gate since 1950. A spirited display is spoiled by a last-minute disallowed goal. Every forward is guilty of at least one miss. 20-year-old Sammy McMillan fades after a bright start. Charlie Mitten's son John plays for City.										
17	A	IPSWICH	18	L	1-4	0-1	McMillan 90 *[Elsworthy 86]*	Gaskell	Brennan	Dunne	Stiles	Foulkes	Setters	Bradley	Giles	Herd	Charlton	McMillan
18/11			*25,755*	*3*	16		*Phillips 25, 67, Crawford 75,*	*Bailey*	*Carberry*	*Compton*	*Baxter*	*Nelson*	*Elsworthy*	*Curtis*	*Moran*	*Crawford*	*Phillips*	*Leadbetter*
							Ref: K Aston	United aren't the first team to succumb to Alf Ramsey's surprise team of misfits. England's boss comes to watch his new man Ray Crawford, who is overshadowed by 20-goal Ted Phillips. United's jittery defence are at sea and the forwards, with David Herd reinstalled, stutter again.										
18	H	BURNLEY	19	L	1-4	1-1	Herd 6 *[Connelly 89]*	Gaskell	Brennan	Dunne	Stiles	Foulkes	Setters	Bradley	Giles	Herd	Quixall	Charlton
25/11			41,029	*1*	16		*Harris 35, Robson 61, Pointer 69,*	*Blacklaw*	*Angus*	*Elder*	*Adamson*	*Cummings*	*Miller*	*Connelly*	*McIlroy*	*Pointer*	*Robson*	*Harris*
							Ref: A Holland	United match the league leaders until the last quarter, when the magical Jimmy McIlroy turns up the heat and they wilt. Connelly and Pointer are the latest Burnley internationals and both show true class. Busby tells the fans he knows the side needs strengthening but to be patient.										
19	A	EVERTON	20	L	**1-5**	0-5	Herd 60 *[Young 38]*	Gaskell	Brennan	Dunne	Nicholson	Foulkes	Setters	**Chisnall**	Giles	Herd	Lawton	Charlton
2/12			*48,099*	*3*	16		*Collins 9, Vernon 11, 32, Fell 15,*	*Dunlop*	*Parker*	*Thomson*	*Gabriel*	*Labone*	*Harris*	*Bingham*	*Collins*	*Young*	*Vernon*	*Fell*
							Ref: J Loynton	Ten games without a win is the longest such run since the war and only Chelsea are below the Reds. Stiles and Quixall are dropped and 19-year -old Phil Chisnall tries hard. Everton ease off after half-time to let United off a massive score. None of the nervous Reds wants the ball.										
20	H	FULHAM	20	W	3-0	1-0	Herd 38, 47, Lawton 79	Gaskell	Brennan	Dunne	Nicholson	Foulkes	Setters	Chisnall	Giles	Herd	Lawton	Charlton
9/12			22,193	*13*	18			*Hewkins*	*Cohen*	*Langley*	*Mullery*	*Dodgin*	*Edwards*	*Key*	*O'Connell*	*Cook*	*Leggat*	*Metchick*
							Ref: M Fussey	A rare unchanged side outclasses a poor Fulham and ends the disastrous run. Herd scores two from Charlton's crosses to end his nightmare. Two more certain goals are saved by stand-in Hewkins. Nobby Lawton can pick his spot after a deflection. Noel Cantwell has a mystery bug.										
21	H	WEST HAM	20	L	1-2	1-0	Herd 18	Gaskell	Brennan	Dunne	Nicholson	Foulkes	Setters	Chisnall	Giles	Herd	Lawton	Charlton
16/12			29,472	*4*	18		*Dick 75, 85*	*Leslie*	*Kirkup*	*Bond*	*Hurst*	*Brown*	*Moore*	*Crawford*	*Woosnam*	*Tindall*	*Dick*	*Musgrove*
							Ref: L Callaghan	West Ham are flying under new boss Greenwood. Herd's goal looks offside. John Dick thunders an equaliser, then, to heap more trouble on United, he converts Musgrove's pass. Poor visibility causes the lights to be switched on early. Hammers' first win at Old Trafford since 1935.										

No	Date	Att	Pos	Pt	F-A	H-T	Scorers, Times, and Referees	1	2	3	4	5	6	7	8	9	10	11
22	H NOTT'M FOREST		18	W	6-3	4-1	Herd 3, Law' 8,30,71, Cha' 24, Bre' 78	Gaskell	Brennan	Dunne	Nicholson	Foulkes	Setters	Chisnall	Giles	Herd	Lawton	Charlton
	26/12	30,822	*19*	20			*Julians 40, Hockey 68, Palmer 81p*	*Grummitt*	*Palmer*	*Grant*	*Whitefoot*	*McKinlay*	*Iley*	*Hockey*	*Booth*	*Julians*	*Quigley*	*Le Flem*
							Ref: J Powell	Vintage United on an icy pitch with Giles, Herd and Lawton starring. Charlton's first goal since September and poor Peter Grummitt, injured in a clash with David Herd, throws the ball straight to Brennan for a rare goal for the full-back. Sloppy Setters gifts lowly Forest two goals.										
23	H BLACKPOOL		19	L	0-1	0-1		Gaskell	Brennan	Dunne	Nicholson	Foulkes	Setters	Chisnall	Giles	Herd	Lawton	Charlton
	13/1	*26,999*	*9*	20			*Hauser 8*	*Waiters*	*Armfield*	*Martin*	*Crawford*	*Gratrix*	*Durie*	*Hill*	*Hauser*	*Charnley*	*Parry*	*Perry*
							Ref: H Wilson	David Herd injures his thigh in the warm-up but Busby declines to replace him and he is soon useless. The heroic Dunne picks up a head injury and United are effectively down to nine men. Despite Foulkes mastering league top scorer Ray Charnley, Ron Suart's boys take advantage.										
24	H ASTON VILLA		17	W	2-0	2-0	Quixall 20, Charlton 25	Gaskell	Brennan	Dunne	Nicholson	Foulkes	Setters	Chisnall	Giles	Quixall	Lawton	Charlton
	15/1	**20,807**	*10*	22				*Sims*	*Lee*	*Aitken*	*Crowe*	*Sleeuwenh'k*	*Tindall*	*McParland*	*Baker*	*Dougan*	*McMorran*	*Burrows*
							Ref: H Wilson	The fans' disillusionment is reflected in the low crowd on a wet and windy night. Both sides fall away after a promising start. Lawton's shot hits the underside of the bar and Quixall is first to react. Charlton drives home Phil Chisnall's shrewd cross. Villa five games without a win.										
25	A TOTTENHAM		16	D	2-2	1-1	Charlton 35, Stiles 65	Gaskell	Brennan	Dunne	Nicholson	Foulkes	Setters	Chisnall	Stiles	Lawton	Giles	Charlton
	20/1	***55,225***	*2*	23			*Greaves 45, 77*	*Brown*	*Baker*	*Henry*	*Blanchflower*	*Norman*	*Marchi*	*Jones*	*Mackay*	*Allen*	*Greaves*	*Dyson*
							Ref: G Roper	A full-blooded head-on clash. Jimmy Greaves' header saves Spurs blushes – they have lost only one home game all season. United are booed for playing offside trap but deserve the point. Charlton's sweet cross-shot is cancelled out by Greaves' shot which goes under Dave Gaskell.										
26	H CARDIFF		14	W	3-0	2-0	Stiles 2, Giles 30, Lawton 89	Gaskell	Brennan	Dunne	Nicholson	Foulkes	Setters	Chisnall	Stiles	Lawton	Giles	Charlton
	3/2	29,200	15	25				*Vearncombe*	*Harrington*	*Milne*	*Gammon*	*Rankmore*	*Baker*	*King P*	*Ward*	*King J*	*Durban*	*Hogg*
							Ref: K Aston	Cardiff, with one win in 10, are sliding down the table. Stiles heads in Charlton's corner and Bobby sets up the livewire Giles. Feisty City fight back but lack punch, apart from Durban's shot that rattles the bar. United's defence with Brennan, called up for England training, is superb.										
27	A MANCHESTER C		14	W	2-0	1-0	Chisnall 34, Herd 68	Gaskell	Brennan	Dunne	Stiles	Setters	Nicholson	Chisnall	Giles	Herd	Lawton	Charlton
	10/2	*49,959*	*19*	27				*Trautmann*	*McDonald*	*Sear*	*Cheetham*	*Leivers*	*Kennedy*	*Young*	*Hannah*	*Dobing*	*Hayes*	*Wagstaffe*
							Ref: J Taylor	City look a poor side and the veteran Bert Trautmann saves them from a drubbing. Slack marking lets Chisnall score and the speedy Herd to score on a breakaway. United's strong defence, with the injured Foulkes missing, is rarely troubled until Bill Leivers moves up near the end.										
28	H WEST BROM		12	W	4-1	0-0	Charl' 52, 75, Setters 57, Quixall 65	Briggs	Brennan	Dunne	Stiles	Foulkes	Setters	Quixall	Giles	Herd	Lawton	Charlton
	24/2	32,456	*16*	29			*Jackson 69*	*Millington*	*Cram*	*Williams S*	*Howe*	*Jones*	*Drury*	*Jackson*	*Burnside*	*Smith*	*Kevan*	*Clark*
							Ref: W Robinson	7-goal Briggs comes in for Gaskell who missed out on an Under 23 cap through injury. After an aimless first half the game comes to life with Charlton back to his best and any relegation thoughts are banished. Millington saves WBA from a bigger loss but can't stop Bobby's bullet.										
29	A WOLVERHAMPTON		11	D	2-2	1-0	Lawton 32, Herd 65	Briggs	Brennan	Dunne	Setters	Foulkes	Nicholson	Quixall	Stiles	Herd	Lawton	Charlton
	28/2	*27,565*	*13*	30			*Murray 68, Crowe 70*	*Davies*	*Stuart*	*Thomson*	*Kirkham*	*Showell*	*Flowers*	*Wharton*	*Crowe*	*Murray*	*Broadbent*	*McParland*
							Ref: H New	United have gone nine games without defeat but squander a point. Charlton sets up Lawton and helps Lawton create Herd's flick. New signing Crowe is the architect of the comeback but Briggs should have held his shot. An uninspiring game with Wolves a shadow of their sides of old.										
30	A BIRMINGHAM		11	D	1-1	0-0	Herd 86	Briggs	Brennan	Dunne	Stiles	Foulkes	Setters	Quixall	Giles	Herd	Lawton	Charlton
	3/3	*25,817*	*14*	31			*Leek 51*	*Schofield*	*Lynn*	*Sissons*	*Hennessey*	*Smith*	*Beard*	*Hellawell*	*Bloomfield*	*Stubbs*	*Leek*	*Auld*
							Ref: G Pullin	A late goal preserves the run on a snow-covered pitch. Blues haven't lost at home since October and lead after Briggs drops Hellawell's cross at Leek's feet. Welshman Ken Leek has scored eleven goals in 12 games. Stiles is limping from the 18th minute. Bradley joins Bury for £6000.										
31	A BOLTON		12	L	0-1	0-0		Briggs	Brennan	Dunne	Nicholson	Foulkes	Setters	Quixall	Giles	Lawton	Stiles	Charlton
	17/3	*34,366*	*18*	31			*Pilkington 46*	*Hopkinson*	*Hartle*	*Farrimond*	*Stanley*	*Edwards*	*Rimmer*	*Holden*	*Hill*	*Davies*	*McGarry*	*Pilkington*
							Ref: H Hackney	The 12-match run is ended at the bogey ground where United have not won since 1949. Wyn Davies and McGarry make their home debuts but it is Hopkinson with three wonder saves in the first 15 mins who stars. This win may keep Bolton up but United's tired attack is out of touch.										

No	Date	Opponent / Att	Pos	Res / Pts	F-A	H-T	Scorers, Times, and Referees	1	2	3	4	5	6	7	8	9	10	11
32	A	NOTT'M FOREST	12	L	0-1	0-1		Briggs	Brennan	Dunne	Nicholson	Foulkes	Setters	Quixall	Giles	Lawton	Stiles	Moir
	20/3	*27,833*	*17*	31			*Vowden 20*	*Grummitt*	*Wilson*	*Gray*	*Winfield*	*McKinlay*	*Iley*	*Rowland*	*Vowden*	*Julians*	*Quigley*	*Le Flem*
							Ref: G McCabe	Forest are pulling away from the drop zone after a fast, scrappy game. Charlton and Herd are missing and United's attack lacks imagination. Geoff Vowden scores as Briggs fails to hold his fierce shot and he follows up. United's defence is solid but Forest could have scored more.										
33	H	SHEFFIELD WED	14	D	1-1	1-0	Charlton 28	Gaskell	Brennan	Dunne	Stiles	Foulkes	Setters	Moir	Giles	Quixall	Lawton	Charlton
	24/3	31,322	*9*	32			*Fantham 61*	*Springett*	*Johnson*	*Megson*	*Hardy*	*Swan*	*Kay*	*Finney*	*Dobson*	*Young*	*Fantham*	*Holliday*
							Ref: J Finney	Wednesday's form has slumped since their Cup exit but they are worth a point against the Reds with one eye on the semi-final. Charlton looks offside with his headed goal. The limping Gerry Young sets up the excellent Fantham for a leveller. Swan is booked after Stiles was pole-axed.										
34	A	LEICESTER	16	L	3-4	2-3	McMillan 39, 43, Quixall 52	Gaskell	Setters	Cantwell	Stiles	Foulkes	Nicholson	Moir	Quixall	Herd	Lawton	McMillan
	4/4	*15,318*	*12*	32			*Cheesebro' 5, 20, Keyworth 37, 57*	*Banks*	*Chalmers*	*Norman*	*McLintock*	*King*	*Appleton*	*Riley*	*Keyworth*	*Walsh*	*Cheesebrough*	*Stringfellow*
							Ref: C Woan	More injuries as Lawton suffers a hairline fracture in a tackle on Riley and Gaskell is limping. Cheesebrough's shooting is deadly but United hit back to level at 3-3. Their defence tightens up after the break but can't grab a draw despite some close shaves. Charlton is on England duty.										
35	H	IPSWICH	14	W	5-0	2-0	Quix' 14,20,48, Setters 80, Stiles 85	Briggs	Brennan	Dunne	Stiles	Foulkes	Setters	Moir	Giles	Quixall	McMillan	Charlton
	7/4	24,976	*2*	34				*Bailey*	*Carberry*	*Compton*	*Baxter*	*Nelson*	*Elsworthy*	*Stephenson*	*Moran*	*Curtis*	*Phillips*	*Leadbetter*
							Ref: R Simons	Heavy pre-match rain turns the pitch into a quagmire but can't stop an irrepressible United ripping the league leaders apart. Roy Bailey saves Ipswich from a double-figure defeat. Quixall is in top form and scores a left-footer from 25 yards. Charlton and McMillan hit the woodwork.										
36	A	BLACKBURN	14	L	0-3	0-2		Gaskell	Brennan	Dunne	Stiles	Foulkes	Setters	Moir	Giles	Cantwell	Pearson	McMillan
	10/4	***14,623***	*9*	34			*Clayton 10, Pickering 17, Ratcliffe 84*	*Jones*	*Taylor*	*Bray*	*Clayton*	*Newton*	*McGrath*	*Ratcliffe*	*Lawther*	*Pickering*	*Byrom*	*Haverty*
							Ref: F Stringer	Reshuffled United succumb to a strong display from Rovers. Quixall, Herd and Charlton are injured or on international duty and Foulkes plays with flu. Ronnie Clayton's deceptive shot and Pickering's poaching gives Rovers an early lead before Ratcliffe scores direct from a corner.										
37	A	BURNLEY	15	W	3-1	1-0	Cantwell 40, Brennan 64p, Herd 88	Briggs	Brennan	Dunne	Stiles	Foulkes	Setters	Giles	Pearson	Cantwell	Herd	McMillan
	14/4	*36,240*	*2*	36			*Pointer 65*	*Blacklaw*	*Angus*	*Elder*	*Walker*	*Cummings*	*Joyce*	*Connelly*	*Towers*	*Pointer*	*Robson*	*Harris*
							Ref: T Reynolds	Many think Burnley are Britain's best, but United damage their title hopes. Twin centre-forwards cause the damage with Pearson the schemer in charge in the absence of Burnley's McIlroy. Harris and Giles are booked as the game threatens to boil over. Charlton is on England duty.										
38	H	ARSENAL	15	L	2-3	1-2	McMillan 35, Cantwell 71	Briggs	Brennan	Cantwell	Stiles	Foulkes	Setters	Giles	Pearson	Herd	McMillan	Charlton
	16/4	24,258	*8*	36			*East'm 12, Cant' 32 (og), Skirton 79*	*Kelsey*	*Magill*	*McCullough*	*Brown*	*Neill*	*Petts*	*MacLeod*	*Griffiths*	*Strong*	*Eastham*	*Skirton*
							Ref: P Bye	Arsenal's first double over United since 1930-31 is well deserved. Their speed is too much for a harassed United defence and Eastham's mazy run and goal sets the tone. A fight-back sees the Reds draw level but an unmarked Skirton gives the Gunners a deserved win. Briggs is dodgy.										
39	H	EVERTON	16	D	1-1	1-1	Herd 38	Gaskell	Brennan	Dunne	Stiles	Foulkes	Setters	Giles	Pearson	Cantwell	Herd	Charlton
	21/4	31,926	*4*	37			*Stevens 44*	*West*	*Meagan*	*Thomson*	*Gabriel*	*Labone*	*Harris*	*Lill*	*Stevens*	*Young*	*Vernon*	*Temple*
							Ref: P Rhodes	Harry Catterick's blend of local home-grown talent and expensive stars is having a good season. There is plenty of action for an end of season game and Stiles' boob sets up new signing Dennis Stevens to equalise Herd's thunderous shot. The irascible Stiles is cautioned for dissent.										
40	H	SHEFFIELD UTD	16	L	0-1	0-1		Gaskell	Brennan	Dunne	Stiles	Foulkes	Setters	Giles	Pearson	Herd	McMillan	Charlton
	23/4	30,073	*4*	37			*Pace 11*	*Hodgkinson*	*Coldwell*	*Shaw G*	*Richardson*	*Shaw*	*Matthewson*	*Allchurch*	*Kettleborough*	*Pace*	*Hodgson*	*Simpson*
							Ref: J Loynton	Promoted Blades are having their best season since the 1920s. Pace's scrambled goal on a hard pitch is sufficient to win a mistake-riddled Bank Holiday game in the sunshine. Too many Reds look off-colour, especially Setters and Pearson. Cantwell is out with a shoulder injury.										
41	A	SHEFFIELD UTD	15	W	3-2	0-0	McMillan 75, 89, Stiles 78	Gaskell	Brennan	Dunne	Nicholson	Foulkes	Setters	Giles	Pearson	McMillan	Stiles	Charlton
	24/4	*25,324*	*5*	39			*Pace 47, Hodgson 58*	*Hodgkinson*	*Coldwell*	*Shaw G*	*Richardson*	*Shaw*	*Matthewson*	*Allchurch*	*Kettleborough*	*Pace*	*Hodgson*	*Simpson*
							Ref: R Langdale	A fine comeback after United were outplayed for an hour. Hodgson lobs for Pace, then heads in Coldwell's free-kick. A bloodied McMillan steers in Giles' pass and scores the late winner. Alan Hodgkinson can't hold Stiles' wicked shot and Nobby nets. United keen on Dennis Law.										
42	A	FULHAM	15	L	0-2	0-2		Gaskell	Brennan	Dunne	Nicholson	Foulkes	Setters	Giles	Pearson	McMillan	Stiles	Charlton
	28/4	*40,113*	*20*	39			*Cook 3, Leggat 21*	*Macedo*	*Cohen*	*Langley*	*Mullery*	*Dodgin*	*Lowe*	*Leggat*	*Henderson*	*Cook*	*Haynes*	*O'Connell*
	Home	Away					Ref: H Horner	Fulham save themselves from relegation on the final day as Cardiff lose badly at Everton. United's first defeat at Fulham since 1949 is forged by England captain Johnnie Haynes. Ipswich clinch the title and United lose their record of finishing in the top half every year since the war.										
Average	33,491	33,964																

FA Cup					F-A	H-T	Scorers, Times, and Referees	1	2	3	4	5	6	7	8	9	10	11
3	H	BOLTON	18	W	2-1	0-1	Herd 83, Nicholson 90	Gaskell	Brennan	Dunne	Nicholson	Foulkes	Setters	Chisnall	Giles	Herd	Lawton	Bradley
	6/1	42,202	*17*				*Stevens 35*	*Hopkinson*	*Hartle*	*Farrimond*	*Threlfall*	*Edwards*	*Rimmer*	*Holden*	*Deakin*	*Stevens*	*Hill*	*Pilkington*
							Ref: D Howell	At a fog-shrouded stadium Bolton look certs to win courtesy of Stevens following up Deakin's header. Then Herd, looking well offside, levels and Nicholson's long-range effort goes in off the post in injury time. At last some luck for the Reds, whose goals come from a direct route.										
4	H	ARSENAL	16	W	1-0	1-0	Setters 28	Gaskell	Brennan	Dunne	Nicholson	Foulkes	Setters	Chisnall	Stiles	Lawton	Giles	Charlton
	31/1	54,082	*8*					*Kelsey*	*Bacuzzi*	*McCullough*	*Snedden*	*Brown*	*Clamp*	*Skirton*	*Barnwell*	*Charles*	*Eastham*	*MacLeod*
							Ref: E Crawford	Charlton smashes the dressing room mirror but it fails to bring United bad luck. On a pitch like a paddy field, Setters' header from Chisnall's corner is vital. Eastham-inspired Arsenal throw everything at the Reds in a tense finale, with Foulkes winning the key battle with Mel Charles.										
5	H	SHEFFIELD WED	14	D	0-0	0-0		Gaskell	Brennan	Dunne	Setters	Foulkes	Nicholson	Chisnall	Giles	Herd	Lawton	Charlton
	17/2	65,263	*7*					*Springett*	*Johnson*	*Megson*	*McAnearney*	*Swan*	*Kay*	*Wilkinson*	*Craig*	*Ellis*	*Fantham*	*Finney*
							Ref: J Finney	Everyone wants to see these teams meeting for the third successive year in the FA Cup. Both defences are superb, with the agile England goal-keeper Springett brilliant as the Reds turn up the heat. Setters is back to his best but survives strong penalty claims when he collides with Ellis.										
5R	A	SHEFFIELD WED	14	W	2-0	1-0	Giles 8, Charlton 73	Gaskell	Brennan	Dunne	Stiles	Foulkes	Setters	Quixall	Giles	Herd	Lawton	Charlton
	21/2	*65,009*	*7*					*Springett*	*Johnson*	*Megson*	*McAnearney*	*Swan*	*Kay*	*Wilkinson*	*Craig*	*Ellis*	*Fantham*	*Finney*
							Ref: J Finney	Giles and Herd's one-two gives well-organised United an early lead which they gamely defend. The Owls' constant pressure is soaked up by a Setters-inspired show. As the tide seems to be turning, Charlton's solo goal, his 100th, silences the massive crowd and wraps up a famous win.										
QF	A	PRESTON	12	D	0-0	0-0		Gaskell	Brennan	Dunne	Nicholson	Foulkes	Setters	Chisnall	Giles	Cantwell	Lawton	Charlton
	10/3	*37,521*	*2:14*					*Kelly*	*Cunningham*	*Ross*	*Wylie*	*Singleton*	*Smith*	*Wilson D*	*Biggs*	*Dawson*	*Spavin*	*Thompson*
							Ref: G McCabe	An all-ticket crowd see proud Preston push the injury-hit Reds to the limit with a gutsy display. They hit the bar, miss three good chances, and have a goal disallowed. Ex-Red Dawson causes lots of problems and is booked for retaliation. The gamble of playing Cantwell up front fails.										
QF R	H	PRESTON	12	W	2-1	2-0	Charlton 27, Herd 37	Gaskell	Brennan	Dunne	Stiles	Foulkes	Setters	Quixall	Giles	Herd	Lawton	Charlton
	14/3	63,468	*2:14*				*Spavin 70*	*Kelly*	*Wilson R*	*Ross*	*Wylie*	*Singleton*	*Smith*	*Wilson D*	*Biggs*	*Dawson*	*Spavin*	*Thompson*
							Ref: G McCabe	Full-strength United scrape home in a thriller. Cunningham is injured and Charlton has more room. He scores the first and David Herd adds a magnificent second. In an electric atmosphere Preston fight to the end, with Spavin volleying home and Thompson almost forcing extra-time.										
SF	N	TOTTENHAM	14	L	1-3	0-2	Herd 80	Gaskell	Dunne	Cantwell	Stiles	Foulkes	Setters	Quixall	Giles	Herd	Lawton	Charlton
	31/3	*65,000*	*3*				*Greaves 4, Jones 23, Medwin 85*	*Brown*	*Baker*	*Henry*	*Blanchflower*	*Norman*	*Mackay*	*Medwin*	*White*	*Smith R*	*Greaves*	*Jones*
		(at Hillsborough)					Ref: R Langdale	Arrogant Spurs sweep United aside in sporadic hailstorms to reach the final for the second year running. Smith nods down for Greaves and Jones heads in White's long ball. Herd sparks some hope from Charlton's rebound but Medwin heads in a third. Ever-present Brennan injured.										

		Home					Away					
	P	W	D	L	F	A	W	D	L	F	A	Pts
1 Ipswich	42	17	2	2	58	28	7	6	8	35	39	56
2 Burnley	42	14	4	3	57	26	7	7	7	44	41	53
3 Tottenham	42	14	4	3	59	34	7	6	8	29	35	52
4 Everton	42	17	2	2	64	21	3	9	9	24	33	51
5 Sheffield U	42	13	5	3	37	23	6	4	11	24	46	47
6 Sheffield W	42	14	4	3	47	23	6	2	13	25	35	46
7 Aston Villa	42	13	5	3	45	20	5	3	13	20	36	44
8 West Ham	42	11	6	4	49	37	6	4	11	27	45	44
9 West Brom	42	10	7	4	50	23	5	6	10	33	44	43
10 Arsenal	42	9	6	6	39	31	7	5	9	32	41	43
11 Bolton	42	11	7	3	35	22	5	3	13	27	44	42
12 Manchester C	42	11	3	7	46	38	6	4	11	32	43	41
13 Blackpool	42	10	4	7	41	30	5	7	9	29	45	41
14 Leicester	42	12	2	7	38	27	5	4	12	34	44	40
15 MAN UNITED	42	10	3	8	44	31	5	6	10	28	44	39
16 Blackburn	42	10	6	5	33	22	4	5	12	17	36	39
17 Birmingham	42	9	6	6	37	35	5	4	12	28	46	38
18 Wolves	42	8	7	6	38	34	5	3	13	35	52	36
19 Nott'm Forest	42	12	4	5	39	23	1	6	14	24	56	36
20 Fulham	42	8	3	10	38	34	5	4	12	28	40	33
21 Cardiff	42	6	9	6	30	33	3	5	13	20	48	32
22 Chelsea	42	7	7	7	34	29	2	3	16	29	65	28
	924	246	106	110	958	624	110	106	246	624	958	924

Odds & ends

Double wins: (2) Cardiff, Man City.
Double losses: (2) Bolton, Arsenal.

Won from behind: (2) Sheff United (a), Bolton FAC (a).
Lost from in front: (2) Burnley (h), West Ham (h).

High spots: Good FA Cup run.
Excellent start to the season.
Good wins over the top teams; Ipswich, Spurs and Burnley.
12-game unbeaten run in the New Year.

Low spots: 10-game run without a win in Autumn.
Eight home defeats – the most since 1933-34.
Inconsistent form of many top players.

Red cards (United): (0).
Red cards (Opponents): (0).
Ever-presents: (0).
Hat-tricks: (2) Lawton, Quixall.
Opposing hat-tricks: (0).
Leading scorer: (17) Herd.

	Appearances		Goals		
	Lge	FAC	Lge	FAC	Tot
Bradley, Warren	**6**	1			
Brennan, Shay	**41**	6	2		**2**
Briggs, Ronnie	**8**				
Cantwell, Noel	**17**	2	2		**2**
Charlton, Bobby	**37**	6	8	2	**10**
Chisnall, Phil	**9**	4	1		**1**
Dawson, Alex	**4**		2		**2**
Dunne, Tony	**28**	7			
Foulkes, Bill	**40**	7			
Gaskell, Dave	**21**	7			
Giles, Johnny	**30**	7	2	1	**3**
Gregg, Harry	**13**				
Haydock, Frank	**1**				
Herd, David	**27**	5	14	3	**17**
Lawton, Nobby	**20**	7	6		**6**
McMillan, Sammy	**11**		6		**6**
Moir, Ian	**9**				
Nicholson, Jimmy	**17**	4		1	**1**
Pearson, Mark	**17**		1		**1**
Quixall, Albert	**21**	3	10		**10**
Setters, Maurice	**38**	7	3	1	**4**
Stiles, Nobby	**34**	4	7		**7**
Viollet, Dennis	**13**		7		**7**
(own-goals)			1		**1**
23 players used	**462**	**77**	**72**	**8**	**80**

No		Date	Att	Pos	Pt	F-A	H-T	Scorers, Times, and Referees	1	2	3	4	5	6	7	8	9	10	11
1	H	WEST BROM			D	2-2	2-0	Herd 2, Law 7	Gaskell	Brennan	Dunne	Stiles	Foulkes	Setters	Giles	Quixall	Herd	Law	Moir
		18/8	51,896		1			*Kevan 75, Smith 85*	*Millington*	*Howe*	*Williams G*	*Williams S*	*Jones*	*Drury*	*Jackson*	*Burnside*	*Smith*	*Kevan*	*Clark*
								Ref: A Sparling	Herd's goal from Stiles' quick free-kick and Law's flicked header makes for a dream start. United fizzle out and persistent Albion force their way back. Setters' woeful back-pass hands the Baggies the equaliser. The fans even start a slow handclap. Charlton is out for three months.										
2	A	EVERTON			L	1-3	0-3	Moir 61	Gaskell	Brennan	Dunne	Stiles	Foulkes	Setters	Giles	Pearson	Herd	Law	Moir
		22/8	***69,500***		1			*Young 13, 14, Parker 44*	*West*	*Parker*	*Thomson*	*Gabriel*	*Labone*	*Harris*	*Bingham*	*Stevens*	*Young*	*Vernon*	*Veall*
								Ref: A Holland	The fourth largest away crowd since the war ensures a £70 per man bonus. Slick Everton show their title credentials and destroy a shaky Reds defence with fast skilful football. Quixall is dropped as Busby gets tough and Moir sparks a vain mini revival. Young's first goal is a classic.										
3	A	ARSENAL		11	W	3-1	0-0	Herd 58, 74, Chisnall 71	Gaskell	Brennan	Dunne	Nicholson	Foulkes	Lawton	Giles	Chisnall	Herd	Law	Moir
		25/8	*62,203*	*8*	3			*Clamp 88*	*McKechnie*	*Magill*	*McCullough*	*Clamp*	*Brown*	*Snedden*	*Armstrong*	*Eastham*	*Strong*	*Barnwell*	*Skirton*
								Ref: M Fussey	Busby wields the axe, with Setters, Stiles and Pearson rested. All London seem to want to see the dazzling Law and the gates are locked. Giles changes his boots at the break and makes all three goals with Herd grabbing two, a glancing header and a thunderbolt shot, against his old club.										
4	H	EVERTON		13	L	0-1	0-0		Gaskell	Brennan	Dunne	Nicholson	Foulkes	Lawton	Giles	Chisnall	Herd	Law	Moir
		29/8	**63,675**	*1*	3			*Vernon 78p*	*West*	*Parker*	*Thomson*	*Gabriel*	*Labone*	*Harris*	*Bingham*	*Stevens*	*Young*	*Vernon*	*Morrissey*
								Ref: A Jobling	Harry Catterick's expensive Everton team haven't lost a league game since March and look strong championship contenders. Their winner, a penalty, is felt to be harsh as Brennan fouls Morrissey. In an entertaining game the Toffees' strong half-back line proves to be the difference.										
5	H	BIRMINGHAM		9	W	2-0	1-0	Giles 7, Herd 51	Gaskell	Brennan	Dunne	Nicholson	Foulkes	Lawton	Giles	Chisnall	Herd	Law	Moir
		1/9	40,618	*20*	5				*Schofield*	*Lynn*	*Sissons*	*Hennessey*	*Smith*	*Beard*	*Hellawell*	*Bloomfield*	*Harris*	*Leek*	*Auld*
								Ref: L Callaghan	Blues' poor start to the season continues against a mediocre Reds, with Law sluggish. The form shown against Everton disappears but they are grateful for the points. Smith's clearance goes straight to Giles, and Moir's run sets up Herd. Blues have two strong penalty claims rejected.										
6	A	BOLTON		14	L	0-3	0-2		Gaskell	Brennan	Dunne	Nicholson	Foulkes	Lawton	Giles	Quixall	Herd	Law	Moir
		5/9	*45,097*	*10*	5			*Davies 6, Pilkington 32p, Hill 77*	*Hopkinson*	*Hartle*	*Farrimond*	*Threlfall*	*Edwards*	*Rimmer*	*Holden*	*Hill*	*Davies*	*McGarry*	*Pilkington*
								Ref: J Cowell	Bill Ridding's physical Bolton rattle United and the Burnden bogey continues with no win there in 13 visits. Giles injured shoulder means punch-less United are down to ten for the second half. Gaskell's slip helps Wyn Davies, and Brennan fouls Brian Pilkington for the spot-kick.										
7	A	LEYTON ORIENT		18	L	0-1	0-0		Gaskell	Brennan	Dunne	Nicholson	Foulkes	Lawton	Moir	Setters	Herd	Law	McMillan
		8/9	*25,101*	*17*	5			*McDonald 89*	*Robertson*	*Charlton*	*Lewis*	*Lucas*	*Bishop*	*Lee*	*Deeley*	*Bolland*	*Dunmore*	*Graham*	*McDonald*
								Ref: J Osbourne	Orient's first ever season in Div 1 has started well, with Johnny Carey in charge. McDonald's swerving right-foot shot is all that beats the brilliant Gaskell all day and it sparks a good-natured pitch invasion. Ex-Red, Eddie Lewis, now a full-back, is excellent. Quixall is axed again.										
8	H	BOLTON		10	W	3-0	1-0	Cantwell 35, Herd 70, 89	Gaskell	Brennan	Dunne	Stiles	Foulkes	Setters	Giles	Lawton	Herd	Law	Cantwell
		12/9	37,951	*14*	7				*Hopkinson*	*Hartle*	*Cooper*	*Threlfall*	*Edwards*	*Hatton*	*Holden*	*Hill*	*Davies*	*Deakin*	*Pilkington*
								Ref: K Howley	Busby makes five more changes as he seeks the right blend. Giles and Stiles are outstanding and Mr Versatile Noel Cantwell has a blinder on the left wing. Gaskell's long clearances cause a panic in Bolton's defence. Albert Quixall is considering a move to Second Division Stoke City.										
9	H	MANCHESTER C		14	L	2-3	0-2	Law 46, 70	Gaskell	Brennan	Dunne	Stiles	Foulkes	Nicholson	Giles	Lawton	Herd	Law	Cantwell
		15/9	49,455	*20*	7			*Dobing 17p, Hayes 23, Harley 90*	*Trautmann*	*Betts*	*Sear*	*Kennedy*	*Leivers*	*Chadwick*	*Young*	*Dobing*	*Harley*	*Hayes*	*Wagstaffe*
								Ref: L Tirebuck	New signing Alex Harley wins the derby with the last kick of the match and gives City their first win at Old Trafford since 1955. United are let down by a jittery defence, with Bill Foulkes at fault for two goals and handling for the penalty. 38-year-old Bert Trautmann gifts Law a goal.										
10	H	BURNLEY		16	L	2-5	0-3	Stiles 58, Law 64 *[McIlroy 43]*	Gaskell	Brennan	Dunne	Stiles	Foulkes	Lawton	Giles	Law	Herd	Pearson	Moir
		22/9	46,176	*5*	7			*Lochhead 5, Connelly 35, 75, 80,*	*Blacklaw*	*Angus*	*Elder*	*Walker*	*Talbut*	*Miller*	*Connelly*	*Pointer*	*Lochhead*	*McIlroy*	*Harris*
								Ref: A Luty	Burnley look likely to score every time they attack as they notch their fourth win in five at Old Trafford. Gaskell looks unhappy behind a shaky defence, as England man Connelly rips it apart. Law scores a brilliant goal and lays on Stiles'. Blacklaw saves Shay Brennan's weak penalty.										

No	Venue / Date	Opponent / Att	Pos	Res	Score	H-T	Scorers, Times, Referees	1	2	3	4	5	6	7	8	9	10	11
11	A	SHEFFIELD WED	19	L	0-1	0-0		Gregg	Brennan	Dunne	Stiles	Foulkes	Lawton	Giles	Law	Quixall	Chisnall	McMillan
	29/9	*38,410*	*6*	7			*Kay 85*	*Springett*	*Horrobin*	*Megson*	*Eustace*	*Swan*	*Kay*	*Wilkinson*	*Dobson*	*Layne*	*Young*	*Holliday*
							Ref: P Brandwood	Gregg returns after ten months out with shoulder injuries and has lost none of his talent. The Owls may be one of the country's top sides, but struggle against a poor United who miss the injured Herd. Kay's close-range effort wins the game after the home fans had jeered their players.										
12	A	BLACKPOOL	18	D	2-2	2-1	Herd 2, 39	Gregg	Brennan	Dunne	Stiles	Foulkes	Nicholson	Giles	Law	Herd	Lawton	McMillan
	6/10	*33,242*	*13*	8			*McPhee 30, Charnley 75*	*Waiters*	*Armfield*	*Martin*	*Crawford*	*Gratrix*	*Durie*	*Watt*	*McPhee*	*Charnley*	*Parry*	*Horne*
							Ref: K Stokes	An improved performance sees United lead twice but pegged back by new England cap Ray Charnley. Herd borrows Cantwell's boots to good effect as the impressive Giles lays on both goals. Dennis Law gifts McPhee his goal and United upset the home fans with time-wasting tactics.										
13	H	BLACKBURN	20	L	0-3	0-2		Gregg	Brennan	Dunne	Stiles	Foulkes	Nicholson	Giles	Law	Herd	Charlton	McMillan
	13/10	42,923	*16*	8			*McGrath 12, Harrison 37, Lawth' 58*	*Else*	*Bray*	*Newton*	*Clayton*	*Woods*	*McGrath*	*Ratcliffe*	*Lawther*	*Pickering*	*Douglas*	*Harrison*
							Ref: K Seddon	The third home defeat in a row is worrying for Busby, and Blackburn also miss a penalty and finish with ten men. Bryan Douglas is supreme in a midfield role. Charlton returns from his hernia op but looks a way off match fitness. Law's petulance earns his second booking of the season.										
14	A	TOTTENHAM	22	L	**2-6**	0-3	Herd 83, Quixall 87p *[Jones 70]*	Gregg	Brennan	Cantwell	Stiles	Foulkes	Setters	Giles	Quixall	Herd	Law	Charlton
	24/10	*51,314*	*1*	8			*Greaves 15, 50, 78, Medwin 28, 40,*	*Brown*	*Baker*	*Henry*	*Blanchflower*	*Norman*	*Mackay*	*Medwin*	*White*	*Allen*	*Greaves*	*Jones*
							Ref: N Burtenshaw	Busby makes five more changes and fields his strongest team, but they can't contain slick Spurs who have scored 49 goals in 14 games. Setters returns from his appendix operation and for once is fleeced by Jimmy Greaves, who also misses easy chances. United continue to play football.										
15	H	WEST HAM	20	W	3-1	2-1	Quixall 17p, 41, Law 79	Gregg	Brennan	Cantwell	Stiles	Foulkes	Setters	Giles	Quixall	Herd	Law	Charlton
	27/10	29,419	*12*	10			*Musgrove 29*	*Leslie*	*Burkett*	*Lyall*	*Peters*	*Brown*	*Moore*	*Brabrook*	*Woosnam*	*Sealey*	*Byrne*	*Musgrove*
							Ref: D Howell	United climb off the bottom with an important win. Leslie sends Nobby Stiles spinning inside the box and Quixall nets the penalty. Following Musgrove's equaliser Sealey misses an open goal and new signing Brabrook hits the bar. Leslie pushes out Giles' centre to the lurking Quixall.										
16	A	IPSWICH	18	W	5-3	4-1	Law 2, 9, 19, 85, Herd 33	Gregg	Brennan	Cantwell	Stiles	Foulkes	Setters	Giles	Quixall	Herd	Law	Charlton
	3/11	*18,475*	*21*	12			*Crawford 8, Blackwood 46, 59*	*Hall*	*Carberry*	*Malcolm*	*Baxter*	*Nelson*	*Pickett*	*Stephenson*	*Moran*	*Crawford*	*Blackwood*	*Leadbetter*
							Ref: E Jennings	The champions are without a win in nine and their boss Ramsey has just been appointed England manager. Law shows his value and outshines England cap Crawford, who is shackled by Foulkes. Ipswich's brave fight-back is nipped in the bud by Dennis's fourth as the rain pours down.										
17	H	LIVERPOOL	18	D	3-3	1-0	Herd 39, Quixall 69p, Giles 90	Gregg	Brennan	Cantwell	Stiles	Foulkes	Setters	Giles	Quixall	Herd	Law	Charlton
	10/11	44,045	*19*	13			*St John 51, Melia 85, Moran 89*	*Lawrence*	*Byrne*	*Moran*	*Milne*	*Yeats*	*Stevenson*	*Callaghan*	*Hunt*	*St John*	*Melia*	*A'Court*
							Ref: J Carr	New signings Lawrence and Stevenson almost complete Shankley's jigsaw. In a thrilling last five minutes United salvage a point when two looked certain. Pool's kick and run style, with Milne and Callaghan shackling Law and Charlton, works but Quixall is the star, creating Herd's.										
18	A	WOLVERHAMPTON	16	W	3-2	0-2	Herd 62, Law 68, 75	Gregg	Brennan	Cantwell	Stiles	Foulkes	Setters	Giles	Quixall	Herd	Law	Charlton
	17/11	*37,305*	*7*	15			*Stobart 12, 41*	*Davies*	*Showell*	*Thomson*	*Kirkham*	*Woodfield*	*Flowers*	*Wharton*	*Crowe*	*Stobart*	*Broadbent*	*Hinton*
							Ref: N Burtenshaw	Suddenly United look unbeatable. The heads don't drop as they go two down and they show their resilience. After an unbeaten 11-game start, Wolves have gone seven without a win. Law is superb but Setters is booked for a third time and faces a ban. New England man Hinton is quiet.										
19	H	ASTON VILLA	19	D	2-2	1-1	Quixall 28p, 55	Gregg	Brennan	Cantwell	Stiles	Foulkes	Setters	Giles	Quixall	Herd	Law	Charlton
	24/11	37,747	*7*	16			*Cantwell 4(og), Dougan 57*	*Sidebottom*	*Fraser*	*Aitken*	*Crowe*	*Sleeuwenh'k*	*Tindall*	*MacEwan*	*Baker*	*Dougan*	*O'Neill*	*Burrows*
							Ref: H Hackney	10-man United – Law is off after a Crowe tackle –deserve the point in a rough game. Villa's tackles are blood-curdling but Quixall rises above the melee to score his fourth pen in six games, after Fraser handled, and heads the second. Sidebottom saves Joe Mercer's men from defeat.										
20	A	SHEFFIELD UTD	17	D	1-1	1-1	Charlton 19	Gregg	Brennan	Cantwell	Stiles	Foulkes	Setters	Giles	Quixall	Herd	Lawton	Charlton
	1/12	*25,173*	*12*	17			*Simpson 25p*	*Hodgkinson*	*Coldwell*	*Shaw G*	*Richardson*	*Shaw J*	*Summera*	*Allchurch*	*Kettleborough*	*Shiels*	*Hodgson*	*Simpson*
							Ref: J Loynton	Another rough game, with Setters one of four Reds booked for a bad foul on Keith Kettleborough, as the ref implements a new tough FA edict. Charlton cuts in from the left and hits a screamer to bring back memories. Harry Gregg saves a second Simpson penalty in the same place.										
21	H	NOTT'M FOREST	14	W	**5-1**	3-1	Herd 10, 22, Charlton 25, Giles 72, [Law 88]	Gregg	Brennan	Cantwell	Nicholson	Foulkes	Lawton	Giles	Quixall	Herd	Law	Charlton
	8/12	**27,615**	*6*	19			*Addison 18*	*Armstrong*	*Wilson J*	*Gray*	*Whitefoot*	*McKinlay*	*Palmer*	*Hockey*	*Addison*	*Julians*	*Quigley*	*Le Flem*
							Ref: J Powell	Noel Cantwell is captain for the first time in the banned absence of Setters. United look well-balanced and exceedingly dangerous as they make it seven without loss. Law gets married the following day and nets a late effort. Albert Quixall is the architect with his defence-splitting passes.										

No	Date		Att	Pos	Pt	F-A	H-T	Scorers, Times, and Referees	1	2	3	4	5	6	7	8	9	10	11
22	A	WEST BROM		15	L	0-3	0-1		Gregg	Brennan	Cantwell	Stiles	Foulkes	Nicholson	Giles	Quixall	Herd	Law	Moir
	15/12		*18,113*	*10*	19			*Cram 37, Smith 49, Jackson 69*	*Potter*	*Howe*	*Williams G*	*Cram*	*Jones*	*Drury*	*Jackson*	*Fenton*	*Smith*	*Kevan*	*Clark*
								Ref: G Pullin	The run ends on a slippery Hawthorns pitch but the score flatters Albion. Law misses good chances, Quixall seizes up, and Charlton is missing injured. Cram's 35-yarder is out of the blue and Gregg is at fault for two goals. Only Giles looks useful as Law accuses the ref of heckling him.										
23	A	FULHAM		12	W	1-0	1-0	Charlton 40	Gregg	Brennan	Cantwell	Stiles	Foulkes	Setters	Giles	Quixall	Herd	Law	Charlton
	26/12		*23,338*	*21*	21				*Macedo*	*Cohen*	*Langley*	*Mullery*	*Keetch*	*Watson*	*Leggat*	*Cook*	*Brown S*	*Robson*	*Stratton*
								Ref: H New	Fulham are without a home win since September when captain Johnny Haynes was injured in a car crash. On a rock hard frosty surface the Reds are always too good for the struggling Londoners. Quixall misses an early penalty but Charlton's thunderous ground shot wins the game.										
24	H	BLACKPOOL		14	D	1-1	0-0	Herd 68	Gregg	Brennan	Cantwell	**Crerand**	Foulkes	Setters	Giles	Quixall	Herd	Chisnall	Charlton
	23/2		43,121	*19*	22			*Charnley 72p*	*Waiters*	*Armfield*	*Martin*	*McPhee*	*Gratrix*	*Durie*	*Hill*	*Quinn*	*Napier*	*Charnley*	*Horne*
								Ref: J Carr	The weather relents for the first time in two months but the 6ft 4in blue track-suit bottomed Waiters keeps United at bay and saves a Quixall penalty. New-boy Pat Crerand looks a good buy as he prompts classy United's attacks but Law is sorely missed. The fixture backlog is huge.										
25	A	BLACKBURN		13	D	2-2	1-0	Law 25, Charlton 75	Gregg	Brennan	Cantwell	Crerand	Foulkes	Setters	Giles	Quixall	Herd	Law	Charlton
	2/3		*27,924*	*14*	23			*Byrom 60, Pickering 65*	*Else*	*Bray*	*Newton*	*Clayton*	*Woods*	*McGrath*	*Ferguson*	*Douglas*	*Pickering*	*Byrom*	*Harrison*
								Ref: K Stokes	The pitch is not fully thawed and defenders struggle with their footing. Law, back in the team, scores when Else boobs. United fail to capitalise on their superiority and are made to pay. Quixall's poor pass-back lets in Fred Pickering before Bobby rescues the point from Crerand's pass.										
26	H	TOTTENHAM		14	L	0-2	0-1		Gregg	Brennan	Cantwell	Crerand	Foulkes	Stiles	Giles	Quixall	Herd	Law	Charlton
	9/3		53,416	1	23			*Jones 32, Saul 65*	*Brown*	*Hopkins*	*Henry*	*Marchi*	*Norman*	*Mackay*	*Saul*	*White*	*Smith*	*Greaves*	*Jones*
								Ref: P Baldwin	Leaders Spurs, unbeaten in seven, are lucky to beat the Reds, who miss at least eight good chances. Charlton and Herd are the worst culprits. Jones heads in from 18 yards with Gregg stranded, and Frank Saul is ideally placed to slot home Greaves' cross to cap a strong team display.										
27	A	WEST HAM		15	L	1-3	0-1	Herd 76	Gregg	Brennan	Cantwell	Crerand	Foulkes	Setters	Giles	Stiles	Herd	Law	Charlton
	18/3		*28,950*	*11*	23			*Brown 36, Sealey 78, Brennan 89(og)*	*Rhodes*	*Kirkup*	*Burkett*	*Bovington*	*Brown*	*Moore*	*Brabrook*	*Boyce*	*Sealey*	*Hurst*	*Scott*
								Ref: A Moore	Hammers' first home win in five months. Ken Brown bundles in Alan Sealey's free-kick. David Herd hits the bar before heading the equaliser but Eddie Bovington then passes over Foulkes' head for Sealey to restore the lead. After six games in seventeen days, the Reds look weary.										
28	H	IPSWICH		18	L	0-1	0-1		Gregg	Brennan	Cantwell	Crerand	Foulkes	Setters	Giles	Quixall	Herd	Law	Charlton
	23/3		32,798	*20*	23			*Leadbetter 31*	*Bailey*	*Carberry*	*Compton*	*Baxter*	*Nelson*	*Elsworthy*	*Stephenson*	*Blackwood*	*Crawford*	*Phillips*	*Leadbetter*
								Ref: R Windle	Despite Cup success, United are given the slow handclap during a dire display. Ipswich, under new boss Jackie Milburn, get their first win for three months and increase pressure on United. Leadbetter, nicknamed 'Steptoe', scores from Crawford's header and Town pack their defence.										
29	H	FULHAM		17	L	0-2	0-1		Gregg	Brennan	Dunne	Crerand	Foulkes	Setters	Giles	Chisnall	Quixall	Law	Charlton
	1/4		28,124	*10*	23			*O'Connell 12, Leggat 79*	*Macedo*	*Cohen*	*Langley*	*Mullery*	*Keetch*	*Robson*	*Key*	*Leggat*	*Cook*	*Brown S*	*O'Connell*
								Ref: W Downey	Seven straight wins have pulled Fulham out of certain relegation and United are tired after their tough game at Coventry. Tony Macedo stems the early Red tide and Graham Leggat's 25-yarder seals a famous first ever win at the ground to increase the relegation pressure on the Reds.										
30	A	ASTON VILLA		18	W	2-1	1-0	Stiles 25, Charlton 60	Gregg	Brennan	Cantwell	Crerand	Foulkes	Setters	Giles	Stiles	Herd	Quixall	Charlton
	9/4		*26,895*	*11*	25			*Thomson 75*	*Gavan*	*Fraser*	*Aitken*	*Crowe*	*Sleeuwenh'k*	*Tindall*	*Baker*	*Thomson*	*Dougan*	*Woosnam*	*Burrows*
								Ref: J Finney	The first league win since Boxing Day relieves some relegation nerves but only after a late barrage. Bobby Charlton, poor for England against Scotland last week, has a storming game and his goal is impossible to see, let alone stop. Villa's season is drifting after five defeats in a row.										
31	A	LIVERPOOL		19	L	0-1	0-0		Gregg	Brennan	Dunne	Crerand	Foulkes	Setters	Giles	Stiles	Quixall	Law	Charlton
	13/4		*51,529*	*6*	25			*St John 72*	*Lawrence*	*Jones*	*Moran*	*Milne*	*Yeats*	*Stevenson*	*Callaghan*	*Hunt*	*St John*	*Arrowsmith*	*Melia*
								Ref: H Hackney	Liverpool have lost one in 23 games and are potential Cup final rivals. Jimmy Melia, newly capped by England, is in superb form but Pool waste chances. There is no love lost – Nobby Stiles gives two fingers to the Kop and Scotland team-mates Law and Ian St John have fisticuffs.										

No	Venue	Opponent / Date	Att	Pos	Res	FT	HT	Scorers, Times, and Referees	1	2	3	4	5	6	7	8	9	10	11
32	H	LEICESTER		19	D	2-2	1-0	Herd 16, Charlton 62	Gregg	Brennan	Dunne	Crerand	Foulkes	Setters	Quixall	Stiles	Herd	Law	Charlton
		15/4	49,973	*2*	26			*Cross 53, Norman 64*	*Banks*	*Sjoberg*	*Norman*	*McLintock*	*King*	*Appleton*	*Riley*	*Cross*	*Keyworth*	*Gibson*	*Cheesebrough*
								Ref: R Harper	Leicester's renowned blanket defence is breached as Herd's shot deflects off Sjoberg and more goals look likely, with United on top. The visitors' title challenge is no fluke and they come back and deserve a draw. Quixall touches a free-kick to Charlton, who nets from 20 yards.										
33	A	LEICESTER		19	L	3-4	1-1	Law 31, 52, 69	Gregg	Brennan	Dunne	Crerand	Foulkes	Setters	Quixall	Stiles	Herd	Law	Charlton
		16/4	*37,002*	*1*	26			*Heath 30, Keyworth 50, 54, 55*	*Banks*	*Sjoberg*	*Norman*	*Cross*	*King*	*Appleton*	*Riley*	*Heath*	*Keyworth*	*McLintock*	*Cheesebrough*
								Ref: A Moore	The gates are locked with thousands outside. Leicester go top and the double is a possibility. United boss a nervous City until Ken Keyworth scores three identical headers from Riley crosses. Law completes his hat-trick with a magical overhead kick, but City keep their heads in front.										
34	H	SHEFFIELD UTD		20	D	1-1	0-1	Law 81	Gregg	Brennan	Dunne	Crerand	Foulkes	Setters	Quixall	Stiles	Herd	Law	Charlton
		20/4	31,179	*9*	27			*Hartle 12*	*Hodgkinson*	*Coldwell*	*Shaw G*	*Richardson*	*Shaw J*	*Summers*	*Allchurch*	*Wagstaff*	*Pace*	*Jones*	*Hartle*
								Ref: W Handley	Law's late diving header is vital as Man City and Ipswich win away to close the gap. Charlton misses a penalty and the fitful Reds are lucky to be still in the game. The defence is jittery, especially Gregg and Brennan and 17-year-old debutant Mick Jones causes havoc. Stiles alone stars.										
35	H	WOLVES		18	W	2-1	2-1	Herd 5, Law 40	Gaskell	Brennan	Dunne	Crerand	Foulkes	Setters	Quixall	Stiles	Herd	Law	Charlton
		22/4	36,147	*4*	29			*Dunne 25 (og)*	*Davies*	*Showell*	*Thomson*	*Kirkham*	*Woodfield*	*Goodwin*	*Crowe*	*Murray*	*Stobart*	*Broadbent*	*Wharton*
								Ref: R Tinkler	Despite having one eye on next week's semi final, United end Wolves' seven-game run and their slim title hopes. It's the Reds' best display for weeks with Herd heading in Quixall's cross and Law ending a delightful move. Tony Dunne can't avoid heading in Goodwin's free-kick.										
36	H	SHEFFIELD WED		19	L	1-3	0-3	Setters 83	Gaskell	Brennan	Cantwell	Crerand	Foulkes	Setters	Quixall	Stiles	Herd	Law	Charlton
		1/5	31,875	*7*	29			*Finney 25, Quinn 30, Megson 38*	*Springett*	*Johnson*	*Megson*	*McAnearney*	*Swan*	*Young*	*Finney*	*Quinn*	*Layne*	*Fantham*	*Dobson*
								Ref: K Howley	The semi-final win is forgotten as a workmanlike Wednesday coast to a victory. Giles is surprisingly dropped and Colin Dobson creates the first two goals, a header and a tap-in. Megson's 25-yarder dips under the bar before Setters' late header. England-reject Peter Swan is a giant.										
37	A	BURNLEY		18	W	1-0	0-0	Law 69	Gaskell	Dunne	Cantwell	Crerand	Foulkes	Setters	Giles	Stiles	Quixall	Law	Charlton
		4/5	*30,266*	*5*	31				*Blacklaw*	*Angus*	*Elder*	*O'Neill*	*Talbut*	*Miller*	*Connelly*	*Robson*	*Lochhead*	*Simpson*	*Harris*
								Ref: E Crawford	A shock win for the Reds as, after a tentative start, they look like a team for the first time in weeks. Simpson's shot rattles the bar but United survive and Law heads in Albert Quixall's cross for the points. Andy Lochead and Bill Foulkes get too physical and almost get sent off.										
38	H	ARSENAL		18	L	2-3	0-1	Law 54, 63	Gaskell	Dunne	Cantwell	Crerand	Foulkes	Setters	Giles	Stiles	Quixall	Law	Charlton
		6/5	35,999	*8*	31			*Baker 32, Strong 50, Skirton 62*	*McClelland*	*Magill*	*Clarke*	*Barnwell*	*Brown*	*McCullough*	*MacLeod*	*Strong*	*Baker*	*Sammels*	*Skirton*
								Ref: T Reynolds	Billy Wright in his first season in charge at Highbury has had a fair season. Joe Baker in his first season back from Italy scores his 26th goal of the season but a draw would have been fairer. Law has a third goal ruled offside. Maurice Setters twists an ankle and is doubtful for Wembley.										
39	A	BIRMINGHAM		19	L	1-2	0-1	Law 76	Gaskell	Dunne	Cantwell	Crerand	Foulkes	Stiles	Quixall	Giles	Herd	Law	Charlton
		10/5	*21,855*	*20*	31			*Bloomfield 22, Leek 75*	*Withers*	*Lynn*	*Green*	*Hennessey*	*Smith*	*Beard*	*Hellawell*	*Bloomfield*	*Harris*	*Leek*	*Auld*
								Ref: L Callaghan	Birmingham's relegation revival continues on a miserably wet Friday night and United are slipping too close to the drop zone for comfort. Inspired by the transfer listed Jimmy Bloomfield Blues deserve the win. United are disjointed and cut up rough in a tension-ridden second half.										
40	A	MANCHESTER C		18	D	1-1	0-1	Quixall 84p	Gaskell	Dunne	Cantwell	Crerand	Foulkes	Stiles	Quixall	Giles	Herd	Law	Charlton
		15/5	*52,452*	*21*	32			*Harley 8*	*Dowd*	*Kennedy*	*Sear*	*Oakes*	*Leivers*	*Gray*	*Young*	*Dobing*	*Harley*	*Hayes*	*Wagstaffe*
								Ref: G McCabe	The locked gates are broken down at the biggest derby game since the war and many see the game for nothing. Both teams are desperate for points and City are set to win until David Wagstaff's back-pass puts Dowd in trouble. Law falls for a doubtful penalty and City look doomed.										
41	H	LEYTON ORIENT		18	W	3-1	0-1	Charl' S 52 (og), Law 81, Charl' R 85	Gaskell	Dunne	Cantwell	Crerand	Foulkes	Setters	Quixall	Giles	Herd	Law	Charlton
		18/5	32,759	*22*	34			*Dunmore 9*	*George*	*Charlton S*	*Taylor*	*Lucas*	*Bishop*	*Lee*	*Mason*	*Gibbs*	*Dunmore*	*Bolland*	*Musgrove*
								Ref: H Horner	Johnny Carey's Orient's one season of glory is over – they are already relegated – but give sloppy United a shock. The fans jeer the Reds, who rely on Stan Charlton's diving header from Bobby's cross. Late goals breach Orient's tight defence and United are safe from relegation.										
42	A	NOTT'M FOREST		19	L	2-3	1-1	Giles 2, Herd 50	Gaskell	Dunne	Cantwell	Crerand	Haydock	Brennan	Quixall	Stiles	Herd	Giles	**Walker**
		20/5	***16,130***	*9*	34			*Addison 39, Mochan 65, Julians 80*	*Grummitt*	*Baird*	*Mochan*	*Whitefoot*	*McKinlay*	*Winfield*	*Hockey*	*Addison*	*Julians*	*Quigley*	*Le Flem*
		Home / Average 40,329	Away / 35,251					Ref: J Carr	United rest key players five days before the final and deservedly lead twice. Forest, unbeaten in six games, roar back to claim the points. Len Julians' winner comes after Gaskell's feeble punch. Frank Haydock and Dennis Walker look promising. Injured Stiles will miss the Cup final.										

FA Cup					F-A	H-T	Scorers, Times, and Referees	1	2	3	4	5	6	7	8	9	10	11
3	H	HUDDERSFIELD	13	W	5-0	4-0	Quixall 3, Law 11, 32, 88, Giles 20	Gregg	Brennan	Cantwell	Stiles	Foulkes	Setters	Giles	Quixall	Herd	Law	Charlton
	4/3	47,703	*2:9*					*Wood*	*Atkins*	*Parker*	*Bettany*	*Taylor*	*Dinsdale*	*McHale*	*White*	*Stokes*	*Massie*	*O'Grady*
							Ref: K Howley	United's Cup campaign gets under way two months late because of the big freeze. Huddersfield are eliminated in a one-sided massacre and ex-Red Ray Wood is put through the mill. The impudent Law is too quick for his former team, who miss their injured England full-back Wilson.										
4	H	ASTON VILLA	14	W	1-0	1-0	Quixall 36	Gregg	Brennan	Cantwell	Stiles	Foulkes	Setters	Giles	Quixall	Herd	Law	Charlton
	11/3	52,265	*7*					*Sidebottom*	*Fraser*	*Aitken*	*Tindall*	*Crowe*	*Deakin*	*MacEwan*	*Wylie*	*Thomson*	*Woosnam*	*Burrows*
							Ref: A Sparling	The games are coming thick and fast as the backlog of games is cleared. Pat Crerand is ineligible and Setters and Ron Wylie mix it in midfield. Quixall's shot goes under a despairing Sidebottom and a far from impressive United survive Villa's powder-puff late assaults to go through.										
5	H	CHELSEA	15	W	2-1	1-0	Law 17, Quixall 46	Gregg	Brennan	Cantwell	Stiles	Foulkes	Setters	Giles	Quixall	Herd	Law	Charlton
	16/3	48,298	*2:1*				*Sorrell 69*	*Bonetti*	*Shellito*	*McCreadie*	*Venables*	*Mortimore*	*Upton*	*Murray*	*Tambling*	*Moore*	*Sorrell*	*Blunstone*
							Ref: L Callaghan	The third FA Cup-tie in less than a fortnight and the Reds are unconvincing against Tommy Docherty's Blues. Law bundles in Quixall's cross before Bonetti becomes the hero and villain. He misreads Albert's shot but then keeps Chelsea alive with several saves before Sorrell's tap-in.										
QF	A	COVENTRY	17	W	3-1	1-1	Charlton 27, 49, Quixall 72	Gregg	Brennan	Dunne	Crerand	Foulkes	Setters	Giles	Quixall	Herd	Law	Charlton
	30/3	*44,000*	*3:4*				*Bly 5*	*Wesson*	*Sillett*	*Kearns*	*Hill*	*Curtis*	*Bruck*	*Humphries*	*Barr*	*Bly*	*Whitehouse*	*Rees*
							Ref: E Crawford	Jimmy Hill has started the Sky Blue revolution and his Third Division team give United a fright on a sand and sawdust surface. Charlton is at his best and scores two stunners before a Bruck and Wesson mix-up ends their 23-game unbeaten run. City never give up and Bly hits the bar.										
SF	N	SOUTHAMPTON	19	W	1-0	1-0	Law 22	Gaskell	Dunne	Cantwell	Crerand	Foulkes	Setters	Giles	Stiles	Herd	Law	Charlton
	27/4	*68,312*	*2:16*					*Reynolds*	*Williams*	*Traynor*	*Wimshurst*	*Knapp*	*Huxford*	*Paine*	*O'Brien*	*Kirby*	*Burnside*	*Sydenham*
		(at Villa Park)					Ref: G McCabe	The Saints have beaten Div 1 Forest and Sheff U but lose a featureless game to a scrappy goal. Defences are on top in a grim, hard match. Law misses Herd's cross with his head but scrambles the ball in. O'Brien goes close near the end but Ted Bates' unadventurous side deserve little.										
F	N	LEICESTER	19	W	3-1	1-0	Law 29, Herd 57, 85	Gaskell	Dunne	Cantwell	Crerand	Foulkes	Setters	Giles	Quixall	Herd	Law	Charlton
	25/5	*100,000*	*4*				*Keyworth 80*	*Banks*	*Sjoberg*	*Norman*	*McLintock*	*King*	*Appleton*	*Riley*	*Cross*	*Keyworth*	*Gibson*	*Stringfellow*
		(at Wembley)					Ref: K Aston	United deservedly win their first Wembley final since 1948 in what is a shock result. Off-colour Leicester are three time losers. Law scores an opportunistic first then Banks fails to hold Charlton's shot and Herd nets. Unusually Banks drops a cross for No.3. Crerand and Law are super.										

	P	W	D	L	F	A	W	D	L	F	A	Pts
		Home					Away					
1 Everton	42	14	7	0	48	17	11	4	6	36	25	61
2 Tottenham	42	14	6	1	72	28	9	3	9	39	34	55
3 Burnley	42	14	4	3	41	17	8	6	7	37	40	54
4 Leicester	42	14	6	1	53	23	6	6	9	26	30	52
5 Wolves	42	11	6	4	51	25	9	4	8	42	40	50
6 Sheffield Wed	42	10	5	6	38	26	9	5	7	39	37	48
7 Arsenal	42	11	4	6	44	33	7	6	8	42	44	46
8 Liverpool	42	13	3	5	45	22	4	7	10	26	37	44
9 Nott'm Forest	42	12	4	5	39	28	5	6	10	28	41	44
10 Sheffield Utd	42	11	7	3	33	20	5	5	11	25	40	44
11 Blackburn	42	11	4	6	55	34	4	8	9	24	37	42
12 West Ham	42	8	6	7	39	34	6	6	9	34	35	40
13 Blackpool	42	8	7	6	34	27	5	7	9	24	37	40
14 West Brom	42	11	1	9	40	37	5	6	10	31	42	39
15 Aston Villa	42	12	2	7	38	23	3	6	12	24	45	38
16 Fulham	42	8	6	7	28	30	6	4	11	22	41	38
17 Ipswich	42	5	8	8	34	39	7	3	11	25	39	35
18 Bolton	42	13	3	5	35	18	2	2	17	20	57	35
19 MAN UNITED	42	6	6	9	36	38	6	4	11	31	43	34
20 Birmingham	42	6	8	7	40	40	4	5	12	23	50	33
21 Manchester C	42	7	5	9	30	45	3	6	12	28	57	31
22 Leyton Orient	42	4	5	12	22	37	2	4	15	15	44	21
	924	223	113	126	895	641	126	113	223	641	895	924

Odds & ends

Double wins: (1) Arsenal.
Double losses: (3) Everton, Tottenham, Sheff Wed.

Won from behind: (3) Wolves (a), Leyton O (h), Coventry FAC (a).
Lost from in front: (1) Nottm Forest (a).

High spots: FA Cup victory.
7-game unbeaten run in November-December.
Excellent form of Law and Stiles.

Low spots: Worst league finish since 1937.
Nine home defeats – equalling the worst ever.
Woeful start to the season, culminating in 2-6 thrashing at Spurs.

Red cards (United): (0).
Red cards (Opponents): (0).
Ever-presents: (0).
Hat-tricks: (3) Law (3).
Opposing hat-tricks: (3) Connelly (Burnley), Greaves (Tottenham), and Keyworth (Leicester).
Leading Scorer: Law (29).

	Appearances Lge	Appearances FAC	Goals Lge	Goals FAC	Tot
Brennan, Shay	37	4			
Cantwell, Noel	25	5	1		1
Charlton, Bobby	28	6	7	2	9
Chisnall, Phil	6		1		1
Crerand, Pat	19	3			
Dunne, Tony	25	3			
Foulkes, Bill	41	6			
Gaskell, Dave	18	2			
Giles, Johnny	36	6	4	1	5
Gregg, Harry	24	4			
Haydock, Frank	1				
Herd, David	37	6	19	2	21
Law, Dennis	38	6	23	6	29
Lawton, Nobby	12				
McMillan, Sammy	4				
Moir, Ian	9		1		1
Nicholson, Jimmy	10				
Pearson, Mark	2				
Quixall, Albert	31	5	7	4	11
Setters, Maurice	27	6	1		1
Stiles, Nobby	31	4	2		2
Walker, Dennis	1				
(own-goals)			1		1
	462	**66**	**67**	**15**	**82**

No	Date		Att	Pos	Pt	F-A	H-T	Scorers, Times, and Referees	1	2	3	4	5	6	7	8	9	10	11
1	A	SHEFFIELD WED			D	3-3	1-2	Moir 38, Charlton 52, 78	Gregg	Dunne	Cantwell	Crerand	Foulkes	Setters	Moir	Chisnall	**Sadler**	Law	Charlton
	24/8		*34,035*		1			*Quinn 10, McAnear' 26p, Holliday 65*	*Springett*	*Johnson*	*Megson*	*McAnearney*	*Swan*	*Young*	*Finney*	*Quinn*	*Ellis*	*Fantham*	*Holliday*
								Ref: K Burns	A battling comeback gains United's first point at Hillsborough since 1954. 17-year-old Sadler plays after one reserve game and Moir atones for conceding a penalty with a goal. Law is booked and booed for fouling Megson. Giles, Herd and Quixall dropped after Charity Shield debacle.										
2	H	IPSWICH			W	2-0	0-0	Law 56, 83	Gregg	Dunne	Cantwell	Crerand	Foulkes	Setters	Moir	Chisnall	Sadler	Law	Charlton
	28/8		39,921		3				*Bailey*	*Bolton*	*Compton*	*Baxter*	*Nelson*	*Elsworthy*	*Stephenson*	*Moran*	*Crawford*	*Phillips*	*Blackwood*
								Ref: V James	Ipswich's defensive tactics thwart a lively United. Gregg saves Phillips' penalty, his first miss in three years, after Setters' handball. Law takes over and his quick thinking wins the game. Ipswich are lucky to not lose more heavily. Giles set to join Leeds. Quixall also wants a transfer.										
3	H	EVERTON		2	W	5-1	2-1	Chisnall 25, 32, Sadler 52, Law 70, 80	Gregg	Dunne	Cantwell	Crerand	Foulkes	Stiles	Moir	Chisnall	Sadler	Law	Charlton
	31/8		**63,206**	*14*	5			*Vernon 8*	*West*	*Parker*	*Meagan*	*Gabriel*	*Labone*	*Kay*	*Scott*	*Stevens*	*Young*	*Vernon*	*Temple*
								Ref: K Howley	United defy their critics with a comprehensive revenge over Everton for the Charity Shield. Charlton and Law are on top form and the injured Setters is not missed. They mimic Everton by playing keep-ball at the end and Law scores almost at will. Tony Dunne claims Vernon's goal.										
4	A	IPSWICH		1	W	**7-2**	3-0	Sadler 4, Law 35, 62p, 84, Setters 40,	Gregg	Dunne	Cantwell	Crerand	Foulkes	Setters	Moir	Chisnall	Sadler	Law	Charlton
	3/9		*28,113*	*14*	7			*Moran 47, 86* [Moir 59, Chisnall 67]	*Bailey*	*Bolton*	*Compton*	*Baxter*	*Nelson*	*Elsworthy*	*Stephenson*	*Moran*	*Crawford*	*Phillips*	*Blackwood*
								Ref: P Bye	No contest, as United notch their biggest away win since 1937. Battered Ipswich look like relegation certs and boss Milburn tips United for the title. Gregg again saves Phillips' spot-kick but otherwise the Reds are irrepressible. Law makes it successive hat-tricks at Portman Road.										
5	A	BIRMINGHAM		1	D	1-1	1-0	Chisnall 5	Gregg	Dunne	Cantwell	Crerand	Foulkes	Setters	Moir	Chisnall	Sadler	Law	Charlton
	7/9		*36,874*	*15*	8			*Harley 78*	*Withers*	*Lynn*	*Green*	*Hennessey*	*Smith*	*Beard*	*Hellawell*	*Bloomfield*	*Harley*	*Leek*	*Auld*
								Ref: D Roper	Chisnall's deflected shot is all United have for their first-half domination, thanks to Withers' super saves. Blues come back after the break and the expensive Harley nets his first goal. Charlton beats Lynn with ease but can't deliver a final ball. Cantwell is booked again and faces action.										
6	H	BLACKPOOL		1	W	3-0	1-0	Law 44, Charlton 62, 78	Gregg	Dunne	Cantwell	Crerand	Foulkes	Setters	Moir	Chisnall	Sadler	Law	Charlton
	11/9		47,363	*21*	10				*Waiters*	*Armfield*	*Martin*	*Green*	*Gratrix*	*Durie*	*Lea*	*Quinn*	*Charnley*	*McPhee*	*Parry*
								Ref: M Fussey	Tony Waiters fights a one-man battle against United's pulsating attack and saves struggling Pool from a cricket score. The Reds are in form and Law is unlucky not to score more. Bobby scores one with his left foot and the second when Waiters makes his only mistake, with his right.										
7	H	WEST BROM		1	W	1-0	0-0	Sadler 64	Gregg	Dunne	Cantwell	Crerand	Foulkes	Setters	**Best**	Stiles	Sadler	Chisnall	Charlton
	14/9		51,624	*2*	12				*Potter*	*Crawford*	*Williams G*	*Howe*	*Jones*	*Simpson*	*Foggo*	*Cram*	*Readfern*	*Fenton*	*Clark*
								Ref: G Grundy	Jimmy Hagan's Albion's 4-game winning sequence has put them up with the leaders, which flatters them. Injured Law is missed and Sadler's left-foot drive is the winner. 17-year-old George Best gets his chance after three reserve games and shines despite ankle-taps from Williams.										
8	A	BLACKPOOL		1	L	0-1	0-1		Gregg	Dunne	Cantwell	Crerand	Foulkes	Setters	Moir	Stiles	Sadler	Chisnall	Charlton
	16/9		*29,806*	*21*	12			*Charnley 30*	*Harvey*	*Armfield*	*Martin*	*Crawford*	*Gratrix*	*Cranston*	*Horne*	*Ball*	*Charnley*	*Quinn*	*Oates*
								Ref: H Hackney	Blackpool follow up a win at Anfield with a fine result after introducing six kids. Their waspish style harries United into errors and Charnley's close-range goal created by Ball and Oates is deserved. Setters is pushed forward to little effect as the attack fails. Waiters has a broken finger.										
9	A	ARSENAL		2	L	1-2	1-1	Herd 17	Gregg	Dunne	Cantwell	Crerand	Foulkes	Setters	Herd	Chisnall	Sadler	Law	Charlton
	21/9		***56,826***	*8*	12			*Eastham 25p, Baker 81*	*McKechnie*	*Magill*	*McCullough*	*Brown*	*Ure*	*Groves*	*MacLeod*	*Strong*	*Baker*	*Eastham*	*Armstrong*
								Ref: J Finney	Billy Wright's team notch a fourth straight win but only after controversy. McKechnie punches Charlton's corner into his own net and the ball bounces out, but the ref is unsighted and waves play on. Joe Baker's stunning volley decides the rip-roaring game with Denis Law in top form.										
10	H	LEICESTER		1	W	3-1	3-0	Setters 23, Herd 26, 29	Gregg	Dunne	Cantwell	Crerand	Foulkes	Setters	Moir	Chisnall	Sadler	Herd	Charlton
	28/9		41,873	*11*	14			*Gibson 75*	*Banks*	*Sjoberg*	*Norman*	*McLintock*	*King*	*Roberts*	*Riley*	*Cross*	*Keyworth*	*Gibson*	*Hodgson*
								Ref: A Luty	The recalled Herd is in top form for watching Scottish boss McColl, and the injured Law is barely missed. United ease up after an exciting first half, but Leicester rarely trouble them. Bobby Roberts has a fine debut but McLintock ends limping. Setters, Dunne and Cantwell impressive.										

No	Venue	Opponent	Att / Pos	Res	F-A	H-T	Scorers, Ref	1	2	3	4	5	6	7	8	9	10	11
11	A	CHELSEA	1	D	1-1	1-0	Setters 15	Gregg	Dunne	Cantwell	Crerand	Foulkes	Setters	Moir	Chisnall	Sadler	Herd	Charlton
	2/10		*45,351* *17* 15				*Brown 70*	*Bonetti*	*Harris A*	*McCreadie*	*Venables*	*Mortimore*	*Harris R*	*Brown*	*Tambling*	*Bridges*	*Moore*	*Blunstone*
							Ref: L Callaghan	Dennis 'Bullets' Brown heads a dream debut goal to give Chelsea a deserved point. The defence has to be in top form, as Tommy Docherty's newly promoted team pile on the pressure. Gregg saves well from Graham Moore and Tambling misses two gifts. The attack is off-colour.										
12	A	BOLTON	1	W	1-0	0-0	Herd 82	Gregg	Dunne	Cantwell	Crerand	Foulkes	Setters	Herd	Chisnall	Sadler	Stiles	Charlton
	5/10		*36,183* *21* 17					*Smith*	*Hartle*	*Hatton*	*Rimmer*	*Hulme*	*Lennard*	*Birch*	*Lee*	*Davies*	*Taylor*	*Butler*
							Ref: J Carr	Bill Ridding's fledgling side is struggling but deserve a point after foiling the Reds for long periods. Wyn Davies and Setters are booked in a stormy first half before Charlton's burst of speed sets up the first win at Bolton since 1949. Harry Gregg is recalled by Ireland after two years.										
13	A	NOTT'M FOREST	1	W	2-1	1-1	Chisnall 7, Quixall 70	Gregg	Dunne	Cantwell	Crerand	Foulkes	Setters	Quixall	Chisnall	Herd	Law	Charlton
	19/10		*41,426* *7* 19				*Wignall 22*	*Grummitt*	*Wilson J*	*Mochan*	*Whitefoot*	*McKinlay*	*Winfield*	*Hockey*	*Addison*	*Wignall*	*Quigley*	*Le Flem*
							Ref: J Cooke	Carey is new boss at Forest but United are first winners at the City Ground since the opening day. Forest have more of the play but Quixall's lucky goal decides the game. The Reds get stuck in traffic and arrive ten minutes before the kick-off. Two points separate the top ten sides.										
14	H	WEST HAM	2	L	0-1	0-1		Gregg	Dunne	Cantwell	Crerand	Foulkes	Setters	Moir	Chisnall	Herd	Law	Charlton
	26/10		46,333 *13* 19				*Britt 36*	*Standen*	*Bond*	*Burkett*	*Peters*	*Brown*	*Moore*	*Sealey*	*Boyce*	*Britt*	*Hurst*	*Brabrook*
							Ref: J Thacker	United are welcomed onto the pitch by the majorettes but are knocked off the top of the table and lose their 100% home record to Martin Britt's goal. Hurst hits the bar, but the ball bounces into Gregg's arms. Sealey is injured as West Ham finish with ten men and under the cosh.										
15	H	BLACKBURN	2	D	2-2	2-1	Quixall 5, 44	Gregg	Dunne	Cantwell	Crerand	Foulkes	Stiles	Moir	Chisnall	Quixall	Law	Charlton
	28/10		41,436 *8* 20				*Harrison 4, McEvoy 90*	*Else*	*Bray*	*Newton*	*Clayton*	*England*	*McGrath*	*Ferguson*	*McEvoy*	*Pickering*	*Douglas*	*Harrison*
							Ref: A Sparling	Enigmatic Rovers grab a late undeserved point after United take their foot off the pedal in an excellent game. Herd is dropped again and Setters injured. Law is matched for skill by Bryan Douglas. Quixall, back in favour, knows little about the second goal that rebounds off his head.										
16	A	WOLVERHAMPTON	3	L	0-2	0-0		Gregg	Dunne	Cantwell	Crerand	Foulkes	Setters	Moir	Chisnall	Quixall	Law	Charlton
	2/11		*34,159* *14* 20				*Wharton 49, Crawford 58*	*Davies*	*Showell*	*Thomson*	*Goodwin*	*Woodfield*	*Flowers*	*Wharton*	*Knowles*	*Crawford*	*Broadbent*	*Hinton*
							Ref: S Stoakes	Wolves have recovered from a dire start and are unbeaten in eight. Crawford, a big signing from Ipswich causes the damage whilst 18-year-old Peter Knowles looks a star in the making. The attack threatens but can't deliver and Busby will sign Chelsea's Graham Moore to bolster things.										
17	H	TOTTENHAM	3	W	4-1	1-0	Law 42, 80, 85, Herd 56	Gregg	Dunne	Cantwell	Crerand	Foulkes	Setters	Quixall	**Moore**	Herd	Law	Charlton
	9/11		57,513 *5* 22				*Gregg 72 (og)*	*Brown*	*Baker*	*Henry*	*Blanchflower*	*Norman*	*Mackay*	*Jones*	*White*	*Smith*	*Greaves*	*Dyson*
							Ref: G McCabe	The double side is showing signs of strain but they are still scoring goals for fun and have 47 in 16 games. Blanchflower's two errors signal the end of his career. Law returns from scoring four for Scotland and nets three after the Reds miss eleven good chances before the first goal.										
18	A	ASTON VILLA	6	L	0-4	0-2		Gregg	Dunne	Cantwell	Crerand	Foulkes	Setters	Quixall	Moore	Herd	Law!	Charlton
	16/11		*36,276* *18* 22				*Hateley 1,48, Deakin 17, Burrows 89*	*Sidebottom*	*Wright*	*Aitken*	*Deakin*	*Sleeuwenh'k*	*Pountney*	*MacEwan*	*Ewing*	*Hateley*	*Wylie*	*Burrows*
							Ref: J Carr	Tony Hateley's 35-second goal sets Villa on the way to their biggest win over Man U since 1930. Deakin's 35-yard shot for No 2 is sublime. Law's dismissal for striking Deakin after 33 mins sparks crowd trouble. Hateley exposes Foulkes in the air as an abysmal defence collapses.										
19	H	LIVERPOOL	8	L	0-1	0-0		Gregg	Dunne	Cantwell	Crerand	Foulkes	Setters	Quixall	Moore	Herd	Law	Charlton
	23/11		54,884 *1* 22				*Yeats 75*	*Lawrence*	*Ferns*	*Moran*	*Milne*	*Yeats*	*Stevenson*	*Callaghan*	*Hunt*	*St John*	*Melia*	*Thompson*
							Ref: E Jennings	Superb defences are on top in a gripping game as Shankley's men hit the top. Gregg's collar-bone is broken in a clash with the physical Ron Yeats and the Scottish defender thunders a header past stand-in keeper Herd to help Pool to win at Old Trafford for the first time since 1936.										
20	A	SHEFFIELD UTD	5	W	2-1	1-0	Law 19, 70	Gaskell	Dunne	Cantwell	Crerand	Foulkes	Setters	Quixall	Moore	Herd	Law	Charlton
	30/11		*30,615* *6* 24				*Docherty 81p*	*Thompson*	*Coldwell*	*Shaw B*	*Richardson*	*Shaw J*	*Summers*	*Docherty*	*Allchurch*	*Pace*	*Wagstaff*	*Simpson*
							Ref: W Gow	With Gregg injured, Gaskell plays with a strapped wrist but his defence protect him. Law is on best behaviour, awaiting his trial, but is deadly in the box. Setters fouls Len Allchurch to concede another penalty. Blades' injury crisis means keeper Des Thompson is on loan from Buxton.										
21	H	STOKE	4	W	5-2	2-0	Herd 4, Law 8, 76, 78, 88	Gaskell	Dunne	Cantwell	Crerand	Foulkes	Setters	Quixall	Moore	Herd	Law	Charlton
	7/12		52,530 *17* 26				*Ritchie 60, Dobing 85*	*Leslie*	*Skeels*	*Allen*	*Kinnell*	*Stuart*	*Palmer*	*Matthews*	*Viollet*	*Ritchie*	*Dobing*	*Bebbington*
							Ref: K Stokes	48-year-old Stan Matthews has led Stoke back to Div 1 after ten years away, but is overshadowed by Law, who starts a 28-day suspension on Monday and goes out with a bang. The ubiquitous Law gets a standing ovation from the crowd and Stoke's players after a wonderful display.										

No	Date		Att	Pos	Pt	F-A	H-T	Scorers, Times, and Referees	1	2	3	4	5	6	7	8	9	10	11
22	H	SHEFFIELD WED		5	W	3-1	2-0	Herd 28, 43,73	Gaskell	Brennan	Dunne	Crerand	Foulkes	Setters	Chisnall	Moore	Sadler	Herd	Charlton
	14/12		36,002	*9*	28			*Layne 77*	*McLaren*	*Hill*	*Megson*	*McAnearney*	*Swan*	*Young*	*Finney*	*Dobson*	*Layne*	*Pearson*	*Holliday*
								Ref: R Langdale	David Herd answers his critics with an emphatic hat-trick in a comfortable win. Owls suffer their first defeat in 9 games despite the presence of ex-Red Pearson who is warmly greeted. Crerand and Setters dominate midfield and provide Herd's ammunition. Nobby Stiles wants a transfer.										
23	A	EVERTON		5	L	0-4	0-0	*[Stevens 78]*	Gaskell	Dunne	Cantwell	Crerand	Foulkes	Setters	Moir	Moore	Sadler	Herd	Charlton
	21/12		*48,027*	*6*	28			*Temple 55, Vernon 61, Harris 65,*	*Rankin*	*Brown*	*Meagan*	*Gabriel*	*Heslop*	*Harris*	*Scott*	*Stevens*	*Young*	*Vernon*	*Temple*
								Ref: A Jobling	Bill Foulkes deserves better after a brave display in his 400th league game. The attack is poor and the defence does well to hold tight until after the break. Brave Setters, hobbling for most of the match, can do little to stem the Toffee-tide, for whom Stevens and Temple are sheer class.										
24	A	BURNLEY		6	L	**1-6**	1-2	Herd 30	Gaskell	Dunne	Cantwell	Crerand!	Foulkes	Setters	Quixall	Moore	Charlton	Herd	Brennan
	26/12		*35,766*	*7*	28			*Lochh'd 7, 42, 72, 85, Morgan 66, 82*	*Blacklaw*	*Angus*	*Elder*	*O'Neill*	*Talbut*	*Miller*	*Morgan*	*Pointer*	*Lochhead*	*Harris*	*Towers*
								Ref: M Fussey	A typical Turf Moor mudbath makes balance difficult for the Reds' woeful defence, but not Andy Lochhead, who is the first man to score four against them since the war. 18-year-old Willie Morgan fleeces Cantwell but Pat Crerand is dismissed for elbowing Towers in a clean game.										
25	H	BURNLEY		5	W	5-1	3-0	Herd 11, 70, Moore 25, 68, Best 38	Gaskell	Dunne	Cantwell	Crerand	Foulkes	Setters	**Anderson**	Moore	Charlton	Herd	Best
	28/12		48,035	*9*	30			*Lochhead 87*	*Blacklaw*	*Angus*	*Elder*	*O'Neill*	*Talbut*	*Miller*	*Morgan*	*Pointer*	*Lochhead*	*Robson*	*Price*
								Ref: G McCabe	Busby brings in the teenage wingers to gain revenge after a shaky opening. Setters and Crerand take control and Charlton excels in his new deep-lying role. Bobby's miskick lets in the precocious 17-year-old Best for his first goal, taken with cool aplomb. Foulkes shackles Lochhead.										
26	H	BIRMINGHAM		6	L	1-2	1-1	Sadler 29	Gaskell	Dunne	Cantwell	Crerand	Foulkes	Setters	Herd	Moore	Sadler	Law	Best
	11/1		44,919	18	30			*Harley 4, Bullock M 47*	*Withers*	*Lynn*	*Martin*	*Hennessey*	*Smith*	*Beard*	*Anderson*	*Harley*	*Bullock M*	*Thomson*	*Auld*
								Ref: G Grundy	Law returns from suspension and looks rusty as United struggle against solid Blues who record their second successive away win. The chances go begging as Gil Merrick's team hang on for a shock win. The game witnesses one of the first instances of crowd violence at Old Trafford.										
27	A	WEST BROM		6	W	4-1	1-1	Charlton 19, Best 49, Law 51, 89	Gaskell	Dunne	Cantwell	Crerand	Foulkes	Setters	Herd	Moore	Charlton	Law	Best
	18/1		***25,624***	*10*	32			*Simpson 40*	*Potter*	*Howe*	*Williams G*	*Fraser*	*Jones*	*Simpson*	*Clark*	*Fenton*	*Kaye*	*Fudge*	*Carter*
								Ref: G Davies	West Brom's seven-game run without defeat is smashed on a cold day. Don Howe wears gloves as the temperature drops but is bamboozled by Best, who dribbles in the second. Charlton ends his goal-drought by slamming in Herd's cross and Simpson's 35-yard equaliser raises the roof.										
28	H	ARSENAL		4	W	3-1	1-1	Herd 4, Setters 76, Law 82	Gaskell	Brennan	Dunne	Stiles	Foulkes	Setters	Herd	Moore	Charlton	Law	Best
	½		49,618	*7*	34			*McCullough 16*	*Furnell*	*Magill*	*McCullough*	*Groves*	*Ure*	*Snedden*	*Skirton*	*Strong*	*Baker*	*Eastham*	*Armstrong*
								Ref: A Holland	Arsenal look set for a well-earned point until a late flurry. With Cantwell suspended Law captains the side and sets up Herd. Billy McCullough breaks the offside trap to level. Foulkes blots out Joe Baker, and England man Eastham is out of sorts as United's title hopes are rejuvenated.										
29	A	LEICESTER		7	L	2-3	1-1	Law 2, Herd 77	Gaskell	Brennan	Dunne	Crerand	Foulkes	Setters	Herd	Moore	Charlton	Law	Best
	8/2		*35,538*	*9*	34			*Stringfellow 23, Hodgson 56, 68*	*Banks*	*Sjoberg*	*Norman*	*Cross*	*King*	*Appleton*	*Hodgson*	*Roberts*	*Keyworth*	*Gibson*	*Stringfellow*
								Ref: K Burns	Another Filbert Street thriller but six straight defeats at their bogey ground. Sloppy defending with Gaskell at fault for No 3, means they are chasing the game. Although always looking capable of scoring, time runs out. Charlton hits the bar and Best has one ruled out in a frantic end.										
30	H	BOLTON		4	W	5-0	2-0	Best 3, 72, Herd 7, 89, Charlton 80	Gaskell	Brennan	Dunne	Crerand	Foulkes	Setters	Herd	Stiles	Charlton	Law	Best
	19/2		33,426	*21*	36				*Hopkinson*	*Hartle*	*Farrimond*	*Stanley*	*Edwards*	*Lennard*	*Dawson*	*Lee*	*Deakin*	*Hill*	*Taylor*
								Ref: K Howley	Bolton are heading for the drop and are blooding young players. United show no mercy and are never troubled. Law even misses a penalty after the diminutive Best is brought down by the tormented Hartle. Charlton's is a 25-yard special. Wanderers' 29-year stay in Div 1 is ending.										
31	A	BLACKBURN		3	W	3-1	1-0	Chisnall 38, Law 69, 78	Gaskell	Brennan	Dunne	Crerand	Foulkes	Setters	Herd	Chisnall	Charlton	Law	Best
	22/2		*37,526*	*4*	38			*Pickering 67*	*Else*	*Bray*	*Sims*	*Clayton*	*England*	*McGrath*	*Ferguson*	*McEvoy*	*Pickering*	*Douglas*	*Harrison*
								Ref: J Taylor	Traffic chaos hits Blackburn as everyone wants to see Busby's team. Under-23 cap Chisnall is recalled and scores against the run of play. Pickering's equaliser wakes United up and Law strikes. The boy Best is devastating and leaves Bray shell-shocked. United are in the title race.										

No	Venue	Opponent	Att	Pos	Pts	Res	F-A	H-T	Scorers, Times, Referees	1	2	3	4	5	6	7	8	9	10	11
32	A	WEST HAM		5		W	2-0	0-0	Sadler 72, Herd 86	Gaskell	Brennan	Dunne	Crerand	**Tranter**	Stiles	Anderson	Chisnall	Sadler	Herd	Moir
	7/3		*27,177*	*14*	40					*Standen*	*Bond*	*Burkett*	*Bovington*	*Brown*	*Moore*	*Brabrook*	*Boyce*	*Byrne*	*Hurst*	*Sissons*
									Ref: W Clements	The teams warm up for the semi-final next week and West Ham are all at sea. A draw might have been fair but for John Bond's silly back-pass that lets in Sadler. As the Hammers push forward, Herd exploits the gaps and races clear for No 2. United's first win at Upton Park since 1936.										
33	A	TOTTENHAM		5		W	3-2	3-1	Law 25, Moore 29, Charlton 36	Gaskell	Brennan	Dunne	Crerand	Foulkes	Stiles	Best	Moore	Sadler	Law	Charlton
	21/3		*56,292*	*3*	42				*Brown 28, Greaves 89p*	*Hollowbread*	*Baker*	*Henry*	*Mullery*	*Norman*	*Marchi*	*Jones*	*White*	*Brown L*	*Greaves*	*Dyson*
									Ref: J Finney	After shattering defeats in Sheffield and Lisbon, United pick themselves up to destroy Spurs on a muddy pitch. Blanchflower's replacement, £72,500 Alan Mullery, is bemused by Law, who scores from a tight angle. The Reds are four points behind Everton with two games in hand.										
34	H	CHELSEA		5		D	1-1	1-0	Law 44	Gaskell	Brennan	Dunne	Crerand	Foulkes	Stiles	Best	Moore	Sadler	Law	Charlton
	23/3		43,172	*7*	43				*Murray 61*	*Bonetti*	*Shellito*	*McCreadie*	*Harris R*	*Mortimore*	*Upton*	*Murray*	*Tambling*	*Bridges*	*Venables*	*Blunstone*
									Ref: P Rhodes	Tommy Docherty's Chelsea are hard to beat and defend with style. Bonetti saves well from Law, and Sadler fires over before Law's turn and shot makes it 1-0. Bert Murray heads a deserved equaliser after Bridges headed against the bar. Ken Shellito carried off after a clash with Law.										
35	A	FULHAM		3		D	2-2	2-1	Herd 24, Law 29	Gaskell	Brennan	Dunne	Crerand	Foulkes	Stiles	Best	Moore	Herd	Law	Charlton
	27/3		*41,770*	*15*	44				*Haynes 10, Earle 82*	*Macedo*	*Cohen*	*Langley*	*Robson*	*Keetch*	*Callaghan*	*Earle*	*Leggat*	*Stratton*	*Haynes*	*O'Connell*
									Ref: J Osbourne	18-year-old Steve Earle has made a big impression and scores again. Only two sides have won at the Cottage but, with Mullery sold, Fulham stutter. Haynes hits a superb volley after his free-kick is cleared. Herd nets from Charlton's corner and Denis poaches No 2. End-to-end action.										
36	H	WOLVERHAMPTON		3		D	2-2	1-1	Herd 19, Charlton 48	Gregg	Brennan	Cantwell	Crerand	Foulkes	Stiles	Best	Chisnall	Herd	Setters	Charlton
	28/3		44,789	*16*	45				*Crawford 25, 62*	*Davies*	*Showell*	*Thomson*	*Flowers*	*Woodfield*	*Woodruff*	*Wharton*	*Melia*	*Crawford*	*Broadbent*	*Le Flem*
									Ref: R Harper	Crawford is the buy of the season with 18 goals since signing from Ipswich. His first is from a rebound, the second from a Woodruff long throw which the fit again Gregg punches poorly. Setters is booked for a silly foul on Davies. Scrappy game, which United can't afford to draw.										
37	H	FULHAM		3		W	3-0	1-0	Crerand 26, Foulkes 75, Herd 82	Gregg	Brennan	Dunne	Crerand	Foulkes	Stiles	Moir	Moore	Herd	Law	Charlton
	30/3		42,495	*15*	47					*Underwood*	*Cohen*	*Drake*	*Brown*	*Robson*	*Callaghan*	*Earle*	*Cook*	*Stratton*	*Haynes*	*O'Connell*
									Ref: W Downey	George Cohen apart, Fulham have little to offer. United are unconvincing. Moore is limping after 20 minutes. Crerand strikes from 25 yards, Foulkes forces in a corner, and Law feeds Herd. Earle has Fulham's best effort but Gregg saves. Manager Jezzard unhappy at Mullery's sale.										
38	A	LIVERPOOL		3		L	0-3	0-2		Gregg	Brennan	Dunne	Crerand	Foulkes	Setters	Best	Stiles	Herd	Law	Charlton
	4/4		*52,559*	*1*	47				*Callaghan 6, Arrowsmith 42, 52*	*Lawrence*	*Byrne*	*Moran*	*Milne*	*Yeats*	*Stevenson*	*Callaghan*	*Hunt*	*St John*	*Arrowsmith*	*Thompson*
									Ref: H Hackney	Barring miracles the title is going to Anfield. Arrowsmith's 12 goals in 13 games since his call-up have virtually sealed the title for Pool. Yeats upsets Gregg again and Law is the butt of the crowd after his misses and a booking. United are steamrollered as the Kop sing Beatles' songs.										
39	H	ASTON VILLA		3		W	1-0	1-0	Law 30	Gregg	Brennan	Dunne	Crerand	Foulkes	Stiles	Best	Charlton	Herd	Law	Moir
	6/4		**26,072**	*16*	49					*Wilson*	*Fraser*	*Aitken*	*Tindall*	*Sleeuwenh'k*	*Pountney*	*Baker*	*Wylie*	*Home*	*Chatterley*	*Burrows*
									Ref: A Sparling	A pitifully low crowd sees Law, with one moment of inspiration, lift the game above mediocrity. Villa's offside tactics are roundly booed. Charlton's thunderbolt is spilled by Wilson, and Law is on it in a flash. Maurice Setters is dropped to make way for Nobby Stiles. A dire game.										
40	H	SHEFFIELD UTD		2		W	2-1	1-1	Law 42, Moir 72	Gregg	Brennan	Cantwell	Crerand	Foulkes	Stiles	Best	Charlton	Herd	Law	Moir
	13/4		28,626	*11*	51				*Jones 23*	*Hodgkinson*	*Badger*	*Shaw B*	*Richardson*	*Shaw J*	*Matthewson*	*Docherty*	*Kettleborough*	*Jones*	*Wagstaff*	*Simpson*
									Ref: H Wilson	Outstanding displays from the two centre-halves are the highlight. The young Blades take a shock lead when Mick Jones scores at the second attempt and the blond striker also hits wood. Law nets after Charlton hits the post and Ian Moir scores with a cheeky left-footer from 18 yards.										
41	A	STOKE		2		L	1-3	1-2	Charlton 26	Gregg	Brennan	Dunne	Crerand	Foulkes	Stiles	Best	Charlton	Sadler	Herd	Moir
	18/4		*45,697*	*17*	51				*Palmer 18, Viollet 21, Ritchie 76*	*Irvine*	*Asprey*	*Allen*	*Palmer*	*Kinnell*	*Skeels*	*Dobing*	*Viollet*	*Ritchie*	*McIlroy*	*Bebbington*
									Ref: D Smith	Nothing to play for, but Stoke play like demons on a grass-less Victoria Ground. Dobing and Viollet are on top form and Palmer catches Gregg out with a long shot. United always have an uphill struggle without the injured Law, and they splutter against Waddington's experienced men.										
42	H	NOTT'M FOREST		2		W	3-1	2-1	Law 9, 56, Moore 34	Gaskell	Brennan	Dunne	Crerand	Foulkes	Setters	Best	Moore	Herd	Law	Charlton
	25/4		32,786	*13*	53				*Hinton 37*	*Grummitt*	*Wilson J*	*Mochan*	*Newton*	*McKinlay*	*Whitefoot*	*Storey-Moore*	*Addison*	*Wignall*	*Barnwell*	*Hinton*
		Home	Away						Ref: P Baldwin	Denis Law finishes two short of Dennis Viollet's scoring record with a header and a half-volley despite hurting his hip. An Inter Cities Fairs Cup place is secured in a carnival atmosphere. Johnny Carey is building a strong team with 19-year-old Storey-Moore a promising newcomer.										
Average		44,125	38,840																	

Charity Shield

Match	Pos	Res	F-A	H-T	Scorers, Times, and Referees	1	2	3	4	5	6	7	8	9	10	11
A EVERTON		L	0-4	0-1	*[Temple 75]*	Gaskell	Dunne	Cantwell	Crerand	Foulkes	Setters	Giles	Quixall	Herd	Law	Charlton
17/8 *54,840*					*Gabriel 42, Vernon 54p, Stevens 62,*	*West*	*Parker*	*Meagan*	*Gabriel*	*Labone*	*Kay*	*Scott*	*Stevens*	*Young*	*Vernon*	*Temple*
					Ref: E Crawford	A stroll for classy Everton, but only after a farcical thrice-taken penalty. Stevens and Vernon are in top form, with the former's dribble creating No 3 and the latter's pile-driver free-kick being too much for Gaskell to hold, as Temple flicks in No 4. Tempers are frayed in the sunshine.										

European Cup-Winners' Cup

Match	Pos	Res	F-A	H-T	Scorers, Times, and Referees	1	2	3	4	5	6	7	8	9	10	11
1:1 A WILLEM II	2	D	1-1	1-1	Herd 12	Gregg	Dunne	Cantwell	Crerand	Foulkes	Setters	Herd!	Chisnall	Sadler	Law	Charlton
25/9 (Holland) *20,000*					*Louer 9*	*Dijkmans*	*Van Dormalen*	*Brooymann*	*Walhout*	*Vriens*	*De Wit*	*Senders*	*Kerestes*	*Koopal*	*Timmermans*	*Louer*
					Ref: M Tricot (France)	A disappointing game against a Dutch Second Division side from Tilburg, played in Rotterdam. After the early goals the only excitement is Charlton's header which hits the post and Koopal's shot which Gregg grabs on the line. David Herd retaliates and is sent off after 80 minutes.										
1:2 H WILLEM II	1	W	6-1	3-1	Setters 7, Law 12, 29, 68, Charlton 64,	Gregg	Dunne	Cantwell	Crerand	Foulkes	Setters	Quixall	Chisnall	Herd	Law	Charlton
15/10 46,272					*Cantwell 36(og)* [Chisnall 65]	*Dijkmans*	*Verwyst*	*Brooymann*	*Walhout*	*Vriens*	*Van Elderen*	*Senders*	*De Wit*	*Koopal*	*Timmermans*	*Louer*
					Ref: H Faucheux (France) (United win 7-2 on aggregate)	Herd's suspension is waived as UEFA bend the rules. Law returns from injury and is unstoppable as a ruthless United coast home against the outclassed part-timers. Charlton's scissors-kick is the pick of the goals, although Noel Cantwell's super shot past Gregg takes some beating.										
2:1 A TOTTENHAM	5	L	0-2	0-0		Gaskell	Dunne	Cantwell	Crerand	Foulkes	Setters	Quixall	Stiles	Herd	Law	Charlton
3/12 *57,447*	*3*				*Mackay 67, Dyson 87*	*Brown*	*Baker*	*Henry*	*Marchi*	*Norman*	*Mackay*	*Jones*	*White*	*Smith*	*Greaves*	*Dyson*
					Ref: H Phillips (Scotland)	A brave defensive display just fails to get a draw and Dyson's late goal after Dunne's dire back-pass makes it an uphill battle in the second leg. The holders Spurs dominate and Dave Mackay's wonder goal is worth the entrance fee. The belligerent Setters marks Greaves out of the game.										
2:2 H TOTTENHAM	4	W	4-1	1-0	Herd 6, 57, Charlton 80, 89	Gaskell	Dunne	Cantwell	Crerand	Foulkes	Setters	Quixall	Chisnall	Sadler	Herd	Charlton
10/12 (England) 48,639	*3*				*Greaves 58*	*Brown*	*Baker*	*Henry*	*Marchi*	*Norman*	*Mackay*	*Jones*	*White*	*Smith*	*Greaves*	*Dyson*
					Ref: L Callaghan (Wales) (United win 4-3 on aggregate)	A memorable night and a thrilling finish as Charlton's late goal avoids a play-off at Villa Park. The fans roar United on and rise to Charlton's finest hour. Dave Mackay breaks his leg in a clash with Cantwell after eight minutes. Setters goes off for a spell for stitches to a cut head.										
3:1 H SPORTING LISBON	3	W	4-1	2-0	Law 22, 60p, 70p, Charlton 39	Gaskell	Brennan	Dunne	Crerand	Foulkes	Setters	Herd	Stiles	Charlton	Law	Best
26/2 (Portugal) 60,000					*Osvaldo 66*	*Carvalho*	*Gomes*	*Hilario*	*Jose Carlos*	*Baptista*	*Alfredo*	*Osvaldo*	*Mendes*	*Figueiredo*	*Geo*	*Morais*
					Ref: J Martens (Netherlands)	The skilful Portuguese in their green-hooped shirts are unlucky to concede two penalties. Stiles falls over for the first, but the second, when Charlton is tripped, looks clear cut. Osvaldo's 25-yarder is the best of the night and United miss two costly gilt-edged chances near the end.										
3:2 A SPORTING LISBON	5	L	0-5	0-2		Gaskell	Brennan	Dunne	Crerand	Foulkes	Setters	Herd	Chisnall	Charlton	Law	Best
18/3 *40,000*					*Osvaldo 2p, 13, 54, Geo 46, Morais 51*	*Carvalho*	*Gomes*	*Hilario*	*Jose Carlos*	*Baptista*	*Mendes*	*Figueiredo*	*Osvaldo*	*Mascarenhas*	*Geo*	*Morais*
					Ref: M Kitabdjan (France) (United lose 4-6 on aggregate)	Full strength United are completely out of touch from the start at the Avalade Stadium. They look a yard slower than their dazzling opponents. Dunne handles for the penalty and Osvaldo completes his hat-trick with a bending 35-yard free-kick around the wall past a statuesque Gaskell.										

FA Cup

Match	Pos	Res	F-A	H-T	Scorers, Times, and Referees	1	2	3	4	5	6	7	8	9	10	11
3 A SOUTHAMPTON	5	W	3-2	0-2	Moore 48, Herd 62, Crerand 85	Gaskell	Dunne	Cantwell	Crerand	Foulkes	Setters	Anderson	Moore	Charlton	Herd	Best
4/1 *29,164*	*2:7*				*Chivers 44, Paine 45*	*Godfrey*	*Davies*	*Traynor*	*McGuigan*	*Knapp*	*Huxford*	*Paine*	*Chivers*	*Kirby*	*White*	*Sydenham*
					Ref: W Clements	Prodigious teenage wingers Best and Willie Anderson spark a thrilling comeback after the Saints had stormed the Cup holders. In a ding-dong battle, Moore heads home and Pat Crerand drives in from Herd's loose ball. Saints wear gold shirts. United 'fans' wreck trains returning home.										
4 H BRISTOL ROVERS	6	W	4-1	2-0	Law 11, 63, 84, Herd 29	Gaskell	Dunne	Cantwell	Crerand	Foulkes	Setters	Herd	Chisnall	Charlton	Law	Best
25/1 55,772	*3:12*				*Crerand 72(og)*	*Hall*	*Hillard*	*Jones*	*Oldfield*	*Davies*	*Mabbutt*	*Jarman*	*Brown*	*Biggs*	*Hamilton*	*Bradford*
					Ref: H Horner	Ten-man United – Cantwell has a back strain – end Rovers' Cup dreams. Despite an 8,000 following, Rovers boss Bert Tann, architect of the win in 1956, has no answer for 'King' Denis, who has 25 in 22 games. The third goal, a Law header from Bobby's cross, is a sublime move.										
5 A BARNSLEY	7	W	4-0	1-0	Best 25, Law 47, 56, Herd 49	Gaskell	Brennan	Dunne	Crerand	Foulkes	Setters	Herd	Stiles	Charlton	Law	Best
15/2 *38,076*	*3:20*					*Williamson*	*Hopper*	*Brookes*	*Wood*	*Winstanley*	*Houghton*	*Sheavills*	*Byrne*	*Leighton*	*Kerr*	*O'Hara*
					Ref: A Sparling	In the biggest day in Barnsley's history for a long time, but the Reds spoil the party at misty Oakwell. Danger-man Tony Leighton is quelled and United go on the rampage with Stiles superb. Best is a genius, scoring one and cheekily dribbling round the goalkeeper before Law taps in.										

Continued on next page

Rd	Ven	Opponent	Pos	Res	Score	HT	Scorers	1	2	3	4	5	6	7	8	9	10	11
QF	H	SUNDERLAND	4	D	3-3	0-1	Hurley 55(og), Charlton 86, Best 88	Gaskell	Brennan	Dunne	Crerand	Foulkes	Setters	Herd	Stiles	Charlton	Law	Best
29/2		63,700	*2:1*				*Mulhall 41, Crossan 49, 60p*	*Montgomery*	*Irwin*	*Ashurst*	*Harvey*	*Hurley*	*Elliott*	*Usher*	*Herd*	*Sharkey*	*Crossan*	*Mulhall*
							Ref: A Holland	The Second Division leaders come close to a major shock, with a cultured display. Mulhall heads in Usher's cross and Crossan runs from the halfway line to score. Hurley's header cheers United before Brennan fouls Crossan for a penalty. A Red tide sweeps in and Law almost wins it.										
QF R	A	SUNDERLAND	5	D	2-2	0-1	Law 70, Charlton 118	Gaskell	Brennan	Dunne	Crerand	Foulkes	Setters	Herd	Chisnall	Charlton	Law	Best
4/3		*46,727*	*2:1*		*aet*		*Sharkey 40, Setters 91(og)*	*Montgomery*	*Irwin*	*Ashurst*	*Harvey*	*Hurley*	*Elliott*	*Usher*	*Herd*	*Sharkey*	*Crossan*	*Mulhall*
							Ref: E Crawford	A gate collapses and the crowd is estimated at 70,000 with 30,000 outside. Sunderland again take the initiative in a fairy tale story and are desperately unlucky after twice leading. Setters can't control the wet ball and nets but Charlton's header at the death means another replay.										
QF RR	N	SUNDERLAND	5	W	5-1	0-0	Law 48, 52p, 61, Chisnall 49, Herd 67	Gaskell	Brennan	Dunne	Crerand	Foulkes	Setters	Herd	Chisnall	Charlton	Law	Best
9/3		*54,952*	*2:1*				*Sharkey 47*	*Montgomery*	*Irwin*	*Ashurst*	*Harvey*	*Hurley*	*Elliott*	*Usher*	*Herd*	*Sharkey*	*Crossan*	*Mulhall*
		(at Huddersfield)					Ref: E Crawford	Five minutes of magic ends plucky Sunderland's resistance with Law and Best at the heart of things. Herd sets up the first for Denis and is then tripped for the penalty. Best's mazy dribble creates Law's third goal before Herd's fierce drive. Tired players lose their cool near the end.										
SF	N	WEST HAM	5	L	1-3	0-0	Law 78	Gaskell	Brennan	Dunne	Crerand	Foulkes	Setters	Herd	Chisnall	Charlton	Law	Best
14/3		*65,000*	*15*				*Boyce 56, 63, Hurst 80*	*Standen*	*Bond*	*Burkett*	*Bovington*	*Brown*	*Moore*	*Brabrook*	*Boyce*	*Byrne*	*Hurst*	*Sissons*
		(at Hillsborough)					Ref: K Stokes	West Ham reach their first FA Cup final since 1923, overturning last week's league defeat on a mud-heap of a pitch. Boyce lets rip from 25 yards past the stranded Gaskell, then adds another from a short-corner. Law lunges feet-first into Jim Standen. Moore is a Trojan in defence.										

		Home						Away					
	P	W	D	L	F	A	W	D	L	F	A	Pts
1 Liverpool	42	16	0	5	60	18	10	5	6	32	27	57
2 MAN UNITED	42	15	3	3	54	19	8	4	9	36	43	53
3 Everton	42	14	4	3	53	26	7	6	8	31	38	52
4 Tottenham	42	13	3	5	54	31	9	4	8	43	50	51
5 Chelsea	42	12	3	6	36	24	8	7	6	36	32	50
6 Sheffield Wed	42	15	3	3	50	24	4	8	9	34	43	49
7 Blackburn	42	10	4	7	44	28	8	6	7	45	37	46
8 Arsenal	42	10	7	4	56	37	7	4	10	34	45	45
9 Burnley	42	14	3	4	46	23	3	7	11	25	41	44
10 West Brom	42	9	6	6	43	35	7	5	9	27	26	43
11 Leicester	42	9	4	8	33	27	7	7	7	28	31	43
12 Sheffield Utd	42	10	6	5	35	22	6	5	10	26	42	43
13 Nott'm Forest	42	9	5	7	34	24	7	4	10	30	44	41
14 West Ham	42	8	7	6	45	38	6	5	10	24	36	40
15 Fulham	42	11	8	2	45	23	2	5	14	13	42	39
16 Wolves	42	6	9	6	36	34	6	6	9	34	46	39
17 Stoke	42	9	6	6	49	33	5	4	12	28	45	38
18 Blackpool	42	8	6	7	26	29	5	3	13	26	44	35
19 Aston Villa	42	8	6	7	35	29	3	6	12	27	42	34
20 Birmingham	42	7	7	7	33	32	4	0	17	21	60	29
21 Bolton	42	6	5	10	30	35	4	3	14	18	45	28
22 Ipswich	42	9	3	9	38	45	0	4	17	18	76	25
	924	228	108	126	935	636	126	108	228	636	935	924

Odds & ends

Double wins: (6) Ipswich, Bolton, Nott'm Forest, Sheff Utd, West Brom, Tottenham.
Double losses: (1) Liverpool.

Won from behind: (4) Everton (h), Sheffield U (h), Southampton FAC (a), Sunderland FAC (n).
Lost from in front: (2) Arsenal (a), Leicester (a).

High spots: Law's remarkable scoring record.
Three FA Cup matches with Sunderland.
Emergence of George Best.

Low spots: Defeat at Hillsborough in the FA Cup semi-final.
Heavy defeat in Lisbon.
Boxing Day defeat at Burnley.

Red cards (United): (3) Herd (Willem a), Law (Aston Villa a), Crerand (Burnley a).
Red cards (Opponents): (0).
Ever-presents: (0).
Hat-tricks: (8) Law (7), Herd.
Opposing hat-tricks: (2) Lochhead (Burnley), Osvaldo (Sporting Lisbon).
Leading scorer: (46) Law.

	Appearances			Goals			
	Lge	FAC	Eur	Lge	FAC	Eur	Tot
Anderson, Willie	2	1					
Best, George	17	7	2	4	2		6
Brennan, Shay	17	5	2				
Cantwell, Noel	28	2	4				
Charlton, Bobby	40	7	6	9	2	4	15
Chisnall, Phil	20	4	4	6	1	1	8
Crerand, Pat	41	7	6	1	1		2
Dunne, Tony	40	7	6				
Foulkes, Bill	41	7	6	1			1
Gaskell, Dave	17	7	4				
Gregg, Harry	25		2				
Herd, David	30	7	6	20	4	3	27
Law, Denis	30	6	5	30	10	6	46
Moir, Ian	18			3			3
Moore, Graham	18	1		4	1		5
Quixall, Albert	9		3	3			3
Sadler, David	19		2	5			5
Setters, Maurice	32	7	6	4		1	5
Stiles, Nobby	17	2	2				
Tranter, Wilf	1						
(own-goals)					1		1
20 players used	**462**	**77**	**66**	**90**	**22**	**15**	**127**

LEAGUE DIVISION 1

Manager: Matt Busby

SEASON 1964-65

No	Date		Att	Pos	Pt	F-A	H-T	Scorers, Times, and Referees	1	2	3	4	5	6	7	8	9	10	11
1	H	WEST BROM			D	2-2	2-2	Law 21, Charlton 38	Gaskell	Brennan	Dunne A	Setters	Foulkes	Stiles	**Connelly**	Charlton	Herd	Law	Best
	24/8		52,268		1			*Brown 14, Foulkes 41 (og)*	*Potter*	*Cram*	*Williams*	*Fraser*	*Jones*	*Simpson*	*Foggo*	*Brown*	*Kaye*	*Hope*	*Clark*
								Ref: M Fussey	The season starts full of promise in all departments. Desperate defending keeps United at bay after debutant Connelly crosses for Law and Charlton hits a left-foot rocket. 18-year-old Tony Brown nets and looks a great prospect. Law has a goal disallowed and Herd is sadly booed.										
2	A	WEST HAM			L	**1-3**	0-2	Law 79	Gaskell	Brennan	Dunne A	Setters	Foulkes	Stiles	Connelly	Charlton	Herd	Law	Best
	24/8		*37,298*		1			*Byrne 4, Sissons 19, Hurst 85*	*Standen*	*Bond*	*Burkett*	*Bovington*	*Brown*	*Moore*	*Brabrook*	*Boyce*	*Byrne*	*Hurst*	*Sissons*
								Ref: K Burns	The Cup holders are given a rapturous reception by their largest crowd for five years. United play the last 30 mins with ten men after Boyce's studs sliced through Setters' boot. Byrne scores when Sissons' shot is blocked. Sissons lobs a second. Law's header sets up a furious climax.										
3	A	LEICESTER		17	D	2-2	0-1	Sadler 71, Law 88	Gaskell	Brennan	Dunne A	Crerand	Foulkes	Stiles	Connelly	Charlton	Sadler	Law	Best
	29/8		*32,373*	*8*	2			*Keyworth 10, Appleton 84*	*Banks*	*Sjoberg*	*Cross*	*McLintock*	*King*	*Appleton*	*Riley*	*Sweenie*	*Keyworth*	*Gibson*	*Stringfellow*
								Ref: D Wells	United gain their first point at Filbert Street since 1957, courtesy of a late Law goal. Keyworth catches United cold from close range before Sadler's neat header from Best's cross. Appleton dribbles through to score what looks like the winner, but United's heavy pressure pays off.										
4	H	WEST HAM		12	W	3-1	2-1	Connelly 1, Law 28, Best 53	Gaskell	Brennan	Dunne A	Crerand	Foulkes	Stiles	Connelly	Charlton	Sadler	Law	Best
	2/9		45,415	*14*	4			*Stiles 6 (og)*	*Standen*	*Bond*	*Burkett*	*Bovington*	*Brown*	*Moore*	*Brabrook*	*Boyce*	*Byrne*	*Hurst*	*Sissons*
								Ref: H Wilson	First win of the season after Connolly's 45-second goal, set up by Best, who dummies Bond, not once but twice. Stiles turns Byrne's cross past Gaskell, but United turn up the heat. They create chances galore but only take two of them. England captain Bobby Moore given the bird.										
5	A	FULHAM		16	L	1-2	1-0	Connelly 45	Gaskell	Brennan	Dunne A	Crerand	Foulkes	Stiles	Connelly	Charlton	Sadler	Law	Best
	5/9		*36,291*	*9*	4			*Brennan 52 (og), Haynes 78*	*Macedo*	*Cohen*	*Langley*	*Robson*	*Keetch*	*Callaghan*	*Key*	*Metchick*	*Marsh*	*Haynes*	*O'Connell*
								Ref: J Cooke	Lively Fulham snatch a surprise win after United had dominated for long periods. Connelly's shot goes in off the post after the agile Macedo had starred. Stiles' clearance bounces off Brennan and Haynes' soft shot creeps in as Gaskell dives late. Tempers become frayed at the end.										
6	A	EVERTON		16	D	3-3	2-0	Law 4, Herd 25, Connelly 78	**Dunne P**	Brennan	Dunne A	Crerand	Foulkes	Stiles	Connelly	Charlton	Herd	Law	Best
	8/9		***63,465***	*2*	5			*Pickering 51, 59, Young 84*	*Rankin*	*Parker*	*Brown*	*Gabriel*	*Labone*	*Harris*	*Scott*	*Young*	*Pickering*	*Vernon*	*Temple*
								Ref: K Howley	Former Everton reserve Pat Dunne debuts after five reserve games. On a wet night, United take early command, with Law's header and John Connelly's left-foot shot. Pickering's persistence is rewarded. Connelly seems to have won the game until the classy Alex Young glides one in.										
7	H	NOTT'M FOREST		14	W	3-0	3-0	Herd 2, 24, Connelly 18	Dunne P	Brennan	Dunne A	Crerand	Foulkes	Setters	Connelly	Charlton	Herd	Stiles	Best
	12/9		46,437	*13*	7				*Grummitt*	*Wilson J*	*Mochan*	*Newton*	*McKinlay*	*Whitefoot*	*Crowe*	*Addison*	*Wilson D*	*Barnwell*	*Hinton*
								Ref: W Handley	Early goals deflate shaky Forest. Herd is the villain turned hero, and Stiles' incisive pass breaks the offside trap for David to run 40 yards for his second. Leading scorers Law and Wignall both miss out with injury. Albert Quixall has gone to Oldham and Charlton deputises as skipper.										
8	H	EVERTON		10	W	2-1	2-1	Best 12, Law 21	Dunne P	Brennan	Dunne A	Crerand	Foulkes	Stiles	Connelly	Charlton	Herd	Law	Best
	16/9		50,286	*2*	9			*Pickering 40*	*Rankin*	*Harris*	*Brown*	*Gabriel*	*Labone*	*Stevens*	*Scott*	*Young*	*Pickering*	*Harvey*	*Temple*
								Ref: J Carr	An exciting match is marred by petty feuds, with Crerand and Pickering the main protagonists. Referee Carr calls the teams together after four bookings and the air cools. Law's header is disallowed before Best's shot flies in off Harris's boot. Law's 40-yard run upsets Labone for No 2.										
9	A	STOKE		7	W	2-1	0-1	Herd 48, Connelly 69	Dunne P	Brennan	Dunne A	Crerand	Foulkes	Setters	Connelly	Charlton	Herd	Stiles	Best
	19/9		*40,064*	*15*	11			*Ritchie 10*	*Leslie*	*Asprey*	*Allen*	*Skeels*	*Kinnell*	*Philpott*	*Dobing*	*Viollet*	*Ritchie*	*McIlroy*	*Bebbington*
								Ref: A Sparling	United, playing in their new blue shirts, win at Stoke for the first time since 1947. They bounce back from Ritchie's header, that Pat Dunne should have held, to win with Connelly's shot off the underside of the bar. Best and Connelly are super and the defence hang on for the points.										
10	H	TOTTENHAM		4	W	4-1	1-0	Crerand 17, 56, Law 59, 89	Dunne P	Brennan	Dunne A	Crerand	Foulkes	Stiles	Connelly	Charlton	Herd	Law	Best
	26/9		53,362	*10*	13			*Robertson 80*	*Jennings*	*Knowles*	*Henry*	*Mullery*	*Brown L*	*Marchi*	*Robertson*	*Greaves*	*Saul*	*Jones*	*Dyson*
								Ref: A Luty	Bill Nicholson's Spurs are in a period of transition and are comprehensively beaten. Crerand's 20-yarder and a jammy shot through Jennings' legs put the Reds in command. Law nets after twice being played onside by sloppy play. A heavy downpour at half-time soaks the terrace fans.										

No	H/A	Opponent / Att	Pos	Res / Pts	F-A	H-T	Scorers / Ref											
11	A	CHELSEA	2	W	2-0	1-0	Best 32, Law 73	Dunne P	Brennan	Dunne A	Crerand	Foulkes	Stiles	Connelly	Charlton	Herd	Law	Best
30/9		60,769	1	15				Bonetti	Shellito	McCreadie	Hollins	Hinton	Harris R	Murray	Tambling	Bridges	Venables	Houseman
							Ref: P Bye	United end Chelsea's ten-game unbeaten start with a professional display that impresses the London press. They withstand a furious opening before McCreadie's back-pass gifts a goal to the ubiquitous Best. Law's flicked header wraps up the points as Bonetti only parried Best's lob.										
12	A	BURNLEY	2	D	0-0	0-0		Dunne P	Brennan	Dunne A	Crerand	Foulkes	Stiles	Connelly	Charlton	Herd	Law	Best
6/10		31,056	18	16				Blacklaw	Angus	Elder	Todd	Talbut	Miller	Morgan	Irvine	Lochhead	Bellamy	Towers
							Ref: G McCabe	Burnley have made their worst start for many years but deserve a point. The bad blood between the teams continues in a niggly game. Adam Blacklaw plays his 150th successive game for the Clarets but has little to do. Law's header hits the bar and Willie Irvine misses an open goal.										
13	H	SUNDERLAND	2	W	1-0	0-0	Herd 77	Dunne P	Brennan	Dunne A	Crerand	Foulkes	Stiles	Connelly	Charlton	Herd	Law	Best
10/10		48,862	20	18				McLaughlan	Irwin	Ashurst	Harvey	Hurley	Elliott	Usher	Herd	Sharkey	Mitchinson	Mulhall
							Ref: D Lyden	Newly promoted but managerless Sunderland have won only once. They defend stoutly before David Herd's header from Connelly's corner. Best is the darling of the fans and can do no wrong, but Charlton misses three good chances as United fail to press home their vast superiority.										
14	A	WOLVES	2	W	4-2	4-1	Law 15, 44, Harris 22 (og), Herd 35	Dunne P	Brennan	Dunne A	Crerand	Foulkes	Stiles	Connelly	Charlton	Herd	Law	Best
17/10		26,763	22	20			Crawford 42, 58	Davies	Thomson	Harris	Flowers	Showell	Woodruff	Wharton	Broadbent	Woodfield	Crawford	Buckley
							Ref: H New	Wolves have won 1 game in 13 and sacked long-serving boss Stan Cullis. They are overrun by rampant United. Harris can't avoid Connelly's cross, Herd can't miss and Law grabs two opportunist goals. Brave Wolves never give up and Harris wallops the bar at 4-2. Crerand is the star.										
15	H	ASTON VILLA	2	W	**7-0**	2-0	Herd 17, 77, Law 20, 50, 65, 89, [Connelly 56]	Dunne P	Brennan	Dunne A	Crerand	Foulkes	Setters	Connelly	Stiles	Herd	Law	Best
24/10		37,233	21	22				Sidebottom	Wright	Aitken	Tindall	Sleeuwenh'k	Pountney	MacLeod	Woosnam	Hateley	Wylie	Burrows
							Ref: P Baldwin	Villa's biggest defeat since 1950, at Old Trafford! Five defeats in a row for new boss Dick Taylor and they haven't won away for over a year. After Villa missed two good chances, the wingers destroy a shaky defence. Law makes it 15 goals in 13 games with four close-range efforts.										
16	A	LIVERPOOL	1	W	2-0	1-0	Herd 35, Crerand 59	Dunne P	Brennan	Dunne A	Crerand	Foulkes	Stiles	Connelly	Charlton	Herd	Law	Best
31/10		52,402	18	24				Lawrence	Lawler	Byrne	Milne	Yeats	Stevenson	Callaghan	Hunt	St John	Graham	Thompson
							Ref: J Taylor	The champions have started badly. This is their third home defeat but they give the Reds a hard time. The full house sees a pulsating game won by a stern defence and rapier-like attacks. Dunne is cool in front of the baiting Kop, but Yeats and Law have a dust-up before Yeats butts Herd.										
17	H	SHEFFIELD WED	1	W	1-0	1-0	Herd 15	Dunne P	Brennan	Dunne A	Crerand	Foulkes	Stiles	Connelly	Charlton	Herd	Law	Best
7/11		50,446	9	26				Springett R	Hill	Megson	Eustace	Mobley	Young	Finney	Quinn	Wilkinson	Fantham	Dobson
							Ref: P Brandwood	United survive Wednesday's rough tactics and long-ball game to win. Herd picks up Hill's sliced clearance, shrugs off three challenges and beats Springett with a low shot. Young and Law have a running battle. With Stiles and Crerand in top form, Setters is set for a move to Stoke.										
18	A	BLACKPOOL	1	W	2-1	1-1	Herd 4, Connelly 48	Dunne P	Brennan	Dunne A	Crerand	Foulkes	Stiles	Connelly	Charlton	Herd	Law !	Moir
14/11		31,129	6	28			Oates 28	Waiters	Armfield	Thompson	McPhee	Rowe	Green	Lea	Ball	Charnley	Oates	Horne
							Ref: P Rhodes	Blackpool's good start is fizzling out and United's ten men hang on for a vital win. Law is sent off just before half-time for swearing at the ref. Crerand is booked and there is crowd trouble. Feisty Alan Ball creates an equaliser to Herd's dipping shot, but Connelly's header wins the day.										
19	H	BLACKBURN	1	W	3-0	0-0	Best 52, Connelly 65, Herd 76	Dunne P	Brennan	Dunne A	Crerand	Foulkes	Stiles	Connelly	Charlton	Herd	Law	Best
21/11		49,928	5	30				Else	Newton	Joyce	Clayton	Mulvaney	McGrath	Ferguson	McEvoy	Byrom	Douglas	Harrison
							Ref: E Jennings	Seventeen games unbeaten since Pat Dunne came into the side, with Herd scoring in each of the last seven. After an even first half, Blackburn crack once Charlton unlocks the defence to set up Best. United finish an entertaining and sporting game on top. A major rival is well beaten.										
20	A	ARSENAL	1	W	3-2	3-1	Law 4, 29, Connelly 17	Dunne P	Brennan	Dunne A	Crerand	Foulkes	Stiles	Connelly	Charlton	Herd	Law	Best
28/11		59,637	13	32			Anderson 35, Eastham 75	Burns	Howe	McCullough	Snedden	Neil	Court	Anderson	McLintock	Baker	Eastham	Armstrong
							Ref: W Clements	United thrill London again with a devastating first half. Law is impossible to handle and flashes in two glorious goals to make a nonsense of Billy Wright's plans to shackle him. Eastham-inspired Arsenal fight back strongly and in a ding-dong climax both sides have chances to score.										
21	H	LEEDS	1	L	0-1	0-0		Dunne P	Brennan	Dunne A	Crerand	Foulkes	Stiles	Connelly	Charlton	Herd	Law	Best
5/12		53,651	3	32			Collins 55	Sprake	Reaney	Bell	Bremner	Charlton	Hunter	Giles	Johnson	Storrie	Collins	Cooper
							Ref: J Finney	Revie's promoted Leeds make it nine wins in ten, and win at Old Trafford for the first time since 1931. They defend doggedly and Bremner finds Collins unmarked for the goal. As the fog descends the ref takes the teams off for seven minutes near the end but play restarts as it abates.										

No	Date	Att	Pos	Pt	F-A	H-T	Scorers, Times, and Referees	1	2	3	4	5	6	7	8	9	10	11
22	A WEST BROM		2	D	1-1	1-1	Law 15	Dunne P	Brennan	Dunne A	Crerand	Foulkes	Stiles	Connelly	Charlton	Herd	Law	Best
	12/12	*28,126*	*15*	33			*Kaye 35*	*Potter*	*Fairfax*	*Williams*	*Fraser*	*Jones*	*Simpson*	*Foggo*	*Kaye*	*Astle*	*Hope*	*Clark*
							Ref: G Davis	Law's final game before his 28-day ban starts and he signs off with a typical goal – sliding in Charlton's cross. John Kaye scrambles an equaliser and United fail to convert the chances that would have given them a deserved win. Pat Crerand takes a knock and limps on the wing.										
23	H BIRMINGHAM		1	D	1-1	1-0	Charlton 38p	Dunne P	Brennan	Dunne A	Crerand	Foulkes	Stiles	Connelly	Charlton	Sadler	Herd	Best
	16/12	**25,938**	*19*	34			*Thwaites 75*	*Schofield*	*Lynn*	*Green*	*Hennessey*	*Foster*	*Beard*	*Jackson*	*Sharples*	*Thomson*	*Vowden*	*Thwaites*
							Ref: H Hackney	Joe Mallett's struggling team frustrate United with their negative tactics. On a rock-hard pitch Hennessey handles for captain Charlton to score from the spot. Thwaites' mazy run and shot earns the point after Schofield had saved well from Charlton and Herd, and Sadler had hit the bar.										
24	A SHEFFIELD UTD		1	W	1-0	1-0	Best 12	Dunne P	Brennan	Dunne A	Crerand	Foulkes	Stiles	Connelly	Charlton	Sadler	Herd	Best
	26/12	*37,295*	*14*	36				*Hodgkinson*	*Badger*	*Shaw G*	*Richardson*	*Shaw J*	*Matthewson*	*Woodward*	*Kettleborough*	*Jones*	*Wagstaff T*	*Hartle*
							Ref: W Handley	Best's early goal is enough on a treacherous icy pitch. His duel with 19-year old Len Badger is fascinating and deemed a draw. His goal is from the top drawer as he keeps his feet as the Blades defence slithers and coolly beats the keeper. Blades contain the Reds but threaten little.										
25	H SHEFFIELD UTD		1	D	1-1	0-0	Herd 53	Dunne P	Brennan	Dunne A	Crerand	Foulkes	Stiles	Connelly	Charlton	Sadler	Herd	Best
	28/12	42,219	*14*	37			*Woodward 60*	*Hodgkinson*	*Badger*	*Shaw G*	*Richardson*	*Shaw J*	*Matthewson*	*Woodward*	*Kettleborough*	*Jones*	*Birchenall*	*Hartle*
							Ref: K Howley	United frustrated at home again but an entertaining match on a frosty surface. A fair result, with Hodgkinson deceived by Stiles' lob and Herd heading home. Pat Dunne, harassed by the excellent Mick Jones, drops the ball and Alan Woodward nets. Sheffield finish the stronger side.										
26	A NOTT'M FOREST		3	D	2-2	2-2	Law 3, 31	Dunne P	Brennan	Dunne A	Crerand	Foulkes	Stiles	Connelly	Charlton	Herd	Law	Best
	16/1	*43,009*	5	38			*Hinton 15, 23*	*Grummitt*	*Hindley*	*Mochan*	*Newton*	*McKinlay*	*Whitefoot*	*Storey-Moore*	*Addison*	*Crowe*	*Barnwell*	*Hinton*
							Ref: G Grundy	Law returns from suspension and scores after a clever free-kick. Forest's biggest crowd of the season drool at a thriller with England-man Alan Hinton the home star. His mazy run and bullet shot levels things, but he looked offside for No 2. The King pounces after Herd's shot is spilled.										
27	H STOKE		3	D	1-1	1-1	Law 21	Dunne P	Brennan	Dunne A	Crerand	Foulkes	Stiles	Connelly	Charlton	Herd	Law	Best
	23/1	51,978	*12*	39			*Bloor 10*	*Leslie*	*Asprey*	*Allen*	*Setters*	*Kinnell*	*Bloor*	*Palmer*	*Skeels*	*Ritchie*	*Viollet*	*McIlroy*
							Ref: M Fussey	Setters returns to a warm reception as the teams warm up for the FA Cup-tie next week with a tough, no-nonsense game. Stoke have only lost one in nine since Maurice signed, and he marshals a superb scrooge-like defence. United's siege culminates with late penalty appeals in vain.										
28	A TOTTENHAM		3	L	0-1	0-1		Dunne P	Brennan	Dunne A	Crerand	Foulkes	Stiles	Connelly	Charlton	Herd	Law	Best
	6/2	*58,639*	*4*	39			*Henry 19*	*Brown W*	*Knowles*	*Henry*	*Mullery*	*Norman*	*Clayton*	*Robertson*	*Greaves*	*Gilzean*	*Jones*	*Dyson*
							Ref: L Callaghan	The gates are locked and Spurs maintain their 18-match unbeaten home run, inflicting United's first away defeat since September. On a sticky pitch, Dunne palms Dyson's cross to Henry, who scores with a 30-yarder for his first ever league goal after 234 games. Law misses a sitter.										
29	H BURNLEY		3	W	3-2	2-0	Best 10, Herd 34, Charlton 50	Dunne P	Brennan	Dunne A	Crerand	Foulkes	Stiles	Connelly	Charlton	Herd	Law	Best
	13/2	39,135	*15*	41			*Walker 47, Irvine 88*	*Blacklaw*	*Smith*	*Elder*	*O'Neill*	*Miller*	*Walker*	*Towers*	*Bellamy*	*Irvine*	*Harris*	*Latcham*
							Ref: K Stokes	United notch their first league win at home since November against next week's injury-hit Cup rivals. Best is in sublime form, shooting low past Blacklaw and laying on the second for Herd. Charlton's thunderbolt wraps it up but Willie Irvine's late header has Reds' fans sweating.										
30	A SUNDERLAND		3	L	0-1	0-1		Dunne P	Brennan	Dunne A	Crerand	Foulkes	**Fitzpatrick**	Connelly	Charlton	Herd	Law	Best
	24/2	*51,336*	*19*	41			*Hood 10*	*McLaughlan*	*Parke*	*Black*	*Harvey*	*Hurley*	*McNab*	*Hellawell*	*Herd*	*Hood*	*Sharkey*	*Mulhall*
							Ref: H Hackney	Former England captain George Hardwick is struggling to get Sunderland out of relegation trouble. His team are up for it against a tired and lethargic United. Hood's volley is the decider but not before a frantic last fifteen minutes. United are three points behind leaders Chelsea.										
31	H WOLVERHAMPTON		3	W	3-0	1-0	Connelly 4, Charlton 69, 87	Dunne P	Brennan	Dunne A	Crerand	Foulkes	Stiles	Connelly	Best	Herd	Law	Charlton
	27/2	38,587	*22*	43				*Davies*	*Thomson*	*Harris*	*Flowers*	*Woodfield*	*Kirkham*	*Wharton*	*Woodruff*	*Miller*	*Knowles*	*Wagstaffe*
							Ref: A Luty	Wolves are eight points adrift of safety and are heading to Div 2. Best and Charlton are switched to good effect, but Nobby Stiles is the star, fresh from a successful first Under-23 cap. Charlton sets up Connelly's tap-in before scoring one with each foot in another Cup rehearsal.										

No	Venue / Date	Opponent	Att	Pos	Pts	F-A	H-T	Scorers, Times, and Referees	1	2	3	4	5	6	7	8	9	10	11
32	H	CHELSEA		3	W	4-0	2-0	Best 3, Herd 23, 50, Law 75	Dunne P	Brennan	Dunne A	Crerand	Foulkes	Stiles	Connelly	Charlton	Herd	Law	Best
	13/3		**57,662**	*1*	45				*Bonetti*	*Hinton*	*McCreadie*	*Hollins*	*Mortimore*	*Harris R*	*Murray*	*Graham*	*Bridges*	*Venables*	*Tambling*
								Ref: G McCabe	The big games keep on coming and Chelsea suffer their biggest defeat for three years as the gates are locked with thousands outside. Best's superb lob beats the over-worked Bonetti to start the rout. Pat Crerand is the boss in a stylish display, with Tommy Docherty's men outclassed.										
33	H	FULHAM		3	W	4-1	3-1	Herd 9, 24, Connelly 43, 49	Dunne P	Brennan	Dunne A	Crerand	Foulkes	Stiles	Connelly	Charlton	Herd	Law	Best
	15/3		45,631	*19*	47			*Marsh 4*	*Macedo*	*Cohen*	*Langley*	*Robson*	*Keetch*	*Brown*	*Key*	*Marsh*	*Cook*	*Haynes*	*Leggat*
								Ref: E Crawford	Fulham are outclassed and fall to their seventh straight away defeat as United make it 13 goals in five days. Charlton and Crerand are almost perfection, once Rodney Marsh's goal is cancelled out. Fulham never give up and have some good chances, but Cohen's slip lets in Connelly.										
34	A	SHEFFIELD WED		3	L	0-1	0-0		Dunne P	Brennan	Dunne A	Crerand	Foulkes	Stiles	Connelly	Charlton	Herd	Law	Best
	20/3		*32,782*	*6*	47			*Fantham 64*	*Springett R*	*Hill*	*Megson*	*Eustace*	*Mobley*	*Smith*	*Wilkinson*	*Quinn*	*Hickton*	*Fantham*	*Dobson*
								Ref: K Howley	United have won only once in 11 visits to Hillsborough but are unlucky today. The rain and sleet make for a dreadful surface that hampers the skilful players. Fantham's flashing header dents the title hopes, leaving United three points behind Leeds. Springett keeps Law and Best at bay.										
35	H	BLACKPOOL		3	W	2-0	0-0	Law 68, 70	Dunne P	Brennan	Dunne A	Crerand	Foulkes	Stiles	Connelly	Charlton	Herd	Law	Best
	22/3		42,586	*18*	49				*Waiters*	*Armfield*	*Thompson*	*McPhee*	*James*	*Green*	*Moir*	*Ball*	*Waddell*	*Robson*	*Oates*
								Ref: A Sparling	Ron Stuart's struggling Seasiders are unlucky to lose after they dominate for long periods. Alan Ball is in superb form and comes out on top in the battle with Stiles. Ex-Red Moir fires over a good chance, Robson heads onto the crossbar and Dunne saves well from Waddell. A vital win.										
36	A	BLACKBURN		3	W	5-0	0-0	Charlton 47, 65, 76, Connelly 54, [Herd 62]	Dunne P	Brennan	Dunne A	Crerand	Foulkes	Stiles	Connelly	Charlton	Herd	Law	Best
	3/4		*29,363*	*9*	51				*Else*	*Wilson*	*Newton*	*Clayton*	*England*	*Joyce*	*Ferguson*	*McEvoy*	*Byrom*	*Douglas*	*Harrison*
								Ref: E Jennings	Rovers suffer for United's semi-final defeat with their biggest home defeat since 1947. The sunshine is glorious and there is no warning of the damage to come in an even first half. Everything clicks for 18 minutes as a fluent United run riot with dead-eye Charlton's shooting awesome.										
37	H	LEICESTER		3	W	1-0	0-0	Herd 49	Dunne P	Brennan	Dunne A	Crerand	Foulkes	Stiles	Connelly	Charlton	Herd	Best	**Aston**
	12/4		35,906	*17*	53				*Banks*	*Walker*	*Norman*	*Roberts*	*Sjoberg*	*Cross*	*Hodgson*	*Gibson*	*Goodfellow*	*Sweenie*	*Stringfellow*
								Ref: J Carr	Law is missing injured after the England v Scotland game and is missed. Leicester are suffering after a Cup semi-final defeat and barely trouble Dunne. Herd cuts in and beats England's No 1 Banks from a narrow angle. England hero Charlton is very effective in a deep lying role.										
38	A	LEEDS		3	W	1-0	1-0	Connelly 14	Dunne P	Brennan	Dunne A	Crerand	Foulkes	Stiles	Connelly	Charlton	Herd	Law	Best
	17/4		*52,368*	*2*	55				*Sprake*	*Reaney*	*Bell*	*Greenhoff*	*Charlton*	*Hunter*	*Giles*	*Weston*	*Peacock*	*Collins*	*Cooper*
								Ref: K Stokes	The result of a tense battle leaves Leeds one point ahead but United have the psychological advantage. Leeds face Liverpool in FA Cup final in two weeks and the hectic programme is beginning to tell. Connelly's ground shot ends their 25-game unbeaten run and the defence holds firm.										
39	A	BIRMINGHAM		1	W	4-2	1-1	Best 13, 63, Charlton 65, Cantwell 75	Dunne P	Brennan	Dunne A	Crerand	Foulkes	Stiles	Connelly	Charlton	Cantwell	Law	Best
	19/4		*28,914*	*22*	57			*Thwaites 27, Vowden 62*	*Schofield*	*Lynn*	*Sharples*	*Hennessey*	*Foster*	*Page*	*Jackson*	*Fraser*	*Vowden*	*Beard*	*Thwaites*
								Ref: P Bye	Blues give United a major fright before skill wins the day and they are relegated. Leeds lose at Hillsborough and the title is within the Reds' grasp. A biting wind and flurries of snow can't halt United's surge in the last half hour. The joyous fans invade the pitch after the fourth goal.										
40	H	LIVERPOOL		2	W	3-0	1-0	Law 40, 57, Connelly 81	Dunne P	Brennan	Dunne A	Crerand	Foulkes	Stiles	Connelly	Charlton	Cantwell	Law	Best
	24/4		56,058	*10*	59				*Lawrence*	*Lawler*	*Byrne*	*Smith*	*Yeats*	*Stevenson*	*Graham*	*Hunt*	*Strong*	*Chisnall*	*Thompson*
								Ref: D Smith	Shankly's team are in the FA Cup final next week and, with one eye on Wembley, rest a few stars. United are set for the championship after Law buries Yeats' unconvincing header and poaches a second that leaves him injured and off. Charlton is on song and hits the post twice.										
41	H	ARSENAL		1	W	3-1	1-0	Best 6, Law 60, 85	Dunne P	Brennan	Dunne A	Crerand	Foulkes	Stiles	Connelly	Charlton	Herd	Law	Best
	26/4		53,350	*13*	61			*Eastham 66*	*Furnell*	*Howe*	*McCullough*	*Neil*	*Ure*	*McLintock*	*Sammels*	*Court*	*Baker*	*Eastham*	*Armstrong*
								Ref: W Clements	On a tense evening, Leeds draw at St Andrews, making United champions. Arsenal fight hard but Best's goal settles the nerves. Dunne saves Eastham's penalty but the schemer follows up to score. Law's close-range effort, after Herd had hit the bar, sparks the noisy celebrations.										
42	A	ASTON VILLA		1	L	1-2	0-2	Charlton 58	Dunne P	Brennan	Dunne A	Fitzpatrick	Foulkes	Stiles	Connelly	Charlton	Herd	Law	Best
	28/4		*36,005*	*16*	61			*Baker 6, Park 35*	*Withers*	*Wright*	*Aitken*	*Parken*	*Pountney*	*Deakin*	*Baker*	*Chatterley*	*Hateley*	*Park*	*MacLeod*
		Home	Away					Ref: W Holian	Villa extend their unbeaten run to eight games in a meaningless final game. Dick Taylor's young team win with Baker's hard drive and Park's tap-in after Dunne's faux-pas. Charlton raises the roof with a mazy run past six men and a low finish. A late barrage on the Villa goal just fails.										
Average		46,521	41,385																

Inter-Cities Fairs Cup				F-A	H-T	Scorers, Times, and Referees	1	2	3	4	5	6	7	8	9	10	11
1:1 A DJURGAARDENS IF	7	D		1-1	0-1	Herd 87	Dunne P	Brennan	Dunne A	Crerand	Foulkes	Stiles	Connelly	Charlton	Herd	Setters	Best
23/9 (Sweden)	*6,537*					*Johansson 8*	*Arvidsson*	*Karlsson J*	*Arnesson*	*Fururkrantz*	*Mild*	*Sandberg*	*Andersson*	*Karlsson H*	*Eriksson*	*Nilsson*	*Johansson*
						Ref: E Poulsen (Denmark)	On a cold, wet night United put on a sloppy display. The Swedish part-timers attack with vigour and miss three good chances after Johansson's early shot from Andersson's cross. Herd's late header saves the blushes. United are open to offers for five, including Setters, Moir and Moore.										
1:2 H DJURGAARDENS IF	2	W		6-1	1-0	Law 20, 63, 66p, Charlton 61, 70,	Dunne P	Brennan	Dunne A	Crerand	Foulkes	Stiles	Connelly	Charlton	Herd	Law	Best
27/10	38,437					*Karlsson H 90* [Best 85]	*Arvidsson*	*Karlsson J*	*Arnesson*	*Fururkrantz*	*Mild*	*Sandberg*	*Andersson*	*Karlsson H*	*Eriksson*	*Persson*	*Johansson*
						Ref: F Geluck (Belgium) (United win 7-2 on aggregate)	Despite the scoreline, United are unimpressive against the new champions of Sweden. Four goals in nine minutes end the game as a contest as the Swedes tire. Poor Karlsson is run ragged by the impish Best and fouls him for the penalty. Law's first is the best – from a clever free-kick.										
2:1 A BORUSSIA DORT	1	W		6-1	2-0	Herd 12, Charlton 30, 79, 89,	Dunne P	Brennan	Dunne A	Crerand	Foulkes	Stiles	Connelly	Charlton	Herd	Law	Best
11/11 (W Germany)	*25,000*					*Kurrat 52p* /Best 50, Law 77]	*Wessel*	*Cyliax*	*Redder*	*Kurrat*	*Paul*	*Sturm*	*Wosab*	*Brungs*	*Beyer*	*Konietzka*	*Emmerich*
						Ref: L Rigato (Italy)	Arguably one of United's finest European nights, as Borussia, near the top of the Bundesliga, are thrashed. Herd's low drive starts the rout and Dortmund collapse after the third, a brilliant solo from the mesmerising Best. One blot is Crerand's rash challenge on Kurrat for the penalty.										
2:2 H BORUSSIA DORT	1	W		4-0	2-0	Charlton 1, 18, Law 65, Connelly 79	Dunne P	Brennan	Dunne A	Crerand	Foulkes	Stiles	Connelly	Charlton	Herd	Law	Best
2/12	31,896						*Tilkowski*	*Busmuller*	*Pfeifer*	*Cyliax*	*Paul*	*Straschitz*	*Sturm*	*Schmidt*	*Brungs*	*Beyer*	*Wosab*
						Ref: G Loraux (Belgium) (United win 10-1 on aggregate)	An easy victory against much-changed Borussia, who never offer a serious challenge. In driving rain control is difficult but Charlton is superb, scoring with a 20-yarder and a rare header. Dennis Law's lob lifts the tedium as United make it 19 games unbeaten and eleven straight wins.										
3:1 H EVERTON	3	D		1-1	1-1	Connelly 33	Dunne P	Brennan	Dunne A	Crerand	Foulkes	Stiles	Connelly	Charlton	Herd	Law	Best
20/1 (England)	49,075	*8*				*Pickering 14*	*West*	*Wright*	*Wilson*	*Gabriel*	*Labone*	*Stevens*	*Scott*	*Harvey*	*Pickering*	*Temple*	*Morrissey*
						Ref: G Schulenberg (W Germany)	Despite territorial superiority, United may rue their missed chances and the saves of Gordon West. Both goals come from errors. Bill Foulkes' miskick lets in England cap Fred Pickering, who finishes clinically. Jimmy Gabriel's back-pass is pounced upon by the sharp John Connelly.										
3:2 A EVERTON	3	W		2-1	1-0	Connelly 6, Herd 69	Dunne P	Brennan	Dunne A	Crerand	Foulkes	Stiles	Connelly	Charlton	Herd	Law	Best
9/2	*54,397*	*11*				*Pickering 54*	*West*	*Wright*	*Wilson*	*Gabriel*	*Labone*	*Stevens*	*Scott*	*Harvey*	*Pickering*	*Vernon*	*Temple*
						Ref: T Wharton (Scotland) (United win 3-2 on aggregate)	United advance to the quarter-final with an impressive win after soaking up Everton's considerable pressure. Connelly is the hero, outpacing England full-back Ray Wilson to net, and forcing West to spill a shot that Herd forces in. Pickering's vicious free-kick is deflected past Dunne.										
QF 1 A RC STRASBOURG	1	W		5-0	2-0	Connelly 19, Herd 40, Law 61, 89,	Dunne P	Brennan	Dunne A	Crerand	Foulkes	Stiles	Connelly	Charlton	Herd	Law	Best
12/5 (France)	*29,000*					[Charlton 72]	*Schuth*	*Hauss*	*Gonzalez*	*Stieber*	*Devaux*	*Kaelbel*	*Heine*	*Merschel*	*Gress*	*Szepaniak*	*Hausser*
						Ref: H Baumgarter (W Germany)	A poor French side are swept aside by a masterly United in a friendly atmosphere. On a bumpy and thickly grassed pitch it is exhibition football with Dennis Law's two headers the pick of the bunch. Strasbourg have only two shots in 90 minutes and the tie is as good as over.										
QF 2 H RC STRASBOURG	1	D		0-0	0-0		Dunne P	Brennan	Dunne A	Crerand	Foulkes	Stiles	Connelly	Charlton	Herd	Law	Best
19/5	34,188						*Schuth*	*Gonzalez*	*Sbaiz*	*Stieber*	*Devaux*	*Kaelbel*	*Gress*	*Merschel*	*Biernet*	*Szepaniak*	*Hausser*
						Ref: F Geluck (Belgium) (United win 5-0 on aggregate)	The league championship trophy is presented before the match, with Law's European Footballer of the year award. The pace is like a practice match and a heap of Red chances go missing. The crowd is low as TV shows West Ham v TSV Munich live in the Cup-Winners' Cup final.										

SF	H	FERENCVAROS	1	W	3·2	1·1	Law 35p, Herd 61, 69	Dunne P	Brennan	Dunne A	Crerand	Foulkes	Stiles	Connelly	Charlton	Herd	Law	Best
1	31/5	(Hungary) 39,902					*Novak 23, Rakosi 78*	*Geczi*	*Novak*	*Horvath*	*Orosz*	*Matrai*	*Juhasz*	*Ratkai*	*Varga*	*Albert*	*Rakosi*	*Fenyvesi M*
							Ref: M Burguet (France)	Things threaten to get out of hand at the end of a niggly first half on a raw, cold night. Novak's free-kick pierces United's wall and Horvath handles for the penalty. United are finally rewarded for a strong attacking display but sloppy defending costs a vital second goal near the end.										
SF	A	FERENCVAROS	1	L	0·1	0·1		Dunne P	Brennan	Dunne A	Crerand!	Foulkes	Stiles	Connelly	Charlton	Herd	Law	Best
2	6/6	*60,000*					*Novak 44p*	*Geczi*	*Novak*	*Horvath*	*Juhasz*	*Matrai*	*Orosz!*	*Fenyvesi J*	*Varga*	*Albert*	*Rakosi*	*Fenyvesi M*
							Ref: M Kitabdjan (France) (United draw 3-3 on aggregate)	United's defensive tactics hold out until Stiles handles in the area. A bad tempered game spills over after seventy five minutes and Crerand and Orosz are sent off for fighting. The Nepstadion pitch is in a poor state after heavy rain. Matrai's well-drilled defence holds out for a play-off.										
SF	A	FERENCVAROS	1	L	1·2	0·1	Connelly 85	Dunne P	Brennan	Dunne A	Crerand	Foulkes	Stiles	Connelly	Charlton	Herd	Law	Best
P/O	16/6	*90,000*					*Karaba 44, Fenyvesi 54*	*Geczi*	*Novak*	*Horvath*	*Juhasz*	*Matrai*	*Orosz*	*Karaba*	*Varga*	*Albert*	*Rakosi*	*Fenyvesi M*
							Ref: G Schulenberg (W Germany)	The sun is out and the bad feeling has subsided. The Magyars again score at a crucial time as Rakosi, one of eight internationals, hits a swirling 30-yarder past a sleepy Dunne. Fenyvesi's half-volley seals a final tie with Juventus. Connelly's goal after Geczi spilled Herd's shot is too late.										

FA Cup						F-A	H-T	Scorers, Times, and Referees	1	2	3	4	5	6	7	8	9	10	11
3	H	CHESTER		2	W	2-1	0-1	Best 56, Kinsey 59	Dunne P	Brennan	Dunne A	Crerand	Foulkes	Stiles	Connelly	Charlton	Herd	**Kinsey**	Best
	9/1		45,660	*4:8*				*Humes 9*	*Reeves*	*Jones*	*Sharkey*	*Hauser*	*Butler*	*Durie*	*Humes*	*Metcalf*	*Talbot*	*Ryden*	*Morris*
								Ref: J Taylor	Albert Kinsey scores a point-blank winner on his one and only first team appearance, after Humes' early header had rocked the Reds. Peter Hauser's heroes are roared on by their fans in the pouring rain and for a time a shock looks on. Once United are ahead there is only one winner.										
4	A	STOKE		3	D	0-0	0-0		Dunne P	Brennan	Dunne A	Crerand	Foulkes	Stiles	Connelly	Charlton	Herd	Law	Best
	30/1		*49,032*	*12*					*Leslie*	*Asprey*	*Allen*	*Setters*	*Kinnell*	*Bloor*	*Palmer*	*Skeels*	*Ritchie*	*Viollet*	*McIlroy*
								Ref: L Callaghan	A minute's silence for the late Winston Churchill is disrupted by banal chants and sets the tone. Stoke are unyielding and there are vicious challenges on both sides, with Setters and Crerand the main culprits. George Best goes closest to scoring, hitting the bar with a cross-cum-shot.										
4R	H	STOKE		3	W	1-0	0-0	Herd 73	Dunne P	Brennan	Dunne A	Crerand	Foulkes	Stiles	Connelly	Charlton	Herd	Law	Best
	3/2		50,814	*12*					*Leslie*	*Asprey*	*Allen*	*Setters*	*Kinnell*	*Bloor*	*Palmer*	*Skeels*	*Ritchie*	*Viollet*	*McIlroy*
								Ref: L Callaghan	Stoke's brave rearguard action holds out until Herd nets. He is on his knees to glance in Tony Dunne's cross-shot with his head. The thick descending mist threatens the game. Stoke rarely trouble Pat Dunne. Best's penalty claim is rejected before Herd fires over from three yards.										
5	H	BURNLEY		3	W	2-1	0-1	Law 81, Crerand 82	Dunne P	Brennan	Dunne A	Crerand	Foulkes	Stiles	Connelly	Charlton	Herd	Law	Best
	20/2		54,000	*15*				*Lochhead 17*	*Blacklaw*	*Smith*	*Elder*	*O'Neill*	*Talbut*	*Miller*	*Bellamy*	*Lochhead*	*Irvine*	*Harris*	*Latcham*
								Ref: G McCabe	Harry Potts' disciplined defensive plans foil United in front of an all-ticket full house. After Lochhead's goal Burnley have another disallowed. Finally a boot-less Best crosses for Law's spectacular overhead kick. Soon after, Crerand's 30-yarder seals the tie with Blacklaw unsighted.										
QF	A	WOLVERHAMPTON		3	W	5-3	1-2	Law 42, 75, Herd 51, Best 61,	Dunne P	Brennan	Dunne A	Crerand	Foulkes	Stiles	Connelly	Charlton	Herd	Law	Best
	10/3		*53,581*	*22*				*McIlm' 3, 15, Know' 87* [Crerand 67]	*Davies*	*Thomson*	*Harris*	*Flowers*	*Woodfield*	*Miller*	*Wharton*	*Woodruff*	*McIlmoyle*	*Knowles*	*Wagstaffe*
								Ref: L Callaghan	Relegation-threatened Wolves give United a massive fright before the Reds take control in a fast, furious game, and rip the home side apart. Best's goal, direct from a corner, and Law's wicked, swerving free-kick, are the highlights. 'Double' talk is rife in the city, but also in Leeds.										
SF	N	LEEDS		3	D	0-0	0-0		Dunne P	Brennan	Dunne A	Crerand	Foulkes	Stiles	Connelly	Charlton	Herd	Law	Best
	27/3		*65,000*	*2*					*Sprake*	*Reaney*	*Bell*	*Bremner*	*Charlton*	*Hunter*	*Giles*	*Storrie*	*Peacock*	*Collins*	*Johanneson*
		(at Hillsborough)						Ref: R Windle	A week after a league defeat on the ground, United struggle again on a ploughed field. A gruelling game is full of malice and it is amazing no one is sent off. Law and Jack Charlton spark off a mass brawl in a game best forgotten. Man United on top early on, but Leeds finish stronger.										
SF	N	LEEDS		3	L	0-1	0-0		Dunne P	Brennan	Dunne A	Crerand	Foulkes	Stiles	Connelly	Charlton	Herd	Law	Best
R	31/3		*46,300*	*2*				*Bremner 89*	*Sprake*	*Reaney*	*Bell*	*Bremner*	*Charlton*	*Hunter*	*Giles*	*Storrie*	*Peacock*	*Collins*	*Cooper*
		(at Nott'm Forest)						Ref: R Windle	The battle moves to Nottingham and Billy Bremner's header from Giles' floated free-kick sends Don Revie's team to their first Cup final. United dominate the second half but the agile Sprake, the woodwork, and poor finishing foil the Reds. Revie's fulsome praise is scant reward.										

		Home						Away					
	P	W	D	L	F	A	W	D	L	F	A	Pts
1 MAN UNITED	42	16	4	1	52	13	10	5	6	37	26	61
2 Leeds	42	16	3	2	53	23	10	6	5	30	29	61
3 Chelsea	42	15	2	4	48	19	9	6	6	41	35	56
4 Everton	42	9	10	2	37	22	8	5	8	32	38	49
5 Nott'm Forest	42	10	7	4	45	33	7	6	8	26	34	47
6 Tottenham	42	18	3	0	65	20	1	4	16	22	51	45
7 Liverpool	42	12	5	4	42	33	5	5	11	25	40	44
8 Sheffield Wed	42	13	5	3	37	15	3	6	12	20	40	43
9 West Ham	42	14	2	5	48	25	5	2	14	34	46	42
10 Blackburn	42	12	2	7	46	33	4	8	9	37	46	42
11 Stoke	42	11	4	6	40	27	5	6	10	27	39	42
12 Burnley	42	9	9	3	39	26	7	1	13	31	44	42
13 Arsenal	42	11	5	5	42	31	6	2	13	27	44	41
14 West Brom	42	10	5	6	45	25	3	8	10	25	40	39
15 Sunderland	42	12	6	3	45	26	2	3	16	19	48	37
16 Aston Villa	42	14	1	6	36	24	2	4	15	21	58	37
17 Blackpool	42	9	7	5	41	28	3	4	14	26	50	35
18 Leicester	42	9	6	6	43	36	2	7	12	26	49	35
19 Sheffield Utd	42	7	5	9	30	29	5	6	10	20	35	35
20 Fulham	42	10	5	6	44	32	1	7	13	16	46	34
21 Wolves	42	8	2	11	33	36	5	2	14	26	53	30
22 Birmingham	42	6	8	7	36	40	2	3	16	28	56	27
	924	251	106	105	947	596	105	106	251	596	947	924

Odds & ends

Double wins: (6) Chelsea, Wolves, Liverpool, Blackpool, Arsenal, Blackburn.
Double losses: (0).

Won from behind: (7) Stoke (a), Fulham (h), Birm'm (a), Chester FAC (a), Burnley FAC (h), Wolves FAC (a), Ferencvaros ICFC (h).
Lost from in front: (1) Fulham (a).

High spots: First league title since 1957.
19-game unbeaten run in the autumn.
Form of wingers Connelly and Best.
Eleven successive wins in October-November.

Low spots: Losing FA Cup and Fairs Cup semi-finals.

Red cards: Law (Blackpool a), Crerand (Ferencvaros a).
Red cards (Opponents): (1) Orosz (Ferencvaros).
Ever-presents: (4) Brennan, Dunne (A), Foulkes, Connelly.
Hat-tricks: (4) Law (2), Charlton (2).
Opposing hat-tricks: (0).
Leading scorer: (39) Law.

	Appearances			Goals			
	Lge	FAC	Eur	Lge	FAC	Eur	Tot
Aston, John	**1**						
Best, George	**41**	7	11	**10**	2	2	**14**
Brennan, Shay	**42**	7	11				
Cantwell, Noel	**2**			**1**			**1**
Charlton, Bobby	**41**	7	11	**10**		8	**18**
Connelly, John	**42**	7	11	**15**		5	**20**
Crerand, Pat	**39**	7	11	**3**	2		**5**
Dunne, Pat	**37**	7	11				
Dunne, Tony	**42**	7	11				
Fitzpatrick, John	**2**						
Foulkes, Bill	**42**	7	11				
Gaskell, Dave	**5**						
Herd, David	**37**	7	11	**20**	2	6	**28**
Kinsey, Albert		1			1		**1**
Law, Dennis	**36**	6	10	**28**	3	8	**39**
Moir, Ian	**1**						
Sadler, David	**6**			**1**			**1**
Setters, Maurice	**5**		1				
Stiles, Nobby	**41**	7	11				
(own-goals)				**1**			**1**
18 players used	**462**	**77**	**121**	**89**	**10**	**29**	**128**

No	Date		Att	Pos	Pt	F-A	H-T	Scorers, Times, and Referees	1	2	3	4	5	6	7	8	9	10	11	12 sub used
1	H	SHEFFIELD WED			W	1-0	1-0	Herd 23	Dunne P	Brennan	Dunne A	Crerand	Foulkes	Stiles	Anderson	Charlton	Herd	Best	Aston	
	21/8		37,524		2				*Springett R*	*Hill*	*Megson*	*Eustace*	*Mobley*	*Young*	*Usher*	*Quinn*	*Hickton*	*Fantham*	*Dobson*	
								Ref: P Brandwood	An opening-day win for the first time in seven years, despite a strong Owls rally in the second half. With Law injured, Aston comes in to form a young attack that sadly runs out of steam. Herd's thunderous shot from Stiles' cheeky chip seals the points and the impish Best impresses.											
2	A	NOTT'M FOREST			L	2-4	0-3	Aston 66, Best 80	Dunne P	Brennan	Dunne A	Crerand	Foulkes	Stiles	Connelly	Charlton	Herd	Best	Aston	
	24/8		*33,744*		2			*Wignall 8, Addison 28, 44, Hinton 62*	*Grummitt*	*Hindley*	*Mochan*	*Newton*	*McKinlay*	*Whitefoot*	*Crowe*	*Addison*	*Wignall*	*Barnwell*	*Hinton*	
								Ref: R Harper	Bobby McKinlay celebrates his 280th successive appearance for Forest with a solid win. United's defence is ripped apart, with Alan Hinton scoring one and making the first two. Pat Dunne is at fault for two goals, and a late rally is in vain. Forest celebrate their centenary in style.											
3	A	NORTHAMPTON		13	D	1-1	1-0	Connelly 10	Gaskell	Dunne A	Cantwell	Crerand	Foulkes	Stiles	Connelly	Charlton	Herd	Law	Best	
	28/8		*21,245*	*17*	3			*Hunt 83*	*Harvey*	*Foley*	*Cockcroft*	*Leck*	*Carr*	*Kiernan*	*Walden*	*Hunt*	*Brown*	*Lines*	*Robson*	
								Ref: D Brady	Seven years ago the Cobblers were in Division 4 and now they are in Div 1 for the first time. In a cup-tie atmosphere, Charlton's through-ball is slotted home by Connelly. On a slippery pitch, casual United pay when Hunt volleys home and the wild but happy crowd invade the pitch.											
4	H	NOTT'M FOREST		12	D	0-0	0-0		Gaskell	Brennan	Dunne A	Crerand	Foulkes	Stiles	Connelly	Charlton	Herd	Law	Best	
	1/9		40,027	*3*	4				*Grummitt*	*Hindley*	*Mochan*	*Newton*	*McKinlay*	*Whitefoot*	*Crowe*	*Addison*	*Wignall*	*Barnwell*	*Hinton*	
								Ref: D Payne	Forest are lucky to retain their unbeaten record with a dour defensive display. United penetrate the blanket often, but miss good chances in a lacklustre match. John Connelly hits the bar and Peter Grummitt punches Crerand's 30-yarder onto the bar in a late siege on the visitors' goal.											
5	H	STOKE		13	D	1-1	0-1	Herd 73	Gaskell	Brennan	Dunne A	Crerand	Foulkes	Stiles	Connelly	Charlton	Herd	Law	Best	
	4/9		37,764	*11*	5			*Dobing 42*	*Leslie*	*Palmer*	*Skeels*	*Setters*	*Kinnell*	*Bloor*	*Bridgew'd**	*Dobing*	*Viollet*	*Vernon*	*Burrows*	*McIlroy*
								Ref: H Wilson	United move with more purpose against a hard Stoke, for whom Setters and Leslie are outstanding. They keep the rampant Reds at bay in a siege. Law and Setters are constantly grappling, but it's supposedly friendly! Herd's close-range goal after good play by Law is scant reward.											
6	A	NEWCASTLE		9	W	2-1	1-0	Herd 25, Law 68	Gaskell	Brennan	Dunne A	Crerand	Foulkes	Stiles	Connelly	Charlton	Herd	Law	Best	
	8/9		*57,436*	*10*	7			*Hockey 85*	*Marshall*	*Craig*	*Clark*	*Anderson*	*McGrath*	*Iley*	*Hockey*	*McGarry*	*Cummings*	*Hilley*	*Suddick*	
								Ref: J Thacker	Joe Harvey's newly promoted team are on top for long periods but are let down by basic errors. Gordon Marshall fails to hold Best's centre and Herd taps in. Then, Jim Iley's bungled clearance lets in Dennis Law. As the rain pours down, Trevor Hockey's header is too little and too late.											
7	A	BURNLEY		13	L	0-3	0-1		Gaskell	Brennan	Dunne A	Crerand	Foulkes	Stiles	Connelly	Charlton	Herd	Law	Best	
	11/9		*30,137*	*1*	7			*Harris 6, 47, Elder 89p*	*Thomson*	*Angus*	*Elder*	*O'Neill*	*Talbut*	*Miller*	*Morgan*	*Lochhead*	*Irvine*	*Harris*	*Latcham*	
								Ref: K Howley	Harry Potts' Burnley have lost only once. They soak up Red pressure and counter-attack with venom. Gaskell is wrong-footed for Harris' free-kick and Morgan's raid sets up Harris with the defence at sea. Foulkes concedes a penalty for dangerous play. United fans cause crowd trouble.											
8	H	NEWCASTLE		12	D	1-1	0-1	Stiles 85	Gaskell	Brennan	Dunne A	Crerand	Foulkes	Stiles	Connelly	Charlton	Herd	Law	Best	
	15/9		30,636	*17*	8			*McGarry 42p*	*Marshall*	*Burton*	*Clark*	*Anderson*	*Moncur*	*Iley*	*Hockey*	*Bennett*	*McGarry*	*Hilley*	*Knox*	
								Ref: K Stokes	United's goal-touch is eluding them. Stiles fouls Bennett for a penalty against the run of play but redeems himself by driving home Charlton's cross. Newcastle's time-wasting upsets the fans but ultimately fail. Bobby Charlton is booked for the first time for comments to the referee.											
9	H	CHELSEA		10	W	4-1	1-1	Charlton 33, Law 61, 73, 78	Gaskell	Brennan	Dunne A	Crerand	Foulkes	Stiles	Connelly	Charlton	Herd	Law	Aston	
	18/9		38,183	*12*	10			*Venables 22*	*Bonetti*	*Shellito*	*McCreadie*	*Hollins*	*Young*	*Harris R*	*Murray*	*Graham*	*Bridges*	*Venables*	*Fascione*	
								Ref: V James	Chelsea have lost only one game, but lack the bite of last season. Tommy Docherty's team buckle in the last half hour to three Law headers. John Aston, in for the injured Best, has a superb game on a slippery pitch. United click at last to get their title challenge belatedly on the move.											
10	A	ARSENAL		13	L	2-4	1-2	Charlton 25, Aston 68 *[Eastham 77]*	Dunne P	Brennan	Dunne A	Crerand	Foulkes	Stiles	Connelly	Charlton	Herd	Law	Aston	
	25/9		*56,757*	*10*	10			*Baker 29, Radford 42, Armstrong 58,*	*Furnell*	*Howe*	*McCullough*	*McLintock*	*Neill*	*Court*	*Armstrong*	*Radford*	*Baker*	*Sammels*	*Eastham*	
								Ref: R Tinkler	Bobby Charlton is in England class and his rare header gives the Reds a short-lived lead. Billy Wright's men's finishing is top class, especially Armstrong's 25-yarder. 18-year-old John Aston's shot is too hot for Jim Furnell, but a hard-fought game is won by George Eastham's header.											
11	H	LIVERPOOL		11	W	2-0	2-0	Best 18, Law 37	Dunne P	Brennan	Dunne A	Crerand	Foulkes	Stiles	Connelly	Best	Charlton	Law	Aston	
	9/10		58,461	6	12				*Lawrence*	*Lawler*	*Byrne*	*Strong*	*Yeats*	*Stevenson*	*Callaghan*	*Hunt*	*St John*	*Smith*	*Thompson*	
								Ref: M Fussey	Best returns with a bang. He nips in to score when Yeats' header puts Lawrence in trouble and is denied a penalty for Strong's heavy tackle. Law's opportunism seals the win before Tommy Smith clatters Best after the Irish wizard fools him. Pool fans throw missiles at United's men.											

12	A	TOTTENHAM		13	L	1-5	0-2	Charlton 74 *[Clay' 60, Roberts'n 77]*	Dunne P	Brennan	Dunne A	Crerand	Foulkes	Stiles	Connelly	Best	Charlton	Law*	Aston	Fitzpatrick
	16/10		*58,051*	*4*	12			*Gilzean 25, Johnson 38, Greaves 58,*	*Jennings*	*Norman*	*Knowles*	*Mullery*	*Brown L*	*Mackay*	*Johnson*	*Clayton*	*Gilzean*	*Greaves*	*Robertson*	
								Ref: E Wallace	Busby's 20th anniversary as boss is marred by a thumping. A full-house watch Spurs extend their unbeaten home record to eighteen months with ease. Greaves' goal is out of this world – he beats five Reds before slotting home. Fitzpatrick is United's first sub: on for the injured Law.											
13	H	FULHAM		12	W	4-1	1-0	Herd 24, 59, 89, Charlton 88	Dunne P	Brennan	Dunne A	Crerand	Foulkes	Stiles	Connelly	Best	Charlton	Herd	Aston	
	23/10		34,417	*19*	14			*Dempsey 51*	*Macedo*	*Cohen*	*Nicholls*	*Pearson*	*Keetch*	*Robson*	*Key*	*Marsh*	*Dempsey*	*Haynes*	*Dyson*	
								Ref: J Carr	Herd celebrates his recall with a hat-trick in an unimpressive win over struggling Fulham. Pancho Pearson makes a nostalgic return and ex-Spur Terry Dyson hits the bar before Dempsey's header. Macedo can't hold Crerand's stinging shot and Herd nets. Late goals flatter the Reds.											
14	A	BLACKPOOL		12	W	2-1	0-1	Herd 75, 89	Gregg	Brennan	Dunne A	Crerand	Foulkes	Stiles	Connelly	Best	Charlton	Herd	Aston	
	30/10		*24,703*	*16*	16			*Ball 33*	*Waiters**	*Prentis*	*Thompson*	*Turner*	*James*	*Green*	*Moir*	*Ball*	*Charnley*	*Robson*	*Oates*	*McPhee*
								Ref: E Crawford	Turner replaces the injured Waiters in goal for the last 20 minutes and United take advantage. On a blustery day the effervescent Ball had been in charge and left the recalled Gregg standing with a glorious goal. Herd, with a header and a dribble through a static defence, wins the day.											
15	H	BLACKBURN		10	D	2-2	1-0	Charlton 38, Law 88	Gregg!	Brennan	Dunne A	Crerand	Foulkes	Stiles	Best	Law	Charlton	Herd	Aston*	Connelly
	6/11		39,093	*22*	17			*Harrison 83p, 90*	*Else*	*Newton*	*Wilson*	*Sharples*	*Mulvaney*	*Clayton*	*Ferguson*	*McEvoy*	*England*	*McGrath**	*Harrison*	*Byrom*
								Ref: W Clements	A Polio epidemic in Blackburn has forced several Rovers' games to be postponed. A poor start is getting worse by the game but they earn a fighting point with Harrison's deflected shot. Gregg, who has glass thrown at him, is off after kicking Mike England and Herd is beaten twice.											
16	A	LEICESTER		7	W	5-0	3-0	Connelly 11, Herd 31, 44, Charlton 70, [Best 73]	Gregg	Dunne A	Cantwell	Crerand	Foulkes	Stiles	Best	Law	Charlton	Herd	Connelly	
	13/11		*34,551*	*14*	19				*Banks*	*Sjoberg*	*Norman*	*Roberts*	*King*	*Cross*	*Sinclair*	*Goodfellow*	*Dougan*	*Gibson*	*Stringfellow*	
								Ref: L Callaghan	The first win at Filbert Street since 1957 ends the bogey in style. Connelly returns from England duty to net and Herd's 30-yard rocket soars past Banks. A Herd header, a Charlton cracker off the bar and a Best special seal it for white-shirted United. Crerand corners a wayward dog.											
17	H	SHEFFIELD UTD		6	W	3-1	3-1	Best 8, 38, Law 40	Gregg	Dunne A	Cantwell	Crerand	Sadler	Stiles	Best	Law	Charlton	Herd	Connelly	
	20/11		38,216	*8*	21			*Jones 22*	*Widdowson*	*Badger*	*Mallender*	*Matthewson*	*Shaw J*	*Wagstaff B*	*Woodward*	*Kettlebor'gh*	*Jones*	*Wagstaff T*	*Reece*	
								Ref: W Gow	United receive a standing ovation at half-time after an impressive display. Mick Jones' half-volley levels Best's vicious shot and George's header from Connelly's cross puts United ahead. Herd sets up Law to complete the scoring and the Blades rarely threaten after the break.											
18	H	WEST HAM		8	D	0-0	0-0		Dunne P	Dunne A	Cantwell	Crerand	Foulkes	Stiles	Best	Law	Charlton	Herd	Connelly	
	4/12		33,172	*17*	22				*Standen*	*Kirkup*	*Charles*	*Bovington*	*Brown*	*Moore*	*Brabrook*	*Peters*	*Byrne*	*Hurst*	*Sissons*	
								Ref: K Burns	Former Hammer Cantwell plays his 100th league game for United. West Ham, well marshalled by the cool Moore, play a blanket defence but Byrne twice hits the woodwork to almost end United's unbeaten home record. A new by-law allows throwers of toilet rolls to be prosecuted.											
19	A	SUNDERLAND		7	W	3-2	2-1	Best 15, 35, Herd 59	Dunne P	Dunne A	Cantwell	Crerand	Foulkes	Stiles	Best	Law	Charlton	Herd	Connelly	
	11/12		*37,417*	*16*	24			*Martin 7, 75*	*McLaughlan*	*Irwin*	*Ashurst*	*Harvey*	*Hurley*	*Baxter*	*Hellawell**	*Herd*	*Moore*	*Martin*	*Mulhall*	*Elliott*
								Ref: V James	Three away wins in a row lift United amongst the leaders. This is a rough game and it is amazing no one is sent off. Herd and Ashurst raise fists but stay on. New signing Neil Martin nets two good goals but is eclipsed by the irrepressible Best who jinks through for two special goals.											
20	H	EVERTON		3	W	3-0	1-0	Best 30, Herd 50, Charlton 52	Gregg	Dunne A	Cantwell	Crerand	Foulkes	Stiles	Best	Law	Charlton	Herd	Connelly	
	15/12		32,896	*11*	26				*Barnett*	*Wright*	*Wilson*	*Harvey*	*Labone*	*Harris*	*Scott*	*Gabriel*	*Pickering*	*Hurst*	*Temple*	
								Ref: E Crawford	After several good seasons, Harry Catterick's Everton are having a poor league season. They are on top early on but go home empty handed. Best's genius, allied to his never-say die-attitude, are a potent mix. He cheekily scores one and sets up simple tap-ins for Herd and Charlton.											
21	H	TOTTENHAM		3	W	5-1	3-0	Charlton 20, Law 21, 81, Beal 36 (og), [Herd 49]	Gregg	Dunne A	Cantwell	Crerand	Foulkes	Stiles	Best	Law	Charlton	Herd	Connelly	
	18/12		39,511	*5*	28			*Jones 47*	*Jennings*	*Beal*	*Knowles*	*Mullery*	*Brown L*	*Mackay*	*Robertson*	*Clayton*	*Saul*	*Gilzean*	*Jones*	
								Ref: K Howley	A revenge win over Nicholson's Spurs lifts United four points behind Liverpool with a game in hand. Busby is away watching Benfica and misses a Charlton special and a rampant team display that earns a standing ovation. Luckily the ref misses Law and Brown having a spat.											
22	H	WEST BROM		3	D	1-1	0-0	Law 60p	Gregg	Dunne A	Cantwell	Crerand	Foulkes	Stiles	Best	Law	Charlton	Herd	Connelly	
	27/12		54,370	*7*	29			*Crawford 65*	*Potter*	*Cram*	*Fairfax*	*Lovett*	*Jones*	*Fraser*	*Foggo*	*Crawford*	*Kaye*	*Hope*	*Clark*	
								Ref: H Davey	Bill Foulkes equals Joe Spence's record 481 league games. On a heavily sanded pitch, Law is fouled by Stan Jones and scores from the spot. Charlton's uncharacteristic back-pass tees up Ray Crawford. In the final minute Stiles turns John Kaye's goal-bound shot onto the crossbar.											
23	A	LIVERPOOL		5	L	1-2	1-1	Law 2	Gregg	Dunne A	Cantwell	Crerand	Foulkes	Stiles	Best	Law	Charlton	Herd	Connelly	
	1/1		53,970	*1*	29			*Smith 39, Milne 88*	*Lawrence*	*Lawler*	*Byrne*	*Milne*	*Yeats*	*Stevenson*	*Callaghan*	*Hunt*	*St John*	*Smith*	*Thompson*	
								Ref: R Harper	A defining result in the title race as United suffer a first defeat in ten. 10,000 are locked out and the Kop are in full voice but Law silences them. United are on top in a thriller but Smith's 20-yarder sneaks past the unsighted Gregg and Milne gets a touch on Byrne's fierce shot.											

No	Date		Att	Pos	Pt	F-A	H-T	Scorers, Times, and Referees	1	2	3	4	5	6	7	8	9	10	11	12 sub used
24	H	SUNDERLAND		4	D	1-1	1-0	Best 7	Gregg	Dunne A	Cantwell	Crerand	Foulkes	Stiles	Best	Law	Charlton	Herd	Aston	
	8/1		39,410	15	30			O'Hare 61	Montgomery	Irwin	Ashurst	Harvey	McNab	Elliott	Hellawell	Herd	O'Hare	Moore	Mulhall	
								Ref: D Corbett	Injury-hit Sunderland are without big signing Jim Baxter and captain Charlie Hurley but gain a vital draw against a casual home side. John O'Hare's close-range goal stings United and cancels out Best's full-blooded shot. The Reds have three strong penalty claims turned down.											
25	A	LEEDS		4	D	1-1	0-1	Herd 60	Gregg	Dunne A	Cantwell	Crerand	Foulkes	Stiles	Best	Law	Charlton	Herd	Aston	
	12/1		49,672	3	31			Storrie 23	Sprake	Reaney	Bell	Bremner	Charlton	Hunter	Greenhoff	Storrie	Peacock	Giles	O'Grady	
								Ref: K Stokes	A fair result in a tense clash. Leeds are on top in the first half. Gregg twice saves well from Giles but can't stop Jack Charlton's looping header that Storrie nets. Gary Sprake parries Bobby's stinger and Herd is first to the ball. United finish stronger but only Liverpool have won at Leeds.											
26	A	FULHAM		4	W	1-0	1-0	Charlton 27	Gregg	Dunne A	Cantwell	Crerand	Foulkes	Stiles	Best	Law	Charlton	Herd	Aston	
	15/1		33,018	22	33				Macedo	Cohen	O'Connell	Robson	Dempsey	Brown	Key	Keetch	Leggat	Haynes	Parmenter	
								Ref: P Brandwood	Vic Buckingham's fighting Fulham never give up and the result is always in doubt. United show greater skill on the icy surface with Best peerless. Law and Best create Charlton's strong shot. Johnny Haynes is denied a penalty but they have now lost eight of their last nine games.											
27	A	SHEFFIELD WED		3	D	0-0	0-0		Gregg	Dunne A	Cantwell	Crerand	Foulkes	Stiles	Best	Law	Charlton	Herd	Aston	
	29/1		37,628	15	34				Springett R	Smith	Megson	Eustace	Mobley	Young	Usher	Fantham	McCalliog	Hickton*	Dobson	Quinn
								Ref: R Tinkler	The Hillsborough bogey continues – no league win since 1954 – and Wednesday deserve to win. Herd hits the bar in a below-par performance. Brian Usher has a fine shot tipped over by Gregg and another cleared off the line by Cantwell. Liverpool are now seven points clear of United.											
28	H	NORTHAMPTON		3	W	6-2	4-1	Law 6, 46, Connelly 10,	Gregg	Dunne A	Cantwell	Crerand	Foulkes	Stiles	Best	Law	Charlton	Herd	Connelly	
	5/2		35,273	20	36			Moore 22, Martin 75 [Charl' 27,31,84]	Coe	Foley	Everitt	Kurila	Carr	Kiernan	Broadfoot	Moore	Hall	Martin	Lines	
								Ref: H Hackney	Dave Bowen's Cobblers have conceded 65 goals as they struggle against the drop and are blitzed by United's rampaging forwards. Graham Moore, sold to Northampton in December, scores a good goal before Bobby's show. United are the first team to reach 1,000 points since 1945.											
29	A	STOKE		4	D	2-2	1-0	Herd 39, Connelly 58	Gregg	Brennan	Dunne A	Crerand	Foulkes	Stiles	Connelly	Best	Charlton	Herd	Aston	
	19/2		36,885	8	37			Ritchie 64, Vernon 70	Farmer	Palmer	Allen	Bloor*	Setters	Skeels	Bebbington	Viollet	Ritchie	Vernon	Jones	Kinnell
								Ref: D Smith	On a sea of mud United feel the effects of their tie at Rotherham, and Stoke come from behind. 18-year-old keeper John Farmer stars but can't stop Herd's fierce drive, his 100th United goal, nor Connelly's near-post header. Ritchie's header and Vernon's solo effort seal a merited draw.											
30	H	BURNLEY		2	W	4-2	2-1	Charlton 3, Herd 40, 63, 67	Gregg	Brennan	Dunne A	Crerand	Foulkes	Stiles	Best	Law	Charlton	Herd	Connelly	
	26/2		50,188	4	39			Lochhead 8, Irvine 50	Thomson	Angus	Buxton	O'Neill	Miller	Merrington	Morgan	Lochhead	Irvine	Harris	Coates	
								Ref: G McCabe	United deservedly win a high quality game that has a nasty undercurrent after recent games between these clubs. Nobby Stiles, fresh from his England goal against Germany, stars and Herd outshines Law on a wet, miserable day. Lochhead rattles Gregg, who boobs for the second goal.											
31	A	CHELSEA		4	L	0-2	0-2		Gregg	Brennan	Dunne A	Crerand	Foulkes	Stiles	Best	Law	Charlton	Herd	Connelly	
	12/3		**60,296**	6	39			Tambling 1, Graham 4	Bonetti	Kirkup	McCreadie	Hollins	Hinton	Harris R	Bridges	Graham	Osgood	Venables	Tambling	
								Ref: K Howley	Everyone wants to see the Lisbon heroes and the gates are shut at 2.15. Chelsea catch United cold as George Graham nods down for Tambling and then curls a lob in. Best and Osgood vie for the 'entertainer' award, and both are superb. Chelsea defend the lead well, and deserve a win.											
32	H	ARSENAL		4	W	2-1	2-0	Law 2, Stiles 29	Gregg	Brennan	Dunne A	Crerand	Foulkes	Stiles	Best	Law	Charlton	Herd	Connelly	
	19/3		47,532	12	41			Walley 88	Furnell	Storey	McCullough*	McLintock	Neill	Ure	Armstrong	Sammels	Radford	Court	Walley	Simpson
								Ref: J Finney	Arsenal have only one win in 11 and manager Billy Wright is under pressure. The first half is one-sided with Best at the peak of his powers. Two headers put United ahead, Law from Neill's deflection and Stiles from Connelly's cross. Arsenal improve but rarely trouble Harry Gregg.											
33	A	ASTON VILLA		4	D	1-1	0-0	Cantwell 63	Gaskell	Brennan	Dunne A	Crerand	Foulkes	Fitzpatrick	Connelly	Law	Anderson	Cantwell	Aston	
	6/4		28,222	16	42			MacEwan 64	Withers	Bradley	Aitken	Pountney	Sleeuwenh'k	Deakin	MacEwan	Hamilton	Hateley	Woosnam	Scott	
								Ref: E Wallace	United start a run of nine games in April and rest some key players. Villa, without a win in six, are lacking in confidence. Stand-in striker Noel Cantwell scores after good work by Crerand and Connelly. McEwan squares a humdrum game with a shot which seems to take a deflection.											
34	H	LEICESTER		4	L	1-2	0-2	Connelly 81	Gregg	Brennan	**Noble**	Crerand	Sadler	Stiles	Best	Anderson	Charlton	Herd	Connelly	
	9/4		41,961	7	42			Stringfellow 24, 25	Banks	Rodrigues	Norman	Roberts	Cross	Appleton	Sinclair	Goodfellow	Dougan	Gibson	Stringfellow	
								Ref: W Handley	The unbeaten run of 39 home league and cup games is ended and Liverpool are now 13 points ahead. Best is limping and several players are missing injured. Banks saves City before Davie Gibson makes both the goals. In a frantic finish United go close to grabbing a deserved draw.											

35 A SHEFFIELD UTD 5 L 1-3 0-1 Sadler 71 *[Woodward 79]*
16/4 *22,330* *10* 42 *Fenoughty 23, Birchenall 67,*
Ref: D Corbett

Gregg, Brennan, Cantwell, Fitzpatrick, Foulkes, Stiles, Connelly, Anderson, Sadler, Herd, Aston
Hodgkinson, Badger, Shaw B, Barlow, Matthewson, Wagstaff B, Woodward, Wagstaff T, Jones, Birchenall, Fenoughty

Six players are rested for the Partizan second leg, including Best who is seriously hurt. United are unlucky to lose as the Blades score their first against the run of play. Sadler's header is not enough against Birchenall-inspired Blades. A Fairs Cup place is now slipping out of their grasp.

---

36 A EVERTON 6 D 0-0 0-0
25/4 *50,843* *9* 43
Ref: L Callaghan

Gregg, Brennan, Dunne A, Crerand, Cantwell, Stiles, Anderson, Law, Sadler, Charlton, Aston
West, Brown, Wilson, Gabriel, Labone, Harris, Scott, Hurst, Pickering, Trebilcock, Temple

Two days after their Cup semi-final, the teams meet again. The defence takes the honours with Cantwell blotting out Pickering. Nobby Stiles is booed constantly and is warned for gesticulating to the crowd. Gabriel hits the post and United create half-chances but the game peters out.

---

37 H BLACKPOOL 5 W 2-1 2-0 Law 18, Charlton 30
27/4 26,953 *16* 45 *Ball 80*
Ref: J Thacker

Gregg, Brennan, Dunne A, Crerand, Cantwell, Stiles, Connelly, Law, Sadler, Charlton, Aston
Waiters, Armfield, Thompson, Fisher, James, McPhee, Lea, Ball, Charnley, Waddell, Horne, Robson*

United are compassionate to Ron Suart's poor Blackpool side, who rely too much on leading scorer Alan Ball. They should have won by more than Law's header and Charlton's easy second after a great cross by John Aston. Liverpool are close to regaining the league title from United.

---

38 A WEST HAM 6 L 2-3 0-2 Cantwell 63, Aston 78
30/4 *36,423* *11* 45 *Hurst 28, 73, Byrne 42p*
Ref: P Bye

Gregg, Brennan, Dunne A*, Crerand, Cantwell, Stiles, Connelly, Law, Sadler, Charlton, Aston, Herd
Standen, Burnett, Charles, Peters, Bickles, Moore, Brabrook, Boyce, Byrne, Hurst, Sissons

Alf Ramsey casts his eyes over six players contesting places for England's match with Yugoslavia including leading league scorer Geoff Hurst. Cantwell is hissed by the fans for writing an article slagging off West Ham. Brennan brings down Peters for the penalty. Serious crowd trouble.

---

39 A WEST BROM 6 D 3-3 1-1 Herd 27, Aston 49, Dunne A 70
4/5 *22,609* *5* 46 *Clark 30, Lovett 55, Kaye 88*
Ref: J Finney

Gregg, Brennan, Dunne A, Crerand, Cantwell, Fitzpatrick*, **Ryan**, Law, Sadler, Herd, Aston, Anderson
Potter, Fairfax, Williams, Lovett, Jones, Fraser, Brown, Astle, Kaye, Hope, Clark

Jimmy Hagan's Albion are unbeaten in eight and are the division's top scorers. Stiles, Connelly and Charlton are on England duty. Three times United lead, only to be pegged back by the League Cup winners. David Herd heads a superb first and John Aston shoots in from a tight angle.

---

40 A BLACKBURN 6 W 4-1 3-1 Herd 3, 27, Charlton 31, Sadler 70
7/5 ***14,513*** *22* 48 *Harrison 36*
Ref: H Davey

Gregg, Brennan, Dunne A, Crerand, Cantwell, Stiles, Ryan, Charlton, Sadler, Herd, Aston
Roberts, Newton, Joyce, Clayton, Mulvaney, England, Ferguson, Byrom, Jones, Douglas, Harrison, Darling*

Blackburn are relegated and are 13 points adrift of 21st place. They suffer a sixth home defeat in a row after goalkeeper Roberts is stretchered off with the score at 3-1. United take pity on poor Rovers and add only one more goal. The lowest league crowd to watch United since 1955.

---

41 H ASTON VILLA 4 W **6-1** 3-0 Herd 12, 73 Sadler 15, 55, Ryan 18,
9/5 **23,205** *16* 50 *Woosnam 77* [Charlton 83]
Ref: R Windle

Gregg, Brennan, Dunne A, Crerand, Cantwell, Stiles, Ryan, Herd, Sadler, Charlton, Aston
Withers, Bradley, Aitken, Pountney, Sleeuwenh'k, Deakin, Baker, Hamilton, Hateley, Woosnam, MacLeod

Dick Taylor's Villa have stayed up, thanks to Hateley's 27 goals, but can only stand and admire as United rip them apart. Withers stops the score going into double figures with endless saves. Herd and Charlton are dazzling and Bobby's pile-driver is the best of an exquisite night.

---

42 H LEEDS 4 D 1-1 0-0 Herd 50
19/5 35,348 2 51 *Reaney 55*
Ref: A Sparling

Home Away
Average 38,768 38,117

Gregg, Brennan, Noble, Crerand, Cantwell, Dunne A, Ryan, Herd, Sadler, Law, Aston
Sprake, Reaney, Greenhoff, Bremner, Bell, O'Grady, Storrie, Giles, Belfitt, Collins, Johanneson

Leeds have again finished with nothing to show for a good season. Considering the 'previous' between the clubs, it is a placid and clean game. England players are resting before the finals. Herd volleys in Ryan's free-kick and Reaney heads in Storrie's cross. The game then fizzles out.

Charity Shield

H LIVERPOOL D 2-2 1-1 Best 29, Herd 82
14/8 48,502 *Stevenson 38, Yeats 86*
Ref: J Finney

Dunne P, Brennan, Dunne A, Crerand, Cantwell, Stiles, Best, Charlton, Herd, Law*, Aston, Anderson
Lawrence, Lawler, Byrne, Milne, Yeats, Stevenson, Callaghan, Hunt, St John, Smith, Strong

A thrilling game lifts the occasion out of the friendly class. Law limps off after 19 minutes with tendon injury. Best's breakaway and lob over Lawrence is classy. Herd's rocket seems to have won it but Big Ron Yeats heads home and the trophy is shared. Most of the new stand is open.

European Cup

PR 1 A HJK HELSINKI (Finland) 10 W 3-2 3-1 Herd 1, Connelly 15, Law 37
22/9 *25,000* *Pahlman 34, Peltoniemi 70*
Ref: R Banasiuk (Poland)

Gaskell, Brennan, Dunne A, Fitzpatrick, Foulkes, Stiles, Connelly, Charlton, Herd, Law, Aston
Heinonen, Jalava, Murtovaara, Kaupinnen, Laine, Peltoniemi, Pajo, Kaartinen, Lethtolainen, Pahlman, Lindhal

The amateur Finns emerge with a respectable scoreline after Herd's 30-second goal. United ease off after a good start. Gaskell fails to hold Pahlman's swerving free-kick and 17-year-old Peltoniemi scores in only his second game. Fitzpatrick, in for the injured Crerand, is impressive.

PR 2 H HJK HELSINKI 13 W 6-0 2-0 Connelly 13, 47, 71, Best 44, 50,
6/10 30,388 [Charlton 60]
Ref: M Rodrigues (Portugal)
(United win 9-2 on aggregate)

Dunne P, Brennan, Dunne A, Crerand, Foulkes, Stiles, Connelly, Best, Charlton, Law, Aston
Heinonen, Jalava, Murtovaara, Kokko, Laine, Peltoniemi, Rytkonen, Kaupinnen, Lethtolainen, Pahlman, Lindhal

The new stand executive boxes are fully operational. Poor Helsinki are there for the experience not the result and are never in the game. Keeper Heinonen is hampered after a collision with Best and his elementary errors let United romp home. Wingers Best and Connelly run rampant.

European Cup (cont.)	Att			F-A	H-T	Scorers, Times, and Referees	1	2	3	4	5	6	7	8	9	10	11	12 sub used
1:1 A ASK VORWARTS		7	W	2-0	0-0	Law 72, Connelly 80	Gregg	Dunne A	Cantwell	Crerand	Foulkes	Stiles	Best	Law	Charlton	Herd	Connelly	
17/11 (E Germany)	*35,000*						*Weiss*	*Fraessdorf*	*Krampe*	*Kuipel*	*Unger*	*Koerner*	*Nachtigall*	*Noeldner*	*Vogt*	*Begerad*	*Piepenburg*	
						Ref: H Carlsson (Sweden)	No English servicemen are allowed into East Berlin to see United play the Army side at the Walter Ulbricht stadium. United adopt defensive tactics on an icy pitch and catch the Germans on the break. They live dangerously, before Law scores with a header and sets up John Connelly.											
1:2 H ASK VORWARTS		6	W	3-1	2-0	Herd 12, 40, 90	Dunne P	Dunne A	Cantwell	Crerand	Foulkes	Stiles	Best	Law	Charlton	Herd	Connelly	
1/12	30,082					*Piepenburg 86*	*Zulkowski*	*Fraessdorf*	*Krampe*	*Kuipel*	*Unger*	*Koerner*	*Piepenburg*	*Kalinke*	*Vogt*	*Begerad*	*Grossheim*	
						Ref: J Gardeazabal (Spain) (United win 5-1 on aggregate)	Gregg's suspension lets the mistake-ridden Pat Dunne in for a recall. Herd's early goal seals the victory at a foggy Old Trafford, with Law setting up both first-half goals and hitting a post. Professional United ease off after the break and Piepenburg scores the best goal of the night.											
QF 1 H BENFICA		3	W	3-2	2-1	Herd 37, Law 42, Foulkes 60	Gregg	Dunne A	Cantwell	Crerand	Foulkes	Stiles	Best	Law	Charlton	Herd	Connelly	
2/2 (Portugal)	64,035					*Augusto 30, Torres 70*	*Costa Pereira*	*Raul*	*Cruz*	*Coluna*	*Germano*	*Pinto*	*Augusto*	*Pedras*	*Torres*	*Eusebio*	*Simoes*	
						Ref: K Galba (Czechoslovakia)	Last year's beaten finalists are a strong team and play their part in a thriller. On a night of high passion, United bounce back to take a two-goal lead, only for Gregg to blunder and fail to reach the lanky Torres' header. Eusebio and Stiles have a real battle. Record receipts of £30,000.											
QF 2 A BENFICA		2	W	5-1	3-0	Best 6, 12, Connelly 16, Crerand 80,	Gregg	Brennan	Dunne A	Crerand	Foulkes	Stiles	Best	Law	Charlton	Herd	Connelly	
9/3	*75,000*					*Brennan 52(og)* [Charlton 89]	*Costa Pereira*	*Cavem*	*Cruz*	*Coluna*	*Germano*	*Pinto*	*Augusto*	*Silva*	*Torres*	*Eusebio*	*Simoes*	
						Ref: M Lobello (Italy) (United win 8-3 on aggregate)	A memorable night in the Stadium of Light as Benfica's nine-year unbeaten home record is shattered. Best is the star of a fantastic attacking display and makes European Footballer of the Year Eusebio look ordinary. Best scores a header, a brilliant solo, and makes No 3 for Connelly.											
SF 1 A PARTIZ BELGRADE		4	L	0-2	0-0		Gregg	Brennan	Dunne A	Crerand	Foulkes	Stiles	Best	Law	Charlton	Herd	Connelly	
13/4 (Yugoslavia)	*55,000*					*Hasanagic 47, Becejac 69*	*Soskic*	*Jusufi*	*Mihajlovic*	*Becejac*	*Rasovic*	*Vasovic*	*Bajic*	*Kovacevic*	*Hasanagic*	*Miladinovic*	*Pirmajer*	
						Ref: J Tschenscher (W Germany)	A strange, lifeless display in the Red Army stadium. United are caught out by a quick throw-in they think is theirs for the first goal and never recover. Soskic has little to do against a punchless attack well held by a Partizan defence that has not conceded a home goal in the competition.											
SF 2 H PARTIZ BELGRADE		5	W	1-0	0-0	Stiles 73	Gregg	Brennan	Dunne A	Crerand !	Foulkes	Stiles	Anderson	Law	Charlton	Herd	Connelly	
20/4	62,500						*Soskic*	*Jusufi*	*Mihajlovic*	*Becejac*	*Rasovic*	*Vasovic*	*Bajic*	*Davidovic*	*Hasanagic*	*Miladinovic !*	*Pirmajer*	
						Ref: G Dienst (Switzerland) (United lose 1-2 on aggregate)	On a frenzied night United fail to make the early breakthrough. They swarm around the Partizan goal but the unrelenting defence holds firm. Crerand and Miladinovic are ordered off for fighting. Finally Stiles scores, despite Soskic's brave save but Partizan hang on to reach the final.											

FA Cup	Att			F-A	H-T	Scorers, Times, and Referees	1	2	3	4	5	6	7	8	9	10	11
3 A DERBY		4	W	5-2	3-2	Law 13, 73p, Best 16, 25, Herd 76	Gregg	Dunne A	Cantwell	Crerand	Foulkes	Stiles	Best	Law	Charlton	Herd	Aston
22/1	*33,827 2:7*					*Richardson 29p, Upton 42*	*Matthews*	*Richardson*	*Daniel*	*Webster*	*Saxton*	*Upton*	*Hughes*	*Thomas*	*Buxton*	*Durban*	*Hodgson*
						Ref: M Fussey	Derby's biggest crowd since 1960 witness an impressive away win. On a rock-hard pitch with pools of water United start like a train but are pegged back when Gregg knocks out Buxton with his shoulder. Law, who is felled by Matthews for the penalty, nets a record 30th Cup goal.										
4 H ROTHERHAM		3	D	0-0	0-0		Gregg	Dunne A	Cantwell	Crerand	Foulkes	Stiles	Best	Law	Charlton	Herd	Connelly
12/2	54,263 *2:9*						*Jones*	*Wilcockson*	*Clish*	*Rabjohn*	*Haselden*	*Tiler*	*Lyons*	*Chappell*	*Galley*	*Casper*	*Pring*
						Ref: J Taylor	Jack Mansell's young team come to attack and are applauded warmly. They restrict United's space and fully deserve a draw. Pring twice hits the post and ex-Red junior Rod Jones is in brilliant form. 12,000 away fans roar on their heroes on their first visit to Old Trafford since 1922.										
4R A ROTHERHAM		3	W	1-0	0-0	Connelly 115	Gregg	Brennan	Dunne A	Crerand	Foulkes	Stiles	Best	Law	Charlton	Herd	Connelly
15/2	*23,500 2:9*			*aet*			*Jones*	*Wilcockson*	*Clish*	*Rabjohn*	*Haselden*	*Tiler*	*Lyons*	*Chappell*	*Galley*	*Casper*	*Pring*
						Ref: J Taylor	On a slippery, muddy surface, fighting Rotherham feel they are robbed after Chappell's 'goal' is disallowed. Soon after, Stiles clears when the ball looks over the line and a packed Millmoor goes mad. Connelly goes on to wreck the Millers dream and the players finish covered in mud.										
5 A WOLVERHAMPTON		2	W	4-2	1-2	Law 22, 61, Best 72, Herd 87	Gregg	Brennan	Dunne A	Crerand	Foulkes	Stiles	Best	Law	Charlton	Herd	Connelly
5/3	*53,428 2:4*					*Wharton 2p, 9p*	*MacLaren*	*Wilson*	*Thomson*	*Flowers*	*Woodfield*	*Holsgrove*	*Wharton*	*Hunt*	*McIlmoyle*	*Knowles*	*Wagstaffe*
						Ref: K Howley	A foul on Hunt and a Foulkes handball give Ronnie Allen's lively team a dream two-goal start. Two Dennis Law headers haul United back. Best raises the roof by running half the length of the pitch to score before setting up David Herd for No 4. United are now Cup favourites.										

QF	A	PRESTON		4	D	1-1	0-1	Herd 47	Gregg	Brennan	Dunne A	Crerand	Foulkes	Stiles	Best	Law	Charlton	Herd	Connelly
	26/3		*37,876*	*2:14*				*Dawson 40*	*Kelly*	*Ross*	*Smith*	*Lawton*	*Singleton*	*Kendall*	*Hannigan*	*Godfrey*	*Dawson*	*Spavin*	*Lee*
								Ref: J Finney	Another full house and a delayed start because a wall collapses. Feisty Preston refuse to buckle to United's class and deserve the draw. Dawson has the defence at sea as he nets, but Herd shoots through Kelly's legs after being put through by Best. A replay is not what United need.										
QF R	H	PRESTON		4	W	3-1	1-0	Law 30, 87, Connelly 89	Gregg	Brennan	Dunne A	Crerand	Foulkes	Stiles	Connelly	Law	Charlton	Herd	Aston
	30/3		60,433	*2:14*				*Singleton 69*	*Barton*	*Ross*	*Smith*	*Lawton*	*Singleton*	*Kendall*	*Hannigan*	*Godfrey*	*Dawson*	*Spavin*	*Lee*
								Ref: E Crawford	Best is out with a knee injury and he is missed by an off-colour United. Skilful but unlucky Preston look more likely winners until Law's poached second. He scores the first, after Barton and Kendall's mix-up before Tony Singleton scores only the second goal of his career.										
SF	N	EVERTON		7	L	0-1	0-0		Gregg	Brennan	Dunne A	Crerand	Foulkes	Stiles	Anderson	Law	Charlton	Herd	Connelly
	23/4		*60,000*	*10*				*Harvey 78*	*West*	*Brown*	*Wilson*	*Gabriel*	*Labone*	*Harris*	*Scott*	*Trebilcock*	*Young*	*Harvey*	*Temple*
		(at Burnden Park)						Ref: E Jennings	United's fifth consecutive FA Cup semi-final is a dour affair and they lose their second semi-final in a week. They do all the attacking but can't break down Everton's solid defence and create little. Derek Temple's break catches United napping and Colin Harvey's low shot creeps in.										

			Home						Away					
	P	W	D	L	F	A	W	D	L	F	A	Pts
1 Liverpool	42	17	2	2	52	15	9	7	5	27	19	61
2 Leeds	42	14	4	3	49	15	9	5	7	30	23	55
3 Burnley	42	15	3	3	45	20	9	4	8	34	27	55
4 MAN UNITED	42	12	8	1	50	20	6	7	8	34	39	51
5 Chelsea	42	11	4	6	30	21	11	3	7	35	32	51
6 West Brom	42	11	6	4	58	34	8	6	7	33	35	50
7 Leicester	42	12	4	5	40	28	9	3	9	40	37	49
8 Tottenham	42	11	6	4	55	37	5	6	10	20	29	44
9 Sheffield Utd	42	11	6	4	37	25	5	5	11	19	34	43
10 Stoke	42	12	6	3	42	22	3	6	12	23	42	42
11 Everton	42	12	6	3	39	19	3	5	13	17	43	41
12 West Ham	42	12	5	4	46	33	3	4	14	24	50	39
13 Blackpool	42	9	5	7	36	29	5	4	12	19	36	37
14 Arsenal	42	8	8	5	36	31	4	5	12	26	44	37
15 Newcastle	42	10	5	6	26	20	4	4	13	24	43	37
16 Aston Villa	42	10	3	8	39	34	5	3	13	30	46	36
17 Sheffield Wed	42	11	6	4	35	18	3	2	16	21	48	36
18 Nott'm Forest	42	11	3	7	31	26	3	5	13	25	46	36
19 Sunderland	42	13	2	6	36	28	1	6	14	15	44	36
20 Fulham	42	9	4	8	34	37	5	3	13	33	48	35
21 Northampton	42	8	6	7	31	32	2	7	12	24	60	33
22 Blackburn	42	6	1	14	30	36	2	3	16	27	52	20
	924	245	103	114	877	580	114	103	245	580	877	924

Odds & ends

Double wins: (2) Blackpool, Fulham.
Double losses: (0).

Won from behind: (5) Chelsea (h), Blackpool (a), Sunderland (a).
Benfica (h), Wolves FAC (a).
Lost from in front: (2) Arsenal (a), Liverpool (a).

High spots: 10-game unbeaten league run in the autumn.
Strong home form.
A great European Cup win in Lisbon.

Low spots: Semi-final defeat to Partizan.
Semi-final defeat to Everton.
Poor away form.

Red cards (United): (2) Gregg (Blackburn h), Crerand (Partizan h).
Red cards (Opponents): (1) Miladinovic (Partizan h).
Ever-presents: (4).
Hat-tricks: (6) Herd (3), Law, Charlton, Connelly.
Opposing hat-tricks: (0).
Leading scorer: (32) Herd.

	Appearances						Goals			
	Lge	*Sub*	FAC	*Sub*	EC	*Sub*	Lge	FAC	EC	Tot
Anderson, Willie	5	*1*	1		1					
Aston, John	23		2		2		4			4
Best, George	31		5		6		9	3	4	16
Brennan, Shay	28		5		5					
Cantwell, Noel	23		2		3		2			2
Charlton, Bobby	38		7		8		16		2	18
Connelly, John	31	*1*	6		8		5	2	6	13
Crerand, Pat	41		7		7					
Dunne, Pat	8				2					
Dunne, Tony	40		7		8		1			1
Fitzpatrick, John	3	*1*			1					
Foulkes, Bill	33		7		8				1	1
Gaskell, Dave	8				1					
Gregg, Harry	26		7		5					
Herd, David	36	*1*	7		7		24	3	5	32
Law, Dennis	33		7		8		15	6	3	24
Noble, Bobby	2									
Ryan, Jimmy	4						1			1
Sadler, David	10						4			4
Stiles, Nobby	39		7		8		2		1	3
(own-goals)							1			1
20 players used	**462**	*4*	**77**		**88**		**84**	**14**	**22**	**120**

LEAGUE DIVISION 1 — Manager: Matt Busby — SEASON 1966-67

No	Date	Att	Pos	Pt	F-A	H-T	Scorers, Times, and Referees	1	2	3	4	5	6	7	8	9	10	11	12 sub used
1	H WEST BROM			W	5-3	5-1	Best 1, Stiles 8, Law 16, 22, Herd 17	Gaskell	Brennan	Dunne A	Fitzpatrick	Foulkes	Stiles	Best	Law	Charlton	Herd	Connelly	
	20/8	**41,543**		2			*Hope 10, Clark 46, 87*	*Potter*	*Cram*	*Fairfax*	*Williams*	*Jones*	*Fraser*	*Brown*	*Astle*	*Kaye*	*Hope*	*Clark*	
							Ref: M Fussey	Best has recovered from a cartilage operation and scores the quickest goal of the day. Under a hot sun, United run rampant after the World Cup heroes and Jimmy Murphy are given ovations, the latter for 20 years' service. The game is an anti-climax after the mesmerising first half hour.											
2	A EVERTON			W	2-1	0-0	Law 63, 89	Gaskell	Brennan	Dunne A	Fitzpatrick	Foulkes	Stiles	Best	Law	Charlton	Herd	Connelly	
	23/8	*60,657*		4			*Temple 58*	*West*	*Wright*	*Wilson*	*Gabriel*	*Labone*	*Harvey*	*Scott*	*Ball*	*Pickering*	*Young*	*Temple*	
							Ref: J Finney	£110,000 Alan Ball's home debut for the Cup winners is overshadowed by the sublime Law. The 'King' heads in from an impossible angle and poaches his 100th United goal to snatch the win. Everton fail to press home superiority and the Reds get their first win at Goodison since 1956.											
3	A LEEDS		10	L	1-3	0-2	Best 58	Gaskell	Brennan	Dunne A	Fitzpatrick	Foulkes	Stiles	Best	Law	Charlton	Herd	Connelly	
	27/8	*45,092*	*9*	4			*Madeley 5, Reaney 35, Lorimer 79*	*Sprake*	*Reaney*	*Cooper*	*Bremner*	*Bell*	*Hunter*	*Lorimer*	*Gray*	*Madeley*	*Giles*	*Johanneson*	
							Ref: K Howley	Injury-hit Leeds beat United at home for the first time since 1939. They run themselves into the ground, with ex-Red Giles the star. Stand-in striker Madeley has Gaskell at sea with a header and Reaney heads No 2. Best scores from a tight angle, but Lorimer's 30-yarder seals matters.											
4	H EVERTON		6	W	3-0	1-0	Foulkes 44, Connelly 55, Law 60	Gaskell	Brennan	Dunne A	Crerand	Foulkes	Stiles	Connelly	Law	Charlton	Herd	Best	
	31/8	61,114	*15*	6				*West*	*Wright*	*Wilson*	*Gabriel*	*Labone*	*Harvey*	*Scott*	*Ball*	*Young*	*Trebilcock*	*Temple*	
							Ref: J Carr	United answer their critics with a comprehensive scoreline but unlucky Everton rue their missed chances, especially Mike Trebilcock who hits the post. John Connelly is in top form and crosses for Bill Foulkes before scoring number two. Law heads home from an impossible angle.											
5	H NEWCASTLE		5	W	3-2	0-0	Herd 60, Connelly 68, Law 79	Gregg	Brennan	Dunne A	Crerand	Foulkes	Stiles	Connelly	Law	Charlton	Herd	Best	
	3/9	44,438	*11*	8			*McGarry 63, Craig 86*	*Marshall*	*Craig*	*Clark*	*Burton*	*Thompson*	*Iley*	*Suddick*	*Kettlebor'gh*	*McGarry*	*Hilley*	*Knox*	
							Ref: D Lyden	Newcastle's goal leads a charmed life as United hit form. Best hits wood twice and Charlton's header is disallowed. Then the Magpies defence caves in. Herd grabs a fine individual goal, Best lays on No 2 for Connelly and Law nods in from point-blank range for his sixth in five games.											
6	A STOKE		12	L	0-3	0-2		Gregg	Brennan	Dunne A	Crerand	Foulkes	Stiles	Connelly	Law	Charlton	Herd	Best	
	7/9	*44,420*	*5*	8			*Ritchie 32, 46, Palmer 36*	*Farmer*	*Palmer*	*Skeels*	*Viollet*	*Bloor*	*Philpott*	*Bridgewood*	*Dobing*	*Ritchie*	*Eastham*	*Burrows*	
							Ref: H Davies	Despite injuries, Stoke continue their impressive early season form with a 14-minute blitz. Palmer's forays cause United problems and he creates the first before heading No 2. The cool Eastham creates No 3 for Tony Waddington's team of veterans. United give up the ghost.											
7	A TOTTENHAM		8	L	1-2	1-0	Law 43	Gaskell	Brennan	Dunne A	Crerand	Foulkes	Stiles	Best	Law	Sadler*	Herd	Charlton	Aston
	10/9	*56,295*	*4*	8			*Gilzean 86, Greaves 88*	*Jennings*	*Kinnear*	*Knowles*	*Mullery*	*England*	*Beal**	*Robertson*	*Greaves*	*Gilzean*	*Venables*	*Weller*	*Clayton*
							Ref: P Walters	Spurs, with £95,000 Mike England, are a good title bet. The gates are locked on a sun-drenched, shirt-sleeved crowd. In a sloppy game, Law heads a classic against the run of play before Gilzean nods in from Weller. Greaves' goal sparks a pitch invasion. Foulkes' 500th league game.											
8	H MANCHESTER C		9	W	1-0	1-0	Law 39	**Stepney**	Brennan	Dunne A	Crerand	Foulkes	Stiles	Best	Law	Sadler	Charlton	Aston	
	17/9	62,085	*16*	10				*Dowd*	*Book*	*Kennedy**	*Horne*	*Heslop*	*Oakes*	*Connor*	*Bell*	*Summerbee*	*Pardoe*	*Young*	*Doyle*
							Ref: J Taylor	Mercer and Allison have steered City back to Div 1. Flags and banners are banned from the ground but there is lots of trouble. In the first derby since 1963, Connor marks Best like a limpet. Aston and Law combine for the winner. City fight hard but rarely trouble new signing Stepney.											
9	H BURNLEY		5	W	4-1	1-1	Law 39, Herd 50, Crerand 86, [Sadler 89]	Stepney	Brennan	Dunne A	Crerand	Foulkes	Stiles	Herd	Law*	Sadler	Charlton	Best	Aston
	24/9	52,717	*6*	12			*Lochhead 44*	*Blacklaw*	*Angus*	*Talbut*	*O'Neill*	*Miller*	*Bellamy*	*Morgan*	*Lochhead*	*Irvine*	*Harris*	*Coates*	
							Ref: D Smith	Burnley's eight-match unbeaten start is ended by a superb performance. Law's scissors-kick brings the house down and Herd scores his 100th league goal and the 203rd of his career. Crerand is the star and his, and David Sadler's goals, make the scoreline reflect United's domination.											
10	A NOTT'M FOREST		8	L	**1-4**	0-3	Charlton 72	Stepney	Brennan	Dunne A	Crerand	Foulkes	Stiles	Best	Herd	Sadler	Charlton	Aston	
	1/10	*41,854*	*7*	12			*Crowe 1, 44, 55p, Wignall 30*	*Grummitt*	*Hindley*	*Winfield*	*Hennessey*	*McKinlay*	*Newton*	*Crowe*	*Barnwell**	*Baker*	*Wignall*	*Storey-M're*	*Taylor*
							Ref: N Burtenshaw	Chris Crowe's 30-second header sets the tone. Stepney and Dunne collide allowing Wignall an open goal as Forest push home their advantage. Best is kicked incessantly, but still bemuses Winfield. Stepney's weak punch and Stiles' trip on Baker allows Crowe to complete his hat-trick.											

11	A	BLACKPOOL	6	W	2-1	1-1	Law 23, 88p	Stepney	Dunne A	**Noble**	Crerand	Cantwell	Stiles	Herd	Law	Sadler	Charlton	Best	
	8/10	*33,555*	22	14			*Charnley 3*	*Waiters*	*Thompson*	*Hughes*	*Fisher*	*James**	*McPhee*	*Brown*	*Robson*	*Charnley*	*Moir*	*Lea*	*Craven*
							Ref: K Stokes	Pool have yet to win a game – it is their worst ever start. Starman Ball has gone and they look relegation certs. Cantwell boobs in his first game of the season and lets Charnley net. Law deflects in Best's shot and ends the five-game losing away run when Emlyn Hughes up-ends Best.											
12	H	CHELSEA	6	D	1-1	0-0	Law 78	Stepney	Dunne A	Noble	Crerand	Cantwell	Stiles	Herd	Law	Sadler	Charlton	Best	
	15/10	56,789	*2*	15			*Crerand 51(og)*	*Bonetti*	*Kirkup*	*McCreadie**	*Hollins*	*Hinton*	*Harris R*	*Boyle*	*Houseman*	*Baldwin*	*Cooke*	*Tambling*	*Harris A*
							Ref: N Callender	Tommy Docherty's one-defeat side are on top for long periods and defend with style. John Boyle's shot spins in off Crerand and United look clueless. Finally, Law saves the day with his lightning reaction to a rebound. Boy-wonder Peter Osgood is missing, having broken his leg.											
13	H	ARSENAL	5	W	1-0	1-0	Sadler 30	Stepney	Dunne A	Noble	Crerand	Cantwell	Stiles	Herd	Law	Sadler	Charlton	Best	
	29/10	45,417	*15*	17				*Furnell*	*McNab*	*Storey*	*McLintock*	*Neill*	*Simpson*	*Sammels*	*Addison*	*Graham*	*Radford*	*Armstrong*	
							Ref: W Holian	Bertie Mee's men defend well but can't stop David Sadler's header from a half-clearance after Herd's shot was stopped on the line. United dominate despite a quiet game from George Best, who had a petulant game for Ireland v England last week. Alex Stepney's best game so far.											
14	A	CHELSEA	4	W	3-1	1-0	Aston 43, 75, Best 63	Stepney	Brennan	Noble	Crerand	Foulkes	Stiles	Herd	Aston	Sadler	Charlton	Best	
	5/11	*56,452*	*1*	19			*Hollins 73*	*Bonetti*	*Kirkup*	*McCreadie*	*Hollins*	*Hinton*	*Harris R*	*Boyle*	*Baldwin*	*Hateley*	*Cooke*	*Tambling**	*Houseman*
							Ref: J Taylor	The league leaders are given a footballing lesson by the Reds. Bonetti spills Crerand's stinger and Aston pounces. After the break, United besiege the Chelsea goal. Sadler makes No 2 for Best, who turns on the magic to make Aston's second. Hollins' 30-yarder eludes Stepney.											
15	H	SHEFFIELD WED	2	W	2-0	2-0	Charlton 12, Herd 26	Stepney	Dunne A	Noble	Crerand	Foulkes*	Stiles	Herd	Law	Sadler	Charlton	Best	Aston
	12/11	46,946	*14*	21				*Springett R*	*Smith*	*Megson*	*Eustace*	*Ellis*	*Young*	*Pugh*	*McCalliog*	*Ritchie*	*Ford*	*Quinn*	
							Ref: K Howley	On a drab and drizzly afternoon, United ease off after a job well done. Charlton hits a 25-yard lazy lob and Herd heads home Crerand's centre. Wednesday's big signing John Ritchie has a quiet debut despite his marker Foulkes limping off. Law and Megson have a niggly personal feud.											
16	A	SOUTHAMPTON	3	W	2-1	2-1	Charlton 1, 37	Stepney	Dunne A	Noble	Crerand	Cantwell*	Stiles	Herd	Law	Sadler	Charlton	Best	Aston
	19/11	***29,458***	*16*	23			*Davies 23*	*MacLaren*	*Webb*	*Jones*	*Wimshurst*	*Knapp*	*Walker*	*Paine*	*Chivers*	*Davies*	*Melia*	*Thompson*	
							Ref: J Finney	Ted Bates' Saints are in Div 1 for the first time. 18-goal Ron Davies scores but is generally well held by Sadler, switched because of Noel Cantwell's cut head. United rarely look troubled after Bobby's 50-second low drive off the post and are now one point behind leaders Chelsea.											
17	H	SUNDERLAND	2	W	5-0	2-0	Herd 20, 44, 80, 88, Law 48	Stepney	Dunne A	Noble	Crerand	Sadler	Stiles	Best	Law	Charlton	Herd	Aston	
	26/11	44,687	*14*	25				*Montgom'y**	*Irwin*	*Ashurst*	*Elliott*	*Hurley*	*Kinnell*	*Herd*	*O'Hare*	*Martin*	*Baxter*	*Mulhall*	*Parke*
							Ref: E Jennings	A concussed Jim Montgomery is off after 32 minutes, after diving at Dunne's feet. First Hurley takes over, then Parke, but to no avail. The formidable Herd, playing more down the middle, has had his shots measured at 72mph. The first goal is faster; the fourth and fifth are gifts.											
18	A	LEICESTER	1	W	2-1	1-0	Law 22, Best 55	Stepney	Dunne A	Noble	Crerand	Sadler	Stiles	Best	Law	Charlton	Herd	Aston	
	30/11	*39,014*	*5*	27			*Gibson 87*	*Banks*	*Rodrigues*	*Norman*	*Roberts*	*Sjoberg*	*Cross*	*Sinclair*	*Sharkey*	*Dougan*	*Gibson*	*Stringfellow*	
							Ref: R Prichard	The gates are locked and City's unbeaten home record goes. Law's shot skids through the mud past Banks. Best beats several defenders with a mazy dribble and hits a stunning shot that Banks doesn't even move for. He almost repeats the feat 10 minutes later. McGuinness is 12th man.											
19	A	ASTON VILLA	1	L	1-2	0-1	Herd 75	Stepney	Dunne A	Noble	Crerand	Sadler	Stiles	Best	Law	Charlton	Herd	Aston	
	3/12	*40,016*	*19*	27			*Scott 21, Chatterley 79*	*Withers*	*Bradley*	*Aitken*	*Tindall*	*Sleeuwenh'k*	*Deakin*	*Roberts*	*Broadbent*	*Chatterley*	*Scott*	*MacLeod*	
							Ref: L Callaghan	United's non-stop attacking is in vain as they squander lots of chances. Villa fight like demons after Scott's scrappy goal on a wet and slippy pitch. Herd's drive seems to have done the trick, but Stepney spills a cross and Lew Chatterley scores the winner. Nobby Stiles booked again.											
20	H	LIVERPOOL	1	D	2-2	2-2	Best 18, 29p	Stepney	Brennan	Noble	Crerand	Sadler	Dunne A*	Best	Ryan	Charlton	Herd	Aston	Anderson
	10/12	61,768	*3*	28			*St John 15, 45*	*Lawrence*	*Lawler*	*Milne*	*Smith*	*Yeats*	*Stevenson*	*Callaghan*	*Hunt*	*St John*	*Strong*	*Thompson*	
							Ref: W Crossley	Despite Stiles and Law being injured, reshuffled United get a deserved point. The precocious Best is outstanding but is booked for pushing Yeats. In a thrilling match, Yeats lunges at Ryan for the penalty. The second half is end-to-end action and United stay a point clear at the top.											
21	A	WEST BROM	1	W	4-3	4-3	Herd 5, 13, 41, Law 33	Stepney	Brennan	Noble	Crerand	Sadler	Stiles	Best	Law	Charlton	Herd	Aston	
	17/12	*32,080*	*21*	30			*Astle 8, 43, Kaye 20*	*Potter*	*Fairfax*	*Collard**	*Howshall*	*Jones*	*Fraser*	*Brown*	*Astle*	*Kaye*	*Hope*	*Clark*	*Williams*
							Ref: W Gow	Albion have the worst defence in Division 1 but United match them for mistakes in a thriller. Stepney is at fault for two goals as Albion expose United's Achilles heel with long crosses. The ubiquitous Law only scores one, but creates two of Herd's goals. The score could have been 7-7.											

No	Date			Att	Pos	Pt	F-A	H-T	Scorers, Times, and Referees	1	2	3	4	5	6	7	8	9	10	11	12 sub used
22	26/12	A	SHEFFIELD UTD	42,752	13	30	L 1-2	1-1	Herd 44	Stepney	Dunne A	Noble	Crerand	Foulkes	Sadler	Best	Law	Charlton	Herd	Aston	
									Birchenall 42, Jones 59	*Hodgkinson*	*Badger*	*Shaw B*	*Mallender*	*Matthewson*	*Wagstaff B*	*Woodward*	*Fenoughty*	*Jones*	*Birchenall*	*Punton*	
									Ref: R Tinkler	A young Blades team end an eight-game run without a win after exposing United's aerial frailty. Stepney's boob lets in Birchenall for a header. Herd replies immediately with a thunderous shot. Mick Jones wins the game from Woodward's teasing free-kick. Noble booked for fighting.											
23	27/12	H	SHEFFIELD UTD	59,392	15	32	W 2-0	1-0	Crerand 35, Herd 60	Stepney	Dunne A	Noble	Crerand	Foulkes	Sadler	Best	Law	Charlton	Herd	Aston	
										Hodgkinson	*Badger*	*Shaw B*	*Mallender*	*Matthewson*	*Wagstaff B*	*Woodward*	*Barlow*	*Jones*	*Birchenall*	*Wagstaff T*	
									Ref: D Corbett	A big Christmas crowd is let down by a poor game of misplaced passes. Crerand's 30-yarder stuns everyone. Things improve after half-time and United deservedly win. Bill Foulkes blots out Jones and Aston's pace frightens the Blades' defence. Herd scores his tenth goal in seven.											
24	31/12	H	LEEDS	51,578	6	33	D 0-0	0-0		Stepney	Dunne A	Noble	Crerand	Foulkes	Sadler	Best	Law	Charlton	Herd	Aston	
										Sprake	*Reaney*	*Bell*	*Bremner*	*Charlton*	*Hunter*	*O'Grady*	*Lorimer*	*Greenhoff**	*Gray*	*Johanneson*	*Cooper*
									Ref: W Handley	An exciting goalless draw, as Leeds emerge on top in the first half, twice hitting the bar, only for United to finish stronger. Leeds' defence is awesome, with Reaney having Best in his pocket. Irish Footballer of the Year Dunne makes his 200th league appearance. Stiles is suspended.											
25	14/1	H	TOTTENHAM	57,365	7	35	W 1-0	0-0	Herd 73	Stepney	Dunne A	Noble	Crerand	Foulkes	Sadler	Best	Ryan	Charlton	Herd	Aston	
										Jennings	*Beal*	*Knowles*	*Mullery*	*England*	*Clayton*	*Robertson*	*Greaves*	*Saul*	*Venables*	*Weller*	
									Ref: P Baldwin	Two attacking sides in good form put on an exciting spectacle. Law is injured in training and United miss him. Both keepers are in fine form with Stepney saving a certain Greaves goal. Sadler is more than a match for Greaves, and Herd wins the game with a shot through a crowd.											
26	21/1	A	MANCHESTER C	62,983	17	36	D 1-1	0-0	Foulkes 76	Stepney	Dunne A	Noble	Crerand	Foulkes	Stiles	Ryan	Charlton	Sadler	Herd	Best	
									Stiles 89(og)	*Ogley*	*Book*	*Pardoe*	*Horne*	*Heslop*	*Oakes*	*Summerbee*	*Connor*	*Bell*	*Doyle*	*Young*	
									Ref: K Howley	City, without a win in six, raise their game for the derby in atrocious muddy conditions. City coach Allison throws his overcoat into the mud after Summerbee fails to win a penalty. Foulkes' header from Ryan's corner dips under the bar before City hero Stiles heads in Bell's shot.											
27	4/2	A	BURNLEY	40,265	12	37	D 1-1	1-0	Sadler 33	Stepney	Dunne A	Noble	Crerand	Foulkes	Stiles	Best	Law	Sadler	Herd	Charlton	
									Harris 89p	*Thomson*	*Smith*	*Latcham*	*O'Neill*	*Miller*	*Merrington*	*Morgan*	*Lochhead*	*Blant*	*Harris*	*Coates*	
									Ref: J Carr	Burnley's form is poor but as usual they give United a buffeting at Turf Moor and deserve their late point. Sadler celebrates his 21st birthday with a shot on the run, but is adjudged to have handled, and Gordon Harris nets from the spot. Biggest league gate at the ground in four years.											
28	11/2	H	NOTT'M FOREST	**62,727**	3	39	W 1-0	0-0	Law 85	Stepney	Dunne A	Noble	Crerand	Foulkes*	Stiles	Best	Law	Sadler	Herd	Charlton	Ryan
										Grummitt	*Hindley*	*Winfield*	*Hennessey*	*McKinlay*	*Newton*	*Lyons*	*Barnwell*	*Baker**	*Wignall*	*Storey-M're*	*Hinton*
									Ref: D Lyden	United end Johnny Carey's Forest's 13-game unbeaten run. The clash between two title contenders is billed as the showdown. United are now a point behind Liverpool with a game in hand. Law is airbourne as he volleys past Forest hero Grummitt. Sadler tames the dangerous Wignall.											
29	25/2	H	BLACKPOOL	47,157	22	41	W 4-0	1-0	Law 30, Charlton 49, 87, [Hughes 57(og)]	Stepney	Dunne A	Noble	Crerand	Foulkes	Stiles	Best	Law	Sadler	Charlton	Aston	
										Waiters	*Thompson*	*Hughes*	*Armfield*	*James*	*Craven*	*Skirton*	*Suddick*	*Charnley*	*Robson*	*Oates*	
									Ref: G McCabe	After five straight defeats, Stan Mortensen has replaced Suart as desperate Pool's manager. Once Law scores with a perfect header, United are never in danger. Two memorable Charlton goals and an own-goal from 19-year-old Emlyn Hughes, who is set to join Liverpool, seal a big win.											
30	3/3	A	ARSENAL	**63,563**	13	42	D 1-1	0-1	Aston 54	Stepney	Dunne A	Noble	Crerand	Foulkes	Stiles	Best	Law	Sadler	Charlton	Aston	
									Sammels 42p	*Furnell*	*McNab*	*Storey*	*McLintock**	*Neill*	*Simpson*	*Addison*	*Radford*	*Graham*	*Sammels*	*Armstrong*	*Court*
									Ref: D Smith	Highbury's biggest crowd for three years and another 28,000 watching on giant screens at Old Trafford see an enthralling game. Stepney keeps Arsenal at bay until Law fouls Sammels for the penalty. Aston nets when Furnell fumbles Best's cross and Furnell's late saves earn a point.											
31	11/3	A	NEWCASTLE	38,202	21	43	D 0-0	0-0		Stepney	Dunne A	Noble	Crerand	Foulkes	Stiles	Best	Law	Sadler	Charlton	Aston	
										Marshall	*Craig*	*Clark*	*Elliott*	*McNamee*	*Iley*	*Bennett*	*Noble*	*Davies*	*Hilley*	*Robson B*	
									Ref: M Fussey	Without showing top form, United knock Liverpool of the top. A fierce wind ruins the game against a Newcastle side desperate for points. Mighty Wyn Davies troubles Foulkes but the defence holds out. The attack struggles and Bobby Noble has a goal disallowed for offside.											

No	Venue / Date	Opponent	Att	Pos	Res / Pts	F-A	H-T	Scorers, Times, and Referees	1	2	3	4	5	6	7	8	9	10	11	12 sub used
32	H	LEICESTER		1	W	5-2	2-0	Herd 2, Charl' 10, Aston 48, Law 58,	Stepney	Dunne A	Noble	Crerand	Foulkes	Stiles	Best	Law	Charlton	Herd*	Aston	Sadler
	18/3		50,281	*9*	45			*Sinclair 61, 65* [Sadler 85]	*Banks*	*Rodrigues*	*Norman*	*Roberts*	*Cross*	*Nish*	*Matthews*	*Goodfellow*	*Stringfellow*	*Gibson*	*Sinclair*	
								Ref: V James	Burnley beat Liverpool, but a crucial day in the title race is marred by David Herd's broken leg as he scores in 90 seconds. The attack is back in top form with Best exquisite. Charlton's ground shot makes it 2-0 and Law chips Banks for a stunning fourth, before sub Sadler's header.											
33	A	LIVERPOOL		1	D	0-0	0-0		Stepney	Dunne A	Noble	Crerand	Foulkes	Stiles	Best	Law	Sadler	Charlton	Aston	
	25/3		*53,813*	*2*	46				*Lawrence*	*Lawler*	*Hughes*	*Smith*	*Yeats*	*Stevenson*	*Callaghan*	*Hunt*	*St John*	*Strong*	*Thompson*	
								Ref: E Jennings	In a game of few chances defences are on top. The potential title decider is a psychological victory for United. Nerves affect both sides in front of a noisy, all-ticket crowd. Stepney is a hero, tipping Ian Callaghan's shot over the bar before being laid out in a collision with Ian St John.											
34	A	FULHAM		1	D	2-2	1-1	Best 25, Stiles 83	Stepney	Dunne A	Noble	Crerand	Foulkes	Stiles	Best	Law	Sadler	Charlton	Aston	
	27/3		*47,290*	*16*	47			*Clarke 18, Barratt 53*	*Macedo*	*Cohen*	*Dempsey*	*Robson*	*Callaghan*	*Conway*	*Haynes*	*Brown*	*Pearson*	*Clarke*	*Barratt*	
								Ref: G Roper	United are given a hard time in front of Fulham's biggest crowd since the war. Johnny Haynes inspires the Cottagers, who lead twice. His free-kick is nodded in by Allan Clarke, and his pass sets up Barratt's goal. Stiles grabs a late equaliser then hits the side netting in the last minute.											
35	H	FULHAM		1	W	2-1	0-0	Stiles 69, Foulkes 86	Stepney	Dunne A	Noble	Crerand	Foulkes	Stiles	Best	Law	Sadler	Charlton	Aston	
	28/3		51,673	*17*	49			*Earle 81*	*Seymour*	*Cohen*	*Dempsey*	*Robson*	*Callaghan*	*Conway*	*Haynes*	*Brown*	*Pearson**	*Clarke*	*Barratt*	*Earle*
								Ref: H Williams	Brave Fulham are unlucky after again thwarting United for long periods. Seymour's memorable debut is ruined by the majestic Stiles, who steers in a header from Crerand's cross. David Sadler's miskick is punished by Steve Earle, but Bill Foulkes' header seals a vital two points.											
36	H	WEST HAM		1	W	3-0	1-0	Charlton 3, Best 86, Law 89	Stepney	Dunne A	Noble	Crerand	Foulkes	Stiles	Best	Law	Sadler	Charlton	Aston	
	1/4		61,308	*11*	51				*Standen*	*Charles*	*Kitchener*	*Bovington*	*Heffer*	*Moore*	*Redknapp*	*Boyce*	*Peters*	*Hurst*	*Brabrook*	
								Ref: W Handley	In a one-sided affair, West Ham trail through league leading scorer Hurst's wayward pass until the closing minutes. Charles fouls Best but Law hits the post from the spot. Best's volley and Law's hook seal an easy win. Liverpool lose and Forest are now the main threat, two points back.											
37	A	SHEFFIELD WED		1	D	2-2	2-0	Charlton 36, 38	Stepney	Dunne A	Noble	Crerand	Foulkes	Stiles	Best	Law	Sadler	Charlton	Aston	
	10/4		*50,315*	*13*	52			*Fantham 49, Ritchie 57*	*Springett R*	*Smith*	*Megson*	*Mobley*	*Ellis*	*Quinn*	*Fantham*	*McCalliog*	*Ritchie*	*Usher*	*Pugh*	
								Ref: M Fussey	The Owls bounce back from an FA Cup exit last week. They trail to two Charlton goals. The first after Best had tricked four men and crossed, the second from Dunne's centre. Wednesday deservedly reply and look more likely winners at the end. United are 15 league games unbeaten.											
38	H	SOUTHAMPTON		1	W	3-0	0-0	Charlton 53, Law 67, Sadler 80	Stepney	Dunne A	Noble	Crerand	Foulkes	Stiles	Best	Law	Sadler	Charlton	Aston	
	18/4		55,121	*19*	54				*Martin*	*Hollywood*	*Jones*	*Fisher*	*Knapp*	*Walker*	*Paine*	*Chivers*	*Davies*	*Melia*	*Byrne*	
								Ref: K Burns	Despite Ron Davies' fantastic 33-goal haul, Saints have had a hard relegation battle. The Saints keep the Reds at bay until after the break. Law makes a goal for Charlton, who reciprocates before Sadler heads in. Six goals would not flatter United. The home gates soar past one million.											
39	A	SUNDERLAND		1	D	0-0	0-0		Stepney	Dunne A	Noble	Crerand	Foulkes	Stiles	Best	Law	Sadler	Charlton	Aston	
	22/4		*43,570*	*16*	55				*Montgomery*	*Irwin*	*Ashurst*	*Todd*	*Kinnell*	*Baxter*	*Suggett*	*O'Hare*	*Martin*	*Herd*	*Gauden*	
								Ref: V James	An eighth successive away draw nudges United towards the championship. Scot Jim Baxter, England's tormentor at Wembley last week, has a similar effect on United. Keeper Jim Montgomery is in fine form and in the last minute he grabs the ball of the hesitant Bobby Charlton's toe.											
40	H	ASTON VILLA		1	W	3-1	0-1	Aston 56, Law 62, Best 80	Stepney	Brennan	Dunne A	Crerand	Foulkes	Stiles	Best	Law	Sadler	Charlton	Aston	
	29/4		55,763	*21*	57			*Anderson 15*	*Withers*	*Bradley*	*Aitken*	*Chatterley*	*Sleeuwenh'k*	*Pountney*	*Anderson*	*Deakin*	*Stobart*	*Broadbent*	*MacLeod**	*Park*
								Ref: H Davey	United clinch the title as physical Villa slide towards Division 2 after seven games without a win. Old boy Anderson nets after Stobart's shot rebounded off a post. Aston scores in a melee to settle the nerves, Law heads in off the bar, and is booked for petulance and Best curls in No 3.											
41	A	WEST HAM		1	W	**6-1**	4-0	Charlton 2, Crerand 7, Foulkes 10,	Stepney	Brennan	Dunne A	Crerand	Foulkes	Stiles	Best	Law	Sadler	Charlton	Aston	
	6/5		*38,424*	*17*	59			*Charles 46* [Best 25, Law 63p, 79]	*Macklew'th*	*Burkett*	*Charles*	*Peters*	*Heffer*	*Moore*	*Redknapp*	*Bennett*	*Boyce*	*Hurst*	*Sissons*	
								Ref: R Spittle	The title is clinched in front of Upton Park's biggest crowd since the war. Burkett makes a hash of a clearance and Charlton nets. It was soon 0-4. Charles concedes a penalty for No 5, pushing Law after he had been slapped around the face. Serious crowd trouble erupts at the end.											
42	H	STOKE		1	D	0-0	0-0		Stepney	Brennan	Dunne A	Crerand	Foulkes	Stiles	Ryan	Best	Sadler	Charlton	Aston	
	13/5		61,071	*12*	60				*Banks*	*Skeels*	*Bentley*	*Bernard*	*Bloor*	*Allen*	*Burrows*	*Dobing*	*Mahoney*	*Vernon*	*Eastham*	
	Home		Away					Ref: P Partridge	United extend their unbeaten run to 20 and have not lost at home. Amazingly it is a niggly game and Law and Dobing are lucky to stay on after punches and spittle fly. The trophy is presented but the game is like flat champagne. The team salutes the Stretford End on a lap of honour.											
Average	53,854		45,718																	

League Cup	Att			F-A	H-T	Scorers, Times, and Referees	1	2	3	4	5	6	7	8	9	10	11	12 sub used
2 A BLACKPOOL		8	L	1-5	1-4	Herd 37	Dunne P	Brennan	Dunne A	Crerand	Foulkes	Stiles	Connelly	Best	Sadler	Herd	Aston	
14/9	*15,570*	*22*				*Charnley 9p, 10, 79, Lea 30, [Waddell 44]*	*Waiters*	*Armfield**	*Thompson*	*Hughes*	*James*	*Green J*	*Brown*	*Waddell*	*Charnley*	*Oates*	*Lea*	*Fisher*
						Ref: J Carr	In pouring rain, struggling Blackpool skim over the slippery surface. Foulkes handles for the penalty and Pat Dunne fails to hold Brown's shot and Lea scores No 3. As the rain eases off, United, without Law and Charlton, fight back but Charnley fleeces Foulkes to complete a hat-trick.											

FA Cup	Att			F-A	H-T	Scorers, Times, and Referees	1	2	3	4	5	6	7	8	9	10	11	12 sub used
3 H STOKE		2	W	2-0	1-0	Law 34, Herd 73	Stepney	Dunne A	Noble	Crerand	Foulkes	Stiles	Best	Law	Sadler	Herd	Charlton	
28/1	63,497	*4*					*Farmer*	*Palmer*	*Skeels*	*Viollet*	*Setters*	*Bloor*	*Philpott*	*Dobing*	*Vernon*	*Eastham*	*Burrows*	
						Ref: J Finney	Stoke, roared on by 21,000 fans, hold United for a nervy 30 minutes. Then Law breaks the FA Cup scoring record with his 31st goal, a header from Best's cross. United live dangerously until Herd's 30-yard shot fools Farmer. 33-year-old Viollet captains Stoke against his old club.											
4 H NORWICH		2	L	1-2	1-1	Law 34	Stepney	Dunne A	Noble	Crerand	Sadler	Stiles	Ryan	Law	Charlton	Herd	Best	
18/2	63,409	*2:21*				*Heath 26, Bolland 65*	*Keelan*	*Stringer*	*Mullett*	*Lucas*	*Brown*	*Allcock*	*Kenning*	*Heath*	*Bryceland*	*Bolland*	*Anderson*	
						Ref: W Gow	The injured Foulkes misses his first Cup-tie for 13 years as the Canaries' dour defence and fast breakaways end United's record of five straight semi-finals. The long balls are United's undoing with Dunne and Stepney in a pickle for the second goal. Reds' 'fans' stone Norwich coaches.											

		Home						Away					
	P	W	D	L	F	A	W	D	L	F	A	Pts
1 MAN UNITED	42	17	4	0	51	13	7	8	6	33	32	60
2 Nott'm Forest	42	16	4	1	41	13	7	6	8	23	28	56
3 Tottenham	42	15	3	3	44	21	9	5	7	27	27	56
4 Leeds	42	15	4	2	41	17	7	7	7	21	25	55
5 Liverpool	42	12	7	2	36	17	7	6	8	28	30	51
6 Everton	42	11	4	6	39	22	8	6	7	26	24	48
7 Arsenal	42	11	6	4	32	20	5	8	8	26	27	46
8 Leicester	42	12	4	5	47	28	6	4	11	31	43	44
9 Chelsea	42	7	9	5	33	29	8	5	8	34	33	44
10 Sheffield Utd	42	11	5	5	34	22	5	5	11	18	37	42
11 Sheffield Wed	42	9	7	5	39	19	5	6	10	17	28	41
12 Stoke	42	11	5	5	40	21	6	2	13	23	37	41
13 West Brom	42	11	1	9	40	28	5	6	10	37	45	39
14 Burnley	42	11	4	6	43	28	4	5	12	23	48	39
15 Manchester C	42	8	9	4	27	25	4	6	11	16	27	39
16 West Ham	42	8	6	7	40	31	6	2	13	40	53	36
17 Sunderland	42	12	3	6	39	26	2	5	14	19	46	36
18 Fulham	42	8	7	6	49	34	3	5	13	22	49	34
19 Southampton	42	10	3	8	49	41	4	3	14	25	51	34
20 Newcastle	42	9	5	7	24	27	3	4	14	15	54	33
21 Aston Villa	42	7	5	9	30	33	4	2	15	24	52	29
22 Blackpool	42	1	5	15	18	36	5	4	12	23	40	21
	924	232	110	120	836	551	120	110	232	551	836	924

Odds & ends

Double wins: (6) Everton, Blackpool, Southampton, Leicester, West Brom, West Ham.
Double losses: (0).

Won from behind: (3) Everton (a), Blackpool (a), Aston Villa (h).
Lost from in front: (1) Tottenham (a).

High spots: 20-game unbeaten league run from Christmas.
Unbeaten home record.
Solid defence and goalkeeper.
Bobby Charlton's European Footballer of the Year award.

Low spots: FA Cup exit to 2nd Division Norwich.
Poor start.
Shock League Cup defeat at Blackpool.

Red cards (United): (0).
Red cards (Opponents): (0).
Ever-presents: (2) Best, Charlton.
Hat-tricks: (2) Herd (2).
Opposing hat-tricks: (2) Crowe (Nott'm Forest), Charnley (Blackpool LC).
Leading scorer: (25) Law.

	Appearances						Goals			
	Lge	*Sub*	LC	*Sub*	FAC	*Sub*	Lge	LC	FAC	Tot
Anderson, Willie		*1*								
Aston, John	**26**	*4*	1				**5**			**5**
Best, George	**42**		1		2		**10**			**10**
Brennan, Shay	**16**		1							
Cantwell, Noel	**4**									
Charlton, Bobby	**42**				2		**12**			**12**
Connelly, John	**6**		1				**2**			**2**
Crerand, Pat	**39**		1		2		**3**			**3**
Dunne, Pat			1							
Dunne, Tony	**40**		1		2					
Fitzpatrick, John	**3**									
Foulkes, Bill	**33**		1		1		**4**			**4**
Gaskell, Dave	**5**									
Gregg, Harry	**2**									
Herd, David	**28**		1		2		**16**	1	1	**18**
Law, Dennis	**36**				2		**23**		2	**25**
Noble, Bobby	**29**				2					
Ryan, Jimmy	**4**	*1*			1					
Sadler, David	**35**	*1*	1		2		**5**			**5**
Stepney, Alex	**35**				2					
Stiles, Nobby	**37**		1		2		**3**			**3**
(own-goals)							**1**			**1**
21 players used	**462**	*7*	**11**		**22**		**84**	**1**	**3**	**88**

No	Date		Att	Pos	Pt	F-A	H-T	Scorers, Times, and Referees	1	2	3	4	5	6	7	8	9	10	11	12 sub used
1	A	EVERTON			L	1-3	0-1	Charlton 86	Stepney	Brennan	Dunne	Crerand*	Foulkes	Stiles	Best	Law	Charlton	**Kidd**	Aston	Sadler
	19/8		*61,452*		0			*Ball 13, 66, Young 68*	*West*	*Wright*	*Wilson*	*Kendall*	*Labone*	*Harvey*	*Young*	*Ball*	*Royle*	*Hurst*	*Morrissey*	
								Ref: D Smith	Everton bombard the Reds from first to last and deserve their win. Ball's two close-range goals sparks crowd trouble and woeful United slip to their first league defeat in 20 since Boxing Day. By the finish, slick Everton are in teasing mood and Charlton's 20-yarder is a consolation.											
2	H	LEEDS			W	1-0	0-0	Charlton 60	Stepney	Brennan	Dunne	Crerand	Foulkes	Stiles	Ryan	Law	Charlton	Kidd	Aston	
	23/8		52,986		2				*Sprake*	*Reaney*	*Madeley*	*Bremner*	*Charlton*	*Hunter*	*O'Grady*	*Lorimer*	*Gray*	*Giles*	*Cooper*	
								Ref: J Finney	A typically hard game against Revie's Leeds. Stiles is immaculate in a wild midfield in heatwave conditions. Both keepers are in top form but Sprake cracks first and spills Aston's shot for Bobby Charlton to net. Stepney's late save from Peter Lorimer seals the win over unlucky Leeds.											
3	H	LEICESTER		11	D	1-1	0-0	Foulkes 63	Stepney	Brennan	Dunne	Sadler	Foulkes	Stiles	Best	Law	Charlton	Kidd	Aston	
	26/8		51,256	*18*	3			*Stringfellow 54*	*Shilton**	*Rodrigues*	*Norman*	*Roberts*	*Woollett*	*Cross*	*Sinclair*	*Nish*	*Sjoberg*	*Gibson*	*Stringfellow*	*Tewley*
								Ref: P Partridge	United are struggling to find their form and Crerand is out injured. 17-year-old Peter Shilton looks classy until he is carried off – Roberts goes in goal. Stepney falls foul of the new four-step rule and Gibson's free-kick is tapped in by Stringfellow. Foulkes heads in Charlton's corner.											
4	A	WEST HAM		8	W	3-1	0-0	Kidd 54, Sadler 59, Ryan 82	Stepney	Dunne	**Burns**	Crerand	Foulkes	Stiles	Ryan	Sadler	Charlton	Kidd	Best	
	2/9		*36,562*	*20*	5			*Peters 79*	*Ferguson*	*Bonds**	*Charles*	*Peters*	*Cushley*	*Moore*	*Redknapp*	*Dear*	*Hurst*	*Boyce*	*Sissons*	*Brooking*
								Ref: E Jennings	West Ham have the better of the first half but Hurst and Dear miss chances. When Charlton hooks over Cushley's head to Kidd for his first senior goal, the die is cast. Peters heads in Redknapp's corner to set up a thrilling finale. 18-year-old Brooking makes his second appearance.											
5	A	SUNDERLAND		9	D	1-1	1-1	Kidd 5	Stepney	Dunne	Burns	Crerand	Foulkes	Stiles*	Ryan	Sadler	Charlton	Kidd	Best	Fitzpatrick
	6/9		*51,527*	*3*	6			*Suggett 6*	*Montgomery*	*Parke*	*Ashurst*	*Todd*	*Kinnell*	*Baxter*	*Herd*	*Suggett*	*Brand*	*Heslop*	*Mullhall*	
								Ref: J Thacker	Sunderland's best start for years is continued with a deserved draw. Kidd's header from Crerand's cross is cancelled out by Suggett's fifth goal in five from Baxter's pass. Montgomery saves well from Best, Sadler and Kidd before the tables are turned and the home side finish strongly.											
6	H	BURNLEY		10	D	2-2	0-1	Burns 86, Crerand 90	Stepney	Dunne	Burns	Crerand	Foulkes	Fitzpatrick*	Ryan	Sadler	Charlton	Kidd	Best	**Kopel**
	9/9		55,809	*12*	7			*Lochhead 44, 61*	*Thomson*	*Smith*	*Latcham*	*O'Neill*	*Angus*	*Bellamy*	*Morgan*	*Casper*	*Lochhead*	*Harris*	*Coates*	
								Ref: N Burtenshaw	Late goals save the 27-game unbeaten home run. Lochhead's powerful headers had left Foulkes and United bemused until Burns hammers in Kidd's pull-back and Best repeats the move for Crerand in the second minute of injury time. 19-year-old Kopel on for a concussed Fitzpatrick.											
7	A	SHEFFIELD WED		10	D	1-1	0-1	Best 75	Stepney	Dunne	Burns	Crerand	Foulkes	Stiles	Best	Sadler	Charlton	Law	Kidd	
	16/9		*46,626*	*4*	8			*Usher 32*	*Springett P*	*Quinn*	*Smith*	*Mobley*	*Ellis*	*Young*	*Eustace*	*Fantham**	*Ritchie*	*McCalliog*	*Usher*	*Whitham*
								Ref: K Wynn	In a game of two halves, Wednesday are on top until the break. Usher scores his first goal for two years. Burn's free-kick is headed into the top of the net by Best and United deserve a point in an incident-packed match at their bogey ground. Near misses at both ends in a frantic finish.											
8	H	TOTTENHAM		7	W	3-1	1-1	Best 6, 87, Law 85	Stepney	Dunne	Burns	Crerand	Foulkes	Stiles	Best	Sadler	Charlton	Law	Kidd	
	23/9		58,779	*6*	10			*Gilzean 1*	*Jennings*	*Kinnear*	*Knowles*	*Mullery*	*England*	*Beal*	*Robertson*	*Greaves*	*Gilzean*	*Clayton*	*Saul*	
								Ref: G Kew	An astonishing start and a whirlwind finish. Law misses a penalty soon after Gilzean's opener before Best equalises with a fierce shot. Stiles is the master of Greaves. Dogged but talented Spurs somehow survive until the last five minutes. Law's header and Best's drive seals the win.											
9	A	MANCHESTER C		5	W	2-1	2-1	Charlton 22, 35	Stepney	Dunne	Burns	Crerand	Foulkes*	Stiles	Best	Sadler	Charlton	Law	Kidd	Aston
	30/9		***62,942***	*7*	12			*Bell 5*	*Mulhearn*	*Book*	*Pardoe*	*Doyle*	*Heslop*	*Oakes*	*Bowles*	*Bell*	*Summerbee*	*Young**	*Coleman*	*Horne*
								Ref: K Howley	A fortunate win, with City denied two good penalty appeals. In a niggly match the partisan fans are kept apart. Kidd and Stan Bowles exchange blows and are lucky not to be sent off. Charlton is the man of the match, with Summerbee, who leads Foulkes a merry dance, not far behind.											
10	H	ARSENAL		3	W	1-0	0-0	Aston 76	Stepney	Dunne	Burns	Crerand	Sadler	Stiles	Best	Kidd	Charlton	Law!	Aston	
	7/10		60,201	*6*	14				*Furnell*	*Storey*	*McNab*	*McLintock*	*Neill*	*Ure!*	*Radford*	*Simpson*	*Graham*	*Sammels*	*Armstrong*	
								Ref: G McCabe	A disgraceful game with petty feuds erupting all over the pitch. Ian Ure and Law are sent off for fighting and Kidd and McLintock are lucky to stay on. Kidd's pass finds Crerand, who dummies and crosses for Aston to coolly head in. Stepney makes a save of a lifetime to foil Simpson.											

No		Opponent / Date	Att	Pos	Res / Pt	F-A	H-T	Scorers, Times, and Referees	1	2	3	4	5	6	7	8	9	10	11	12
11	A	SHEFFIELD UTD		3	W	3-0	0-0	Kidd 64, Aston 75, Law 87p	Stepney	Dunne	Burns	Crerand	Sadler	Stiles*	Best	Kidd	Charlton	Law	Aston	Fitzpatrick
		14/10	***29,170***	21	16				*Hodgkinson*	*Badger*	*Shaw B*	*Munks*	*Mallender*	*Barlow*	*Hill*	*Carlin*	*Birchenall*	*Fenoughty*	*Reece*	
								Ref: K Burns	The Blades' dire start is compounded by a smooth second half display from the Reds on a wet pitch. Mick Jones' sale to Leeds has further depressed the Blades faithful. Carlin's error lets in Kidd. John Aston, for once, gets away from Len Badger and then is fouled for the penalty.											
12	H	COVENTRY		2	W	**4-0**	2-0	Aston 31, 58, Best 33, Charlton 68	Stepney	Dunne	Burns	Crerand	Sadler	Fitzpatrick	Best	Kidd	Charlton	Law	Aston	
		25/10	54,253	*20*	18				*Glazier*	*Coop*	*Hill**	*Kearns*	*Knapp*	*Clements*	*Lewis*	*Machin*	*Tudor*	*Gibson*	*Rees*	*Morrissey*
								Ref: J Carr	Noel Cantwell's first game in charge of Coventry, in their first ever season in Division 1. City battled well but in the second half United tear them apart. The best goal is Charlton's 30-yarder, which the crowd applauds for over two minutes. Bill Glazier saves Law's late twice-taken penalty.											
13	A	NOTT'M FOREST		2	L	1-3	0-2	Best 71	Stepney	Kopel	Burns	Crerand	Sadler	Fitzpatrick	Best	Kidd	Charlton	Law	Aston	
		28/10	*49,946*	*7*	18			*Baker 26, 40, Wignall 59*	*Grummitt*	*Hindley*	*Winfield*	*Hennessey*	*McKinlay*	*Newton*	*Lyons*	*Barnwell*	*Baker*	*Wignall*	*Storey-M're*	
								Ref: V James	The City Ground is becoming a bogey ground for United. A record crowd watches them lose to Carey's boys for the third year running. The speedy Joe Baker has too much guile for John Fitzpatrick, and Law has two markers at all times. Best's impudent goal is too little, too late.											
14	H	STOKE		2	W	1-0	0-0	Charlton 75	Stepney	Dunne	Burns	Crerand	Foulkes	Sadler	Ryan	Kidd	Charlton	Best	Aston	
		4/11	51,141	*13*	20				*Banks*	*Elder*	*Bentley*	*Skeels*	*Bloor*	*Allen*	*Bernard*	*Palmer*	*Dobing*	*Eastham*	*Burrows*	
								Ref: M Fussey	Dennis Law starts his six-week ban and with Charlton off-colour the hard work is left to Best. Calvin Palmer's dire back-pass is pounced on by George and when Banks can only parry the shot Bobby nets. Tony Waddington's vintage collection move with confidence but lack goal power.											
15	A	LEEDS		2	L	0-1	0-1		Stepney	Dunne	Burns	Crerand	Foulkes	Sadler	Ryan*	Kidd	Charlton	Best	Aston	Fitzpatrick
		8/11	*43,999*	*4*	20			*Greenhoff 25*	*Sprake*	*Reaney*	*Cooper*	*Bremner*	*Charlton*	*Hunter*	*Greenhoff*	*Lorimer*	*Madeley*	*Gray*	*Johanneson*	
								Ref: J Taylor	United miss their chance to go top with a lacklustre performance at foggy Elland Road. Billy Bremner returns to inspire a Leeds win as Greenhoff's shot catches Stepney off-guard. The tackles fly in and the Reds barely have a chance. Johanneson misses, thinking he is offside.											
16	A	LIVERPOOL		1	W	2-1	2-0	Best 18, 40	Stepney	Dunne	Burns	Crerand	Foulkes	Sadler	Fitzpatrick	Kidd	Charlton	Best	Aston	
		11/11	*54,515*	*2*	22			*Hunt 83*	*Lawrence*	*Lawler*	*Byrne*	*Smith*	*Yeats*	*Hughes*	*Callaghan*	*Hunt*	*Hateley*	*St John*	*Thompson*	
								Ref: W Handley	Liverpool's 100% home record is smashed and the Kop silenced by a great team performance. Best shows his big-game temperament again with two super goals. A glancing header from Aston's cross and a clinical finish as Lawrence hesitates. Pool come back strongly near the end.											
17	H	SOUTHAMPTON		1	W	3-2	3-1	Aston 15, Kidd 26, Charlton 41	Stepney	Dunne	Burns	Crerand	Foulkes	Sadler	Fitzpatrick	Kidd	Charlton	Best	Aston	
		18/11	**48,732**	*16*	24			*Davies 35, Chivers 57*	*Martin*	*Jones*	*Byrne*	*Gabriel*	*Webb*	*Walker*	*Paine*	*Chivers*	*Davies*	*Melia*	*Channon*	
								Ref: P Baldwin	Ted Bates' Saints are earning a reputation for being hard. Tony Byrne upsets the Stretford End and Best by kicking, hacking and barging the Irish imp. Davies and Chivers, linked with big moves, embarrass the Reds' defence. Charlton's thunderbolt is worthy of winning any match.											
18	A	CHELSEA		1	D	1-1	1-1	Kidd 33	Stepney	Brennan	Dunne	Crerand	Foulkes	Sadler	Burns	Kidd	Charlton	Best	Aston	
		25/11	*54,712*	*18*	25			*Baldwin 21*	*Bonetti*	*Kirkup*	*McCreadie*	*Hollins*	*Hinton*	*Harris R*	*Fascione*	*Baldwin*	*Osgood*	*Boyle*	*Cooke*	
								Ref: J Taylor	Dave Sexton has succeeded Docherty and steadied a shaky Chelsea ship. This is their best display of the season, with Charlie Cooke inspiring. Baldwin scores a trademark breakaway before Kidd's header. Ron Harris mercilessly chops Best. David Sadler celebrates an England call-up.											
19	H	WEST BROM		1	W	2-1	2-0	Best 21, 26	Stepney	Brennan	Dunne	Crerand	Foulkes	Sadler	Burns	Kidd	Charlton	Best	Aston	
		2/12	52,897	*13*	27			*Kaye 75*	*Osbourne*	*Colquhoun*	*Williams*	*Brown*	*Talbut*	*Fraser*	*Krzywicki*	*Kaye*	*Astle*	*Hope*	*Clark*	
								Ref: R Tinkler	Albion have lost only one game in 8 and are the best side to visit Old Trafford. Two more wonder goals from Best – a shot from an acute angle and header from Aston's corner – clinch a good win. With Prime Minister Wilson in attendance, Albion's Jeff Astle goes close to an equaliser.											
20	A	NEWCASTLE		1	D	2-2	0-0	Kidd 82, Dunne 89	Stepney	Brennan	Dunne	Crerand	Foulkes	Sadler	Burns	Kidd	Charlton	Best	Aston	
		9/12	*48,639*	*8*	28			*Iley 47, Robson 57*	*Marshall*	*Burton*	*Clark*	*Elliott*	*McNamee*	*Moncur*	*Scott*	*Bennett*	*Davies*	*Iley*	*Robson T*	
								Ref: R Harper	A football feast on a treacherous icy pitch. Newcastle are unbeaten in 17 home games and look home and dry, but in a frantic last fifteen minutes the Geordies buckle. Best sets up Kidd then Tony Dunne's cross looks too long but swerves and goes in off a post with Marshall static.											
21	H	EVERTON		1	W	3-1	1-0	Sadler 3, Aston 52, Law 64	Stepney	Dunne	Burns	Crerand	Foulkes	Sadler	Best	Kidd	Charlton	Law	Aston	
		16/12	57,078	*9*	30			*Young 75*	*West*	*Wright*	*Wilson*	*Kendall*	*Labone*	*Harvey*	*Young*	*Ball*	*Royle*	*Hurst*	*Morrissey*	
								Ref: W Handley	Revenge for the opening-day defeat as Everton wilt after half-time. Law returns, avoids trouble, makes the second goal and beats four men to score No 3. Alex Young's immaculate free-kick causes some flutters and Stepney pulls off a super save from Joe Royle's header near the end.											

No Date	Att	Pos	Pt	F-A	H-T	Scorers, Times, and Referees	1	2	3	4	5	6	7	8	9	10	11	12 sub used
22 A LEICESTER		1	D	2-2	0-0	Charlton 60, Law 69	Stepney	Dunne	Burns	Crerand	Foulkes	Sadler	Best	Kidd	Charlton	Law	Aston	
23/12	*40,138*	*15*	31			*Sjoberg 52, Tewley 87*	*Shilton*	*Rodrigues*	*Bell*	*Roberts*	*Sjoberg*	*Nish*	*Tewley*	*Large*	*Stringfellow*	*Gibson*	*Glover*	
						Ref: A Dimond	Leicester's biggest crowd since 1963 see a thriller. United come from behind and look home and dry before Willie Bell's shot rebounds to Alan Tewley to hammer home. Shilton is superb but cannot stop Charlton's 20-yarder and Law's rebound. Pat Crerand's 200th league game.											
23 H WOLVERHAMPTON		1	W	4-0	3-0	Best 10, 42, Kidd 30, Charlton 50	Stepney	Dunne	Burns	Crerand	Foulkes	Sadler	Best	Kidd	Charlton	Law	Aston	
26/12	**63,450**	*14*	33				*Williams*	*Taylor*	*Thomson*	*Bailey*	*Hawkins*	*Holsgrove*	*Wilson*	*Evans*	*Knowles*	*Burnside*	*Wagstaffe*	
						Ref: K Styles	United go three points clear and look unstoppable. The scoreline does not flatter them in front of a full house. Best carves a weakened Wolves side who miss the injured Dougan and whose defence fall asleep for two of the goals. The cool Francis Burns looks a long-standing veteran.											
24 A WOLVERHAMPTON		1	W	3-2	0-1	Charlton 46, Aston 50, Kidd 60	Stepney	Dunne	Burns	Crerand	Foulkes	Sadler	Best	Kidd	Charlton	Law	Aston	
30/12	*53,940*	*15*	35			*Buckley 1, Bailey 67*	*Williams*	*Wilson*	*Thomson*	*Bailey*	*Hawkins*	*Holsgrove*	*Evans*	*Knowles*	*Buckley*	*Ross*	*Wagstaffe*	
						Ref: K Walker	Lively Wolves give United a fright for 30 minutes and lead through Buckley's 25-second goal. Then Best, for whom superlatives are running out, takes control. After Charlton's shot from a tight angle, he makes goals for Aston and Kidd. Mike Bailey's 35-yard shot gives some hope.											
25 H WEST HAM		1	W	3-1	1-1	Charlton 11, Best 51, Aston 77	Stepney	Dunne	Burns	Crerand	Sadler	Fitzpatrick	Best	Kidd	Charlton	Law	Aston	
6/1	59,516	*15*	37			*Brooking 22*	*Ferguson*	*Bonds*	*Lampard*	*Peters*	*Cushley*	*Moore*	*Dear*	*Boyce*	*Brooking*	*Hurst*	*Sissons*	
						Ref: K Howley	Bobby Charlton celebrates his 400th league game with a goal from 20 yards. Ron Greenwood's inconsistent team give United a good game. Dear sets up Brooking. Best heads in despite being surrounded before Aston's low drive. The win means they are unbeaten in 36 home games.											
26 H SHEFFIELD WED		1	W	4-2	1-0	Best 16, 56, Charlton 64, Kidd 67	Stepney	Dunne	Burns	Crerand	Sadler	Fitzpatrick	Best	Kidd	Charlton	Law	Aston	
20/1	56,254	*11*	39			*Whitham 77, 88*	*Springett P*	*Smith*	*Megson*	*Branfoot*	*Mobley*	*Young**	*Fantham*	*Symm*	*Ritchie*	*McCalliog*	*Usher*	*Whitham*
						Ref: L Callaghan	The Owls' great start has fizzled out and they have just one win in 11. United are in top form with Best at his zenith. John Fitzpatrick has a blinder. Charlton hits a special and Kidd glances in a header. Sub Jack Whitham scores two to take the gloss off and has another disallowed.											
27 A TOTTENHAM		1	W	2-1	1-1	Best 18, Charlton 88	Stepney	Dunne	Burns	Crerand	Sadler	Fitzpatrick	Best	Kidd	Charlton	Herd	Aston	
3/2	*57,690*	*7*	41			*Chivers 2*	*Jennings*	*Kinnear*	*Knowles*	*Mullery*	*England*	*Beal*	*Robertson*	*Greaves*	*Chivers*	*Venables*	*Jones*	
						Ref: N Burtenshaw	United deservedly win the third meeting with Spurs in a week. Chivers' goal looks offside but Best cancels it out despite being surrounded by five defenders. Knowles fouls Best but Charlton misses the spot-kick. He atones by running half the pitch to score the winner of a classic.											
28 A BURNLEY		1	L	1-2	1-0	Best 8	Stepney	Dunne	Burns	Crerand	Sadler	Stiles	Best	Kidd	Charlton	Law	Aston	
17/2	*32,165*	*11*	41			*O'Neill 61, Dobson 68*	*Thomson*	*Angus*	*Latcham*	*Todd*	*Waldron*	*Merrington*	*Morgan*	*Lochhead**	*Casper !*	*O'Neill*	*Coates*	*Dobson*
						Ref: W Handley	The 12-game unbeaten run is ended, despite Law and Stiles' return from injury. Best's early lead, after hesitation in the home defence, looks enough until Brian O'Neill's rising drive goes in off a post and Dobson finishes coolly. Frank Casper floors Francis Burns and gets sent off.											
29 A ARSENAL		1	W	2-0	1-0	Storey 23 (og), Best 56	Stepney	Dunne	Burns	Crerand	Sadler	Stiles	Best	Kidd	Fitzpatrick	Law	Aston	
24/2	*46,417*	*10*	43				*Furnell*	*Storey*	*McNab*	*McLintock*	*Neill*	*Simpson*	*Jenkins*	*Gould*	*Graham*	*Sammels*	*Armstrong*	
						Ref: D Lyden	Arsenal's 27-match unbeaten home run is ended. Charlton, on England duty, is not missed and Best is not distracted by his growing modelling activities. Best harries Storey into an own-goal and then creates an opening out of nothing. Arsenal will play Leeds in the League Cup final.											
30 H CHELSEA		1	L	1-3	0-1	Kidd 52	Stepney	Dunne	Burns	Crerand	Sadler	Stiles	Best	Kidd	Charlton	Ryan	Aston	
2/3	62,471	*10*	43			*Tambling 16, Baldwin 59, Osgood 78*	*Bonetti*	*Boyle*	*Thomson*	*Cooke*	*Webb*	*Harris R*	*Houseman*	*Baldwin*	*Osgood*	*Birchenall*	*Tambling*	
						Ref: M Fussey	United's 37-match unbeaten home run is ended by an impressive Chelsea. Stepney is limping from an early stage and can't dive for Osgood's shot. Cooke is the man of the match and his dazzling run tees up Tambling's goal. Baldwin looks offside but United have a Euro hangover.											
31 A COVENTRY		2	L	0-2	0-1		Stepney	Brennan	Burns	Crerand	Sadler	Stiles	Best	Kidd*	Charlton	Fitzpatrick	Herd	Aston
16/3	*47,111*	*20*	43			*Machin 34, Setters 52*	*Glazier*	*Bruck*	*Cattlin*	*Machin*	*Setters*	*Clements*	*Hannigan*	*Hunt*	*Martin*	*Tudor*	*Carr*	
						Ref: H New	Although City's main stand is closed because of the fire, the gate is their second biggest ever. Two transfer deadline purchases, Cattlin and Hunt, play their part in knocking United off the top. Machin's 30-yard volley sparks a pitch invasion and ex-Red Maurice Setters heads a second.											

No	H/A	Opponent / Date	Att	Pos	Res	Pts	F-A	H-T	Scorers, Times, and Referees	1	2	3	4	5	6	7	8	9	10	11	12 sub used
32	H	NOTT'M FOREST		2	W		3-0	2-0	Herd 15, Brennan 29, Burns 69	Stepney	Brennan	Burns	Crerand	Sadler	Stiles	Fitzpatrick	Herd	Charlton	Best	Aston	
		23/3	61,978	*10*		45				*Williamson*	*Hindley*	*Winfield*	*Hennessey*	*McKinlay*	*Newton*	*Barnwell*	*Baxter**	*Baker*	*Chapman*	*Hilley*	*Lyons*
									Ref: D Corbett	Forest's form has deserted them. Herd nets his first goal since his broken leg a year ago. Shay Brennan scores as reserve keeper Williamson lets a shot slither through his hands. Burns' wild shot deflects off McKinlay. Forest fade after a bright start, with Jim Baxter anonymous.											
33	H	MANCHESTER C		3	L		1-3	1-1	Best 1	Stepney	Brennan	Burns	Crerand	Sadler	Stiles	Fitzpatrick	Law	Charlton	Best	Herd*	Aston
		27/3	62,243	*2*		45			*Bell 18, Heslop 57, Lee 82p*	*Mulhearn*	*Book*	*Pardoe*	*Doyle*	*Heslop*	*Oakes*	*Lee*	*Bell**	*Summerbee*	*Young*	*Coleman*	*Connor*
									Ref: D Smith	Leeds and the two Manchester clubs are all on 45 points after a full-blooded game which is never dirty. After Best's 35-second goal City are in charge. Bell bemuses Fitzpatrick to score and Heslop heads his first City goal from Coleman's free-kick. Burns brings down Bell for a penalty.											
34	A	STOKE		1	W		4-2	2-2	Best 2, Gowling 23, Aston 69, Ryan 78	Stepney	Brennan	Burns	Crerand	Sadler	Fitzpatrick	Best	**Gowling**	Charlton	Herd*	Aston	Ryan
		30/3	*32,549*	*16*		47			*Eastham 9, Dobing 37*	*Banks*	*Elder**	*Bentley*	*Moore*	*Bloor*	*Allen*	*Vernon*	*Stevenson*	*Dobing*	*Eastham*	*Burrows*	*Bernard*
									Ref: V James	Stoke's fourth defeat in a row sends them sliding towards the drop zone. United deservedly win a fast-flowing thriller. Kidd is suspended and his stand-in, England Amateur international Alan Gowling, is the star, scoring with a volley and fooling Banks for the impressive Aston to net.											
35	H	LIVERPOOL		2	L		1-2	1-2	Best 2	Stepney	Dunne	Burns	Crerand	Sadler	Fitzpatrick	Best	Gowling	Charlton	Herd	Aston	
		6/4	60,714	*4*		47			*Yeats 9, Hunt 17*	*Lawrence*	*Lawler*	*Hughes*	*Ross*	*Yeats*	*Strong*	*Callaghan*	*Hunt*	*Hateley**	*St John*	*Thompson*	*Arrowsmith*
									Ref: K Dagnall	The third defeat in four home games is disastrous as City leapfrog the Reds. Composed Liverpool bounce back from an FA Cup defeat to West Brom and an early Best goal. Yeats jabs home after his header rebounds off a post. Roger Hunt and Tony Hateley's one-two seals a vital win.											
36	A	FULHAM		1	W		4-0	3-0	Best 20, 34, Kidd 40, Law 50	Stepney	Dunne	Burns	Crerand	Sadler	Stiles	Best	Kidd	Charlton	Law	Aston	
		12/4	*40,154*	*22*		49				*Macedo*	*Conway*	*Dempsey*	*Ryan*	*Callaghan*	*Haynes*	*Brown*	*Clarke*	*Byrne*	*Barrett*	*Salvage*	
									Ref: E Wallace	Fulham are almost doomed to the drop and the reason is obvious. Their defence is statuesque as United notch four goals without reply. New manager Bobby Robson has had little impact on a poor side. United barely raise a sweat and create so many chances it could have been 8-0.											
37	A	SOUTHAMPTON		1	D		2-2	2-2	Charlton 42, Best 44	Stepney	Dunne	Burns	Crerand	Foulkes	Sadler	Best	Kidd	Charlton	Gowling	Aston	
		13/4	*30,079*	*13*		50			*Paine 13, Davies 34*	*Martin*	*Kirkup*	*Hollywood*	*Fisher*	*McGrath*	*Gabriel**	*Paine*	*Channon*	*Davies*	*Melia*	*Saul*	*Walker*
									Ref: J Yates	A locked-gates full house go wild as the home side take a two-goal lead, with Big Ron Davies causing the recalled Foulkes real problems. United fight back well and Burns sets up both goals for Charlton and the subdued Best who is given some strong treatment by the tough Saints.											
38	H	FULHAM		1	W		3-0	2-0	Charlton 12, Best 35, Aston 86	**Rimmer**	Dunne	Burns	Crerand	Foulkes	Sadler	Best	Kidd	Charlton	Law	Aston	
		15/4	60,865	*22*		52				*Seymour*	*Mealand*	*Dempsey*	*Ryan*	*Callaghan**	*Brown*	*Conway*	*Clarke*	*Earle*	*Barrett*	*Gilroy*	*Nichols*
									Ref: R Harmer	A compassionate United take pity on relegated Fulham, who have gone eight games without a win. 20-year-old Jimmy Rimmer has little to do on his debut. Charlton beats six men before hitting a glorious opener. Best scores from an impossible angle. Allan Clarke misses a sitter.											
39	H	SHEFFIELD UTD		1	W		1-0	1-0	Law 5	Stepney	Brennan	Dunne	Crerand	Sadler	Stiles	Best	Kidd	Charlton	Law	Aston	
		20/4	55,033	*13*		54				*Hodgkinson*	*Badger*	*Shaw B*	*Munks*	*Mallender*	*Barlow*	*Woodward*	*Carlin*	*Fenoughty*	*Currie*	*Reece*	
									Ref: J Taylor	Relegation-threatened Blades cause a few scares as the Reds have their minds on the Real game. United are one point ahead of Leeds who have a game in hand. Law scores a classic header from Brian Kidd's cross. In the heat, United switch to v-necked short-sleeved shirts at half-time.											
40	A	WEST BROM		2	L		**3-6**	0-2	Law 60p, Kidd 80, 88 *[Hartford 70]*	Stepney	Dunne	Burns	Crerand	Sadler	Stiles	Best	Kidd	Charlton	Law	Aston	
		29/4	*45,992*	*8*		54			*Astle 10, 59, 75, Rees 39, Brown 58p,*	*Osborne*	*Clarke*	*Williams*	*Brown*	*Talbut*	*Fraser*	*Rees**	*Collard*	*Astle*	*Hope*	*Hartford*	
									Ref: H Davey	United's defence is ripped apart by an Albion side celebrating reaching the FA Cup semi-final and Jeff Astle, one of the best strikers in the land. The first two goals come from poor back-passes and then United throw caution to the wind. 17-year-old Asa Hartford nets his first goal.											
41	H	NEWCASTLE		2	W		**6-0**	3-0	Kidd 10, 60, Best 23, 27p, 55p, [Sadler 65]	Stepney	Brennan	Dunne	Crerand	Foulkes	Sadler	Best	Kidd	Charlton	Gowling	Aston	
		4/5	59,976	*9*		56				*McFaul*	*Craig*	*Clark*	*Burton*	*Winstanley**	*Moncur*	*Sinclair*	*Scott*	*Davies*	*Elliott*	*Robson T*	*Iley*
									Ref: D Lyden	Despite a big win, United's goal-difference is inferior to leaders Man City. Best scores his first hat-trick with a brilliant solo display. Robson fouls Kidd for the first penalty and Winstanley emulates him by leaning on George. Dennis Law enters hospital for an exploratory operation.											
42	H	SUNDERLAND		2	L		1-2	1-2	Best 44	Stepney	Brennan	Dunne	Crerand	Foulkes*	Stiles	Best	Kidd	Charlton	Sadler	Aston	Gowling
		11/5	62,963	*15*		56			*Suggett 14, Mulhall 32*	*Montgomery*	*Harvey*	*Ashurst*	*Hurley*	*Todd*	*Porterfield*	*Harris*	*Herd*	*Stuckey*	*Suggett*	*Mulhall*	
		Home	Away						Ref: J Clarke	Two soft goals condemn United to a shock defeat that hands the title to City, who win 4-3 at Newcastle. Newly anointed Footballer of the Year Best tries to rally the troops, but they are goal-shy with one eye on the big game in Madrid. United set a new seasonal attendance record.											
Average		57,552	46,015																		

Charity Shield	Att	Pos	Res	F-A	H-T	Scorers, Times, and Referees	1	2	3	4	5	6	7	8	9	10	11	12 sub used
H TOTTENHAM 12/8	54,106		D	3-3	2-2	Charlton 18, 20, Law 72	Stepney	Brennan	Dunne	Crerand	Foulkes	Stiles	Best	Law	Charlton	Kidd	Aston	
						Robertson 2, Jennings 5, Saul 49	*Jennings*	*Kinnear*	*Knowles*	*Mullery*	*England*	*Mackay*	*Robertson*	*Greaves*	*Gilzean*	*Venables*	*Saul*	
						Ref: E Jennings	On a wet afternoon, this is a great advert for the game. Spurs, who start like a train, are pegged back by two Charlton specials, The second is a brilliant move involving Law and the ubiquitous Kidd, who sets Bobby up for a thunderous shot. Pat Jennings' kick bounces over Stepney.											

European Cup	Att	Pos	Res	F-A	H-T	Scorers, Times, and Referees	1	2	3	4	5	6	7	8	9	10	11	12 sub used
1:1 H HIBERNIANS 20/9 (Malta)	43,912	10	W	4-0	2-0	Sadler 12, 58 Law 42, 62	Stepney	Dunne	Burns	Crerand	Foulkes	Stiles	Best	Sadler	Charlton	Law	Kidd	
							Mizzi	*Privitera*	*Gatt*	*Mallia*	*Caruana*	*Theobald*	*Mifsud*	*Scerri*	*Cassar*	*Delia*	*Young*	
						Ref: J Ferreira (Portugal)	United's shooting practice against the plucky Maltese part-timers is unimpressive. Only Maltese Footballer of the Year Eddie Theobald looks Football league class. Sadler scores with a header, Mizzi fumbles Law's 30-yard shot, Best's dribble creates No 3, and Law taps in a fourth.											
1:2 A HIBERNIANS 27/9	*25,000*	7	D	0-0	0-0		Stepney	Dunne	Burns	Crerand	Foulkes	Stiles	Best	Sadler	Charlton	Law	Kidd	
							Mizzi	*Privitera*	*Gatt*	*Mallia*	*Caruana*	*Theobald*	*Attard*	*Scerri*	*Cassar*	*Delia*	*Young*	
						Ref: B de Marchi (Italy) (United win 4-0 an aggregate)	United fail to live up to their reputation in the Gzira Stadium. They never master a sand and gravel pitch, although Mizzi makes several good saves, Charlton hits the bar and Theobald heads off the line. The best chance falls to the locals and Stepney saves well from Francis Scerri.											
2:1 A FC SARAJEVO 15/11 (Yugoslavia)	*45,000*	1	D	0-0	0-0		Stepney	Dunne	Burns	Crerand	Foulkes	Sadler	Fitzpatrick	Kidd	Charlton	Best	Aston	
							Muftic	*Fazlagic*	*Blazevic*	*Jesenkovic*	*Vujovic*	*Bajic*	*Prodanovic*	*Siljkut*	*Musemic*	*Prijaca*	*Antic*	
						Ref: F Franceschini (Italy)	The physical Slavs severely provoke the Reds in front of a record crowd at the Kosovo Stadium. Musemic looks to have scored in the 27th minute before Stepney grabs the ball on the line. Prodanovic limps off after half an hour and Sarajevo do all the pressing but United hold firm.											
2:2 H FC SARAJEVO 29/11	62,801	1	W	2-1	1-0	Aston 14, Best 63	Stepney	Brennan	Dunne	Crerand	Foulkes	Sadler	Burns	Kidd	Charlton	Best	Aston	
						Delalic 88	*Muftic*	*Fazlagic*	*Blazevic*	*Jesenkovic*	*Vujovic*	*Bajic*	*Delalic*	*Siljkut*	*Musemic*	*Prijaca !*	*Antic*	
						Ref: R Machin (France) (United win 2-1 on aggregate)	Another rough house, with three Slavs booked and Prijaca sent off for chopping down Best. George himself is lucky not to have an early bath after a swing at the keeper but his spark is undimmed. His header is palmed out to Aston, and he later seals the win. Battling Slavs are unlucky.											
QF 1 H GORNIK ZABRZE 28/2 (Poland)	63,456	1	W	2-0	0-0	Florenski 60(og), Kidd 89	Stepney	Dunne	Burns	Crerand	Sadler	Stiles	Best	Kidd	Charlton	Ryan	Aston	
							Kostka	*Kuchta*	*Oslizlo*	*Latocha*	*Florenski*	*Szoltysik*	*Wilczek*	*Olek*	*Deja*	*Lubanski*	*Musialek*	
						Ref: O de Mendibil (Spain)	A sporting and entertaining tie with United nosing in front. The Gornik defence are superb and look set for a 0-0 draw until Best's acute angled shot flies in off Florenski. Pat Crerand and Charlton continue to drive the Reds forward, and Kidd's late cheeky back-heel gives them hope.											
QF 2 A GORNIK ZABRZE 13/3	*105,000*	1	L	0-1	0-0		Stepney	Dunne	Burns	Crerand	Sadler	Stiles	Fitzpatrick	Kidd	Charlton	Best	Herd	
						Lentner 70	*Kostka*	*Kuchta*	*Oslizlo*	*Latocha*	*Florenski*	*Deja*	*Wilczek*	*Olek*	*Lentner*	*Lubanski*	*Musialek*	
						Ref: C Lo Bello (Italy) (United win 2-1 on aggregate)	Played before a full house in the snowbound Slaski Stadium in Chorzow. A brave defence do their job and restrict Gornik to one goal. Stepney is penalised in the box and Kuchta's free-kick is slotted home by Lentner. It is the first away goal conceded in the competition by United.											
SF 1 H REAL MADRID 24/4 (Spain)	63,500	1	W	1-0	1-0	Best 35	Stepney	Dunne	Burns	Crerand	Sadler	Stiles	Best	Kidd	Charlton	Law	Aston	
							Betancourt	*Gonzalez*	*Sanchis*	*Pirri*	*Zunzunegui*	*Zoco*	*Perez*	*Jose Luiz*	*Grosso*	*Velazquez*	*Gento*	
						Ref: T Bakhramov	Newly crowned Spanish champions Real are not the side of old. They defend stoutly, with the agile Betancourt superb, but rarely threaten Stepney. Best's full-blooded shot from Aston's cross creates a slender lead. Perez is unlucky not to win a penalty when upended by Stiles.											
SF 2 A REAL MADRID 15/5	*125,000*	2	D	3-3	1-3	Zoco 43 (og), Sadler 75, Foulkes 78	Stepney	Brennan	Dunne	Crerand	Foulkes	Stiles	Best	Kidd	Charlton	Sadler	Aston	
						Pirri 32, Gento 42, Amancio 45	*Betancourt*	*Gonzalez*	*Sanchis*	*Pirri*	*Zunzunegui*	*Zoco*	*Perez*	*Grosso*	*Amancio*	*Velazquez*	*Gento*	
						Ref: A Sbardella (Italy) (United win 4-3 on aggregate)	One of the greatest nights in the club's history as United come back from the dead. After a horrendous first half, United stun the home fans with two goals after a bold attacking display. Sadler is moved into attack and scores; then Foulkes appears from nowhere to meet Best's cross.											
F N BENFICA 29/5 (Portugal) (at Wembley)	*100,000*	2	W	4-1 *aet*	0-0	Charlton 53, 99, Best 92, Kidd 93	Stepney	Brennan	Dunne	Crerand	Foulkes	Stiles	Best	Kidd	Charlton	Sadler	Aston	
						Graca 80	*Henrique*	*Adolfo*	*Humberto*	*Jacinto*	*Cruz*	*Graca*	*Coluna*	*Augusto*	*Torres*	*Eusebio*	*Simoes*	
						Ref: C Lo Bello (Italy)	Most of the crowd support United who deservedly win the Cup. Charlton's glancing header is cancelled out by Graca, and Stepney's two saves from Eusebio earns extra-time. United come to life and Best dribbles through, Kidd heads in a rebound of the bar, and Charlton, aptly, seals it.											

FA Cup

Rd		Opponent		Res	Score	H-T	Scorers, Times, and Referees	1	2	3	4	5	6	7	8	9	10	11	subs used
3	H	TOTTENHAM	1	D	2-2	1-1	Best 4, Charlton 73	Stepney	Dunne	Burns	Crerand	Sadler	Fitzpatrick	Best	Kidd	Charlton	Law	Aston	
27/1		63,500	*6*				*Chivers 2, 89*	*Jennings*	*Kinnear*	*Knowles*	*Mullery*	*England*	*Mackay*	*Robertson*	*Gilzean*	*Chivers*	*Venables**	*Beal*	*Jones*
							Ref: J Finney	A storming Cup tie ends all-square. Spurs' £125,000 new man, Martin Chivers, nets after Fitzpatrick's boob and then earns a replay from close range. In between, United are the better side with Spurs always dangerous on the break. Best's charge down of Jennings' clearance riles Spurs.											
3R	A	TOTTENHAM	1	L	0-1	0-0		Stepney	Dunne	Burns	Crerand	Sadler	Fitzpatrick	Best	Kidd !	Charlton	Herd	Aston	
31/1		*57,200*	*6*		*aet*		*Robertson 104*	*Jennings*	*Kinnear !*	*Knowles*	*Mullery*	*England*	*Mackay*	*Robertson*	*Gilzean**	*Chivers*	*Greaves*	*Beal*	*Venables*
							Ref: J Taylor	Spurs maintain their record of not losing a home FA Cup replay since 1911 with a controversial winner as England heads Greaves' corner onto the bar and Robertson forces in the rebound. A full-blooded game, with chances at both ends. Brian Kidd and Joe Kinnear sent off for fighting.											

			Home					Away					
		P	W	D	L	F	A	W	D	L	F	A	Pts
1	Manchester C	42	17	2	2	52	16	9	4	8	34	27	58
2	MAN UNITED	42	15	2	4	49	21	9	6	6	40	34	56
3	Liverpool	42	17	2	2	51	17	5	9	7	20	23	55
4	Leeds	42	17	3	1	49	14	5	6	10	22	27	53
5	Everton	42	18	1	2	43	13	5	5	11	24	27	52
6	Chelsea	42	11	7	3	34	25	7	5	9	28	43	48
7	Tottenham	42	11	7	3	44	20	8	2	11	26	39	47
8	West Brom	42	12	4	5	45	25	5	8	8	30	37	46
9	Arsenal	42	12	6	3	37	23	5	4	12	23	33	44
10	Newcastle	42	12	7	2	38	20	1	8	12	16	47	41
11	Nott'm Forest	42	11	6	4	34	22	3	5	13	18	42	39
12	West Ham	42	8	5	8	43	30	6	5	10	30	39	38
13	Leicester	42	7	7	7	37	34	6	5	10	27	35	38
14	Burnley	42	12	7	2	38	16	2	3	16	26	55	38
15	Sunderland	42	8	7	6	28	28	5	4	12	23	33	37
16	Southampton	42	9	8	4	37	31	4	3	14	29	52	37
17	Wolves	42	10	4	7	45	36	4	4	13	21	39	36
18	Stoke	42	10	3	8	30	29	4	4	13	20	44	35
19	Sheffield Wed	42	6	10	5	32	24	5	2	14	19	39	34
20	Coventry	42	8	5	8	32	32	1	10	10	19	39	33
21	Sheffield Utd	42	7	4	10	25	31	4	6	11	24	39	32
22	Fulham	42	6	4	11	27	41	4	3	14	29	57	27
		924	244	111	107	850	548	107	111	244	548	850	924

Odds & ends

Double wins: (7) West Ham, Sheffield U, Wolves, Tottenham, Arsenal, Stoke, Fulham.
Double losses: (0).

Won from behind: (4) Tottenham (h), Man City (a), Wolves (a), Spurs (a).
Lost from in front: (3) Burnley (a), Man City (h), Liverpool (h).

High spots: Winning the European Cup at Wembley.
Outstanding form of new boy Brian Kidd.
Best's brilliant form that won him the European Footballer of the Year.
The league form up to February with only three defeats in 27 games.

Low spots: League collapse in February and March, which lost the title.
Early FA Cup exit.
Injury to Dennis Law that cost him a European Cup final place.

Red cards (United): (2) Law (Arsenal h), Kidd (Tottenham FAC a).
Red cards (Opponents): (4) Ure (Arsenal h), Casper (Burnley a), Kinnear (Tottenham FAC a) Prijaca (Sarajevo h).
Ever-presents: (0).
Hat-tricks: (1) Best.
Opposing hat-tricks: (1) Astle (West Brom).
Leading scorer: (32) Best.

	Appearances						Goals			
	Lge	*Sub*	FAC	*Sub*	EC	*Sub*	Lge	FAC	EC	Tot
Aston, John	34	*3*	2		6		10		1	11
Best, George	41		2		9		28	1	3	32
Brennan, Shay	13				3		1			1
Burns, Francis	36		2		7		2			2
Charlton, Bobby	41		2		9		15	1	2	18
Crerand, Pat	41		2		9		1			1
Dunne, Tony	37		2		9		1			1
Fitzpatrick, John	14	*3*	2		2					
Foulkes, Bill	24				6		1		1	2
Gowling, Alan	4	*1*					1			1
Herd, David	6		1		1		1			1
Kidd, Brian	38		2		9		15		2	17
Kopel, Frank	1	*1*								
Law, Dennis	23		1		3		7		2	9
Rimmer, Jimmy	1									
Ryan, Jimmy	7	*1*			1		2			2
Sadler, David	40	*1*	2		9		3		3	6
Stepney, Alex	41		2		9					
Stiles, Nobby	20				7					
(own-goals)							1		2	3
19 players used	462	*10*	22		99		89	2	16	107

LEAGUE DIVISION 1

Manager: Matt Busby

SEASON 1968-69

No	Date		Att	Pos	Pt	F-A	H-T	Scorers, Times, and Referees	1	2	3	4	5	6	7	8	9	10	11	12 sub used
1	H	EVERTON			W	2-1	2-1	Best 21, Charlton 28	Stepney	Brennan	Dunne	Crerand	Foulkes	Stiles	Best	Kidd	Charlton	Law	Aston	
	10/8		61,311		2			Ball 25	West	Wright	Brown	Kendall	Labone	Harvey	Husband	Ball	Royle	Hurst	Morrissey	
								Ref: M Fussey	Everton are unlucky to lose on a scorching hot day. 36-year-old Foulkes is given a torrid time by Royle, and Stiles is off-colour. Best scores against the run of play and sets up Charlton's bullet. He 'scores' a third after Law's header rebounds off a post, but the ref has blown for time.											
2	A	WEST BROM			L	1-3	1-3	Charlton 42	Stepney	Brennan	Dunne	Crerand	Foulkes*	Stiles	Best	Kidd	Charlton	Law	Aston	Sadler
	14/8		38,299		2			Astle 5, 18, Brown 8	Sheppard	Fraser	Williams	Brown	Talbut	Kaye	Krzywicki	Collard	Astle	Hope	Rees	
								Ref: W Gow	Albion make a blistering start and Astle makes it five in two games against the Reds. Indecisive defending undoes United, especially on long crosses. Best leads the comeback with a one-man show but despite long periods of domination little impression is made on Albion's defence.											
3	A	MANCHESTER C		11	D	0-0	0-0		Stepney	Kopel	Dunne	Fitzpatrick	Sadler	Stiles	Best	Gowling	Charlton	Kidd	Aston*	Burns
	17/8		63,052	8	3				Mulhearn	Kennedy	Pardoe	Doyle	Heslop	Oakes	Lee	Bell	Summerbee	Owen	Young	
								Ref: D Smith	Busby drops Brennan and Crerand, and Law and Foulkes are injured. The defence looks more secure but is lucky to survive City's strong second-half performance. Bell is denied a penalty appeal and Young's goal is ruled out for offside. Aston collides with Lee and breaks his leg.											
4	H	COVENTRY		8	W	1-0	1-0	Ryan 16	Stepney	Kopel	Dunne	Fitzpatrick	Sadler	Stiles	Ryan	Kidd	Charlton	Burns	Best	
	21/8		51,201	22	5				Glazier	Bruck	Cattlin	Hill*	Setters	Clements	Hannigan	Hunt	Tudor	Machin	Carr	Gibson
								Ref: K Walker	A dull game and a poor performance. Coventry never threaten to pull back the early deficit, and Alex Stepney is under-employed. The jury is still out on United's reshuffled defence. Bill Glazier makes four outstanding saves after Ryan connects with a high-bouncing ball to score.											
5	H	CHELSEA		12	L	0-4	0-3	[Birchenall 65]	Stepney	Kopel	Dunne	Crerand	Sadler	Stiles	Ryan	Kidd	Charlton	Burns	Best	
	24/8		55,114	7	5			Baldwin 1, 38, Tambling 14,	Bonetti	Harris	McCreadie	Hollins	Webb	Boyle	Baldwin	Tambling	Osgood	Birchenall	Houseman	
								Ref: P Baldwin	Willie Morgan has signed from Burnley but has to sit and watch his team slump to efficient Chelsea. Baldwin is unmarked for two goals, the first in 40 seconds, and Tambling scores his fourth in four games. United have little to offer in attack; it's their biggest home defeat since 1959.											
6	H	TOTTENHAM		7	W	3-1	1-0	Fitzpatrick 14, 48, Beal 65(og)	Stepney	Brennan	Dunne	Fitzpatrick	Sadler	Stiles	Morgan	Kidd	Charlton	Law	Best	
	28/8		62,649	19	7			Greaves 58	Jennings	Kinnear	Knowles	Mullery	England	Beal	Robertson	Greaves	Chivers	Venables	Gilzean*	Jones
								Ref: K Howley	Spurs have had their worst start for years but play their part in a fine game. New-boy Morgan and returning Dennis Law are the heroes of a good win. Fitzpatrick heads home a Dunne cross and hits a powerful 35-yarder. Greaves' classic goal gives some hope until Beal heads in.											
7	A	SHEFFIELD WED		11	L	4-5	4-3	Best 10, Law 12, 26, Charlton 36	Stepney	Brennan	Dunne*	Fitzpatrick	Sadler	Stiles	Morgan	Kidd	Charlton	Law	Best	Burns
	31/8		50,490	4	7			Whit' 2,45,72, Ritch' 15, Stiles47(og)	Springett P	Young	Megson	Ellis	Mobley	Eustace	Whitham	McCalliog	Ritchie	Ford	Fantham	
								Ref: W Castle	A sporting game, riddled with defensive errors. United recover from the early goal to lead 4-2, with Law, playing his 200th game, netting twice. Wednesday's fast flowing football catches the Reds' defence asleep. They restore parity and then Jack Whitham pounces for the winner.											
8	H	WEST HAM		9	D	1-1	0-0	Law 59	Stepney	Dunne	Burns	Fitzpatrick	Foulkes	Stiles	Morgan	Sadler	Charlton	Law	Best	
	7/9		63,274	3	8			Hurst 67	Ferguson	Bonds	Charles	Peters	Stephenson	Moore	Redknapp	Boyce	Brooking	Hurst	Sissons	
								Ref: E Jennings	West Ham labour under an inferiority complex for more than an hour. George Best bamboozles Bonds and chips a gem of a pass to the far post where Law heads in, but Redknapp loads the gun for the impressive Hurst's equaliser. Charlton, Law and Best not at their best, but Moore is.											
9	A	BURNLEY		9	L	0-1	0-0		Stepney	Dunne	Burns	Fitzpatrick	Foulkes	Stiles	Morgan	Sadler	Charlton	Law	Best	
	14/9		32,935	11	8			O'Neill 88	Thomson	Murray	Latcham	O'Neill	Waldron	Merrington	Coates	Lochhead	Casper	Bellamy*	Thomas	Blant
								Ref: J Finney	Burnley bounce back from a 0-7 drubbing at Spurs. They have done their homework and win the personal battles. Latcham marks Best superbly and Merrington quashes Morgan. Transfer-listed Brian O'Neill breaks the deadlock with a 25-yard arrowed shot past Stepney.											
10	H	NEWCASTLE		10	W	3-1	3-0	Best 16, 17, Law 28	Stepney	Dunne	Burns	Crerand*	Sadler	Stiles	Morgan	Fitzpatrick	Charlton	Law	Best	Kidd
	21/9		47,262	20	10			Gibb 70	McFaul	Craig	Guthrie	Gibb	Burton	Elliott	Sinclair*	Duffy	Scott	Robson B	Allen	Iley
								Ref: L Callaghan	After a bright start it turns into a bore. United have one eye on the trip to Argentina. Newcastle are woeful, with only one win in 10. In driving rain, Best floats a superb goal from the by-line, scores a cheeky second, and sets up Law's 30-yarder. Sadler's error lets in Tommy Gibb.											

11	H	ARSENAL		10	D	0-0	0-0		Stepney	Dunne	Burns	Crerand	Foulkes	Stiles	Morgan	Fitzpatrick	Charlton	Law	Best	
	5/10		61,843	2	11				*Wilson*	*Storey*	*McNab*	*McLintock*	*Neill*	*Simpson*	*Radford*	*Sammels*	*Gould*	*Court*	*Jenkins*	
								Ref: K Burns	Bertie Mee's aggressive, defensive team have had their best start for years – they have only lost once. The Stretford End chants 'We want football'. Best is a victim of strong tackling, and Storey and Fitzpatrick are villains. The ref threatens to abandon as coins rain on Bob Wilson.											
12	A	TOTTENHAM		10	D	2-2	1-2	Crerand 35, Law 53	Stepney	Dunne	Burns*	Crerand	Foulkes	Stiles	Morgan	Fitzpatrick	Charlton	Law	Best	**Sartori**
	9/10		*56,205*	*8*	12			*Jones 9, Gilzean 21*	*Jennings*	*Kinnear*	*Want*	*Mullery*	*England*	*Beal*	*Jones*	*Greaves*	*Pearce*	*Venables*	*Gilzean*	
								Ref: H New	Spurs unbeaten in seven are pegged back in a thriller by United, back to their best. The comeback is almost completed with a debut goal from Sartori, but England clears off the line. Cliff Jones's lash and Gilzean's header are cancelled out by Crerand's volley and Law's poached goal.											
13	A	LIVERPOOL		14	L	0-2	0-1		Stepney	Brennan	Kopel	Crerand	**James**	Stiles	Ryan	Fitzpatrick	Charlton	Gowling	Sartori	
	12/10		*53,392*	*2*	12			*St John 14, Evans 82*	*Lawrence*	*Lawler*	*Strong*	*Smith*	*Yeats*	*Hughes*	*Callaghan*	*Hunt*	*Evans*	*St John*	*Thompson*	
								Ref: R Harper	Steve James has an intimidating debut but comes through with flying colours. Injury-hit Reds put up a fighting display but are sunk by Bill Shankly's men. Ian St John heads in Thompson's cross and Alun Evans sidefoots in Callaghan's centre. United are four points off the bottom.											
14	H	SOUTHAMPTON		15	L	1-2	1-1	Best 27	Stepney	Kopel	Dunne	Crerand	Foulkes*	Stiles	Morgan	Sadler	Charlton	Sartori	Best	Fitzpatrick
	19/10		46,426	*17*	12			*Saul 18, Davies 49*	*Gurr*	*Kirkup*	*Jones*	*Kemp*	*McGrath*	*Gabriel*	*Paine*	*Channon*	*Davies*	*Walker*	*Saul*	
								Ref: D Lyden	There is a feeling of anti-climax after the Estudiantes game. Ron Davies and Mick Channon are a constant thorn and the ageing Bill Foulkes is at fault for both goals and subbed. Best scores after Gerry Gurr pushes his first shot onto the bar. Saints' first win at Old Trafford since 1937.											
15	A	QP RANGERS		14	W	3-2	1-0	Best 26, 57, Law 84	Stepney	Brennan	Dunne	Crerand	Sadler	Stiles	Morgan	Kidd	Charlton	Law	Best	
	26/10		*31,138*	*20*	14			*Leach 58, Wilks 88*	*Kelly*	*Watson*	*Harris*	*Keen*	*Hunt*	*Hazell*	*Bridges*	*Leach*	*Allen*	*Wilks*	*Morgan R*	
								Ref: R Johnson	A record crowd packs into Loftus Road to see Bill Dodgin's newly promoted side given a football lesson. Rangers rebound from two down and the result is in doubt until the end. Best scores from an impossible angle and crosses for Hunt's goal. Law finishes of a slick move for No 3.											
16	H	LEEDS		14	D	0-0	0-0		Stepney	Brennan	Dunne	Crerand	Sadler	Stiles	Morgan	Kidd	Charlton	Law	Best	
	2/11		53,839	*3*	15				*Sprake*	*Reaney*	*Madeley*	*Bremner*	*Charlton*	*Hunter*	*Lorimer*	*Bates*	*Jones*	*Giles*	*O'Grady*	
								Ref: D Smith	The usual tight game with Revie's men, on a drizzly Manchester day. Leeds have only lost once and are impressive. Kidd and Hunter have a running battle and Norman is booked. The two centre-halves, Sadler and Jack Charlton, are in great form. Sprake denies Law a deserved goal.											
17	A	SUNDERLAND		13	D	1-1	0-1	Hurley 88(og)	Stepney	Brennan	Dunne	Crerand	Sadler	Stiles	Morgan	Kidd	Charlton	Sartori	Best	
	9/11		*33,151*	*11*	16			*Harris 22*	*Montgomery*	*Irwin*	*Harvey*	*Hurley*	*Todd*	*Palmer*	*Herd*	*Harris*	*Hughes*	*Suggett*	*Mulhall*	
								Ref: J Taylor	United attack adventurously and, after several near misses, get their reward when Stiles' vicious shot hits Hurley and curls over Montgomery. Gordon Harris gave Alan Brown's team the lead with a glorious drive from a long throw-in. In a sporting match Law is missing injured again.											
18	H	IPSWICH		13	D	0-0	0-0		Stepney	Brennan	Dunne	Crerand	James	Stiles	Morgan	Kidd*	Charlton	Law	Best	Kopel
	16/11		45,796	*17*	17				*Hancock*	*Mills*	*Houghton*	*Morris*	*Baxter*	*Jefferson*	*Hegan*	*Viljoen*	*Crawford**	*O'Rourke*	*Brogan*	*Carroll*
								Ref: D Corbett	Newly promoted Ipswich are on the verge of losing their manager Bill McGarry to Wolves. His team put up a determined fight, despite losing Ray Crawford, injured after nine minutes. Brian Kidd limps off with a twisted ankle and United's finishing is a letdown. A draw is a fair result.											
19	A	STOKE		14	D	0-0	0-0		Stepney	Kopel	Dunne	Crerand	James	Stiles	Morgan	Sartori	Charlton	Fitzpatrick	Best	
	23/11		*30,562*	*18*	18				*Banks*	*Marsh*	*Elder*	*Skeels*	*Bloor*	*Stevenson*	*Mahoney*	*Conroy*	*Herd*	*Dobing*	*Burrows*	
								Ref: K Burns	It's 366 minutes since a United player scored a league goal. On a mud-bath, a weakened side create many chances but can't finish, with Bobby Charlton, without a goal in three months, the biggest culprit. David Herd is captain against his old club. Morgan is out of touch on the wing.											
20	H	WOLVERHAMPTON		12	W	2-0	0-0	Best 59, Law 80	Stepney	Kopel	Dunne	Crerand	Sadler	Stiles*	Morgan	Sartori	Charlton	Law	Best	Fitzpatrick
	30/11		50,165	*14*	20				*Parkes*	*Parkin*	*Thomson*	*Bailey*	*Woodfield**	*Holsgrove*	*Wignall*	*Knowles*	*Dougan*	*Wilson*	*Wagstaffe*	*Kenning*
								Ref: N Graham	McGarry is the new boss at Molineux, but suffers defeat in his first game. Another 0-0 looks certain until Crerand sends Best through and the magical Irishman beats Parkes in a one-on-one. Law's classy header from Morgan's cross seals a win. Sadler and Dougan in a bruising battle.											
21	A	LEICESTER		15	L	1-2	1-1	Law 15p	Stepney	Dunne	Burns	Crerand	Sadler	Stiles	Morgan	Sartori	Charlton	Law	Best	
	7/12		*36,303*	*20*	20			*Nish 17p, Fern 50*	*Shilton*	*Rodrigues*	*Woollett*	*Roberts*	*Sjoberg*	*Nish*	*Glover*	*Cross*	*Lochhead*	*Fern*	*Stringfellow*	
								Ref: A Dimond	Struggling Leicester rebound from a 1-7 defeat at Everton to register their first home win over the Reds in five years. It is manager Gillies' swansong. Law nets after Best was fouled by Rodrigues. Burns fouls Lochhead, who causes terror for the defence and hits the bar near the end.											

No	Date		Att	Pos	Pt	F-A	H-T	Scorers, Times, and Referees	1	2	3	4	5	6	7	8	9	10	11	12 sub used
22	H	LIVERPOOL		13	W	1-0	0-0	Law 53	Stepney	Dunne	Burns	Crerand	James	Stiles	Best	Sadler	Charlton	Law	Sartori	
	14/12		55,354	*1*	22				*Lawrence*	*Lawler*	*Strong*	*Smith*	*Yeats*	*Hughes*	*Callaghan*	*Hunt*	*Evans*	*St John*	*Thompson*	
								Ref: K Howley	United raise their game and defeat the leaders in a stirring game. They end Pool's six-game winning streak as Best and Sartori revel in the icy conditions. Tommy Lawrence keeps them out, but can't stop Law's fine effort. Willie Morgan is dropped and Busby is scouting in Vienna.											
23	A	SOUTHAMPTON		16	L	0-2	0-2		Stepney	Dunne	Burns	Crerand	James	Stiles	Best	Sadler	Charlton	Law	Sartori	
	21/12		*26,194*	*12*	22			*Davies 5, Channon 6*	*Gurr*	*Kirkup*	*Jones**	*Gabriel*	*McGrath*	*Byrne*	*Paine*	*Channon*	*Davies*	*Walker*	*Saul*	*Kemp*
								Ref: N Burtenshaw	The negative Saints pack their defence after the early goals and a frustrated United lose friends with an ill-tempered performance. Nobby Stiles and Pat Crerand are booked, the former for retaliation for Fred Kemp's stamp on him. The Reds dominate Ted Bates' team but get no reward.											
24	A	ARSENAL		16	L	**0-3**	0-0		Stepney	Dunne	Burns	Crerand*	James	Stiles	Best	Sadler	Charlton	Law	Kidd	Sartori
	26/12		*62,300*	*3*	22			*Armstrong 60, Court 61, Radford 77*	*Wilson*	*Storey*	*McNab*	*McLintock*	*Ure*	*Simpson*	*Radford*	*Graham*	*Court*	*Gould*	*Armstrong*	
								Ref: M Fussey	Bertie Mee is building a formidable side – they have won five in a row – and look strong title contenders. United's early flurry deserves a goal before three headers, all from left wing crosses, does for them. United fail to score at Highbury for the first time since 1950. Crerand limps off.											
25	A	LEEDS		16	L	1-2	0-1	Charlton 52	Stepney	Dunne	Burns	Crerand	James	Stiles	Best	Fitzpatrick	Charlton	Law	Sartori	
	11/1		*48,145*	*2*	22			*Jones 28, O'Grady 75*	*Sprake*	*Reaney*	*Madeley*	*Bremner*	*Charlton*	*Hunter*	*O'Grady*	*Lorimer*	*Jones*	*Giles*	*Gray**	*Cooper*
								Ref: W Gow	Controversy at Elland Road. At 1-1, Best's 'goal' from a free-kick is ruled out as the referee says it was indirect. Stepney fails to catch Peter Lorimer's cross and Jones heads in. Charlton's goal-drought ends. As United look the likely winners, Mike O'Grady hits a stunning winner.											
26	H	SUNDERLAND		15	W	4-1	1-0	Law 23, 48, 53, Best 88	Rimmer	Dunne	Burns	Fitzpatrick	James	Stiles	Morgan	Best	Charlton	Law	Sartori	
	18/1		45,670	*16*	24			*Mulhall 72*	*Montgomery*	*Palmer*	*Harvey*	*Hurley*	*Todd*	*Harris*	*Herd*	*Kerr*	*Stuckey*	*Suggett*	*Mulhall*	
								Ref: J Finney	As the rain pours down, United finally find their shooting boots. Law notches his first league hat-trick for 3½ years with three cool finishes. He also has two disallowed. The spies from Rapid and Watford are given plenty of food for thought. Colin Todd is forced to rip Best's shorts off.											
27	A	IPSWICH		17	L	0-1	0-0		Stepney	Fitzpatrick	Dunne	Crerand	James	Stiles	Morgan	Kidd	Charlton	Law	Best	
	½		*30,837*	*16*	24			*Dunne 79(og)*	*Best*	*Mills*	*Houghton*	*Morris*	*Baxter*	*McNeil*	*Hegan*	*Barnard*	*Crawford**	*O'Rourke*	*Brogan*	*Woods*
								Ref: G Hill	A record crowd watch new manager Bobby Robson's first home game. The star-studded attack lets United down and when Dunne and Barnard tussle for the ball it sails softly over the recalled Stepney's head. Best and Bill Baxter are lucky not to be ordered off after trading punches.											
28	A	WOLVERHAMPTON		15	D	2-2	0-2	Charlton 46, Best 68	Stepney	Fitzpatrick	Dunne	Crerand	James	Sadler	Morgan	Kidd	Charlton	Sartori*	Best	Foulkes
	15/2		*44,023*	*13*	25			*Dougan 29, Curran 44*	*Parkes*	*Parkin*	*Thomson*	*Bailey*	*Woodfield*	*Taylor*	*Wilson*	*Knowles*	*Dougan*	*Curran*	*Wagstaffe*	
								Ref: B Homewood	On a treacherous snowy pitch, United's fight-back is thrilling. Dougan heads over an unsighted Stepney and new signing Curran pounces as Best dallies in the area. Charlton's low drive and Best's graceful header pegs back Mike Bailey-inspired Wolves. Either side could have won.											
29	H	MANCHESTER C		17	L	0-1	0-1		Stepney	Brennan	Fitzpatrick	Crerand	Foulkes	Stiles	Morgan	Kidd	Charlton	Sadler	Best	
	8/3		63,264	*13*	25			*Summerbee 38*	*Dowd*	*Book*	*Pardoe*	*Doyle*	*Booth*	*Oakes*	*Summerbee*	*Bell*	*Lee**	*Young*	*Coleman*	*Owen*
								Ref: W Handley	City are in the FA Cup semi-final, but their league form is patchy. They boss the first half and Mike Summerbee scores at the second attempt – his first goal for six months. United are on top after the break and Morgan hits Dowd's legs and Kidd hits the post. Best's 200th league game.											
30	A	EVERTON		17	D	0-0	0-0		Stepney	Brennan*	Dunne	Crerand	James	Stiles	Best	Kidd	Fitzpatrick	Sadler	Aston	Foulkes
	10/3		*57,514*	*3*	26				*West*	*Wright*	*Brown*	*Jackson*	*Labone*	*Hurst*	*Husband*	*Ball*	*Royle*	*Whittle*	*Morrissey*	
								Ref: E Jennings	Harry Catterick's Everton are unbeaten in 13 League and Cup games. In a niggly, petulant match, Best and Fitzpatrick are booked and United are booed off. 'We want football,' chant the Goodison Park faithful. United up the pace after half-time and go close, but a draw is a fair result.											
31	A	CHELSEA		17	L	2-3	1-2	James 31, Law 63p	Stepney	Fitzpatrick	Dunne	Crerand	James	Stiles	Morgan	Kidd	Sadler	Law	Best	
	15/3		*60,436*	*5*	26			*Webb 1, Hutchison 27, Tambling 56*	*Bonetti*	*Webb*	*McCreadie*	*Hollins*	*Dempsey*	*Harris*	*Boyle*	*Tambling*	*Hutchinson*	*Osgood*	*Houseman*	
								Ref: G McCabe	The gates are locked on Chelsea's biggest crowd for four years. Reds are always chasing the game after Webb's 60-second goal but could have won a point. Tempers are frayed on a muddy pitch and Fitzpatrick may face suspension as he is booked for the third time. One win in nine.											

No	Date	Opposition	Att	Pos	Pts	Result	F-A	H-T	Scorers, Times, and Referees	1	2	3	4	5	6	7	8	9	10	11	12 sub used
32	H	QP RANGERS		16		W	**8-1**	1-0	Morgan 30, 75, 86, Best 47, 67,	Stepney	Fitzpatrick	Dunne	Crerand	James	Stiles	Morgan	Kidd	Aston	Law	Best	
	19/3		**36,638**	22	28				Marsh 64 [Stiles 85, Kidd 88, Aston89]	Spratley	Watson	Clement	Hazell	Hunt	Sibley	Morgan I	Leach	Clarke*	Marsh	Glover	Keetch
									Ref: H Davey	Les Allen's Rangers are without a win since November and are heading for a fast return to Division 2. John Aston returns from injury to make Morgan's first league goal. The scoreline, United's biggest league win since 1898, is flattered by Rangers' capitulation in the last five minutes.											
33	H	SHEFFIELD WED		13		W	1-0	1-0	Best 33	Stepney	Fitzpatrick	Dunne	Crerand	James	Stiles	Morgan	Kidd	Aston	Law	Best	
	22/3		45,527	11	30					Springett P	Smith	Burton	Eustace	Mobley	Young	Irvine	McCalliog	Fantham	Pugh	Woodall*	Ellis
									Ref: R Kirkpatrick	Owls, with one win in nine, are sliding down the table. Manager Jack Marshall has resigned and Tom McAnearney is caretaker. United miss chances before Best scores from a free-kick. On a bitterly cold day, Law's penalty, from Ellis's foul on Morgan, is saved by Peter Springett.											
34	H	STOKE		11		D	1-1	1-0	Aston 38	Stepney	Fitzpatrick	Dunne	Crerand	James	Stiles	Morgan*	Kidd	Aston	Law	Best	Sadler
	24/3		39,931	18	31				Stevenson 85	Banks	Marsh	Elder	Bernard	Smith	Stevenson	Herd	Dobing	Conroy	Mahoney	Eastham*	Vernon
									Ref: R Tinkler	Stoke have not won away all season and are desperate for points. Stevenson's late scrambled goal is reward for a gutsy performance, with Gordon Banks in top form in goal. One save from Law is world-class. Stepney also has to be at his best to keep Stoke's veteran attack at bay.											
35	A	WEST HAM		11		D	0-0	0-0		Stepney	Fitzpatrick	Dunne*	Crerand	James	Stiles	Ryan	Kidd	Aston	Law	Best	Sadler
	29/3		41,546	5	32					Ferguson	Charles	Howe	Peters	Stephenson	Moore	Bonds	Boyce	Brooking	Hurst	Sissons	
									Ref: I Jones	Despite United's poor away form the crowds flock to see them. A record crowd see an action packed goal-less draw under the eyes of Alf Ramsey. A game of few fouls but plenty of injuries. Dunne fractures his jaw when colliding with Stephenson, and Crerand breaks his nose.											
36	A	NOTT'M FOREST		10		W	1-0	0-0	Best 50p	Stepney	Fitzpatrick	Stiles	Crerand	James	Sadler	Ryan	Kidd	Aston	Law	Best	
	31/3		41,892	18	34					Hill	Hindley	Winfield	McKinlay	Hennessey	Newton	Lyons	Baxter	Hall	Hilley	Rees*	Barnwell
									Ref: R Spittle	Forest's disastrous season has left them struggling against relegation. Johnny Carey has made way for Matt Gillies as manager. On a greasy, wet surface Best is a constant thorn in Forest's side and scores from a fiercely disputed penalty after McKinlay obstructs Kidd. Forest are poor.											
37	H	WEST BROM		9		W	2-1	0-0	Best 66, 89	Stepney	Fitzpatrick	Stiles	Crerand	James	Sadler	Morgan	Ryan*	Aston	Kidd	Best	Foulkes
	2/4		38,846	16	36				Astle 51	Osborne	Fraser	Wilson	Brown	Talbut	Kaye	Krzywicki	Lovett	Astle	Hope	Clark	
									Ref: M Fussey	Albion's attractive football deserves a point. Jeff Astle nets after good work by the energetic Tony Brown. The magical Best comes to the rescue. A mistake by Talbut and Osborne sets up the first, and Best scores the winner in a congested penalty area. Aston looks back to his best.											
38	H	NOTT'M FOREST		9		W	3-1	1-1	Morgan 11, 63, Best 52	Stepney	Fitzpatrick	Stiles	Crerand	James	Sadler	Morgan	Kidd	Aston	Law	Best	
	5/4		51,952	19	38				Hilley 41	Hill	Hindley	Winfield	Richardson	Hennessey	Newton	Lyons	Baxter	Baker	Barnwell*	Hilley	Hall
									Ref: V James	A third game in a week as United clear their fixtures for Euro glory. United beat relegation-threatened Forest with ease, once Stepney saves Baker's early penalty. Alex has little else to do as Morgan scrambles in Aston's cross and the improving Kidd sets up Best and Morgan.											
39	A	COVENTRY		9		L	1-2	0-1	Fitzpatrick 69	Stepney	Fitzpatrick	Stiles	Crerand	James	Sadler	Morgan	Kidd	Aston	Charlton	Best	
	8/4		45,402	20	38				Curtis 3, Martin 48	Glazier	Coop	Cattlin	Machin	Curtis	Blockley	Baker*	Hunt	Martin	Carr	Hill	Hannigan
									Ref: H New	The seven-game unbeaten run is ended by relegation-fighting City. Stepney can only parry Curtis's header over the line. Martin hits a post before half-time and fires home when Stepney drops the ball. Fitzpatrick drives in after Kidd's run. United lay siege till the end, but the score is fair.											
40	A	NEWCASTLE		11		L	0-2	0-1		Rimmer	Fitzpatrick	Stiles	Crerand	James	Sadler	Morgan	Kidd	Charlton	Law	Best	
	12/4		46,379	10	38				Robson B 8p, Foggon 84	McFaul	Craggs	Clark	Gibb	McNamee	Moncur	Robson B	Horsfield*	Davies	Arentoft	Foggon	Sinclair
									Ref: L Cussons	Newcastle demonstrate why they are in the Fairs Cup semi-final. United, who drop Stepney, are rarely in the game after James trips Gibb for the penalty. Best hits the bar but struggles against the rugged home defence. Milan's Cesare Maldini spies on United and must feel confident.											
41	H	BURNLEY		10		W	2-0	0-0	Best 56, Waldron 59(og)	Rimmer	Brennan	Fitzpatrick	Crerand	Foulkes	Stiles	Morgan	Kidd	Aston	Law	Best	
	19/4		52,626	12	40					Thomson	Merrington	Latcham	Docherty	Waldron	Blant	Thomas	Coates	Casper	Probert	Collins	
									Ref: E Wallace	Best receives the European Footballer of the Year award and Stiles is booked for the third time. United step up the pace after half-time and deserve to win a niggly game. Best heads in Crerand's floated cross and Morgan's centre is nodded in by Waldron. The title is going to Leeds.											
42	H	LEICESTER		11		W	3-2	2-1	Best 3, Morgan 4, Law 47	Rimmer	Brennan	Burns	Crerand	Foulkes	Stiles	Morgan	Kidd	Charlton	Law	Best	
	17/5		45,860	21	42				Nish 1, Fern 71	Shilton	Rodrigues	Woollett	Nish	Manley	Cross	Fern*	Gibson	Lochhead	Clarke	Glover	Matthews
	Home	Away							Ref: P Baldwin	Leicester have lost the FA Cup final and need a win to retain their Division 1 status. They briefly threaten to ruin Busby's farewell party with a brave display. Best and Morgan are brilliant though, with George's stunning 20-yarder the pick of the goals. Noel Cantwell's Coventry stay up.											
Average	51,169	44,295																			

European Cup	Att			F-A	H-T	Scorers, Times, and Referees	1	2	3	4	5	6	7	8	9	10	11	12 sub used
1:1 A WATERFORD		9	W	3-1	2-0	Law 8, 37, 55	Stepney*	Dunne	Burns	Crerand	Foulkes	Stiles	Best	Sadler	Charlton	Law	Kidd	Rimmer
18/9 (Eire)	*48,000*					*Matthews 64*	*Thomas*	*Bryan*	*Griffin*	*Maguire*	*Morley*	*McGeough*	*Casey*	*Hale*	*O'Neill*	*Coad*	*Matthews*	
(at Landsdown Rd)						Ref: W Mullen (Scotland)	A memorable night in Dublin for the Irish part-timers, who match United for fitness and endeavour but lack the skill to seriously trouble them. Hat-trick 'King' Dennis is back to his best, but misses a penalty after Best is fouled. Exuberant Waterford fans invade the pitch several times.											
1:2 H WATERFORD		10	W	7-1	2-0	Stiles 36, Law 40,47,60,72, Burns 66, [Charlton 87]	Stepney	Dunne	Burns	Crerand	Foulkes	Stiles	Best	Sadler	Charlton	Law	Kidd	
2/10	41,750					*Casey 69*	*Thomas*	*Bryan*	*Griffin*	*Morrissey*	*Morley*	*McGeough*	*Casey*	*Hale*	*O'Neill*	*Coad*	*Matthews*	
						Ref: J F Campos (Portugal) (United win 10-2 on aggregate)	Waterford put up a stubborn first-half resistance, but then the floodgates open. Only the agile Thomas keeps the score in single figures, with Law running riot in the Irish penalty area. Casey's dipping shot is a nice consolation and the team are given a marvellous ovation at the end.											
2:1 H ANDERLECHT		13	W	3-0	0-0	Kidd 51, Law 70, 78	Stepney	Brennan	Dunne	Crerand	Sadler	Stiles	Ryan	Kidd	Charlton	Law	Sartori	
13/11 (Belgium)	51,000						*Trappeniers*	*Heylens*	*Cornelis*	*Herbert*	*Kialunda*	*Peteers*	*Bergholtz*	*Volbers*	*Devrindt*	*Nordahl*	*Puis*	
						Ref: A Oliveira (Portugal)	With Best suspended and Morgan ineligible, United are anxious against the fast, clever Belgians. Law misses a first-half penalty – four misses in the last six. The Reds have some close shaves before Kidd's soaring header. Law's flicked header and a stab home in a scramble seal a win.											
2:2 A ANDERLECHT		14	L	1-3	1-1	Sartori 8	Stepney	Kopel	Dunne	Crerand	Foulkes	Stiles	Fitzpatrick	Sadler	Charlton	Law	Sartori	
27/11	*40,000*					*Mulder 18, Bergholtz 58, 70*	*Trappeniers*	*Heylens*	*Cornelis*	*Hanon*	*Kialunda*	*Devrindt*	*Bergholtz*	*Van Himst*	*Mulder*	*Nordahl*	*Puis*	
						Ref: O de Mendibil (United win 4-3 on aggregate)	At the Parc Astrid, Sartori's goal seems to put the tie out of Anderlecht's reach. The Belgians throw seven men into attack and Bergholtz's two headers have United quivering. The defence holds firm and Stepney's save from Mulder earns the aggregate victory. Stiles booed incessantly.											
QF 1 H RAPID VIENNA		15	W	3-0	1-0	Best 43, 70, Morgan 66	Stepney	Fitzpatrick	Dunne	Crerand	James	Stiles	Morgan	Kidd	Charlton	Law	Best	
26/2 (Austria)	63,188						*Fuchsbichler*	*Gebhardt*	*Fritsch*	*Glechner*	*Fak*	*Bjerregaard*	*Uullmann*	*Kaltenbrun'r*	*Graumann*	*Floegel*	*Sondergaard*	
						Ref: B Botic (Yugoslavia)	Rapid Vienna are to be respected after knocking out Real Madrid but seem overawed. Their spirited display fades out in the second half. Willie Morgan scores on his European debut whilst George Best is at his peak and pounces on a back-pass for No 2, before netting a stunning third.											
QF 2 A RAPID VIENNA		16	D	0-0	0-0		Stepney	Fitzpatrick	Dunne	Crerand	James	Stiles	Morgan	Kidd	Charlton	Sadler	Best	
5/3	*52,000*						*Fuchsbichler*	*Gebhardt*	*Fritsch*	*Glechner*	*Fak*	*Bjerregaard*	*Lindmann*	*Kaltenbrun'r*	*Graumann*	*Floegel*	*Sondergaard*	
						Ref: L van Ravens (Holland) (United win 3-0 on aggregate)	In the Prater Stadium, United defend well with a calm, confident display. There are a few close shaves, but Stepney is in top form. Bjerregaard, top scorer in Austria, is quiet, whilst Charlton goes close with three long-range efforts. United go through to a fifth European Cup semi-final.											
SF 2 A AC MILAN (Italy)		10	L	0-2	0-1		Rimmer	Brennan	Fitzpatrick!	Crerand	Foulkes	Stiles*	Morgan	Kidd	Charlton	Law	Best	Burns
23/4	*80,000*					*Sormani 34, Hamrin 50*	*Cudicini*	*Anquilletti*	*Schnellinger*	*Rosato^*	*Malatrasi*	*Trapattoni*	*Hamrin*	*Lodetti*	*Sormani*	*Rivera**	*Prati*	*Fogli/Maldera*
						Ref: J Krnavac (Czechoslovakia)	Cool, compact Milan are a classy side. They miss two good chances before Stiles limps off to loud booing. Sormani appears to handle before scoring the first goal. When poor United do mount attacks, they find a resolute defence. Fitzpatrick is sent off after kicking Hamrin off the ball.											
SF 2 H AC MILAN		11	W	1-0	0-0	Charlton 70	Rimmer	Brennan	Burns	Crerand	Foulkes	Stiles	Morgan	Kidd	Charlton	Law	Best	
15/5	63,103						*Cudicini*	*Anquilletti*	*Schnellinger*	*Rosato**	*Malatrasi*	*Maldera*	*Hamrin*	*Lodetti*	*Sormani*	*Rivera*	*Prati*	*Santin*
						Ref: R Machin (France) (United lose 1-2 on aggregate)	United, in their all-white kit, find Milan's defensive blanket impossible to break down. There are several chances and Law has a goal ruled out. Finally, Best's cheeky run sets up Charlton to score from an acute angle. Despite constant pressure there are no further goals. A sporting game.											

World Club Championship

							1	2	3	4	5	6	7	8	9	10	11	12
F:1	A	ESTUDIANTES	10	L	0-1	0-1	Stepney	Dunne	Burns	Crerand	Foulkes	Stiles!	Morgan	Sadler	Charlton	Law	Best	
25/9		(Argentina) *55,000*				*Togneri 29*	*Poletti*	*Malbernat*	*Medina*	*Bilardo*	*Suarez*	*Madero*	*Ribaudo*	*Togneri*	*Coniglario*	*Pachame*	*Veron*	
						Ref: S Miranda (Paraguay)	In the Boca Stadium, United are tolerant under severe provocation. Stiles is targeted for punches and butts before he gesticulates and is sent off. Others are given brutal treatment by an aggressive and violent home side. Sadler's header is disallowed, but very little football is played.											
F:2	H	ESTUDIANTES	14	D	1-1	0-1	Stepney	Brennan	Dunne	Crerand	Foulkes	Sadler	Morgan	Kidd	Charlton	Law*	Best!	Sartori
16/10		63,500				Morgan 88	*Poletti*	*Malbernat*	*Medina!*	*Bilardo*	*Suarez*	*Madero*	*Ribaudo**	*Togneri*	*Coniglario*	*Pachame*	*Veron*	*Echecopar*
						Veron 5												
						Ref: K Zecevic (Yugoslavia) (United lose 1-2 on aggregate)	Another unsavoury game, but tamer than the first. Veron's early header makes it an uphill task and Poletti twice saves from Law before the 'King' departs injured. Near the end, Best and Medina are sent off for fighting, Morgan equalises and Kidd nets, but the final whistle had gone.											

FA Cup

Rd	Venue	Opponent / Date	Att	Pos	Res	F-A	H-T	Scorers, Times, and Referees	1	2	3	4	5	6	7	8	9	10	11	12 sub used
3	A	EXETER		16	W	3-1	1-1	Fitzpatr'k 44, Newman 60(og), Kidd 61	Stepney	Dunne	Burns	Fitzpatrick	James	Stiles	Best*	Kidd	Charlton	Law	Sartori	Sadler
		4/1	*18,500*	*4:23*				*Banks 15*	*Shearing*	*Smyth*	*Blain*	*Harvey**	*Sharples*	*Newman*	*Corr*	*Banks*	*Pinkney*	*Mitten*	*Balson*	*Pleat*
								Ref: E Wallace	A big shock looks on, as Banks' header puts Exeter ahead. The 91st club in the league can't hold out, though. Tony Dunne's teasing crosses create for Fitzpatrick and Newman's unsighted header. Best limps off after harsh treatment. Charlie Mitten's son, John, plays for the Grecians.											
4	H	WATFORD		15	D	1-1	0-1	Law 60	Rimmer	Kopel	Dunne	Fitzpatrick	James	Stiles	Morgan	Best	Charlton	Law	Sartori	
		25/1	63,498	*3:1*				*Scullion 3*	*Walker*	*Welbourne*	*Williams*	*Eddy*	*Garvey*	*Walley*	*Scullion*	*Hale*	*Garbett*	*Endean**	*Owen*	*Green*
								Ref: W Handley	Watford are heading for Div 2 for the first time and have the best defence in the league. Their 10,000 fans go home happy. It takes an hour for United to crack the yellow-shirted line and cancel out the early goal. Mike Walker drops Dunne's curling cross and Fitzpatrick sets up Law.											
4R	A	WATFORD		17	W	2-0	1-0	Law 31, 87	Stepney	Fitzpatrick	Dunne	Crerand	James	Stiles	Morgan	Kidd	Charlton	Law	Best	
		3/2	*34,099*	*3:1*					*Walker*	*Welbourne*	*Williams*	*Hale*	*Eddy*	*Walley*	*Scullion*	*Garbett*	*Green*	*Endean*	*Owen*	
								Ref: W Handley	The predatory Law's 30th goal overtakes Rowley's record total of FA Cup goals. In a packed ground, United's defence earn their corn against strong late pressure from the Hornets. Watford have conceded only four goals at home all season but a smash-and-grab display beats them.											
5	A	BIRMINGHAM		17	D	2-2	0-0	Law 61, Best 80	Stepney	Fitzpatrick	Dunne	Crerand	James	Stiles	Morgan	Kidd	Charlton	Law	Best	
		11/2	*52,500*	*2:15*				*Beard 66, Robinson 86p*	*Herriot*	*Martin*	*Green*	*Page*	*Robinson*	*Wylie*	*Vincent*	*Greenhoff*	*Pickering*	*Hockey*	*Thwaites**	*Beard*
								Ref: D Smith	Snow puts the game in doubt until just before the kick-off. Blues live dangerously and Herriot is in dazzling form. Law heads in Kidd's cross, only for Beard to level a minute after coming on. Best crashes in the best of the night, but handles for 20-year-old Robinson to earn a replay.											
5R	H	BIRMINGHAM		17	W	6-2	3-1	Law 16p, 26, 74, Crerand 22, Kidd 75,	Stepney	Fitzpatrick	Dunne	Crerand	James	Stiles	Morgan	Kidd	Charlton	Law	Best	
		24/2	61,932	*2:15*				*Green'f 4, Summerill 80* [Morgan 85]	*Herriot*	*Martin*	*Green*	*Page*	*Robinson*	*Wylie*	*Vincent*	*Greenhoff**	*Pickering*	*Hockey*	*Beard*	*Summerill*
								Ref: D Smith	After two postponements, the pitch is a quagmire. United show Stan Cullis's boys no mercy, despite Jimmy Greenhoff's early goal. Law is in deadly form and scores a penalty after Beard trips Fitzpatrick. United go for goals and don't ease up. The first of three home games in six days.											
QF	H	EVERTON		17	L	0-1	0-0		Stepney	Fitzpatrick	Dunne	Crerand	James	Stiles	Morgan	Kidd	Charlton	Law	Best	
		1/3	63,464	*3*				*Royle 77*	*West*	*Wright*	*Brown*	*Jackson*	*Labone*	*Harvey**	*Husband*	*Ball*	*Royle*	*Hurst*	*Morrissey*	*Kenyon*
								Ref: P Partridge	A tired United play their third game in six days. Everton defend like demons and score against the run of play. Only Jimmy Greaves has scored more goals than 26-goal Royle who stabs in at the far post after James misjudges a cross. Best punches Johnny Morrissey but gets away with it.											

		Home					Away					
	P	W	D	L	F	A	W	D	L	F	A	Pts
1 Leeds	42	18	3	0	41	9	9	10	2	25	17	67
2 Liverpool	42	16	4	1	36	10	9	7	5	27	14	61
3 Everton	42	14	5	2	43	10	7	10	4	34	26	57
4 Arsenal	42	12	6	3	31	12	10	6	5	25	15	56
5 Chelsea	42	11	7	3	40	24	9	3	9	33	29	50
6 Tottenham	42	10	8	3	39	22	4	9	8	22	29	45
7 Southampton	42	13	5	3	41	21	3	8	10	16	27	45
8 West Ham	42	10	8	3	47	22	3	10	8	19	28	44
9 Newcastle	42	12	7	2	40	20	3	7	11	21	35	44
10 West Brom	42	11	7	3	43	26	5	4	12	21	41	43
11 MAN UNITED	42	13	5	3	38	18	2	7	12	19	35	42
12 Ipswich	42	10	4	7	32	26	5	7	9	27	34	41
13 Manchester C	42	13	6	2	49	20	2	4	15	15	35	40
14 Burnley	42	11	6	4	36	25	4	3	14	19	57	39
15 Sheffield Wed	42	7	9	5	27	26	3	7	11	14	28	36
16 Wolves	42	7	10	4	26	22	3	5	13	15	36	35
17 Sunderland	42	10	6	5	28	18	1	6	14	15	49	34
18 Nott'm Forest	42	6	6	9	17	22	4	7	10	28	35	33
19 Stoke	42	9	7	5	24	24	0	8	13	16	39	33
20 Coventry	42	8	6	7	32	22	2	5	14	14	42	31
21 Leicester	42	8	8	5	27	24	1	4	16	12	44	30
22 QP Rangers	42	4	7	10	20	33	0	3	18	19	62	18
	924	233	140	89	757	456	89	140	233	456	757	924

Odds & ends

Double wins: (2) QP Rangers, Nott'm Forest.
Double losses: (2) Chelsea, Southampton.

Won from behind: (4) West Brom (h), Leicester (h) Exeter FAC (a), Birmingham FAC (h).
Lost from in front: (3) Sheff Wed (a), Leicester (a), Anderlecht EC (a).

High spots: European Cup run.
Good FA Cup form.
Home win over Liverpool.

Low spots: Poor league form especially away from home.
FA Cup quarter-final exit to Everton.
European Cup semi-final exit to AC Milan.
Defeat by Estudiantes in the World Club Championship.

Red cards (United): (3) Stiles (Estudiantes a), Best (Estudiantes (h), and Fitzpatrick (AC Milan a).
Red cards (Opponents): (1) Medina (Estudiantes h).
Ever-presents: (0).
Hat-tricks: (5) Law (4), Morgan.
Opposing hat-tricks: (1) Whitham (Sheff Wed).
Leading scorer: (30) Law.

	Appearances								Goals				
	Lge	*Sub*	WC	*Sub*	FAC	*Sub*	EC	Sub	**Lge**	WC	FAC	EC	**Tot**
Aston, John	**13**								**2**				**2**
Best, George	**41**		2		6		6		**19**		1	2	**22**
Brennan, Shay	**13**		1				3						
Burns, Francis	**14**	*2*	1		1		3	*1*				1	**1**
Charlton, Bobby	**32**		2		6		8		**5**			2	**7**
Crerand, Pat	**35**		2		4		8		**1**		1		**2**
Dunne, Tony	**33**		2		6		6						
Fitzpatrick, John	**28**	*2*			6		4		**3**		1		**4**
Foulkes, Bill	**10**	*3*	2				5						
Gowling, Alan	**2**												
James, Steve	**21**				6		2		**1**				**1**
Kidd, Brian	**28**	*1*	1		5		7		**1**		2	1	**4**
Kopel, Frank	**7**	*1*			1		1						
Law, Dennis	**30**		2		6		7		**14**		7	9	**30**
Morgan, Willie	**29**		2		5		4		**6**	1	1	1	**9**
Rimmer, Jimmy	**4**				1		2	*1*					
Ryan, Jimmy	**6**						1		**1**				**1**
Sadler, David	**26**	*3*	2			*1*	5						
Sartori, Carlo	**11**	*2*		*1*	2		2					1	**1**
Stepney, Alex	**38**		2		5		6						
Stiles, Nobby	**41**		1		6		8		**1**			1	**2**
(own-goals)									**3**		1		**4**
21 players used	**462**	*14*	22	*1*	66	*1*	88	2	**57**	1	14	18	**90**

No	Date	Att	Pos	Pt	F-A	H-T	Scorers, Times, and Referees	1	2	3	4	5	6	7	8	9	10	11	12 sub used
24	A CHELSEA		15	W	2-1	0-0	Morgan 77p, Gowling 86	Stepney	Fitzpatrick	Dunne	Crerand	Edwards	Stiles	Morgan	Law	Charlton	Gowling	Aston	
	9/1	*53,482*	*5*				*Hudson 59*	*Bonetti*	*Boyle*	*Harris*	*Hollins*	*Hinton*	*Webb*	*Hudson*	*Baldwin*	*Smethurst*	*Cooke*	*Houseman*	
							Ref: H New	United's best performance for months as Chelsea's style-kings are beaten. It looks bad when Crerand's poor pass lets in Hudson, but in a great fight-back Boyle fouls Law for a penalty and Gowling's gangly run ends with a shot which Bonetti can't hold and the ball creeps over the line.											
25	H BURNLEY		14	D	1-1	0-0	Aston 47	Stepney	Fitzpatrick	Dunne	Crerand	Edwards	Stiles	Morgan	Law	Charlton	Gowling	Aston	
	16/1	38,796	*22*				*Dobson 78*	*Waiters*	*Angus*	*Merrington*	*Docherty*	*Waldron*	*Dobson*	*Thomas*	*Coates*	*Probert*	*Kindon*	*Casper**	*Wilson*
							Ref: R Johnson	Burnley have won only twice all season and deserve a win. Inspired by Coates and Thomas, they pummel a confidence-less United, who are without Best, suspended for missing training. Burnley argue that Aston handled before scoring. Dobson swept home after Edwards' mistake.											
26	A HUDDERSFIELD		14	W	2-1	1-1	Law 26, Aston 46	Stepney	Fitzpatrick	Burns	Crerand	Edwards	Sadler	Morgan	Law*	Charlton	Gowling	Best	Aston
	30/1	*41,464*	*15*				*Worthington 35p*	*Lawson D*	*Clarke*	*Hutt*	*Nicholson*	*Ellam*	*Cherry*	*Smith*	*Greenhalgh*	*Worthington*	*McGill*	*Chapman*	
							Ref: L Callaghan	Old boy Ian Greaves' Terriers are fresh from beating Arsenal. United look like a team again and deserve the win. Best returns with an unselfish display but Law limps off. Stepney's last-minute save from Greenhalgh earns the win. Ex-Red Nicholson stars for Town who never give up.											
27	H TOTTENHAM		13	W	2-1	2-1	Best 15, Morgan 24p	Stepney	Fitzpatrick	Burns	Crerand	Edwards	Sadler	Morgan	Kidd	Charlton	Gowling	Best	
	6/2	48,416	*5*				*Peters 27*	*Jennings*	*Evans*	*Knowles*	*Mullery*	*Collins*	*Beal*	*Gilzean*	*Perryman*	*Chivers*	*Peters*	*Neighbour*	
							Ref: G Kew	The first home win for 3½ months makes it eight home wins in a row over Spurs. Gowling upsets the Londoners' defence and Best neatly lobs over Jennings and three defenders after Jennings' poor punch. Kidd is fouled by Peter Collins for a penalty. Charlton's bad pass lets in Peters.											
28	H SOUTHAMPTON		13	W	5-1	4-0	Morgan 26, Gowling 35, 42, 44, 88	Stepney	Fitzpatrick	Burns	Crerand	Edwards	Sadler	Morgan	Best	Charlton	Gowling	Aston	
	20/2	34,720	*8*				*Gabriel 67*	*Davie*	*Kirkup*	*Hollywood*	*Fisher*	*McGrath*	*Gabriel*	*Paine*	*Channon*	*Davies*	*O'Neill*	*Walker*	
							Ref: C Thomas	Gowling wrecks Sandy Davie's only ever appearance for the Saints with a nine-minute hat-trick. Aston creates three of the goals, two headers and two shots. The defence is rarely troubled by the poor visitors. The violent John McGrath is booked after four fouls in the first 11 minutes.											
29	A EVERTON		14	L	0-1	0-1		Stepney	Fitzpatrick	Dunne	Crerand	Edwards	Sadler	Morgan	Best	Charlton	Gowling*	Aston	Burns
	23/2	*52,544*	*9*				*Wright 22*	*West*	*Wright*	*Newton H*	*Kendall*	*Kenyon*	*Harvey*	*Morrissey*	*Ball*	*Royle*	*Hurst*	*Johnson*	
							Ref: K Styles	Everton's season is improving and they are in the last eight of the European Cup. In an exciting game, Busby's six-game unbeaten league run is ended. Stepney drops a corner and Tommy Wright stabs home. Aston hits the bar and Crerand, Fitzpatrick and Sadler are outstanding.											
30	H NEWCASTLE		12	W	1-0	1-0	Kidd 43	Stepney	Fitzpatrick	Dunne	Crerand	Edwards	Sadler	Morgan	Best	Charlton	Kidd	Aston	
	27/2	41,170	*15*					*McFaul*	*Craig*	*Guthrie*	*Gibb*	*Burton*	*Moncur*	*Mitchell*	*Tudor*	*Davies*	*Smith*	*Young*	
							Ref: K Wynn	The Geordies have sold Pop Robson to the fans' disgust and miss his guile up front. Tonight is Best's house-warming party, and the showbiz celebrities are out in force. George vies with Jim Smith for the most skilful player. Brian Kidd nets after Charlton's shot rebounds off a post.											
31	A WEST BROM		13	L	3-4	1-1	Best 18, Aston 50, Kidd 60	Stepney	Fitzpatrick	Dunne	Crerand	Edwards	Sadler	Morgan	Best	Charlton	Kidd	Aston	
	6/3	*41,134*	*15*				*Brown 31, 47, 54, Wile 62*	*Cumbes*	*Kaye*	*Wilson*	*Lovett*	*Wile*	*Merrick*	*McVitie*	*Brown*	*Astle*	*Hope*	*Hartford*	
							Ref: J Daniels	United are beaten after looking the better side in the first half. Albion have conceded 58 goals, more than any team in the top three leagues. But they have the deadly Tony Brown, whose 24 goals have forced him to the verge of the England team. A standing ovation for a football feast.											
32	H NOTT'M FOREST		11	W	2-0	2-0	Law 12, Best 43	Stepney	Fitzpatrick	Dunne	Crerand	Edwards	Sadler	Morgan	Best	Charlton	Law	Aston*	Burns
	13/3	39,339	*19*					*Barron*	*Hindley*	*Winfield*	*Chapman*	*O'Kane*	*Fraser*	*Lyons*	*Richardson*	*Martin*	*Cormack*	*Moore*	
							Ref: D Smith	United are well in control against a poor Forest side. Aston's headed pass sets up Law for the first. Best heads in Charlton's perfect corner for No 2. Three goals are disallowed for offside. Neil Martin misses Forest's best chance before limping off. Fitzpatrick is a star, snapping at heels.											
33	A STOKE		9	W	2-1	2-0	Best 23, 34	Stepney	Fitzpatrick	Dunne	Crerand	Edwards	Sadler	Morgan	Best	Charlton	Law	Aston	
	20/3	*40,005*	*12*				*Ritchie 77*	*Banks*	*Marsh*	*Pejic*	*Skeels*	*Smith*	*Bloor*	*Greenhoff*	*Bernard*	*Ritchie*	*Conroy*	*Burrows*	
							Ref: W Gow	Stoke boss Tony Waddington is the Manager of the Month for his club's FA Cup efforts. His team have next week's semi-final on their minds and succumb to Best's silky skills. He scores from an acute angle, then cheekily dribbles around Gordon Banks. Later he is booked for dissent.											

No	Venue	Opponent / Date	Att / Pos	Res	F-A	H-T	Scorers, Times, Referees	1	2	3	4	5	6	7	8	9	10	11	12
34	A	WEST HAM	10	L	1-2	0-2	Best 56	Stepney	Fitzpatrick	Dunne	Crerand	Edwards	Sadler*	Morgan	Best	Charlton	Law	Aston	Burns
	1/4	*38,507*	*20*				*Hurst 4, Robson 10*	*Ferguson*	*McDowell*	*Lampard*	*Bonds*	*Taylor*	*Moore*	*Redknapp*	*Boyce*	*Hurst*	*Robson*	*Greaves*	
							Ref: D Lyden	West Ham's first win over United for five years. They could have had four in first 10 minutes. Hurst's fierce shot and Robson's deft placement has Upton Park roaring. Aston's cross deflects off the ref into Best's path. Bobby Moore handles but Ferguson saves Morgan's poor penalty.											
35	H	DERBY	11	L	1-2	0-1	Law 70	Stepney	Dunne	Burns	Crerand	Edwards	Stiles	Morgan	Best	Charlton	Law	Aston*	Gowling
	10/4	44,203	*12*				*O'Hare 38, 48*	*Boulton*	*Todd*	*Robson*	*Durban*	*McFarland*	*Mackay*	*McGovern*	*Gemmill*	*O'Hare*	*Hector*	*Hinton*	
							Ref: P Partridge	Two defeats have wrecked United's European hopes. Derby are far sharper and faster than the Reds. O'Hare scores with a diving header and a low shot. Roy McFarland and Dave Mackay are impenetrable and new boy Colin Todd looks classy. Stiles replaces Sadler but struggles.											
36	H	WOLVERHAMPTON	11	W	1-0	1-0	Gowling 42	Stepney	Dunne	Burns	Crerand	Edwards	Stiles	Best	Gowling	Charlton	Law*	Morgan	Kidd
	12/4	39,584	*4*					*Parkes*	*Shaw*	*Parkin*	*Bailey*	*Munro*	*McAlle*	*McCalliog*	*Hibbitt**	*Gould*	*Curran*	*Wagstaffe*	*O'Grady*
							Ref: R Kirkpatrick	Wolves head for a European place but fail to impress. United have little to play for but pride. Gowling returns and scores again. Kenny Hibbitt and Frank Munro dally and Crerand nips in to set up the goal. Wolves hit woodwork twice but lack guile. Kidd is unhappy at being left out.											
37	A	COVENTRY	12	L	1-2	0-1	Best 60	Stepney	Dunne	Burns	Crerand	Edwards	Stiles	Best	Gowling	Charlton	Kidd	Morgan	
	13/4	*33,849*	*10*				*Hunt 5, 49*	*Glazier*	*Smith*	*Cattlin*	*Machin*	*Blockley*	*Strong*	*Alderson**	*Carr*	*Rafferty*	*Hunt*	*Clements*	*Mortimer*
							Ref: K Walker	Ernie Hunt ends City's five-game goal-drought with a crisp shot after United fail to clear a corner. His second is an exquisite volley from 15 yards. Best then comes to life and ghosts in to volley home Crerand's cross. City deservedly survive, despite Best dominating the second half.											
38	A	CRYSTAL PALACE	10	W	5-3	1-2	Law 43, 48,66, Best 58, 65	Stepney	Fitzpatrick	Dunne	Crerand*	Edwards	Sadler	Best	Gowling	Charlton	Law	Morgan	Burns
	17/4	*39,145*	*18*				*Birchenall 4, Tambling 23, Queen 82*	*Jackson*	*Payne*	*Wall*	*Hoadley*	*McCormick*	*Taylor*	*Wharton**	*Kember*	*Tambling*	*Birchenall*	*Scott*	*Queen*
							Ref: D Turner	United give Palace a two-goal lead, then massacre Bert Head's team in an entertaining game. Palace, despite only one win in 11, are safe from relegation but let Charlton and Crerand run the game and it is so easy for Best and Law. The reliable John Jackson is at fault for goal No 4.											
39	H	LIVERPOOL	10	L	0-2	0-1		Stepney	Dunne	Burns	Crerand	Edwards	Sadler	Best	Gowling	Charlton	Law	Morgan	
	19/4	43,066	*5*				*Heighway 19, Edwards 60(og)*	*Clemence*	*Lawler*	*Yeats*	*Smith*	*Ross*	*McLaughlin*	*Callaghan*	*Thompson*	*Heighway*	*Toshack*	*Hall*	
							Ref: K Styles	Liverpool are in the FA Cup final and the UEFA semi-final and rest key players. Clemence brilliantly saves from Best on several occasions and looks ready for an England cap. Heighway and Hall cause the problems on the flanks. Paul Edwards' glancing header is a classic own-goal.											
40	H	IPSWICH	9	W	3-2	2-1	Best 27p, Charlton 40, Kidd 76	Stepney	Dunne	Burns	Crerand	James	Sadler*	Law	Gowling	Charlton	Kidd	Best	Sartori
	24/4	31,662	*19*				*Morris 18, Clarke 82*	*Best*	*Hammond**	*Harper*	*Morris*	*Bell*	*Jefferson*	*Robertson*	*Hill*	*Clarke*	*Mills*	*Miller*	*Woods*
							Ref: H Williams	Busby's last home game in charge is a damp squib and memorable only for the goals. Morris's 25-yarder fizzes past Stepney, and Best nets a penalty after Kidd is fouled. Charlton scores his first for six months before Kidd restores his standing. Clarke's goal keeps United on their toes.											
41	A	BLACKPOOL	11	D	1-1	1-1	Law 6	Stepney	Dunne	Burns	Crerand!	James	Sadler	Law	Gowling	Charlton	Kidd	Best	
	1/5	*29,857*	*22*				*Green 26*	*Burridge*	*Armfield*	*Hatton*	*Johnston**	*James*	*Alcock*	*Burns*	*Green*	*Craven!*	*Wann*	*Hutchison*	*Bentley*
							Ref: H Davey	United fans run riot in Blackpool before the game. Armfield plays his final game for the relegated Seasiders in a scrappy game full of brawls. The ref loses patience and Crerand and John Craven get marching orders. Tony Green's goal is fabulous whilst Hutchison is man of the match.											
42	A	MANCHESTER C	8	W	4-3	3-0	Charlton 15, Law 30, Best 31, 75	Stepney	**O'Neill**	Burns	Crerand	James	Sadler*	Law	Gowling	Charlton	Kidd	Best	
	5/5	*43,623*	*11*				*Hill 46, Lee 80, Mellor 82*	*Healey*	*Book*	*Connor*	*Towers*	*Heslop*	*Donachie*	*Carter*	*Hill*	*Lee*	*Young*	*Mellor*	
	Home	Away					Ref: C Thomas	A glorious end to Busby's career as United roar into a 3-0 lead but are almost pegged back by a makeshift City, who have won only one of 17 games. The exhilarating game is the highest scoring derby game since 1926 and the teams deserve their standing ovation. Best is awesome.											
Average	45,021	41,317																	

FA Cup

No	Venue	Opponent / Date	Att / Pos	Res	F-A	H-T	Scorers, Times, Referees	1	2	3	4	5	6	7	8	9	10	11	12
3	H	MIDDLESBROUGH	18	D	0-0	0-0		Rimmer	Fitzpatrick	Dunne	Crerand	Ure	Sadler	Morgan	Best	Charlton	Kidd	Law	
	2/1	47,824	*2:8*					*Whigham*	*Smith A*	*Jones*	*Moody*	*Gates*	*Spraggon*	*Downing*	*McMordie*	*McIlmoyle*	*Hickton*	*Laidlaw*	
							Ref: G Hill	Busby is back in charge and at least stems the flow of goals conceded. An icy surface does not suit United and Boro run rings around them but spurn good chances. 17-goal Hickton hits the post. The Stretford End has been reduced to try to cut out missile throwing and it seems to work.											
3R	A	MIDDLESBROUGH	18	L	1-2	0-1	Best 89	Rimmer	Fitzpatrick	Dunne	Crerand	Edwards	Sadler	Morgan	Best	Charlton	Kidd*	Law	Gowling
	5/1	*40,040*	*2:8*				*McIlmoyle 7, Downing 73*	*Whigham*	*Smith A*	*Jones*	*Smith G*	*Gates*	*Spraggon*	*Downing*	*McMordie*	*McIlmoyle*	*Hickton*	*Laidlaw*	
							Ref: G Hill	Boro avenge their two defeats last season at snowbound Ayresome Park. They deserve to win after United fade in the second half. Rimmer misses a cross and Hugh McIlmoyle heads in. Eric McMordie's clever dribble sets up Derrick Downing. Best's consolation header is too late.											

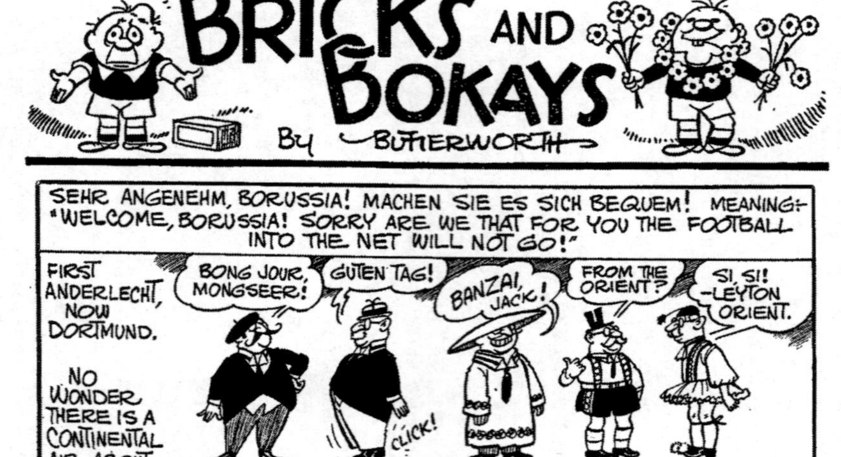

This cartoon appeared in the United Review, the match programme for the visit of Borussia Dortmund in the European Cup, October 1956